For Referen D0941476

Not to be taken from this room

Historical Dictionaries of Literature and the Arts
Jon Woronoff, Series Editor

Historical Dictionary of the Broadway Musical

William A. Everett
Paul R. Laird

*Historical Dictionaries of Literature
and the Arts, No. 22*

The Scarecrow Press, Inc.
Lanham, Maryland • Toronto • Plymouth, UK
2008

SCARECROW PRESS, INC.

Published in the United States of America
by Scarecrow Press, Inc.
A wholly owned subsidiary of
The Rowman & Littlefield Publishing Group, Inc.
4501 Forbes Boulevard, Suite 200, Lanham, Maryland 20706
www.scarecrowpress.com

Estover Road
Plymouth PL6 7PY
United Kingdom

British Library Cataloguing in Publication Information Available

Library of Congress Cataloging-in-Publication Data
Everett, William A., 1962–
   Historical dictionary of the Broadway musical / William A. Everett, Paul
R. Laird.
      p. cm. — (Historical dictionaries of literature and the arts ; No. 22)
   Includes bibliographical references (p.   ).
   ISBN-13: 978-0-8108-6054-4 (hardcover : alk. paper)
   ISBN-10: 0-8108-6054-6 (hardcover : alk. paper)
      1. Musicals—New York (State)—New York—Dictionaries. I. Laird, Paul R.
II. Title.

ML102.M88E94 2008
782.1'409747103—dc22   2007037712

∞™ The paper used in this publication meets the minimum requirements of
American National Standard for Information Sciences—Permanence of Paper
for Printed Library Materials, ANSI/NISO Z39.48-1992.
Manufactured in the United States of America.

Contents

Editor's Foreword

Everybody knows what a Broadway musical is—that is, until they try to define it. Broadway is the easy part, although it actually has less to do with geography than with size. But the "musical" part of the term can vary incredibly, defining different types of music and dance; comedy, romance, and tragedy; talented performers; and creative authors. These types of performances have also varied considerably in the past, with early ones being simple and even naive compared to the palette of emotions evoked and topics broached more recently, while individual songs that were once impervious to the surrounding action have increasingly been woven into the plot. Broadway musicals cover quite a range, from high brow to low brow, opera and operetta to musical comedies, and musical plays to revues and vaudeville. The musical styles have also fluctuated; they were once closer to ballads and waltzes but today are more related to jazz, pop, and rock. Still, it's not that hard to tell a Broadway musical when you see it, even if it's not on Broadway.

It's also hard to forget a Broadway musical once you've seen it and been captivated by it, even if that was decades ago. This *Historical Dictionary of the Broadway Musical* is an indispensable record of who wrote or composed what, who sang or danced what, what the plot was, and how the critics responded, to say nothing of how long it ran and where it was staged. Its chronology tracing the Broadway musical's evolution over a century and a half and an introduction places the musical in context, providing an overview of the history and current status of the art form. The dictionary contains facts and figures, with entries on important people, places, events, and—of course—musicals. The bibliography provides additional sources so you can track down anything else.

This volume was compiled by two authorities on musicals, William A. Everett and Paul Laird. Both live far from Broadway, the former teaching at the University of Missouri–Kansas City and the latter at the University of Kansas–Lawrence. They're both musicologists, teach music history, and have a special interest in the musical. This is expressed, among other things, by their publications. Dr. Everett has written books on Rudolf Friml and Sigmund Romberg, and Dr. Laird wrote a book on Leonard Bernstein; together they edited *The Cambridge Companion to the Musical*. They avidly attend and deeply appreciate musicals, evidenced by this informative and fascinating guide, which will help others gain more from an art form that is hard to define but incredibly easy to enjoy.

Jon Woronoff
Series Editor

Preface

Creating a reference work about the venerable American institution known as the Broadway musical is a challenging endeavor. Our first task was to define the term "Broadway musical," as opposed to "musical theater" or even *American* musical theater." For the sake of what could be contained in a single volume, we decided to focus on musicals that played on Broadway, New York's theater district, most of which is centered around the Times Square area. Furthermore, we defined a "Broadway" house according to the criteria used by Actors Equity (the union for Broadway performers) as one that has at least 500 seats. Because of these admittedly narrow parameters, this volume focuses on one dimension, albeit a primary one, of the popular musical theater. There are some off-Broadway shows of special importance included, and it should be noted that a number of Broadway shows actually first ran at a smaller house, identified by Actors Equity as off-Broadway or off-off-Broadway, depending upon the theater's capacity. Even with these limitations, however, we have had to be selective about what we included. We have chosen what we feel to be the most significant shows and people in the genre's history, but recognize that our criteria might not be the same that others writing such a dictionary might have used.

We begin our coverage with *The Black Crook* (1866), considered by many to be the "first Broadway musical" (if one can be so bold as to use such a loaded and controversial term) because of its long run in the same theater. We end 140 years later, in 2006, with shows such as *Mary Poppins* and *Spring Awakening*, two works that demonstrate substantially different approaches to the genre. For shows that are still playing on Broadway in early 2007, we provide the number of performances as of 31 December 2006.

Entries in this dictionary are of three types: shows, people, and terms. The show entries include information on the original Broadway run and principal creators followed by material on the show itself. Entries on people focus on the subject's Broadway contributions. In the terms category, we included various types of Broadway musicals (such as revue, operetta, musical comedy, megamusical, rock musical, and jukebox musical) and the types of roles of people involved with mounting a Broadway musical (including producer, director, choreographer, orchestrator, etc.). Since they appear so frequently, titles of professions are not bolded for cross-referencing when they appear in other entries. We also address terms related to music (e.g., chorus, refrain, verse) and societal or social dimensions of the genre (e.g., African American musicals, homosexuality, Orientalism). The book includes a highly selective bibliography on the ever-growing literature about the Broadway musical.

We would like to thank all those who helped bring this book to fruition, especially Jon Woronoff for approaching us to create the volume, the production staff at Scarecrow Press, the librarians at our universities, the University of Kansas and the University of Missouri—Kansas City, our graduate students who proofread and double-checked information, and our families for their support of this project. We also thank Douglas M. Laird for his assistance with the entries on the musicals of Rodgers and Hammerstein.

Chronology

1866 **12 September:** *The Black Crook*, one of the most spectacular shows of its age and often considered one of the first important Broadway musicals, opens at Niblo's Garden and runs 475 performances. **13 September:** *The Doctor of Alcantara*, with a libretto by Benjamin Woolf (a significant writer for the musical stage), opens at the French Theater, one of three productions of the show to open in New York that season.

1867 **24 September:** *La Grande Duchesse de Gérolstein*, by Jacques Offenbach and sung in French, opens at the French Theater and plays 156 performances that season at various houses.

1868 **17 January:** *The White Fawn*, a sequel to *The Black Crook*, opens at Niblo's Garden, but is not as successful. **10 March:** *Humpty Dumpty*, one of the most important of American pantomimes, opens at the Olympic Theater with George Lafayette Fox as its star and librettist.

1870 **11 July:** *Fritz, Our Cousin German* opens at Wallack's Theater starring Joseph K. Emmet, a prominent actor specializing in German character types.

1871 **8 April:** *The Black Crook* opens at Niblo's Garden in its first revival and runs 122 performances.

1872 **30 November:** *Leo and Lotos*, a ballet extravaganza in the tradition of *The Black Crook*, opens at Niblo's Garden and runs four months.

1874   **27 July:** *Evangeline*, one of the most popular pieces of American musical theater in the last three decades of the 19th century, opens at Niblo's Garden.

1875   **August:** Competing versions of *Around the World in Eighty Days* open at the Grand Opera House and the Academy of Music.

1876   **18 September:** *Baba*, another work in *The Black Crook* tradition, opens at Niblo's Garden for a three-month run.

1877   **3 September:** *Old Lavender*, one of Edward Harrigan's most enduring shows (and personal roles, as he played the title character), opens.

1879   **13 January:** *The Mulligan Guards' Ball*, a popular collaboration of Harrigan and Tony Hart, opens at the Theatre Comique. **15 January:** Gilbert and Sullivan's *H.M.S. Pinafore* premieres at the Standard Theater and becomes enormously successful in the United States. **31 December:** Gilbert and Sullivan's *The Pirates of Penzance* opens at the Fifth Avenue Theater.

1880   **22 November:** Harrigan and Hart bring back their Irish character types in the successful *The Mulligan Guards' Nominee*, which opens at the Theatre Comique.

1881   **22 September:** *Patience*, the latest offering from Gilbert and Sullivan, opens at the Standard Theater. Other productions of the show appeared later in the season, one of which starred Lillian Russell, a famed comic opera performer of the era.

1882   **9 January:** Harrigan and Hart open their *Squatter Sovereignty* at the Theatre Comique.

1883   **9 July:** *Prince Methusalem* by Johann Strauss opens at the Casino Theater with Lillian Russell playing the male title role in trousers (a typical practice of the day) and runs for three months.

1884   **4 September:** *Adonis*, starring Henry E. Dixey, opens at the Bijou Theater and plays for 603 performances, the longest run in Broadway history to that point.

1885   19 August: Richard D'Oyly Carte opens the official production of Gilbert and Sullivan's *The Mikado* at the Fifth Avenue Theater, where it settles in for a 250-performance run.

1886   15 February: Harrigan's *The Leather Patch* opens at the Park Theater and Johann Strauss's *The Gypsy Baron* debuts at the Casino Theater.

1887   21 November: *The Begum*, with libretto by Harry B. Smith and music by Reginald De Koven, opens at the Fifth Avenue Theater, beginning the career of two of Broadway's most important creators of the period.

1888   17 October: Gilbert and Sullivan's *Yeoman of the Guard* made its New York debut at the Casino Theater, running for 100 performances.

1889   22 April: *Fritz in a Madhouse*, a new German vehicle for Joseph K. Emmet, opens at the 14th Street Theater.

1890   5 May: *Castles in the Air*, starring De Wolf Hopper, premieres at the Broadway Theater and plays 105 performances.

1891   4 May: *Wang*, a show that remained popular for several seasons, opens at the Broadway Theater and runs through the summer. **22 September:** *Robin Hood*, a spectacularly successful comic opera with libretto by Harry B. Smith and music by Reginald De Koven, opens at the Standard Theater. **9 November:** *A Trip to Chinatown*, a musical comedy that included an unusual integration between music and plot for the time, opens at the Madison Square Theater and runs 657 performances, the longest run for a musical at that point.

1892   14 November: *The Fencing Master*, the next show from Smith and De Koven, opens at the Casino Theater and runs for more than three months.

1893   25 October: Lillian Russell is the star of *Princess Nicotine*, which debuts at the Casino Theater and stays for three months.

1894   12 May: *The Passing Show*, Broadway's first revue, opens at the Casino Theater. **18 September:** *The Gaiety Girl*, a British import, opens at Daly's Theater.

1895   4 November: *The Wizard of the Nile*, the first collaboration between composer Victor Herbert and librettist Harry B. Smith, premieres at the Casino Theater and runs for 105 performances.

1896   20 April: *El Capitan*, with music by John Philip Sousa and starring De Wolf Hopper, opens at the Broadway Theater and runs for 112 performances.

1897   16 March: *The Serenade*, an outstanding success for composer Victor Herbert and librettist Harry B. Smith, opens at the Knickerbocker Theater and runs for two months as part of its national tour.

1898   5 July: *Clorindy; or, The Origin of the Cakewalk*, with a score by African American composer Will Marion Cook and librettist Paul Laurence Dunbar, opens as an afterpiece to *Rice's Summer Nights* on the roof of the Casino Theater, the first musical by African American creators to play in (or on) a major Broadway house.

1899   21 September: *Whirl-i-gig*, a musical starring the comedy team Joe Weber and Lew Fields that they produced at their own Music Hall with Lillian Russell as the female star, opens and runs for 264 performances.

1900   10 November: *Floradora*, a hit show from London, premieres at the Casino Theater and plays for 505 performances.

1901   25 February: George M. Cohan makes his Broadway debut when *The Governor's Son*, an expansion of a sketch from the family's vaudeville act, opens at the Savoy Theater for a run of 32 performances.

1902   11 September: Weber and Fields open another hit, *Twirly-Whirly*, at their Music Hall, this one running for 244 performances.

1903   20 January: *The Wizard of Oz*, adapted by author L. Frank Baum into a musical, opens at the Majestic Theater starring the comedy team of Dave Montgomery and Fred Stone. **18 February:** *In Dahomey*, the first full-length Broadway musical created by African Americans to play in a major Broadway house, opens at the New York Theater. **13 October:** *Babes in Toyland*, with a popular score by Victor Herbert, debuts at the Majestic Theater.

1904 **19 September:** *Mr. Wix of Wickham*, the first musical with most of its score by Jerome Kern, opens at the Bijou Theater for a short run. **7 November:** *Little Johnny Jones*, George M. Cohan's first successful Broadway show, opens at the Liberty Theater. **24 December:** *Lady Teazle*, a vehicle for Lillian Russell, premieres at the Casino Theater and is the first musical produced by the Shubert Brothers.

1905 **14 January:** *Fantana*, the hit of the season, opens at the Lyric Theater with a young Douglas Fairbanks playing a small role. **25 December:** *Mlle. Modiste*, one of Victor Herbert's most successful shows, debuts at the Hippodrome starring the famed singer Fritzi Scheff.

1906 **1 January:** George M. Cohan opens one of his finest shows, *Forty-five Minutes from Broadway*, at the New Amsterdam Theater, starring Fay Templeton and including such hits as the title tune and "Mary is a Grand Old Name." **24 September:** *The Red Mill*, with a score by Victor Herbert (including "The Streets Of New York") and the antics of Montgomery and Stone, opens at the Knickerbocker Theater.

1907 **8 July:** *The Follies of 1907*, the first revue that Florenz Ziegfeld produced, opens at the Jardin de Paris, also known as the New York Theater Roof. **21 October:** *The Merry Widow*, an operetta with music by Franz Lehár that was a triumph in Europe, opens at the New Amsterdam Theater and takes New York by storm.

1908 **30 November:** *Miss Innocence*, a risqué vehicle for Florenz Ziegfeld's wife, Anna Held, opens at the New York Theater for a run of 176 performances.

1909 **13 September:** *The Chocolate Soldier* by Oscar Straus premieres at the Lyric Theater, demonstrating the continuing popularity of Continental operettas with a run of 296 performances.

1910   20 June: *The Ziegfeld Follies of 1910*, which included the Broadway debut of Fanny Brice, opens at the Jardin de Paris. **7 November:** *Naughty Marietta*, featuring one of Victor Herbert's best scores and starring Emma Trentini, opens at the New York Theater.

1911   13 March: *The Pink Lady*, a hugely successful vehicle for the star Hazel Dawn, debuts at the New Amsterdam Theater and runs for eighteen months. **20 March:** *La Belle Paree*, featuring the Broadway debut of Al Jolson, opens at the Winter Garden Theater.

1912   2 December: *The Firefly*, starring Emma Trentini and with the first Broadway score by Rudolf Friml, opens at the Lyric Theater for a run of 120 performances.

1913   10 December: *High Jinks*, Friml's second Broadway score, premieres at the Lyric Theater.

1914   10 January: *The Whirl of the World*, a revue, opens at the Winter Garden Theater, the first Broadway show with a score by Sigmund Romberg. **8 December:** *Watch Your Step*, with a score entirely of songs by Irving Berlin, debuts at the New Amsterdam Theater.

1915   20 April: *Nobody Home*, one of the "Princess Theatre musicals" with music by Jerome Kern and book by Guy Bolton, opens for a run of 135 performances. **5 August:** *The Blue Paradise*, with a score by Romberg and the new star Vivienne Segal leading the cast, opens at the Casino Theater. **23 December:** *Very Good Eddie*, another of the "Princess Theater musicals," premieres and runs for nearly a year.

1916   6 November: *The Century Girl*, with a score by Herbert and the combined production team of Ziegfeld and Charles Dillingham, opens at the Century Theater and runs for 200 performances.

1917   20 February: *Oh, Boy!*, another of the famous "Princess Theatre musicals" with a score by Kern, premieres at that small house. **16 August:** *Maytime*, with Romberg's score, opens at the Shubert Theater and runs for 492 performances. **28 November:** *Over the Top*, a revue that included the debut of Fred and Adele Astaire, opens at the 44th Street Roof Garden.

1918 **1 February:** *Oh, Lady! Lady!!*, another "Princess Theatre musical" and Kern's third Broadway score in four months, premieres to rapturous reviews. **19 August:** *Yip! Yip! Yaphank!*, a soldier's show with a score by Irving Berlin (including "Oh, How I Hate to Get Up in the Morning!"), opens at the Century Theater.

1919 **26 May:** *La, La, Lucille*, the first show with a complete score by George Gershwin, debuts at the Henry Miller Theater. **18 November:** *Irene*, a Cinderella story about a shop girl who marries an heir, opens at the Vanderbilt Theater and plays for 675 performances, at the time the longest run in Broadway history.

1920 **5 January:** *Always You*, the first musical with book and lyrics by Oscar Hammerstein II, premieres at the Central Theater. **28 July:** *Poor Little Ritz Girl*, the first show with a score by Richard Rodgers and Lorenz Hart (much of it replaced with songs by Romberg and Alex Gerber before the show opened), premieres at the Central Theater. **21 December:** *Sally*, which made a star of Marilyn Miller, opens at the New Amsterdam Theater and plays 561 performances.

1921 **23 May:** *Shuffle Along*, the first widely popular show created by African Americans, debuts at the 63rd Street Music Hall. **29 September:** *Blossom Time*, with a score by Dorothy Donnelly and Romberg and based on the music of Franz Schubert, opens at the Ambassador Theater. The show was a touring staple for years.

1922 **19 September:** *Orange Blossoms*, the last Broadway show to open during Victor Herbert's lifetime for which he supplied the score, premieres at the Fulton Theater.

1923 **7 May:** *Wildflower*, an operetta that included the first orchestrations by Robert Russell Bennett, opens at the Casino Theater.

1924 **19 May:** The Marx Brothers make their Broadway debuts in *I'll Say She Is!*, which opens at the Casino Theater. **2 September:** *Rose Marie*, a hugely successful operetta with a score by Friml, premieres at the Imperial Theater for a 557-performance run. **1 December:** *Lady, Be Good!*, with one of Broadway's first jazz-influenced scores by George and Ira Gershwin, opens at the Liberty Theater for a run of 330 performances. **2 December:** *The Student Prince*, with a score by Romberg, opens at the Jolson Theater. At 608 performances, it was the longest running musical of the decade.

1925   17 May: Rodgers and Hart supply seven songs (including "Manhattan") for the revue *The Garrick Gaieties*, presented by the Theater Guild with great success. **16 September:** *No, No, Nanette*, perhaps the prototypical musical comedy of the era with a score by Vincent Youmans (including "Tea for Two" and "I Want to Be Happy"), debuts at the Globe Theater for a run of 321 performances. **18 September:** *Dearest Enemy*, the first successful book musical with a score by Rodgers and Hart, opens at the Knickerbocker Theater. **21 September:** *The Vagabond King*, another popular operetta with a score by Friml, premieres at the Casino Theater for a run of 511 performances. **22 September:** *Sunny*, a vehicle for Marilyn Miller with a score by Kern, opens at the New Amsterdam Theater for a run of 517 performances. **8 December:** *The Cocoanuts*, starring the Marx Brothers and with a script by George S. Kaufman (and an unacknowledged Morrie Ryskind) and score by Berlin, premieres at the Lyric Theater.

1926   4 October: *Deep River*, a "native opera," opens at the Imperial Theater, but it is well ahead of its time in terms of its seriousness and racial attitudes and closes in four weeks. **8 November:** *Oh, Kay!*, with a score by George and Ira Gershwin (including "Someone to Watch over Me") and starring Gertrude Lawrence, opens at the Imperial Theater. **30 November:** *The Desert Song*, with music by Romberg and lyrics and book by Otto Harbach and Oscar Hammerstein II, debuts at the Casino Theater and runs for 471 performances.

1927   2 February: *Rio Rita*, an operetta based on older models, opens the spectacular Ziegfeld Theater and runs for nearly a year. **16 August:** *The Ziegfeld Follies of 1927*, starring Eddie Cantor and with a score by Berlin, premieres at the New Amsterdam Theater. Ziegfeld is said to have spent $289,000 producing the revue. **6 September:** *Good News*, a typical 1920s musical comedy, opens at the 46th Street Theater and runs for 557 performances. **3 November:** *A Connecticut Yankee*, with a fine score by Rodgers and Hart, debuts at the Vanderbilt Theater. **22 November:** *Funny Face*, with a score by George and Ira Gershwin and starring Fred and Adele Astaire, is the first show to play at the Alvin Theater. **27 December:** *Show Boat*, considered by many Broadway's first musical play, premieres at the Ziegfeld Theater. Kern wrote the music; Hammerstein wrote the lyrics and book; Ziegfeld produced.

1928   **9 May:** *Blackbirds of 1928*, a show with an African American cast and a score by Dorothy Fields and Jimmy McHugh (including "I Can't Give You Anything But Love"), opens at the Liberty Theater and runs for 518 performances. **19 September:** *The New Moon*, an operetta with music by Romberg and lyrics by Hammerstein, debuts at the Imperial Theater and runs for 509 performances.

1929   **5 November:** *Bitter Sweet*, with score and libretto by Noel Coward and starring Evelyn Laye, opens at the Ziegfeld Theater, running 159 performances. **27 November:** *Fifty Million Frenchmen*, the first major hit with music and lyrics by Cole Porter, premieres at the Lyric Theater and plays for 254 performances.

1930   **23 September:** *Fine and Dandy*, with music by Kay Swift and lyrics by Paul James, opens at the Erlanger Theater, one of the few musicals of the period by a female composer. **14 October:** *Girl Crazy*, featuring the debut of Ethel Merman and a score by George and Ira Gershwin (including "I Got Rhythm" and "Embraceable You"), premieres at the Alvin Theater.

1931   **15 October:** *The Cat and the Fiddle*, with music by Kern and lyrics by Harbach, opens at the Globe Theater, playing 395 performances. **26 December:** *Of Thee I Sing*, a highly successful musical satire with a score by George and Ira Gershwin, opens at the Music Box Theater.

1932   **17 February:** *Face the Music*, with score by Berlin and satirical book by Moss Hart, debuts at the New Amsterdam Theater, running for 165 performances. **8 November:** *Music in the Air*, with music by Kern and libretto by Hammerstein, opens at the Alvin Theater for a successful run of 342 performances.

1933   30 September: *As Thousands Cheer*, a satirical revue with score by Berlin and book by Moss Hart, premieres at the Music Box Theater, running 400 performances. **21 October:** *Let 'Em Eat Cake*, the unsuccessful sequel to *Of Thee I Sing*, opens at the Imperial Theater.

1934   21 November: *Anything Goes*, with a score by Porter and starring Ethel Merman, debuts at the Alvin Theater. Its book was the first collaboration of Howard Lindsay and Russel Crouse.

1935   10 October: *Porgy and Bess*, George Gershwin's opera, opens at the Alvin Theater. **16 November:** *Jumbo*, a circus musical with a score by Rodgers and Hart and starring Jimmy Durante in the midst of animals and circus acts, premieres at the Hippodrome and runs for 233 performances.

1936   11 April: *On Your Toes*—featuring memorable use of dance, Ray Bolger in a starring role, and a score by Rodgers and Hart—opens at the Imperial Theater. **19 November:** *Johnny Johnson*, Kurt Weill's first score for Broadway following his move to the United States, debuts at the 44th Street Theater for a short run.

1937   14 April: *Babes in Arms*, with a score by Rodgers and Hart (including "My Funny Valentine" and "The Lady Is a Tramp"), opens at the Shubert and runs for 289 performances. **2 November:** *I'd Rather Be Right*, a political satire with a score by Rodgers and Hart and George M. Cohan (his last major work on Broadway) starring as President Franklin D. Roosevelt, premieres at the Alvin Theater. **27 November:** *Pins and Needles*, a revue produced by the International Ladies' Garment Workers Union and the Broadway debut of composer Harold Rome, opens at the Labor Stage (Princess Theater) and becomes for a time the longest-running Broadway musical with a run of 1,108 performances.

1938   22 September: *Hellzapoppin'*, a revue based on old vaudeville humor, debuts at the 46th Street Theater and runs for a then-record 1,404 performances. **9 November:** *Leave It to Me!*, which featured the Broadway debut of Mary Martin and a score by Porter, opens at the Imperial Theater. **23 November:** *The Boys from Syracuse*, another Rodgers and Hart hit directed by George Abbott, premieres at the Alvin Theater.

1939 **17 November:** *Very Warm for May*, with a score by Kern and Hammerstein that includes the song "All the Things You Are," opens at the Alvin Theater. **6 December:** *Du Barry Was a Lady*, with score by Porter and starring Merman and Bert Lahr, premieres at the 46th Street Theater and runs 408 performances.

1940 **28 May:** *Louisiana Purchase*, with a score by Berlin and starring Victor Moore and William Gaxton, debuts at the Imperial Theater and runs for 444 performances. **25 October:** *Cabin in the Sky*, a fantasy that took place among African Americans in the South and starring Ethel Waters, opens at the Martin Beck Theater. **30 October:** *Panama Hattie*, another collaboration starring Merman with a score by Porter, premieres at the 46th Street Theater and runs for 501 performances. **25 December:** *Pal Joey*, with a score by Rodgers and Hart and Gene Kelly playing the anti-hero of the title, opens at the Barrymore Theater for a run of 374 performances.

1941 **23 January:** *Lady in the Dark*, a musical about psychoanalysis with score by Kurt Weill and Ira Gershwin, book by Moss Hart, and starring Gertrude Lawrence, opens at the Alvin Theater for a run of 467 performances.

1942 **3 June:** *By Jupiter*, the last new show with a score by Rodgers and Hart and starring Ray Bolger, premieres at the Shubert Theater. **4 July:** *This Is the Army*, Berlin's famed tribute to the troops that toured the world until late 1945, opens at the Broadway Theater.

1943 **7 January:** Once again pairing a Porter score with Merman as the star, *Something for the Boys* opens at the Alvin Theater for a run of 422 performances. **31 March:** *Oklahoma!*, the first collaboration of Richard Rodgers and Oscar Hammerstein II, opens at the St. James Theater. Its level of integration of plot, music, and dance was a huge influence on later musicals, and its run of 2,212 performances was unprecedented for a musical. **7 October:** *One Touch of Venus*, with a score by Weill and Ogden Nash and starring Mary Martin, premieres at the Imperial Theater and runs for 567 performances. **11 November:** *What's Up*, the first show combining the talents of librettist Alan Jay Lerner and composer Frederick Loewe, opens at the National Theater but only runs 63 performances. **2 December:** *Carmen Jones*, Hammerstein's version of Bizet's opera with fresh lyrics and an African American cast, debuts at the Broadway Theater for a run of 503 performances.

1944   **21 August:** *Song of Norway*, Robert Wright's and George Forrest's adaptation of Edvard Grieg's music into a fictionalized biography of the composer's life, opens at the Imperial Theater and runs 860 performances. **5 October:** *Bloomer Girl*, with a score by composer Harold Arlen and lyricist E. Y. Harburg, premieres at the Shubert Theater and runs for 654 performances. **28 December:** *On the Town* opens at the Adelphi Theater and features the Broadway debuts of Leonard Bernstein as composer, Jerome Robbins as choreographer, and Betty Comden and Adolph Green as lyricists and book writers.

1945   **27 January:** *Up in Central Park*, the first new musical in years with a score by Romberg, opens at the Century Theater and runs for 504 performances. **19 April:** Rodgers and Hammerstein confirm their innovations in the musical play with the appearance of *Carousel* at the Majestic Theater.

1946   **30 March:** *St. Louis Woman*, a show for an African American cast (including Pearl Bailey) with score by composer Harold Arlen and lyricist Johnny Mercer, debuts at the Martin Beck Theater. **18 April:** *Call Me Mister*, a humorous look at postwar demobilization with a score by Harold Rome, opens at the National Theater and runs for 734 performances. **16 May:** *Annie Get Your Gun*, one of Berlin's most successful musicals and another great role for Ethel Merman, opens at the Imperial Theater.

1947   **9 January:** *Street Scene*, an opera with music by Weill and lyrics by Langston Hughes, premieres at the Adelphi Theater and runs for 148 performances. **10 January:** *Finian's Rainbow*, a fantasy with music by Burton Lane and lyrics by Harburg and Fred Saidy and the song "How Are Things in Glocca Morra?," opens at the 46th Street Theater and runs for 725 performances. **13 March:** *Brigadoon*, another fantasy and the first hit for Lerner and Loewe, opens at the Ziegfeld Theater and runs for 581 performances. **9 October:** *High Button Shoes*, starring Phil Silvers and with a score by Jule Styne (his first work for Broadway) and Sammy Cahn, opens at the Century Theater and runs for

727 performances. **10 October:** *Allegro*, one of Rodgers and Hammerstein's less popular shows, opens at the Majestic Theater.

1948 **7 October:** *Love Life*, an unusual show that foreshadowed the later idea of the "concept musical" with music by Weill and libretto by Lerner, premieres at the 46th Street Theater and runs for 252 performances. **11 October:** *Where's Charley?*, the first Broadway show with music and lyrics by Frank Loesser and starring Bolger, debuts at the St. James Theater and runs for 792 performances. **30 December:** *Kiss Me, Kate*, one of Porter's finest shows, opens at the New Century Theater.

1949 **7 April:** *South Pacific*, one of Rodgers and Hammerstein's strongest musical plays and starring Mary Martin and Ezio Pinza, premieres at the Majestic Theater. **30 October:** *Lost in the Stars*, a serious musical play based on the novel *Cry, the Beloved Country* by Alan Paton with music by Kurt Weill and libretto by Maxwell Anderson, opens at the Music Box Theater for a run of 273 performances. **8 December:** *Gentlemen Prefer Blondes*, featuring a young Carol Channing singing "Diamonds Are a Girl's Best Friend," debuts at the Ziegfeld Theater.

1950 **12 October:** *Call Me Madam*, with a score by Berlin and starring Merman, opens at the Imperial Theater and runs 644 performances. **24 November:** *Guys and Dolls*, a brilliant musical comedy with a score by Loesser and book by Abe Burrows, premieres at the 46th Street Theater.

1951 **29 March:** Rodgers and Hammerstein's *The King and I*, starring Gertrude Lawrence and Yul Brynner, opens at the St. James Theater. **12 November:** *Paint Your Wagon*, the latest show from Lerner and Loewe, opens at the Shubert Theater and plays 289 performances.

1952 **25 June:** *Wish You Were Here*, a musical about a Jewish summer camp with a score by Rome and an actual swimming pool on stage, debuts at the Imperial Theater for a run of 598 performances.

1953 **25 February:** *Wonderful Town*, with a score by Bernstein and libretto by Comden and Green and starring Rosalind Russell, opens at the Winter Garden Theater, running 559 performances. **7 May:** *Can-Can*, featuring a score by Porter (with such songs as "I Love Paris") and dancer Gwen Verdon's first role in a Broadway hit, premieres at the Shubert Theater. **28 May:** *Me and Juliet*, one of Rodgers and Hammerstein's less successful shows, opens at the Majestic Theater. **3 December:** *Kismet*, an Arabian tale with Robert Wright and George Forrest adding lyrics to Alexander Borodin's music, debuts at the Ziegfeld Theater for a run of 583 performances.

1954   **13 May:** *The Pajama Game*, the Broadway debut of choreographer Bob Fosse and first score for a book musical by Richard Adler and Jerry Ross, opens at the St. James Theater. **30 September:** *The Boy Friend*, featuring the Broadway debut of Julie Andrews, opens at the Royale Theater. **20 October:** *Peter Pan*, with an iconic performance by Mary Martin that became famous in television versions, premieres at the Winter Garden Theater. **4 November:** *Fanny*, with a score by Rome and starring Ezio Pinza and Walter Slezak, opens at the Majestic Theater and runs 888 performances.

1955   **24 February:** *Silk Stockings*, a musical with score by Porter and a plot based on the Cold War, debuts at the Imperial Theater and runs 478 performances. **5 May:** *Damn Yankees*, a baseball musical starring Gwen Verdon with a score by Adler and Ross, opens at the 46th Street Theater for 1,019 performances. **20 September:** *The Threepenny Opera*, in Marc Blitzstein's translation of the German original by dramatist Bertolt Brecht and composer Kurt Weill, opens off-Broadway at the Theater de Lys and runs for 2,611 performances, briefly the longest run of an American musical.

1956   **15 March:** *My Fair Lady*, the greatest hit from Lerner and Loewe, premieres at the Mark Hellinger Theater. Its run of 2,717 performances sets the Broadway record for the time. **3 May:** *The Most Happy Fella*, a musical filled with a huge amount of music by Loesser (including "Standing On the Corner"), opens at the Imperial Theater for a run of 676 performances. **15 November:** *Li'l Abner*, based on the famous comic strip, debuts at the St. James Theater for a run of 693 performances. **29 November:** *Bells Are Ringing*, starring Judy Holliday and with a score by Styne, Comden, and Green, opens at the Shubert Theater and runs for 924 performances. **1 December:** *Candide*, a failure in its initial run but remaining popular because of Bernstein's ebullient score, opens at the Martin Beck Theater.

1957   26 September: *West Side Story* premieres at the Winter Garden Theater, demonstrating a complete synthesis of Jerome Robbins's direction and choreography, Arthur Laurents's book, Leonard Bernstein's music, and Stephen Sondheim's lyrics. **19 December:** *The Music Man*, with a score and libretto by Meredith Willson and starring Robert Preston, opens at the Majestic Theater and runs for 1,375 performances.

1958   1 December: *Flower Drum Song*, a musical by Rodgers and Hammerstein taking place in San Francisco's Chinatown, debuts at the St. James Theater and runs 600 performances.

1959   5 February: *Redhead*, starring Gwen Verdon with direction and choreography by Bob Fosse, premieres at the 46th Street Theater for a run of 452 performances. **11 May:** *Once upon a Mattress*, Carol Burnett's Broadway debut, opens at the Phoenix Theater. **21 May:** *Gypsy*, featuring one of Ethel Merman's finest roles, opens at the Broadway Theater. **16 November:** *The Sound of Music*, Rodgers and Hammerstein's final collaboration, premieres at the Lunt-Fontanne Theater. **23 November:** *Fiorello!*, which won the Pulitzer Prize for best drama in 1960, opens at the Broadhurst Theater.

1960   14 April: *Bye Bye Birdie*, a show lampooning Elvis Presley's entrance into the army starring Dick Van Dyke, debuts at the Martin Beck Theater and runs 607 performances. **3 May:** *The Fantasticks*, the longest running musical in the history of the American musical theater, opens at the Sullivan Street Playhouse. Its run of 17,162 performances was entirely off-Broadway. **3 November:** *The Unsinkable Molly Brown*, with score by Willson and starring Tammy Grimes, opens at the Winter Garden Theater and runs for 532 performances. **3 December:** *Camelot*, starring Richard Burton and Julie Andrews and created by Lerner and Loewe, debuts at the Majestic Theater and runs for 873 performances.

1961   13 April: *Carnival!*, the first show to open with Jerry Orbach in a lead role, premieres at the Imperial Theater. **14 October:** *How to*

Succeed in Business Without Really Trying, with score by Loesser and book by Abe Burrows, opens at the 46th Street Theater, running 1,416 performances.

1962 **15 March:** *No Strings*, the only show for which Rodgers wrote music and lyrics, opens at the 54th Street Theater and runs for 580 performances. **22 March:** *I Can Get It for You Wholesale*, featuring the Broadway debut of Barbra Streisand, opens at the Shubert Theater. **8 May:** *A Funny Thing Happened on the Way to the Forum*, the first Broadway show with music and lyrics by Sondheim, opens at the Alvin Theater. **20 October:** *Mr. President*, the last original show with a score by Berlin, premieres at the St. James Theater.

1963 **6 January:** *Oliver!*, a British musical with a score and libretto by Lionel Bart and based on Dickens's *Oliver Twist*, opens at the Imperial Theater for a run of 774 performances.

1964 **16 January:** *Hello, Dolly!*, in which Carol Channing became an icon in the starring role, debuts at the St. James Theater. Its run of 2,844 performances was briefly Broadway's longest. **22 September:** *Fiddler on the Roof*, featuring a great performance by Zero Mostel, bows at the Imperial Theater. Its run of 3,242 performances quickly broke the record set by *Hello, Dolly!*.

1965 **17 October:** *On a Clear Day You Can See Forever*, with a popular title song, music by Burton Lane and libretto by Lerner, opens at the Mark Hellinger Theater and runs for 280 performances. **22 November:** *Man of La Mancha*, starring Richard Kiley, debuts at the ANTA Washington Square Theater, running 2,328 performances.

1966 **29 January:** *Sweet Charity*, starring Gwen Verdon and staged by Fosse with a score by Cy Coleman and Dorothy Fields (including "Big Spender"), opens at the Palace Theater and runs 608 performances. **24 May:** *Mame*, with music and lyrics by Jerry Herman and starring Angela Lansbury, bows at the Winter Garden Theater and runs for 1,508 performances. **20 November:** *Cabaret*, Hal Prince's first hit as a director and Joel Grey's first starring role, opens at the Broadhurst Theater. **5 December:** *I Do! I Do!*, starring Mary Martin and Robert Preston, premieres at the 46th Street Theater and plays 560 performances.

1967   **7 March:** *You're a Good Man, Charlie Brown*, based on the *Peanuts* comic strip, opens off-Broadway at the 80 St. Marks Theater.

1968   **29 April:** *Hair*, the first important rock musical, premieres at the Biltmore Theater. **17 November:** *Zorba*, with music by John Kander, lyrics by Fred Ebb, and book by Joseph Stein, opens at the Imperial Theater and runs 305 performances. **1 December:** *Promises, Promises*, with book by Neil Simon and score by composer Burt Bacharach and lyricist Hal David (including "I'll Never Fall in Love Again"), debuts at the Shubert Theater and runs 1,281 performances.

1969   **16 March:** *1776*, a musical about the writing of the Declaration of Independence with music and lyrics by Sherman Edwards and book by Peter Stone, bows at the 46th Street Theater and runs for 1,217 performances. **18 December:** *Coco*, starring Katherine Hepburn, opens at the Mark Hellinger Theater and runs 329 performances.

1970   **15 March:** *Purlie*, an African American musical starring Cleavon Little and Melba Moore, premieres at the Broadway Theater and runs 688 performances. **30 March:** *Applause*, starring Lauren Bacall, opens at the Palace Theater and plays for 896 performances. **26 April:** *Company*, a musical about marriage with a score by Sondheim and produced by Prince, bows at the Alvin Theater and runs for 705 performances.

1971   **4 April:** *Follies*, the next collaboration by Sondheim and Prince, opens at the Winter Garden Theater. **17 May:** *Godspell*, with a score by Stephen Schwartz, debuts off-Broadway at the Cherry Lane Theater for a long run. **12 October:** *Jesus Christ Superstar*, featuring the Broadway debut of composer Andrew Lloyd Webber and lyricist Tim Rice, opens at the Mark Hellinger Theater.

1972   **14 February:** *Grease*, a nostalgic look at the 1950s that set a Broadway musical record with a run of 3,388 performances, bows at the Eden Theater. **23 October:** *Pippin*, starring Ben Vereen, directed by Fosse, and with a score by Schwartz, opens at the Imperial Theater for a run of 1,944 performances.

1973   25 February: *A Little Night Music*, one of Sondheim's major successes, produced and directed by Prince, premieres at the Shubert Theater.

1974   10 March: A revival of *Candide*, with Hugh Wheeler's new book, Bernstein's score, and Prince's imaginative production, opens at the Broadway Theater and runs 740 performances.

1975   5 January: *The Wiz*, an African American adaptation of *The Wizard of Oz* with a popular score, debuts at the Majestic Theater and runs for 1,672 performances. **7 January:** *Shenandoah*, starring John Cullum, opens at the Alvin Theater and runs for 1,050 performances. **3 June:** *Chicago*, a hugely successful show with score by Kander and Ebb, bows at the 46th Street Theater. **25 July:** After running off-Broadway, *A Chorus Line* opens at the Shubert Theater, directed and choreographed by Michael Bennett. The show ran for 6,137 performances, shattering the existing record.

1976   22 December: *Your Arms Too Short to Box with God*, a gospel-inspired trip through the New Testament book of St. Matthew, premieres at the Lyceum Theater and plays for 429 performances.

1977   29 April: *Annie*, inspired by the comic strip *Little Orphan Annie* and with a score by composer Charles Strouse and lyricist Martin Charnin (including "Tomorrow"), opens at the Alvin Theater and runs for 2,377 performances.

1978   27 March: *Dancin'*, an evening of Fosse's choreography, bows at the Broadhurst Theater and runs for 1,774 performances. **19 June:** *The Best Little Whorehouse in Texas*, one of the most successful shows with musical numbers staged by Tommy Tune, opens at the 46th Street Theater.

1979   11 February: *They're Playing Our Song*, with a book by Neil Simon, premieres at the Imperial Theater and runs for 1,082 performances. **1 March:** *Sweeney Todd: The Demon Barber of Fleet Street*, with music and lyrics by Sondheim and book by Hugh Wheeler and starring Len Cariou and Angela Lansbury, opens at the

Uris Theater and runs for 557 performances. **25 September:** *Evita*, featuring an iconic role for Patti LuPone and Mandy Patinkin's debut in a Broadway musical, bows at the Broadway Theater. **8 October:** *Sugar Babies*, a tribute to old-time vaudeville starring Ann Miller and Mickey Rooney, opens at the Mark Hellinger Theater and runs for 1,208 performances.

1980   25 August: *42nd Street*, directed and choreographed by Gower Champion, opens at the Winter Garden Theater and runs 3,486 performances.

1981   1 March: *Sophisticated Ladies*, a tribute to the music of Duke Ellington starring Gregory Hines, premieres at the Lunt-Fontanne Theater, running 767 performances. **29 March:** *Woman of the Year*, with score by Kander and Ebb and a book by Peter Stone and starring Lauren Bacall, debuts at the Palace Theater and runs 770 performances. **20 December:** *Dreamgirls*, the last show created by director and choreographer Michael Bennett, opens at the Imperial Theater and plays for 1,521 performances.

1982   4 February: *Joseph and the Amazing Technicolor Dreamcoat*, Lloyd Webber and Rice's look at the famous story from Genesis, opens at the Royale Theater and runs for 747 performances. **7 October:** *Cats*, Lloyd Webber's hugely popular adaptation of a children's book by T. S. Eliot, debuts at the Winter Garden Theater and runs for a record 7,485 performances.

1983   21 August: *La Cage aux Folles*, with a score by Herman and one of Broadway's first frank looks at a homosexual relationship, opens at the Palace Theater and runs for 1,761 performances.

1984   2 May: *Sunday in the Park with George*, featuring a score by Sondheim with Bernadette Peters and Mandy Patinkin in the lead roles, opens at the Booth Theater.

1985   25 April: *Big River*, a show based on Twain's *Huckleberry Finn* with a score by Roger Miller, opens at the O'Neill Theater for a run of 1,005 performances.

1986　**10 August:** *Me and My Girl*, a British show from the 1920s that had been recently revived in London, premieres at the Marquis Theater, running 1,420 performances.

1987　**12 March:** *Les Misérables*, adapted from Victor Hugo's novel and produced by Cameron Mackintosh with a score by Claude-Michel Schönberg and Alain Boublil, opens at the Broadway Theater and runs for 6,680 performances. **15 March:** *Starlight Express*, Andrew Lloyd Webber's megamusical about racing trains, bows at the Gershwin Theater and runs for 761 performances. **5 November:** *Into the Woods*, with score by Sondheim and book by James Lapine, opens at the Martin Beck Theater and runs for 765 performances.

1988　**26 January:** *The Phantom of the Opera*, Lloyd Webber's spectacular adaptation of the famous tale, debuts at the Majestic Theater and becomes the longest-running show in Broadway history.

1989　**26 February:** *Jerome Robbins' Broadway*, a retrospective of segments from the director/choreographer's many shows, opens at the Imperial Theater and runs for 633 performances. **12 November:** *Grand Hotel*, staged by Tommy Tune, bows at the Martin Beck Theater and runs for 1,017 performances. **11 December:** *City of Angels*, with book by Larry Gelbart and score by composer Cy Coleman and lyricist David Zippel, opens at the Virginia Theater and runs for 879 performances.

1990　**8 April:** *Aspects of Love*, with music by Lloyd Webber, debuts at the Broadway Theater and runs for 377 performances.

1991　**11 April:** *Miss Saigon*, a modern retelling of the story of Giacomo Puccini's *Madama Butterfly*, premieres at the Broadway Theater for a 10-year run. **25 April:** *The Secret Garden*, based on the famous children's book by the same name, opens at the St. James Theater, playing for 709 performances. **1 May:** *The Will Rogers Follies*, with music by Cy Coleman, lyrics by Comden and Green, and staging by Tommy Tune, premieres at the Palace Theater for a run of 981 performances.

1992　**26 April:** *Jelly's Last Jam*, a fantasy on Jelly Roll Morton's last day on earth starring Gregory Hines, opens at the Virginia Theater for a run of 569 performances.

1993   **22 April:** *The Who's Tommy*, a rock musical based on the film *Tommy*, bows at the St. James Theater and plays for 899 performances. **25 April:** *Blood Brothers*, a British musical about class distinctions, opens at the Music Box Theater and runs for 840 performances. **3 May:** *Kiss of the Spider Woman*, starring Chita Rivera in the title role and staged by Hal Prince, premieres at the Broadhurst Theater and runs for 904 performances.

1994   **18 April:** *Beauty and the Beast*, Disney's first foray into the Broadway musical, opens at the Palace Theater for a long run. **17 November:** *Sunset Boulevard*, with music by Lloyd Webber and starring Glenn Close, debuts at the Minskoff Theater and runs for 977 performances.

1995   **2 March:** *Smokey Joe's Café*, a jukebox musical of 1950s-60s rock-and-roll songs by Jerry Lieber and Mike Stoller, opens at the Virginia Theater for a run of 2,036 performances. **25 October:** *Victor/Victoria*, marking the return of Julie Andrews to Broadway after an absence of more than 30 years, premieres at the Marquis Theater and plays for 734 performances.

1996   **25 April:** *Bring in 'da Noise, Bring in 'da Funk*, offering tap dancing as a metaphor for the African American experience in the United States and starring Savion Glover, opens at the Ambassador Theater and plays for 1,135 performances. **29 April:** *Rent*, Jonathan Larson's popular modern retelling of Giacomo Puccini's *La Bohème*, bows at the Nederlander Theater for a long run. **14 November:** The award-winning and long-running revival of *Chicago* premieres at the Richard Rodgers Theater.

1997   **23 April:** *Titanic*, with book by Peter Stone and score by Maury Yeston, debuts at the Lunt-Fontanne Theater, playing for 804 performances. **28 April:** *Jekyll and Hyde*, with music by Frank Wildhorn and libretto by Leslie Bricusse, opens at the Plymouth Theater and runs for 1,543 performances. **13 November:** *The Lion King*, Disney's second long-running musical, premieres at the refurbished New Amsterdam Theater.

1998 **18 January:** *Ragtime*, with book by Terrence McNally and score by Stephen Flaherty and Lynn Ahrens, opens at the Ford Center and runs for 834 performances. **19 March:** A revival of *Cabaret* debuts at the Kit Kat Club (Henry Miller's Theater) and runs for 2,377 performances. **22 October:** *Footloose*, based on the film of the same name, opens at the Richard Rodgers Theater and runs for 709 performances.

1999 **14 January:** *Fosse*, an anthology of dances from Fosse's shows, premieres at the Broadhurst Theater and runs for 1,093 performances. **7 October:** *Contact*, an evening of dances choreographed by Susan Stroman, bows at the Newhouse Theater and moves to the Broadway-sized Vivian Beaumont Theater on 30 March 2000, where it runs for 1,010 performances.

2000 **23 March:** *Aida*, with music by Elton John and lyrics by Rice, opens at the Palace Theater and runs for 1,852 performances.

2001 **19 April:** *The Producers*, created by Mel Brooks and based on his film of the same name, premieres at the St. James Theater and begins a long run. **2 May:** A revival of *42nd Street* opens at the Ford Center and runs for 1,524 performances. **11 September:** Terrorist attacks on the World Trade Center towers kill more than 2,700 people. Subsequent lack of tourism in New York City produces a huge economic challenge for Broadway. **20 September:** *Urinetown*, a musical created by Mark Hollmann and Greg Kotis about a water shortage, bows at Henry Miller's Theater and runs 965 performances. **18 October:** *Mamma Mia!*, a jukebox musical based on the hits of ABBA, settles in at the Winter Garden Theater for a long run.

2002 **18 April:** *Thoroughly Modern Millie*, based on the 1967 film of the same name, opens at the Marquis Theater and plays for 903 performances. **15 August:** *Hairspray*, based on the 1988 film by John Waters, debuts at the Neil Simon Theater and begins a long run. **24 October:** *Movin' Out*, a jukebox musical based on the songs of Billy Joel with direction and choreography by Twyla Tharp, opens at the Richard Rodgers Theater and runs 1,303 performances.

2003   **1 May:** *Gypsy*, in a revival starring Bernadette Peters, premieres at the Shubert Theater and runs 451 performances. **31 July:** *Avenue Q*, a musical with actors and puppets but with an adult sensibility, opens at the John Golden Theater and begins a long run. **30 October:** *Wicked*, with music and lyrics by Schwartz and starring Kristin Chenoweth, Idina Menzel, and Joel Grey, debuts at the Gershwin Theater. **23 November:** *Wonderful Town* opens at the Al Hirschfeld Theater in a revival starring Donna Murphy, running 497 performances.

2004   **26 February:** A revival of *Fiddler on the Roof* bows at the Minskoff Theater and runs for 781 performances.

2005   **17 March:** *Monty Python's Spamalot*, based on the 1975 film *Monty Python and the Holy Grail*, opens at the Shubert Theater and begins a successful run. **17 March:** *The Light in the Piazza*, with book by Craig Lucas and score by Adam Guettel, premieres at the Vivian Beaumont Theater and runs for 504 performances. **2 May:** *The 25th Annual Putnam County Spelling Bee*, with book by Rachel Sheinkin and score by William Finn, opens at the Circle in the Square Theater and begins a successful run. **6 November:** *Jersey Boys*, a jukebox musical based on Frankie Valli and The Four Seasons, debuts at the August Wilson Theater and begins an extended run. **1 December:** *The Color Purple*, based on the novel and film of the same name, opens at the Broadway Theater.

2006   **1 May:** *The Drowsy Chaperone*, a show that evokes the style of the 1920s, premieres at the Marquis Theater. **9 November:** *Les Misérables* opens in a revival at the Broadhurst Theater. **16 November:** *Mary Poppins*, in a version based on the Disney film, transfers from London and bows at the New Amsterdam Theater. **10 December:** *Spring Awakening*, a show that explores issues of teen sexuality with a rock-based score, opens at the Eugene O'Neill Theater.

Introduction

The Broadway musical has greatly influenced American (and world) culture and likewise has also been influenced by historical forces such as two world wars, the civil rights movement, times of economic prosperity and decline, and, most recently, the terrorist attacks of 11 September 2001. Shows such as *Oklahoma!* and *Annie Get Your Gun* are as "American as apple pie," while the long runs of imports such as *Cats*, *The Phantom of the Opera*, and *Les Misérables* have broken records. Broadway has produced cultural icons such as Ethel Merman, Yul Brynner, and Julie Andrews, and composers such as Irving Berlin, Sigmund Romberg, George Gershwin, Cole Porter, Richard Rodgers, Frank Loesser, Leonard Bernstein, Stephen Sondheim, Andrew Lloyd Webber, and many others have had their melodies sung on its stages. Visionaries including George Abbott, Agnes de Mille, Jerome Robbins, Bob Fosse, Tommy Tune, and Susan Stroman have brought productions to life through their innovative direction and choreography. Through it all, the musical has proven that people want to see music and lyrics applied to life's general sentiments, as characters sing about their pleasures and frustrations. Since the latter part of the 19th century, the Broadway musical has remained one of the most popular genres in entertainment. In the early 21st century, its appeal and draw have become increasingly international.

A SKETCH HISTORY

The Broadway musical was born in substantial confusion in the 19th century, when most American theater was musical, with many plays including interpolated songs and dances, and often an instrumental group in the pit. A number of genres of musical theater existed at the time, but definitions were not hard and fast, and there was considerable overlap between types. The minstrel show, with comedy, songs, and dancing performed by white actors in blackface, existed for most of the 19th century and continued into the 20th. Pantomime had a French flavor, and ballet was popular as well. Musicals with lavish sets and costumes sometimes were called spectacles, a moniker that included such early shows as *The Black Crook* (1866), and shows with more of a comic element were dubbed burlesques, a famous example being *Evangeline* (1874). Operettas from various traditions were also popular, including those from France by such composers as Jacques Offenbach and from Vienna by Johann Strauss II and others. Gilbert and Sullivan's Savoy Operas were especially popular in the United States and extremely influential on the Broadway musical's development.

In the decades around 1900, three major Broadway musical genres gained prominence. The operetta remained important, with a significant exponent of the genre in the United States being Irish-born Victor Herbert. The modern musical comedy—in which comedy and stars were at the forefront—started to appear in the 1890s with such examples as *A Trip to Chinatown* (1891). George M. Cohan codified the type shortly after 1900 with shows like *Little Johnny Jones* (1904), which featured Tin Pan Alley tunes, rampant flag-waving, praise for the Irish, and Cohan's own persona as the fast-talking leading man who sang and danced his way through the evening and always got the girl. Musical comedies often took place in the here and now, in contrast to operettas, which tended to occur in exotic locales and had scores with more demanding singing roles. *The Passing Show* (1894) was the first revue, an evening of skits, songs, and dances based on a central theme and often showing French influence in terms of content. These three genres dominated Broadway stages until about 1930. An important step in the integration of the Broadway musical, where music and dance start to become more important in the storytelling, appeared in the "Princess Theatre Musicals" of the 1910s, nearly all with music by Jerome Kern, lyrics by P. G. Wodehouse, and book by Guy Bolton.

These three genres—musical comedy, operetta, and revue—continued into the 1920s, along with the emergence of the musical play. Dozens of musical comedies appeared each year with scores by songwriters such as Richard Rodgers and Lorenz Hart, George and Ira Gershwin, and Cole Porter. The stories were generally inconsequential, but audiences came to hear new hit songs and appreciated the charisma and talents of such stars as Marilyn Miller, Gertrude Lawrence, and Fred and Adele Astaire. It was also an important decade for operetta, for it not only included the end of Victor Herbert's career (who died in 1924) but was also the era for new, popular hits including *The Student Prince of Heidelberg* (1924) by Sigmund Romberg and *Rose Marie* (1924) by Rudolf Friml. The operetta more or less disappeared from Broadway in the early 1930s, but its popularity continued in Hollywood at least for another decade. A new type of show from the 1920s was *Show Boat* (1927), with music by Jerome Kern and words by Oscar Hammerstein II. It told a serious story with carefully placed songs and dances, making it an early example of the musical play. A continuing development in the 1920s was the revue, often with an emphasis on displaying the female form along with popular singers and dancers. Some producers launched their revues in an annual series, the most famous version of which was the *Ziegfeld Follies*.

The 1930s was a challenging decade for Broadway, with harder economic conditions, but was a time of significant new stars, including Ethel Merman and Mary Martin, and continued brilliant songwriting. Although Hollywood lured several creative teams away from New York, many were bicoastal. The Gershwins did some of their best work in the satirical *Of Thee I Sing* (1931) and their opera *Porgy and Bess* (1935), the latter a financial failure but an enduring contribution to American music. It was also a successful decade for Cole Porter, who wrote, among other works, *Anything Goes* (1934). Toward the end of the decade, Rodgers and Hart produced a series of sophisticated musicals with notable integration of elements, topped off with *On Your Toes* (1936), with its significant use of dance, and *Pal Joey* (1940), one of the first musicals to have an antihero as a male lead. It was also a decade of political agitation on Broadway with the union-produced revue *Pins and Needles* (1937) and Marc Blitzstein's controversial *The Cradle Will Rock* (1938).

The musical play became more important in the 1940s, largely through the efforts of Richard Rodgers and Oscar Hammerstein II, who worked together for the first time on *Oklahoma!* (1943). Before writing a word or a note of the show, Rodgers and Hammerstein discussed the plot in detail and decided where songs and dances could most effectively contribute to the storytelling. The dances, choreographed by

Agnes de Mille, were a major part of the effect. The influence of this type of writing, confirmed by Rodgers and Hammerstein in later shows such as *Carousel* (1945) and *South Pacific* (1949), was immediate. Careful placement of songs and dances and a distinctive sense of music developing from the plot can be observed in many shows over the next few decades from a variety of creators, including, for example: Leonard Bernstein, Betty Comden, and Adolph Green in *On the Town* (1944) and *Wonderful Town* (1953); Irving Berlin in *Annie Get Your Gun* (1946); Alan Jay Lerner and Frederick Loewe in *Brigadoon* (1947) and *My Fair Lady* (1956); Frank Loesser in *Guys and Dolls* (1950) and *The Most Happy Fella* (1956); and Jerry Bock and Sheldon Harnick in *Fiorello!* (1959) and *Fiddler on the Roof* (1964). Broadway producers were faced with an audience's expectation for dramatic stories with a sophisticated use of music and dance. While comedic silliness remained important on Broadway, in many ways the musical play took the Broadway theater away from offering pure entertainment and turned it more toward art. New important major stars emerged as well, including Julie Andrews.

The passing of what could be seen as the Rodgers and Hammerstein era happened gradually in a process that began while that team continued to work. The team's last Broadway show was *The Sound of Music* (1959), which, although somewhat "old-fashioned" when it opened, had a successful run because it effectively exemplified the traits that had come to define the musical play. The new sensibility appeared in what some have called the "concept musical," which can be loosely defined as a show in which linear storytelling becomes less important than the show's overall message, which involves a psychological perception or common life event. Often unusual theatrical devices are used to underline that message. In some ways the category of "concept musical" can be applied to such a large number of shows that its meaning becomes blurred, but it is useful as a way of seeing how the musical play changed. One of the first concept musicals was *Love Life* (1948) by Kurt Weill and Alan Jay Lerner, which was the story of a marriage that lasts for well over a century. Interpolated vaudeville acts commented upon the drama in an effort to help make the point. *Love Life* had limited success, but it illustrated the types of shows that creators wished to try. Rodgers and Hammerstein themselves wrote a sort of concept musical in *Allegro* (1947), but it was unsuccessful and they abandoned such experimentation.

The increased importance of dance and choreographers in musicals in the 1940s and 1950s encouraged experimentation in other directions, finally resulting in *West Side Story* (1957), a show in which the director/choreographer Jerome Robbins told much of the story through dance. The show tells a linear story, but the largely inarticulate characters express themselves primarily through motion, making dance part of the show's "concept."

Experimentation in terms of form and content became even more important in the 1960s and 1970s, finally moving past the concept musical to entirely new types of shows. It should be remembered that traditional musicals, such as *Hello, Dolly!* (1963), also remained popular. An especially innovative concept musical was *Cabaret* (1966), which was directed by Harold Prince and told a compelling story from Berlin in the early 1930s during the Nazis' rise in popularity. Consistent commentary on the plot took place in cabaret acts mostly starring the Master of Ceremonies, who otherwise had no role in the more conventional part of the show. Another well-known concept musical was Stephen Sondheim's *Company* (1970), also directed by Prince. It featured a gleaming, modernistic set of chrome and glass, and commented on the contemporary state of marriage. Sondheim and Prince followed *Company* with *Follies* (1971), a show about the passing of youth. By this time, critics discussed the "plotless musical," an ideal that reached maturity in *A Chorus Line* (1975). In this exceptionally successful tour de force directed and choreographed by Michael Bennett, storytelling was abandoned in favor of musical numbers and monologues for dancers auditioning for a Broadway musical. The audience gets to know several characters exceptionally well, and accepts them singing and dancing about their lives and dreams because that is what they do for a living. Yet another important concept musical from about the same time was *Chicago* (1975), choreographed and directed by Bob Fosse and including production numbers that exist in the characters' imaginations.

A highly experimental show from the late 1960s was *Hair* (1968), one of Broadway's first rock musicals, which also featured nontraditional staging by director Tom O'Horgan, including improvisatory elements, suspension of the "fourth wall" as action came right into the audience, a nude scene, and cast members singing into handheld microphones in the style of a rock concert. *Hair* told a story but also resembled a 1960s communal "happening" with many references to drugs and sex, in effect providing "safe" exposure to the counterculture for middle-class audiences. Despite the show's success, rock has had a checkered history on Broadway with few shows having scores fully in the style. A more recent show billed as a rock musical is *Rent*, but its score also includes a number of other popular styles.

Many Broadway musicals played in London during the 20th century, but few shows that originated in the West End had notable Broadway success before the 1970s. Since that time, Broadway has become an international phenomenon. Earlier British shows that made it on Broadway included *The Boy Friend* (1954) and *Oliver!* (1963), but many believed that the true "invasion" came with the shows with music by Andrew Lloyd Webber, an astoundingly successful composer who has worked with several lyricists. His earliest shows with wordsmith Tim Rice include *Jesus Christ Superstar* (1971) and *Evita* (1979), both solid successes in New York. Lloyd Webber struck gold with *Cats* (1982), a show based on poems by T. S. Eliot. Combining elements of the revue and concept musical and presenting a fantastic world in which fabulously costumed human cats dance and sing in a junkyard, *Cats* played for almost eighteen years in New York and toured endlessly. Lloyd Webber's next major hit, *The Phantom of the Opera* (1988), with lyrics by Charles Hart, was a more conventional show in terms of storytelling, but possessed a huge set and grand sense of spectacle. Like most of Lloyd Webber's shows, *Phantom* is nearly sung throughout, and there are many moments that approach the operatic.

The other major international successes on Broadway have been the shows of composer Claude-Michel Schönberg and lyricist Alain Boublil. Their major hits have been *Les Misérables* (1987) and *Miss Saigon* (1991), both of which are sung throughout and present hard-hitting, dramatic stories. Schönberg shows a wide musical range, from nearly operatic music to pop ballads, and his best tunes rank with some of the finest heard on Broadway. An important collaborator for both *Les Misérables* and *Miss Saigon*, as well as many of Lloyd Webber's shows, is British producer Cameron Mackintosh, a major figure in the development of the so-called megamusical.

The Broadway musical theater of the past two decades has come to depend more on its past glories, and is characterized by many revivals of bankable shows. There have, for example, been long-running new productions of *Chicago* (opened 1996) and *Cabaret* (1998–2004), the latter also representative of the so-called "revisical," a version of a canonical show with strong rethinking in terms of focus and theatrical devices. There will always be interest in reviving previously successful shows with today's major stars, such as *Gypsy* with Tyne Daly (1989) and Bernadette Peters (2003) or *Man of La Mancha* with Brian Stokes Mitchell (2002). Film versions of Broadway musicals have been around since the advent of synchronized sound of film, and in the early 21st century, there has been a renewed interest in the genre as demonstrated in film versions of *Chicago* (2002), *The Phantom of the Opera* (2004), and *Rent* (2005), among others. Various television productions have demonstrated the continued vitality of Broadway shows that are decades old and in musical styles that many consider dated, such as *South Pacific* (2001) and *The Music Man* (2003), but, like Broadway revivals, such projects often involve considerable rethinking of the material. The historic Broadway repertory at this point is like the opera repertory, full of works that remain appealing and will continue to be reconsidered by new generations.

This does not mean, however, that new creativity has been drained from the Broadway stage. Despite those who have been preaching the demise of the American musical (a possibility that has been trumpeted by somebody in each generation for a century or more!), new shows continue to appear, and some are extremely successful. There are fewer new shows, and financial realities make a new musical a bigger risk than it was five decades ago, but Broadway still has producers and creative teams willing to take chances. Broadway's embrace of popular music has included the new "jukebox musicals," where hit songs by a particular songwriter, or those associated with a certain group, comprise the score for a show. Not all such attempts pan out, of course, but several have proven their commercial worth. Successful recent examples of such a show are *Mamma Mia!* (2001) and *Jersey Boys* (2005). Adaptations of films, both live action and animated, have become especially popular, with Disney's Broadway participation causing the opening of such long-running hits as *Beauty and the Beast* (1994) and *The Lion King* (1997). Other recent, successful examples of films that have become stage musicals outside of Disney's camp include *The Producers* (2001), *Hairspray* (2002), *Monty Python's Spamalot* (2005), and *Mary Poppins* (2006). One must observe, however, that the current Broadway scene continues to include new shows based on plays or other creative ideas that find an audience, such as *Avenue Q* (2003), *Wicked* (2003), *The 25th Annual Putnam County Spelling Bee* (2005), and *Spring Awakening* (2006). The huge differences between these four shows alone testify to the continuing vitality and diversity of the Broadway musical stage.

COMPLEXITY AND SPECIALTIES

Few forms of entertainment or art reach the complexity of the musical in terms of the number of specialists involved in its production. Opera is an obvious comparison, but there one does not find as wide a variety of musical types. Film relies on many different specialties as well, but there one does not have the added factor of live theatrical action that must be re-created eight times per week. Major creative figures in a musical include (sometimes with one person performing more than one of these tasks) the composer, the lyricist, the book writer, the director, the choreographer, the set designer, the costume designer, the lighting designer, the conductor, and the orchestrator, not to mention the cast, musicians, and stage crew. The producer oversees the efforts of each specialist, and also raises money and keeps the production within a budget. Some famous Broadway producers have included Cheryl Crawford, David Merrick, and Florenz Ziegfeld.

Broadway composers (such as Irving Berlin, George Gershwin, John Kander, Frederick Loewe, and Richard Rodgers) have traditionally written a piano/vocal score; the musical arrangement for the pit musicians is done by the orchestrator (the most famous in Broadway history to date has been Robert Russell Bennett), and sometimes a separate person creates choral arrangements. Music for dances is often the work of a dance arranger (such as Trude Rittman), who usually draws from themes the composer has already written for the show. Some composers have assisted with orchestrations and/or dance arrangements, such as Leonard Bernstein, Victor Herbert, and Kurt Weill, but usually in the time crunch of producing a musical, when new songs continue to be written well into the rehearsal process, it is not possible for one person to accomplish all the necessary musical tasks.

Some composers also have written lyrics, such as Cole Porter, Stephen Schwartz, Stephen Sondheim, and Meredith Willson, but for most creators Broadway wordsmithing is a separate discipline. Many lyricists, such as Alan Jay Lerner, Oscar Hammerstein II, and the team of Betty Comden and Adolph Green, have often written the entire libretto for a show, including both song lyrics and spoken dialogue (the latter sometimes identified as the book). Other writers have tended to concentrate on books, such as the team of Howard Lindsay and Russel Crouse or Joseph Stein. Directors often have a huge influence on what characters say on stage, and a number of directors, such as George Abbott, either write the book for a show or collaborate on it, sometimes in an uncredited capacity. A major change in the position of director came in the 1940s with the advent of the choreographer/director. Figures such as Bob Fosse, Agnes de Mille, Michael Kidd, Jerome Robbins, Susan Stroman, and Tommy Tune helped make dance a far more important part of the musical by integrating their choreography with other aspects of the show. Harold Prince has been very influential as a Broadway director, although his theatrical career began as a producer.

There have been major figures as well in each of the other creative areas one encounters in a musical. Oliver Smith was a significant set designer who worked on many different shows, as well as having a related career in the ballet world. Jo Meilziner was both a set and lighting designer who worked on many of Broadway's most famous shows. Perhaps Broadway's most storied costume designer was Irene Sharaff. The work of these designers can have major influence on a show's success, and these are components that most critics notice. One considers, for example, the raves at the time accorded to Cecil Beaton's costumes for *My Fair Lady* or the role of Howard Bay's memorable set and lighting design in *Man of La Mancha*. Directors are frequently intimately involved with the designing process.

ART VS. THE BOTTOM LINE

One can never lose sight of the fact that the Broadway musical is both a commercial venture and an art form. The final test of any show is not what it sounds like or looks like, but whether it fills the seats. The genre's history is littered with shows that many respected but few saw, and the temptation to aim too high on an artistic plane for the usual audience member has threatened many Broadway careers. Despite other successes, Harold Prince has acknowledged that his lofty and expensive sets and concepts for *Company* (1970) and *Follies* (1971) hampered their commercial success, and that his career as a producer and director might have been over if *A Little Night Music* (1973) had failed to be a hit. Stephen Sondheim, the composer/lyricist for each of those shows, has long been considered one of Broadway's leading artists, but few of his shows have been moneymakers because of the heavy expectations that he places upon the audience with his sophisticated music and lyrics. Few Broadway creators have enjoyed the commercial success of Andrew Lloyd Webber, but many critics have been reluctant to call him one of the genre's better composers. Histories of individual shows prove that one never really knows whether a particular endeavor will be a hit, but one could generalize that the most successful musicals are those where the creators find a workable balance between artistic and commercial concerns.

Despite the perilous investment history that plagues the Broadway musical, shows continue to open. It is true that millions of dollars are lost when a show closes after a few weeks, but major successes such as *The Phantom of the Opera* and *Wicked* demonstrate that a hit, with the New York production, productions in other major cities, tours, recordings, and sales of souvenirs and other show-related merchandise, can reap huge profits. With the increasingly multinational profile of the musical theater, with both international shows coming to Broadway and American shows playing throughout the world, profits on some of these shows have exceeded what anyone might dare dream. The Broadway musical has changed greatly since the 1860s but remains a viable commodity and beloved type of entertainment in the global environment of the early 21st century.

The Dictionary

– A –

AARONS, ALEXANDER A. (ALSO KNOWN AS ALEX A. AARONS, 1891–1943). Producer, who, with **Vinton Freedley**, worked closely with **George** and **Ira Gershwin**, and brought many of their shows to the stage, including *Lady, Be Good!* (1924), *Oh, Kay!* (1926), and *Girl Crazy* (1930). At the height of the producers' success, they built the Alvin Theater, creating its name from the first letters of their first names (AL + VIN).

ABBOTT, GEORGE (1887–1995). One of the most important directors and producers, "Mr. Abbott," as he was called out of great respect, worked on more than 130 Broadway musicals, from *Jumbo* in 1933 to reworking the book of *Damn Yankees* for the show's 1994 revival. His nearly 107 years on planet Earth had a significant impact on the concept and development of the Broadway musical. He increased the pace of **musical comedy** during the 1930s, and throughout his career worked to increase the integrated role of dance in a Broadway musical, working with legendary choreographers **George Balanchine**, **Jerome Robbins**, and **Bob Fosse** on shows such as *On Your Toes* (1936), *On the Town* (1944), *The Pajama Game* (1954), and *Damn Yankees* (1955). Abbott insisted on creative control, often rewriting a book (with or without credit), and he ruthlessly cut dialogue, songs, and dances that slowed down the proceedings. His approach to the musical influenced noted directors Robbins, Fosse, and **Hal Prince**.

***ABYSSINIA* (20 FEBRUARY 1906, MAJESTIC, 31 PERFORMANCES).** Music by **Will Marion Cook** and **Bert Williams**, lyrics and book by J. A. Shipp and Alex Rogers. The second African

1

American show that the comic team of Bert Williams and **George Walker** brought to Broadway, following *In Dahomey* (1903). In *Abyssinia*, they travel to the African country by that name, where they encounter idealized Africans who speak the King's English. These images were far from the minstrelsy figures that Williams and Walker typically portrayed. The review in the *New York Times* found much to admire: "The piece is far in advance of their last vehicle . . . in costumes, scenery, and effects, while the work of the singers, especially in the choruses, surpasses all their previous efforts." The critic reports that the large audience was very appreciative. Scenic effects, including a live waterfall and re-creation of an African marketplace, were lavish, and the review foretold a long run. This did not materialize, however, and long-running **African American musicals** on Broadway were still a few decades away.

THE ACT **(29 OCTOBER 1977, MAJESTIC, 233 PERFORMANCES).** Music by **John Kander**, lyrics by **Fred Ebb**, book by George Furth, directed by Martin Scorsese. Conceived as a vehicle for **Liza Minnelli**, *The Act* offered what appeared to be a dazzling live performance but became consumed by controversy when the press learned that Minnelli had prerecorded some of the songs so she could simply mouth them in performance. She played Michelle Craig, a film star whose career collapses after her marriage disintegrates but who resurrects herself as a nightclub performer in Las Vegas. George Furth's book was slight, but the creators knew that the audience came to hear Minnelli. Although Martin Scorsese carried director credit, **Gower Champion** replaced him before opening night. Richard Eder panned the book in the *New York Times*, but said of the show, "It is an act, and a splendid one." He called Minnelli's voice a "force," and added that her "strength is her improbability. In full voice she is a great bell in an insecure belfry."

ADAMS, EDITH (BORN ELIZABETH EDITH ENKE, ALSO KNOWN AS EDIE ADAMS, 1927–). Comic actress and singer who created the roles of Eileen Sherwood in *Wonderful Town* (1953), appearing opposite **Rosalind Russell**, and Daisy Mae in *Li'l Abner* (1956), for which she won a **Tony Award** for Best Featured Actress in a Musical.

ADAMS, LEE (1924–). Lyricist and librettist whose credits include *Bye Bye Birdie* (1960); *It's a Bird, It's a Plane, It's Superman!*, a failure from 1966; *Applause* (1970); *Bring Back Birdie* (1981), an ill-fated sequel to *Bye Bye Birdie*; and *Ain't Broadway Grand* (1993), a show based on the life of producer Michael Todd that had a short run. Adams's Broadway shows evoke earlier times in 20th-century American history.

ADLER, RICHARD (1921–). Composer, lyricist, and producer, who, with Jerry Ross, wrote *The Pajama Game* (1954) and *Damn Yankees* (1955). He was producer for a handful of ill-fated shows, including **Richard Rodgers**'s *Rex* (1972), and wrote music and lyrics for *Kwamina* (1961), a show that pleaded for racial tolerance in South Africa and starred his then-wife, **Sally Ann Howes**.

AFRICAN AMERICAN MUSICALS. Shows involving African Americans as either creators or performers or concerning experiences of African Americans have been a mainstay of the Broadway musical throughout the 20th century and into the 21st. *Clorindy, The Origin of the Cakewalk* (1898), *In Dahomey* (1903), and *Abyssinia* (1906) were vehicles for the comic team of **Bert Williams** and **George Walker** and introduced African American elements with increasing dignity to white audiences. **Will Marion Cook** provided music for the productions. *Shuffle Along* (1921), developed from a **vaudeville** sketch, was extremely popular, and its score with music by **Eubie Blake** and lyrics by Noble Sissle included "I'm Just Wild about Harry." African American performers, including **Josephine Baker**, **Adelaide Hall**, **Lena Horne**, and **Ethel Waters**, also appeared in **revue**s, some of which, such as *Blackbirds of 1928* and others in the series, featured all-African American casts. **Jerome Kern** and **Oscar Hammerstein II**'s *Show Boat* (1927) presented a racially integrated cast and had subplots that concerned African American experiences. **George** and **Ira Gershwin**'s *Porgy and Bess* (1935) also dealt with experiences of African Americans and featured an almost exclusively African American cast, though its creators were white. Another white-conceived show involving African Americans was *Cabin in the Sky* (1940, music by **Vernon Duke**); and *Lost in the Stars* (1949, music by **Kurt Weill**) concerned South African apartheid.

More recent **book musical**s with African American dimensions include **Bring In 'Da Noise, Bring In 'Da Funk** (1996), **Ragtime** (1998), **Marie Christine** (1999), and **Caroline, or Change** (2004). **Jukebox musicals** showcasing music and performances by African Americans such as **Ain't Misbehavin'** (1978, featuring the music of Thomas "Fats" Waller) and **Jelly's Last Jam** (1992, featuring the music of Jelly Roll Morton) have been extremely successful. All-black **revivals** of several musicals have also appeared on Broadway, including **Guys and Dolls** in 1976, and the cast of the long-running **Hello, Dolly!** became African American in 1967.

See also BAILEY, PEARL; BATTLE, HINTON; *BIG DEAL*; BLEDSOE, JULES; *BLOOMER GIRL*; *BUBBLING BROWN SUGAR*; *CARMEN JONES*; CARROLL, DIAHANN; *THE COLOR PURPLE*; COOK, WILL MARION; DAVIS, SAMMY, JR.; *DON'T BOTHER ME, I CAN'T COPE*; *DREAMGIRLS*; DUNBAR, PAUL LAWRENCE; DUNCAN, TODD; *FINIAN'S RAINBOW*; *GOLDEN BOY*; *HALLELUJAH, BABY!*; HINES, GREGORY; *JAMAICA*; LITTLE, CLEAVON; McDONALD, AUDRA; MITCHELL, BRIAN STOKES; *THE MULLIGAN GUARDS' BALL*; *NO STRINGS*; PINKINS, TONYA; *PURLIE*; *RAGTIME*; *RAISIN*; *ST. LOUIS WOMAN*; *THE TAP DANCE KID*; UGGAMS, LESLIE; VEREEN, BEN; WILLIAMS, VANESSA; *THE WIZ*; *YOUR ARMS TOO SHORT TO BOX WITH GOD*.

AHRENS, LYNN (1948–). Composer, lyricist, and librettist whose collaborations with composer **Stephen Flaherty** include *Once on This Island* (1990), *My Favorite Year* (1972), **Ragtime** (1998), *Seussical* (2000), and new songs for *Chita Rivera: A Singer's Life* (2005). Flaherty and Ahrens's songs possess a strong sense of dramatic purpose that allow them to be fully integrated into the plot as well as exist as independent entities outside of their original larger contexts.

AIDA (23 MARCH 2000, PALACE, 1,852 PERFORMANCES). Music by **Elton John**; lyrics by **Tim Rice**; book by Linda Woolverton, Robert Falls, and David Henry Hwang; directed by Falls; choreography by Wayne Cilento. Hyperion Theatricals, a division of **Disney Theatrical Productions**, brought the story of Giuseppe Verdi's

opera to Broadway, but with none of its famous score. For the music and lyrics, they turned to pop music giants, helping Disney to strike commercial gold with a show that took a critical drubbing. The new version kept the love triangle of Aida, Amneris, and Rademes, and encased it with a frame story set in a present-day Egyptian museum gallery. **Heather Headley**, as the title character, was one of the few things *New York Times* reviewer **Ben Brantley** liked about the show. He wrote that she had "It—that ineffable, sensual glow . . ." When she sings, according to the critic, "the show springs into vital life, only to sag into its torpor again when she leaves the stage." Brantley's major complaint is the show's lack of consistency of tone, careening between campiness and tragedy. As has often been the case in the era of the **megamusical**, however, the sophisticated Broadway critic did not appreciate the show. The public loved Tim Rice's lyrics and Elton John's score, which Brantley felt was "too similar throughout." Brantley also disliked the book, but its very blandness guaranteed a pleasing result for the average audience member. Brantley compared the set to Las Vegas, but people love such glitz. (One of the show's visual highlights was a vertical swimming pool on the stage's back wall.) *Aida* was a commercial triumph that played for more than four years, a critic-proof show designed for such a distinction.

***AIN'T MISBEHAVIN'* (9 MAY 1978, LONGACRE, 1,604 PERFORMANCES).** Primarily based on music and lyrics by Fats Waller, music supervision by pianist Luther Henderson. A highly successful revue of tunes that Fats Waller either wrote or performed. Conceived by Murray Horowitz and Richard Malty Jr., *Ain't Misbehavin'* achieved its long run and wide appeal on the strength of Waller's appealing songs and a cast of energetic performers, including pianist Luther Henderson, who also did the arrangements and orchestrations. In his review in the *New York Times*, Richard Eder singled out cast members Nell Carter, Armelia McQueen, and **Ken Page** for special praise. The songs appeared as either independent songs or in skits. The functional set consisted of Henderson and his moving piano. Eder found the show to be "a whole cluster of marvels" and "heartstopping," a show that "no self-respecting audience could let . . . go on without interrupting it continuously." *See also* AFRICAN AMERICAN MUSICALS.

ALBERT, EDDIE (BORN EDWARD ALBERT HEIMBERGER, 1906–2005). Although perhaps best known as the star of the 1960s sitcom *Green Acres*, Albert possessed a strong high baritone voice (as heard in the theme song for *Green Acres*). He appeared in *The Boys from Syracuse* (1938), where his songs included "This Can't Be Love" and "Dear Old Syracuse"; and *Miss Liberty* (1949), introducing the **Irving Berlin** standard "Let's Take an Old-Fashioned Walk."

ALDA, ROBERT (1914–1986). With a career rooted in **vaudeville**, radio, and film, Alda was also active on Broadway and appeared in two musicals. He won the **Tony Award** for Best Actor in a Musical in 1951 for his portrayal of Sky Masterson in *Guys and Dolls* and played Al Manhaim in *What Makes Sammy Run?* (1964).

ALEXANDER, JASON (BORN JASON SCOTT GREENSPAN, 1959–). Actor known for his work on television, film, and stage who won the 1989 **Tony Award** for Best Actor in a Musical for *Jerome Robbins' Broadway*. He also appeared in *Merrily We Roll Along* (1981) and *The Rink* (1984). He is best known for playing George Constanza on the television series *Seinfeld*.

***ALLEGRO* (10 OCTOBER 1947, MAJESTIC, 315 PERFORMANCES).** Music by **Richard Rodgers**, lyrics and book by **Oscar Hammerstein II**, choreographed and directed by **Agnes de Mille**, produced by Lawrence Langner and Theresa Helburn. Although it was Rodgers and Hammerstein's first show with an original book (by Hammerstein) and included a number of innovative features, *Allegro* was one of the team's least successful works. The show broke ground as the first "concept" musical (even before the idea had been described) but never lived up to expectations or its record advance ticket sales as the "next" R&H musical. Hammerstein's original story, partially based on his own experiences, chronicled the life of physician Joseph Taylor Jr. (John Battles) from birth through middle age. (Hammerstein had originally conceived a cradle-to-grave story.) The show's "concept" included minimal sets, rear screen projections, a Greek chorus, and songs wrapped in dialogue (patterned after "If I Loved You" from *Carousel*). Agnes de Mille, as one of the first director-choreographers, helped to pave the way for **Bob Fosse** and

Jerome Robbins but struggled with the enormous cast of *Allegro*. The New York critics were mixed, but **Brooks Atkinson** of the *New York Times* appreciated the show: "Before the mood breaks after the first act it is full of a kind of unexploited glory." He proclaimed that the show comes close to "the final splendor of a perfect work of art." Dance critics applauded de Mille's choreography. The score included "So Far" and "The Gentleman Is a Dope." *Allegro* has seldom been revived, and Hammerstein was reworking the play for television at the time of his death.

ALLEN, FRED (1894–1956). Comedian who began his career in **vaudeville** before appearing on Broadway in **revues**, including *The Passing Show* of 1922, *The Little Show* (1929), and *Three's A Crowd* (1930), and achieving tremendous fame as a radio humorist.

ALLEN, PETER (1944–1992). Composer, lyricist, and performer whose Broadway musical *Legs Diamond* (1988) was a colossal flop but whose life and songs (including "I Honestly Love You" and "Don't Cry Out Loud") formed the basis for *The Boy from Oz* (1998, Sydney; 2003, New York), in which **Hugh Jackman** made his Broadway debut.

ALL SHOOK UP **(24 MARCH 2005, PALACE, 213 PERFOR-MANCES).** Book by Joe DiPietro. A **jukebox musical** featuring the songs of Elvis Presley, the show takes place during a 24-hour period in summer 1995 in a "small, you-never-heard-of-it town somewhere in the Midwest."

ALLYSON, JUNE (BORN ELEANOR GEISMAN, 1917–2006). Singing actress on stage and screen whose Broadway credits include multiple roles in the **revue** *Sing Out the News* (1938), June in *Very Warm for May* (1939, music by **Jerome Kern**), Dancing Girl in *Panama Hattie* (1940), and Minerva in *Best Foot Forward* (1941).

ALTON, ROBERT (ROBERT ALTON HART, 1897–1957). A dancer and choreographer who was one of the first to use the term "choreographer" as opposed to "dance director." He broke up the tra-ditional chorus line, replacing it and filling the stage with small groups of people doing different things. Credits include *Anything Goes* (1934), *Leave It to Me!* (1938), *Panama Hattie* (1940), *Pal Joey* (1940), and *By Jupiter* (1942). In addition to his work on Broadway, Alton choreographed several films, including many of MGM's classic movie musicals of the 1940s.

AMERICA'S SWEETHEART (10 FEBRUARY 1931, BROAD-HURST, 135 PERFORMANCES). Music by **Richard Rodgers**, lyrics by **Lorenz Hart**, book by **Herbert Fields**. Although not one of Rodgers and Hart's best shows, *America's Sweetheart* managed to have a decent run. The plot is a satire of Hollywood that follows a leading man and woman who are in love and are trying to make the transition from silent films to talkies. Geraldine March (Harriette Lake, known as Ann Sothern in Hollywood) reveals a lisp and cannot speak on film, while Michael Perry (Jack Whiting) finds success with sound. He shows his continuing loyalty to Geraldine by escorting her to his latest premiere. Fields's book took a satirical look at Hollywood, but reviewer J. Brooks Atkinson in the *New York Times* found problems, noting that the plot compared unfavorably to *Once in a Lifetime* by Moss Hart and George S. Kaufman, also a Hollywood satire. He was most critical of the second act, which "falls pretty well to pieces." Atkinson felt that Rodgers and Hart "have acquitted themselves most creditably. There is a rush about the music and a mocking touch in the lyrics . . ."

ANDERSON, JOHN MURRAY (1886–1954). Dancer and society emcee who directed and staged sumptuous productions between the 1910s and 1950s, including *The Greenwich Village Follies* (1919–24) and *Dearest Enemy* (1925).

ANDERSON, MAXWELL (1888–1959). Author, playwright, and librettist who worked with **Kurt Weill** on *Knickerbocker Holiday* (1938) and *Lost in the Stars* (1949). He addressed contemporary sociopolitical issues in his libretti and lyrics, namely Franklin D. Roosevelt and his cabinet in *Knickerbocker Holiday* and South African apartheid in *Lost in the Stars*.

ANDREWS, JULIE (BORN JULIA WELLS, 1935–). Her four-octave range and crystalline sound, along with her classic beauty and

impeccable sense of timing, made her one of the leading musical theater actresses of all time. Born in England, she made her Broadway
debut in *The Boy Friend* (1954). **Alan Jay Lerner** and **Frederick
Loewe** were among the many captivated by her talents, and she
starred in two of their most famous shows, *My Fair Lady* (1956, as
Eliza Doolittle) and *Camelot* (1960, as Guenevere). She was also
popular in Hollywood, starring in **Richard Rodgers** and **Oscar
Hammerstein II**'s television musical *Cinderella*, *Mary Poppins*, and
the film version of *The Sound of Music*. She returned to Broadway
in 1993 in the **Stephen Sondheim revue** *Putting It Together*, and in
1996, reprised the title role she created in the film *Victor/Victoria*.
Her precise intonation and innate ability to shape a musical line have
garnered her immense respect.

ANIMAL CRACKERS **(23 OCTOBER 1928, 44TH STREET, 191
PERFORMANCES).** Music and lyrics by Bert Kalmar and Harry
Ruby, book by **George S. Kaufman** and **Morrie Ryskind**, produced
by **Sam H. Harris**. The monument to the Marx Brothers and their inspired clowning is most famous from its 1930 film version. Kaufman
and Ryskind knew that their material would be subjected to the star
family's improvisatory spirit, and songs would be of secondary importance. As **J. Brooks Atkinson** reported in the *New York Times*,
"Whatever the plot or background might be these scurrilous mimes
remain very much themselves." One famous song from the show was
"Hooray for Captain Spalding," which remained associated with
Groucho Marx throughout his career.

ANNIE **(21 APRIL 1977, ALVIN, 2,377 PERFORMANCES).** Music
by Charles Strouse, lyrics and direction by Martin Charnin, book by
Thomas Meehan, choreography by Peter Gennaro. Based upon the
comic strip *Little Orphan Annie*, *Annie* took audiences on a nostalgic
trip back to 1933, when a little orphan goes all the way to President
Franklin Delano Roosevelt's cabinet, where she helps launch the
New Deal. Annie, played by **Andrea McArdle**, is just another unfortunate orphan in the care of Miss Hannigan (**Dorothy Loudon**),
who detests her charges. Annie remains certain that her parents are
alive and searching for her; she plots an escape (when she meets her
dog, Sandy), but is unsuccessful. She avoids Miss Hannigan's reprisal
because of a visit from Grace Farrell (Sandy Faison), secretary to

billionaire Oliver Warbucks (**Reid Shelton**). Warbucks wants an orphan with whom to share Christmas, and Farrell chooses Annie. She completely wins Warbucks over, and he decides to adopt her. Annie, however, is unwilling as long as there is hope that her parents survive. Warbucks launches a campaign to find them, causing Miss Hannigan's shifty brother and his girlfriend to pose as her parents to collect the reward. With the help of President Roosevelt and J. Edgar Hoover of the Federal Bureau of Investigation (FBI), Warbucks discovers that Annie's parents have died, so the imposters fail and Warbucks adopts Annie.

It is a sentimental story that involves cute little girls, a dog, and Christmas—enough to send a cynic running for cover—but the creators made it work with many light scenes, laughs, and a dash of social commentary. The seven orphans sang and danced through several numbers and offered other enjoyable moments. Of the adults, Dorothy Loudon was memorable as the leering, boozing Miss Hannigan, and Reid Shelton was a steady and appealing Warbucks. Writing in the *New York Times*, Clive Barnes admitted that he usually shares W. C. Fields's attitude about children and dogs on stage, but he described *Annie* as "whimsically charming" and "an intensely likable musical." He comments on the many "cute but appealing references to the period" in the book and describes the music as "tuneful and supportive . . . neither unduly inventive nor memorable, but . . . distinctly pleasing." Barnes only disliked Charnin's lyrics, which he found "bland."

Barnes was not overwhelmed by Charles Strouse's score, but the song "Tomorrow" is one of the biggest hits to emanate from Broadway in the past three decades. There were other songs that assisted greatly with characterization, including Annie's "Maybe," the orphans' "The Hard-Knock Life," and Miss Hannigan's "Little Girls." The reprise of "Tomorrow" with Roosevelt's cabinet could have been one of the campier moments in Broadway history, but instead is genial and funny, an example of the show's irresistible spirit that kept the Alvin Theater filled for more than five years. An off-Broadway sequel, *Annie Warbucks*, appeared in 1993.

***ANNIE GET YOUR GUN* (16 MAY 1946, IMPERIAL, 1,147 PERFORMANCES).** Music and lyrics by **Irving Berlin**, book by **Her-**

bert and **Dorothy Fields**, directed by **Joshua Logan**, produced by **Richard Rodgers** and **Oscar Hammerstein II**. Conceived as a vehicle for **Ethel Merman**, *Annie Get Your Gun* proved a great success in its own right, and remained in the professional repertory for decades without its famed star. Producers Rodgers and Hammerstein asked **Jerome Kern** to write the score, but the composer's unexpected death kept this plan from materializing. Instead, Irving Berlin came in and wrote his finest dramatic score. Herbert and Dorothy Fields penned an effective book with interesting characterization and situations based upon the life of Annie Oakley, the famous sharpshooter who became a star in Buffalo Bill Cody's "Wild West Show." She falls in love with marksman Frank Butler (**Ray Middleton**), but he is unable to look past her superior shooting ability. Chief Sitting Bull (Harry Bellaver), also in the "Wild West Show" and a friend of Annie's, convinces her that she will have to lose a shooting contest with Frank to win his heart. She does, and the story ends happily.

Critics for the most part raved about *Annie Get Your Gun*, citing the fabulous score (with many true hits), the carefully crafted book, Merman's strong presence, a good supporting cast, and fine production values. Writing for the *New York Times*, Lewis Nichols admitted most of these things (except he disliked the book), but much of the show he damned with faint praise. He called it a "good professional Broadway musical" with a "pleasant score" that provides an "agreeable evening on the town." Nichols admits that *Annie Get Your Gun* will run for "many months" with "Ethel Merman to roll her eyes and to shout down the rafters."

Berlin was worried when he decided to write the score that he could fulfill what he saw as new expectations in making songs fit a plot. This was after Rodgers's and Hammerstein's *Oklahoma!* and *Carousel*. Berlin need not have worried. *Annie Get Your Gun* is an old-fashioned musical comedy but one whose songs meet the dramatic needs of the libretto. This is apparent in "Doin' What Comes Natur'lly," where we meet an innocent and uneducated Annie trying to provide for her siblings with her shooting ability. Another song that fits its dramatic needs is "I'm an Indian Too," although this song is problematic today because of its negative Native American stereotypes. The songs between Annie and Frank work extremely well, with "Anything You Can Do" being the humorous highlight. "There's

No Business Like Show Business" has become an anthem for the entire entertainment industry, yet another of Berlin's songs to become a ubiquitous part of popular culture.

ANTHOLOGY MUSICAL. *See* JUKEBOX MUSICAL/ANTHOLOGY MUSICAL.

ANYONE CAN WHISTLE **(4 APRIL 1964, MAJESTIC, 9 PERFORMANCES).** Music and lyrics by **Stephen Sondheim**, book and staging by **Arthur Laurents**, choreography by Herbert Ross. An early failure for Sondheim, Laurents's original story involved a town with little industry that fabricates a miracle of water pouring from a rock. Inmates from the local asylum, seeking a cure, discover the ruse, showing how one can learn from madness. **Howard Taubman** in the *New York Times* found that "Laurents's book lacks the fantasy that would make the idea work . . ." He praised Ross's choreography and the cast, which included **Angela Lansbury** and Lee Remick, and noted that Sondheim wrote "several pleasing songs but not enough of them to give the musical wings."

ANYTHING GOES **(21 NOVEMBER 1934, ALVIN, 420 PERFORMANCES).** Music and lyrics by **Cole Porter**, book by **Guy Bolton** and **P. G. Wodehouse** and revised by **Howard Lindsay** and **Russel Crouse**, staged by Lindsay, dances and ensembles arranged by **Robert Alton**, produced by **Vinton Freedley**. One of the most memorable musical comedies of the 1930s with Cole Porter's overall best score before *Kiss Me, Kate* and a famous performance by **Ethel Merman**, *Anything Goes* suffered a difficult production history. Guy Bolton and P. G. Woodhouse wrote a book about a shipwreck, but then the *Morro Castle* burned off Asbury Park, killing 125 people and making their book unusable. Bolton and Woodhouse, meanwhile, had moved on to another show. Howard Lindsay and Russel Crouse then came together, launching a hugely successful joint writing career that later included *Life with Father*. They revised the book around existing songs, sets, and principals, producing a show full of smart comedy, good characters, and some dreadful puns. Public Enemy No. 13 (**Victor Moore**), dressed as a minister, has boarded the ship and provides some hilarious clowning. Joining him are a famous ex-evangelist and current bar hostess, Reno Sweeney (Ethel Merman), a society girl named Hope Harcourt (Bettina Hall) who is engaged to an English nobleman (Leslie Barrie) who Reno Sweeney ends up marrying, and the stowaway Billy Crocker (**William Gaxton**) who loves Hope. All ends happily for these couples, and Public Enemy No. 13 at the end of the show has been removed from the "Most Wanted" list because he has been classified as harmless.

A major contributor to the show's success was Donald Oenslager's set, which presented the ship on three different levels, allowing, among other things, ample room for chorus girls in bathing suits to dance. Porter's score encompassed a number of hits such as the jaunty title number, the revival anthem "Blow, Gabriel, Blow," the Latin-tinged "All Through the Night," the ballad "I Get a Kick Out of You," and "You're the Top," a truly wonderful list song. **Brooks Atkinson** raved about the show in the *New York Times*. He praised all of the creators for producing "a show . . . off the top shelf of the pantry cupboard" with material so well suited to the performers that the cast seems to have produced it themselves. Victor Moore is "tremendously funny" and Ethel Merman sings with "swaggering authority." William Gaxton goes through many disguises, "fairly dances with high spirits," and forms a wonderful duet with Merman in "You're the Top," which is "one of the most congenial songs" that Porter has ever written. He also appreciates Bettina Hall, the fine soprano who sang "All Through the Night," the chorus, the costumes, and the sets.

APPLAUSE (30 MARCH 1970, PALACE, 896 PERFORMANCES). Music by Charles Strouse, lyrics by Lee Adams, book by **Betty Comden** and **Adolph Green**. Based on the film *All About Eve*, *Applause* was a vehicle for **Lauren Bacall**. She plays Margo Channing, a star who helps a young actress, Eve Harrington (Penny Fuller). Eve cleverly works her way into most facets of Margo's life and cozies up to her friends. She becomes Margo's understudy and eventually takes away her lead role. Margo retires and marries her director, Bill Sampson (**Len Cariou**). The book by Comden and Green was cynical and effective, including many of what **Clive Barnes** called in the *New York Times* "bitchily inspired show-biz wisecracks," helping to make the overall effect "bright, witty, direct and nicely punchy." They gave Lauren Bacall a rich role. Barnes terms her "a sensation" who "sings with all the misty beauty of an on-tune foghorn" and carries herself like an experienced star. Bacall's rival, Penny Fuller, projected the right level of ambition. Barnes finds the main problem to be Strouse's music, which is simple and not adequately interesting. The one song from *Applause* that reached a level of popularity was the title tune, but another memorable moment was the musical scene surrounding "But Alive," when Margo Channing goes to a gay bar to find some solace.

THE APPLE TREE **(18 OCTOBER 1966, SHUBERT, 463 PERFORMANCES).** Music by **Jerry Bock**, lyrics by **Sheldon Harnick**, book by Harnick and Bock with additional material by Jerome Coopersmith. An unusual evening of three short musicals based on short stories, *The Apple Tree* ran for almost 14 months. The source for the first half was Mark Twain's "The Diary of Adam and Eve," with Alan Alda and **Barbara Harris** in the title roles and Larry Blyden as the snake. The second half included the other two shorts, the first based on Frank R. Stockton's "The Lady and the Tiger" and the second on Jules Feiffer's "Passionella." Most critics preferred the first half, with Alda playing a nervous husband who must make a living and Harris a housewife who tries to make their lives more interesting. A **revival** starring **Kristin Chenoweth** and Brian d'Arcy James opened in December 2006.

ARDEN, EVE (BORN EUNICE QUEDENS, 1908–1990). Comic actress known primarily for her screen roles who made her Broadway debut in *Ziegfeld Follies* of 1934. She also appeared in the 1936 edition of the *Follies* and other **revues**. She played Winnie Spofford in the **musical comedy** *Very Warm for May* (1939) and Maggie Watson in *Let's Face It!* (1941).

ARLEN, HAROLD (BORN HYMAN ARLUCK, 1905–1986). Arlen began his Broadway career as a rehearsal pianist and collaborated with lyricist Ted Koehler on songs such as "Stormy Weather" and "I've Got a Right to Sing the Blues" that were sometimes used as **interpolations** in **revues**. His first Broadway show, with lyrics by **E. Y. Harburg**, was *Life Begins at 8:40* (1934). After time in Hollywood writing songs for movie musicals, including "Over the Rainbow" for

The Wizard of Oz (1939), he returned to Broadway, where his work included *House of Flowers* (1954), for which he wrote the music and collaborated with Truman Capote on the lyrics, and the **Lena Horne** vehicle *Jamaica* (1957). He is especially remembered for his sophisticated melodies and range of evocative musical styles.

ARONSON, BORIS (ca. 1900–1980). Innovative scenic designer who won **Tony Awards** for the musicals *Cabaret* (1966), *Zorba* (1968), *Company* (1970), *Follies* (1971), and *Pacific Overtures* (1976). He designed sets for many shows from the 1930s through the 1970s, including *Cabin in the Sky* (1940), *Love Life* (1948), *Do Re Mi* (1960), *Fiddler on the Roof* (1964), and *A Little Night Music* (1973).

ARTHUR, BEATRICE (BORN BERNICE FRANKEL, ALSO KNOWN AS BEA ARTHUR, 1923–). The versatile comic actress with a distinctive low range created the roles of Yente the matchmaker in *Fiddler on the Roof* (1964) and Vera Charles in *Mame* (1966). She won a **Tony Award** for *Mame*, in which she sang "The Man in the Moon Is a Lady" and, with **Angela Lansbury**, "Bosom Buddies." She is also known for television work, including lead roles in *Maude* and *The Golden Girls*.

ASHMAN, HOWARD (1951–1991). Lyricist, librettist, playwright, and director whose greatest work lies in fantasy-based moralities on which he collaborated with composer **Alan Menken**: *Little Shop of Horrors* (1982) and *Beauty and the Beast* (1994). Ashman's lyrics blended the fantastic elements of the shows with contemporary reality. Also with Menken, he wrote lyrics for the **Disney** film *The Little Mermaid* (1989).

ASPECTS OF LOVE (8 APRIL 1990, BROADHURST, 377 PER-FORMANCES). Music by **Andrew Lloyd Webber**, lyrics by Don Black and Charles Hart, directed by **Trevor Nunn**, choreography by **Gillian Lynne**. Based on David Garnett's 1955 novella, *Aspects of Love*, which opened in London in 1989, was a show about four bed-hopping Europeans in the years following World War II. A middle-aged English playboy (Kevin Colson) and his nephew (**Michael Ball**, who created the role in London) cavort variously with a French actress (Ann Crumb), her daughter (Danielle Du Clos), and an Italian artist (Kathleen Rowe McAllen). The couplings are both straight and lesbian, but Frank Rich noted in the *New York Times* that "What neither Mr. Lloyd Webber nor his collaborators can provide is a semblance of the humanity that is also, to some, an aspect of love." He finds a streak of misogyny in Lloyd Webber's shows and sees it quite on display in *Aspects of Love*. The show is sung throughout, with the most recognizable song emerging from the score being "Love Changes Everything." As is his wont, Lloyd Webber reprised the tunes regularly, causing one reviewer to count the repetitions.

ASSASSINS **(22 APRIL 2004, STUDIO 54, 101 PERFORMANCES).** Music and lyrics by **Stephen Sondheim**, book by John Weidman. Although it first appeared at Playwrights Horizons in 1990, *Assassins* did not play on Broadway until 2004. A production was scheduled for fall 2001, but was canceled after the 9/11 attacks on the World Trade Center. Incorporating aspects of both the **revue** and the **concept musical**, the show tells the tales of people who have attempted, both successfully and unsuccessfully, to assassinate American presidents. Each assassin's story is told through song and spoken dialogue. The show gravitates toward "Another National Anthem," in which the assassins collectively assert their identity as the outsiders of American society. The rage of the assassins consumes the folksy Balladeer (Neil Patrick Harris), who had been helping tell their stories. He is reborn in the final scene as Lee Harvey Oswald as the assassins surround him, encouraging him to fire on John Fitzgerald Kennedy's motorcade and bringing meaning to their collective identity. The various assassins' tales are set to music appropriate of their eras, such as the vapid 1970s-style ballad "Unworthy of Your Love," sung by John Hinckley to Jodie Foster and Squeaky Fromme to Charles Manson. Other songs join the characters together across time and space—a notable example being "Gun Song," a bubbly waltz with lyrics about the power of a gun to change the world, and "Everybody's Got the Right," the revue-like number that opens and closes the show. **Michael Cerveris** won the 2004 **Tony Award** for Best Actor in a Musical for his portrayal of John Wilkes Booth, and the production won several other Tonys, including Best Revival of a Musical.

ASTAIRE, ADELE (BORN ADELE AUSTERLITZ, 1896?–1981). After establishing herself as a significant star with her brother, **Fred Astaire**, Adele retired from the stage to marry Lord Charles Cavendish after the successful run of *The Bandwagon* (1931). *See also* **ASTAIRE, FRED**.

ASTAIRE, FRED (BORN FREDERICK AUSTERLITZ, 1899–1987). The legendary dancer began his Broadway career with his sister, **Adele Astaire**. The team starred in **revues**, including *Over the Top* (1917) and *The Passing Show of 1918*, and **musical comedies** such as *Lady, Be Good!* (1924) and *Funny Face* (1927). Astaire's nimble and virtuosic dancing and silky vocal style made him one of the greatest stage and screen actors of the 20th century. After his sister left the stage in the early 1930s, he became a dancing-singing star of film musicals, partnering most famously with **Ginger Rogers**.

AS THOUSANDS CHEER (30 SEPTEMBER 1933, MUSIC BOX, 400 PERFORMANCES). Music and lyrics by **Irving Berlin**, book by **Moss Hart**, staged and lighted by **Hassard Short**, produced by **Sam H. Harris**. Produced in the midst of the Great Depression, *As Thousands Cheer* was a brilliant success that ran nearly a year. The stars included **Marilyn Miller**, **Clifton Webb**, Helen Broderick, and **Ethel Waters**. Hart's assorted and inspired skits included President and Mrs. Herbert Hoover in their last bitter days in office, John D. Rockefeller Jr. trying to give his father Radio City Music Hall for his 94th birthday, **Noel Coward** causing problems for a hotel staff, and an **African American** woman (Waters) lamenting her husband's lynching. The introduction to each skit was a projected newspaper headline. **Brooks Atkinson**, writing in the *New York Times*, noted that "Mr. Hart has never turned his wit with such economical precision." Berlin's score was one of his finest, and featured the songs "Easter Parade," "Heat Wave," Not for All the Rice in China," and "Supper Time," the latter serving as Ethel Waters's lament.

ATKINSON, BROOKS (ALSO KNOWN AS J. BROOKS ATKINSON, 1894–1984). Theater critic for the *New York Times* from 1925 to 1960. Atkinson was known for his commitment to theatrical innovations and was a strong advocate of **off-Broadway** during the 1950s. In 1960, the year he retired, the Mansfield Theatre at 256 W. 47th St. was renamed the Brooks Atkinson Theatre.

ATTERIDGE, HAROLD (1886–1938). Staff lyricist and librettist for the **Shuberts** who contributed to their **revues**, including various editions of *The Passing Show*, and **musical comedies**, including several starring **Al Jolson** (*The Honeymoon Express* [1913], *Sinbad* [1918], and *Bombo* [1921]). He also worked on adaptations of Central European **operettas** for Broadway such as *The Blue Paradise* (1915). Among his musical collaborators were composers **Harry Carroll** and **Sigmund Romberg**.

AUBERJONOIS, RENE (1940–). Actor who created the role of Sebastian Baye, Broadway's first openly gay character, in *Coco* (1969) and received a **Tony Award** for Best Featured Actor in a Musical for his performance. Noted for his comic abilities and nimble physique, other musical roles include The Duke in *Big River* (1985), Irving S. Irving in *City of Angels* (1989), and Professor Abronsius in *Dance of the Vampires* (2002). He is also known for his nonmusical roles and his work on television, including the series *Benson* (Clayton) and *Star Trek: Deep Space Nine* (Odo).

AVENUE Q **(31 JULY 2003, GOLDEN, 1,428 PERFORMANCES AS OF 31 DECEMBER 2006).** Music and lyrics by Robert Lopez and Jeff Marx, book by Jeff Whitty. The winner of the 2003 **Tony Awards** for Best Musical and Best Score, *Avenue Q* is a witty, entertaining musical geared toward urbanites in their twenties and thirties who grew up with *Sesame Street*. The combination of puppets and humans address themes such as **racism**, **homosexuality**, and social responsibility. The appealing score evokes the song styles of *Sesame Street*, albeit with adult-oriented lyrics. Songs such as "What Do You Do with a B.A. in English?," "It Sucks to Be Me," "If You Were Gay," "Everyone's A Little Bit Racist," "The Internet Is for Porn," and "Schadenfreude" have easily memorable tunes and lyrics and capture the overall spirit of the show. *See also* SOCIAL JUSTICE/INJUSTICE.

AVIAN, BOB (ALSO KNOWN AS ROBERT AVIAN). Choreographer, producer, director, and performer who won **Tony Awards** for Best Choreography for *A Chorus Line* (1975) and *Ballroom* (1978). He also played the Grand Duke Alexandrovitch in *Coco* (1969), produced *Dreamgirls* (1981), conceived the musical staging for *Miss Saigon* (1991) and *Sunset Boulevard* (1994), and directed the 2006 revival of *A Chorus Line*.

– B –

BABES IN ARMS **(14 APRIL 1937, SHUBERT, 289 PERFORMANCES).** Music by **Richard Rodgers**, lyrics by **Lorenz Hart**, book by Rodgers and Hart, choreography by **George Balanchine**. *Babes in Arms* featured one of Rodgers and Hart's best scores in the service of young talent. The simple plot worked wonders. Children of vaudeville performers have the choice of putting on a show or going to a work farm. They put on the show, but it is a financial failure and they end up at the work farm anyway. Their savior is a French aviator who completes his transatlantic flight with an emergency landing on the farm. The cast included **Alfred Drake**, **Mitzi Green**, Ray Heatherton, **Robert Rounseville**, Dan Dailey, and others. In addition to the show-within-a-show, there was also a dream ballet (one of Balanchine's major contributions) in which the kids met major Hollywood stars. **Brooks Atkinson** wrote an appreciative review in the *New York Times*, offering the following unlikely praise because he finds the show so very fresh: "There is very little of Broadway in it." He believes that the book is "not inspired," but "full of good feeling." He called the music "one of the most contagious scores Rodgers and Hart have written," not surprising since the show included such classics as "Where or When," "The Lady Is a Tramp," "Johnny One Note," "My Funny Valentine," and "I Wish I Were in Love Again."

BABES IN TOYLAND **(13 OCTOBER 1903, MAJESTIC, 192 PERFORMANCES).** Music by **Victor Herbert**, lyrics and book by Glen MacDonough, directed by **Julian Mitchell**. One of Herbert's most enduring scores, *Babes in Toyland* was also a substantial commercial success and appreciated by critics. The plot concerned the nefarious

Uncle Barnaby (George H. Denham), who wishes to steal the inheritance of his nephew Allan (William Norris) and niece Jane (Mabel Barrison). He pays thugs to kidnap the rightful heirs, but the young adults escape to Mary Contrary's garden, where they encounter nursery rhyme characters. Allan falls in love with Mary (Amy Ricard), and his uncle is his competition for her heart. All of course works out in the end because the Mother Goose characters help foil the uncle's plans. The unsigned review in the *New York Times* was an unqualified rave, opening with a report on the show's reception, noting that the audience wanted more after it was over. Part of this certainly had to do with the glorious spectacle and exceptionally large number of sets and set changes. The critic declares that the show "is as full of good things as Jack Horner's Christmas pie was popularly supposed to have been," a sensible way to praise a show based on nursery rhymes. The reviewer asserts that Herbert's score was one of the best heard on Broadway in some time. Herbert's score included the evergreen "March of the Toys" and "Toyland."

BACALL, LAUREN (BORN BETTY JOAN PERSKE, 1924–). Hollywood icon, former model, and original member of the "Rat Pack" with a distinctively husky voice who won **Tony Awards** for Best Actress in a Musical for her renditions of Margo Channing in *Applause* (1970) and Tess Harding in *Woman of the Year* (1981).

BAILEY, PEARL (1918–1990). Legendary singer who starred on Broadway in *St. Louis Woman* (1946) and an all-black version of *Hello, Dolly!* (1967). *See also* AFRICAN AMERICAN MUSICALS.

BAKER, JOSEPHINE (1906–1975). African American dancer, actress, and singer who achieved her greatest fame in Paris, where she was known for her erotic dancing and minimal clothing. She became a French citizen in 1937, and was an active supporter of the French Resistance during World War II and the American civil rights movement. Before emigrating, she appeared in **vaudeville** and was in the chorus for the **revues** *Shuffle Along* (1921) and *The Chocolate Dandies* (1924). She returned to Broadway in the *Ziegfeld Follies* of 1936 and the star-centered *Josephine Baker* (1964) and *An Evening with Josephine Baker* (1973).

BALANCHINE, GEORGE (BORN GEORGES BAL-ANCHIVADZE, 1904–1983). The Russian-born choreographer was known primarily for his work in ballet and brought that style to Broadway in shows such as *On Your Toes* (1936), *Song of Norway* (1944), and *Where's Charley?* (1948). His extended ballet sequences became increasingly integrated into the shows and helped develop their plots.

BALL, LUCILLE (1911–1989). The "Queen of Comedy" and star of *I Love Lucy* (1951–1957) drew sell-out audiences in her one-and-only Broadway musical appearance when she starred as Wildcat Jackson in *Wildcat* (1960), with music by **Cy Coleman**. She returned to her television projects after the musical closed.

BALL, MICHAEL (1962–). A leading singing actor and concert and recording artist in Great Britain, Ball created the roles of Marius in *Les Misérables* (1985), Alex in *Aspects of Love* (1989), and Caractacus Potts in *Chitty Chitty Bang Bang* (2002), all in London's West End. He reprised the part of Alex when *Aspects of Love* transferred to Broadway in 1990, and in 2005, played Count Fosco in *The Woman in White*.

BARNES, CLIVE (1927–). Born in London and educated at Oxford, Barnes was Dance and Theater critic for the *New York Times* from 1965 to 1977. He left the *Times* to become Dance and Drama critic at the *New York Post*.

***BARNUM* (30 APRIL 1980, ST. JAMES, 854 PERFORMANCES).** Music by **Cy Coleman**, lyrics by **Michael Stewart**, book by Mark Bramble, directed and staged by Joe Layton. An entertaining show starring the versatile and irrepressible **Jim Dale** and many circus acts, but with a very thin book. The larger-than-life story of P. T. Barnum would seem ideal for the musical theater, and *Barnum* enjoyed a two-year run. As the title character, Dale made a huge impression, prompting **Frank Rich** to open his *New York Times* review with a rhetorical question: "Is there anything that Jim Dale can't do?" Rich praises his singing, dancing, leaping on a trampoline, riding a unicycle, walking a tightrope, conducting a marching band, and playing a clown. Rich clearly found Dale to be most of the show: "he . . .

transforms a gargantuan circus of a show into his own joyous playpen."

BARRETT, BRENT (1957–). Tenor who has successfully recorded many Broadway standards and starred in the London revival of *Kiss Me, Kate* (2002), which was released on DVD. He took over major roles in the long-running Broadway revivals of *Chicago* and *Annie Get Your Gun.*

BART, LIONEL (1930–1999). English composer and lyricist whose *Oliver!* (1963) is filled with memorable songs such as "Food, Glorious Food" and "As Long as He Needs Me." In his best work, Bart combined simple and direct melodies with lyrics that hint at social and political injustices. *See also* SOCIAL JUSTICE/INJUSTICE.

BATTLE, HINTON (1956–). Versatile **African American** dancer, actor, and singer who won three **Tony Award**s for Best Featured Actor in a Musical: the first for *Sophisticated Ladies* (1981), the second for Dipsey in *The Tap Dance Kid* (1983), and the third for John in *Miss Saigon* (1991). He also created the role of the Scarecrow in *The Wiz* (1975).

BEACH, GARY (1947–). A fine baritone with a strong sense of comedy, Beach created the roles of Lumière in *Beauty and the Beast* (1994), leading "Be Our Guest," and Roger DeBris in *The Producers* (2001), delighting audiences with "Keep It Gay" and "Springtime for Hitler." He received a **Tony Award** for his manic portrayal of DeBris and reprised the role in the show's screen version. He also starred in the 2005 revival of *La Cage aux Folles* and played Thénardier in the 2006 revival of *Les Misérables.*

BEAUTY AND THE BEAST (18 APRIL 1994, PALACE, 5,221 PERFORMANCES AS OF 31 DECEMBER 2006). Music by **Alan Menken**, lyrics by **Howard Ashman** and **Tim Rice**, book by Linda Woolverton, presented by Walt Disney Productions (a.k.a. **Disney Theatrical Productions**). Disney's first Broadway musical, *Beauty and the Beast* is a faithful re-creation of the popular 1991 film and has become one of Manhattan's major tourist attractions. The true star of the show is the special effects, which, as David Richards reported in the *New York Times*, are so good that, paradoxically, they remove some of the wonder from the proceedings: "Nothing has been left to the imagination. . . . There is no room for dreaming." Especially memorable are the visual effects that occur in the song "Be Our Guest" and in the final transformation of the beast into a human. For many, of course, the complexity and completeness of the proceedings is what makes *Beauty and the Beast* one of Broadway's all-time great hits and productions. The plot is very famous. **Terrence Mann** starred as the Beast, and Richards found his work most memorable because even under his huge costume he can "convey the delicacy of awak ning love." **Susan Egan** played the heroine, Belle, and her father was Broadway veteran **Tom Bosley**. Gaston, the handsome villain who wants to marry Belle, was played by Burke Moses; Richards found Moses very effective as the animated buffoon, comparing him to a balloon in Macy's Thanksgiving Day Parade.

The staging of *Beauty and the Beast* included a number of showstoppers, including the huge "Be Our Guest," when the castle's objects show their happiness at Belle's arrival, the event that might end their enchantment. Richards was almost dazed by the spectacle, comparing it to "Busby Berkeley on magic mushrooms." The production overwhelmed the plot, making Linda Woolverton's book almost unnecessary. The score included the familiar songs from the animated film, as well as seven new songs. Since the film's lyricist Howard Ashman died in 1991, Tim Rice assumed the role for the added musical numbers. Several of the songs, including "Belle," "Be Our Guest," "Gaston," and the haunting title tune are delightfully reminiscent of Broadway's golden age of the 1950s.

BEECHMAN, LAURIE (1954–1998). Singing actress who made her Broadway debut in five small roles in *Annie* (1977) before appearing as the Narrator in *Joseph and the Amazing Technicolor Dreamcoat* (1982). She played Grizabella in the First National Company (touring production) of *Cats* and joined the show's Broadway production in 1984, singing the role for more than four years. In 1990, she sang Fantine in *Les Misérables*. Her voice was both powerful and nuanced, and she brought deeply felt interpretations to "Memory" (*Cats*) and "I Dreamed a Dream" (*Les Misérables*).

BELLS ARE RINGING (**29 NOVEMBER 1956, SHUBERT, 924 PERFORMANCES**). Music by **Jule Styne**, lyrics and book by **Betty Comden** and **Adolph Green**, directed by **Jerome Robbins**, choreography by Robbins and **Bob Fosse**. Based on an original story about a telephone answering service, *Bells Are Ringing* found its popularity largely in its appealing star, **Judy Holliday**. She played Ella Peterson, who worked for "Susanswerphone" and got mixed up in her clients' lives. She listens to a contentious call between playwright Jeff Moss (Sydney Chaplin) and a producer, and then goes to the writer's apartment to encourage him. They fall in love and, after complications, are together at the end. The show was a simple, funny musical comedy that audiences loved. **Brooks Atkinson**, writing in the *New York Times*, believed that any success *Bells Are Ringing* might enjoy would come from Judy Holliday's efforts. He noted that "she sings, dances, clowns and also carries on her shoulders one of the most antiquated plots of the season." *Bells Are Ringing* included several fine songs. Easily the score's most popular was the moving "The Party's Over," sung by Ella at a low point in her relationship with Jeff. Other musical highlights included "Just in Time" and "I'm Goin' Back." **Faith Prince** starred in the 2001 revival.

BENNETT, MICHAEL (1943–1987). Choreographer-director primarily remembered for *A Chorus Line* (1975) who also envisioned the lively dances and continuous stage movement in *Promises, Promises* (1968), *Coco* (1969), *Company* (1970), and *Follies* (1971). *A Chorus Line* memorably told the story of Broadway dancers and included many striking solo and ensemble dance pieces. Bennett surrounded himself with such talents as **Bob Avian** and **Donna McKechnie** and allowed them to design choreography, but the result remained true to Bennett's vision. His last successful show was *Dreamgirls* (1981).

BENNETT, ROBERT RUSSELL (1894–1981). Composer, arranger, and conductor who was the leading orchestrator on Broadway from the 1920s to the 1960s and whose credits include *Rose Marie* (1924), *Show Boat* (1927), *Girl Crazy* (1930), *Of Thee I Sing* (1931), *Lady in the Dark* (1941), **Lerner and Loewe**'s *My Fair Lady* (1956) and *Camelot* (1960), and **Rodgers and Hammerstein**'s *Oklahoma!* (1943), *Carousel* (1945), *South Pacific* (1949), *The King and I*

(1951), and *The Sound of Music* (1959). Bennett was largely responsible for creating the lush orchestral sound and subtle colorings that characterize Broadway's "Golden Age."

BENZELL, MIMI (1924–1971). Metropolitan Opera soprano who created the role of Ruth in *Milk and Honey* (1961). She also appeared in nightclubs and on television.

BERKELEY, BUSBY (BORN WILLIAM BERKELEY ENOS, 1895–1976). Choreographer and director who honed his flair for presenting the female form and using human bodies to create geometric designs in shows such as *The Wild Rose* (1926) and *A Connecticut Yankee* (1927) before achieving tremendous fame in Hollywood with such films as *42nd Street* (1933). He supervised the 1971 revival of *No, No, Nanette.*

BERLIN, IRVING (BORN ISRAEL BALINE, 1888–1989). One of the most important American songwriters of the 20th century, Berlin helped define the quintessential Broadway style of the 1910s. He wrote more than 1,500 songs during his lifetime, many of them becoming exemplars of American popular song. **Jerome Kern** once said of him: "Irving Berlin has no place in American music; he *is* American music." Furthermore, **Cole Porter** included "a Berlin ballad" among the superlatives lavishly listed in his alliterative lyrics for "You're the Top." A Russian immigrant and son of a Jewish cantor, Berlin achieved tremendous fame in 1911 for "Alexander's Ragtime Band." He began his Broadway career writing for **revues**, creating well-known songs such as "Play a Simple Melody" (1914), "I Love a Piano" (1915), "Oh, How I Hate to Get Up in the Morning" (1918), and "A Pretty Girl Is Like a Melody," the last for the 1919 edition of *Ziegfeld Follies*. Berlin was also active as a producer during the early 1920s with his own series of *Music Box Revues*. He also created other classic **musical comedy** and **revue** scores such as *Face the Music* (1932), *As Thousands Cheer* (1933, featuring "Heat Wave" and "Easter Parade"), *Annie Get Your Gun* (1946, with "There's No Business Like Show Business"), *Miss Liberty* (1949), *Call Me Madam* (1950), and *Mr. President* (1962). In both his words and his music, Berlin spoke in middle-class vernacular, unless he was creating a song in dialect or attempting to evoke a specific atmosphere in his music. He proved the versatility and effectiveness of the **verse-refrain** form, and had a strong working relationship with legendary singers such as **Ethel Merman**, who became famous as a singer of his songs (she starred in *Annie Get Your Gun* and *Call Me Madam*). His famous transposing piano (Berlin could neither read music nor play the piano in more than one key) is now at the Smithsonian Institution's Museum of American History.

BERNSTEIN, LEONARD (1918–1990). Legendary American conductor, pianist, composer, educator, and writer who wrote five Broadway scores: *On the Town* (1944), *Wonderful Town* (1953), *Candide* (1956), *West Side Story* (1957), and *1600 Pennsylvania Avenue* (1976). Bernstein brought a sophistication and extremely high level of craftsmanship to his work for Broadway. He incorporated popular dance idioms into many of his scores, as well as a range of vocal styles spanning comic speech-singing ("Gee, Officer Krupke" from *West Side Story*) to operatic coloratura ("Glitter and Be Gay" from *Candide*). Bernstein created some of Broadway's most famous ballads, including "A Little Bit in Love" from *Wonderful Town* and "Maria," "Tonight," and "Somewhere" from *West Side Story*.

***BEST FOOT FORWARD* (1 OCTOBER 1941, ETHEL BARRYMORE, 326 PERFORMANCES).** Music and lyrics by Hugh Martin and Ralph Blane, book by John Cecil Holm, production staged and produced by **George Abbott**, dances arranged by **Gene Kelly**. Another one of Abbott's college-themed musicals that starred relatively unknown talents, *Best Foot Forward* ran for 10 months and launched the Broadway career of **Nancy Walker**. It was the first new musical to open in eight months. The show took place at Winsocki College, where Bud Hooper (Gil Stratton Jr.) cheekily invites Hollywood starlet Gale Joy (Rosemary Lane) to the prom, hardly expecting her to accept. With her career at a low point, she does come, setting the college astir. At the dance, Bud's girlfriend, Helen Schlessinger (Maureen Cannon) tears off part of Joy's gown, causing a wave of souvenir seekers who nearly strip her naked. The star leaves, and Bud and Helen reunite. Nancy Walker played Blind Date, the girl nobody wants; she made a major impression singing "Just a

Little Joint with a Juke Box." **Brooks Atkinson** called the show "good-humoured," the book "good," the music and lyrics "excellent," providing "all of the beguilements of a well-turned evening." Nancy Walker "is a hard-boiled skirt who is tremendously funny." Another unknown, **June Allyson**, had "considerable charm." He never implied that the show was exceptional, but praised the lyrics, music, and production. Martin and Blane, who later wrote the score to the 1944 MGM film musical *Meet Me in St. Louis*, produced one major hit in *Best Foot Forward*: "Buckle Down, Winsocki." During the war it took on new life as "Buckle Down, Buck Private."

THE BEST LITTLE WHOREHOUSE IN TEXAS (17 APRIL 1978, ENTERMEDIA, 1,703 PERFORMANCES). Music and lyrics by Carol Hall, book by Larry L. King and Peter Masterson, directed by Masterson and **Tommy Tune**, musical numbers staged by Tune. Perhaps most famous for its suggestive title, *The Best Little Whorehouse in Texas* combined a pleasant country-tinged score with Tommy Tune's showmanship to carve out a stunning four-year run. The show's basis was Larry L. King's magazine article about the closing of a long-tolerated brothel in a Texas town when a crusading minister causes a political furor. The minister, a hypocritical television evangelist, is Melvin P. Thorpe (Clint Allmon). The house's madam, Mona Stangley (Carlin Glynn), runs a community-minded business that befriends the sheriff and, thanks to an alumni gift, provides its services gratis to the college football team. The sheriff is Ed Earl Dodd (Henderson Forsythe), a potty-mouthed "good ol' boy" who tries to get rid of the evangelist, but the preacher's influence proves too powerful. Tune overcame any hokiness with his hugely effective show-biz sense, bringing style and fun to the proceedings. Among his best dances was one featuring six live football cheerleaders, each carrying two life-sized dolls with legs that kicked wildly. Richard Eder, reviewing the show's off-Broadway opening for the *New York Times*, calls the routine "hilarious." Each live dancer and doll was a blue-eyed blonde, conveying the empty-headed spectacle of cheerleading. The show's producers reveled in the naughty title, running advertisements that said only "whorehouse," but the musical was primarily harmless fun. Some of the better songs were "The Sidestep," where the governor evades questions at a press conference; the direct

"Texas Has a Whorehouse in It"; and the duet "No Lies." A sequel, *The Best Little Whorehouse Goes Public*, ran for only two weeks in May 1994.

BETSY **(28 DECEMBER 1926, NEW AMSTERDAM, 39 PER-FORMANCES).** Music by **Richard Rodgers**, lyrics by **Lorenz Hart**, book by **Irving Caesar** and David Freedman, produced by **Florenz Ziegfeld**. A failure despite a good Rodgers and Hart score, a popular vaudeville star in the cast, and the interpolation of **Irving Berlin**'s famous "Blue Skies," the show was saddled with an unworkable plot, which the *New York Times* reported "became of less and less consequence as the night wore on . . ." The cast's vaudeville star was Belle Baker, playing the title character, whose Jewish mother would not allow her other children to marry before "Betsy." The *Times* reports that she was applauded heartily, especially after "Blue Skies"—when even Berlin took a bow—but she seldom "added to the gayety of the occasion."

BIG DEAL **(10 APRIL 1986, BROADWAY, 69 PERFORMANCES).** Written, directed, and choreographed by **Bob Fosse**, the Broadway legend's last musical, based upon the film *Big Deal on Madonna Street*, was a failure on several levels. He replaced the Italian gang who bungle a robbery in the film with an African American cast on Chicago's South Side. He chose famous songs of the 1930s but could not overcome what Frank Rich in the *New York Times* called his "static and mirthless" story. The songs included such former hits as "Beat Me Daddy Eight to the Bar," "I'm Just Wild about Harry," and "Me and My Shadow." Despite Fosse's deserved reputation as a showman, Rich found the work's only "show stopper" to be "Beat Me Daddy," the first-act finale. *See also* AFRICAN AMERICAN MUSICALS.

BIG RIVER **(25 MAY 1985, EUGENE O'NEILL, 1,005 PERFOR-MANCES).** Music and lyrics by Roger Miller, book by William Hauptman. Based on Mark Twain's novel *Huckleberry Finn*, *Big River* came at the end of a disappointing Broadway season and brought sufficient charms to run for about two and a half years. *Big River* also won several **Tony Awards**, including Best Musical. Roger

Miller, a country musician and composer, supplied an accessible and tuneful score that worked well within the context of the show. Major songs were "Muddy Water," "Waitin' for the Light to Shine," "How Blest We Are," and "River in the Rain." The scenery was lovely, especially backdrops showing the Mississippi River. *Big River* returned to Broadway in an innovative production with deaf and hearing-impaired actors using American Sign Language that ran for two months at the American Airlines Theater in the summer of 2003.

BIG: THE MUSICAL **(28 APRIL 1996, SHUBERT, 193 PERFORMANCES).** With music by David Shire, lyrics by **Richard Maltby Jr.**, and book by **John Weidman**. The musical version of the 1988 film starring Tom Hanks about Josh, a boy who, after having a fortune-telling automaton at a carnival grant his wish to become a 20-something man, included a vibrant musical score that captured the humor and drama of the story. Daniel Jenkins starred in the short-lived production.

BIKEL, THEODORE (1924–). Viennese-born actor, folk singer, radio host, activist, and spokesperson who created the role of Captain Georg von Trapp in *The Sound of Music* (1959). He is also closely associated with the role of Tevye in *Fiddler on the Roof*, having played the part more than 2,000 times. Bikel was president of Actor's Equity Association from 1973 to 1982.

BILLION DOLLAR BABY **(21 DECEMBER 1945, ALVIN, 219 PERFORMANCES).** Music by Morton Gould, book and lyrics by **Betty Comden** and **Adolph Green**, production staged by **George Abbott**, choreography and musical numbers staged by **Jerome Robbins**. A recreation of the 1920s that had only limited success; many of the same creators recalled the 1930s in the previous year's *On the Town*. The only major change was the composer: Morton Gould replaced **Leonard Bernstein**. Lewis Nichols in the *New York Times* called Gould's score "serviceable rather than outstandingly brilliant." Such limited praise described much of the show, which Nichols found "one of those affairs which doesn't completely come off." The plot concerned a young woman (Joan McCracken) rising from her Staten Island roots, having a series of boyfriends, and finding herself in various comic situations.

***BITTER SWEET* (5 NOVEMBER 1929, ZIEGFELD, 159 PER-FORMANCES).** Music, lyrics, book, and staging by **Noel Coward**; presented by **Florenz Ziegfeld** and Arch Selwyn. An **operetta** that was extremely popular in London, *Bitter Sweet* received appreciative notices in New York but did not enjoy a long run. The show demonstrated Coward's wide versatility. Not only did he do everything listed above, but he also played many of the roles. The plot involved the Marchioness of Chayne (Evelyn Laye, who created the role in London) recounting her complicated life to her granddaughter in an effort to help the young woman decide whom she should marry. **Brooks Atkinson**, writing in the *New York Times*, found the book "not highly inventive" but "with sufficient dramatic quality to carry the burden of his theme." The score included "I'll See You Again," one of Coward's greatest hits, along with the songs "Tell Me What Is Love," "The Last Dance," and "Zigeuner." Atkinson praised every aspect of Laye's performance, including her "fragile beauty" and "the daintiness with which she acts and sings."

***BLACKBIRDS OF 1928* (9 MAY 1928, LIBERTY, 518 PERFOR-MANCES).** Music by **Jimmy McHugh**, lyrics by **Dorothy Fields**. One of the longer-running **revues** of the period, *Blackbirds of 1928* featured many moments that made for satisfying entertainment at the time but today could not go on stage because of derogatory racial allusions. The show starred important African American performers such as Tim Moore, **Adelaide Hall**, and Alda Ward. McHugh and Fields's score included the standards "I Can't Give You Anything But Love" and "Diga Diga Doo." Skits included one about an actor afraid of a skeleton and a number set in Harlem, such as a "burlesque boxing match" and a poker game. One of the show's highlights was the dancing, especially an extended number by the famous tap dancer Bill Robinson. *See also* AFRICAN AMERICAN MUSICALS.

***THE BLACK CROOK* (12 SEPTEMBER 1866, NIBLO'S GARDEN, 475 PERFORMANCES).** Music and lyrics by various writers, book by Charles M. Barras, produced by **William Wheatley** and Henry Jarrett. Often cited as the first example of a Broadway musical, *The Black Crook* was a hugely popular spectacle that brought together a plot, music, dancing, and extravagant stage effects. It was hardly the first musical in New York, with ballad operas going back into the first half of the 18th century, but the show's great appeal and especially its long run at the same theater seems to mark the beginning of a new era for the musical in New York City. The show's apocryphal origins came about when the Academy of Music burned down, leaving a French ballet troupe stranded in New York without a theater. Wheatley, the producer at Niblo's Garden, then supposedly stuck them into what he considered a slow melodrama opening at his theater. Barras's story for *The Black Crook* includes elements reminiscent of *Der Freischütz*, with the satanic character Zamiel (E. B. Holmes) forcing Hertzog (C. H. Morton), "The Black Crook," to bring him one soul every New Year's Eve. A painter, Rudolf (G. C. Boniface), has been imprisoned by Count Wolfenstein (J. W. Blaisdell), but Hertzog arranges his escape, saying that he will lead him to some gold. Rudolf later saves a dove who is really Stalacta (Annie Kemp Bowler), "Queen of the Golden Realm." She warns Rudolf of the fate that awaits him and conducts him instead to a fairyland where he finds love with Amina (Rose Morton). The book was not the evening's highlight, and today's audience would find the dialogue hopelessly stilted. The music used in *The Black Crook* changed during the run, and included such songs as "You Naughty, Naughty Men," "March of the Amazons," and "Dare I Tell?," along with extensive ballet music. Extravagant production values appeared in the painted backdrops and flats and in the material used in the costumes and drapery.

The unsigned review in the *New York Times* opens with a description of the improvements that Wheatley had made at Niblo's Garden. *The Black Crook* is called an "original spectacular drama." The opening act is "trashy" but allows for plenty of spectacle and use of the "English and French ballet troupes." The reviewer names some dancers, one described "as light as a feather." The critic's praise of the dancers was effusive: "No similar exhibition has been made in an American stage that we remember, certainly none where such a combination of youth, grace, beauty and *élan* was found." Overall, the show "is decidedly the event of this spectacular age." Not all observers found the show "spectacular." Given the dancers' flesh-colored tights, some flocked to *The Black Crook* to see what at the time seemed to be the unadorned female anatomy. Preachers condemned the show, giving it marvelous publicity. **Sigmund Romberg**'s musical *The Girl in Pink Tights* (1954) was loosely based on the events surrounding the production.

BLAINE, VIVIAN (BORN VIVIAN STAPLETON, 1921–1995). Actress who created Miss Adelaide in *Guys and Dolls* (1950) and played the character in the 1955 film. Her portrayal of the heroine plagued by a psychosomatic illness caused by her 14-year engagement left an indelible impression upon the character's future depictions.

BLAKE, EUBIE (1883–1983). African American ragtime pianist and composer who collaborated with vaudeville partner Noble Sissle to create *Shuffle Along* (1921), the hit song from which, "I'm Just Wild about Harry," remained extremely popular for decades and boosted Harry S. Truman's 1948 election campaign. *See also* AFRICAN AMERICAN MUSICALS.

BLEDSOE, JULES (1898–1943). African American operatic baritone who created the role of Joe in *Show Boat* (1927), introducing "Ol' Man River," after Paul Robeson had to withdraw from the production because of scheduling conflicts. The previous year, Bledsoe appeared in Frank Harling's Broadway **opera** *Deep River*.

BLITZSTEIN, MARC (1905–1964). Composer, lyricist, and critic whose iconoclastic works for Broadway approached the operatic and typically emphasized his left-wing politics. His most famous Broadway score is *The Cradle Will Rock* (1938), although he also wrote the music for *Regina* (1949, along with the libretto) and *Juno* (1959, along with the lyrics). He wrote the book for *Pins and Needles* (1937) and adapted the book and lyrics of **Kurt Weill**'s *The Threepenny Opera* for Broadway (1954). Blitzstein also wrote songs and incidental music for various Broadway plays and **revues**.

***BLOOD BROTHERS* (25 APRIL 1993, MUSIC BOX, 840 PERFORMANCES).** Music, lyrics, and book by Willy Russell. A show that has been running for more than two decades in London, *Blood Brothers* managed a fairly long run in New York through the casting of brothers and pop stars David and Shaun Cassidy. It opened in New York a decade after its London premiere. The show tells the tragic tale of twins who were separated at birth. One remains with his poor mother (Stephanie Lawrence, who played the role for two years in London) and the other becomes a child of privilege through adoption. Their reunion later in life leads to horrific results. The show's overt social commentary on the problems of the British class system may have been lost on many American audience members. Writing in the *New York Times*, **Frank Rich** found the show notably lacking in "Broadway glitz," very different from many West End transplants. He wondered how well the show would do in New York with its bare-bones atmosphere and "melodramatic tale peopled with agitprop characters." He praises the score as "tuneful," but complains that there are far too many reprises, and that "the evening seems to have too little music and too much talk." The show's outstanding musical numbers include the hard rock "The Devil's Got Your Number," the ballad-like "Marilyn Monroe," "Easy Terms," and "Light Romance," and the dramatic finale, "Tell Me It's Not True." *See also* SOCIAL JUSTICE/INJUSTICE.

BLOOMER GIRL (5 OCTOBER 1944, SHUBERT, 654 PERFOR-MANCES). Music by **Harold Arlen**, lyrics by **E. Y. Harburg**, book by Sig Herzig and **Fred Saidy**, production staged by Harburg, choreography by **Agnes de Mille**. Eighteen months after *Oklahoma!* opened, some of the same creators and cast returned to the American past and again found success, although the result was not as memorable. The story takes place in 1861. **Celeste Holm**, Ado Annie from *Oklahoma!*, starred as Evelina, daughter of a hoop skirt manufacturer (Matt Briggs), in her first lead role. Evelina follows the lead of her aunt, the real-life Dolly Bloomer (Margaret Douglass), who argues for female comfort with the garment that bears her name. The show included a number of reflections of its period, among them Pompey (Dooley Wilson), an **African American** character who sings "The Eagle and Me," a call for better **race relations**. The show also included a play-within-a-play featuring part of *Uncle Tom's Cabin*. An especially poignant moment was de Mille's "Civil War Ballet," where mournful women watch their men go off to fight. Although Arlen's score has always been considered excellent, it included few lasting standards. A duet for the lovers, "Right as the Rain," is a fine ballad, and "Evelina" drew positive comment.

BLOSSOM, HENRY (ca. 1866–1919). Librettist and lyricist best remembered for his collaborations with **Victor Herbert**, including *Mlle. Modiste* (1905), *The Red Mill* (1906), *The Princess Pat* (1915), and *Eileen* (1917).

BLOSSOM TIME **(29 SEPTEMBER 1921, AMBASSADOR, 516 PERFORMANCES).** Lyrics and book by **Dorothy Donnelly**, music by **Sigmund Romberg**, after Franz Schubert and Heinrich Berté. An adaptation of the Viennese success *Das Dreimäderlhaus*, the fictional romantic story about Franz Schubert (Bertram Peacock) and Mitzi (Olga Cook) included Broadway versions of music by the 19th-century Viennese composer in the score. Among its most famous songs were the waltz "Song of Love" (the refrain of which was based on a theme from the first movement of Schubert's Eighth Symphony) and the "Serenade" (a version of "Ständchen"), which was sung by Baron Schober (**Howard Marsh**). Numerous road companies of *Blossom Time* traveled across the United States in the middle part of the century and became synonymous with cheap tours that had ratty costumes and sets and a general level of mediocrity.

THE BLUE PARADISE **(5 AUGUST 1915, CASINO, 356 PERFORMANCES).** Music by Edmund Eysler with additional music by Leo Edwards, Cecil Lean, and **Sigmund Romberg**; lyrics by Herbert Reynolds; book by Edgar Smith. An adaptation of the Viennese **operetta** *Ein Tag im Paradis*, the score included Romberg's first successful song, the waltz "Auf Wiedersehn." The plot about a man whose nostalgic longings are so strong that he imagines himself to have returned to the inn where he spent many hours as a youth resonated strongly with Romberg and the **Shuberts**, who produced the show. **Vivienne Segal** made her Broadway debut in the operetta.

BOCK, JERRY (1928–). Composer who, with lyricist **Sheldon Harnick**, wrote the scores to *The Body Beautiful* (1958), a musical about boxing, *Fiorello!* (1959), *Tenderloin* (1960), *She Loves Me* (1963), *Fiddler on the Roof* (1964), *Baker Street* (1965), *The Apple Tree*

(1966), and *The Rothschilds* (1970). Bock effectively synthesizes the mainstream Broadway idiom with particular time-, place-, and ethnic-specific references, as is evident in the New York of *Fiorello!*, the Russian-Jewish village of Anatevka in *Fiddler on the Roof*, or 18th-century Frankfurt and London in *The Rothschilds*.

BOLGER, RAY (1904–1987). Dancer, actor, and singer who played Junior Dolan in *On Your Toes* (1936) before going to Hollywood and starring in MGM films, most notably as the Scarecrow in *The Wizard of Oz* (1939). He returned to Broadway, creating Sapiens in *By Jupiter* (1942) and winning the **Tony Award** for Best Actor in a Musical for his portrayal of Oxford undergraduate Charley Wykeham in *Where's Charley?* (1948). As part of the show, Bolger, as Charley, disguised himself as his aunt "from Brazil, where the nuts come from," and also led the audience in a sing-along of "Once in Love with Amy."

BOLTON, GUY (1884–1979). British librettist and lyricist who collaborated with **P. G. Wodehouse** and **Jerome Kern** to create the legendary **Princess Theatre musicals**. He went on to work on important **musical comedies** such as *Very Good Eddie* (1915), *Sally* (1920), *Lady, Be Good!* (1924), *Oh, Kay!* (1926), *Girl Crazy* (1930), *Anything Goes* (1934), and *Follow the Girls* (1944). Bolton was able to capture the effervescent spirit of musical comedy and was one of the genre's greatest wordsmiths.

***BOMBAY DREAMS* (29 APRIL 2004, BROADWAY, 284 PERFORMANCES).** Music by **A. R. Rahman**, lyrics by Don Black, book by Meera Syal and Thomas Meehan, directed by Steven Pimlott. A London import, where it was produced by **Andrew Lloyd Webber**'s **Really Useful Company** in 2002, the show was a live-action Bollywood musical. The plot was of Akaash (Manu Narayan), whose rags-to-riches story takes place in Mumbai, beginning in the slums and ending when Akaash is with Priya (Anisha Nagarajan), a major Bollywood star. Indian musical styles fill the score, including tablas (traditional Indian drums) in the orchestra. Dazzling production numbers such as "Shakalaka Baby" and "Salaam Bombay" appear alongside power ballads like "Love's Never Easy" (sung by the eunuch

Sweetie) and "How Many Stars?" For the Broadway production, some of the strongly ethnic Indian dimensions were softened and the main love story received a happy ending.

BOMBO **(6 OCTOBER 1921, JOLSON'S, 218 PERFOR-MANCES).** Music by **Sigmund Romberg** and others, book and lyrics by **Harold Atteridge**. An **Al Jolson** vehicle with a framing story in which American explorer Jack Christopher and his cook, Gus (Jolson, in blackface), are visiting an Italian castle, and after participating in some magic tricks, are transformed into Christopher Columbus and his servant, Bombo. At some performances, Jolson asked the audience if they wanted the show to continue or just have him perform a solo act. They invariably voted in his favor, and the rest of the cast was dismissed.

BOOK MUSICAL. A musical with a dramatic plot, or "book." *See also* MUSICAL COMEDY; MUSICAL PLAY; OPERETTA.

BOOTH, SHIRLEY (1898–1992). Comedienne with a distinctive character voice and mannerisms whose Broadway musical credits include Cissy in *A Tree Grows in Brooklyn* (1951) and the title role in **Marc Blitzstein's** *Juno* (1959). She also appeared in many Broadway plays as well as on film and television, and is perhaps best remembered for playing the title character, a housekeeper, in the sitcom *Hazel* (1961–1966).

BOSLEY, TOM (1927–). Singing actor with a comforting paternal stage presence who won a **Tony Award** for Best Featured Actor in a Musical for the title role in *Fiorello!* (1959). He created the title role in *The Education of H*Y*M*A*N K*A*P*L*A*N* (1968) and Maurice in *Beauty and the Beast* (1994). In 2002–2003, he was a **replacement** for Herr Schultz in the **revival** of *Cabaret*. He is famous for his television roles, including Howard Cunningham on *Happy Days*, Sheriff Amos Tupper on *Murder, She Wrote* (appearing with **Angela Lansbury**), and Father Frank Dowling on *Father Dowling Mysteries*.

BOSTWICK, BARRY (1946–). Most famous for his work on television and cult film (including Brad in *The Rocky Horror Picture Show*

[1975]), Bostwick created the role of Danny Zuko in *Grease* (1972) and won a **Tony Award** for his portrayal of Jamie Lockhart in *The Robber Bridegroom* (1976). He also played Nick Charles in *Nick & Nora* (1991).

BOUBLIL, ALAIN (1941–). Tunis-born librettist and lyricist who, with composer Claude-Michel Schönberg, created the **megamusicals** *Les Misérables* (1985, London; 1987, New York) and *Miss Saigon* (1989, London; 1991, New York). The romantic tales both have French associations, 1830s France in *Les Misérables* and Indochina, a former French colony, in *Miss Saigon*, though the show concerns Americans at the end of the Vietnam War.

***THE BOY FRIEND* (30 SEPTEMBER 1954, ROYALE, 485 PERFORMANCES).** Music, lyrics, and book by Sandy Wilson. A satirical but loving look at the musicals of the 1920s that introduced **Julie Andrews** to Broadway, and one of the most successful British exports to New York musical theater before the age of **Andrew Lloyd Webber**. Although not nearly as successful in New York as it had been in London, *The Boy Friend* reminded New York audiences how silly 1920s musicals had been, while also beguiling audiences with its own charm. As creator of book, lyrics, and music, Wilson evoked most of the decade's memorable signifiers while telling a simple story about two British children of privilege, Polly (Julie Andrews) and Tony (John Hower), who feign to be of lower social class to draw romantic interest from the other. Wilson's score is rooted firmly in the 1920s, drawing on the Charleston and jazzy syncopations, and his lyrics were gloriously evocative, with the harmless innocence of many of the period's songs. Writing in the *New York Times*, **Brooks Atkinson** understood the satire and spoke for those who remember the decade when he said: "Was the musical stage as silly as this in Twenties? Well, it was." His nearly rave review included praise for Broadway newcomer Andrews ("But it is probably Julie Andrews . . . who gives 'The Boy Friend' its special quality."), although he did not mention her singing.

***THE BOY FROM OZ* (16 OCTOBER 2003, IMPERIAL, 364 PERFORMANCES).** Music and lyrics by **Peter Allen**, book by Martin

Sherman (original book by Nick Enright). The **jukebox musical** based on the life and work of **Peter Allen (Hugh Jackman)** included characters from Allen's life such as Judy Garland, **Liza Minnelli**, and Greg Connell, the love of his life, in supporting roles. The extravagant show originated in Sydney in 1998 and was the first Australian musical to transfer to Broadway. It included such memorable songs as "Quiet Please, There's a Lady on Stage," "Not the Boy Next Door," "I Honestly Love You," "Once Before I Go," and the grand finale, "I Go to Rio." *See also* HOMOSEXUALITY.

THE BOYS FROM SYRACUSE **(23 NOVEMBER 1938, ALVIN, 235 PERFORMANCES).** Music by **Richard Rodgers**; lyrics by **Lorenz Hart**; book, staging, and produced by **George Abbott**; choreography by **George Balanchine**. A long-remembered show based on Shakespeare's *The Comedy of Errors* with the memorable participation of George Abbott and an excellent score by Rodgers and Hart. If **Rodgers and Hammerstein** had never collaborated, Rodgers and Hart would receive more credit for integrating music more fully into the storyline because of this Broadway musical. In crafting his book, Abbott borrowed Shakespeare's plot of two sets of twins separated at birth, both of whom find themselves in Ephesus, ignorant of the other pair, and entirely confusing the good Ephesians. The two masters, both named Antipholus, were played by Ronald Graham and **Eddie Albert**, and the two servants Dromio were Teddy Hart (brother of the lyricist) and Jimmy Savo. Abbott retained the story but wrote the dialogue in the modern vernacular, and brought his usual frenetic pace to the proceedings. **Brooks Atkinson**, writing in the *New York Times*, commented on the show's "freshness, spontaneity and spinning pace." Five years before *Oklahoma!* and its famous ballets, Atkinson also praised Balanchine's dances and his two principal dancers, Betty Bruce and Heidi Vosseler, "who can translate the revelry of a musical rumpus into dainty beauty." Rodgers and Hart's score included several memorable songs that showed various sides of the team's personality: "This Can't Be Love," one of their all-time hits; the melancholy waltz "Falling in Love with Love"; the sarcastic and cutting "What Can You Do with a Man?"; and the show-stopping ballad "Sing for Your Supper," sung by a female trio.

BRANTLEY, BEN (ALSO KNOWN AS BENJAMIN D. BRANT-LEY, 1954–). Chief theater critic of the *New York Times* since 1996. Prior to joining the *Times* in 1993 as drama critic, he wrote for *The New Yorker* and *Vanity Fair*, reviewed films for *Elle*, and was European editor, publisher, and Paris bureau chief for *Women's Wear Daily*. He edited *The New York Times Book of Broadway* (2001), a collection of reviews from the paper.

BRICE, FANNY (BORN FANNY BORACH, 1891–1951). Comedienne and singer who was one of the greatest stars to emerge from *Ziegfeld Follies*. Especially gifted at physical humor, dialect comedy, and parody, she could also deliver heartbreaking renditions of love laments. Among her most famous songs was "Second Hand Rose." Her life was the subject of the musical *Funny Girl* (1964).

BRICUSSE, LESLIE (1931–). London-born composer, lyricist, and librettist who collaborated with singer-songwriter Anthony Newley on *Stop the World—I Want to Get Off* (1962) and *The Roar of the Greasepaint—The Smell of the Crowd* (1965), two shows that share the theme of an individual taking on the world. He created the book and lyrics for **Frank Wildhorn**'s *Jekyll & Hyde* (1997) and worked on the stage version of the film *Victor/Victoria* (1995), for which he and Henry Mancini wrote the Academy Award-winning score.

***BRIGADOON* (13 MARCH 1947, ZIEGFELD, 581 PERFORMANCES).** Music by **Frederick Loewe**, lyrics and book by **Alan Jay Lerner**, choreographed by **Agnes de Mille**. A fantasy musical that takes place in the Scottish highlands, *Brigadoon* was Lerner and Loewe's first hit. Inspired by the phrase that "faith can move mountains" and, perhaps a German short story, Lerner conceived this musical play about a Scottish village that only appears for one day each century. The New York critics toasted the show for its seamless integration of plot, song, and dance. *Brigadoon* opened two months after *Finian's Rainbow*, placing two comparable fantasies on Broadway simultaneously. In his score, Loewe captured a Scottish flavor in his songs and dances, including folk devices such as the pentatonic scale and drones suggestive of bagpipes. He also satisfied traditional

Broadway demands for lovely ballads ("The Heather on the Hill"), rhythmic numbers ("I'll Go Home with Bonnie Jean"), and comic songs ("My Mother's Wedding Day"). Lerner created the elegant and expressive lyrics for which he became famous in later scores, and with Loewe managed a symbiotic relationship between words and music, especially evident in "It's Almost Like Being in Love." *New York Times* critic **Brooks Atkinson** loved de Mille's dances, including the second act chase and the funeral sword dance. The cast was filled with young actors who were not yet famous, including David Brooks as the male lead, Tommy Albright; George Keane as his comic sidekick, Jeff Douglas; Marion Bell (who for a while was Mrs. Alan Jay Lerner) as Tommy's love, Fiona MacLaren; and Pamela Britton as the randy Meg Brockie.

BRIGHTMAN, SARAH (1960–). English singer, actress, and dancer who can achieve vocal timbres of either an operatic soprano or a pop artist. While married to **Andrew Lloyd Webber**, he wrote the role of Christine Daaé in *The Phantom of the Opera* (1986, London; 1988, New York) especially for her. She created the part in both London and New York. She was a **replacement** Rose in the Broadway production of *Aspects of Love* (1990), another Lloyd Webber show.

BRING IN 'DA NOISE, BRING IN 'DA FUNK **(25 APRIL 1996, AMBASSADOR, 1,523 PERFORMANCES).** Music by Daryl Waters, Zane Mark, and Ann Duquesnay, book by Reg E. Gaines. Based on an idea by George C. Wolfe and Savion Glover, *Bring in 'da Noise, Bring in 'da Funk* told the history of African Americans in the United States through the medium of tap dancing. The show opened off-Broadway at the tiny Public Theater, but transferred to Broadway and ran for almost four years. Glover, who had starred on Broadway as a 12-year-old tap dancer in *Jelly's Last Jam*, was a remarkable presence in the show as both dancer and choreographer. According to **Ben Brantley** in the *New York Times*, his dances carried a feeling of viewing "the creative process," moving from "tentativeness to full-blown, assured performances." Jeffrey Wright appeared as a narrator in a white jacket, and opened the show by reciting names of slave ships while Glover shuffled slowly across the stage. Later numbers showed Glover manacled on a ship, slaves on the plantation using their feet for communication because their drums were banned, and dancers in 20th-century Chicago becoming part of a large machine. Brantley compared Glover with **Fred Astaire** in terms of his "prodigious inventiveness" and "nimble elegance," and praised the dancer's charisma and ability to change characters. *See also* AFRICAN AMERICAN MUSICALS.

BRODERICK, MATTHEW (1962–). Actor who won a **Tony Award** for his first singing role on Broadway, J. Pierrepont Finch in the 1995 revival of *How to Succeed in Business without Really Trying* (as **Robert Morse** did when he originated the role in 1961). He created the part of Leo Bloom in *The Producers* (2001), appearing opposite **Nathan Lane**. Broderick reprised Bloom in the 2005 film version of *The Producers.*

BROWN, LEW (BORN LOUIS BROWNSTEIN, 1893–1958). Lyricist who collaborated with **B. G. De Sylva** and **Ray Henderson** on the 1925 and 1926 editions of *George White's Scandals* and 11 **musical comedies**, including the trilogy *Good News!* (1927), *Hold Everything!* (1928), and *Flying High* (1930). He was also active as a director and producer in the 1930s.

BRYNNER, YUL (BORN TAIDJE KHANO, ALSO KNOWN AS YOUL BRYNER, 1911 OR 1915–1985). He made his Broadway debut in *Lute Song* (1946) opposite **Mary Martin**, who encouraged **Richard Rodgers** and **Oscar Hammerstein II** to consider him for the role of King Mongkut in *The King and I* (1951). They cast him in the role opposite **Gertrude Lawrence**, and he won a **Tony Award** for his legendary performance. He immortalized the role in the 1956 film version of *The King and I*, winning an Academy Award. He played the part of the King, with which his fame is inextricably linked, more than 4,000 times.

***BUBBLING BROWN SUGAR* (2 MARCH 1976, ANTA, 766 PERFORMANCES).** Music and lyrics by many figures, book by Loften Mitchell. An African American **revue** of music and dances from Harlem's past and present, *Bubbling Brown Sugar* included memorable performances of many songs by composers such as **Eubie**

Blake, Duke Ellington, and Fats Waller. There were some new songs in the score as well. The thin book involves a supposed tour of Harlem's musical history for two couples, one white and one African American. Predictably, both couples enjoy the tour. The stars of the cast included Avon Long, Josephine Premice, Vivian Reed, Vernon Washington, and Joseph Attles. Highlights included impersonations of African American stars from the past, including Washington's turn at playing Bill Robinson as a tap dancer and Long's singing of **Bert Williams**'s trademark number "Nobody." **Clive Barnes** raved about the show in the *New York Times*, noting that it includes "some of the most likable and lovable music around . . . and performances that take off with the noise, speed and dazzle of the Concorde." *See also* AFRICAN AMERICAN MUSICALS.

BUCK, GENE (EDWARD EUGENE BUCK, 1885–1957). Lyricist, librettist, and sometimes director who wrote for *Ziegfeld Follies* and other revues. He also worked with **Victor Herbert** and **Jerome Kern**.

BUCKLEY, BETTY (1947–). Singing actress whose high-profile Broadway debut was as Martha Jefferson in *1776* (1969), in which she sang "He Plays the Violin." She won a **Tony Award** for her riveting performance as Grizabella in *Cats* (1982) introducing "Memory" to Broadway. In male drag, she created the title role in *The Mystery of Edwin Drood* (1985), and took over the part of Norma Desmond in *Sunset Boulevard* in both London and New York. Her clear vocal tone coupled with her strong acting ability allows her to bring dramatic depth to each character she plays and every song she sings.

BURLESQUE. Theatrical form that originated in the 1840s and was based on satire, parody, and performance art. Female performers, such as the famous Gypsy Rose Lee, employed lush colorful costumes, novelty acts, and striptease to entertain their audiences. Music and dance segments were included, and humor was typically low-brow and mocked high society. The genre was especially popular in the decades surrounding the turn of the 20th century.

BURNETT, CAROL (1933–). Comic actress who made her Broadway debut as Princess Winnifred in *Once Upon a Mattress* (1959) and also appeared in *Fade Out—Fade In* (1965) and as Carlotta Campion in the **Stephen Sondheim** tribute *Follies* in Concert (1985), where she gave an unforgettable rendition of "I'm Still Here." *New York Times* critic **Howard Taubman** said of her performance in *Fade Out—Fade In*, "there is no exhausting this girl's amiable zest or genial comic impudence." In addition to programs with **Julie Andrews**, Burnett's *The Carol Burnett Show* (1967–1978) included homages to and parodies of Broadway musicals.

BURROWS, ABE (1910–1985). Librettist and director whose first Broadway libretto was for **Frank Loesser**'s *Guys and Dolls* (1950), the success of which catapulted him to fame. He wrote the book for **Cole Porter**'s *Can-Can* (1953), which he also directed. He repeated his dual roles as librettist and director for **Loesser**'s *How to Succeed in Business without Really Trying* (1961). Other credits include *Silk Stockings* (1955, librettist) and *What Makes Sammy Run?* (1964, director).

BURTON, RICHARD (1925–1984). British dramatic actor who won the 1961 **Tony Award** for Best Actor in a Musical for his portrayal of King Arthur in *Camelot*. He reprised the role on Broadway in the 1980 revival.

BY JEEVES (28 OCTOBER 2001, HELEN HAYES, 73 PERFORMANCES). Music by **Andrew Lloyd Webber**, lyrics and book by Alan Ayckbourn. A reworking of Lloyd Webber's *Jeeves* (1975), the musical based on the "Jeeves" stories by **P. G. Wodehouse** did not fare well on Broadway. Lloyd Webber's score captured the spirit of **musical comedy** with songs such as the opening number, "Wooster Will Entertain You"; the catchy title song; the slightly syncopated ballad "When Love Arrives"; and the company finale, "Wizard Rainbow Banjo Mix."

BY JUPITER (2 JUNE 1942, SHUBERT, 427 PERFORMANCES). Music by **Richard Rodgers**, lyrics by **Lorenz Hart**, book by

Rodgers and Hart, staged by **Joshua Logan**, dances by **Robert Alton**. Based on Julian F. Thompson's play *The Warrior's Husband* and the last collaboration between Rodgers and Hart (except for new songs for a revival of *A Connecticut Yankee* in 1943), *By Jupiter* was a successful vehicle for **Ray Bolger**. The bawdy tale takes place in ancient Pontus where the women, led by Queen Hippolyta (Benay Venuta), rule over the men, including her husband, King Sapiens (Bolger). This all ends when Hippolyta loses her magic girdle and the Greeks, hoping to restore the natural order, send an invading force led by Theseus (Ronald Graham) and Hercules (Ralph Dumke). King Sapiens returns to his throne, and Theseus wins the hand of Antiope (Constance Moore). Memorable songs include "Nobody's Heart," "Wait Till You See Her," "Ev'rything I've Got," "Jupiter Forbid," "The Gateway of the Temple of Minerva," "Life with Father," and "Bottoms Up."

BYE BYE BIRDIE **(14 APRIL 1960, MARTIN BECK, 607 PERFORMANCES).** Music by **Charles Strouse**, lyrics by **Lee Adams**, book by **Michael Stewart**, directed and choreographed by **Gower Champion**. Inspired by Elvis Presley's entry into the U.S. Army a few years before, *Bye Bye Birdie* has found immortality in many productions by youthful companies. When a pop singer is drafted, he leaves behind a manager, Albert Peterson (**Dick Van Dyke**), and Albert's girlfriend and secretary, Rose Grant (**Chita Rivera**). Kay Medford played Albert's mother, who is given to histrionics whenever her son mentions Rose or marriage. Rose hatches a plan to write one last hit song for their star, Conrad Birdie (Dick Gautier), and then marry and live off the royalties. They invade a small town in Ohio, where Birdie is to sing the song to a local girl on *The Ed Sullivan Show*; Paul Lynde was the local girl's father. Women of all ages faint over Birdie's performances. Despite the obvious possibilities for rock and roll in the score, Strouse wrote firmly in the Broadway style. The kids sang the "A Lot of Livin' to Do," a delightful tune full of pop-style rhythms. Among Albert's tunes was "Put on a Happy Face," a song with coyly optimistic lyrics and an unpredictable melody. The show's other outstanding song was the jaunty "Kids," sung memorably by Paul Lynde and other parents. Strouse's fairly conventional tunes for Conrad Birdie were "Honestly Sincere" and "One Last Kiss." Champion provided several memorable dances, especially the "Shriner's Ballet," where Rose crashes a staid Masonic meeting. That *Bye Bye Birdie* became a hit could not have been predicted by **Brooks Atkinson**'s review in the *New York Times*. He found the show "uneven," with too many holes in the story, praised Van Dyke, Rivera, and Medford, but concluded that the show "is neither fish, fowl nor good **musical comedy**."

– C –

CABARET (20 NOVEMBER 1966, BROADHURST, 1,165 PERFORMANCES). Music by **John Kander**, lyrics by **Fred Ebb**, book by Joe Masteroff, directed and produced by **Harold Prince**. Based on John Van Druten's play *I Am a Camera* (which came from Christopher Isherwood's stories of an American in Berlin during the Weimar Republic), *Cabaret* was a serious and influential musical play. Numbers inside the cabaret reflected the events occurring on the outside. Bert Convy was Clifford Bradshaw, the American writer coming to live in Berlin. He meets Ernst Ludwig (Edward Winter), who smuggles to earn money for the growing Nazi Party. Clifford goes to the Kit Kat Club, where he encounters the empty-headed singer, Englishwoman Sally Bowles (Jill Haworth), who ends up in his apartment and bed. They part when she aborts the child they had conceived. He lives in the boarding house of Fraulein Schneider (**Lotte Lenya**), who seems ready to marry one of her boarders, Herr Schultz (Jack Gilford), a Jewish grocer. The Nazis, however, prevent the match by spooking Fraulein Schneider with demonstrations of disapproval. Woven through the story are musical numbers at the Kit Kat Club, most featuring **Joel Grey** as the smarmy "Master of Ceremonies," who wears garish make-up and slinks through his songs in a nearly obscene reflection of the real world. He makes fun of Nazis and Jews, Germans and foreigners, encouraging the live-for-today attitude that appears all around him while Germany stumbles down the path that leads to Hitler. The characters seemed real, as did their urge to live the unexamined life at the Kit Kat Club.

Cabaret showed clear influence from the theatrical works of **Kurt Weill** and Bertolt Brecht, a feeling reinforced by the presence of

Lenya, Weill's widow and the original Jenny in *Die Dreigroschenoper*. The show carried a consistent sense and tone, making it Hal Prince's strongest contribution to the **concept musical**. **Walter Kerr** reviewed *Cabaret* for the *New York Times*. He liked almost everything except Jill Haworth as Sally Bowles, whom he terms a "flavorless ingenue" and considers her Prince's major error in the production. He calls Grey's character "cheerful, charming, soulless and conspiratorially wicked" while Lenya "has never been better." He praises other members of the cast as well and finds the show, overall, to be "brilliantly conceived" with an excellent sense of style. Grey's performance has become one of Broadway's archetypal blends of actor and part.

Kander's and Ebb's score for *Cabaret* was a rich blending of period and modern idioms. The songs within the Kit Kat Club included the famous opening "Willkommen" and seamy "The Money Song." Other numbers are particularly disturbing, especially the seemingly innocuous "If You Could See Her," where the Master of Ceremonies parades around with a gorilla that he says he has fallen in love with, but at the end we learn she is Jewish. Among Sally's numbers sung from the stage, the sexy and very 1930s "Don't Tell Mama" and hedonistic title number stand out. Gilford sang the delightfully comic "Meeskite" at the end of the first act. Frau Schneider sums up the attitude of just about everyone with the song "So What?," a perverse waltz that carries a strong hint of Weill. The effective Nazi hymn, first sung by the Master of Ceremonies, is "Tomorrow Belongs to Me." Clifford and Sally sing the light "Perfectly Marvelous," somewhat like a **musical comedy** number from the 1920s. The 1972 film version starred Grey and **Liza Minnelli**, and the much-publicized 1998 Broadway revival, with **Alan Cumming** as the Master of Ceremonies, ran for 2,377 performances.

CABIN IN THE SKY (25 OCTOBER 1940, MARTIN BECK, 156 PERFORMANCES). Music by **Vernon Duke**, lyrics by John Latouche, book by Lynn Root, directed by **George Balanchine**. Although the fantasy about African Americans in the South did not enjoy a very long run, it is remembered as a Broadway highlight and for its star, **Ethel Waters**. It was similar to *Porgy and Bess* in that it was primarily created by whites for a black cast, but *Cabin in the Sky*

was not an opera. The plot involved the devout Petunia (Waters) trying to redeem before God her ne'er-do-well husband, "Little Joe"
Jackson (Dooley Wilson). Because Petunia is so favored in heaven,
God sends "The Lawd's General" (**Todd Duncan**) to give Little Joe
another chance. Joe argues with Petunia and shoots her, but heaven
admits them both after Petunia pleads for her husband's soul. In his
New York Times review, **Brooks Atkinson** called Lynn Root's book
"extraordinarily fresh" and praised as well Balanchine's "lyrical direction" and "the excellent performance by a singularly well-chosen
Negro cast." Although elements of Atkinson's review make for em-
barrassing reading today, they reflect their time and his love of the
production. *Cabin in the Sky* was the most impressive moment of
Ethel Waters's outstanding career. Atkinson notes that she "captures
all the innocence and humor of a storybook character" and rhapsodized about her singing of "Taking a Chance on Love." Vernon
Duke's memorable score included the title song, "Boogy-Woogy,"
"Honey in the Honeycomb," and others. *See also* AFRICAN
AMERICAN MUSICALS.

CAESAR, IRVING (1895–1996). Primarily known as a lyricist, Caesar was also a composer, librettist, and producer. Among his best
known lyrics are those for "Swanee" (music by **George Gershwin**)
and *No, No, Nanette* (music by **Vincent Youmans**), the show that
included "Tea for Two," "I Want to Be Happy," and the sprightly title song. He created music and lyrics for *Polly* (1929) and the short-
lived *My Dear Public* (1943), for which he also was producer and librettist.

LA CAGE AUX FOLLES **(21 AUGUST 1983, PALACE, 1,761 PER-
FORMANCES).** Music and lyrics by **Jerry Herman**, book by **Harvey Fierstein**, directed by **Arthur Laurents**. A sign of changing
times, *La Cage Aux Folles* was the first Broadway musical to focus
on the lives of a **homosexual** couple, but in many ways was in the
same aesthetic as *Hello, Dolly!* and *Mame*, Herman's other hits. The
show's model was the French film of the same name, which was
based on a French play by Jean Poiret. Albin (**George Hearn**) is the
star of a drag show that plays at a nightclub owned by his lover,
Georges (Gene Barry). They have been together for two decades, but

Albin has started to notice that he is aging, something that is extremely unnerving for a performer. They have a son, however, Jean-Michel (John Weiner), the result of Georges's one-night heterosexual stand from years before. Jean-Michel has fallen in love with a young woman whose father is a politician crusading against homosexuals. Georges asks Albin to disappear when the prospective in-laws come to visit. Act 1 closes as Albin, in the full drag of the nightclub show, angrily sings "I Am What I Am," one of the most powerful moments in a Herman musical. **Frank Rich** noted in the *New York Times* that "Hearn acts the song as searingly as he sings it." Especially memorable songs in the score, in addition to "I Am What I Am," include "Song on the Sand," "Look Over There," and "With You on My Arm." The show was revived in 2004.

CAHILL, MARIE (1874–1933). Musical comedy and silent film star whose Broadway credits include Vera von Lahn in *The Wild Rose* (1902), Sally in *Sally in Our Alley* (1902), and Katherine Peepfogle in *It Happened in Nordland* (1904). Decades later, she played Gloria Wentworth in **Cole Porter**'s *The New Yorkers* (1930).

CALL ME MADAM **(12 OCTOBER 1950, IMPERIAL, 644 PERFORMANCES).** Music and lyrics by **Irving Berlin**, book by **Howard Lindsay** and **Russel Crouse**, staged by **George Abbott**, dances and musical numbers staged by **Jerome Robbins**. A highly successful musical that showed Irving Berlin at the top of his game and brought **Ethel Merman** back to the stage. For his second term, Harry Truman appointed major Democratic donor and famed party hostess Perle Mesta ambassador to Luxembourg. Inspired by this true story, the creators of *Call Me Madam* made Ethel Merman into "Sally Adams," ambassador to the fictional country of Lichtenburg. Her lack of preparedness is ludicrous, but, as Merman memorably sang, she is "The Hostess with The Mostes' on the Ball." She falls in love with Lichtenberg's prime minister (Paul Lukas) and begins to offer her considerable fortune to his country. Her presence is resented by the parliamentary opposition, who manage to have her recalled to Washington, but all works out in the end. The sub-plot involved Sally's bookish assistant, Kenneth Gibson (Russell Nype), falling in love with Princess Maria (Galina Talva). He thinks he is ill, but Sally tells him "You're Just In Love." *New York Times* critic **Brooks Atkinson** called this one of Berlin's "most enchanting scores, fresh, light, and beguiling." The score's most famous song was "They Like Ike," sung before the famous general on opening night and later used as his Presidential campaign song.

CALL ME MISTER **(18 APRIL 1946, NATIONAL, 734 PERFORMANCES).** Music and lyrics by **Harold Rome**, sketches by Arnold Auerbach. An energetic revue that poked fun at demobilization and other issues after the war became one of its season's hits. The war's influence on Broadway musicals hardly ended with victory, and *Call Me Mister* showed that there was a great deal of fun to be had with the long process of bringing the boys home. The clear star was **Betty Garrett**, who plays, among other things, a drugstore waitress who wonders "What's to Become of Little Surplus Me?" and, in the major hit of the show, declares how tired she is of Latin American dances such as the conga in "South America, Take It Away." Reflection on the late, wartime president came in "The Face On The Dime." In his *New York Times* review, Lewis Nichols found composer and lyricist Harold Rome "one of the heroes of the evening," a creator whose songs are "singable and light." Nichols called *Call Me Mister* "an engaging revue and a credit to Selective Service."

CAMELOT **(3 DECEMBER 1960, MAJESTIC, 873 PERFORMANCES).** Music by **Frederick Loewe**; lyrics and book by **Alan Jay Lerner**; directed by **Moss Hart**; choreographed by **Hanya Holm**; produced by Lerner, Loewe, and Hart. A treatment of the Arthurian legend that, despite its tortured production history, has become a beloved musical. Lerner and Loewe directly followed *My Fair Lady* with the film *Gigi*. The inspiration for their next Broadway project came from T. H. White's novel *The Once and Future King*. Finding the principal actors—**Richard Burton**, **Julie Andrews**, **Robert Goulet**, **Roddy McDowall**, and Robert Coote—was comparatively simple, but problems began with Lerner's book. The second act, concerning the love triangle between Arthur, Guenevere, and Lancelot, made for a depressing ending, and the show was more than four hours long on opening night. During tryouts in Toronto, plagued by technical problems in a brand new theater, Lerner had a bleeding ulcer and Hart suffered a heart attack. The show went to Broadway with a huge advance sale, but critics reacted variably. **Brooks Atkinson** in the *Times* found the show visually "a thing of beauty," but felt it was "weighed down by the burden of its book." He was lukewarm about the score. *Camelot* ran until Hart could come back and help to fix it. An appearance on *The Ed Sullivan Show* brought much-needed publicity, and *Camelot* settled in for a two-year run.

The score, an especially fine effort by Loewe the melodist, has aged well. In previous scores with Lerner, one hears Loewe deliberately imitating specific musical styles, but *Camelot* includes no music that sounds medieval. One finds instead Loewe's great range within the traditional arena of the theater song. The title song is a straight-forward AABA form with a jaunty, simple melody defined by the opening ascending octave and then primarily conjunct motion. He brought a directness to Guenevere's wistful "The Simple Joys of Maidenhood" and a lovely sense of nostalgia to Arthur's "How to Handle a Woman." Full romantic melody appears in "If Ever I Would Leave You" and "I Loved You Once in Silence." Lerner's words cover a wide range in tone and manner, not unlike White's book, which is full of anachronisms. Whether the changes in tone work for Lerner's lyrics has been a matter of debate, but they usually supply an elegant complement to Loewe's music. The lavish film version appeared in 1967.

CAN-CAN (7 MAY 1953, SHUBERT, 892 PERFORMANCES). Music and lyrics by **Cole Porter**, book and staging by **Abe Burrows**, choreography by **Michael Kidd**, produced by **Cy Feuer** and Ernest Martin. Based on an original story concerning the famed 19th-century Parisian dance, *Can-Can* opened to tepid notices but became a substantial hit. The plot involved a judge, Aristide Forestier (Peter Cookson), who investigates the morality of the dancing at a Montmartre café. He falls in love with the owner, La Mome Pistache (Lilo), whom he marries and subsequently assists in legalizing the dance. One of the dancers, Claudine (**Gwen Verdon**), sparks the interest of two patrons, allowing for a comic subplot that eventually leads to a comic duel. Lilo came from Paris to star in the work and received appreciative notices, but many raved even more about Verdon in Michael Kidd's dances. **Brooks Atkinson**, writing in the *New*

York Times, had mixed feelings. He called Burrows's book and direction "heavy-handed facetiousness from the past" and heard in Porter's score "recognizable clichés" but a bevy of stylistic references. When Lilo sang, however, he noted that "she raises the temperature of the theatre perceptibly." Atkinson believed that it was choreographer Kidd who "picks 'Can-Can' out of the old **operetta** routines and turns it into a modern show," and he praised Verdon's role in each of the main dances. Porter's exquisite score included "C'est Magnifique," "I Love Paris," and "It's All Right with Me," among others. Sometimes it takes a few years for the cream to rise to the top, but *Can-Can* would still be remembered if it had only launched "I Love Paris."

CANDIDE **(1 DECEMBER 1956, MARTIN BECK, 73 PERFORMANCES).** Music by **Leonard Bernstein**, lyrics by Richard Wilbur, additional lyrics by John Latouche and **Dorothy Parker**, book by Lillian Hellman, staged by Tyrone Guthrie. Although the initial production was a noble failure, Bernstein's ebullient score has caused the frequent revival of this comic **operetta**. Hellman set out to comment on McCarthyism and what she viewed as an apathetic America in the mid-1950s, and produced a heavy-handed satire based on Voltaire's novella. Bernstein, on the other hand, wrote a light operetta score that had moments of intense sarcasm, but was primarily frothy and based largely upon old European dance rhythms. Hellman and Bernstein never resolved these conceptual differences, and none of the other creators could fix the problems. The cast included **Robert Rounseville** as Candide and a very young **Barbara Cook** as Cunegonde, both wonderful singers, and the production values were indeed splendid. Reviews were mixed and hardly warm enough to imagine that a long run would have been possible, but some critics were impressed. **Brooks Atkinson** wrote in the *Times* that it was "the first musical of the season that has distinction." He noted the disconnect between Bernstein's score and the play, however, stating that he wrote "a score that skips gaily over the Voltaire theme." One could not deny, however, the effectiveness of the Overture or such songs as "Glitter and Be Gay" and "Make Our Garden Grow," merely high points in a score of uncommon richness. It was this music that inspired **Harold Prince** to bring *Candide* back to Broadway on 10

March 1974 (when he moved the production from Brooklyn's Chelsea Theater Center) with a new book by Hugh Wheeler, a completely new conception, and some new lyrics by **Stephen Sondheim**. Hellman hated this production, but it did show the public what was possible with the property. There have been numerous other reworkings, and Bernstein recorded a concert version in 1989.

CANTOR, EDDIE (BORN EDWARD ISRAEL ISKOWITZ, 1892–1964). Singer, dancer, and comedian who starred in *Ziegfeld Follies* before starring in the **musical comedies** *Kid Boots* (1923), in which he introduced "If You Knew Susie," and *Whoopee* (1928), with the hit song "Makin' Whoopee." He appeared in many Hollywood films and was a radio celebrity; his last Broadway appearance was in *Banjo Eyes* (1941). He brought a Jewish cantoral tradition to the musical theater, and occasionally appeared in blackface.

THE CAPEMAN **(29 JANUARY 1998, MARQUIS, 68 PERFORMANCES).** Music, lyrics, and book by Paul Simon; lyrics and book by Derek Walcott; direction and choreography by Mark Morris. A spectacular failure with an admirable score by a pop legend, *The Capeman* showed that a sung-through musical must pay attention to the dramatic element. The plot, based on a true story, concerned Salvador Agron, a Puerto Rican who grew up in New York under appalling conditions, joined a street gang (where he wore a cape, hence the title), and committed a notorious double murder in 1959 at age 16. He learns to read in prison, studies poetry and philosophy, and becomes a compelling figure. He died in 1986, seven years after his release. Simon discovered the story and released an album of songs, but could not effectively bring the idea to the stage. Writing for the *New York Times*, **Ben Brantley** stated "that no one has been able to find the visual and verbal equivalents to Mr. Simon's multilayered score."

EL CAPITAN **(20 APRIL 1896, BROADWAY, 112 PERFORMANCES).** Music by **John Philip Sousa**, lyrics by Sousa and Tom Frost, book by Charles Klein, produced by De Wolf Hopper. The most enduring of Sousa's **operettas**, *El Capitan* played for about four months in New York, followed by a national tour of four years and a six-month run in London. As important as was Sousa's participation, probably more significant for its success was its star, comic actor De Wolf Hopper. Praise for Hopper dominates the opening of the *New York Times* review. Hopper played Don Medigua, the Viceroy of Peru, who captures El Capitan, the leader of a rebel band. After having the rebel leader executed, Medigua takes his place. Many complications ensue, but all turns out to the advantage of right and lovers in the end. Sousa's songs, some with music borrowed from earlier shows, included "The Legend of the Frogs," "Sweetheart, I'm Waiting," and "El Capitan's Song," the latter the basis for the famous "El Capitan March."

CARIOU, LEN (1939–). The Canadian actor's Broadway credits include Bill Sampson in *Applause* (1970), Fredrik in *A Little Night Music* (1973), and the title character in *Sweeney Todd: The Demon Barber of Fleet Street* (1979). He won a **Tony Award** for his portrayal of the murderous Sweeney Todd. His strengths as a character actor and his excellent diction and resonant sound allow him to bring an unusually strong dramatic effect to all his roles.

CARMEN JONES **(2 DECEMBER 1943, BROADWAY, 502 PERFORMANCES).** Music by Georges Bizet, with new orchestral arrangements by **Robert Russell Bennett**, lyrics and book by **Oscar Hammerstein II**, staging by **Hassard Short**, choreography by **Eugene Loring**, produced by **Billy Rose**. An inspired retelling and African American version of Bizet's *Carmen* that moved the story to a parachute factory in the southern United States, *Carmen Jones* became a surprise hit that demonstrated Hammerstein's ability to write fine lyrics for an existing score and, perhaps, the effectiveness of Billy Rose as a publicist. Except for changing the locale and updating situations, Hammerstein did not change the plot, moving through the opera's libretto scene by scene. He presented the plot with the requisite seriousness and did not write a parody. His changes include making the bullfighter a prizefighter. The show remained an opera, necessitating that major roles be double-cast because of the strenuous singing. Lewis Nichols raved in the *New York Times*: "It is beautifully done in every way," with beautiful sets, ballets, and "singers who can sing." Of Hammerstein lyrics, Nichols noted they "are light, but there are no Broadway gags." He praised the principals, such as Muriel

Smith in the title role, who "looked sultry" and had a wonderful voice, while the chorus, directed by a young Robert Shaw, was "perfect." He also loved the various production elements, especially the colorful costumes by Raoul Pene du Bois. Hammerstein's lyrics for *Carmen Jones* are most effective. The African American dialect that he adopted is believable, and he seems to have captured every beat and accent of Bizet's music. The famous "Habanera" becomes "Dat's Love," as sexy and coquettish as the original. Carmen's invitation to Don Jose to meet her, "Près des remparts de Seville" in the original, became "Dere's a Café on de Corner," the "Toreador Song" is now "Stan' Up and Fight," a song about boxing. *Carmen Jones* might now raise racial issues in revival, but in terms of artistic merit, it certainly deserves to be heard. A film version appeared in 1954. *See also* AFRICAN AMERICAN MUSICALS.

CARNIVAL! (13 APRIL 1961, IMPERIAL, 719 PERFORMANCES). Music and lyrics by **Bob Merrill**, book by **Michael Stewart**, staged and choreographed by **Gower Champion**, presented by **David Merrick**. Based upon material by Helen Deutsch from Paul Gallico's story "The Seven Seals of Clement O'Reilly," which had recently been made into the successful film *Lili*, *Carnival!* combined Gower Champion's brilliant staging with the naïve charm of Anna Maria Alberghetti. The story involves the arrival of Lili (Alberghetti), an orphan, at a European carnival, where she seeks a friend of her dead father. The carnival workers take her in. Potential romantic matches include Marco the Magnificent (James Mitchell) and the puppeteer, Paul Bethalet (**Jerry Orbach**). Marco at first beguiles Lili, but she finds love with Paul. She becomes the figure in the show that speaks with his puppets and brings out the best in the disabled and gruff puppeteer. The show included a real carnival, with jugglers, barkers, acrobats, and other figures often performing onstage and in the audience. The choreography was lively and involved many cast members, and the lack of a curtain made the audience feel like part of the show. **Howard Taubman** of the *New York Times* reviewed *Carnival!* favorably and placed the principal appeal of the show in "the constant interplay of Lili's sweet simplicity and the strident artificiality of carnival life." He praised many elements of the show, but reserved his strongest praise for Champion, who took all of the diverse elements and brought them together into a whole of "polish and exuberance." Taubman dismissed Merrill's score as "workmanlike," but one hit, "Love Makes the World Go 'Round," emerged from the show.

CAROLINE, OR CHANGE **(2 MAY 2004, EUGENE O'NEILL, 136 PERFORMANCES).** Music by **Jeanine Tesori**, lyrics and book by Tony Kushner, directed by George C. Wolfe. **Tonya Pinkins** played Caroline Thibodeaux, a 39-year-old **African American** maid who works for a white, Jewish, southern family in November and December 1963. The show deals with issues of racism, religion, war, poverty, divorce, domestic violence, John F. Kennedy's assassination, and above all, the challenges of change. A nearly sung-through musical, Caroline sings in her basement with The Washing Machine (Capathia Jenkins), The Dryer (Chuck Cooper), and The Radio (Tracy Nicole Chapman, Marva Hicks, and Ramona Keller), a female trio with Motown roots; outside, The Moon (Aisha de Haas) offers her advice. Among the show's many outstanding moments are the opening "Washer/Dryer" scene, the emotive JFK sequence, including the lament sung by The Bus (Cooper), and Caroline's powerful act 2 soliloquy "Lot's Wife." The score's eclectic musical style, innovative staging and dramaturgy, and themes of **social justice and injustice**, along with convincing performances, gave it an extremely distinctive character that challenged its audience.

CAROUSEL **(19 APRIL 1945, MAJESTIC, 890 PERFOR-MANCES).** Music by **Richard Rodgers**, lyrics and book by **Oscar Hammerstein II**, directed by **Rouben Mamoulian**, choreographed by **Agnes de Mille**, produced by Lawrence Langner and Theresa Helburn. The second **musical play** by Rodgers and Hammerstein that confirmed their innovative work in *Oklahoma!* was based on playwright Ferenc Molnár's fantasy *Liliom*. Moving the setting from Budapest to 19th-century Maine, Hammerstein made a few substantive changes in Molnár's story. *Carousel* opened with a pantomime set to the "Carousel Waltz" that told the story and relationship between mill worker Julie Jordan and carnival barker Billy Bigelow. Billy and Julie discover their love during a 16-minute musical scene ("Bench Scene," including "If I Loved You"), confirming the integration of plot and music that they had explored in *Oklahoma!*. The couple elopes, but Billy does not adjust well to married life, especially after learning that Julie is pregnant. While Billy delivers an alternately joyous and contemplative "Soliloquy" concerning what he hopes to be his unborn son, he realizes that he needs to find money and agrees to help in a robbery that results in his death. In the second act, Billy returns briefly from heaven to help his now teenaged daughter, Louise, who has been shunned because of her father's reputation. After one unsuccessful attempt to assist her, he manages to instill some hope and dignity in her at her graduation. Julie's friend Carrie Pipperidge and capitalist Enoch Snow provide the secondary leads, both of whom are foils for the antiestablishment Julie and Billy.

Tryouts started in New Haven and then moved to Boston. Concerned about an overly long second act, Rodgers and Hammerstein reworked the sequence in heaven and cut Agnes de Mille's opening ballet that chronicled Louise's life. In New York, however, the restored ballet stopped the show. Lewis Nichols of the *New York Times* felt that *Carousel* could do no wrong: "The Majestic is across the street from the St. James, where 'Oklahoma!' is stationed . . . (and they) . . . will be able to wink at one another for a long time to come." Richard Rodgers considered *Carousel* his most satisfying score because of the wide variety of songs. It was filled with songs that became standards, including "We'll Have a Real Nice Clambake," "June is Bustin' Out All Over," and the anthem "You'll Never Walk Alone." *Carousel*'s cast consisted mostly of unknowns, including **Jan Clayton** as Julie and **John Raitt** as Billy. Bambi Linn, the original "Dream Laurie" in *Oklahoma!*, played Louise. The film version appeared in 1956, and the show was revived at London's National Theatre in 1993. The London production transferred to Broadway the next year and featured **Audra McDonald** as Carrie, the role for which she won her first **Tony Award**.

CARROLL, DIAHANN (BORN CAROL DIAHANN JOHNSON, 1935–). African American film and television star who starred in *House of Flowers* (1954) and won a **Tony Award** for her performance as Barbara Woodruff in **Richard Rodgers**'s *No Strings* (1962). She created the role of Norma Desmond in the Canadian production of **Andrew Lloyd Webber**'s *Sunset Boulevard*.

CARROLL, EARL (1892–1948). A songwriter from Pittsburgh who wrote "Isle D' Amour" for the *Ziegfeld Follies* of 1913 and songs for other shows, Carroll produced several **revues** under other titles before the first that he named after himself, *Earl Carroll Vanities*, in 1923. His major financial backer was William R. Edrington, a Texas oil tycoon who figured in many of Carroll's activities, such as the construction of a new Art Deco theater that seated 3,000 people and hosted its first edition of the *Vanities* in 1931. (The house was too large for Broadway-style entertainment, however, and soon was demolished.) It was during a birthday party for Edrington during the fourth *Vanities* that some of the girls allegedly took a bath in champagne. Carroll spent four months in prison for violating Prohibition laws. In addition to his *Vanities*, Carroll also produced two shows called *Earl Carroll's Sketch Book* that opened on 1 July 1929 and 4 June 1935, running 392 and 207 performances. When the Broadway revue format died, Carroll took his shows to a Hollywood dinner theater for a number of years. In 1940 he returned to New York for another version of the *Vanities*, but it ran for less than a month. *See also EARL CARROLL VANITIES.*

CARROLL, HARRY (1892–1962). Self-taught composer whose music appeared in **revues** during the 1910s and early 1920s. He contributed songs to *Ziegfeld Follies* (1910, 1916, and 1921) and to the **Shubert**-produced *The Passing Show* of 1914 (including "By the Beautiful Sea"), *Dancing Around* (1914), and *Maid in America* (1915). He wrote and produced *Oh, Look!* in 1918, which included the famous "I'm Always Chasing Rainbows," the melody of which came from Chopin's *Fantasie-Impromptu in C sharp minor*.

CARVER, BRENT (1951–). Actor known for his emotive portrayals of characters in distress. He won a **Tony Award** for playing the **homosexual** window dresser, Molina, in *Kiss of the Spider Woman* (1993), and also appeared as Leo Frank, the troubled hero who is jailed on false charges and lynched before his release, in *Parade* (1998).

CARYLL, IVAN (BORN FELIX TILKINS, 1861–1921). Born in Belgium, Caryll established his reputation as a musical theater composer in London before relocating to New York in 1911. His works, which follow in the general style of **W. S. Gilbert** and **Arthur Sullivan**, include *The Pink Lady* (1911), *Oh! Oh! Delphine* (1912), *The Belle of Bond Street* (1914), *Chin Chin* (1914), and *Kissing Time* (1920).

THE CAT AND THE FIDDLE **(15 OCTOBER 1931, GLOBE, 395 PERFORMANCES).** Music by **Jerome Kern**, lyrics and book by **Otto Harbach**, ensemble dances arranged by **Albertina Rasch**, presented by Max Gordon in association with Erlanger Productions, Inc. Billed as a "musical love story," *The Cat and the Fiddle* resembled the European-based **operettas** that had fallen somewhat out of favor. Rumanian composer Victor Florescu (George Metaxa) and American songwriter Shirley Sheridan meet in Brussels. He has written an opera and resists Shirley for various reasons, but they come together in the end; all the while Victor endures professional problems with his opera's lead female singer. Kern's score was a wonderful blend of the sounds of American popular music and the European operetta, a common stylistic mixture for the composer, and the show's delightful songs included "She Didn't Say Yes," "The Night Was Made for Love," and "Try to Forget." **J. Brooks Atkinson**, reviewing the show for the *New York Times*, lauded the creators for trying "to break free of the stereotyped **musical comedy** patterns," but takes issue with George Metaxa as the romantic lead because of the "metallic quality in his singing." He noted that Harbach provided an "appropriate background," Kern's score is "genuine and infectiously romantic," and the "production is entrancing." The show managed to run for nearly a year at a time when Broadway was suffering the effects of the 1929 Stock Market Crash and Great Depression.

CATS **(7 OCTOBER 1982, WINTER GARDEN, 7,485 PERFORMANCES).** Music by **Andrew Lloyd Webber**, lyrics by T. S. Eliot and **Trevor Nunn**, directed by Nunn, choreography by **Gillian Lynne**, presented by **Cameron Mackintosh**, **The Really Useful Company**, David Geffen, and the **Shubert Organization**. The longest-running show in Broadway history until *The Phantom of the Opera* surpassed it in January 2006, *Cats* was based on T. S. Eliot's book of children's poetry *Old Possum's Book of Practical Cats*. It had played in London for 17 months before opening in New York. Although its staging was nothing short of spectacular, *Cats* is in many ways a simple show based on a consistent theme. The single setting is a junkyard of oversized objects, making humans look the size of cats. The show is **revue**-like in structure, with different Jellicle Cats presenting songs and dances of various types. Old Deuteronomy (**Ken Page**) introduces the slim plot: At the end of the Jellicle Ball he will choose the cat to be reborn in "the heaviside layer." The audience meets various cats who might deserve another life, but it seems fairly obvious from early in the show that it will be Grizabella (**Betty Buckley**), the tawdriest and saddest cat, who will ascend. When she sings "Memory," the show's major hit near the end, it is clear that she will be resurrected. In the show's glitziest effect, a paw-shaped ladder descends like a spaceship and Grizabella heads toward the offstage light. Many members of the cast emerge with individual personalities, but among the more distinctive are Munkustrap (**Harry Groener**), the mischievous duo Mungojerrie (Rene Clemente) and Rumpleteaser (Christine Langer), the tap-dancing Jennyanydots (Anna McNeeley), the conjuring Mistoffolees (Timothy Scott), the evil Macavity (Kenneth Ard), the strutting, rockstar-like Rum Tum Tugger (**Terrence V. Mann**), the railroad cat Skimbleshanks (Reed Jones), the fat cat that frequents clubs, Bustopher Jones, and the theater cat Asparagus (both played by Stephen Hanan).

The show is sung throughout with musical sequences of considerable contrast. For example, "Gus: The Theater Cat" is a simple and nostalgic number that leads into a parody of Italian opera, "Growltiger's Last Stand." Shorter, but memorable, is the spirited "Skimbleshanks: The Railway Cat," accompanied by the cat chorus assembling a train out of junk. "Macavity: The Mystery Cat" is a sexy number with choreography reminiscent of **Bob Fosse**. "The Old Gumbie Cat," a tap dance, likewise recalls the style of songs from the 1930s. Lloyd Webber makes considerable use of reprise, with "Memory" playing a major role in delineating the character and fate of Grizabella. Gillian Lynne, the British choreographer, made *Cats* a dancing show. In comparison to previous West End shows, she was highly successful, but some critics in the United States found the dance vocabulary limited when compared to shows choreographed by **Jerome Robbins**, Fosse, **Gower Champion**, and others.

Frank Rich wrote a mixed review for the *New York Times*. He found the show's best feature to be the way it "transports the audience into a complete fantasy world," a journey that too rarely happens in the theater, but he does not call it a "brilliant musical" or one filled with ideas. He compared the playful spirit of Eliot's poems to *Alice in Wonderland* and believed that this playfulness made it into the theater. He appreciated **John Napier**'s set and costume designs, the former made the Winter Garden Theater "unrecognizable"; the latter "completes the illusion." Nunn and Lynne managed to give each cat a personality through movement, and Rich considered this their "highest achievement." He cited Hanan and Buckley as providing the show's "emotional pull." Rich wished for a bit more feeling from the show, but lauded its spectacle and the special world that it evokes. It was that special world that kept audiences coming to the Winter Garden for almost 18 years.

THE CENTURY GIRL **(6 NOVEMBER 1916, CENTURY, 200 PERFORMANCES).** Music by **Victor Herbert** and **Irving Berlin**, book by "Everyman," produced by **Charles Dillingham** and **Florenz Ziegfeld**. An opulent **revue** offered at an enormous theater by two of Broadway's biggest producers, *The Century Girl* was a star-studded affair that played for about six months. On opening night, the show ran more than four hours because of the wealth of material. It consisted mostly of **vaudeville** routines intermingled with the spectacle of huge chorus numbers, some of the latter taking place on staircases, a later Ziegfeld trademark. The cast included some of the era's biggest stars, including Elsie Janis, Marie Dressler, Leon Errol, Harry Kelly, Hazel Dawn, and the team of Van and Schenck. Although two leading composers, Herbert and Berlin, wrote the music, there were few hits. Two songs, "When Uncle Sam Is Ruler of the Sea" and "Uncle Sam's Children," showed the growing patriotism before the United States entered World War I. A comic skit included actors portraying Herbert and Berlin competing with **operetta** and ragtime tunes, and another offered humorous dancing of a "stone age romance" to Stravinskian dissonances like those in *The Rite of Spring*. The unsigned review in the *New York Times* is glowing, the author even asking whether the producers "can afford to give such prodigal entertainment on so staggering a scale." The show was simply "altogether like nothing else" of the time.

CERVERIS, MICHAEL (1960–). Singing actor with a commanding stage presence who played the 18-year-old Tommy in *The Who's Tommy* (1993) and Thomas Andrews in *Titanic* (1997). He won a **Tony Award** for Best Featured Actor in a Musical for his portrayal of John Wilkes Booth in *Assassins* (2004) and continued his exploration of murderous characters in the title role of **John Doyle**'s **revival** of *Sweeney Todd: The Demon Barber of Fleet Street* (2005).

CHAMPION, GOWER (1919–1980). Influential director and choreographer who began his Broadway career in the late 1930s as a dancer and choreographer. He won a **Tony Award** for his staging of *Lend an Ear* (1948). Other credits included *Bye Bye Birdie* (1960), *Carnival!* (1961), and *Hello, Dolly!* (1964). His final show was *42nd Street* (1980); tragically, Champion died hours before the show opened. Famous examples of his work include the "Shriner's Ballet" in *Bye Bye Birdie*, the riotous stage motion around **Carol Channing** in *Hello, Dolly!*, and the brilliant evocation of 1930s tap dancing in *42nd Street*.

CHANNING, CAROL (1921–). Channing made her stage debut in *No for an Answer* (1941), created Lorelei Lee in *Gentlemen Prefer Blondes* (1949) and introduced "Diamonds Are a Girl's Best Friend," succeeded **Rosalind Russell** as Ruth Sherwood in *Wonderful Town* (1953), and originated the immortal role of Dolly Gallagher Levi in *Hello, Dolly!* (1964). She received a **Tony Award** and the *Variety* Drama Critics' Award for Dolly. She returned to Broadway as Lorelei Lee in *Lorelei* (1973). **Brooks Atkinson**, in his review of *Gentlemen Prefer Blondes*, said that Channing resembled "a dazed automaton . . . looking out on a confused world through big, wide, starry eyes." Although she started as a soprano, the Broadway icon evolved into a true belter and emphasized her lower chest register and nasal quality to tremendous character effect. Her wide eyes and big smile have become as legendary and unmistakable as her voice.

CHARNIN, MARTIN (1934–). Lyricist and director whose most successful show was *Annie* (1977, with music by **Charles Strouse**), for which he both wrote lyrics and directed. He began his Broadway career playing Big Deal, one of the Jets, in the original production of *West Side Story* (1957). As a lyricist, he collaborated with **Mary**

Rodgers on *Hot Spot* (1963) and with **Richard Rodgers** on *Two by Two* (1971) and *I Remember Mama* (1979).

CHENOWETH, KRISTIN (1968–). Singing actress who made her Broadway debut as Precious McGuire in *Steel Pier* (1997), going on to win the **Tony Award** for Best Featured Actress in a Musical for her portrayal of Sally in the 1999 **revival** of *You're a Good Man, Charlie Brown*. She created the role of Galinda (later Glinda) in *Wicked* (2003) and dazzled audiences as Cunegunde in the New York Philharmonic's semi-staged version of *Candide* (2004). Chenoweth starred in the 2006 revival of *The Apple Tree*.

CHERRY BLOSSOMS (28 MARCH 1927, 44TH STREET, 56 PERFORMANCES). Music by **Sigmund Romberg**, book and lyrics by **Harry B. Smith**. Set in Japan, the Pygmalion-derived tale (based on the play *The Willow Tree*) recalls David Belasco's *Madame Butterfly* (1900) and Giacomo Puccini's operatic adaptation, *Madama Butterfly* (1904), but without the tragic ending. American Ned Hamilton (Howard Marsh) falls in love with Yo-San (Desiree Ellinger). He returns to Japan 17 years later and meets Yo-San's daughter (also played by Ellinger). The **operetta**'s musical centerpiece is the waltz "My Own Willow Tree," in which Romberg employed musical techniques such as parallel fourths and augmented triads to suggest the sound of Japan. *See also* ORIENTALISM.

CHESS (28 APRIL 1988, IMPERIAL, 68 PERFORMANCES). Music by Benny Andersson and Bjorn Ulvaeus, lyrics by **Tim Rice**, book by Richard Nelson, directed by **Trevor Nunn**. The **rock musical** by the male half of ABBA did very well in London but was not successful on Broadway, perhaps because of the plot's essential anti-Americanism and what was perceived as overamplification of the music. Rice conceived the idea concerning a championship chess match between an immature, self-absorbed American (Philip Casnoff) and a more likable Russian player (David Carroll), complicated by their love triangle with a Hungarian woman (**Judy Kuhn**). The end of the Cold War in effect took place over a chessboard and, as **Frank Rich** noted at length in the *New York Times*, at the top of the actors' lungs: "The show is a suite of temper tantrums, all amplified to a piercing pitch," perhaps more appropriate for "stock-car racing." Rich found great fault with the book, calling it "incoherent." The score included the famous "Anthem," "I Know Him So Well," and "One Night in Bangkok." A revival in 2003 played for a single performance.

CHICAGO (3 JUNE 1975, 46TH STREET, 936 PERFOR-MANCES). Music by **John Kander**, lyrics by **Fred Ebb**, book by Ebb and **Bob Fosse**, directed and choreographed by Fosse. Borrowing a risqué plot from Maurine Watkins's 1926 play *Chicago* that also appeared in the 1942 movie *Roxie Hart* (starring Ginger Rogers), Bob Fosse led a group of talented creators in producing a highly successful, stylish musical that was overshadowed to an extent by the epochal success of *A Chorus Line*, which opened seven weeks after *Chicago*, but audiences were also pleased to frequent the decadent, evocative world of 1920s Chicago. The show's plot involves two glamorous murderesses, Roxie Hart (**Gwen Verdon**) and Velma Kelly (**Chita Rivera**) who, aided by their crooked and smarmy lawyer, Billy Flynn (**Jerry Orbach**), compete for media attention. The three leads, praised lavishly by **Clive Barnes** in the *New York Times* (who in other ways was hardly convinced of the show's merits), brought to *Chicago* true star power. Barnes reported that the heroines danced "their hearts out," with great contrast in the singing between Verdon's "candy innocence . . . yet . . . naughtily suggestive" and Rivera's "blasé worldliness." He called Orbach a "knockout." The show's sleazy sexiness was aided immeasurably by Verdon's and Rivera's willingness to place their well-toned but undeniably middle-aged frames in very scant costumes.

The score and dances in *Chicago* work much like those in *Cabaret*, serving as rich commentary on the outrageous plot, where Flynn plays Chicago's corrupt legal system and out-of-control press like a piano. Clive Barnes noted this similarity with Kander and Ebb's earlier show, stating that both shows stand "aside from a time and a place" with "cynical" indifference. One musical number after another winks at the show's inevitable plot, with its character's despicable machinations and the public's almost maniacal desire to embrace these celebrated killers. Orbach commented on his talented courtroom histrionics in "Razzle Dazzle," a typical Fosse number that is extravagantly overdone. Roxie's husband (Barney Martin) comes to feel invisible in the media circus that surrounds Roxie's trial, a complaint he registers with great irony in the vaudeville number "Mister Cellophane." Rivera and Verdon delivered the tour-de-force "All That Jazz" with unforgettable performances. *Chicago* has been described as being ahead of its time; and renewed popularity came after real-life high-profile celebrity trials in the 1900s. Its long-running Broadway **revival** opened in 1996 (with 4,218 performances as of 31 December 2006), and the 2002 film version starring Renée Zelweger, Catherine Zeta-Jones, and Richard Gere won the Academy Award for Best Motion Picture.

***CHITTY CHITTY BANG BANG* (28 APRIL 2005, HILTON, 285 PERFORMANCES).** Music and lyrics by Richard M. Sherman and Robert B. Sherman, adapted for the stage by Jeremy Sams, directed by Adrian Noble, musical staging and choreography by **Gillian Lynne**. A success in London, the stage adaptation of the classic 1968 children's musical film did not fare so well in New York. **Raúl Esparza** played Caractacus Potts, and Erin Dilly was Truly Scrumptious, but the show's main star was the flying car. The plot was an expanded version of the film's basic storyline, and the score included both songs from the film and newly written numbers such as "Kiddy-Widdy-Winkies" and "The Bombie Samba."

***THE CHOCOLATE SOLDIER* (13 SEPTEMBER 1909, LYRIC, 296 PERFORMANCES).** Music by Oscar Straus, libretto by Rudolph Bernauer and Leopold Jacobson, English version by Stanislaus Stange. Based on George Bernard Shaw's *Arms and the Man*, the operetta appeared in Vienna the previous year; the playwright was distraught at the treatment of his work, which led him to not allow a musicalization of his play *Pygmalion* (something **Lerner and Loewe** eventually did in *My Fair Lady*). On Broadway, the antiwar nature of the plot remained, and focused on Lieutenant Bumerli (J. E. Gardner), who was more interested in eating chocolates than fighting. The show's musical hit was "My Hero."

CHOREOGRAPHER/CHOREOGRAPHY. The designer of dances for a show/dancing in a show. Dance has long been a part of Broadway musicals, becoming a major partner in storytelling with *Oklahoma!* in 1943. Earlier, dance was part of Broadway's quest for variety, sometimes informing the audience about a character; choreographers at the time, such as **Busby Berkeley** and **Albertina Rasch**, often received a commercial credit such as "dances by." Gradually dance played a larger role in shows in the 1930s; notable choreographers of the decade included **George Balanchine** and **Robert Alton**. Dance became increasingly integrated into the overall concept of the Broadway musical in the 1940s. The choreographer for *Oklahoma!* was **Agnes de Mille**, who helped make aspects of ballet, modern dance, and pantomime a major part of the show's story and characterization. She contributed similarly to *Carousel* (1945), and became the first choreographer also to serve as director in *Allegro* (1947). **Jack Cole** was a significant figure in Broadway's dance tradition with imaginative use of steps from vernacular and jazz dancing and acrobatics, as was **Michael Kidd**, who was known for including a wide variety of styles in his work. The legendary career of **Jerome Robbins** spanned from *On the Town* (1944) to *Jerome Robbins' Broadway* (1989), and included the lengthy ballet "The Small House of Uncle Thomas" for *The King and I* (1951). Robbins realized a Broadway landmark as choreographer-director for *West Side Story* (1957). **Bob Fosse** was a protégé of both Abbott and Robbins whose frequent use of overt sensuousness in shows such as *Damn Yankees* (1955), *Sweet Charity* (1966), and *Chicago* (1975) perhaps comes from his early **burlesque** influence. **Gower Champion**, **Michael Bennett**, and **Tommy Tune** were extremely important in the last third of the 20th century, while at the turn of the 21st century, **Susan Stroman**, **Graciela Daniele**, **Twyla Tharp**, and **Kathleen Marshall**, all women, are making their mark.

See also AVIAN, BOB; HANEY, CAROL; HOFFMAN, GERTRUDE; KELLY, GENE; LAYTON, JOE; LORING, EUGENE; LYNNE, GILLIAN; MARSHALL, ROB; MITCHELL, JULIAN; REAMS, LEE ROY; REINKING, ANN; WHITE, ONNA.

CHORUS. (1) The singing and dancing ensemble of a musical can take on various roles. It can be used for spectacle, as in **revues** and other types of musicals, provide aural support for principal singers (as the female chorus does in "I'm Gonna Wash That Man Right Outa My

Hair" in *South Pacific*), offer commentary in the manner of a Greek chorus (as near the end of *Camelot*), or be a fully functioning entity (as in *A Chorus Line*). Many shows rely on the chorus at the beginning of acts to grab the audience's attention through large-scale production numbers, such as the act 1 opening, "We Open in Venice," of *Kiss Me, Kate*, or the act 2 "Honey Bun" from *South Pacific*. Female choruses were especially known in revues such as the *Ziegfeld Follies*, while the male chorus was popularized in operettas such as *The Student Prince* and *The Desert Song*. An especially innovative use of chorus appears in the act 2 opening of *The Phantom of the Opera*, where live actors appear on a spectacular staircase alongside mannequins. (2) *See* REFRAIN.

A CHORUS LINE **(15 APRIL 1975, PUBLIC/NEWMAN AND SHUBERT, 6,137 PERFORMANCES).** Music by **Marvin Hamlisch**; lyrics by **Edward Kleban**; book by James Kirkwood and Nicholas Dante; conceived, choreographed, and directed by **Michael Bennett**, presented by the New York Shakespeare Festival Theater, Joseph Papp, producer. Every fan of Broadway music knows the importance of the **chorus**, but few Broadway musicals explicitly recognized this fact until *A Chorus Line*, a hit that happened when Broadway truly needed one. It was the next logical step in the plotless **concept musical** and was based upon an inspired and simple idea. Some chorus gypsies, originally without Bennett, met to discuss their lives and careers. Compelling material emerged, and Bennett took over the project. The show, assembled in two workshops, included an unlikely but fascinating framing device: dancers at an audition are instructed to talk about themselves. One hears about their careers' phases, pleasures and fears, sex lives, **homosexuality**, what their dreams were, and how they have worked out. Some critics complained about having to listen to other people's problems, but for many the format presented an aura of reality, even though no director would dare ask about an auditioning dancer's life. After eliminating six dancers early in the show, 17 remain, and for each a story and personality emerges. Principal figures include Cassie (**Donna McKechnie**), a former star dancer who was once director Zach's (Robert Lupone) lover and now hopes to catch on with a chorus; Paul (Clive Clerk), a homosexual who describes his humiliating adolescence in a drag revue; and Diana (Priscilla Lopez), a dancer who had an unfortunate experience in a high school drama class. After the eight finalists are selected, the entire cast struts its stuff on stage in full glittering costume for the song "One."

A Chorus Line carried a special sense of integration between the character's lives (rather than the plot), music, and dance. This was partly the result of the workshops, but primarily a tribute to Michael Bennett's vision. He never allowed the focus to move from the dancers. Every element contributes to the audience understanding their individual personalities: rehearsal costumes, the way they stand, the lines they speak from Kirkwood and Dante's taut book, the songs they sing, and the way they dance. Few shows so effectively weave every aspect together into a cohesive whole. Hamlisch and Kleban's score plays a major role in propelling the story forward. It perhaps sounds a bit too much like the 1970s in places, especially the instrumentation, but the songs paint the characters concisely. "Nothing" speaks eloquently of Diana's frustration in acting class, and "Sing" is a humorous look at a dancer who is a poor singer. "Dance: Ten; Looks: Three" tells how another dancer improved her career through plastic surgery. The ensemble sequences are very effective, although the only real song hit to emerge from the show was "What I Did for Love," an anthem for anyone who has ever become dedicated to an art.

A Chorus Line began life at the tiny Public/Newman Theater, soon moving to the Shubert for its record-breaking 15-year run. **Clive Barnes** reviewed it at its first venue and penned a rave. Broadway has heard about innovative shows for years, but Bennett "has really innovated one." Barnes immediately places it in the line of concept musicals, and says that what makes the show work so well "is its honesty of subject matter." He admits that the show is sentimental, although "even the sentimentality is true to form." He praises most elements, but is less than bowled over by Hamlisch's music and Kleban's lyrics. The book is "brilliantly written" and "the cast is 105 percent marvelous." It is Bennett's show, and Barnes believes that nothing the director did could have been better. A Broadway revival opened in fall 2006.

CITY CENTER *ENCORES!* New York City Center *Encores! Great American Musicals in Concert* began in 1994 and features concert versions, with limited staging and performers carrying books, of classic musicals. Many *Encores!* productions have been the impetus for fully staged **revivals**.

CITY OF ANGELS **(11 DECEMBER 1989, VIRGINIA, 879 PERFORMANCES)**. Music by **Cy Coleman**, lyrics by David Zeppel, book by **Larry Gelbart**. Winner of the **Tony Award** for Best Musical in a lackluster season, *City of Angels* was a humorous show about Hollywood in the 1940s with a serviceable score and good production values. Gelbart's constant stream of gags added to the satirical look at Hollywood and detective stores in the 1940s. A novelist, Stine (Gregg Edelman) shops around his screenplay about a detective named Stone (James Naughton), whose story is also enacted on stage. Designer Robin Wagner set the Hollywood story in technicolor and the screenplay in black and white, helping to clarify the action since many actors played double roles. Despite the humor, Gelbart's book also included considerable rage directed at the Hollywood system, personified in the mogul played by **Rene Auberjonois**. *New York Times* critic **Frank Rich** described Coleman's score as "a delirious celebration of jazz and pop styles," brought to life by a swing band in the pit and scat-singing quartet on stage. The score included the clever duet between the creator and the creation, "You're Nothing without Me."

CLARK, VICTORIA. An opera director as well as an actor, Clark appeared as Smitty in the 1995 revival of *How to Succeed in Business without Really Trying* and created the roles of Alice Beane in *Titanic* (1997) and Margaret Johnson in *The Light in the Piazza* (2005), the latter for which she won multiple awards, including a **Tony Award**, a **Drama Desk Award**, and a **New York Outer Critics' Circle Award**. Her extremely fine singing and heartfelt portrayal of an overprotective mother whose marriage has lost its love and who is traveling with her daughter in Italy in *Light* has garnered her tremendous praise. She received special accolades for her revelatory performance of the solo number "Dividing Day."

CLAYTON, JAN (1917–1983). Soprano who created the role of Julie Jordan in *Carousel*. She returned to Broadway in the 1946 revival of *Show Boat*, and also played Christine Crane as a replacement in the original production of *Follies* (1971).

COCA, IMOGENE (1908–2001). Comic screen actress who appeared in Broadway **revues**, including *The Garrick Gaeties* (1930), *Flying Colors* (1932), and *All in Fun* (1940). She starred as Letitia Primrose in the **musical comedy** *On the Twentieth Century* (1978).

COCO **(18 DECEMBER 1969, MARK HELLINGER, 332 PER-FORMANCES).** Music by André Previn, lyrics and book by **Alan Jay Lerner**, staged by Michael Benthall, musical numbers and fashion sequences staged by **Michael Bennett**. A show based on the life of designer Coco Chanel, *Coco* benefited from the star presence of **Katherine Hepburn** and production aspects, but there was insufficient interest to sustain a long run, even though the show had the largest advance sale in Broadway history to that time. The show concerned Coco Chanel's comeback as a fashion designer in America. **Clives Barnes**, writing in the *New York Times*, said of the show's star: "Miss Hepburn is a blithe spirit, a vital flame. . . . Her singing voice is unique—a neat mixture of faith, love and laryngitis, unforgettable." Unfortunately, he found the music completely "unmemorable" and thought that the title of one song described the show: "Fiasco."

THE COCOANUTS **(8 DECEMBER 1925, LYRIC, 276 PERFOR-MANCES).** Music and lyrics by **Irving Berlin**, book by **George S. Kaufman**. A vehicle for the Marx Brothers, what took on place on stage during *The Cocoanuts* sometimes had as much to do with improvisation as it did with the script. Groucho played a crooked hotel owner and developer in Florida, Henry W. Schlemmer, and Harpo and Chico played according to their usual character types. A wealthy guest at the hotel, Mrs. Potter (Margaret Dumont), has some jewels stolen, and the thieves throw the guilt toward her niece's fiancé, but the Marx Brothers find the real culprit. Berlin's score seems almost forgotten in all of the Marxs' fast-paced zaniness, and included the highlights "A Little Bungalow" and "Five o'Clock Tea."

COHAN, GEORGE M. (1878–1942). Performer, songwriter, director, producer, and high-profile patriot who was a central figure in turn-of-the-20th-century **musical comedy**. The son of **vaudevillians**, Cohan wrote book, lyrics, and music for his star vehicles such as *Little Johnny Jones* (1904, which featured "Yankee Doodle Boy" and "Give My Regards To Broadway"). His trademark dance style was a straight-legged strut with his body bent forward, while his vocal style rested somewhere between speaking and true singing. James Cagney portrayed him in the 1942 biopic *Yankee Doodle Dandy*, and **Joel Grey** played him in *George M!* (1968).

COLE, JACK (1914–1974). Dancer, choreographer, and director known for his overtly sensual, jazz-inspired style that included grinding hips and occasionally homoerotic elements. The first show he choreographed on Broadway was *Something for the Boys* (1943), followed by more than a dozen others, including *Kismet* (1953), *Jamaica* (1957), *A Funny Thing Happened on the Way to the Forum* (1962), and *Man of La Mancha* (1965).

COLEMAN, CY (BORN SEYMOUR KAUFMAN, 1929–2004). Composer whose credits include *Wildcat* (1960), *Little Me* (1962), *Sweet Charity* (1966), *On the Twentieth Century* (1978), *Barnum* (1980), *City of Angels* (1989), and *The Life* (1997). For *The Life*, he also served as librettist, producer, and dance arranger. As a composer, Coleman captures the spirit of the "Golden Age" Broadway style, but in more contemporary terms.

COLLINS, JOSE (1887–1958). The impressive British actress was also a star on Broadway, appearing with **Al Jolson** in *The Whirl of Society* in 1912, the 1913 edition of *Ziegfeld Follies*, and *The Passing Show* of 1914.

THE COLOR PURPLE **(1 DECEMBER 2005, BROADWAY, 452 PERFORMANCES AS OF 31 DECEMBER 2006).** Music and lyrics by Brenda Russell, Allee Willis, and Stephen Bray, book by **Marsha Norman**. Based on Alice Walker's 1982 novel and the subsequent 1985 film, the tale of Celie (LaChanze, in a **Tony Award**-winning performance), the long-suffering African American heroine who overcomes poverty, poor self-esteem, and oppression, includes a stirring score that encompasses a wide variety of styles, including gospel, roots, and characteristic Broadway ballads. Among the musical highlights are the situation-setting "Our Prayer," Sofia's defiant "Hell No!," Celie and Shug Avery's emotive duet "What about Love," the energetic and evocative act-2 opening "African Homeland," Celie's revelatory "I'm Here," and the expansive title song. Oprah Winfrey, who played Sofia in the film, headed the list of producers for the musical. *See also* AFRICAN AMERICAN MUSICALS.

COMDEN, BETTY (BORN ELIZABETH COHEN, 1919–2006). Librettist and lyricist who collaborated with **Adolph Green** on musicals such as *On the Town* (1944), *Billion Dollar Baby* (1945), *Wonderful Town* (1953), *Bells Are Ringing* (1956), *Applause* (1970), *On the Twentieth Century* (1978), and *The Will Rogers Follies* (1991). The pair worked together exclusively for more than 50 years, creating words for composers such as **Leonard Bernstein**, **Jule Styne**, and **Cy Coleman**. They formed a theater troupe in the 1930s, the Revuers, and were active as performers. Hence, they created words from a performer's perspective. Their focus was on sparkling **musical comedy**, and their lyrics possess energy, appeal, immediacy, and charm.

COMPANY **(26 APRIL 1970, ALVIN, 706 PERFORMANCES).** Music and lyrics by **Stephen Sondheim**, book by George Furth, directed by **Harold Prince**, musical numbers staged by **Michael Bennett**, presented by Harold Prince in association with Ruth Mitchell. A **concept musical** greeted with mixed feelings during its run but now considered one of Sondheim's most important shows. Along with *A Little Night Music* and *Follies*, *Company* is one of the trilogy of shows that Sondheim created with Harold Prince in the early 1970s. *Company* has no real plot but rather offers a series of related scenes on the theme of modern marriage, mostly demonstrating what the creators considered the institution's sorry state in the modern world. The bachelor Robert/Bobby (**Dean Jones**, replaced after just two weeks by **Larry Kert**) finds a string of girlfriends through his married friends, whose own matrimonies are in various states of happiness. Furth framed the story around Bobby's birthday celebrations, but the guest of honor never shows up for the final surprise party, having decided to strike out on his own. The ensemble cast included a number of memorable performances, including **Elaine Stritch** as Joanne, **Donna McKechnie** as Kathie, Charles Kimbrough as Harry, Steve Elmore as Paul, Charles Braswell as Larry, Pamela Myers as Marta, and Susan Browning as April. The set, designed by **Boris Aronson**, was minimalist, gleaming metal and glass with elevators to move between the levels. The score includes some of Sondheim's most famous songs, including "Being Alive," "Sorry-Grateful," "You Could Drive a Person Crazy," "Barcelona," "The Ladies Who Lunch," and "Another Hundred People." The songs are pure Sondheim, with melodies so closely wedded to the words that one simply cannot think of one without the other. **John Doyle** directed the 2006 Broadway revival, which starred **Raúl Esparza** as Bobby.

COMPOSER. A person who creates music. Most Broadway shows have a single composer, though works with multiple composers also exist. Broadway composers come from a wide range of backgrounds and experiences, and some are also lyricists. Many are Europeans, such as **Arthur Sullivan** (British), **Franz Lehár** (Austro-Hungarian), **Emmerich Kálmán** (Hungarian), **Andrew Lloyd Webber** (British), and **Claude-Michel Schönberg** (French), whose works have been imported to Broadway. Others are European immigrants, including **Victor Herbert, Irving Berlin, Rudolf Friml, Sigmund Romberg, Kurt Weill**, and **Frederick Loewe**. The majority, though, are American-born and trained. **George Gershwin, Jerome Kern, Richard Rodgers, Cole Porter, Frank Loesser, John Kander**, and **Stephen Sondheim** are a handful of the American-born composers whose musical theater works are performed around the world.

Broadway composers employ a diverse array of styles. In the late 19th and early 20th centuries, figures such as **Reginald De Koven, John Philip Sousa**, Friml, and Romberg created **operettas** filled with lush music, coloratura vocal writing, and stirring ensembles. At the same time, people like Berlin and Gershwin, among others, wrote Tin Pan Alley-style songs characterized by syncopation and **verse-refrain form**. In the middle part of the 20th century, composers such as Kern, Rodgers, Loewe, Porter, Loesser, **Jule Styne**, and **Jerry Herman** defined the so-called "Golden Age" of the American musical with immortal songs such as "Oh, What a Beautiful Mornin'" from Rodgers's *Oklahoma!* (1943, lyrics by **Oscar Hammerstein II**) and Styne's "Everything's Coming Up Roses" from *Gypsy* (1959, lyrics by Sondheim). Others such as Weill, **Marc Blitzstein**, and **Leonard Bernstein** infused their scores with a sense of musical sophistication coming from their training in the concert hall tradition.

Still others, including Kander, Sondheim, **Maury Yeston**, **Michael John La Chiusa**, and **Adam Guettel** employ various experimental idioms ranging from pastiches of earlier styles to advanced harmonic and metric techniques.

See also ADLER, RICHARD; AHRENS, LYNN; ALLEN, PETER; BART, LIONEL; BLAKE, EUBIE; BOCK, JERRY; BRICUSSE, LESLIE; CARROLL, HARRY; COLEMAN, CY; COOK, WILL MARION; COWARD, NOEL; DUKE, VERNON; FINN, WILLIAM; FLAHERTY, STEPHEN; FORREST, GEORGE "CHET"; GAY, NOEL; HAMLISCH, MARVIN; HARRIGAN, EDWARD "NED"; HENDERSON, RAY; HOFFMAN, GERTRUDE; HOSCHNA, KARL L.; LANE, BURTON; LARSON, JONATHAN; LEIGH, MITCH; LIBRETTO/LIBRETTIST; LYRICS/LYRICIST; MacDERMOT, GALT; McHUGH, JIMMY; MENKEN, ALAN; MERCER, JOHNNY; MERRILL, BOB; RAHMAN, A. R.; ROME, HAROLD J.; SCHMIDT, HARVEY; SCHWARTZ, ARTHUR; SCHWARTZ, STEPHEN; SIMON, LUCY; STOTHART, HERBERT; STRAUSS, JOHANN, JR.; STROUSE, CHARLES; SWIFT, KAY; TIERNEY, HARRY; WILDHORN, FRANK; WRIGHT, ROBERT; YAZBEK, DAVID; YOUMANS, VINCENT.

CONCEPT MUSICAL. A type of integrated musical theater in which a psychological theme or life event becomes the central unifying device, as opposed to a narrative plot. Examples of the approach include *Cabaret* (1966), *Company* (1970), *Follies* (1971), *Chicago* (1975), and *A Chorus Line* (1975). A descendent of the **revue**, concept musicals often employ songs as soliloquies and stress nonlinear dimensions of time. *See also* ASSASSINS; *LOVE LIFE*; PRINCE, HAROLD; REVUE; SONDHEIM, STEPHEN; *THE WILD PARTY.*

A CONNECTICUT YANKEE **(3 NOVEMBER 1927, VANDERBILT, 418 PERFORMANCES).** Music by **Richard Rodgers**, lyrics by **Lorenz Hart**, book by **Herbert Fields**, dances arranged by **Busby Berkeley**. An adaptation of Mark Twain's famous novel that became one of Rodgers and Hart's early hits. The show began at a bachelor supper for Martin (**William Gaxton**), where his jealous ex-fiancée knocks him out with a champagne bottle. Transported back to the time of King Arthur, he tries to modernize the court. Just as the Twain novel combined 19th-century American vernacular with Arthurian romance, so did Hart's lyrics juxtapose Elizabethan English with 20th-century American slang expressions, evident in the song "Thou Swell." Whereas in Twain, 19th-century inventions are introduced to Arthurian times, in the musical, 20th-century Broadway musical idioms infuse Camelot's soundworld, including the ballad "My Heart Stood Still." The creators added new material for the 1943 revival, including the delightfully morbid "To Keep My Love Alive," written for **Vivienne Segal**, who played the enchantress Morgan le Fay.

CONTACT **(7 OCTOBER 1999, NEWHOUSE, 1,010 PERFOR-MANCES).** Directed and choreographed by **Susan Stroman**, written by **John Weidman**. A **dance musical** set entirely to recorded music (which drew severe criticism from some when it won the **Tony Award** for Best Musical), recalled other dance shows such as *Jerome Robbins' Broadway* and *Dancin'* by **Bob Fosse**. Stroman's effort, however, was not an anthology of great moments from a single director-choreographer but rather an evening of three new dances, not unlike a program of modern dance but with a Broadway sensibility. The first half included two scenes. "Swinging" took its theme from Jean-Honoré Fragonard's painting "The Swing," and was set to period harpsichord music and Stephane Grappelli's jazz violin version of **Rodgers and Hart**'s "My Heart Stood Still." "Did You Move?" featured **Karen Ziemba** as a mousy Italian wife who follows her brutish, gangster husband into a restaurant. While he checks out the buffet, she enters her own dizzy world as a prima ballerina dancing with the headwaiter (David MacGillivry). **Ben Brantley**, writing in the *New York Times*, noted that the segment "brings to mind the Lucille Ball of 'I Love Lucy'." The fantasy ballet sequences included music by classical masters Edvard Grieg ("Anitra's Dance"), Pyotr Ilich Tchaikovsky ("Waltz" from *Eugene Onegin*), and Georges Bizet ("Farandole"). The second act, "Contact," concerned a depressed advertising executive (Boyd Gaines) who considers suicide, but instead goes to a swing dance hall where he sees the Girl in the Yellow Dress (Deborah Yates). He is not a dancer but overcomes this handicap and joins in the revelry in the show's finale, a high-energy dance to Benny Goodman's classic "Sing Sing Sing."

COOK, BARBARA (1927–). Singing actress who brought an operatic technique to Broadway. She created the role of Cunegunde in *Candide* (1956), dazzling audiences with "Glitter And Be Gay" (something she was still doing in a one-woman show in 2002). She was the first Marion Paroo in *The Music Man* (1957), playing opposite **Robert Preston** and singing "Till There Was You" and "Goodnight, My Someone." Subsequent credits include *The Gay Life* (1961) and *She Loves Me* (1963).

COOK, WILL MARION (1869–1944). The first African American composer whose work appeared on Broadway. His credits include *Clorindy* (1898), *In Dahomey* (1903), *Abyssinia* (1906), and *Bandana Land* (1908). Although his shows continued old racial stereotypes, they were the first serious efforts to portray African American characters as multi-dimensional. *See also* AFRICAN AMERICAN MUSICALS.

COOTE, ROBERT (1909–1982). English-born screen and stage actor best known for playing aristocrats and British military officers. He originated roles in two musicals by **Alan Jay Lerner** and **Frederick Loewe**: Colonel Pickering in *My Fair Lady* (1956) and King Pellinore in *Camelot* (1960).

COUNTESS MARITZA **(18 SEPTEMBER 1926, SHUBERT, 321 PERFORMANCES).** Music by **Emmerich Kálmán**; lyrics and book by Julius Brammer and Alfred Grunwald, translated by **Harry B. Smith**. An adaptation of a successful European **operetta** produced by the **Shuberts**, *Countess Maritza* ran for nearly 10 months. The plot concerned a noblewoman with a handsome caretaker. The stars included Walter Woolf and Yvonne D'Arle, among others, and the operetta's major hit was "Play Gypsies—Dance Gypsies." For the American production, the Shuberts interpolated songs by Al Goodman and **Sigmund Romberg**.

COWARD, NOEL (ALSO KNOWN AS NOËL COWARD, 1899–1973). English actor, composer, and playwright whose iconic image in a silk dressing gown touting a cigarette in a holder captures the chic sophistication of his work. Many of his stage works appeared on Broadway, including the **operetta** *Bitter Sweet* (1929), the **revue** *Set to Music* (1939), and the **musical comedy** *Sail Away* (1961). He appeared in **Irving Berlin**'s *As Thousands Cheer* (1933), staged *High Spirits* (1964, based on his play *Blithe Spirit*), and frequently appeared in straight plays with **Gertrude Lawrence**.

THE CRADLE WILL ROCK (3 JANUARY 1938, WINDSOR, 108 PERFORMANCES). Music, lyrics, and book by **Marc Blitzstein**, staged by Orson Welles. A show inspired by left-wing politics and the labor movement, *The Cradle Will Rock* has one of the most intriguing histories of any Broadway musical. Originally planned as a WPA Theater project in Washington, but canceled, *The Cradle Will Rock* came to New York with John Houseman as producer and Orson Welles as director. Political controversy resulted in an injunction against the performance; the unions buckled under the pressure, ordering their members not to appear on stage. Houseman and Welles took everyone to an empty theater, where the actors bought tickets and played their parts from the audience. Blitzstein was the only person on stage, where he played the score at the piano. (The show's genesis is the subject of the 1999 Tim Robbins' film *Cradle Will Rock*, starring Hank Azaria as Blitzstein). The show was presented 20 times in this innovative fashion. The run at the Windsor was more traditional, but still featured Blitzstein alone at the piano. *The Cradle Will Rock* carries the feeling of the agitprop theater with obvious situations and broadly drawn characters. **Howard Da Silva** played Larry Foreman, a foreman in the mill in Steeltown who helps organize his fellow workers. Mr. Mister (Will Geer) runs the town, and with his wife, Mrs. Mister, and children Sister Mister and Brother Mister, represent capitalist ideals. The workers have the support of other members of the underclass in Steeltown, such as the prostitute Moll (Olive Stanton). Blitzstein's score included aspects of both concert music and popular songs with memorable numbers such the title song, "The Freedom of the Press," "Honolulu, "Art for Art's Sake," and "The Nickel under Your Foot."

CRAWFORD, CHERYL (1902–1986). A successful female **producer** from the middle of the 20th century in a profession dominated by men, Crawford made her mark with such artistic successes as *One Touch of Venus* (1943), *Brigadoon* (1947), and *Love Life* (1948).

CRAWFORD, MICHAEL (1942–). Baritone who won the 1988 Tony Award for Best Actor in a Musical for creating the title role in *The Phantom of the Opera*. Crawford brought a combination of human pathos and deeply felt horror to the role. Musical film credits include Hero in *A Funny Thing Happened on the Way to the Forum* (1966) and Cornelius in *Hello, Dolly!* (1969). He starred in the disastrous run of *The Dance of the Vampires* (2002) as Count von Krolock and also played Madam von Krolock, appearing in drag under the pseudonym Dame Edith Shorthouse.

CRAZY FOR YOU (19 FEBRUARY 1992, SHUBERT, 1,622 PERFORMANCES). Music by **George Gershwin**, lyrics by **Ira Gershwin**, book by Ken Ludwig, choreographed by **Susan Stroman**. A reimagining of Gershwin-style musicals and songs for the 1990s, *Crazy for You* proved popular with critics and audiences, introducing some of the greatest Gershwin tunes to new generations. Despite the similarity of the show's title to *Girl Crazy, Crazy for You* was not a mere remake of the classic musical. Of the 18 songs in *Crazy for You*, five were in *Girl Crazy*, including, among others, "I Got Rhythm" and "Embraceable You." The other 13 consist of some of the Gershwin brothers' greatest hits: "Stairway to Paradise," "Nice Work If You Can Get It," "Slap That Bass," and "Someone to Watch over Me," in addition to materials discovered at the **Secaucus Warehouse**. The lightweight plot for *Crazy for You* bears minimal resemblance to *Girl Crazy*, but does involve an Easterner going to the West. Bobby Child (**Harry Groener**), a wealthy New Yorker with interest in the stage but who rarely shows good intentions, finds himself in a poor Nevada mining town where he changes his ways and saves a financially broke theater and wins the heart of Polly Baker (Jodi Benson). A clear star was choreographer Susan Stroman, who showed a sincere love for the material. As **Frank Rich** reported in the *New York Times*, Stroman managed to "reinvent" the dances from the 1930s instead of "piling on exhausting tap routines to steamroll the audience into enjoying itself." Rich placed *Crazy for You* on a high plane, calling it a chance to "grab the musical back from the British," a clear reference to the influence of the **megamusical**.

CRITICS. Critics from major New York newspapers, journals, radio and television stations, and sometimes from the national media as well, review Broadway musicals when they open. Positive reviews often appear in advertising for a show, and all reviews contribute to the "word of mouth" that either helps make or destroy a show's success. Reviews from television and radio are the most ephemeral and are seldom cited by later writers. Within the print media, it is the drama critics of the *New York Times* whose judgments appear most often in later sources, but critics from other newspapers also develop reputations, and some have become major figures. Usually Broadway musicals are reviewed by drama critics, some of whom have limited ability to deal with a show's musical component. Knowledgeable critics can tell one a great deal about a musical, but others sometimes have little to offer in the way of constructive comment. The best critics, such as **Brooks Atkinson**, who wrote for the *New York Times* for decades from the 1920s, write reviews that remain excellent sources of information and comment about a show long after it opened. *See also* BARNES, CLIVE; BLITZSTEIN, MARC; BRANTLEY, BEN; DE KOVEN, REGINALD; DILLINGHAM, CHARLES; KERR, WALTER; RICH, FRANK; TAUBMAN, HOWARD; WOOLL-COTT, ALEXANDER.

CRIVELLO, ANTHONY (1955–). Singing actor known for his convincing characterizations of difficult roles. He made his Broadway debut as a **replacement** Che in the original production of *Evita*. Crivello next appeared on Broadway as a serial killer in *The News* (1985) and played multiple roles in *Les Misérables* (1987), understudying and eventually appearing as Javert. He won a **Tony Award** for Best Featured Actor in a Musical for creating the role of Valentin in *Kiss of the Spider Woman* (1993) and played Dante Keyes in *Marie Christine* (1999).

CROUSE, RUSSEL (1893–1966). Librettist, producer, playwright, and theater owner/operator, Crouse is best known for his collaborations with **Howard Lindsay**. The team revised the libretto for *Anything Goes* (1934) and created the books for *Red, Hot and Blue!* (1936), *Call Me Madam* (1950), and *The Sound of Music* (1959), among others.

CULLUM, JOHN (1930–). Actor who won **Tony Award**s his performances in *Shenandoah* (1975) and *On the Twentieth Century* (1978). He also appeared in *Camelot* (1960), *On a Clear Day You Can See Forever* (1965), *Urinetown* (2001), and *Dr. Seuss' How the Grinch Stole Christmas!* (2006).

CUMMING, ALAN (1965–). Scottish-born actor who won a **Tony Award** for his riveting reinvention of the Master of Ceremonies for the 1996 revival of *Cabaret*. He reprised his iconic black-leather costume for the role of Macheath in the 2006 revival of *The Threepenny Opera*.

CURRY, TIM (1946–). English-born actor who created the role of Frank 'n' Furter in *The Rocky Horror Show* (1975) and whose other Broadway musical credits include Alan Swann in *My Favorite Year* (1992) and King Arthur in *Monty Python's Spamalot* (2005).

– D –

DALE, JIM (1935–). Won 1980 Tony Award for Best Actor in a Musical for *Barnum*. Dale also appeared in the 1997 revival of *Candide* and played Mr. Peachum in the 2006 revival of *The Threepenny Opera*.

***DAMES AT SEA* (20 DECEMBER 1968, THEATRE DE LYS, 575 PERFORMANCES).** Music by Jim Wise, lyrics and book by George Haimsohn and Robin Miller. An off-Broadway success that cast an affectionate eye back on the 1930s, spoofing the movie with Ruby Keeler and Dick Powell and show business clichés from the period. **Bernadette Peters** was the star of the cast of six, playing Ruby, a chorus girl who, in true *42nd Street* fashion, saves the show and becomes a star. Tamara Lang played Mona Kent, the Broadway star, and David Christmas was Dick, a sailor in this following-the-fleet parody, whom Ruby captures in the end. The delight came through the show's knowing look backward, with music and lyrics that parodied **Cole Porter** and others, references to the 1930s, and the right dancing vocabulary and props. **Clive Barnes**, writing for the *New*

York Times, expected to hate the show, but ended up writing nearly a rave. He compared *Dames at Sea* to **The Boy Friend**, noting that it does for the 1930s what the latter did for the 1920s, but he found Dames "much better . . . because it is informed by a genuine love and knowledge for the period."

***DAMN YANKEES* (5 MAY 1955, 46TH STREET, 1,019 PER-FORMANCES).** Music and lyrics by **Richard Adler** and Jerry Ross; book by **George Abbott** and Douglass Wallop; directed by Abbott; dances and musical numbers staged by **Bob Fosse**; presented by Frederick Brisson, Robert E. Griffith, and **Harold S. Prince**, in association with Albert B. Taylor. A hugely successful show that combined the Faust legend with baseball and benefited from a winning score and the memorable presence of dancer **Gwen Verdon**. *Damn Yankees* was a musicalization of Douglass Wallop's popular fantasy, *The Year the Yankees Lost the Pennant*, the first show to take on wholeheartedly what at the time was indisputably America's national sport. It appeared at a time when the Yankees annually dominated the American League; fans in other cities might almost believe that it would take a bargain with the devil to win the pennant. In the plot, a middle-aged fan of the Washington Senators, Joe Boyd (Robert Shafer), mutters after yet another loss to the Yankees that he would sell his soul if the Senators could win a pennant. Mephistopheles appears in the person of Mr. Applegate (**Ray Walston**), who turns Boyd into Joe Hardy (**Stephen Douglass**), a player of supernatural talent. Boyd, however, feels guilty about leaving his wife (Shannon Bolin) and insists on an escape clause. Applegate brings in the lovely witch Lola (Verdon) to convince Boyd to stay with the deal, but in the end she fails and is turned back into an ugly old crone. Boyd reunites with his wife, and the devil loses a soul.

Verdon was an extraordinary dancer, one of Fosse's principal associates, and, for a number of years, his wife. Fosse crafted sexy numbers for her, such as "Whatever Lola Wants," and Verdon brought to them an irresistible spirit. Sex appeal has long been a selling point in the Broadway musical, and the poster campaign for *Damn Yankees* was substantial proof of this. Ticket sales did not really take off until the photo of Verdon in a baseball uniform was replaced with her as the "Black Widow," now the show's recognizable trademark. Walston made his role as the devil outrageously sinister; his song, "Those Were the Good Old Days," was a comic highlight. Fosse's dances, such as the mambo "Who's Got the Pain?," the hoedown "Shoeless Joe from Hannibal, Mo.," and stylized baseball moves in other numbers, were also successful.

DANCE ARRANGER. Person who works with the choreographer to create music for the dance segments in a show. The musical material usually comes from other parts of the show. Often times, the dance arranger is someone other than the main composer. *See also* COLEMAN, CY; FLAHERTY, STEPHEN; RITTMANN, TRUDE; TESORI, JEANINE.

DANCE MUSICAL. A type of musical theater that is based on dance and choreography rather than live singing, sometimes called "dansical." In some of these shows, such as ***Contact*** (2000), plots unfold through dance. Others, such as ***Dancin'*** (1978) and ***Fosse*** (1999), do not have a consistent linear storyline. *See also* FOSSE, BOB; *JEROME ROBBINS' BROADWAY*; MERCER, JOHNNY; *MOVIN' OUT*; STROMAN, SUSAN; THARP, TWYLA.

***DANCIN'* (27 MARCH 1978, BROADHURST, 1,774 PERFORMANCES).** Directed and choreographed by **Bob Fosse**. Fosse had long brought dance and spectacle to book shows, and here he struck out on his own, removing most of the other elements found in a musical. Several of the dances provided dramatic vignettes, but no theme besides dancing united the evening. For the music, Fosse drew upon a wide palate, including Johann Sebastian Bach, **John Philip Sousa**, **George M. Cohan**, **Johnny Mercer**, Cat Stevens, and Benny Goodman, but his own style reigned throughout the show. The star dancer was **Ann Reinking**, about whom Richard Eder wrote in the *New York Times*: "everything she has dances—her hair, her teeth, her expression. Her face dances." Critical reaction was mixed, but audiences knew that Fosse could deliver Broadway pizzazz and flocked to *Dancin'* for about four years. Devotees of Fosse and American show dancing remember *Dancin'* fondly, and elements of it were revived in *Fosse* (1999).

DANIELE, GRACIELA (1939–). Director-choreographer whose gifts at creating high-energy ethnic-inspired dances are evident in *Once on This Island* (1990) and *Ragtime* (1998). Other credits include the 1999 Broadway revival of *Annie Get Your Gun* and *Chita Rivera: A Dancer's Life* (2005).

DA SILVA, HOWARD (BORN HOWARD SILVERBLATT, 1909–1986). Stage and screen actor with a strong dramatic presence who created the roles of Larry Foreman in *The Cradle Will Rock* (1937), Jud Fry in *Oklahoma!* (1943), Ben Marino in *Fiorello!* (1959), and Benjamin Franklin in *1776* (1969). He won a **Tony Award** for Best Featured Actor in a Musical for *Fiorello!*

DAVIS, SAMMY, JR. (1925–1990). Charismatic **African American** nightclub entertainer who created the roles of Charlie Welch in *Mr. Wonderful* (1956) and Joe Wellington in *Golden Boy* (1964). He also played Littlechap in the 1978 revival of *Stop the World—I Want To Get Off*.

THE DAY BEFORE SPRING **(22 NOVEMBER 1945, NATIONAL, 165 PERFORMANCES).** Music by **Frederick Loewe**, lyrics and book by **Alan Jay Lerner**, ballets and musical ensembles arranged by Anthony Tudor. Lerner and Loewe's second Broadway collaboration that, despite showing a number of merits, ultimately failed. Lerner conceived the story that took place at a 10-year college reunion where a married woman (**Irene Manning**) nearly elopes with the same man (Bill Johnson) she almost eloped with a decade earlier. Anthony Tudor's ballets were a substantial part of the show, and it was after the lesson told in one of them that the woman decides not to elope with her former lover.

DAY, EDITH (1896–1971). Stage performer who created the title role in *Irene* (1919), singing "Alice Blue Gown" and ensuring the show a long run. She also appeared in *Going Up* (1917), and *Wildflower* (1923) was conceived as a vehicle for her. She moved to London, where she was known as "The Queen of the Drury Lane Theatre" and played the lead roles in many American imports to the West End in the 1920s.

A DAY IN HOLLYWOOD/A NIGHT IN THE UKRAINE (1 MAY 1980, JOHN GOLDEN AND ROYALE, 588 PERFOR-MANCES). Music by Frank Lazarus, lyrics and book by Dick Vos-burgh, directed and choreographed by **Tommy Tune**. A British revue that took a madcap look at Hollywood of the 1930s, *A Day in Holly-wood/A Night in the Ukraine* became another vehicle in which Tommy Tune demonstrated his ability to please audiences. The first act is a satirical treatment of 1930s Hollywood musicals that is set in the lobby of Grauman's Chinese Theater. In addition to new music by Lazarus, the score included hits from the day and three new songs by **Jerry Herman**. One of Tune's great numbers is "Famous Feet," where male and female dancing feet impersonate Hollywood stars. The second act is based on Anton Chekhov's *The Bear* as it might have been played by the Marx Brothers. According to Mel Gussow's review in the *New York Times*, book author Dick Vosburgh created "a crackling compendium of Marx Brothers comedies . . ." The famous Marx Brothers were there, including Groucho (David Garrison), Harpo (Priscilla Lopez), and Chico (Frank Lazarus), as well as Mar-garet Dumont (Peggy Hewett). Gussow found that Garrison's Grou-cho lacked the original's "devil-may-care quality," but Lopez "is a doll of a Harpo," offering all of the old gags. He finds Lazarus and Hewett most effective in their parts as well, and praises designer Tony Walton for his sets. He concludes, however, with recognition of Tune's accomplishment: ". . . the show is a marvelous directorial feat."

DEAREST ENEMY (18 SEPTEMBER 1925, KNICKERBOCKER, 286 PERFORMANCES). Music by **Richard Rodgers**, lyrics by **Lorenz Hart**, book by **Herbert Fields**, staged by **John Murray An-derson**. Opening the same week as *No, No, Nanette*, *The Vagabond King*, and *Sunny*, *Dearest Enemy* held its own and ran for almost nine months. For this show, their first successful **book musical**, Rodgers and Hart took the idea from a plaque on 37th Street that told the story of a patriotic New York lady during the Revolution who de-tained British officers with charm, cake, and wine, and subsequently allowed 4,000 American soldiers to escape to Harlem. In the show, Mrs. Robert Murray (Flavia Arcaro), detains three British generals. Fields's book included a fictional love story between American Betsy

Burke (**Helen Ford**) and British Captain Sir John Copeland (**Charles Purcell**). Historical figures Aaron Burr and George Washington also appeared in the show. Between Hart's edgy lyrics and some titillating aspects of the book (such as Helen Ford's first appearance wearing nothing but a barrel), *Dearest Enemy* was filled with surprises. The anonymous *New York Times* reviewer found the story "richer" than that of many **musical comedies** of the time and notes that the show "blooms with a fresh charm." Rodgers and Hart's songs include the march "Cheerio," the love duet "Here in My Arms," and the comic "Old Enough to Love."

DE GUZMAN, JOSIE. Lyrical singing actress of Puerto Rican descent who made her Broadway debut in 1978 as Lidia in *Runaways*, a show for which she also provided additional text and English-Spanish translations. She played Maria in the 1980 revival of *West Side Story* and starred as Sarah Brown in the 1992 revival of *Guys and Dolls*.

DE KOVEN, REGINALD (1859–1920). Operetta composer whose important works include *Robin Hood* (1890), *Rob Roy* (1894), and *The Highwayman* (1897). His most famous song is *Robin Hood*'s "O Promise Me," which survived as a wedding standard for most of the 20th century. De Koven was also active as a conductor and music critic.

DE MILLE, AGNES (1905–1993). Legendary dancer and choreographer whose Broadway career began with *Hooray for What!* (1937), on which she worked with **Robert Alton**. Most of de Mille's work was cut by the time the show opened. She made Broadway history with her choreography for *Oklahoma!* (1943). Her dances, such as the "Dream Ballet" ("Laurey Makes Up Her Mind"), were directly related to the plot and integral to its presentation. Subsequent credits on Broadway included *One Touch of Venus* (1943), *Bloomer Girl* (1944, with its "Civil War Ballet"), *Carousel* (1945), *Brigadoon* (1947, including the "Sword Dance" and the "Funeral Dance"), *Allegro* (1947), *Gentlemen Prefer Blondes* (1949), *Paint Your Wagon* (1951), and *110 in the Shade* (1963). De Mille also directed *Allegro*, inspiring the creation of the artistically visionary role of choreographer-director.

THE DESERT SONG **(30 NOVEMBER 1926, CASINO, 471 PER-FORMANCES).** Lyrics and book by **Otto Harbach, Oscar Hammerstein II**, and **Frank Mandel**, music by **Sigmund Romberg**, libretto directed by Arthur Hurley, musical numbers staged by Robert Connolly, settings by Woodman Thompson, produced by **Laurence Schwab** and Mandel. The creators of the **Orientalist operetta** looked to several aspects of popular culture in creating their evocation of disguised heroes and European damsels in Morocco. Among these were Rudolf Valentino, who died weeks before the show opened, Lawrence of Arabia, and the actual Riff Wars in North Africa. In the plot, the bespectacled and clumsy Pierre Birabeau (**Robert Halliday**) is in love with Margot Bonvalet (**Vivienne Segal**), but she is enthralled with the mysterious Red Shadow, who helps the oppressed Riffs rise against the French Imperialists. The plot follows that of Valentino's film *The Sheik* (1921) very closely, including the revelation at the end that the Arab hero is a disguised European; in the case of *The Desert Song*, Pierre is the Red Shadow. The music includes enthralling waltzes ("The Desert Song," "Romance") and rousing marches for the male chorus ("The Riff Song"). It also includes soaring ballads ("One Alone") and even a musical comedy-style number for the secondary leads that is loaded with contemporary sexual references ("It"). Romberg used tonal means to depict the differences between the French and the Arabs, for the French sing and dance in major while the Arabs do so in minor. Of Romberg's major shows, this was the first one to have a happy ending.

Critics loved the show. Charles Brackett wrote in *The New Yorker*: "A great, roaring, splendid musical show. . . . The music is Romberg's best, and in the book it seemed to me that the sheik plot has found at last its really happy medium." *The Desert Song* was filmed in either whole or part four times (1929, 1932, 1943, 1953, all from Warner Brothers), and Nelson Eddy starred in a television version that was broadcast live on NBC in 1955. Of all of Romberg's operettas, *The Desert Song* is the most popular outside of the United States, having appeared successfully in Great Britain, France, Australia, and New Zealand.

DESLYS, GABY (1881–1920). Star dancer of the Paris music hall, Deslys appeared in several Broadway shows under the auspices of

J. J. Shubert, including *The Revue of Revues* (1911), *Vera Violetta* (1911), *The Honeymoon Express* (1913), and *The Belle of Bond Street* (1914). *Vera Violetta* featured Deslys and her partner, Harry Pilcer, in "The Gaby Glide," a syncopated dance that was extremely popular in the 1910s.

DESTRY RIDES AGAIN (23 APRIL 1959, IMPERIAL, 473 PERFORMANCES). Music and lyrics by **Harold Rome**, book by Leonard Gershe, staging and choreography by **Michael Kidd**, presented by **David Merrick**. Based on a story by Max Brand and the film that starred James Stewart and Marlene Dietrich, *Destry Rides Again* ran for 14 months but failed to make any money. Andy Griffith played the title character, the son of a famous Western lawman and the new sheriff in Bottleneck. He does not want to use violence but must resort to it in order to break up the town's dangerous gang. In the meantime he also gets the girl, Frenchy (Dolores Gray). It was a very ordinary story, and some wondered if it was really worth mounting a show based on such a cliché. Michael Kidd's dances were impressive, including several Western-themed ballets, one of which included three dancers with bullwhips. Rome's score included no songs that became hits. **Brooks Atkinson** yawned about the show in his *New York Times* review, lauding individual contributions but finding the story no more than an "old fable." He wrote that Gray's voice "would fill Madison Square Garden" and that Griffith brought "disarming enthusiasm" to his musical numbers.

DE SYLVA, B. G. (ALSO KNOWN AS BUDDY DESYLVA, 1895–1950). Lyricist, librettist, and producer whose early lyrics included "Look for the Silver Lining" (music by **Jerome Kern** and made famous in *Sally*, 1920) and several songs popularized by **Al Jolson**, including "April Showers" and "California, Here I Come." With composer **Ray Henderson** and fellow lyricist **Lew Brown**, he created the scores for the 1925 and 1926 editions of *George White's Scandals* and 11 **musical comedies**, including the sports-themed trilogy *Good News!* (1927), *Hold Everything!* (1928), and *Flying High* (1930). He was also active as a producer, bringing **Cole Porter**'s *Du Barry Was a Lady* (1939) and *Panama Hattie* (1940) to the stage.

DIENER, JOAN (1930–2006). Actress best remembered for creating the dual role of Aldonza/Dulcinea in *The Man of La Mancha* (1966). She reprised the role on Broadway for **revivals** in 1972 and 1992.

DILLINGHAM, CHARLES (1868–1934). Dillingham's theatrical career began as a drama critic, but he became a producer in 1903. His more than 200 Broadway credits (for both plays and musicals) include *Mlle. Modiste* (1905), *The Red Mill* (1906), *The Lady of the Slipper* (1912), *The Century Girl* (1916, with **Florenz Ziegfeld**), *Good Morning Dearie* (1921), and *Sunny* (1925).

DIRECTOR. Person responsible for unifying a musical's various components, including book, acting, music, dance, costumes, set, and lighting. The director's level of influence in a production can vary considerably, depending upon several factors, but the director usually plays a major role in bringing the production to fruition. The director's power tended to increase as the integration of plot, music, and dancing became more important, and from the 1940s onward, a number of successful directors came from the ranks of choreographers, including **Michael Bennett**, **Gower Champion**, **Jack Cole**, **Graciela Daniele**, **Agnes de Mille**, **Bob Fosse**, **Gertrude Hoffman**, **Gene Kelly**, **Michael Kidd**, **Julian Mitchell**, **Ann Reinking**, **Jerome Robbins**, **Susan Stroman**, and **Tommy Tune**. As is the case in the production history of nonmusical plays, many successful directors also wrote part of the show—books, lyrics, or both—but directors have come from a number of different fields in the dramatic arts. Some directors have also served as producers after becoming sufficiently prominent that investors will back their shows.

See also ABBOTT, GEORGE; ASHMAN, HOWARD; AVIAN, BOB; BERKELEY, BUSBY; BROWN, LEW; BUCK, GENE; BURROWS, ABE; CHARNIN, MARTIN; CLARK, VICTORIA; COHAN, GEORGE M.; DOYLE, JOHN; GILBERT, W. S.; HART, MOSS; JONES, TOM; KAUFMAN, GEORGE S.; KERR, WALTER; LAPINE, JAMES; LAURENTS, ARTHUR; LAYTON, JOE; LEIGH, MITCH; LINDSAY, HOWARD; LOGAN, JOSHUA; MALTBY, RICHARD, JR.; MAMOULIAN, ROUBEN; MARSHALL, ROB; McGOWAN, JOHN; MITCHELL, THOMAS;

MOORE, ROBERT; NUNN, TREVOR; O'HORGAN, TOM; PAPP, JOSEPH; PRINCE, HAROLD; PRODUCER; REAMS, LEE ROY; RICE, EDWARD E.; SHORT, HASSARD; WHITE, GEORGE.

DIRTY ROTTEN SCOUNDRELS **(3 MARCH 2005, IMPERIAL, 627 PERFORMANCES).** Music and lyrics by **David Yazbek**, book by Jeffrey Lane. Based on the 1988 film about con artists on the French Riviera, the musical starred Norbert Leo Butz as Freddy Benson (a role for which he won a **Tony Award**), **John Lithgow** as Lawrence Jameson, and Sherrie Rene Scott as Christine Colgate. The show captured the chic sophistication and clever disguises and plot twists typical of classic **musical comedies** from the 1920s and 1930s.

DISNEY THEATRICAL PRODUCTIONS. Also known as The Walt Disney Studios and Walt Disney Productions. Disney's first Broadway musical was *Beauty and the Beast* (1994), through which the corporation became a major presence on Broadway and helped revitalize **Times Square**. Other musical productions include *The Lion King* (1997), which opened the renovated New Amsterdam Theatre, owned and operated by Disney; *Aida* (2000), produced by Hyperion Theatricals, a division of Disney; *Tarzan* (2006); and *Mary Poppins* (2006), a coproduction with **Cameron Mackintosh**.

DO I HEAR A WALTZ? **(18 MARCH 1965, 46TH STREET, 220 PERFORMANCES).** Music and presented by **Richard Rodgers**, lyrics by **Stephen Sondheim**, book by **Arthur Laurents**. Based on Laurents's play *The Time of the Cuckoo*, *Do I Hear a Waltz?* had the shortest run of any musical with music by Richard Rodgers since he had started his collaboration with **Oscar Hammerstein II** more than two decades earlier. The friction between the principal creators has become legendary, but the problems with *Do I Hear a Waltz?* had more to do with a story that was difficult to turn into a musical and an uninspired production. The plot involved a visit to Venice by the American spinster Leona Samish (Elizabeth Allen). She desires romance and meets Renato Di Rossi (Sergio Franchi), a charming but married shopkeeper. The story lacked joy, and the production failed to give its audience a true feeling of being transported to the romantic city of Venice. Howard Taubman, writing in the *New York Times*, remarked that the creators strayed little from the story, but "one cannot suppress a regret that they failed to be bolder. For there are times, particularly in the early stages, when songs are merely decoration." He thought that the play's musical transformation had been accomplished gracefully, but there was little in his review that would make one go see the musical. The score included some fine songs, including the wonderful title number, a delightful waltz, and the comic song "Perfectly Lovely Couple."

DONNELLY, DOROTHY (1880–1928). Lyricist and librettist who began her theatrical career as a stage actress. She is most famous for her four **operetta** collaborations with **Sigmund Romberg**: *Blossom Time* (1921), *The Student Prince* (1924), *My Maryland* (1927), and *My Princess* (1927). She created the book and lyrics for the **musical comedy** *Poppy* (1923), which she also directed and which starred **W. C. Fields**.

DON'T BOTHER ME, I CAN'T COPE **(19 APRIL 1972, PLAYHOUSE, 1,065 PERFORMANCES).** Music, lyrics, and book by Micki Grant; conceived and directed by Vinnette Carroll. A revue that confronted racial attitudes of the time with energetic music and minimal bitterness, *Don't Bother Me, I Can't Cope* ran for about two and a half years. The show first appeared in Washington, D.C., and ran in other theaters in New York City before it made it to Broadway. Micki Grant's music included different styles of African American music, and her lyrics dealt with the realities of urban life, including muggers and numbers rackets. Usually, however, she celebrated hope and African American achievements. **Clive Barnes**, reviewing the show for the *New York Times*, called it "a mixture of a block party and a revival meeting" with a "charming score" that features lyrics of "sweetness and wit." He noted that the production "moves as fast as a carousel," and one of the only mistakes was to leave Micki Grant off the stage until the second act, because "her serene charms" serve as a counterfoil to the chaos all around her. *See also* AFRICAN AMERICAN MUSICALS; RACE RELATIONS.

DO RE MI **(26 DECEMBER 1960, ST. JAMES, 400 PERFORMANCES).** Music by **Jule Styne**, lyrics by **Betty Comden** and

Adolph Green, book and staged by Garson Kanin, choreography by Mark Breaux and Deedee Wood, presented by David Merrick. A somewhat disappointing **musical comedy** partially redeemed by a number of factors, including **Phil Silvers** and **Nancy Walker** in the lead roles. Silvers played Hubert Cram, and Walker was his wife, Kay. The couple occasionally prospered from Hubie's various schemes (including stints as a jukebox magnate and a song producer), but their lives are ultimately mired in the middle class. The score's gems and memorable performances included Silvers's appealingly covetous "It's Legitimate" and Walker's comic "Adventure." For *New York Times* critic **Howard Taubman**, *Do Re Mi* was a decidedly mixed evening. At its worst, he called it "a desperate, lame effort to be '**Guys and Dolls**'." At other moments, however, he found it to be "money in the bank."

DOUGLASS, STEPHEN (BORN STEPHEN FITCH, 1921–). With a career spanning more than 60 years, Douglass made his Broadway debut as Billy Bigelow in the 1949 revival of *Carousel*. The lyrical baritone went on to create the roles of Ulysses in *The Golden Apple* (1954), Joe Hardy in *Damn Yankees* (1955), and File in *110 in the Shade* (1963).

DOYLE, JOHN. British director, costume and set designer whose reworkings of musicals such as *Sweeney Todd: The Demon Barber of Fleet Street* (2005) and *Company* (2006) emphasize techniques of ensemble drama. In Doyle's minimalistic productions, the actors also function as the orchestra (**Patti LuPone** played tuba in *Sweeney Todd*). and remain on stage for the entire performance. Doyle received a **Tony Award** for Best Director for *Sweeney Todd*.

DRAKE, ALFRED (ALFREDO CAPURRO, 1914–1992). A versatile performer who received critical and popular praise for his work in opera, musicals, and dramas, Drake's Broadway roles included Marshall Blackstone and the High Priest in *Babes in Arms* (1937), Curly McLain in *Oklahoma!* (1943), Larry Foreman in *The Cradle Will Rock* (1947 revival), Fred Graham/Petruccio in *Kiss Me, Kate* (1948), and Hajj in *Kismet* (1953). He won the *Variety* New York Drama Critics Poll Award for *Oklahoma!*, the Donaldson award for

Kiss Me, Kate, and the *Variety* New York Drama Critics Poll award, the Donaldson award, and the **Tony Award** for *Kismet*. He was known for the arresting quality of his powerful, resonant baritone voice that he used to enhance his portrayal of strong, forceful characters.

DRAMA DESK AWARDS. Created in 1955, awards are given for shows that appear on Broadway, **off-Broadway**, off-off-Broadway, and in legitimate not-for-profit theaters in New York City. **Tony Awards**, by contrast, are given only to Broadway productions. The categories for Drama Desk Awards were minimal at first but grew over the years to equal those of the Tony Awards. *See also* NEW YORK DRAMA CRITICS' CIRCLE AWARDS; PULITZER PRIZE.

DREAMGIRLS **(20 DECEMBER 1981, IMPERIAL, 1,522 PER-FORMANCES).** Music by Henry Krieger, lyrics and book by Tom Eyen, directed and choreographed by **Michael Bennett**. A show that appeared to be largely based on the story of the Supremes, *Dreamgirls* followed a group called the Dreams as they moved from African American rhythm and blues to white pop. The transition involved inevitable difficulties, such as when manager Curtis (Ben Harney) decides that lead singer (and his lover) Effie (Jennifer Holliday) is too large and has too raw a sound for white audiences: he also wants a new mistress. Her reaction at the end of act 1, "And I Am Telling You I'm Not Going," stopped the show. *Dreamgirls* includes a great deal of music, with nearly 40 distinct numbers and singing taking place during important moments in the plot such as contract negotiations and lover's quarrels. During "It's All Over," as **Frank Rich** noted in his *New York Times* review, "the clashing of seven characters is realized entirely in musical terms." Rich spent the first third of his rave review rhapsodizing about Jennifer Holliday's performance in the act 1 finale. He compared Bennett to **Jerome Robbins**, and said that as far as Robbins's legacy in creating "organic entities" was concerned, "last night the torch was passed, firmly, unquestionably, once and for all." Actors of note, in addition to Holliday, included Sheryl Lee Ralph as the Diana Ross-like lead of Dream and Loretta Devine and Deborah Burrell as the backup singers. *Dreamgirls* showed how sophisticated Broadway creators had become in handling African

American topics, for subtle differences between the black and white musical worlds were clearly illustrated. In this, Bennett's last musical before his untimely death, one could only admire his work as a director and choreographer. The 2006 film version, dedicated to Bennett, starred Jennifer Hudson, Beyoncé Knowles, and Jamie Foxx. *See also* AFRICAN AMERICAN MUSICALS.

THE DROWSY CHAPERONE **(1 MAY 2006, MARQUIS, 280 PERFORMANCES AS OF 31 DECEMBER 2006).** Music and lyrics by Lisa Lambert and Greg Morrison, book by Bob Martin and Don McKellar, directed and choreographed by Casey Nicholaw. A Canadian import billed as "a musical within a comedy" and performed without an intermission, *The Drowsy Chaperone* begins with the Man in a Chair (Bob Martin, of *Second City* fame), who is suffering from a "nonspecific sadness" and puts on an LP of his favorite 1920s **musical comedy**, also called *The Drowsy Chaperone*. The show-within-the-show is the story of a **revue** star, Janet (Sutton Foster), whose impending nuptials are threatened with typical 1920s antics. The Drowsy Chaperone (Beth Leavel, who won a **Tony Award** for her performance) is supposed to keep an eye on Janet until her wedding day. One of the show's other especially entertaining characters is Mrs. Tottendale (Georgia Engel, who played Georgette on *The Mary Tyler Moore Show*), who hosts the wedding. The score is filled with enticing numbers, including Janet's "Show Off" and the duet "Accident Waiting to Happen," performed by the romantic leads on roller skates. The musical won the 2006 **Tony Awards** for Best Book and Best Score.

DR. SEUSS' HOW THE GRINCH STOLE CHRISTMAS! **(8 NOVEMBER 2006, HILTON, 95 PERFORMANCES AS OF 31 DECEMBER 2006).** Music by Mel Marvin, book and lyrics by Timothy Mason. Inspired by the 1966 television special, the **family musical** based on Dr. Seuss's tale starred Patrick Page as The Grinch and **John Cullum** as Old Max. With additional matinees and a Thursday late morning performance for schools, it was the first Broadway musical to play 12 times per week.

DU BARRY WAS A LADY **(6 DECEMBER 1939, 46TH STREET, 408 PERFORMANCES).** Music and lyrics by **Cole Porter**, book by **Herbert Fields** and **B. G. De Sylva**, dances arranged by **Robert Alton**. A vehicle for **Ethel Merman** and **Bert Lahr** that rode its popular stars and humorous book to a respectable run. Porter's score included the perky duet "Friendship," the bawdy "But in the Morning, No!" as well as "Katie Went to Haiti" and "Do I Love You" Merman played May Daly, a cabaret chorus girl, and Lahr was Louis Blore, the washroom attendant who is infatuated with her. After accidentally ingesting knockout drops intended for May's love interest, Louis has an elaborate dream in which he and May are transported back to 18th-century France. After he awakens, Louis realizes that his relationship with May will not work out, and they part friends. In his *New York Times* review, **Brooks Atkinson** saved his greatest praise for Merman and Lahr: "Miss Merman is the perfect musical comedy minstrel. . . . Probably it is a mistake ever to produce a musical show without Bert Lahr."

DUDE **(9 OCTOBER 1972, BROADWAY, 16 PERFORMANCES).** Music by **Galt MacDermot**, lyrics and book by **Gerome Ragni**, directed and staged by **Tom O'Horgan**. A major disappointment from several of *Hair*'s creators, Ragni's rambling story about a young man coming of age with the assistance of many religious and allegorical figures was presented in a completely redesigned Broadway Theater. MacDermot's music was predictably in the rock mold, but included touches of other styles.

DUKE, VERNON (BORN VLADIMIR DUKELSKY, 1903–1969). Russian-born composer who used his real name for his classical compositions and "Vernon Duke" for his works in a popular vein. He wrote mostly for **revues**, including *Walk a Little Faster* (1932), which introduced "April in Paris" (lyrics by **E. Y. Harburg**). Duke wrote the score for *Cabin in the Sky* (1940) with lyricist John Latouche. He possessed a strong command of popular and classical styles, and his two compositional "careers" influenced each other.

DUNBAR, PAUL LAWRENCE (1872–1906). Seminal **African American** poet, novelist, and short story writer known for his evocative use of language, dialect, and rhetoric who was lyricist for *In Dahomey* (1903).

DUNCAN, SANDY (1946–). Energetic singer, dancer, and actress whose Broadway debut included playing several characters in *Canterbury Tales* (1969). In 1979, she flew to rave reviews in the title role of a **revival** of *Peter Pan*. She appeared in *My One and Only* in 1984, and in 1999, took over the role of Roxie Hart in the long-running revival of *Chicago*.

DUNCAN, TODD (1903–1998). African American baritone who, in addition to his work as an opera and concert singer and voice teacher at Howard University, created the character of Porgy in the **Gershwins'** *Porgy and Bess* (1935), singing the part more than 1,800 times. He also originated the dramatically and vocally powerful roles of "The Lawd's General" in *Cabin in the Sky* (1940) and Stephen Kumalo in *Lost in the Stars* (1949).

DURANTE, JIMMY (BORN JAMES FRANCIS DURANTE, 1893–1980). Singing comedian with a raspy voice whose large nose earned him the nickname "Schnozzola," or simply "The Schnozz." Early in life, he was a ragtime pianist, played in a jazz band, and appeared in vaudeville. He performed several of his own songs (music and lyrics) in the **Ziegfeld** production *Show Girl* (1929). Other Broadway credits include Jimmie Deegan in **Cole Porter's** *The New Yorkers* (1930), multiple roles in the **revue** *Strike Me Pink* (1933), Claudius B. Bowers in **Rodgers and Hart's** *Jumbo* (1935), and "Policy" Pinkle in Porter's *Red, Hot and Blue!* (1936). Durante was also a popular radio, television, and film celebrity, and his nose appears in the list of superlatives in Porter's song "You're the Top" from *Anything Goes* (1934).

– E –

EARL CARROLL VANITIES **(EARL CARROLL: 5 JULY 1923, 203 PERFORMANCES; 10 SEPTEMBER 1924, 133 PERFORMANCES; 6 JULY 1925, 390 PERFORMANCES; 28 DECEMBER 1925, ?; 24 AUGUST 1926, ?154 PERFORMANCES; 4 JANUARY 1927, ABOUT 150 PERFORMANCES; 6 AUGUST 1928, 203 PERFORMANCES; 27 AUGUST 1931, 278 PERFOR-**

MANCES; NEW AMSTERDAM: 1 JULY 1930, 215 PERFOR-
MANCES; EARL CARROLL'S BROADWAY: 27 SEPTEMBER
1932, 87 PERFORMANCES; ST. JAMES: 14 JANUARY 1940,
25 PERFORMANCES). The **revue** series *Earl Carroll Vanities* was
most famous for what **Earl Carroll**, the shows' producer, called "the
most beautiful girls in the world." He sometimes had more than 100
of them on stage at one time. A favorite presentation technique was
the "living curtain," where draping would descend around scantily
clad models. Because of these minimal costumes, the police watched
Carroll carefully, something the producer used for publicity. While
the Vanities included comics such as Joe Cook, **W. C. Fields**, Jimmy
Savo, and Milton Berle, musical performances also appeared. Lillian
Roth, Carroll's main singer in the later versions, introduced "I Gotta
Right to Sing the Blues" (by **Harold Arlen** and Ted Koehler) in
1932, one of the few first-class songs to come out of the series. Perhaps the most famous edition in terms of look was the 10th (1932),
for which Vincente Minnelli was the designer. A representative version was the fifth (1926), which **J. Brooks Atkinson** reviewed for the
New York Times. The show was long, lasting until past midnight. The
theater's decorations were in a Spanish motif with gypsy girls acting
as ushers and flower girls and fortune-tellers running around. The
typically eclectic score featured Spanish, Russian, and blues-style
numbers. The production was "generally in good taste," but "dull,"
and Carroll "keeps it moving with difficulty." There were moments
when "Carroll consents to study the feminine form without the im-
pediment of costumery."

EBB, FRED (1932–2004). Librettist and lyricist who, with longtime
collaborator **John Kander**, made his Broadway debut in 1965 with
Flora, the Red Menace, which starred **Liza Minnelli**, an actress
whose career has been strongly linked to songs and shows by Kander
and Ebb. The songwriting team's first major hit was *Cabaret* (1966),
followed by *The Happy Time* (1968), *70, Girls, 70* (1971), *Chicago*
(1975), *The Act* (1977), *Woman of the Year* (1981), *The Rink*
(1984), *Kiss of the Spider Woman* (1993, starring **Chita Rivera**), and
Steel Pier (1997). Ebb's words capture the usually distraught states
of the characters who sing them and evoke the time and place of their
shows' typically historic settings but with a decidedly modern bent.

EBERSOLE, CHRISTINE (1953–). Ebersole won a **Tony Award** for playing Dorothy Brock in the 2001 revival of *42nd Street* and captivated audiences and critics for her riveting lifelike portrayal of the older "Little" Edie Beale and the younger Edith Bouvier Beale in *Grey Gardens* (2006). She is especially known for her ability to recreate musical styles of the past within modern contexts.

EGAN, SUSAN (1970–). Lyrical singing actress who, in her Broadway debut, played Belle in *Beauty and the Beast* (1994). She created the role of Princess Léonide in *Triumph of Love* (1997), played Sally Bowles multiple times in the long-running **revival** of *Cabaret*, and in 2004, was the last actress to appear in the title role of *Thoroughly Modern Millie* on Broadway. She has also garnered praise for her work in film, television, and the recording studio.

ERROL, LEON (BORN LEONCE ERROL SIMMS, 1881–1951). Australian-born comic actor who appeared in several editions of *Ziegfeld Follies* (also directing in 1914 and 1915) and whose **musical comedy** roles include Connie and the Duke of Czechogovinio in *Sally* (1920) and Louie Ketchup in *Louie the 14th* (1925). He made more than 150 films.

ESPARZA, RAÚL. Versatile actor and singer who made his Broadway debut as Riff Raff in *The Rocky Horror Show* (2000), followed by two engagements as the Master of Ceremonies in the long-running revival of *Cabaret* (October 2001 to April 2002, September to December 2002). He created the roles of Philip Sallon in *Taboo* (2003) and Caractacus Potts in *Chitty Chitty Bang Bang* (2005), and played Bobby in the **John Doyle** 2006 revival of *Company*. He brings a convincing portrayal to whatever character type he plays, whether it be the morally (and sexually) ambiguous Master of Ceremonies in *Cabaret* or the idealistic loving father in *Chitty Chitty Bang Bang*.

EVANGELINE (27 JULY 1874, NIBLO'S GARDEN, 16 PERFORMANCES). Music and lyrics by **Edward E. Rice**, book by J. Cheever Goodwin. Suggested by Henry Wadsworth Longfellow's poem by the same name and created in Boston, *Evangeline; or the Belle of Acadie* ran for only two weeks in its original run in New York

City, but it went on to become one of America's favorite musicals until the early 20th century. Like many musicals of the period, it carried several genre labels, including "burlesque," "opera bouffe," and "extravaganza." Most accurately it was a **burlesque**, with a generous dollop of puns, low humor, roles played by actors of the opposite sex, and a dancing heifer formed from two dancers inside the costume. *Evangeline* also carried moments of spectacle, such as a spouting whale and a balloon trip to Arizona. The plot had little to do with Longfellow's poem. Here, Evangeline (Ione Burke, a man) and Gabriel (Connie Thompson, a woman) travel throughout the world and meet in many places that the poet never mentions.

EVITA **(25 SEPTEMBER 1979, BROADWAY, 1,567 PERFORMANCES).** Music by **Andrew Lloyd Webber**, lyrics by **Tim Rice**, directed by **Harold Prince**. *Evita*, like *Jesus Christ Superstar*, began life as a concept album and was successfully staged in London in 1978 before transferring to New York. The show is the story of Eva Perón, a former prostitute who became the wife of Argentinian dictator Juan Perón. Rice and Lloyd Webber explored her public image as opposed to her private reality in an originally conceived manner. Che Guevara (**Mandy Patinkin**) often assumes the role of narrator and also interacts on a psychological level with the title character (**Patti LuPone**), challenging her actions and motivations in marrying Juan Perón (Bob Gunton) and promoting her own career. Guevara, the Cuban leftist revolutionary, was not in Argentina during the Perón era—this was creative license on the part of the authors. Lloyd Webber and Rice portray Eva Perón as a woman desperately wanting to be loved. The show is sung-through, and Lloyd Webber's score includes such memorable songs as "Requiem for Evita," "Oh, What a Circus," "Another Suitcase in Another Hall," "A New Argentina," "High Flying, Adored," "Rainbow High," "Santa Evita," "Waltz for Eva and Che," and the title character's dramatic soliloquy, "Don't Cry for Me Argentina," with its evocative tango rhythmic underpinning. The defining pose of Evita with upwardly stretched arms and head bowed to the side is one of the iconic images of the musical theater. LuPone won her first **Tony Award** for her performance, which *New York Times* critic **Walter Kerr** described as having "rattlesnake vitality." The 1996 film version starred Madonna, Antonio Banderas, and **Jonathan Pryce**.

– F –

FABRAY, NANETTE (BORN NANETTE RUBY BERNADETTE FABARES, 1920–). **Musical comedy**, television, and film actress who appeared in a long line of shows—some successful, others not—during the 1940s and early 1950s, including *Let's Face It!* (1941), *By Jupiter* (1942, **replacement**), *My Dear Public* (1943), *Jackpot* (1944), *Bloomer Girl* (1944, **replacement**), *High Button Shoes* (1947), *Love Life* (1948, for which she won a **Tony Award**), *Arms and the Girl* (1950), and *Make a Wish* (1951). After more than a decade away from Broadway, she returned to play First Lady Nell Henderson in *Mr. President* (1962). The creators whose work she performed on Broadway included **Rodgers and Hart**, **Harold Arlen** and **E. Y. Harburg**, **Kurt Weill** and **Alan Jay Lerner**, Morton Gould and **Dorothy Fields**, and **Irving Berlin**.

FACE THE MUSIC **(17 FEBRUARY 1932, NEW AMSTERDAM, 165 PERFORMANCES).** Music and lyrics by **Irving Berlin**, book by **Moss Hart**, book directed by **George S. Kaufman**, produced by **Sam H. Harris**. After *Strike Up the Band* and *Of Thee I Sing* paved the way for satirical musicals, efforts such as *Face the Music* followed. With a stable of creators that included Berlin, Hart, and Kaufman, one might have expected the show to have a longer run, but *Face the Music* was not a smash hit. The show begins in an automat, where New York's elite eat cheaply because of the Depression. Broadway producer Hal Reisman (Andrew Tombes) comes in to locate backers for his latest production, and finds one in Mrs. Meshbesher (Mary Boland), the wife of Martin van Buren Meshbesher, a wealthy, yet corrupt, policeman. The policemen put their money into the show, *Rhinestones of 1932*, but also face investigations of their own. The show becomes a success only when they make it a bit more risqué. Berlin's score included "Let's Have Another Cup of Coffee," sung in the automat, "Soft Lights and Sweet Music," "Dear Old Crinoline Days," a send-up of **burlesque**, and "A Roof in Manhattan." Berlin's lyrics were not quite as barbed as those of **Ira Gershwin** in *Of Thee I Sing*, a bit of a problem given the biting satire of Hart's book, which took on politics, show business, and the Depression in equal measure. Writing in the *New York Times*, **J.**

Brooks Atkinson remarked that *Face the Music* "is one of the good things in the new vein of song-and-dance arcade."

FADE OUT—FADE IN (26 MAY 1964, MARK HELLINGER, 271 PERFORMANCES). Music by **Jule Styne**, lyrics and book by **Betty Comden** and **Adolph Green**, staged by **George Abbott**. A somewhat disappointing show that nevertheless featured a winning performance by **Carol Burnett**, *Fade Out—Fade In* ran for a total of about eight months in two separate spans. Burnett caused the three-month gap when she became disenchanted with the show, but no substitute could be located, so she returned. She played Hope Springfield, a Broadway chorus girl mistakenly brought to Hollywood to be a star. The studio head who made the error was Lionel Z. Governor (Lou Jacobi), a broad satire on Louis B. Mayer. Hope throws herself at the film's leading man, Byron Prong (**Jack Cassidy**), but instead ends up with one of Governor's nephews, Rudolf (Dick Patterson). Governor decides to shelve the film, but Rudolf arranges a preview. It becomes a hit, and Hope is a star. Lampooning Hollywood in the 1930s was not a new idea on Broadway, but there were memorable moments for Burnett's brand of comedy, and Jacobi was hilarious as a studio head who constantly needs a psychiatrist at his side. Among the score's hits was "Call Me Savage," a send-up of a seduction song sung by Hope after she slips a man's jacket over her embarrassingly slight costume that is festooned with long beads.

FALSETTOS (29 APRIL 1992, JOHN GOLDEN, 486 PERFORMANCES). Music and lyrics by **William Finn**, book by Finn and **James Lapine**, directed by Lapine. The increased visibility of gays and the AIDS crisis (which devastated the theatrical community) inspired two short off-Broadway musicals: *March of the Falsettos* (1981) and *Falsettoland* (1990), both created by Finn and Lapine. The shows were combined and brought to Broadway. Many of the original actors reprised their original roles. The plot revolves around a married Jewish man, Marvin (Michael Rupert), who leaves his wife and son, Jason (Jonathan Kaplan), for a man, Whizzer (Stephen Bogardus). Trina (Barbara Walsh), Marvin's wife, ends up marrying Marvin's psychotheraptist, Mendel (Chip Zien). Marvin is self-absorbed, and naively hopes that his entire "family" can somehow coexist.

Whizzer, however, contracts AIDS, and as he dies, the cast discovers the importance of love. The score included the clever "Four Jews in a Room Bitching," the expansive ballad "Unlikely Lovers," and Trina's seriocomic "I'm Breaking Down." *See also* HOMOSEXU-ALITY.

FAMILY MUSICAL. A style of musical theater developed during the 1990s geared toward children accompanied by adults. **Disney Theatrical Productions** have been a major force in the genre through live-action versions of some of their animated properties such as *Beauty and the Beast* (1994) and *The Lion King* (1997). Other examples include *Seussical* (2000), *A Year with Frog and Toad* (2003), and *Dr. Seuss' How the Grinch Stole Christmas!* (2006).

FANNY **(4 NOVEMBER 1954, MAJESTIC, 888 PERFOR-MANCES).** Music and lyrics by **Harold Rome**, book by S. N. Behrman and **Joshua Logan**, staged by Logan, dances by Helen Tamiris, presented by **David Merrick**. Based on Marcel Pagnol's trilogy of films *Marius*, *Fanny*, and *César*, each telling part of the same story, the musical *Fanny* brought all of the trappings of a major musical to the tale. Some felt this violated the intimate feeling and simplicity of the films, but the result was a hit musical that ultimately had little long-term importance. Fanny (**Florence Henderson**) falls in love with Marius (**William Tabbert**), son of César (**Ezio Pinza**), owner of a Marseilles café. Fanny becomes pregnant by Marius, who flees to become a seaman. Fanny agrees to marry Panisse (**Walter Slezak**), who adopts her son. Years later, Marius returns; Fanny still loves him, but César intervenes to keep Panisse from getting hurt. Panisse, however, is dying, and tells Fanny to marry Marius so that the son, Césario, has a father. The show benefited from fine principal actors, a good score, and plenty of spectacle, including a full-rigged ship and ballets at the circus and under the sea. Writing in the *New York Times*, **Brooks Atkinson** objected only to what he considered a bloated production: "this theatregoer finds himself impatient with Mr. Logan's passion for the supercolossal." Highlights of the score included Pinza's interpretations of "Love Is a Very Light Thing," "Why Be Afraid to Dance?" and "Welcome Home," Slezak's renditions of "To My Wife" and "Panisse and Son," Tabbert's work in

"Restless Heart" and "Fanny," Henderson's performance of "Have to Tell You," and the lovers' act 2 duet, "The Thought of You."

THE FANTASTICKS (**3 MAY 1960, SULLIVAN STREET PLAY-HOUSE, 17,162 PERFORMANCES**). Music by Harvey Schmidt, lyrics and book by Tom Jones. Its entire run was **off-Broadway**, where *The Fantasticks* became the longest-running American musical. Schmidt and Jones based *The Fantasticks* on Rostand's *Les Romantiques*. They created what **Brooks Atkinson** called in the *New York Times* a "dainty masque" in two acts. The story's framing device is the Narrator (**Jerry Orbach**, in his first starring role), who introduces the Girl (Rita Gardner) and the Boy (Kenneth Nelson) to each other. They are neighbors and in love, but they are separated by a wall. They believe their fathers disapprove of their attraction, but the parents actually erected the wall to keep them apart and thus help their hearts to grow fonder. To increase the longing, the fathers hire the Narrator to abduct the Girl. The youngsters discover the ruse, and are together at the end. The simple story is part of the show's charm, as is the fairy-tale atmosphere and archetypal quality of the characters. The score included the waltz "Try to Remember," a major hit, as well as "Soon It's Gonna Rain," another song that became popular on its own. The instrumental ensemble at the tiny theater consisted of just piano and harp. *The Fantasticks* provided a charming evening of theater that played for more than 40 years.

FEUER, CY (BORN SEYMOUR ARNOLD FEUER, 1911–2006). With Ernest Martin, he was the producer for successful shows with scores by **Cole Porter** or **Frank Loesser**, including *Guys and Dolls* (1950), *Can-Can* (1953), *Silk Stockings* (1955), and *How to Succeed in Business without Really Trying* (1961).

FIDDLER ON THE ROOF (**22 SEPTEMBER 1964, IMPERIAL, 3,242 PERFORMANCES**). Music by **Jerry Bock**, lyrics by **Sheldon Harnick**, book by **Joseph Stein**, staged and choreographed by **Jerome Robbins**, presented by **Harold Prince**. Based on short stories by Sholom Aleichem, *Fiddler on the Roof* became the longest-running musical in Broadway history to that point. The work is profoundly Jewish, but also carries a compelling universality. The audience watches the poor residents of the Jewish *shtetl* in Anatevka fight bigotry with humor and strength in Russia of 1905. When the government orders them to evacuate, they respond with the resignation of a people of faith and move on. It is a sentimental story, but involves plausible people the audience comes to understand. The plot surrounds Tevye (**Zero Mostel**), a devout milkman with a penchant for simple philosophy and long conversations with God. His wife, Golde (Maria Karnilova), is blunt and argumentative, but they share an abiding respect for each other. They have five daughters, three of whom are old enough to marry. The busybody Yente (**Beatrice Arthur**) makes the matches, but she is unsuccessful with Tevye's brood. Tzeitel (Joanna Merlin) is matched with the much older butcher, but she is in love with the young tailor, Motel (Austin Pendleton). They convince Tevye, against all traditions, to allow them to marry. The Christians in Anatevka destroy the wedding reception in a brief but nasty pogrom. Tevye's second daughter, Hodel (Julia Migenes), falls in love with Perchik (Bert Convy), a young revolutionary. The couple receive Tevye's blessing, but Perchik is arrested for his antigovernment activities, and Hodel follows him to distant Siberia. The next daughter, Chava (Tanya Everett), elopes with a Christian, which Tevye cannot accept. The show concludes with the Jews' exodus from Anatevka, many of the villagers heading to the United States. *Fiddler* included many memorable performances, but Mostel's was especially captivating. Writing in the *New York Times*, **Howard Taubman** called Tevye "one of the most glowing creations in the history of the musical theater." Taubman extended his extravagant praise to most aspects of the show, finding it a landmark in the genre. He wrote that Jerome Robbins's staging shows "sensitivity and fire," with dance woven into the whole "with subtlety and flaring theatricalism."

Fiddler has remained in the repertory partly because of its unusually fine score, and was revived on Broadway in 2004. Bock managed to weave together elements of popular song with recognizable Jewish idioms, such as the inspired cantillation in "If I Were a Rich Man." "Tradition" is the perfect opening number, identifying all of the characters and illustrating what holds them together. Tevye's "If I Were a Rich Man" epitomizes the character-defining number. The songs for the young people—"Matchmaker," "Miracle of Miracles,"

"Now I Have Everything," and "Far from the Home I Love"—also accentuated aspects of the characters that sing them. "Sabbath Prayer" is simple but heartrending, and "To Life" carries palpable excitement in a suitable ethnic vein. Tevye's snow job for Golde concerning Tzeitel's marriage to Motel, "The Dream," is both humorous and touching. "Sunrise, Sunset" expresses the feelings of all parents as they watch their children age, and the waltz has become the show's most popular tune. Harnick's lyrics in "Do You Love Me?" beautifully capture the feelings of an arranged marriage. The finale, "Anatevka," carries the same elegant simplicity and restraint as "The Sabbath Prayer."

FIELDS, DOROTHY (1905–1974). Prolific librettist and lyricist who wrote words for more than 400 songs on Broadway and in Hollywood. One of her early Broadway successes was "On the Sunny Side of the Street," with music by **Jimmy McHugh**, which appeared in *The International Revue* (1930). After working in Hollywood, she returned to Broadway in 1939 for *Stars in Your Eyes*, with music by **Arthur Schwartz**. With her brother, **Herbert Fields**, she cowrote the books for three shows with music and lyrics by **Cole Porter**, *Let's Face It!* (1941), *Something for the Boys* (1943), and *Mexican Hayride* (1944), as well as for **Irving Berlin**'s *Annie Get Your Gun* (1946) and **Sigmund Romberg**'s *Up in Central Park* (1948), Morton Gould's *Arms and the Girl* (1950), and Albert Hague's *Redhead* (1959). She was also lyricist for *Up in Central Park, Arms and the Girl*, and *Redhead*, and created lyrics for *A Tree Grows in Brooklyn* (1951, music by Schwartz), *Sweet Charity* (1966, music by **Cy Coleman**), and *Seesaw* (1973, music by Coleman), among others. Fields's character-specific lyrics employ vernacular idioms that accentuate particular dimensions of the people who sing them. She was the daughter of **Lew Fields** and sister of **Joseph Fields**.

FIELDS, HERBERT (1897–1958). Performer-turned-librettist who made his Broadway debut on stage in the **revue** *Miss 1917*. He worked with **Richard Rodgers** and **Lorenz Hart** as librettist for *Dearest Enemy* (1925), *The Girl Friend* (1926), *Peggy-Ann* (1926), *A Connecticut Yankee* (1927), and *Present Arms* (1928). Fields created libretti for notable **musical comedies** such as *Hit the Deck*

(1927, music by **Vincent Youmans**), *Fifty Million Frenchmen* (1929, music by **Cole Porter**), *The New Yorkers* (1930, music by Porter), *Pardon My English* (1933, music by **George Gershwin**), and *Du Barry Was a Lady* (1939, music by Porter, cowritten with **B. G. De Sylva**). With his sister, **Dorothy Fields**, he cowrote the books for three more shows with music by Porter, *Let's Face It!* (1941), *Something for the Boys* (1943), and *Mexican Hayride* (1944), as well as for **Irving Berlin**'s *Annie Get Your Gun* (1946) and **Sigmund Romberg**'s *Up in Central Park* (1948), Morton Gould's *Arms and the Girl* (1950), and Albert Hague's *Redhead* (1959). He was the son of **Lew Fields** and brother of **Joseph Fields**.

FIELDS, JOSEPH (1895–1966). Playwright and librettist who created the books for *Gentlemen Prefer Blondes* (1949, music by **Jule Styne**, cowritten with Anita Loos), *Wonderful Town* (1953, music by **Leonard Bernstein**, cowritten with Jerome Chodorov and based on his and Chodorov's play *My Sister Eileen*), and *Flower Drum Song* (1958, music by **Richard Rodgers**, cowritten with **Oscar Hammerstein II**). He was the son of **Lew Fields** and brother of **Dorothy Fields** and **Herbert Fields**.

FIELDS, LEW (BORN MOSES SCHOENFELD, 1867–1941). Actor, comedian, manager, and producer who constituted half of "Weber and Fields," one of the most successful comic duos of the late 19th century. With Joe Weber, he created, among other skits, the "Dutch Act" in which the team portrayed German immigrants. In 1896, they opened the Weber and Fields Music Hall. After the team disbanded in 1904, Fields continued his Broadway career as a performer and producer. Among the works he produced was the **musical comedy** *Poor Little Ritz Girl* (1921), for which he also wrote the book. The show began his collaboration with the team of **Richard Rodgers** and **Lorenz Hart**, which lasted through *Chee-Chee* (1928). Three of his children were notable Broadway wordsmiths: **Dorothy Fields**, **Herbert Fields**, and **Joseph Fields**.

FIELDS, W. C. (BORN WILLIAM CLAUDE DUKENFIELD, 1880–1946). Comic performer with a nasal voice who was active in **vaudeville** as an "eccentric juggler" and appeared in several editions of *Ziegfeld Follies* in addition to other **revues**. He played con man Eustace McGargle in the **musical comedy** *Poppy* (1923); the show's unsigned review in the *New York Times* reported that Fields "has never been quite so amusing as he is in 'Poppy'—nor so versatile," adding that he "creates comedy where certainly none existed in the libretto." Fields was also famous for his work on radio and in film.

FIERSTEIN, HARVEY (1954–). Performer and playwright who wrote the librettos for *La Cage aux Folles* (1983) and *Legs Diamond* (1988). He won a **Tony Award** for his portayal of Edna Turnblad in *Hairspray* (2002), and was a **replacement** Tevye in the 2004 revival of *Fiddler on the Roof*. *See also* HOMOSEXUALITY.

***FIFTY MILLION FRENCHMEN* (27 NOVEMBER 1929, LYRIC, 254 PERFORMANCES).** Music and lyrics by **Cole Porter**, book by **Herbert Fields**, settings by Norman Bel Geddes. Billed as "a musical comedy tour of Paris," *Fifty Million Frenchmen* was Broadway's recognition that many Americans adored the French capital. The show concerns Peter Forbes (**William Gaxton**), a rich young American who falls in love with Looloo Carroll (Genevieve Tobin). He bets his friend Michael Cummins (Jack Thompson) that he can win Looloo's heart without making his wealth known. In various disguises, he manages to lure Looloo away from the Russian aristocrat her parents have picked out for her. **J. Brooks Atkinson**, writing in the *New York Times*, described Gaxton as "enormously amusing with a boyish sort of irresponsibility." Norman Bel Geddes, who worked on Broadway before becoming one of the first famous industrial designers, conceived sets that emerged as among the stars of the show, including the Ritz Bar, Eiffel Tower, and other Parisian haunts. Cole Porter wrote a strong score with such songs as "Find Me a Primitive Man," "So You Want to See Paris?," "I Worship You," "Tale of an Oyster," and "I'm in Love," the last of which inspired a memorable dance routine costumed entirely in black and white.

FILM VERSIONS. *See* SCREEN ADAPTATIONS.

***FINE AND DANDY* (23 SEPTEMBER 1930, ERLANGER'S, 255 PERFORMANCES).** Music by **Kay Swift**, lyrics by Paul James, book by David Ogden Stewart. One of the few musicals from the first half of the 20th century with music by a woman, *Fine and Dandy* was a vehicle for the comedian Joe Cook. He appeared in several versions of *Earl Carroll Vanities* in the 1920s as a rapid-talking comic, a fine acrobat, and a juggler. Cook clearly dominated the show, but there were other high points as well. He played Joe Squibb, a worker for a tool company who becomes general manager through the prurient interest of the founder's widow. Squibb also woos another young lady, even though he has a wife and children at home. His innovations as general manager are too expensive to implement, but the workers appreciated shorter hours and the company picnics. Writing in the *New York Times*, **J. Brooks Atkinson** described the book as "an amiable satire," placed the score "in the fresher vein of musical comedy tunes," and praised **Eleanor Powell** for her dancing. *Fine and Dandy* enjoyed a fine run of about eight months.

FINIAN'S RAINBOW **(10 JANUARY 1947, 46TH STREET, 725 PERFORMANCES).** Music by **Burton Lane**, lyrics by **E. Y. Harburg**, book by Harburg and Fred Saidy, choreography by **Michael Kidd**. *Finian's Rainbow* opened two months before *Brigadoon*, another fantasy-laden tale. After stealing a pot of gold from leprechauns, Finian McLonergan (Albert Sharpe) comes to the United States with his daughter, Sharon (Ella Logan). With a scheme to plant the gold at Fort Knox to see what it might grow, Finian and Sharon end up in Rainbow Valley in the mythical state of Missitucky. The leprechaun, Og (David Wayne), who is trying to recover his gold and also has his eye on Sharon, pursues them. Sharon marries a local man, and Og settles for someone else. In the end, the audience learns that there is no gold and that Finian's hometown of Glocca Morra, Ireland, is nothing more than a fantasy, but it remains real in Finian's dreams as he journeys on. **Brooks Atkinson**, reviewing the show for the *New York Times*, found much of *Finian's Rainbow* irresistible. He had reservations about the first act's "conventional finale," the "tawdry musical show enticements" in the second act that he traced back to **Florenz Ziegfeld**, and the plot's union of make-believe with social commentary when the characters help the plight of **African Americans** in the fictional southern town. For Atkinson, however, these were small problems in a show that "puts the American musical stage several steps forward for the imagination with which it is written" and "the stunning virtuosity" of the actors and production. The score included several memorable songs; "How Are Things in Glocca Morra?" was a huge hit with its soaring melody, and "If This Isn't Love" also became known outside of the theater. *See also* RACE RELATIONS/RACISM.

FINN, WILLIAM (1952–). Composer, lyricist, and librettist who won **Tony Awards** for Best Score and Best Book for *Falsettos* (1992), for which he created music, lyrics, and book. He wrote the music and lyrics for *The 25th Annual Putnam County Spelling Bee* (2005). Finn's music has a directness that allows for the clear declamation of his witty and intelligent words. His lyrics concern life in contemporary America, and include references to **homosexuality**, family, acceptance, and loss. He also wrote the song "Scarlet Pimpernel" for the Broadway play *The Sisters Rosenweig* (1993) and the musical *A New Brain* (1998), produced by **Lincoln Center Theatre**.

FIORELLO! (23 NOVEMBER 1959, BROADHURST, 795 PERFORMANCES). Music by **Jerry Bock**, lyrics by **Sheldon Harnick**, book by Jerome Weidman and **George Abbott**, staged by Abbott, choreography by Peter Gennaro, produced by Robert E. Griffith and **Harold S. Prince**. One of the musicals to win the Pulitzer Prize for Drama, *Fiorello!* remains one of the highlights of Broadway history that was significant in its time but has seldom been performed since. It chronicled the early years of Fiorello La Guardia's political career, when he rose from a lawyer championing the little guy to ward politician and congressman and ends with his second run for mayor, when he defeated Jimmy Walker. **Tom Bosley** played the mayor, and was described by **Brooks Atkinson** in the *New York Times* as having "a kindly face, abundant energy and an explosive personality." Atkinson also noted that the cast could not include better actors and singers. Other members included **Howard Da Silva** as Ben Marino, a Republican party hack of questionable integrity; Patricia Wilson as Marie, La Guardia's secretary and second wife; and Pat Stanley as Dora, Marie's friend and one of the young politician's biggest fans. Atkinson praised Bock's "bouncy score" that shows the considerable influence of **Frank Loesser** and Harnick's "unfailingly humorous" lyrics. The songs were closely allied to the story and its situations, and, with the exception of "When Did I Fall in Love," none achieved success outside of the show.

THE FIREBRAND OF FLORENCE (22 MARCH 1945, ALVIN, 43 PERFORMANCES). Music by **Kurt Weill**, lyrics by **Ira Gershwin**, book by Edwin Justus Mayer. Based on Mayer's play *The Firebrand* (1924) about the life of Benvenuto Cellini, this musical was a dismal, and perhaps undeserved, failure. Lewis Nichols of the *New York Times* describes Gershwin's lyrics as "not outstanding," Weill's score as mostly "casual and not distinguished," the dancing as "brief," but also admits that "the production itself is a beautiful one to see." Weill wrote an enormous score that he orchestrated himself; two of what Nichols considered the catchier songs were "There'll Be Life, Love and Laughter" and "The Nighttime Is No Time for Thinking." The opening sequence of Cellini's scheduled execution and pardon included 20 minutes of continuous music, unusual for a Broadway musical at the time.

THE FIREFLY (2 DECEMBER 1912, LYRIC, 120 PERFORMANCES). Music by **Rudolf Friml**. Lyrics and book by Otto Hauerbach (later **Otto Harbach**). After the success of *Naughty Marietta*, **Victor Herbert** agreed to write another operetta for its leading lady, **Emma Trentini**, and **Arthur Hammerstein**'s company, but the star and composer/conductor had a disagreement over an encore while on tour. Herbert vowed never to write for Trentini again. Hammerstein hired the Czech pianist and composer **Rudolf Friml**, who had never written for Broadway, to create the score. It was an immense success. Trentini played Nina Corelli, a poor Italian street singer who dresses as a cabin boy on a ship bound for Bermuda in order to be near the man she loves, Jack Travers (Craig Campbell). By the end of the show, Nina has become a famous prima donna and Jack has fallen in love with her. The *New York Times* review reported that Friml wrote "one of the most popular scores imaginable," and almost every song of the evening was encored. Highlights of the score included "Sympathy," "Giannina Mia," and "Love Is Like a Firefly." The plot and musical program were completely reworked for the 1937 MGM film starring Jeanette MacDonald and Allan Jones.

FLAHERTY, STEPHEN (1960–). Composer whose collaborations with librettist, lyricist, and composer **Lynn Ahrens** include *Once on This Island* (1990), *My Favorite Year* (1992), *Ragtime* (1998), *Seussical* (2000), and songs for *Chita Rivera: A Singer's Life* (2005). He conceived *Seussical* and is also active as a vocal and dance arranger. Flaherty and Ahrens's songs possess a strong sense of dramatic purpose that allow them to be fully integrated into the plot as well as exist as independent entities outside of their original larger contexts.

FLORADORA (12 NOVEMBER 1900, CASINO, 505 PERFOR-MANCES). A London import with music and lyrics by unnamed songwriters, *Floradora* was the second musical in New York theatrical history to have more than 500 performances. The plot took place on Floradora, an island in the Philippines. Dolores (Fannie Johnston) is an heiress to a perfume fortune, and the evil Cyrus W. Gilfain (R. E. Graham) attempts to cheat her out of her inheritance. With the help of Dolores's fiancé, Frank Albercoed (Bertram Godfrey), and the comic Anthony Tweedledee (Willie Edouin), Dolores foils Gilfain's plans. After a rocky opening with a mixed critical reception, *Floradora* finally took off as the song "Tell Me, Pretty Maiden" became a popular standard.

FLORA, THE RED MENACE (11 MAY 1965, ALVIN, 87 PER-FORMANCES). Music by **John Kander**, lyrics by **Fred Ebb**, book by **George Abbott** and Robert Russell, staged by Abbott, presented by **Harold Prince**. A show created by Broadway songwriting legends and featuring the Broadway debut of **Liza Minnelli**, *Flora, the Red Menace* nevertheless failed. The plot was supposed to be a satire of American Communist Party activities during the 1930s. Flora (Minnelli) is a naive, aspiring fashion designer who joins the Party at the urging of her boyfriend, Harry Toukarain (Bob Deshy). **Howard Taubman**, writing for the *New York Times*, was most impressed by Minnelli, especially her singing, "but her freshly burgeoning talent is not yet overpowering enough to save a faltering production." He cites as specific examples of her good work the songs "A Quiet Thing" and "Sing Happy."

FLOWER DRUM SONG (**1 DECEMBER 1958, ST. JAMES, 600 PERFORMANCES**). Music by **Richard Rodgers**; lyrics by **Oscar Hammerstein II**; book by Hammerstein and Joseph Fields; directed by **Gene Kelly**; choreographed by **Carol Haney**; produced by Rodgers, Hammerstein, and Fields. For their eighth Broadway show, Rodgers and Hammerstein focused on the clash of cultures in the Chinese-American immigrant community in San Francisco as portrayed in C. Y. Lee's popular book *The Flower Drum Song*. It was probably the most contemporary of any of Rodgers and Hammerstein's musicals. The story centered on an arranged marriage between a native Chinese girl, Mei-Li (Miyoshi Umeki), and Americanized Sammy Fong (Larry Blyden), who is in love with nightclub hostess Linda Low (Pat Suzuki). While the scenery and score had a distinctively modern flare, the dancing evoked the style of the previous decade with dream sequences and separate dance sets, eschewing the modern Broadway practice of seamlessly integrating the dancing, as seen, for example, in *West Side Story* the previous year. After some recasting in out-of-town tryouts, Rodgers and Hammerstein decided that the company's combined personality made up for any weaknesses in the show. Gene Kelly was an adequate director, but some commentators felt that he had lost touch with his Broadway roots. **Brooks Atkinson**, writing for the *New York Times*, deemed the show a mixed success: "'Flower Drum Song' is not one of their master works. It is a pleasant interlude among some most agreeable people." The show's hits included "A Hundred Million Miracles" and "I Enjoy Being a Girl," the latter sung by Pat Suzuki. The short-lived 2002 Broadway revival featured a new book by David Henry Hwang and starred **Lea Salonga** as Mei-Li.

FLYING HIGH (**3 MARCH 1930, APOLLO, 357 PERFORMANCES**). Songs by **B. G. De Sylva, Lew Brown**, and **Ray Henderson**; book by De Sylva, Brown, and Jack McGowan; produced by **George White**. Most famous today as the show that **Bert Lahr** was unable to leave so he could play the role written for him in *Girl Crazy*, *Flying High* actually ran nearly three months longer than the Gershwins' more famous show. The plot of *Flying High* involved three couples and men who work around airplanes. Oscar Shaw played the pilot, Tod Addison, who parachutes onto the roof of Eileen

Cassidy (Grace Brinkley), initiating the inevitable love at first sight. Lahr played "Rusty" Krause, Addison's mechanic, whose paramour was Pansy Sparks (**Kate Smith**). **J. Brooks Atkinson**'s review in the *New York Times* opened: "Nearly everything essential to a good Broadway musical comedy . . . is to be found in 'Flying High'." The show's best songs included "Thank Your Father," "Happy Landing," "Without Love," a vehicle for Brinkley, and "Red Hot Chicago," which Kate Smith sang with the volume for which she was famous.

FOLLIES **(4 APRIL 1971, WINTER GARDEN, 522 PERFOR-MANCES).** Music and lyrics by **Stephen Sondheim**, book by James Goldman, directed by **Harold Prince**, presented by Prince in association with Ruth Mitchell. An artistically successful but commercially unsuccessful look at a cast reunion for the *Weismann Follies* (based on the *Ziegfeld Follies*), *Follies* was another serious effort of musical theater from Sondheim and Prince. Those returning to their old theater before it is demolished include Sally and Buddy (Dorothy Collins and Gene Nelson) and Phyllis and Ben (Alexis Smith and John McMartin). In the old days, Sally and Ben had feelings for each other, and now find themselves again attracted to each other, but Ben runs away, just as he did years earlier. The thin plot relied heavily on nostalgia with the older characters also appearing as their youthful selves and ghostly chorus girls parading around as in bygone days. Sondheim's pastiche score evoked the styles of some earlier Broadway creators, particularly those involved with the **revue**. For example, "One More Kiss" was an **operetta** waltz. Other well-known songs from the show include "Waiting for the Girl Upstairs," "Broadway Baby," "In Buddy's Eyes," "Could I Leave You?" and "Losing My Mind." The set design was of a theater in the process of being torn down, an expensive concept that helped cause the show to lose money. *Follies* was a useful barometer on how far what was intended as art could succeed on Broadway in 1971.

FOLLOW THE GIRLS **(8 SEPTEMBER 1944, NEW CENTURY, 882 PERFORMANCES).** Music and lyrics by Dan Shapiro, Milton Pascal, and Phil Charig; book by **Guy Bolton** and Eddie Davis. A show with more than its share of feminine pulchritude, *Follow the Girls* packed in soldiers and sailors on leave and managed a run that lasted a bit more than two years. Gertrude Niesen was Bubbles La Marr, a burlesque star who operates a servicemen's canteen. **Jackie Gleason** played her 4-F boyfriend, Goofy Gale, who dressed as a WAVE to see his love. The loose plot allowed for a number of specialty acts, and the show's most memorable song was Niesen's racy "I Wanna Get Married."

FOLLOW THRU (9 JANUARY 1929, 46TH STREET, 403 PER-
FORMANCES). Music and lyrics by **B. G. De Sylva, Lew Brown**, and **Ray Henderson**; book by **Laurence Schwab** and De Sylva. Created by the team responsible for *Good News!*, *Follow Thru* was another sports-minded hit and ran for a year. This show about golf took place at a country club, where Lora Moore (Irene Delroy) and Ruth Van Horn (Madeline Cameron) vie for both the female championship and the affections of Jerry Downs (John Barker). Ruth loses on both accounts. The delightful subplot had Angie Howard (Zelma O'Neal) running after the less assertive Jack Martin (Jack Haley). In a racy scene, the two male leads ventured into the women's locker room disguised as plumbers. A young **Eleanor Powell** also appeared in the dance-heavy show. **J. Brooks Atkinson** raved in the *New York Times*, calling *Follow Thru* "a frenzied, sufficiently original carnival" that is best when "dancing a mad fandango of humors." He singled out the "vigorous score," which included "Button Up Your Overcoat," "My Lucky Star," and "I Could Give Up Anything But You."

FOOTLOOSE (22 OCTOBER 1998, RICHARD RODGERS, 709
PERFORMANCES). Music by Tom Snow; lyrics by Dean Pitchford; stage adaptation by Pitchford and Walter Bobbie, based on the screenplay by Pitchford; directed by Bobbie. Based on the 1984 film of the same name from 1984, *Footloose* was conceived for the teen market. A teenager named Ren McCormack (Jeremy Kushnier) moves from Chicago to a small town. He is an avid dancer, but finds his favorite activity has been outlawed through the efforts of Rev. Shaw Moore (Stephen Lee Anderson), whose son died in a drunk-driver crash after a dance. Ren agitates against the ban and further complicates matters by falling for the preacher's daughter, Ariel (Jennifer Laura Thompson). Everything works out in the end. The show included a great deal of dancing to music by Kenny Loggins, Eric

Carmen, Sammy Hagar, and Jim Steinman, some of which was heard in the film.

FORD, HELEN (1894–1982). Musical comedy star of the 1920s especially known for creating lead roles in three **Rodgers and Hart** shows: *Dearest Enemy* (1925), *Peggy-Ann* (1926), and *Chee-Chee* (1928).

FORREST, GEORGE "CHET" (1915–1999). Composer and lyricist whose work with **Robert Wright** began in Los Angeles nightclubs before they wrote songs for 58 different films. On Broadway, their best-known shows featured adaptations of famous melodies by earlier composers. These included *Song of Norway* (1944, Edvard Grieg), *Gypsy Lady* (1946, **Victor Herbert**), *Kismet* (1953, Alexander Borodin), and *Anya* (1964, Sergei Rachmaninoff). Their original musical *Grand Hotel*, which closed out of town during its **tryout** in 1958, finally arrived on Broadway in 1989, directed by **Tommy Tune** and with additional music by **Maury Yeston**.

THE FORTUNE TELLER **(26 SEPTEMBER 1898, WALLACK'S, 40 PERFORMANCES).** Music by **Victor Herbert**, lyrics and book by **Harry B. Smith**. An **operetta** in the grand European tradition, *The Fortune Teller* included Herbert's winning score and soprano **Alice Nielsen**, who played three different roles, two of which were look-alike females: Musette, a gypsy who reads fortunes, and Irma, a young heiress and ballet student in Budapest. Nielsen's third role was that of Irma's twin brother. Both girls have trouble with their beaus because of their close physical resemblance, but this ultimately helps Irma marry her suitor. Songs included "Romany Life," "Gypsy Love Song," and "Only in the Play." The brief New York run was part of a national tour, a typical practice of the time.

FORTY-FIVE MINUTES FROM BROADWAY **(1 JANUARY 1906, NEW AMSTERDAM, 90 PERFORMANCES).** Music, lyrics, book, and direction by **George M. Cohan**. Perhaps most famous for its title song, this show was intended as a vehicle for the noted stage personality **Fay Templeton**. She played Mary Jane Jenkins, a faithful maid for many years to a wealthy man. Everyone expects her to inherit his fortune, and she finally does, but only after a number of complications. Another actor in the cast was future star **Victor Moore**, fresh from **vaudeville**. The *New York Times* reviewer disliked the spectacle of placing Fay Templeton in a show where she must be sad. The critic admits, "There are four or five capital songs . . ." In addition to the title song, the score included "So Long, Mary" and "Mary is a Grand Old Name." The *Times* reviewer believed that it was in the songs "where the hand of George M. Cohan apparently shows itself at its best."

42ND STREET (25 AUGUST 1980, WINTER GARDEN, 3,486 PERFORMANCES). Music by Harry Warren, lyrics by **Al Dubin**, direction and dances by **Gower Champion**, presented by **David Merrick**. Based on the 1933 film of the same name, *42nd Street* effectively re-created the world of 1930s popular song and glorious tap dancing. The real star was Gower Champion, who gave his creation a legendary send-off when he died on opening day. Despite battling his final illness while mounting the show, Champion managed what **Frank Rich** called in the *New York Times* a "display of blazing theatrical fireworks." The show was not a parody but rather a semi-serious telling of the story about a chorus girl (Wanda Richert) who fills in for the show's older star (**Tammy Grimes**) and delivers a hit for the desperate director (**Jerry Orbach**). Many lines from the film remained; **Michael Stewart** and Mark Bramble only received credit for "lead-ins and crossovers." Since the film included only a handful of songs, the creators of the stage version interpolated other gems by Warren and Dubin into the score, treating audiences to splendid versions of "42nd Street," "Shuffle off to Buffalo," "Sunny Side to Every Situation," "Lullaby of Broadway," "We're in the Money," and others. The highly successful 2001 revival played for 1,521 performances.

FOSSE (14 JANUARY 1999, BROADHURST, 1,093 PERFORMANCES). Choreography by **Bob Fosse**; conceived by **Richard Maltby Jr.**, Chet Walker, and **Ann Reinking**; choreography re-created by Walker; directed by Maltby; codirected and co-choreographed by Reinking; artistic advice by **Gwen Verdon**. A **Tony Award**-winning musical despite the lack of any new music, dancing, or any book whatsoever, *Fosse* was an exciting tribute to the famed choreographer and director created by dancers who worked with him. The **jukebox musical** (and **dance musical**) demonstrated Fosse's sexually charged, strutting, and singular style. It featured numbers spanning Fosse's career and included work for both Broadway and film; however, the creators did not provide context or chronology. Famous excerpts included "Big Spender" and "The Rich Man's Frug" from *Sweet Charity*, "Shoeless Joe from Hannibal, Mo." from *Damn Yankees*, "Steam Heat" from *The Pajama Game*, "Sing, Sing, Sing" from *Dancin'*, and segments from Fosse's films *All That Jazz* and *Cabaret*. **Ben Brantley** of the *New York Times* appreciated the dancing and cast, but compares the show to "an album of glossy, uncaptioned photographs." They might be lovely, "but it takes your own memories of what they represent to animate those scenes . . . otherwise, they're just pictures."

FOSSE, BOB (1927–1987). Choreographer and director whose distinctive style developed from social and ethnic dances, and demonstrated the influence of **Jack Cole**'s jazz dancing. After choreographing *The Pajama Game* (1954), Fosse worked with **George Abbott** on other projects, including *Damn Yankees* (1955), where he used typical baseball moves and created humorous, sexy dances for star **Gwen Verdon**. Fosse codirected *How to Succeed in Business without Really Trying* (1961) with Abe Burrows. His major successes as director-choreographer were *Sweet Charity* (1966), *Pippin* (1972), and *Chicago* (1975), each including the brilliant stage dances that showed Fosse's blend of demanding choreography and showmanship. In *Dancin'* (1979), he created an anthology of previous dances and new works. The culmination of his late work was *Big Deal* (1986), for which he chose preexisting music but achieved total control of the production. One of the features of his sexually charged choreography was the employment of close-bodied groups of dancers moving across the stage as discrete units.

FOSTER, SUTTON. Singing actress with a youthful exuberance who won a **Tony Award** for her portrayal of the vivacious title role in *Thoroughly Modern Millie* (2002). She also created Jo in *Little Women* (2004) and Janet Van De Fraaff in *The Drowsy Chaperone* (2006).

FREEDLEY, VINTON (1891–1969). Producer, who with **Alexander A. Aarons**, worked closely with **George** and **Ira Gershwin,** and brought many of their shows to the stage, including *Lady, Be Good!* (1924), *Oh, Kay!* (1926), and *Girl Crazy* (1930). At the height of the producers' success, they built the Alvin Theater, creating its name from the first letters of their first names (AL + VIN). In the late 1930s and early 1940s, he produced shows on his own, including *Red, Hot and Blue!* (1936), *Leave It to Me!* (1938), *Cabin in the Sky* (1940), and *Let's Face It!* (1941).

FRIML, RUDOLF (1879–1972). Czech-born pianist and composer who studied with Antonín Dvořák and began his Broadway career with the high-profile *The Firefly* (1912), an **operetta** written for soprano **Emma Trentini** after **Victor Herbert** quit the project. *The Firefly* began a fruitful collaboration with producer **Arthur Hammerstein** and lyricist-librettist **Otto Harbach** that lasted for most of the decade (works included *High Jinks* [1913], *Katinka* [1915], and *Tumble In* [1919]) and into the 1920s. Friml's best-remembered musicals are his spectacular operettas of the 1920s: *Rose Marie* (1924), *The Vagabond King* (1925), and *The Three Musketeers* (1928). In each of these shows, the romantic story is set against a backdrop of oppression or injustice, which, like the challenges facing the lovers, is overcome by the final curtain. Friml continued to compose for Broadway in the 1930s, creating *Luana* (1930) and *Music Hath Charms* (1934), though neither show had a long run. Friml's musical style is firmly rooted in 19th-century Romanticism; the influences of Frederic Chopin and Bedřich Smetana are readily apparent. While his contemporary **Sigmund Romberg** excelled at waltzes, Friml created immortal ballads such as the title song of *Rose Marie* and "Only a Rose" from *The Vagabond King.*

***THE FULL MONTY* (26 OCTOBER 2000, EUGENE O'NEILL, 770 PERFORMANCES).** Music and lyrics by **David Yazbek**, book by **Terrence McNally**. A stage version of the popular British film about unemployed workers in Sheffield who create a male strip show in order to earn money, the setting of the Broadway version was changed to Buffalo, New York. The score includes many appealing songs in a rock style, such as "Scrap," a hard-hitting song of male despondency, "You Rule My World," Dave's love song to his stomach and Harold's to Vicki that is sung as a duet between the two men, and "Let It Go," the striptease finale. *See also* ROCK MUSICALS.

FUNNY FACE (22 NOVEMBER 1927, ALVIN, 250 PERFORMANCES). Music by **George Gershwin**, lyrics by **Ira Gershwin**, book by Fred Thompson and Paul Gerard Smith, produced by **Alexander A. Aarons** and **Vinton Freedley**. A show that involved several Broadway legends and also the first to take place in the Alvin Theater (named after the first syllables of each producer's first name), *Funny Face* had memorable songs and dances, good jokes, and a forgettable plot. **Fred** and **Adele Astaire** starred alongside William Kent, **Victor Moore**, and Allen Kearns, three of Broadway's major male stars of the era. The story involved several teams of robbers trying to break into a jewel safe, but all that really matters is that the right people end up together at the end. This was the first show in which Fred Astaire danced in a tuxedo before a men's **chorus**, here to Gershwin's "High Hat." Other notable songs include "S' Wonderful," "My One and Only," and "Funny Face."

FUNNY GIRL (26 MARCH 1964, WINTER GARDEN, 1,348 PERFORMANCES). Music by **Jule Styne**, lyrics by **Bob Merrill**, book by Isobel Lennart, staging by Garson Kanin, production supervised by **Jerome Robbins**. **Barbra Streisand** became a Hollywood star after starring in *Funny Girl*. She eloquently and memorably recalled the career of **Fanny Brice**, a great Jewish comedienne and stage personality who starred for years in the ***Ziegfeld Follies***. *Funny Girl* followed Brice's early career and her relationship with gambler Nicky Arnstein (**Sydney Chaplin**). The show was sentimental, but Streisand's luminous performance overwhelmed any problems with book or tone. **Howard Taubman**, writing in the *New York Times*, noted Streisand's ability in "recalling the laughter and joy that were Fanny Brice." He found her capable of making the tragic ending work because she "can make a virtue out of suffering, if she is allowed to sing about it." Especially impressive numbers for Streisand included "People," "I'm the Greatest Star," and "Don't Rain on My

Parade." Several production numbers evoked the early 20th century: "Cornet Man," "His Love Makes Me Beautiful," and "Rat-Tat-Tat-Tat." Streisand reprised her role in the film version (1968) and its sequel, *Funny Lady* (1975).

A FUNNY THING HAPPENED ON THE WAY TO THE FORUM **(8 MAY 1962, ALVIN, 964 PERFORMANCES).** Music and lyrics by **Stephen Sondheim**, book by Burt Shevelove and **Larry Gelbart**, staged by **George Abbott**, presented by **Harold Prince**. An outrageous farce based on plays by the ancient writer Plautus, this show included a wickedly funny book, outstanding performances, and an airy score by Sondheim with tons of spirited wordplay. **Zero Mostel** played Pseudolus, a slave trying to earn his freedom by acquiring the lovely courtesan Philia (Preshy Marker) for his master, Hero (Brian Davies). Several conspire to stop the slave's plan, so he announces that Philia has the plague and has died, leading to a madcap funeral. From there the plot descends into total silliness, including Jack Gilford's antics as the memorable Hysterium. *New York Times* critic **Howard Taubman** gleefully described some of the show's more ridiculous situations, such as Jack Gilford "in a shimmering white gown and pretending to be a dead, yet agitated, virgin." This was the first Broadway show for which Sondheim wrote both music and lyrics. Outstanding songs included the raucous opening number "Comedy Tonight" (staged without a credit line for **Jerome Robbins**), "Free," "Lovely" and the male quartet "Everybody Ought to Have a Maid." The film version starring Mostel and featuring **Michael Crawford** as Hero appeared in 1966. **Nathan Lane** played Pseudolus in the 1996 revival and was succeeded in the part by Whoopi Goldberg.

– G –

GAINES, BOYD (1953–). Singer and dancer who won a **Tony Award** for playing Georg Nowack in the 1993 revival of *She Loves Me*. He played Robert in the 1995 revival of *Company* and Michael Wiley in *Contact* (2000).

GALLAGHER, PETER (1956–). Dramatic actor who was a **replacement** Danny Zuko in *Grease* in 1978, won a Theatre World Award for his portrayal of Otto in *A Doll's Life* (1982), played Sky Masterson in the 1992 revival of *Guys and Dolls*, and sang the title role in the **City Center** *Encores!* presentation of *Pal Joey* in 1995.

GARRETT, BETTY (1919–). Actress and dancer who played Mary-Frances in *Something for the Boys* (1943) and understudied **Ethel Merman** in the lead role. Other Broadway credits include multiple roles in the **revue** *Call Me Mister* (1946), in which she sang "South America, Take It Away," a **replacement** Ella in *Bells Are Ringing*, and Hattie Walker in the 2001 **revival** of *Follies*. She is also known for her work in Hollywood and on television, especially the roles of Irene Lorenzo in *All in the Family* (1973–1975) and Edna Babish in *Laverne and Shirley* (1976–1982).

***THE GARRICK GAIETIES* (GARRICK: 17 MAY 1925, 211 PERFORMANCES; 10 MAY 1926, 174 PERFORMANCES; 4 JUNE 1930, 170 PERFORMANCES).** As the **Theatre Guild** was building a new theater, its management asked young writers and actors to put on a show to help raise money for tapestries. They billed the company as the "Junior Group of the Theatre Guild." The show launched a brief series of **revues** and several important careers. Seven songs for the first edition came from the nearly unknown team of **Richard Rodgers** and **Lorenz Hart**, including "Manhattan," their first major hit. The cast included Romney Brent, Sterling Holloway, Philip Loeb, Peggy Conway, and June Cochrane, among others. They mostly lampooned personalities associated with the Guild and their recent plays. The single political skit involved President and Mrs. Coolidge having a quiet evening at the White House, where they listen to the radio and try to be in bed by ten. The anonymous reviewer for the *New York Times* praised the performers and the skits, and noted that Hart's lyrics "were mature and intelligently contrived" and Rodgers's music "tuneful and well adapted to the needs of the entertainment." After the first edition's unexpected run of more than six months, *The Garrick Gaieties* opened with a new version the next May. Several of the cast members, along with Rodgers and Hart, returned. The song writing team's major hit in the show was "Mountain Greenery," but they also created an **operetta** spoof entitled *Rose of Arizona*. The final edition of *The Garrick Gaieties* opened four years later, this time with Sterling Holloway, Philip Loeb, Albert Carroll, and Imogene Coca. **E. Y. Harburg** and **Vernon Duke** supplied three songs, and **Marc Blitzstein** wrote an operetta parody that was eventually replaced with *Rose of Arizona*. The evening's highlight, which **J. Brooks Atkinson** called "one of the best topical satires ever written," was a spoof of ex-police commissioner Grover Whalen, who returns to his earlier job at Wanamaker's Department Store and forces the customers to obey traffic laws within the store. **Kay Swift** and Paul James (her husband, whose real name was James Paul Warburg) created the skit's music and lyrics.

GAXTON, WILLIAM (BORN ARTURO ANTONIO GAXIOLA, 1893–1963). Genre-defining **musical comedy** star who created numerous memorable characters and worked with some of Broadway's finest creators. He played Martin/The Yankee in **Rodgers and Hart**'s *A Connecticut Yankee* (1927), Peter Forbes in **Cole Porter**'s *Fifty Million Frenchmen* (1929), John P. Wintergreen in the **Gershwins'** *Of Thee I Sing* (1931) and its sequel *Let 'Em Eat Cake* (1933), Billy Crocker in Porter's *Anything Goes* (1934), Buckley Joyce Thomas in the same composer's *Leave It to Me!* (1938), and Jim Taylor in **Irving Berlin**'s *Louisiana Purchase* (1940).

GAY DIVORCE **(29 NOVEMBER 1932, ETHEL BARRYMORE, 248 PERFORMANCES).** Music and lyrics by **Cole Porter**, book by Dwight Taylor, staged by **Howard Lindsay**. Perhaps most famous today as the show that introduced Porter's "Night and Day," *Gay Divorce* (without a definite article) was appreciated more by audiences than critics. It was the first show in which **Fred Astaire** appeared without his sister, **Adele**, and his final Broadway role. His costar was Claire Luce, who played Mimi Pratt, a married woman who hopes to get caught in a compromising position. Through a misunderstanding, Astaire (Guy) is the man she is found with, and they fall in love. The score also included "I've Got You on My Mind" and the comic songs "What Will Become of Our England" and "I Still Love the Red, White and Blue." **Brooks Atkinson** observed in the *New York Times* that "Mr. Porter's tunes and lyrics have the proper dash and breeding," but overall he deemed the show a "flat and mirthless entertainment beneath a highly polished exterior." The 1934 film version starring Astaire and **Ginger Rogers** was retitled *The Gay Divorcee*, since a divorce could not be merry according to the mores of the time.

GAY, NOEL (BORN REGINALD ARMITAGE, 1898–1954). British composer of musicals and popular song whose *Me and My Girl* played on Broadway in 1986, nearly a half century after its London premiere in 1937. He was one of the finest British musical theater composers of his era, but his shows did not transfer to New York, as did those of his contemporary **Noel Coward**.

GELBART, LARRY (1928–). Comedy writer for radio, television, film, and stage. He won **Tony Awards** for each of his musical librettos *A Funny Thing Happened on the Way to the Forum* (1962) and *City of Angels* (1989). He was also one of the driving forces behind the television series *M*A*S*H* during its first four seasons (1972–1976).

GENTLEMEN PREFER BLONDES **(8 DECEMBER 1949, ZIEGFELD, 740 PERFORMANCES).** Music by **Jule Styne**, lyrics by **Leo Robin**, book by **Joseph Fields** and Anita Loos, dances and ensembles by **Agnes de Mille**. *Gentlemen Prefer Blondes*, based on Anita Loos's novel of the 1920s, will always be remembered as the beginning of **Carol Channing**'s major stardom with her inimitable rendition of "Diamonds Are a Girl's Best Friend." Channing played Lorelei Lee, the wife of a button manufacturer. She travels to Europe with her friend, Dorothy Shaw (Yvonne Adair), and has some romantic flirtations with wealthy men. Her husband, Gus (Jack McCauley), hears of her adventures and is ready to leave her, but Lorelei is far too shrewd. She not only wins Gus back but also launches a nightclub act. Dorothy, meanwhile, falls in love with Henry Spofford (Eric Brotherson). The score's highlights were Lorelei's two comic songs: "Diamonds" and "A Little Girl from Little Rock." *New York Times* critic **Brooks Atkinson** called Channing's role "the most fabulous comic creation of this dreary period in history."

***GEORGE M!* (10 APRIL 1968, PALACE, 427 PERFORMANCES).**
Music and lyrics by **George M. Cohan**, book by **Michael Stewart**
and John and Fran Pascal, staged and choreographed by **Joe Layton**.
Joel Grey starred in this tribute to George M. Cohan, and, along with
Cohan's great songs, provided much of the show's appeal. The book
was a thin and easily forgotten account of Cohan's life. This did not
matter, because, as **Clive Barnes** wrote in the *New York Times*, "Before you can say they don't write songs like that anymore, they are
singing the next one." *George M!* differed from the famous film *Yankee Doodle Dandy*, telling, for example, about Cohan's first wife, but
the real point of the show was to make production numbers out of
"Give My Regards to Broadway," "Yankee Doodle Dandy," "You're
a Grand Old Flag," "Over There," "Mary," and other well-known Cohan songs. Others in the cast included Jerry Dodge as Cohan's father,
Betty Ann Grove as his mother, and **Bernadette Peters** as his sister,
Josie.

***GEORGE WHITE'S SCANDALS* (LIBERTY: 2 JUNE 1919, 128
PERFORMANCES; 11 JULY 1921, 97 PERFORMANCES;
GLOBE: 7 JUNE 1920, 134 PERFORMANCES; 28 NOVEM-
BER 1922, 89 PERFORMANCES; GLOBE/FULTON: 18 JUNE
1923, 168 PERFORMANCES; APOLLO: 30 JUNE 1924, 196
PERFORMANCES; 22 JUNE 1925, 171 PERFORMANCES; 14
JUNE 1926, 424 PERFORMANCES; 2 JULY 1928, 230 PER-
FORMANCES; 23 SEPTEMBER 1929, 161 PERFORMANCES;
14 SEPTEMBER 1931, 202 PERFORMANCES; NEW AMS-
TERDAM: 25 DECEMBER 1935, 110 PERFORMANCES;
ALVIN: 28 AUGUST 1939, 120 PERFORMANCES).** George
White (born George Weitz) was a dancer who had worked in
Ziegfeld Follies, but he launched his own lavish **revue** in 1919.
White first called his shows simply *Scandals*, finally making the title
eponymous in 1921. Such lighthearted fare had become a summertime Broadway favorite, so White usually opened his show in June or
July. He offered Ziegfeld stiff competition and lured some stars away
from the *Follies*, including **Ann Pennington** and **W. C. Fields**. His
shows were especially noted for the dancing and top-notch composers who wrote the scores. **George Gershwin**, working with various lyricists, provided the songs from 1920 to 1924, when the pro-

ducer decided that the young composer had become too expensive. Among the hits that Gershwin wrote for White were "I'll Build a Stairway to Paradise" in 1922 and "Somebody Loves Me" in 1924. His opera *Blue Monday Blues* opened the second act for one night in 1922, but White decided it was too depressing and cut it. Later scores included music by **Ray Henderson** to the lyrics of **B. G. De Sylva** (until 1928) and **Lew Brown**, and **Ethel Merman**'s famous rendition of "Life Is Just a Bowl of Cherries" in 1931. A regular from 1926 until the end of the series was Willie Howard, an inspired comic who worked with his brother, Eugene. Other name stars in the *Scandals* included **Helen Morgan**, **Ray Bolger**, **Rudy Vallee**, **Ann Miller**, and **Ray Middleton**. White's formula included male and female singers, several dancers and comedians, and a large group of chorus girls with spectacular, if apparently incomplete, costumes. As in Ziegfeld's shows, sets were memorable.

The most successful edition of *George White's Scandals* was that of 1926. The cast featured Ann Pennington, Willie and Eugene Howard, dancer and clown Tom Patricola, singers Harry Richman and Frances Williams, and a chorus led by the comely McCarthy Sisters and Fairbanks Twins. The score by Henderson, De Sylva, and Brown included "The Birth of the Blues" and "The Girl Is You and the Boy Is Me." Ann Pennington danced the "Black Bottom," a wild version of the Charleston. Comic numbers included parodies of **Irving Berlin**'s recent marriage to Ellin Mackay and people who walk the dogs of the rich in New York City.

GERSHWIN, GEORGE (1898–1937). Pianist and composer whose songs from the 1920s and 1930s, often written in collaboration with his brother, **Ira Gershwin,** helped define both **musical comedy** and American popular song of the era. In 1918, **Al Jolson** propelled Gershwin to fame by interpolating "Swanee" (lyrics by Irving Caesar) into his show *Sinbad* (1918). With his brother, Gershwin created scores for some of the finest performers of the time. They wrote *Lady, Be Good!* (1924), which featured "Fascinating Rhythm," for the brother-and-sister team of **Fred** and **Adele Astaire**, and *Oh, Kay!* (1926), with "Someone to Watch Over Me," for **Gertrude Lawrence**. Other shows from the late 1920s include *Funny Face* (1927, again featuring the Astaires) and *Rosalie* (1928, cowritten with **Sigmund Romberg**). The 1930s began with *Strike Up the Band*, then *Girl Crazy*, which starred **Ginger Rogers** and introduced **Ethel Merman** and featured such famous songs as "I Got Rhythm," "But Not for Me," and "Embraceable You." *Of Thee I Sing* (1931) was another hit show, this one a political satire. It fared better than its sequel, *Let 'Em Eat Cake* (1933). The Gershwins challenged Broadway norms by mounting the **opera** *Porgy and Bess* in 1935. Gershwin's musical genius exists on several levels—his incorporation of jazz-inspired rhythms into popular song, his innate gift for creating rhapsodic yet logical melodies, and his consummate ability to integrate aspects of "high" culture with American popular song.

GERSHWIN, IRA (1896–1983). Lyricist who collaborated with his brother, **George Gershwin**, on shows that epitomized the **musical comedy** of the 1920s and 1930s, including *Lady, Be Good!* (1924), *Oh, Kay!* (1926), *Girl Crazy* (1930), and *Of Thee I Sing* (1931). *Of Thee I Sing* was the first musical to receive the **Pulitzer Prize** for drama. *Porgy and Bess* (1935) was in essence an **opera** in musical style, but Ira's lyrics were in the musical theater mold. After the death of his brother, George, Ira continued to write for Broadway, collaborating with **Kurt Weill** on *Lady in the Dark* (1941) and *The Firebrand of Florence* (1945) and with Arthur Schwartz on *Park Avenue* (1946). Gershwin's lyrics are characterized by their juxtaposition of purposeful poor grammar ("I *Got* Rhythm" as opposed to "I *Have* Rhythm") with sophisticated rhyme schemes and chic textual allusions. His creativity is evident in songs such as "'S Wonderful" with its series of phrases that begin with a distinctive "'s" and "Of Thee I Sing, Baby," with its collusion of a phrase from a patriotic song with a slang expression.

GILBERT, W. S. (WILLIAM SCHWENK GILBERT, 1836–1911). British librettist and lyricist whose Savoy operas, collaborations with composer **Arthur Sullivan**, have appeared on Broadway since the late 19th century. *H.M.S. Pinafore* (1879) actually received its world premiere in New York because of international copyright law. Other G&S works to appear on Broadway include *Trial by Jury, The Sorcerer, **The Pirates of Penzance**, Patience, Iolanthe, Princess Ida, The Mikado, Ruddigore, The Yeomen of the Guard*, and *The Gondoliers*.

Gilbert and Sullivan's work had a tremendous influence on Broadway in terms of vocal style (virtuosic soprano writing), effusive marches, comic patter songs, lighthearted waltzes, and various combinations of recitatives, solos, duets, small ensembles, and choral numbers fused together into coherent musical-dramatic scenes. Gilbert was also active as a playwright, director, and literary author.

GIRL CRAZY (14 OCTOBER 1930, ALVIN, 272 PERFORMANCES). Music by **George Gershwin**, lyrics by **Ira Gershwin**, book by **Guy Bolton** and **John McGowan**, produced by **Alex A. Aarons** and **Vinton Freedley**. Perhaps the most famous musical comedy with a score by the Gershwins, *Girl Crazy* featured great songs and several future musical luminaries. Inspired by the trend of vacationing at southwestern dude ranches, the plot involved the removal to Custerville, Arizona, of typical New York musical comedy types: a playboy, a Jewish cab driver, and a bevy of chorus girls. Danny Churchill (Allen Kearns) sets up a New York cabaret in a town that somehow has not seen a woman in 50 years. He falls for the postal worker, Molly Gray (**Ginger Rogers**), who lives in the next town. The other romantic duo was Kate Fothergill (**Ethel Merman**) and her husband, "Slick" (William Kent). It was Rogers's second Broadway show and Merman's first. Both caused a sensation, and Merman became a huge Broadway star. Comic impersonator **Willie Howard** played the cab driver, Gieber Goldfarb. The book, typical of its day, provided the framework of a story on which to hang all of the songs and novelties. The score featured some of the Gershwins' biggest hits: "But Not for Me," "Bidin' My Time," "Embraceable You," "Sam and Delilah," and "I Got Rhythm." "I Got Rhythm" was praised in the *New York Times* review as a tune that "induces a veritable frenzy of dancing." The reviewer called the show "an agreeable diversion which seems destined to find a profitable place among the luxuries of Times Square." The future stars in the production extended into the orchestra pit, and included jazz legends Benny Goodman, Glenn Miller, and Gene Krupa. The show was reworked in 1992 as *Crazy for You.*

GLEASON, JACKIE (1916–1987). Comic actor who appeared in the **revues** *Keep Off the Grass* (1940) and *Along Fifth Avenue* (1949). He also starred in the **musical comedies** *Follow the Girls* (1944) and *Take Me Along* (1959), winning a **Tony Award** for his performance in the latter.

GLEASON, JOANNA (BORN JOANNA HALL, 1950–). Canadian-born singing character actress whose Broadway credits include Monica in *I Love My Wife* (1977), the Baker's Wife in *Into the Woods* (1987), Nora in *Nick & Nora* (1991), and Muriel in *Dirty Rotten Scoundrels* (2005). She won a **Tony Award** for Best Actress in a Musical for *Into the Woods*. Gleason brings a multidimensional complexity to the characters she portrays.

***GODSPELL* (17 MAY 1971, CHERRY LANE; 22 JUNE 1976, THREE BROADWAY THEATERS, 527 PERFORMANCES).** Music and lyrics by **Stephen Schwartz**, conceived and directed by John-Michael Trebelak. After starting its New York life at the experimental Café La Mama, *Godspell* moved to the Cherry Lane Theater, and later went uptown and became a Broadway show. Along with *Jesus Christ Superstar*, it represented an era when the theater showed considerable interest in religious topics. *Godspell* is a modern retelling of the Gospel according to St. Matthew with Jesus and his disciples clothed as clowns. There was a delightful sense of innocence, and Jesus seemed like a regular guy (although he wore a Superman T-shirt), but little blunted the source's religious message. Many appreciated the work's theatricality and its young and energetic cast. Reviewing the off-Broadway opening for the *New York Times*, **Clive Barnes** admitted his lack of interest in such a show, noting that he found the premise rather "nauseating," but he praised Schwartz's music, which he called "eclectic . . . but at its best it provides by far the best part of the entertainment." He thinks the cast worked "with . . . gung-ho vitality," but complained about their singing and lack of discipline. He concluded by admitting that some will see "freshness and originality" in the work. Barnes was clearly of the wrong generation to appreciate *Godspell*.

With a long run off-Broadway, 527 performances on Broadway, and a continuing lively presence in the repertory, the show clearly had its audience. The creators opted for an episodic treatment of the Gospel of St. Matthew based heavily on teachings and parables and allowing music and staging to play a huge role. The crucifixion is by far the most dramatic sequence in the show, considerably advanced through Schwartz's music. The score is a veritable tour through pop musical styles, from the Mae West and 1930s appeal of "Turn Back, O Man," the gospel sound of "Prepare Ye the Way of the Lord," to the folk sound of "On the Willows" and "By My Side." The most famous song was "Day by Day," where Schwartz effectively negotiated the distance between folk and rock through metric changes and shifting accompanimental patterns. The song "Alas for You," aimed at the Pharisees and false prophets, carried considerable effect.

GOING UP (**25 DECEMBER 1917, LIBERTY, 351 PERFORMANCES**). Music by Louis A. Hirsch, lyrics by **Otto Harbach**, book by Harbach and James Montgomery. Based on Montgomery's play *The Aviator*, *Going Up* was a comedy with excellent stage effects that ran for 10 months. Frank Craven played Robert Street, an author who has written a book about flying but has actually never been in an airplane. In order to marry his ladylove, Grace Douglas (**Edith Day**), he needs to win an air race against the French pilot who Grace's father would like to see her marry. Robert somehow wins the race, even after his flying instructor is too drunk to give him lessons. The sets included Robert flying an actual biplane among the clouds on stage. The anonymous critic for the *New York Times* reported that the audience "appeared to enjoy the play from start to finish" and appreciated the efforts of most of the cast and the numbers "Going Up," "I Want a Determined Boy," and "Tickle Toe."

GOLDEN BOY (**20 OCTOBER 1964, MAJESTIC, 569 PERFORMANCES**). Music by **Charles Strouse**, lyrics by Lee Adams, book by Clifford Odets and William Gibson. An adaptation of Clifford Odet's 1938 play of the same name, *Golden Boy* was a snapshot of an ambitious young boxer memorably played by **Sammy Davis Jr.** The play's protagonist was Italian, but by 1964 young boxers were often African American, and Davis was an appealing lead. Odets had begun the adaptation of his play but died in 1963, leaving William Gibson to finish the task. **Howard Taubman**, writing in the *New York Times*, found Gibson's work marked by "conscience and taste" as "the swift, keen-edged lines about the Negro condition have bite and integrity." Taubman was less convinced about the boxer's romance with a white girl played by Paula Wayne. Davis, known as a nightclub performer, made his mark as a singer, actor, and dancer. Taubman praised Davis's ability to "convey the pride that flames inside an intense heart." Although the score left little mark outside of the show, Taubman was simply blown away by the production number "Don't Forget 137th Street," which graphically portrays the problems in Harlem. He also praised "No More," which begins as Davis's defiant soliloquy on his bitterness over lost love, but becomes an "irresistible" choral and dance number.

GOOD MORNING DEARIE **(1 NOVEMBER 1921, GLOBE, 347 PERFORMANCES).** Music by **Jerome Kern**, lyrics and book by Anne Caldwell, produced by **Charles Dillingham**. Yet another show following the success of *Irene* and *Sally* that tells the story of a poor girl who makes good, *Good Morning Dearie* combined a good Kern score with lavish Dillingham production values and lasted ten months. Rose-Marie (Louise Groody), a shop assistant, is the object of affection for the wealthy Billy Van Cortlandt (Oscar Shaw), even though he is engaged to someone else. The skeleton in Rose-Marie's closet is her former boyfriend, Chesty Costello (Harland Dixon), just out of prison and eager to continue his life of crime. The show included a great deal of dancing, especially from Groody and Dixon, and Kern's score boasted fine songs, but only "Kailua" found lasting fame, although the "Blue Danube Blues" was popular at the time. The anonymous *New York Times* critic noted the "baffling likeness" between *Good Morning Dearie* and *Sally*, especially in the "atmosphere and trimmings."

GOOD NEWS! **(6 SEPTEMBER 1927, 46TH STREET, 557 PERFORMANCES).** Music by **Ray Henderson**, lyrics and book by **Laurence Schwab** and **B. G. De Sylva**. In a plot reminiscent of *Leave It to Jane*, *Good News* also mined academia and football for a mirthful evening, and sustained one of the longest runs of the 1920s. At Tait College, Tom Marlowe (John Price Jones), the football star, does not have sufficient understanding to pass his astronomy exam, which he must do to play in the big game on Saturday. Connie Lane (May Lawlor) tutors him and he passes the test. Eventually, of course, she wins his heart as well. *Good News* included the requisite silliness and dancing, and the score rendered no less than five standards: the title song, "The Varsity Drag," "The Best Things in Life Are Free," "Lucky in Love," and "Just Imagine." **Brooks Atkinson** gave the show considerable appreciation in the *New York Times*, noting that "Co-education in America was considerably bucked up at the Forty-sixth Street Theatre last evening." He noted that famed Notre Dame coach Knute Rockne advised the writers on the locker room scene, helping the football elements in the production to "have the ring of gridiron authenticity."

GORDON, MAX (1892–1978). Gordon, famous as the head of Columbia Pictures, was producer for such Broadway shows as *The Cat and the Fiddle* (1931), *Roberta* (1933), and *The Great Waltz* (1934). Famous for his lavish productions, he often invested in other shows.

GOULET, ROBERT (1933–). Singer with a warm baritone voice who created the role of Lancelot Du Lac in *Camelot* (1960). He won a **Tony Award** for his portrayal of Jacques Bonnard in *The Happy Time* (1968). He played Arthur (not Lancelot) in the 1993 revival of *Camelot*, and was a **replacement** Georges in the 2004 revival of *La Cage aux Folles*.

GRAND HOTEL (12 NOVEMBER 1989, BECK, 1,017 PERFOR-MANCES). Music and lyrics by **Robert Wright** and **George Forrest** with additional music and lyrics by **Maury Yeston**, book by Luther Davis, directed and choreographed by **Tommy Tune**. Based on the novel of the same name by Vicki Baum that was made into a movie by MGM in 1932, *Grand Hotel* earned its two-and-a-half-year run on the strength of Tune's brilliant staging. Virtually no other aspect of the production could be called a critical success, but Tony Walton's stunning two-story set brilliantly portrayed the glamour of a first-class hotel in late 1920s Berlin. Tune kept much of the cast on stage all of the time and in constant motion. The main characters include the ballerina at the end of her career (Liliane Montevecchi); a larcenous aristocrat (David Carroll); Otto Kringelein, a Jew dying from an unnamed disease who dances a Charleston near the end of the show (Michael Jeter); and Flaemmchen (Jane Krakowski), a secretary who thinks her amorous talents might lead to Hollywood stardom.

GREASE (14 FEBRUARY 1972, EDEN, 3,388 PERFOR-MANCES). Music, lyrics, and book by Jim Jacobs and Warren Casey. Appearing at a time when nostalgia for the 1950s was reaching a peak, *Grease* was meticulously fashioned to capitalize on the trend and rode it to a record-setting run after starting in Chicago and then off-Broadway. The setting is a high school class reunion for 1959 graduates who relive their earlier days at Rydell High. Danny Zuko (**Barry Bostwick**) is one of the cool boys with slicked-back hair. He falls for Sandy Dumbrowski (Carole Demas), but she is at first uninterested in changing her prim look for him. In the end, she does, a victory for conformity and a defeat for individuality. The show has enjoyed widespread popularity and remains in the repertory. As has often been the case in the past 30 or so years with shows pitched at an unsophisticated audience, some critics did not appreciate it. **Clive Barnes** of the *New York Times*, for example, called it "a parody of one of those old Elvis Presley campus movies," and inviting those who care for such shows to see it. He dismissed the 1950s-style music "as the loud and raucous noise of its time" but thought that many would enjoy the show's "facetious tastelessness." The 1978 film version starred John Travolta and Olivia Newton-John.

THE GREAT WALTZ (22 SEPTEMBER 1934, CENTER, 298 PER-FORMANCES). Music by **Johann Strauss**, father and son, lyrics by Desmond Carter, book by **Moss Hart** adapted from German and English sources by several authors, staging, lighting and mechanical effects by **Hassard Short**, dances and ballets arranged by **Albertina Rasch**, produced by Max Gordon. The sumptuously mounted operetta told a fictional story about two Viennese composers, father and son, both named Johann Strauss. H. Reeves-Smith played the senior Strauss, who would not allow his orchestra to play his son's waltzes. Through the machinations of Countess Olga (Marie Burke), the father gets detained one evening and the younger Strauss (Guy Robertson) triumphs. Among the show's visual highlights was when the orchestra pit left its normal position and rode across the stage, later dividing itself into sets of steps.

GREEN, ADOLPH (1915–2002). Librettist and lyricist who collaborated with **Betty Comden** on musicals such as *On the Town* (1944), *Billion Dollar Baby* (1945), *Wonderful Town* (1953), *Bells Are Ringing* (1956), *Applause* (1970), *On the Twentieth Century* (1978), and *The Will Rogers Follies* (1991). The pair worked together exclusively for more than 50 years, creating words for composers such as **Leonard Bernstein, Jule Styne,** and **Cy Coleman.** They formed a theater troupe in the 1930s, the Revuers, and were active as performers. Hence, they created words from a performer's perspective. Their focus was on sparkling **musical comedy,** and their lyrics possess energy, appeal, immediacy, and charm.

GREEN, MITZI (BORN ELIZABETH KENO, 1920–1969). Hollywood child actor who created the role of Billie Smith in *Babes in Arms* (1937). She played Rhoda Gibson in the **musical comedy** *Walk with Music* (1940) and appeared in the **revue** *Let Freedom Sing* (1942) before creating the role of Georgia Motley in *Billion Dollar Baby* (1945).

GREENWICH VILLAGE FOLLIES **(GREENWICH VILLAGE: 15 JULY 1919, 232 PERFORMANCES; 30 AUGUST 1920, 192 PERFORMANCES; SHUBERT: 31 AUGUST 1921, 167 PERFORMANCES; 12 SEPTEMBER 1922, 209 PERFORMANCES; 16 SEPTEMBER 1924, 127 PERFORMANCES; WINTER GARDEN: 20 SEPTEMBER 1923, 140 PERFORMANCES; 9 APRIL 1928, 158 PERFORMANCES; 46TH STREET: 24 DECEMBER 1925, 180 PERFORMANCES).** After **Florenz Ziegfeld** and others demonstrated the possibilities of annual **revues,** there were of course imitators. **John Murray Anderson,** a ballroom dancer who had put on variety shows at a restaurant, established *Greenwich Village Nights,* but the name soon became *Greenwich Village Follies.* Ziegfeld was furious about the name change, and Anderson's series became serious competition. The first two editions opened at a small theater, but proved sufficiently popular to move uptown. The *Greenwich Village Follies* did not introduce a number of popular songs, and, given the names of its lyricists and composers, Anderson clearly invested his money elsewhere. Only a handful of major songwriters worked on the series. **Cole Porter** wrote the music for the 1924 edition, but it was a major disappointment; the score, however, did include "I'm in Love Again," which became a hit decades later. The *Greenwich Village Follies* were most famous for their comedy routines and spectacles. For several years, the most significant comedy team to appear was Savoy & Brennan. Bert Savoy worked in drag, often talking to his imaginary partner, Margie, or working among the revue's chorus girls and spoofing the proceedings. This particular series had a reputation for providing more intellectual entertainment than its competitors, for it included a fair amount of classical music and ballet. For example, Martha Graham was the main dancer in "The Garden of Kama" in 1923. Like some other annual revues, the *Greenwich Village Follies* included nudity, especially later in its history when the **Shuberts** became more involved with the series' production decisions.

GREENWILLOW (8 MARCH 1960, ALVIN, 95 PERFORMANCES). Music and lyrics by **Frank Loesser**, book by Lesser Samuels and Loesser, directed by George Roy Hill, choreography by **Joe Layton**. A major disappointment from the creator of *Guys and Dolls*, *Greenwillow* was a fantasy about a town in rural America. Based on B. J. Chute's novel of the same name, it ran for only three months. Anthony Perkins played Gideon Briggs, the eldest son of a family whose patriarch cannot seem to stay at home with his family and who returns home sporadically to father another child before his wanderlust carries him off again. Gideon is reluctant to court Dorrie Whitbred (Ellen McCown), but love wins out. **Brooks Atkinson** gave it a good review in the *New York Times*, calling the book "ideal" and music "warm and varied." Among the better songs were "Summertime Love," "Never Will I Marry," "Walking Away Whistling," and "The Sermon," the latter a fine comic number.

GREY GARDENS (2 NOVEMBER 2006, WALTER KERR, 69 PERFORMANCES AS OF 31 DECEMBER 2006). Music by Scott Frankel, lyrics by Michael Korie, book by Doug Wright. **Christine Ebersole** played the dual role of the older "Little" Edie Beale and the younger Edith Bouvier Biele in the musical version of the 1975 documentary *Grey Gardens*, the title of which refers to the 28-room mansion in East Hampton in which Edith Bouvier Beale and her daughter, "Little" Edie (aunt and cousin of Jacqueline Bouvier Kennedy Onassis), were filmed living in squalor. Act 1 takes place in 1941, when the estate and its inhabitants were at their glory, whereas the prologue and act 2 are set in 1973, when the documentary was filmed. Mary Louise Wilson played Edith in the segments set in 1973. The score featured 1940s pastiches, such as "Will You," and haunting numbers based on scenes from the documentary, including "The Revolutionary Costume for Today," "The Cake I Had," and "Around the World."

GREY, JOEL (1932–). Legendary actor, singer, and dancer who created the roles of the Master of Ceremonies in *Cabaret* (1966), **George M. Cohan** in *George M!* (1968), *Goodtime Charley* (1975), *The Grand Tour* (1979), and The Wonderful Wizard of Oz in *Wicked* (2003). His appearance as the formally attired Master of Ceremonies is one of the iconic images of the musical theater. He re-created the Master of Ceremonies in the 1987 revival of *Cabaret* and played Amos Hart in the long-running revival of *Chicago* (1996). He won the 1967 **Tony Award** for Best Featured Actor for *Cabaret* and the 1997 **Drama Desk Award** for Outstanding Featured Actor in a Musical for *Chicago*. Film appearances include the Master of Ceremonies in *Cabaret* (1972) and a cameo in *Dancer in the Dark* (2000).

GRIMES, TAMMY (1934–). Actress who played the title role in **Meredith Willson**'s *The Unsinkable Molly Brown* (1960) for which she won a **Tony Award** for Best Featured Actress in a Musical. She also triumphed as Elvira, the dead wife, in *High Spirits* (1964) and as Dorothy Brock in *42nd Street* (1980). Grimes is known for her strong sense of comic timing, effervescent stage presence, and raspy character voice.

GROENER, HARRY (1951–). Actor, singer, and dancer who played Will Parker in the 1979 **revival** of *Oklahoma!*, created Munkustrap in *Cats* (1982), and was a **replacement** George in *Sunday in the Park with George* before triumphing as Billy Child in *Crazy for You* (1992), where he sang the music of **George Gershwin**. In 2006, he played King Arthur in *Monty Python's Spamalot*. Groener is also known for his work on television, particularly his portrayal of Mayor Wilkins in *Buffy the Vampire Slayer*.

GUETTEL, ADAM (1965–). Won 2005 **Tony Awards** for Best Original Score and Best Orchestrations for his debut Broadway musical, *The Light in the Piazza*. He also wrote the show's lyrics. A third generation Broadway composer, Guettel is the grandson of **Richard Rodgers** and the son of **Mary Rodgers**. His musical language is more advanced than that of the typical Broadway sound, and his expansive melodies (the focus of his scores) are often accompanied by more active arpeggiated rhythmic underpinning.

GUYS AND DOLLS **(24 NOVEMBER 1950, 46TH STREET, 1,200 PERFORMANCES).** Music and lyrics by **Frank Loesser**, book by Jo Swerling and **Abe Burrows**, directed by **George S. Kaufman**, dances and musical numbers staged by **Michael Kidd**, produced by **Cy Feuer** and Ernest H. Martin. One of Broadway's enduring masterpieces, *Guys and Dolls* is a love poem to the colorful residents of midtown Manhattan and a fully integrated evening of entertainment. Based on the memorable and distinctive short stories of Damon Runyon, especially "The Idyll of Miss Sarah Brown," *Guys and Dolls* brought together distinguished creators with solid, comic characters who helped make "New Yawk" rhyme with "tomahawk." Writing in the *New York Times*, **Brooks Atkinson** praised Kaufman, who he asserted was "never . . . in better form in the director's box." Michael Kidd's choreography included both comic ballets and riotous sendups of cheesy nightclub routines in numbers such as "Bushel and a Peck" and "Take Back Your Mink." Atkinson remarked that Loesser's songs "have the same affectionate appreciation of the material as the book" and praised the technical side of the show as well, noting that it "is a work of art." Sam Levene played Nathan Detroit, proprietor of "the oldest established, permanent, floating crap game in New York." He has been engaged for 14 years to Miss Adelaide, star of a nighclub act, played with zany intensity by **Vivian Blaine**, who reprised her role in the film. In an effort to raise cash, Nathan bets the stylish gambler Sky Masterson (**Robert Alda**) that he cannot take a worker from the Save-a-Soul Mission, Sarah Brown (Isobel Bigley), to Havana on a date. Sky wins the bet. Especially memorable supporting characters include Nicely-Nicely Johnson (**Stubby Kaye**) and an older mission worker, Arvide Abernathy (Pat Rooney, Sr.). The show ends with a double wedding for Sky and Sarah and Nathan and Miss Adelaide.

Loesser's songs help propel the plot forward and providing delicious details about personalities and motivations. The "Fugue for Tin Horns," a contrapuntal tour de force, emerges out of the chaos of Kidd's opening ballet that introduces Broadway's underworld. Nathan, Nicely-Nicely, and Benny Southstreet praise their profession in "The Oldest Established Permanent Floating Crap Game in New York," and Nicely-Nicely, leads the revival-style song "Sit Down, You're Rockin' the Boat" near the end of act 2. Loesser uses musical style to distinguish between the pairs of lovers. Miss Adelaide and Nathan are the comic characters, and their music appropriately defines them. "Adelaide's Lament" and the duet "Sue Me" are highlights of the score, as is the more lyrical music of Miss Sarah and Sky, including "I've Never Been in Love Before," one of Loesser's most enduring ballads, and Sky's "My Time of Day." The title song concerns the battle between the sexes from the male point of view, and exudes the same gentle humor that pervades the show. The 1950 film starred Marlon Brando and Frank Sinatra, and the 1992 Broadway **revival** starred **Peter Gallagher**, **Josie de Guzman**, **Nathan Lane**, and Faith Prince.

GYPSY **(21 MAY 1959, BROADWAY, 702 PERFORMANCES).** Music by **Jule Styne**, lyrics by **Stephen Sondheim**, book by **Arthur Laurents**, directed and choreographed by **Jerome Robbins**, presented by **David Merrick** and Leland Hayward. Remembered as the last great vehicle created expressly for **Ethel Merman**, *Gypsy* was also a notable work in the development of the Broadway musical, as it included a close integration of plot and music, a powerful score, and a realistic feel made possible by Robbins's intense direction. Based on the memoirs of Gypsy Rose Lee, the show begins with June and Louise as children, already being driven to stage success by the ultimate stage-door mother, Rose (Merman). The children literally grow up during the number "Let Me Entertain You," becoming young adults played by Lane Bradbury (June) and Sandra Church (Louise). They hope that their mother will marry and lay down roots, but the endless tour continues. Rose finds a boyfriend in Herbie (Jack Klugman), who becomes the act's agent. June has left by this point, running off to marry Tulsa (Paul Wallace), a boy in the act. (Gypsy Rose Lee's real-life sister was the actress June Havoc.) As vaudeville fades from the scene, Rose finds her act booked into a burlesque house. She offers her innocent daughter Louise as a demure young stripper, an act that horrifies Herbie and finally drives him away. Louise receives hilarious advice from older strippers about her need for a gimmick, but decides that her youth and ladylike demeanor are gimmick enough. She strips and talks her way to the top of burlesque, playing Minsky's in New York. Rose cannot stay out of Louise's life, however, and she finally admits in the memorable "Rose's Turn" that her ambition was more for herself than for her daughters. The show ends as Rose and Louise reach a new understanding, but of exactly what kind is left open to interpretation.

Gypsy was in the mold of an old-time musical comedy and paid tribute to America's show business past, one of Robbins's obsessions. But it was also a musical play, with book, score, and dance coming together to tell a story that is advanced and illuminated by the music. *Gypsy* relies on the box-office draw of a huge star in the role of Rose. In the original production, Ethel Merman was omnipresent; **Brooks Atkinson**, writing in the *New York Times*, praised her extravagantly, writing that "her personal magnetism electrifies the whole theatre." Merman's power also extended to aspects of the production. Sondheim had been slated to write the score (music and lyrics) himself, but Merman was unwilling to star in a show with music by an unknown writer, so Styne replaced Sondheim as the composer. Styne wrote effective songs of many types, from the delightful innocence of "Little Lamb," the gentle humor of "If Momma Was Married," and the optimism of "Everything's Coming Up Roses" to such brassy numbers for Merman as "Some People" and "I Had a Dream." The title phrase of the latter became the score's main leitmotif, occurring throughout the show as a unifying device. Rose's dramatic soliloquy "Rose's Turn" has become one of the classic one-woman scenes of the Broadway musical. Recent revelations have suggested that Sondheim played a major role in the music for the number. One of the most dramatic interpretations of the song was that of **Angela Lansbury** in the 1973 London production. Many leading actresses have played the iconic role of Rose, including **Rosalind Russell** in the 1962 film version, Bette Midler in the 1993 television version, and **Bernadette Peters** in the 2003 Broadway **revival**.

– H –

HAIR **(29 APRIL 1968, BILTMORE, 1,742 PERFORMANCES).**
Music by **Galt MacDermot**, lyrics and book by **Gerome Ragni** and
James Rado, staged by **Tom O'Horgan**. One of the most controversial shows in Broadway history, *Hair* was the first successful show in
the genre that has become known, somewhat inaccurately, as a **rock
musical**. It began life in a version by Ragni and Rado that was produced at Ellen Stewart's La Mama Experimental Theatre Club.
Joseph Papp then agreed to an eight-week run at the Public Theater,
for which MacDermot wrote the show's first score. *Hair* moved to
the Cheetah discothèque for 45 performances, and finally started its
Broadway run at the Biltmore Theater in an expanded and altered
version, with 13 new songs and under O'Horgan's expert direction.
In the loose plot, Claude (Rado) tries to decide whether he should
burn his draft card while living in a hippie commune led by Berger
(Ragni). Claude eventually decides to fight in Vietnam, where he is
killed, and his friends mourn his death. The show delivered a "safe"
portrayal of counterculture, allowing the audience to experience it
only for an evening. In addition to the well-publicized (but poorly lit)
nude scene, the show directly approached controversial topics such
as **homosexuality**, drugs, the sexual revolution, poverty, and **race relations**. Profanity infused the book and lyrics. O'Horgan's production was innovative and at times chaotic, with cast members moving
freely throughout the auditorium and amongst the on-stage rock
band. At one point, cast members disguised as policemen burst into
the back of the theater and announced they were raiding the show.
Solo singers used handheld microphones, giving the show an atypical visual look and linking it to the realm of the rock concert. **Clive
Barnes**, writing in the *New York Times*, correctly identified MacDermot's score as "pop-rock" with "the authentic voice of today." He
found the new director, O'Horgan, nearly miraculous, but also
warned followers of Governor Ronald Reagan that they would not
like the show. His conclusion was delicious: "Incidentally, the cast
washes. It also has a delightful sense of self-mockery."
    MacDermot's score became one of the most famous and memo-
rable ever to be heard on Broadway. While the composer employed

the simple chord progressions associated with rock of the mid-1960s (certainly different than those of more traditional musicals) and rock's instruments, amplification, and beat, he also used musical theater's typical **verse-refrain form**, and his melodic sense was far closer to Broadway, or at least the pop world, than to true rock music. Five songs from the show—"Aquarius," "Hair," "Easy To Be Hard," "Good Morning Starshine," and "Let the Sun Shine In"—became Top Forty hits, and "Aquarius" became one of the defining songs of the era.

HAIRSPRAY (15 AUGUST 2002, NEIL SIMON, 1,824 PERFOR-MANCES AS OF 31 DECEMBER 2006). Music by Marc Shaiman, lyrics by Scott Wittman and Shaiman, book by Mark O'Donnell and Thomas Meehan. Based on the 1988 film, *Hairspray* is the story of Tracy Turnblad (Marissa Jaret Winokur), a short, plump, white teenager with a huge hairdo in 1962 who dreams of appearing on the local TV dance program, the *Corny Collins Show*. She achieves her goal and sets out to racially integrate the show, beginning on Mother-Daughter Day. Tracy's mother (cross-dressed **Harvey Fierstein**) is reluctant to appear on the broadcast because of her larger-than-average size, but joins her daughter in the spectacular high-energy finale, "You Can't Stop the Beat," during which the *Corny Collins Show* becomes officially and irreversibly integrated on live television. The musical dealt with aspects of diversity in terms of both race and body type. The vibrant score evoked the styles of early 1960s rock 'n' roll. *Hairspray* won eight **Tony Awards**, including Best Musical, Best Book, Best Original Score, Best Actor (Fierstein), Best Acress (Winokur), and Best Featured Actor (Dick Latessa as Wilbur Turnblad). *See also* RACE RELATIONS/RACISM.

HALEY, JACK (1898–1979). Comic actor with a slightly gruff voice who appeared in the 1925 and 1926 versions of the **revue** *Gay Paree* and the **musical comedies** *Follow Thru* (1929), *Free for All* (1931), and *Take a Chance* (1932) before creating his most famous role, the Tin Man in the 1939 film *The Wizard of Oz*. He returned to Broadway for the musical comedy *Higher and Higher* (1940) and the revue *Inside U.S.A.* (1948).

HALF A SIXPENCE **(25 APRIL 1965, BROADHURST, 512 PER-FORMANCES)**. Music and lyrics by David Heneker, book by Beverly Cross, staged by Gene Saks, choreography by **Onna White**. A successful show in London's West End, *Half a Sixpence* transferred to Broadway, where it played for more than 16 months. Tommy Steele, a teenage heartthrob in England, was Arthur Kipps, a character from the H. G. Wells novel *Kipps*, the work on which the show was based. The plot, which takes place in the seaside town of Folkestone in 1900, is a familiar tale of a poor shop assistant who becomes wealthy and then gets engaged to a girl of high social status. **Howard Taubman**, writing for the *New York Times*, dubbed it a sentimental show, sure to please some, but likely to give others "a touch of indigestion." He enjoyed its "unabashed commitment to sweetness and light" and found Steele to be an appealing lead. Taubman especially liked the dancing in such numbers as "Money to Burn," "If The Rain's Got to Fall," "The Old Military Canal," and "The Party's on the House."

HALL, ADELAIDE (BORN ADALADE LOUISE HALL, 1901–1993). After appearing as Jazz Jasmine in *Shuffle Along* (1921) and other **African American musicals**, Hall achieved tremendous success starring in the **revue *Blackbirds of 1928***. She spent most of her long career in London, but returned to Broadway in 1957 to create the part of Grandma Obeah in *Jamaica* (1957).

HALLELUJAH, BABY! **(26 APRIL 1967, MARTIN BECK, 293 PERFORMANCES)**. Music by **Jule Styne**, lyrics by **Betty Comden** and **Adolph Green**, book by **Arthur Laurents**, directed by Burt Shevelove. Based on an original story, *Hallelujah, Baby!* capitalized on the delightful stage presence of **Leslie Uggams**, who won a **Tony Award** for her performance. Laurents's book traced an **African American** couple and the woman's white lover from the 1920s through the 1960s; however, the principals never age. Georgina (Uggams) leaves home when she learns that her fiancé, Clem (Robert Hooks), has lost their house in a crap game. She becomes a nightclub singer in the 1920s, is destitute during the Great Depression, and reemerges as a nightclub singer during World War II, becoming a star by the 1950s. Resentful of her success with white audiences, Clem loses interest in Georgina, but as the plot reaches the 1960s there is a satisfying close. **Walter Kerr**, writing for the *New York Times*, was unimpressed by the show. He found it politically naive and unsure of its audience, like a "course in Civics One when everyone in the world has already got to Civics Six." He adored Uggams, however, and said that she proceeds through the evening with a "secretive smile." He also liked the score and specifically mentioned the songs "Talking to Yourself," "Another Day," and "Not Mine." In his score, Styne effectively imitated the music of the various decades, thus assisting the audience in keeping up with the plot's temporal shifts.

HALLIDAY, ROBERT (1893–1975). Scottish-born baritone who starred as the romantic freedom-fighting hero in the **operettas** *The Desert Song* (1926), and *The New Moon* (1928) both with scores by **Sigmund Romberg**. He married his costar from *The New Moon*, **Evelyn Herbert**, and the couple starred in the short-lived operetta *Princess Charming* (1930). Halliday also played the lead role in **Rudolf Friml**'s *Music Hath Charms* (1934). His combination of good looks and a beautiful voice made him one of the most famous and most respected male operetta stars.

HAMLISCH, MARVIN (1944–). Composer for stage and screen whose Broadway credits include the **Tony Award**-winning *A Chorus Line* (1975), *They're Playing Our Song* (1979), *Smile* (1986), *The Goodbye Girl* (1993), and *Sweet Smell of Success* (2002). His music is characterized by easily memorable melodies and a strong sense of craftsmanship. He is one of a handful of people to have won all four major American performing arts awards: Tony, Oscar, Emmy, and Grammy.

HAMMERSTEIN, ARTHUR (ca. 1873–1955). Producer who frequently collaborated with composer **Rudolf Friml** and librettist/lyricist **Otto Harbach**. Their shows included *The Firefly* (1912), *High Jinks* (1913), *Katinka* (1915), *You're In Love* (1917), and several others before they created the landmark **operetta** *Rose Marie* (1924). Hammerstein also produced **Jerome Kern** and **Oscar Hammerstein II**'s *Sweet Adeline* (1929) and Friml's *Luana* (1930). His father, Oscar Hammerstein, was a theatrical impresario, and his nephew was the famed wordsmith Oscar Hammerstein II.

HAMMERSTEIN, OSCAR, II (1895–1960). One of Broadway's most important lyricists and librettists, Oscar Greeley Clendenning Hammerstein came from a family of theatrical managers and producers. His father, William, managed the Victoria Theatre; his uncle, **Arthur Hammerstein**, was a producer; and his grandfather, Oscar Hammerstein, was a leading impresario and founded the Manhattan Opera Company. He collaborated with veteran wordsmith **Otto Harbach** on the lyrics and libretto for *Wildflower* (1923, music by **Herbert Stothart** and **Vincent Youmans**), *Rose Marie* (1924, music by **Rudolf Friml**), and *The Desert Song* (1926, music by **Sigmund Romberg**). He created Broadway history in 1927 by writing lyrics for the seminal *Show Boat* to music by **Jerome Kern**. He maintained his ties with **operetta**, creating the words for the last great operetta of the 1920s, *The New Moon* (music by Romberg). After spending a great part of the 1930s in Hollywood, Hammerstein returned to Broadway in the early 1940s and began a new collaboration with **Richard Rodgers**. The legendary partnership resulted in nine musicals, beginning with *Oklahoma!* (1943) and *Carousel* (1945) and ending with *The Sound of Music* (1959). In 1943, he refashioned Georges Bizet's opera *Carmen* as *Carmen Jones* by transferring the opera's setting to America and making its characters African Americans.

Hammerstein, through his treatment of words, helped create the so-called **musical play**, where the storyline and characterization are as important as the music. His lyrics possess immediate appeal through their simplicity and directness. His use of local color in phrases such as "I'm as corny as Kansas in August" (from *South Pacific*'s "Wonderful Guy") or his clever employment of dialect in songs such as "I Cain't Say No" (from *Oklahoma!*) or "Dat's Love" (*Carmen*'s "Habanera" as it appears in *Carmen Jones*) set him apart from his contemporaries.

HANEY, CAROL (1924–1964). Choreographer and performer who won a **Tony Award** for Best Featured Actress in a Musical for her portrayal of Gladys in *The Pajama Game* (1954). She choreographed *Flower Drum Song* (1958), *Bravo Giovanni* (1962), *She Loves Me* (1963), and *Funny Girl* (1964).

THE HAPPY TIME (18 JANUARY 1968, BROADWAY, 286 PER-
FORMANCES). Music by **John Kander**; lyrics by **Fred Ebb**;
book by N. Richard Nash; directed, filmed, and choreographed by
Gower Champion; produced by **David Merrick**. Based on the
book by Robert L. Fontaine and the play by Samuel Taylor, *The
Happy Time* ran for less than nine months, even with David Merrick's substantial publicity campaign. **Michael** (Mike) **Rupert**
played Bibi Bonnard, a French-Canadian coming of age in an unusual family. The show was known for its innovation in dramaturgy,
for **Robert Goulet** played a photographer whose memories carry the
plot and Champion included film clips in his staging. The show's hit
song was "The Life of the Party," sung by David Wayne, the actor
who played Bibi's father.

HARBACH, OTTO (BORN OTTO HAUERBACH, 1873–1963).
Librettist and lyricist who was critical in the serious treatment of
words and story in the Broadway musical. After working on nine musicals with **Karl Hoschna**, Harbach (then working as Hauerbach),
began a successful collaboration with composer **Rudolf Friml** that
included *The Firefly* (1912), *High Jinks* (1913), *Katinka* (1915),
The Little Whopper (1919, the first show written under the abridged
surname Harbach), and, with **Oscar Hammerstein II**, *Rose Marie*
(1924). He worked with **Vincent Youmans** on *Wildflower* (1923) and
No, No, Nanette, **Jerome Kern** on *Sunny* (1925), *The Cat and the
Fiddle* (1931), and *Roberta* (1933), and **Sigmund Romberg** on *The
Desert Song* (1926), *Nina Rosa* (1930), and *Forbidden Melody*
(1948). He served as a mentor to Hammerstein, impressing on the
young wordsmith the importance of integrating music and drama into
an inseparable whole.

HARBURG, E. Y. (EDGAR YIP HARBURG, 1898–1981). Lyricist
who worked with many composers, most notably **Harold Arlen**. His
style of writing, which stemmed from Russian and Yiddish influences, is characterized by onomatopoeia, ingenuity of rhyme, alliteration, and assonance, and comic neologisms. Harburg's lyrics span a
variety of topics, including civil rights, feminism, and pacifism, and
demonstrate an extraordinary gift for creating satire and fantasy.
Among his most important shows are *Hooray for What!* (1937, mu-

sic by Arlen), about an inventor who creates a new laughing gas to end all wars, *Bloomer Girl* (1944), *Finian's Rainbow* (1947), *Flahooley* (1951, music by Sammy Fain), and *Jamaica* (1957).

HARNEY, BEN. Dancer and singer who won a **Tony Award** for his portrayal of Curtis Taylor Jr. in *Dreamgirls* (1981). Other credits include *Don't Bother Me, I Can't Cope* (1972), *Pippin* (1972, **replacement** Leading Player), *The Pajama Game* (1973 **revival**), and *The Wiz* (1975, replacement Tinman).

HARNICK, SHELDON (1924–). Lyricist best known for his collaborations with **Jerry Bock**, including *The Body Beautiful* (1958), *Fiorello!* (1959), *Tenderloin* (1960), *She Loves Me* (1963), *Fiddler on the Roof* (1964), *The Apple Tree* (1966), and *The Rothschilds* (1970). He was lyricist for **Richard Rodgers**'s *Rex* (1976) and also created the book for *The Apple Tree*. His lyrics are characterized by their subtle humor and clever wordplay. A classically trained violinist, Harnick has also composed songs for several Broadway shows: *New Faces of 1952*, *Two's Company* (1952), *Baker Street* (1965), and *The Madwoman of Central Park West* (1979).

HARRIGAN AND HART. Performing team consisting of **Edward Harrigan** and **Tony Hart**. The duo was extremely popular during the 1870s and early 1880s; audiences were distraught when the two men went their separate ways in 1885. Harrigan and Hart were best known for their Mulligan Guard characters, immortalized in *The Mulligan Guards' Ball* (1873). The plots of their shows often involved the Irish in New York City and their relationships with other ethnic populations, especially **African Americans**. The ill-fated Broadway musical *Harrigan and Hart* (1985), which starred **Harry Groener** as Harrigan and Mark Hamill as Hart, was based on the life of the important team.

HARRIGAN, EDWARD "NED" (1844–1911). Actor, playwright, and composer who formed a legendary stage partnership with actor **Tony Hart**, **Harrigan and Hart**. After the team broke up in 1885, Harrigan continued his career as a producer and actor. **George M. Cohan**'s song "Harrigan" was a tribute to this theatrical pioneer.

HARRIS, BARBARA (1935–). Stage and screen actress who starred in *On a Clear Day You Can See Forever* (1965) and who won a **Tony Award** for her performance in *The Apple Tree* (1966).

HARRIS, SAM H. (1872–1941). An extraordinarily active producer who worked on many shows as **George M. Cohan**'s partner as early as *Little Johnny Jones* (1904), and later helping produce *Animal Crackers* (1928), *Of Thee I Sing* (1931), *As Thousands Cheer* (1933), and *Lady in the Dark* (1941).

HARRISON, REX (1908–1990). Stage actor who immortalized Henry Higgins in *My Fair Lady* (1956), a performance for which he won a **Tony Award**. (Harrison won the 1949 Tony for Best Actor [Dramatic] for *Anne of the Thousand Days*.) He reprised Higgins in the 1964 film version and again in the 1981 Broadway **revival**.

HART, LORENZ "LARRY" (1895–1943). Lyricist who collaborated with composer **Richard Rodgers** from 1918, when they first met, until Hart's death in 1943. **Rodgers and Hart** helped define the **musical comedy** of the 1920s and 1930s. Hart had a difficult and unhappy personal life, and turned increasingly to alcohol in his later years. His lyrics can exist on their own as masterpieces and display a brilliance for rhyme scheme, an evocative use of language and metaphor, and overt sexual references, as in "Bewitched, Bothered, Bewildered" from *Pal Joey* (1940). Many of his lyrics depict love not as a happy thing but rather as a malady.

HART, MOSS (1904–1961). Librettist for *As Thousands Cheer* (1933), *Lady in the Dark* (1941), and other musicals who later became a director for such musicals as *Miss Liberty* (1949), *My Fair Lady* (1956), and *Camelot* (1960). Hart was known for his literate, elegant productions with fine casts.

HART, TONY (BORN ANTHONY J. CANNON, 1855–1891). Actor, singer, and comedian who was part of the team **Harrigan and Hart**. Since he was shorter and of a slighter build than his partner, **Edward Harrigan**, Hart often played the female roles in the team's sketches.

HARTMAN, PAUL (1904–1973). Recipient of the first **Tony Award** for Best Actor in a Musical in 1948 for *Angel in the Wings* (1947), a **revue** in which he played several roles.

HAYWARD, LELAND (1902–1971). The Hollywood publicist and agent was also active as a Broadway producer. Credits include *South Pacific* (1949), *Call Me Madam* (1950), and *Wish You Were Here* (1952). In 1959, he simultaneously coproduced *Gypsy* and *The Sound of Music*, and produced his last Broadway musical, **Irving Berlin**'s *Mr. President*, in 1962.

HEADLEY, HEATHER (1974–). Trinidad-born singing actress who created the role of Nala in *The Lion King* (1997) and won a **Tony Award** for the title role in *Aida* (2000). She is also known as a rhythm-and-blues recording artist.

HEARN, GEORGE (1934–). Baritone with a commanding stage presence whose credits include the title role in *Sweeney Todd: The Demon Barber of Fleet Street* (1979, **replacement** on Broadway and subsequent video release), Papa in *I Remember Mama* (1979), Albin in *La Cage aux Folles* (1984, a role for which he won a **Tony Award**), Max in *Sunset Boulevard* (1994), and The Wonderful Wizard of Oz (replacement) in *Wicked* (2003).

HELD, ANNA (ca. 1873–1918). Polish-born *Ziegfeld Follies* star and common-law wife of **Florenz Ziegfeld Jr.** Held's personal exuberance, risqué songs, and attractive legs made her an audience favorite. She appeared in various **revues** and **musical comedies** in the first decade of the century, and played Claire LaTour in *Follow Me* (1916), a show for which she also contributed lyrics. During World War I, she toured France, raising money for the war effort and entertaining troops, and also appeared in **vaudeville**. Songs for which she created both music and words were featured in the revue *Tintypes* (1980).

***HELLO, DOLLY!* (16 JANUARY 1964, ST. JAMES, 2,844 PERFORMANCES).** Music and lyrics by **Jerry Herman**, book by **Michael Stewart**, directed and choreographed by **Gower Champion**, produced by **David Merrick**. For a short time the longest-running musical in Broadway history, *Hello, Dolly!* was a delightful show that combined a strong story, fine score, effective staging, and **Carol Channing**'s unforgettable star presence. Stewart adapted the show from Thornton Wilder's play *The Matchmaker*, which, as **Howard Taubman** wrote in the *New York Times*, "vibrated with unheard melodies and unseen dances." Dolly Levi was one of the more outrageous creations ever to appear on Broadway, and Channing played her magnificently in decades of tours and revivals. As the widow Dolly confesses in her first song, "I Put My Hand in There," she "meddles," providing any service that might be required, from social introductions to instruction in almost anything. She has agreed to introduce Yonkers's wealthiest citizen, Horace Vandergelder (David Burns), to potential wives; he does not know that she is really saving him for herself. In act 2, everyone meets at the Harmonia Gardens Restaurant, where Dolly, although she has not been there in years, is still a legend. Her attention-grabbing arrival at the top of a grand staircase prompts a lavish production number based on the popular title tune. Dolly is also trying to help Vandergelder's niece marry against her uncle's will, and when he spies his niece on the dance floor, a riot ensues and everyone ends up in court. Dolly softens the judge's heart and makes sure Vandergelder receives full blame for everything, her final ammunition in her ultimate plan to make him marry her. Although Taubman took some exception to segments that pandered excessively to popular taste, he pronounced *Hello, Dolly!* "a musical shot through with enchantment."

Herman's score included a number of fine tunes, most of them effectively integrated with the plot, but others that function more in the vein of 1930s **musical comedy**. In addition to the title song, the production number "Before the Parade Passes By" is worthy of the parade that it accompanies and includes some effective harmonic surprises. The show's long run was partly a function of producer David Merrick's heady showmanship. When Channing left the Broadway Company for a national tour, he hired a succession of stars, including **Ginger Rogers**, **Ethel Merman**, and **Pearl Bailey** to play the crafty matchmaker. **Barbra Steisand** starred in the 1969 film version.

HELLZAPOPPIN' **(22 SEPTEMBER 1938, 46TH STREET, 1,404 PERFORMANCES).** Songs by several writers, book author unattributed. An uproarious **revue** of mostly low comedy and vaudeville skits, *Hellzapoppin'* was the longest-running musical in the history of Broadway when it closed. The show's main instigators were Ole Olsen and Chic Johnson, two vaudeville comedians. Writing in the *New York Times*, **Brooks Atkinson** asserted that they found their cast by choosing every third person who walked by on a street corner, discovered their material in an attic where they "swept out all the gags in sight," and then went to an ammunition store to buy blank cartridges to shoot when a joke was told. He also noted that the show "ought to show a higher trace of talent" but admitted that he enjoyed parts of it.

HENDERSON, FLORENCE (1934–). Actress best known for her work on television, particularly as Carol Brady on *The Brady Bunch* (1969–1974), who began her career in musical theater. She made her Broadway debut as "The New Girl" in *Wish You Were Here* (1952) with a one-line role, created the title character in *Fanny* (1954), and played Mary Morgan in *The Girl Who Came to Dinner* (1963).

HENDERSON, RAY (RAYMOND BROST, 1896–1970). Composer who collaborated with lyricists **B. G. De Sylva** and **Lew Brown** on the 1925 and 1926 editions of *George White's Scandals* and 11 **musical comedies**, including the sports-themed trilogy *Good News!* (1927), *Hold Everything!* (1928), and *Flying High* (1930).

HEPBURN, KATHARINE (1907–2003). The legendary actress appeared in one Broadway musical, *Coco* (1969), in which she played the title role of fashion designer Coco Chanel and captivated audiences with her solo number "Always Mademoiselle."

HERBERT, EVELYN (1898–1975). Soprano known for creating lead roles in **operettas** from the 1920s and 1930s including *Princess Flavia* (1925), *My Maryland* (1926), *The New Moon* (1928), and *Melody* (1933), all with scores by **Sigmund Romberg**. She married her costar from *The New Moon*, **Robert Halliday**, and the couple costarred in *Princess Charming* (1930). Herbert's final appearance on Broadway was in the 1934 revival of *Bitter Sweet*. Herbert possessed a fine and agile voice capable of singing the technically challenging music Romberg wrote specifically for her, and coupled with her physical beauty, she epitomized the operetta soprano of the era.

HERBERT, VICTOR (1859–1924). Irish-born and German-trained musician who made his Broadway debut as a composer with *Prince Ananias* (1894). Herbert came to New York in 1886, when his wife, singer Therese Förster, joined the roster of the Metropolitan Opera and Herbert was engaged to play cello in the Metropolitan Opera Orchestra. Herbert was a versatile musician, achieving celebrity as a cellist, conductor, and composer. Many of his most enduring musical theater works, most of which were **operettas**, were written for specific singers. *The Serenade* (1897), *The Fortune Teller* (1898), and *The Singing Girl* (1899) all featured roles tailored for soprano **Alice Nielsen**. He wrote *Mlle. Modiste* (1905) for **Fritzi Scheff**, *Naughty Marietta* (1910) for **Emma Trentini**, and *Sweethearts* (1913) for Christie MacDonald. Other famous scores include *Babes in Toyland* (1903), *It Happened in Nordland* (1904), *The Red Mill* (1906), *The Lady of the Slipper* (1912), *The Only Girl* (1914), *The Princess Pat* (1915), *The Century Girl* (1916), *The Velvet Lady* (1919), *Orange Blossoms* (1922), and *The Dream Girl* (1924). Herbert's musical theater works are noted for their transparency of textures, virtuosic vocal writing, and general effervescence.

***HERE'S LOVE* (3 OCTOBER 1963, SHUBERT, 334 PERFORMANCES).** Music, lyrics, and book by **Meredith Willson**, dances and musical numbers staged by **Michael Kidd**. Based on the classic film *Miracle on 34th Street* (screenplay by George Seaton, based on the novel by Valentine Davies), *Here's Love* was a safe, professional musical that showed little in the way of art but ran for about 10 months. Laurence Naismith played Kris Kringle, and Valerie Lee was the little girl whose belief he earns. Her mother, Doris Walker (Janis Paige), also becomes a believer and ends up loving Fred Gaily (Craig Stevens), Kris's lawyer in his mental competency trial. The popularity of the movie helped the show. **Howard Taubman** reviewed the show for the *New York Times*, qualifying his praise for the family musical. He thought that the songs "seem machine-tooled" and the dances were "reliably colorful and bouncy." Critics expected more from the creator of *The Music Man*.

HERMAN, JERRY (1931–). Composer and lyricist whose songs were featured in the **revue** *From A to Z* (1960) and who wrote music and lyrics for the **musical comedy** *Milk and Honey* (1961) before achieving lasting fame with *Hello, Dolly!* (1964), a star vehicle for **Carol Channing**. This was followed by another show with a strong female lead, *Mame* (1966), which starred **Angela Lansbury** in the title role and also featured **Bea Arthur** as her best friend, Vera. Other musicals include *Dear World* (1969), again starring Lansbury, *Mack & Mabel* (1974), *The Grand Tour* (1979), *La Cage aux Folles* (1983), and *Jerry's Girls* (1985). His songs were featured on Broadway in *A Day in Hollywood/A Night in the Ukraine* (1980), *An Evening with Jerry Herman* (1998), and *Barbara Cook's Broadway* (2004). Herman won **Tony Awards** for *Hello, Dolly!* and *La Cage aux Folles*. His large-scale songs are filled with an exuberant vivacity that captures the colorful personalities of the characters who sing them, while his ballads offer intimate expressions of their singer's emotional state at a specific point in the show.

***HIGH BUTTON SHOES* (9 OCTOBER 1947, NEW CENTURY, 727 PERFORMANCES).** Music and lyrics by **Jule Styne** and **Sammy Cahn**, book by Stephen Longstreet, production directed by **George Abbott**, dances and staging by **Jerome Robbins**. Based on Longstreet's somewhat autobiographical novel *The Sisters Liked Them Handsome*, *High Button Shoes* was a comic romp that ran for almost two years. Its star was the inspired clown **Phil Silvers**, who plays a con man, Harrison Floy, who returns to his hometown of New Brunswick, New Jersey, in 1913 to bilk the unsuspecting citizens in a fraudulent land deal with his assistant, Mr. Pontdue (Joey Faye). The show's most famous moment was Robbins's madcap "Mack Sennett Ballet," inspired by the Keystone Kops routines from silent films. In this sequence, the good citizens of New Brunswick chase Floy and Pontdue until everyone finally falls into a hopeless jumble. **Brooks Atkinson**, reviewing the show for the *New York Times*, calls it "very happy" and "workaday," noting that the creators have "ignored progress in the arts" but offer "excellent family entertainment." The score's two most famous songs are "Papa, Won't You Dance with Me?," a polka, and "I Still Get Jealous," an old-time soft-shoe number.

***HIGH JINKS* (10 DECEMBER 1913, LYRIC, 213 PERFORMANCES).** Music by **Rudolf Friml**, book and lyrics by **Otto**

Harbach, produced by **Arthur Hammerstein**. The self-proclaimed "musical farce," set in a French spa, revolves around the effects of a perfume with opiate qualities. Among the score's highlights were the comic number "Something Seems a Tingle-ingling" and the grand waltz "Love's Own Kiss."

HIGH SPIRITS **(7 APRIL 1964, ALVIN, 375 PERFORMANCES).** Music, lyrics, and book by Hugh Martin and Timothy Gray, staged by **Noel Coward**. Based on Coward's comedy *Blithe Spirit, High Spirits* was a vehicle for **Beatrice Lillie**, one of Broadway's best female comics in the middle decades of the 20th century. Lillie played Madame Arcati, an eccentric medium. Charles Condomine (Edward Woodward) is happily married to his second wife, but to everyone's consternation Madame Arcati brings his first wife, Elvira (**Tammy Grimes**), back from the dead. *High Spirits* had a few fine songs, such as "If I Gave You," but did not include a major hit, a factor that probably hurt its ability to compete with other major musicals of the time such as *Hello, Dolly!* and *Funny Girl.*

HINES, GREGORY (1946–2003). Dancer who appeared in the **jukebox musicals** *Eubie!* (1978), based on the music of Eubie Blake; *Sophisticated Ladies* (1981), which featured the music of Duke Ellington; and *Jelly's Last Jam* (1992), in which he played Jelly Roll Morton and for which he created the tap routines and won a **Tony Award** for Best Actor in a Musical.

HIT THE DECK **(25 APRIL 1927, BELASCO, 352 PERFOR-MANCES).** Music by **Vincent Youmans**, lyrics by **Leo Robin** and Clifford Grey, book by **Herbert Fields**. Based on Hubert Osborne's play *Shore Leave*, the **musical comedy** *Hit the Deck* concerned Bilge (Charles King), a typical sailor who wants a girl in every port. His girl in Newport, Loulou (Louise Groody), owns a coffeehouse frequented by sailors. She falls in love with Bilge, but he will not marry her. Loulou uses her considerable fortune to follow him all over the world, including China, until he decides she is the one. Bilge gets cold feet again when he discovers that she is wealthy, but she wins him in the end by promising to give her fortune to their eldest child. The show included the era's typically large men's and women's choruses and its two most famous songs were "Hallelujah" and "Sometimes I'm Happy."

HOFFMAN, GERTRUDE (1876–1966). Dancer, choreographer, director, and composer famous for her portrayal of Salome and her impersonations of various actors and dancers. The "Hoffman Glide," a social dance, was named after her. Hoffman was also a composer, writing the score for *The Man from Now* (1906) and songs for the *Ziegfeld Follies* of 1907.

HOLD EVERYTHING! **(10 OCTOBER 1928, BROADHURST, 413 PERFORMANCES).** Songs by **Lew Brown**, **B. G. De Sylva**, and **Ray Henderson**, book by De Sylva and **John McGowan**; produced by **Alex A. Aarons** and **Vinton Freedley**. The **musical comedy** that helped make **Bert Lahr** a star and included the song "You're the Cream in My Coffee," *Hold Everything!* was a sports-themed show (like *Good News!*), this time about a welterweight contender, "Sonny Jim" Brooks (Jack Whiting), who has problems with his girlfriend when the boxer refuses to fight for charity. Famous comics in the cast included **Victor Moore**, Nina Olivette, and Lahr, whose routines included knocking himself out with a punch. J. Brooks Atkinson, writing in the *New York Times*, disliked the "annoyingly ubiquitous" book that made little use of Moore, but praises most of the cast and found "the dancing of 'Hold Everything!' more entertaining than the book and chorus." The score also included "Genealogy," "Footwork," and "Don't Hold Everything."

HOLLIDAY, JUDY (BORN JUDY TUVIM, 1921–1965). Actress known for her comic timing who began her theatrical career in 1938 as part of "The Revuers," a nightclub act that also included **Betty Comden** and **Adolph Green**. Comden and Green, with composer **Jule Styne**, created *Bells Are Ringing* (1956) especially for her. Holliday won a **Tony Award** for her portrayal of telephone operator Ella Peterson and also achieved notable fame in Hollywood.

HOLM, CELESTE (1919–). Character actress who created Ado Annie Carnes in *Oklahoma!* (1943) and Evalina in *Bloomer Girl* (1944). In 1967, she took over the title role in the original production of *Mame*. She is also known for her work on film and television, and won an Academy Award for *Gentlemen's Agreement* (1947).

HOMOSEXUALITY. Homosexuality has a considerable kinship with the Broadway musical. Many fans of Broadway are gay, and many leading practitioners of musical theater, including but certainly not limited to **Ethel Merman, Julie Andrews, Liza Minnelli,** and **Bernadette Peters,** are gay icons. Significant Broadway creators and performers have been gay, including **Lorenz Hart, Cole Porter, Noel Coward,** the team of **George Forrest** and **Robert Wright, Harvey Fierstein, William Finn,** and **Stephen Sondheim.** Homosexual themes and characters in Broadway musicals range from clichéd incarnations to real people facing challenging life situations. Broadway's first openly gay character was Sebastian Baye in *Coco* (1969); **Rene Auberjonois,** who played him, received a **Tony Award** for Best Featured Actor in a Musical for his performance. Shows that either have major characters who are homosexual or in which homosexuality is a significant feature of the plot include *Hair* (1968), *Your Own Thing* (1968), *A Chorus Line* (1975), *La Cage aux Folles* (1983), *Falsettos* (1992), *Kiss of the Spider Woman* (1993), *Victor/Victoria* (1995), *Rent* (1996), *The Producers* (2001), *Avenue Q* (2003), *The Boy from Oz* (2003), and *Monty Python's Spamalot* (2005), in which Lancelot (of Arthurian legend) is gay. *See also APPLAUSE; THE 25TH ANNUAL PUTNAM COUNTY SPELLING BEE.*

HOPE, BOB (BORN LESTER TOWNES HOPE, 1903–2003). Famed screen actor, comedian, and entertainer who appeared on Broadway in the 1930s in *Ballyhoo of 1932*, *Roberta* (1933), *Ziegfeld Follies* of 1936, and *Red, Hot and Blue!* (1936).

HORNE, LENA (BORN LENA MARY CALHOUN HORNE, 1917–). **African American** popular singer who worked with many leading jazz musicians and appeared in several MGM film musicals. On Broadway, she played Savannah in the calypso-inspired musical *Jamaica* (1957).

HOSCHNA, KARL L. (1877–1911). Bohemian-born and Viennese-trained composer who collaborated with **Otto Harbach** on *Three*

Twins (1910) and an American adaptation of *Madame Sherry* (1910) called *The Fascinating Widow* (1911), which was a vehicle for female impersonator Julian Eltinge.

HOWARD, WILLIE (1886–1949). Dialect comedian who worked in **vaudeville** with his brother, Eugene. The duo also appeared in **revues**, including editions of *The Passing Show* and *George White's Scandals* as well as *The Show Is On* (1937).

HOWES, SALLY ANN (1930–). English-born soprano who was a replacement for Eliza Doolittle in the original production of *My Fair Lady*, played Fiona MacLaren in the 1963 revival of *Brigadoon*, and created the roles of Kit Sargent in *What Makes Sammy Run?* (1964) and Aunt Julia Morkan in *James Joyce's The Dead* (2000). She is perhaps best known for playing Truly Scrumptious opposite **Dick van Dyke** in the 1968 film musical *Chitty Chitty Bang Bang*.

***HOW TO SUCCEED IN BUSINESS WITHOUT REALLY TRYING* (14 OCTOBER 1961, 46TH STREET, 1,416 PERFORMANCES).** Music and lyrics by **Frank Loesser**, based on Shepherd Mead's book of the same name, adapted by **Abe Burrows**, Jack Weinstock, and Willie Gilbert, directed by Burrows, musical staging by **Bob Fosse**, presented by **Cy Feuer** and Ernest Martin. A satirical look at American business, *How to Succeed in Business without Really Trying* follows Finch (**Robert Morse**) on his run up the corporate ladder. With Mead's book as his guide, Finch quickly gets himself into the mailroom at World Wide Wickets by coyly playing up his "relationship" with the president J. B. Biggley (**Rudy Vallee**), with whom he just collided in the hall. In the mailroom he meets Biggley's nephew, Frump (Charles Nelson Reilly), who threatens to derail Finch's rise. Finch suggests Frump as the new head of the mailroom to replace a retiree, and goes on to a better position himself. On his first day at the company, Finch meets secretary Rosemary Pilkington (Bonnie Scott), who becomes his girl. Finch's secretary is Hedy La Rue (Virginia Martin), who he thinks is Biggley's mistress. This knowledge, and leading the boss to believe that he is a fellow Groundhog from "Grand Old Ivy," gets Finch named advertising director. He needs a worthwhile idea, and produces a television show starring Hedy. She is a disaster, and the chairman of the board comes to clean house. Biggley retires and the chairman appoints Finch to replace him. In the last scene, Finch washes windows at the White House in hopes of another promotion.

Howard Taubman, writing in the *New York Times*, showed boundless enthusiasm for the show, claiming that it "belongs to the blue chips among modern musicals." He noted that Burrows "has directed brilliantly" and Loesser "has written lyrics with an edge and tunes with a grin." Although Loesser's songs contributed greatly to the show's success, few became famous outside of its context. Numbers such as "A Secretary Is Not a Toy" and "I Believe in You," the latter sung by Finch to himself in the washroom mirror, however, were brilliant fun and made Loesser's final Broadway score notable. Many of the creators of *Guys and Dolls* returned for *How to Succeed*. While *How to Succeed* actually ran longer in its initial production, its predecessor has enjoyed a greater legacy. Morse reprised his role for the 1967 film version (with a slightly altered plot), and **Matthew Broderick** starred in the 1995 Broadway revival.

HOYT, CHARLES H. (1860–1900). Prolific librettist and lyricist whose credits include the record-breaking farce *A Trip to Chinatown* (1891). In 1896, he adopted his comedy *A Parlor Match* as a vehicle for **Anna Held**.

– I –

I CAN GET IT FOR YOU WHOLESALE **(22 MARCH 1962, SHUBERT, 300 PERFORMANCES).** Music and lyrics by **Harold Rome**, book by Jerome Weidman, directed by **Arthur Laurents**, presented by **David Merrick**. Based on Weidman's book of the same name, *I Can Get It for You Wholesale* took a jaundiced view of the garment industry and Jewish family life, and provided **Barbra Streisand** with her Broadway debut. Elliott Gould played Harry Bogen, a businessman who runs over everyone on his way up the corporate ladder and ends up bankrupting his firm. Streisand was the secretary Miss Marmelstein, stopping the show every night with a song named after her character. Howard Taubman, writing for the

New York Times, described the show as "keenly professional." The book is "not uplifting," but "honest." He called Streisand "the evening's find" and a "natural comedienne." Among the better songs were the act 1 finale, "Ballad of the Garment Trade," and "Have I Told You Lately."

I DO! I DO! **(5 DECEMBER 1966, 46TH STREET, 584 PERFOR-MANCES).** Music, lyrics, and book by **Harvey Schmidt** and **Tom Jones**, direction and choreography by **Gower Champion**. Based on Jan de Hartog's play *The Fourposter*, *I Do! I Do!* was a two-person show that starred **Mary Martin** and **Robert Preston** and ran for 17 months. The entire musical takes place in the couple's bedroom, from their early married years when Preston sings "I Love My Wife" (while barefoot but strutting in dressing gown with top hat and cane) through his admission of an affair at the end of the first act. Preston sings "A Well Known Fact" about how women cannot resist a mid-dle-aged man. At the show's close, they must sell their large house to a young couple, and leave a bottle of champagne on the pillow for them. A more mirthful moment comes with the birth of a child, marked by the famous song "My Cup Runneth Over." One of Mar-tin's biggest numbers was "Flaming Agnes," during which she put on a feathered hat and declared that she will make herself irresistible to other men. Gower Champion effectively used the limited set and never allowed the action to stop. In the *New York Times*, **Walter Kerr** raved about the performers but found the songs and book "barely passable."

I'D RATHER BE RIGHT **(2 NOVEMBER 1937, ALVIN, 290 PER-FORMANCES).** Music by **Richard Rodgers**, lyrics by **Lorenz Hart**, book by **George S. Kaufman** and **Moss Hart**, book staged by Kaufman, produced by **Sam H. Harris**. An original musical cast in the mold of satires such as *Of Thee I Sing*, *I'd Rather Be Right* fea-tured **George M. Cohan** as President Franklin D. Roosevelt. Two young lovers, Peggy Jones (Joy Hodges) and Phil Barker (Austin Marshall) are in Central Park, lamenting that they cannot marry until receiving pay raises, something that will not happen until Roosevelt balances the budget. Phil falls asleep and dreams that Roosevelt is in the park and that he wants to help the young couple. Along with his cabinet, Roosevelt hatches a number of ludicrous schemes, such as raising the price of postage stamps to one hundred dollars. In the end, Roosevelt cannot balance the budget, but advises Peggy and Phil to marry anyway. In his review in the *New York Times*, **Brooks Atkinson** expressed solid appreciation for Cohan's work in the show, saying he "has never been in better form." Atkinson was less impressed with the book, which he termed "a pleasant-spoken musical comedy." Musical highlights include the love duet "Have You Met Miss Jones?" and Roosevelt's frustrating press conference, "Off the Record." Tensions between Cohan and the team that wrote the score caused many problems, but these did not spill across the footlights, and the show settled in for a nine-month run.

I LOVE MY WIFE **(17 APRIL 1977, ETHEL BARRYMORE, 872 PERFORMANCES).** Music by **Cy Coleman**, lyrics and book by **Michael Stewart**, musical numbers staged by **Onna White**. Based on a French play by Luis Rego, *I Love My Wife* seemed to fit into the age of the sexual revolution with its theme about wife swapping. It was a trendy and smart show that managed a run of more than two years. Wally (**James Naughton**) and Alvin (Lenny Baker), two friends from high school, decide that exchanging wives as bed partners might be fun. Their spouses, played by **Joanna Gleason** and Ilene Graff, enter the project with different degrees of willingness, and complications quickly ensue. Four on-stage musicians, sometimes costumed as devils or wearing pajamas, accompanied and commented on the action. **Clive Barnes**, writing for the *New York Times*, described the plot as "cigarette-paper thin," but he praised it as "light-hearted, light-fingered and original." He found Stewart's lyrics "neat, nifty and very literate," while Coleman's varied music was "tuneful, infectious and slightly impish." He described the cast as "gorgeous . . . just right."

I MARRIED AN ANGEL **(11 MAY 1938, SHUBERT, 338 PERFORMANCES).** Music by **Richard Rodgers**, lyrics by **Lorenz Hart**, book by Rodgers and Hart, staged by **Joshua Logan**, choreography by **George Balanchine**. Based on a Hungarian play by John Vaszary, *I Married an Angel* was one of the literate and forward-looking gems that Rodgers and Hart wrote in the years before World War II. They adapted the book, but Hart's drinking was becoming more serious, so Joshua Logan helped with no credit. Set in Budapest, Willie Palaffi (**Dennis King**) is a banker unlucky in business and love. He ends his relationship with Anna (Audrey Christie) and concludes that he can only marry an angel. Vera Zorina plays the divine messenger sent to him. He marries her, but finds out that an angel too can cause difficult situations. Countess Palaffi (**Vivienne Segal**) teaches the angel how to live in the world and assists Willie in saving his bank from creditors. In addition to their usual fine songs, such as the title number and "Spring Is Here," Rodgers and Hart also wrote extended sequences with rhymed dialogue over music. Balanchine's two ballets depicted the couple's honeymoon in act 1 and an ironic look at the Roxy Music Hall in act 2. Such a lengthy consideration of a New York City theater in a musical that took place in Budapest was unusual, but so clever that the critics were kind about the disjunction. **Brooks Atkinson**, writing for the *New York Times*, called it "one of the best musical comedies for many seasons" with "an extraordinarily beautiful production." He raved about Zorina as the angel, and also appreciated the remainder of the cast, especially Segal, who sang "A Twinkle in Your Eye" with "matchless relish."

I'M GETTING MY ACT TOGETHER AND TAKING IT ON THE ROAD **(14 JUNE 1978, PUBLIC, 1,165 PERFORMANCES).** Music by Nancy Ford; book and lyrics by Gretchen Cryer. Cryer also starred in this show about a middle-aged pop singer trying to make a comeback. She sings for her manager Joe (Joel Fabiani), but he is not impressed. They seem attracted to one another, but Joe returns to his wife and Cryer is left to sing one last song, saying that she has always been lonely. Although Richard Eder called the songs "effortless and not in the best sense of the word" in his *New York Times* review, the show caught on with audiences and ran for almost three years.

IN DAHOMEY **(18 FEBRUARY 1903, NEW YORK, 53 PERFORMANCES).** Music by **Will Marion Cook**, lyrics by **Paul Lawrence Dunbar**, book by J. H. Shipp. The first Broadway **musical comedy** conceived entirely by African Americans, *In Dahomey* shattered a number of conventions but only managed a Broadway run of less than two months. The anonymous *New York Times* critic started the review by recalling the "thunderclouds" that had been gathering since the production's announcement, suggesting that perhaps "trouble-breeders" would use the occasion to start a "race war." Such fears were unfounded, however, and the *Times* reports that the show went off "merrily." The stars were **Bert Williams** and **George Walker**, black **vaudeville** stars making their first foray into Broadway theater. The story concerned some dishonest African Americans from Chicago who plan to make money with a shady scheme involving resettling blacks in the African country of Dahomey. They first send Rareback Pinkerton (Walker) to Florida to swindle a wealthy man out of his fortune. He is accompanied by Shylock Homestead (Williams), a fool with far more money than Pinkerton's intended mark. Pinkerton becomes Homestead's trustee and puts on airs in both Florida and Dahomey. The pair become governors in the African country, setting off a wild, dancing celebration. *In Dahomey* toured for years and played for seven months in London. The *Times* reviewer declared that "the headliners are the whole show," and points out that although the performers were black, the audience was white, and that Williams used burnt cork to make himself darker. That *In Dahomey* enjoyed the success it did in such an atmosphere makes it clear that the show had something to offer. *See also* AFRICAN AMERICAN MUSICALS.

***INSIDE U.S.A.* (30 APRIL 1948, NEW CENTURY, 399 PERFORMANCES).** Music and production by **Arthur Schwartz**, lyrics by **Howard Dietz**, sketches by **Moss Hart** and other writers. A **revue** vehicle for British comic **Beatrice Lillie**, *Inside U.S.A.* took a humorous look at American life and ran for nearly a year. Some of the inspiration came from John Gunther's novel of the same title, but *Inside U.S.A.* was a typical revue with a mixture of comic sketches, dances, and songs. Some critics found the material lacking in wit, but Lillie was her usually uproarious self and **Jack Haley** was a fine leading man. Lillie's characters included, among others, a superstitious maid torturing the actress she works for on an opening night, a mermaid who is unlucky in love, and the queen of a New Orleans Mardi Gras. Among Haley's material was a song where he named important attractions in each state, but "Rhode Island Is Famous for You." The only song to gain popularity outside of the show was "Haunted Heart."

INTERPOLATION. Songs placed into a show that are not part of the original score. Most common in the early decades of the 20th century, the practice typically occurred when stars wanted to sing one of their favorite songs from one show (or a popular standard) in another. This was especially common in **revues** and **musical comedies**, where songs are not necessarily closely tied to the plot. **Al Jolson** was especially famous for interpolations, introducing some of his classic numbers, such as "Swanee" and "California, Here We Come," in this manner.

INTO THE WOODS **(5 NOVEMBER 1987, MARTIN BECK, 765 PERFORMANCES).** Music and lyrics by **Stephen Sondheim**, book and direction by **James Lapine**. Based on familiar fairy tales but with new twists, the show asked the question, "What happens after happily ever after?" Lapine brought together many famous fairy tale characters and added his own tale concerning a baker (**Chip Zien**) and his wife (**Joanna Gleason**) who desire a child but are under the spell of the Witch (**Bernadette Peters**). To undo the curse, they must go "into the woods" to gather specific items. There, they discover more about themselves and how one confronts an adult world. In the woods, they meet Cinderella (Kim Crosby), Jack (of beanstalk fame, Ben Wright), Little Red Ridinghood (Danielle Ferland), and characters from their tales. Their stories are intertwined, and everyone seems ready to live "happily ever after" at the end of act 1. Things change, however, in act 2. The giant's wife comes down the beanstalk to seek revenge on Jack for killing her husband, marital vows fall by the wayside as the baker's wife (**Joanna Gleason**) meets Cinderella's Prince (**Robert Westenberg**), and the characters realize they must work together and that there are no easy answers to life's difficult questions. Writing in the *New York Times*, Frank Rich found the story "wildly overgrown" and wondered if the show needed "less art and more craft." Sondheim's score includes several gems, including "Agony," sung by the two princes, "Hello Little Girl," performed, sometimes with physical gestures, by the sexually charged Wolf, and the songs that represent lessons to be learned, "No One Is Alone" and "Children Will Listen." The show has become a favorite with community and school theater groups, and the 2002

Broadway revival included some new material and starred **Vanessa Williams** as the Witch.

I REMEMBER MAMA **(31 MAY 1979, MAJESTIC, 108 PER-FORMANCES).** Music by **Richard Rodgers**, lyrics by **Martin Charnin**, book by Thomas Meehan. Remembered as Richard Rodgers's Broadway swan song and proof that Liv Ullmann would never be a Broadway musical star, this adaptation of the famous 1944 play of the same name was a major disappointment. Rodgers wrote at least one winning melody in "You Could Not Please Me More," sung beautifully by **George Hearn** as the husband, but little else worked. Richard Eder in the *New York Times* found that the creators "buried most of the strengths under a mass of clichés and a pervading, forced cuteness."

IRENE **(18 NOVEMBER 1919, VANDERBILT, 670 PERFOR-MANCES).** Music by **Harry Tierney**, lyrics by Joseph McCarthy, book by James Montgomery. Based on the unsuccessful play *Irene O'Dare*, also by James Montgomery, *Irene* was the tale of Irene O'-Dare (**Edith Day**), a poor shopgirl of Irish descent, who is sent on an errand to a posh Long Island estate. The estate owner's son, Donald Marshall (Walter Regan), falls in love with her and helps her find a better job. Irene charms his family, and eventually both families ignore their natural prejudices and allow the young couple to marry. *Irene* boasted an unusually strong book that moved back and forth between the two families. The score included the hits "Alice Blue Gown" and "The Last Part of Every Party." **Gower Champion** directed the 1973 revival, which starred **Debbie Reynolds**.

IRMA LA DOUCE **(29 SEPTEMBER 1960, PLYMOUTH, 524 PERFORMANCES).** Music by Marguerite Monnot, French book and lyrics by Alexandre Breffort, English book and lyrics by Julian More, David Haneker, and Monty Norman, choreographed by **Onna White**, produced by **David Merrick**. Long before the shows of Claude-Michel Schönberg and **Alain Boublil** came to Broadway, *Irma La Douce* was a French import that had also been produced in London. Elizabeth Seal played the title role, the famous "prostitute with a heart of gold" who plies her trade in Paris's Place Pigalle. She loses her heart to Nestor-Le-Fripé (Keith Mitchell), a law student, who shares her with an elderly gentleman (also played by Mitchell). **Howard Taubman**'s review in the *New York Times* noted "the Gallic gift for genial satire," which made the red-light district of Place Pigalle "into a kind of cynical fairyland." He stated, however, that "the hearts of all of the creators . . . are well-nigh chaste," even to the point that the English authors avoided many of the double entendres that the book might have offered.

IT HAPPENED IN NORDLAND (5 DECEMBER 1904, LEW FIELDS, 154 PERFORMANCES). Music by **Victor Herbert**, lyrics and book by Glen MacDonough. Written as the opening production for **Lew Fields**'s new theater, *It Happened in Nordland* was a critical and commercial success best remembered for its tension between actors and composers concerning **interpolations**. In the country of Nordland the American ambassador, Katherine Peepfogle (**Marie Cahill**), is the double of the nation's queen, who has disappeared. The ambassador reluctantly takes her place, in the process finding her brother, Hubert (Lew Fields), who has been missing. Disguised as the queen, Katherine is able to get her brother out of several predicaments. Since Herbert failed to include a clause in his contract that forbade interpolations, Cahill brought in extra songs to sing, prompting an ugly incident that resulted in Fields firing her. Fields then fired her replacement, Blanche Ring, for the same reason before the show moved to Boston.

– J –

JACKMAN, HUGH (1968–). The versatile Australian actor won the 2004 Tony Award for his portrayal of **Peter Allen** in *The Boy from Oz*. In the musical, Jackman's first on Broadway, the actor sang in 20 of the show's 27 musical numbers. Previous musical theater credits include Curly in the 1999 National Theatre (London) revival of *Oklahoma!*

JACOBY, MARK (1947–). Resonant baritone who played Vittorio Vidal in the 1986 **revival** of *Sweet Charity* and was a **replacement**

Phantom in *The Phantom of the Opera* in 1991 before appearing as Gaylord Ravenal in the high-profile 1994 **Hal Prince** revival of *Show Boat*. Subsequent roles include Father in *Ragtime* (1998), The Padre in the 2002 revival of *Man of La Mancha*, and Judge Turpin in the 2005 **John Doyle** revival of *Sweeney Todd: The Demon Barber of Fleet Street*.

JAMAICA **(31 OCTOBER 1957, IMPERIAL, 558 PERFORMANCES).** Music by **Harold Arlen**, lyrics by **E. Y. Harburg**, book by Harburg and Fred Saidy, choreography by **Jack Cole**, produced by **David Merrick**. An original **musical comedy** that featured **Lena Horne**, *Jamaica* was a colorful show that ran for 17 months. Horne played Savannah, a resident of Pigeon's Island, off the coast of Jamaica. Her love interest is Koli (Ricardo Montalban), but Savannah wants to leave the island. When Joe Nashua (Joe Adams) comes to the island on business, Savannah plays up to him in hopes that he will take her with him back to New York. However, after Koli saves Savannah's younger brother during a hurricane, Savannah marries him and only gets to New York in a dream ballet. Horne was involved in more than half of the musical numbers, backed by a strong cast and high production values. **Brooks Atkinson**, writing in the *New York Times*, recognized that the creators of *Jamaica* only wished to entertain and assembled "an unpretentious show." He called Horne "a handsome young lady with delicate features, elegant manners and a wonderful glow, to say nothing of a rich singing voice." No songs from *Jamaica* became famous outside of the show, but Horne sang two fine satirical numbers—"Push De Button" (about mechanized society) and "Napoleon" (on the commercial exploitation of famous names)—and there were other highlights that brought a calypso sensibility to Arlen's usual fine craftsmanship. *See also* AFRICAN AMERICAN MUSICALS.

JEKYLL AND HYDE **(28 APRIL 1997, PLYMOUTH, 1,543 PERFORMANCES).** Music by **Frank Wildhorn**, lyrics and book by **Leslie Bricusse**. Based on the famous novella by Robert Louis Stevenson, the creators of *Jekyll and Hyde* helped guarantee the show's Broadway success by a long tour and two recordings of the score before its New York premiere. *Jekyll and Hyde* had a cult following, making it safe from reviewers, who generally panned it. Robert Cuccioli played the two title characters, showing the differences between the good doctor and evil madman with, among other things, a neat ponytail and wild hair. Jekyll's wealthy fiancée, Emma (Christiane Noll), contrasted strongly with the prostitute, Lucy (Linda Eder), for whom Jekyll also develops feelings. Hyde kills Lucy, however, one of a number of people whom he murders in the second act. **Ben Brantley**, writing for the *New York Times*, echoed the typical critical reception for *Jekyll and Hyde*. He made fun of Cucciola's hairstyles, suggesting a **Tony Award** for best use of hair in a musical. Brantley called the book repetitious and similar to what one sees on a late horror movie and was especially cruel toward the music, which he compared to horror film scores. Jekyll's major song was "This Is the Moment," and Eder sang "A New Life" and "Someone Like You" to rapturous audience appreciation.

JELLY'S LAST JAM (26 APRIL 1992, VIRGINIA, 569 PERFORMANCES). Music by Jelly Roll Morton, lyrics by Susan Birkenhead, written and directed by George C. Wolfe, musical adaptation and additional music composed by Luther Henderson. A musical based on the life and work of early jazz musician Jelly Roll Morton, *Jelly's Last Jam* featured **Gregory Hines** in the title role. The show opens in a nightclub between heaven and hell: It is Morton's last day on earth, and Chimney Man (Keith David), a figure representing death, explores his past. It is a frank portrait of an unkind man, but Hines is appealing and made Morton somewhat sympathetic. The production was full of innovative treatments, such as when Morton starts an affair with Anita (**Tonya Pinkins**), a brash nightclub owner. Their first night of passion occurs as the "Hunnies," a Greek chorus of three females, comments on the action while on stage with the lovers. Most of the music was based on Morton's compositions through careful arrangements by Luther Henderson and with Susan Birkenhead's lyrics. Critical response to *Jelly's Last Jam* was mixed; **Frank Rich**, writing in the *New York Times*, was among the kinder critics, calling the show, and especially act 1, "an attempt to remake the Broadway musical in a mythic, African-American image." *See also* AFRICAN AMERICAN MUSICALS.

JEROME ROBBINS' BROADWAY **(26 FEBRUARY 1989, IMPER-IAL, 633 PERFORMANCES).** Music and lyrics by many writers and composers, choreographed and directed by **Jerome Robbins**. A **jukebox musical** consisting of dances taken from throughout Robbins's Broadway career, this production was a substantial hit. The expense of mounting it, however, caused the backers to lose half of their $8 million investment, even after its 18-month run. The show included 15 numbers drawn from *On the Town*, *Fiddler on the Roof*, *A Funny Thing Happened on the Way to the Forum*, *Peter Pan*, *West Side Story*, *Billion Dollar Baby*, *High Button Shoes*, *Gypsy*, and *The King and I*, as well as a number called "Mr. Monotony," which was cut from two **Irving Berlin** musicals during tryouts. **Frank Rich** wrote a long review of the show in the *New York Times* in which he said he savored nearly every moment. He noted that the show recalled "a vanished musical theater" but had "such youthful exuberance" that one almost dreams "that a new generation of Broadway babies may yet be born."

JERSEY BOYS **(6 NOVEMBER 2005, AUGUST WILSON, 481 PERFORMANCES AS OF 31 DECEMBER 2006).** Music by Bob Gaudio, lyrics by Bob Crewe, book by Marshall Brickman and Rick Elice. A **jukebox musical** whose book is a musical biography of Frankie Valli and The Four Seasons, the show includes covers of many of its subjects' famous songs, including "Sherry," "Can't Take My Eyes Off You," and the finale, "Who Loves You." *Jersey Boys* won the 2006 **Tony Award** for Best Musical, and falsetto-singing John Lloyd Young, who played Valli, won the Tony Award for Best Actor in a Musical.

JESUS CHRIST SUPERSTAR **(12 OCTOBER 1971, MARK HELLINGER, 711 PERFORMANCES).** Music by **Andrew Lloyd Webber**, lyrics by **Tim Rice**, conceived and directed by **Tom O'Horgan**. Existing first as a concept album, then as a concert, the show's plot concerned the last seven days in the life of Jesus (Jeff Fenholt), in particular exploring his relationships with Mary Magdalene (Yvonne Elliman) and Judas (**Ben Vereen**). Although some conservative Christians protested that the show was blasphemous and Jewish groups found elements of anti-Semitism, *Jesus Christ Super-*

star made a large splash in the popular culture of the day, and has remained in the repertory. Despite the already popular album, director Tom O'Horgan, famous for his avant-garde work on *Hair*, made sure that the production would be remembered as well. In addition to spectacular staging, such as Jesus on the cross flying over the audience at the end, the singers used handheld microphones, which maintained the spirit of a rock concert. Although billed as a **rock opera**, the show includes a variety of musical styles. The title song, which became hugely popular, was more of a gospel tune, and Mary Magdalene's famous ballad "I Don't Know How to Love Him" is in the spirit of folk music, but with a pop closing. "Everything's Alright" is soft rock, and the outrageously campy "Herod's Song" has roots in **vaudeville**. The character of Judas usually expresses himself in harder rock, as in the song "Damned for All Time." **Clive Barnes**, writing in the *New York Times*, found Lloyd Webber to be a talented musician and believed that the score is one of the finest for an English show in a long time. He is less sanguine about Rice's lyrics, which he calls "doggerel." The 1973 film featured Ted Neeley and Carl Anderson, and the 2000 video version starred Glenn Carter and Jerome Pradon.

JOHN, ELTON (BORN REGINALD KENNETH DWIGHT, 1947–). English pop-rock singer-songwriter who was a dominant force in rock music during the 1970s and who, with lyricist **Tim Rice**, wrote songs for the film and subsequent **Disney**-produced Broadway musical *The Lion King* (1997). Also with Rice, he wrote music for another Disney musical, *Aida* (2000), for which he and Rice won a **Tony Award** for Best Original Score. *Lestat* (2006), based on the Anne Rice vampire novels, was a failure. He also wrote music for the London West End production of *Billy Elliot: The Musical* (2005).

JOHNNY JOHNSON **(19 NOVEMBER 1936, 44TH STREET, 68 PERFORMANCES).** Music by **Kurt Weill**, lyrics and book by Paul Green, staged by Lee Strasberg, produced by the Group Theatre. A meritorious antiwar fable that was produced by a noted left-wing company and which never found an audience, *Johnny Johnson* was the first American production for which Kurt Weill, recently arrived in the United States, wrote the score. It showed the serious intentions and theatricality of his music. The title character (Russell Collins) enlists in World War I, which causes him many problems because of his innocence and good character. Johnson ends up in an asylum, and ultimately returns to his hometown to sell toys of a peaceful nature. *New York Times* critic Brooks Atkinson, a lover of experimental works, called the production "the first departure from polite mediocrity of the season," but added that "new forms cannot be created overnight."

JOHNS, GLYNIS (1923–). South African-born actress who created the role of Desiree Armfeldt in *A Little Night Music* (1973), for which she won a Tony Award and a Drama Desk Award.

JOLSON, AL (BORN ASA YOELSON, 1886–1950). Leading singer and actor of the early 20th century, Jolson starred in revues and musical comedies produced by the Shuberts. Billed as "The World's Greatest Entertainer," Jolson was the first Jewish actor to become a mainstream star in America. His trademark character was the servant, Gus, which he performed in blackface. Jolson played Gus in *The Honeymoon Express* (1913), *Robinson Crusoe, Jr.* (1916), *Sinbad* (1918), and *Bombo* (1921). Each of these shows, even though they featured other cast members and specially written scores, were vehicles for Jolson, and most of the songs he sang were interpolations. He starred in *The Jazz Singer* (1927), one of the earliest "talkies," and went on to a successful film career. Among the songs he made famous were "You Made Me Love You (I Didn't Want to Do It)," "Rock-a-Bye Your Baby with a Dixie Melody," "Swanee" (by George Gershwin), "April Showers," "Toot, Toot, Tootsie, Goodbye," "California, Here I Come," and "Mammy."

JONES, DEAN (1931–). Actor who was famously replaced by Larry Kert as Robert in *Company* (1970) after just two weeks in the role. Jones had already recorded the cast album when the change was made. He is most famous for his appearances in Disney films of the 1960s and 1970s, including *The Love Bug* series.

JONES, TOM (1928–). Lyricist, librettist, and director whose Broadway collaborations with composer Harvey Schmidt include the lyrics for *110 in the Shade* (1963), book and lyrics for *I Do! I Do!*

(1966), and book, lyrics, and direction for *Celebration* (1969). He also wrote book and lyrics for the **off-Broadway** phenomenon *The Fantasticks* (1960).

***JOSEPH AND THE AMAZING TECHNICOLOR DREAMCOAT* (27 JANUARY 1982, ROYALE, 747 PERFORMANCES).** Music by **Andrew Lloyd Webber**, lyrics by **Tim Rice**. A work that started as a brief children's show for a London school in 1968, *Joseph and the Amazing Technicolor Dreamcoat* was later expanded and became increasingly famous after its creators went on to write *Jesus Christ Superstar* and *Evita*. The show opened off-Broadway at the Entermedia Theater on 18 November 1981 and moved uptown to the Royale, where it ran for almost two years. Sung throughout, it faithfully tells the story of Joseph and his brothers with a modern flair that offers a veritable tour of popular musical styles. The Narrator (**Laurie Beechman**) keeps the show moving forward and plays the largest role. Joseph (Bill Hutton) receives the special coat from his father, but his 11 envious brothers sell him into slavery. He ends up serving the Egyptian Pharaoh (Tom Carder), an Elvis impersonator, and saves Egypt from the effects of a famine. Joseph finally gives his family food and moves Jacob and his children to Egypt. It is a breezy and somewhat satirical look at the famous story, and, as Mel Gussow reported in the *New York Times*, "both a pop opera and a Sunday School pageant." He describes several songs along with their musical inspiration, including the country-western "One More Angel in Heaven" and the French cabaret style "Those Canaan Days." The show's big ballads included the optimistic "Any Dream Will Do" and the intense "Close Every Door."

***JUBILEE* (12 OCTOBER 1935, IMPERIAL, 169 PERFORMANCES).** Music and lyrics by **Cole Porter**, book by **Moss Hart**, staged and lighted by **Hassard Short**, dances arranged by **Albertina Rasch**, produced by **Sam H. Harris** and **Max Gordon**. King George V's Silver Jubilee in England inspired Hart to write a story about another royal family that reigned for 25 years. This family flees a potential rebellion and all its members takes the opportunity to live incognito and realize their dreams. The King (Melville Cooper) plays parlor games while his wife (Mary Boland) flirts with a movie ape-man inspired by Johnny Weismuller. The Princess (Margaret Adams) has a romance with a writer much like **Noel Coward** (Derek Williams), and the Prince (Charles Walters) takes a famous dancer to the Café Martinique where they perform the famous "Begin the Beguine." The family's true identities emerge, however, and they return to their royal lives. Critics, including **Brooks Atkinson** of the *New York Times*, liked *Jubilee*. He called it a "rapturous masquerade" and found the story to be "an excellent fable" for musicalization. Besides "Begin The Beguine," the score included the Porter classics "Just One of Those Things" and "Why Shouldn't I?"

JUKEBOX MUSICAL/ANTHOLOGY MUSICAL. A show that features preexistent music, usually associated with the same creators or performers, which is woven around a thin plot. In order to market a Broadway musical to a larger audience, producers sometimes turn to well-known music and capitalize on the fame of a particular artist. Examples include *Jelly's Last Jam* (Jelly Roll Morton), *Mamma Mia!* (ABBA), *Movin' Out* (Billy Joel), *All Shook Up* (Elvis), *Lennon* (John Lennon), and *The Times They Are a'Changin'* (Bob Dylan). The combination of popular musical numbers and a thin plot resemble the **revue**, but at the same time, the live performance aspects, usually with hyperamplification, often strive for the aesthetic of a rock concert.

JULIA, RAUL (1940–1994). Puerto Rican-born stage and screen actor whose Broadway musical credits include the **rock musicals** *Two Gentlemen of Verona* (1971) and *Via Galactica* (1972), Charley in the 1974 **revival** of *Where's Charley?* (1974), and Macheath in the 1976 revival of *The Threepenny Opera*. He received tremendous accolades as Guido Contini in *Nine* (1982) and played Don Quixote/Cervantes in the 1992 revival of *Man of La Mancha*. His suave looks gave him an enticing charm that is readily apparent in his portrayal of Gomez Addams in the first two "Addams Family" films.

***JUMBO* (16 NOVEMBER 1935, HIPPODROME, 233 PERFORMANCES).** Music by **Richard Rodgers**, lyrics by **Lorenz Hart**, libretto by Ben Hecht and Charles MacArthur, entire production staged by **John Murray Anderson**, book directed by **George Abbott**, produced by **Billy Rose**. A **musical comedy** that included an entire circus and was staged in the enormous and renovated but doomed Hippodrome, *Jumbo* was a hugely expensive show that could not recoup its investment even after a seven-month run. The plot involved a failing circus run by John A. Considine (Arthur Sinclair), who has to surrender his troupe to his rival, Matthew Mulligan (W. J. McCarthy). In true musical comedy fashion, Considine's daughter (Gloria Grafton) then falls in love with McCarthy's son (Donald Novis). Considine's press agent, Claudius B. Bowers (**Jimmy Durante**), more or less solves his client's problems. Billy Rose altered the Hippodrome's orchestra seating to install a circus tent. Futhermore, he included many real circus acts with animals galore, and thus sent his costs through the roof. **Brooks Atkinson** wrote in the *New York Times* that *Jumbo* was "one of the most extravagant, crack-brained works of foolishness the town has devised in years." Rodgers and Hart's score included such fine songs as "The Most Beautiful Girl in the World," "Little Girl Blue," and "My Romance."

– K –

KAHN, MADELINE (BORN MADELINE GAIL WOLFSON, 1942–1999). Comic actress who played Goldie in *Two by Two* (1970), topping her song "The Golden Ram" with a memorable high C, and Lily Garland in *On the Twentieth Century* (1978). She is also known for her work on film, including her rendition of "Ah, Sweet Mystery of Life" (from **Victor Herbert**'s *Naughty Marietta*) in *Young Frankenstein* (1974).

KÁLMÁN, EMMERICH (1882–1953). Hungarian **operetta** composer whose works often appeared on Broadway in English-language adaptations, in the first third of the 20th century. His shows (with the years of their Broadway productions) include *The Gay Hussars* (1909), *Sari* (1914, 1930), *Countess Maritza* (1926, 1928), and *The Circus Princess* (1927).

KANDER, JOHN (1927–). Composer who, with longtime lyricist **Fred Ebb**, made his Broadway debut in 1965 with *Flora, The Red*

Menace, which starred **Liza Minnelli**, an actress whose career has been strongly linked to songs and shows by Kander and Ebb. The songwriting team's first major hit was *Cabaret* (1966), followed by *The Happy Time* (1968), *70, Girls, 70* (1971), *Chicago* (1975), *The Act* (1977), *Woman of the Year* (1981), *The Rink* (1984), *Kiss of the Spider Woman* (1993, starring **Chita Rivera**), and *Steel Pier* (1997). Although Kander writes convincingly in many idioms, he is particularly strong when it comes to evoking musical styles of the 1920s and 1930s in more contemporary contexts.

KATINKA **(23 DECEMBER 1915, 45TH STREET, 220 PERFORMANCES).** Music by **Rudolf Friml**, book and lyrics by **Otto Harbach**, produced by **Arthur Hammerstein**. An **operetta** in the Central European mold, *Katinka* featured a romance between two Russians—Katinka (May Naudain) and Ivan (Samuel Ash)—European settings (Yalta, Stamboul, and Vienna), mistaken identities, and **Orientalist** features. Extended dance specialties appear in each of the three acts, and the musical score includes "Allah's Holiday" with its predominantly pentatonic melody, Ivan's lyrical "My Paradise," Katinka and Ivan's romantic waltz "'Tis the End," and the title character's lighthearted "Rackety-Coo."

KAUFMAN, GEORGE S. (1889–1961). In his varied career as a writer, actor, and director, Kaufman directed several important musicals, including *Animal Crackers*, *Of Thee I Sing*, and *Guys and Dolls*.

KAYE, DANNY (BORN DAVID DANIEL KAMINSKI, 1913–1987). Though known principally for his work on film and television, the comic actor, singer, and dancer dazzled audiences with his performance of "Tchaikovsky" in **Kurt Weill** and **Ira Gershwin**'s *Lady in the Dark* (1941), in which he recited the names of 54 Russian composers in 38 seconds. Other Broadway credits include *The Straw Hat Revue* (1939), Jerry Walker in *Let's Face It!* (1941), and Noah in *Two by Two* (1970).

KAYE, JUDY (1948–). Operatic soprano with a comic flair who won a **Tony Award** for her portrayal of opera diva Carlotta in *The Phan-*

tom of the Opera. She also appeared as Emma Goldman in *Ragtime*, Rosie in *Mamma Mia!*, and questionable soprano Florence Foster Jenkins in the play *Souvenir* (2005).

KAYE, STUBBY (1918–1997). Comic actor who created the role of Nicely-Nicely Johnson in *Guys and Dolls*, stopping the show with "Sit Down, You're Rockin' the Boat." He reprised the role in the 1955 film version. Kaye also created the part of Marryin' Sam in *Lil' Abner* to tremendous popular and critical success.

KELLY, GENE (BORN EUGENE CURRAN KELLY, 1912–1996). Dancer, actor, singer, director, choreographer, and producer known for his athletic dancing style and likable screen characters. He made his Broadway debut as the Secretary to Mr. Goodhue in *Leave It to Me!* (1938) and achieved tremendous fame as Joey Evans in *Pal Joey* (1940). He choreographed *Best Foot Forward* (1941) and directed *Flower Drum Song* (1958). Classic film musicals in which he starred and for which he provided choreography include *Anchors Aweigh* (1945) and *Singin' in the Rain* (1952).

KERN, JEROME (1885–1945). Archetypal composer whose work exemplifies many of the innovations apparent in the Broadway musicals of the 1910s, 1920s, and 1930s. His song "They Didn't Believe Me" from *The Girl from Utah* (1914) garnered him great fame. With **Guy Bolton** and **P. G. Wodehouse**, he created the so-called **Princess Theatre musicals**, a group of **musical comedies** (including *Oh, Boy!* [1917]) that strove for intimacy and immediate appeal. He made Broadway history in 1927 with *Show Boat* (lyrics by **Oscar Hammerstein II**), a work that integrated aspects of musical comedy, **revue**, and **operetta** in both plot and music. He continued to write shows that fused different approaches to musical theater during the early 1930s, such as *The Cat and the Fiddle* (1931), *Music in the Air* (1932), and *Roberta* (1933). While working in Hollywood, he wrote *Very Warm for May* (1939) for Broadway; though the show itself was not a success, it included the classic "All the Things You Are." Kern's songs span the gamut of styles, from the sprightly "Look for the Silver Lining" from *Sally* (1920) to the haunting "Ol' Man River" from *Show Boat* and the same show's classic operetta waltz "You Are

Love." Kern's melodies demonstrate a natural ease and grace that make them extremely popular with singers of all styles as well as with jazz musicians.

KERR, WALTER (1913–1996). Theater critic, librettist, and director. He became theater critic for the *New York Herald Tribune* in 1951, and wrote theater reviews for the *New York Times* from 1966 to 1983. He received the **Pulitzer Prize** for criticism in 1978. He was also active as a creator on Broadway. Kerr wrote the books for the **revues** *Count Me In* (1942), *Sing Out, Sweet Land* (1944), and *Touch and Go* (1949), and also directed *Sing Out, Sweet Land* and *Touch and Go*. He created the book and the lyrics for the **musical comedy** *Goldilocks* (1958), which he also directed. In 1990, the Ritz Theater at 219 W. 48th Street was renamed in his honor.

KERT, LARRY (BORN FREDERICK LAWRENCE KERT, 1930–1991). Before creating the role of Tony in *West Side Story* (1957), Kert appeared in the revues *Tickets, Please!* (1950) and *John Murray Anderson's Almanac* (1953). He took over the role of Robert from **Dean Jones** in the original production of *Company* (1970) soon after the show opened and became the first **replacement** cast member to be nominated for a **Tony Award**.

***KID BOOTS* (31 DECEMBER 1923, EARL CARROLL, 479 PER-FORMANCES).** Music by **Harry Tierney**, lyrics by Joseph Mc-Carthy, book by William Anthony McGuire and **Otto Harbach**, produced by **Florenz Ziegfeld**. A vehicle for **Eddie Cantor**, *Kid Boots* was the tale of a caddy master (Cantor) at a Palm Beach golf club who is also a bootlegger and a purveyor of less-than-honest golf balls. The club champion ends up using one of the "special" balls in an important match. Much of the unsigned *New York Times* review was about Cantor, who seemed "a bit more fervent and wide-eyed than he ever has before." The critic reported that Tierney's score included "winners," but no truly popular songs emerged from the show.

KIDD, MICHAEL (1919–). Director-choreographer, dancer, and producer who appeared as The Gangster in the one-act ballet *Filling Station* (1939) and other dance roles before choreographing *Finian's*

Rainbow in 1947 and beginning a career as a choreographer, director-choreographer, or director that lasted until *The Goodbye Girl* in 1993. Credits include *Love Life* (1948), *Guys and Dolls* (1950), *Can-Can* (1953), *Wildcat* (1960), *The Rothschilds* (1970), and the 1980 revival of *The Music Man*, but many consider his greatest creative success to be *Li'l Abner* (1956) with its exuberant Sadie Hawkins' Day scene.

KILEY, RICHARD (1922–1999). Actor with a resonant baritone voice who created the Caliph in *Kismet* (1953), Tom Baxter in *Redhead* (1959), David Jordan in *No Strings* (1962), and Stan the Shpieler in *I Had a Ball* (1964) before immortalizing Don Quixote/Cervantes in *Man of La Mancha* (1965). He reprised the landmark role in 1972 and 1977 Broadway revivals. He won **Tony Awards** for *Redhead* and *Man of La Mancha*.

***THE KING AND I* (29 MARCH 1951, ST. JAMES, 1,246 PER-FORMANCES).** Music by **Richard Rodgers**, lyrics and book by **Oscar Hammerstein II**, choreographed by **Jerome Robbins**, produced by Rodgers and Hammerstein. *The King and I* was Rodgers and Hammerstein's fifth show and one of their greatest successes. The story was based on Margaret Landon's novel *Anna and the King of Siam* and two memoirs by Anna Leonowens, the English teacher who worked at the court of King Mongkut. **Gertrude Lawrence** brought the idea for a show based on Leonowens's life to Rodgers and Hammerstein, asking them to make it into a star vehicle for her. The show also needed a strong male lead, and they offered the part to **Alfred Drake**, **Noel Coward**, and **Rex Harrison**, who all turned it down. Finally, Rodgers and Hammerstein found their king in **Yul Brynner**, a Russian/Mongolian folksinger with a fierce stage presence. In out-of-town tryouts *The King and I* score went through numerous alterations, including the elimination of three songs and the addition of four others.

The story is of British schoolteacher Anna Leonowens who journeys with her son, Louis, to teach the children of King Mongkut. Anna and the King are both strong-willed and match wits over issues including slavery and polygamy. The show ends with the King's death, surrounded by his wives, children, and Anna. The tragic subplot of Tuptim, the King's newest concubine, and her lover, Lun Tha, balances the lightheartedness created by the vast array of children. *The King and I* opened on Broadway to enthusiastic reviews. **Brooks Atkinson** of the *New York Times* found it "an original and beautiful excursion into the rich splendors of the Far East," that had a romantic score and exquisite dancing. Gertrude Lawrence played Anna until she became too ill to continue; she died at the age of 54, 17 months into the run. Brynner became intrinsically associated with the part of the King for 34 years, reprising it in the 1956 film version and numerous revivals. He played the role in 4,625 performances, and won both a **Tony** and an Oscar for his portrayal. The 1996 Broadway **revival** starred **Donna Murphy** and Lou Diamond Phillips.

The score is filled with exquisite songs, including Anna's "I Whistle a Happy Tune" and "Getting to Know You," precursors of "My Favorite Things" and "Do, Re, Mi" in *The Sound of Music*. She also sings the waltz "Hello, Young Lovers," where she compares the young love of Tuptim and Lun Tha with her relationship with her dead husband. Since the show was a vehicle for Gertrude Lawrence, the actress sang most of the show's fine solo numbers. "The Small House of Uncle Thomas," based on *Uncle Tom's Cabin*, is an imaginative ballet with Asian overtones created by Jerome Robbins and dance arranger **Trude Rittmann** that is extremely important in the narrative because of its slavery-related theme. Anna and the King meet as intellectual and emotional equals in "Shall We Dance?" The two leads never kiss in the show; instead, they meet in the world of the dance. Rodgers and Hammerstein used music to define characters in extremely impressive ways. For example, the King never really sings—he intones his songs, with the melody played in the orchestra, as in "A Puzzlement." Furthermore, the Siamese culture is represented by the orchestra itself—no words or songs, but rather sounds. The original cast also included Dorothy Sarnoff playing the Crown Prince Chulalongkorn's mother, Lady Thiang, who sang the vocally demanding "Something Wonderful," along with **Doretta Morrow** as Tuptim and Larry Douglas as Lun Tha, who sang the haunting duet "We Kiss in a Shadow."

The plot of *The King and I* has been scrutinized for its inaccurate and largely unfavorable impression of Siam and its great kings Mongkut and Chulalongkorn and has also been interpreted as an allegory for Western influence in Asia. *See also* ORIENTALISM.

KISMET **(3 DECEMBER 1953, ZIEGFELD, 583 PERFOR-MANCES).** Music by Alexander Borodin, musical adaptation and lyrics by **Robert Wright** and **George Forrest**, book by Charles Lederer and Luther Davis, choreography by **Jack Cole**. Based on Edward Knoblock's 1911 play of the same name, *Kismet* starred **Alfred Drake** as "A Public Poet" named Hajj, who in a single day becomes an Emir and sees his daughter, Marsinah (**Doretta Morrow**), marry the Caliph (**Richard Kiley**). *New York Times* critic **Brooks Atkinson** was not amused, feeling that the show was "assembled from a storehouse of spare parts," which is "no substitute for creation." He savaged the lyrics, calling them "some of the most fearful poetry of our time." Wright and Forrest created *Kismet*'s score from the melodies of Russian composer Alexander Borodin, similar to what they had done for *Song of Norway* with Edvard Grieg's music. What Atkinson might have missed in his opening-night review is the beauty of Borodin's exotic melodies, which make songs like "Strangers in Paradise" and "Baubles, Bangles, and Beads" some of the loveliest ever heard on the Broadway stage. *See also* ORIENTALISM.

KING, DENNIS (BORN DENNIS PRATT, 1897–1971). English-born singing actor with a resonant baritone voice who created the male leads in **Rudolf Friml**'s three principal **operettas** from the 1920s: Jim Kenyon in *Rose Marie* (1924), François Villon in *The Vagabond King* (1925), and D'Artagnan in *The Three Musketeers* (1928). He also created Count Willy Palarffi in **Rodgers and Hart**'s *I Married An Angel* (1938) and appeared on stage and screen in numerous nonmusical roles.

KISS ME, KATE **(30 DECEMBER 1948, NEW CENTURY, 1,077 PERFORMANCES).** Music and lyrics by **Cole Porter**, book by **Bella and Samuel Spewack**, choreography by Hanya Holm. A fine musical combining Shakespeare's *The Taming of the Shrew* with a plot involving the performers appearing in it, *Kiss Me, Kate* was the highlight of the latter part of Porter's career. With a tuneful, varied score, a wonderful book, and lively dances, *Kiss Me, Kate* was one of the best integrated musical plays of the period. Each of the characters seemed to be a living, breathing person who brought realistic, if humorous, reactions to situations. **Alfred Drake** played Fred Graham/Petruchio, the lead and director in a musical adaptation of *The*

Taming of the Shrew that is opening that day in Baltimore. *Kiss Me, Kate* shifts between the production itself and the backstage antics. The female lead is his ex-wife Lilli Vanessi/Katherine (**Patricia Morison**). They still love each other but constantly argue, and Lilli is now engaged to someone else. Following dictates of **musical comedy**, the secondary pair of lovers are Bill Calhoun (Harold Lang) and Lois Lane (Lisa Kirk), both of whom are actors in the troupe. Bill has lost all of his money while gambling and signed Fred's name to an IOU. Two gangsters come to the theater to collect their money. In the end, Lilli and Fred recognize their love for each other, as do Bill and Lois, and the gangsters announce that their boss has been killed, erasing the debt, and confess their new interest in Shakespeare. Porter's score includes the energetic opening number, "Another Op'nin', Another Show," the sultry "Too Darn Hot," the **operetta**-style waltz "So in Love," and the riotous "Brush Up Your Shakespeare." Songs that take place within the musical version of *The Taming of the Shrew* include Katherine's "I Hate Men" and "I Am Ashamed That Women Are So Simple," Petruccio's "Were Thine That Special Face" and "Where Is the Life That Late I Led," and the ensemble numbers "I've Come to Wive It Wealthily in Padua" and "Kiss Me, Kate." **Brian Stokes Mitchell** and **Marin Mazzie** starred in the 1999 Broadway **revival**.

KISS OF THE SPIDER WOMAN (**3 MAY 1993, BROADHURST, 906 PERFORMANCES**). Music by **John Kander**, lyrics by **Fred Ebb**, book by **Terrence McNally**, directed by **Harold Prince**. Based on the novel by Manuel Puig (which also was the basis for the 1985 film starring William Hurt), *Kiss of the Spider Woman* told the story of the homosexual window dresser Molina (**Brent Carver**) and the political revolutionary Valentin (**Anthony Crivello**), a character similar to Che Guevara in *Evita*, who are held in the same prison cell in an unnamed Latin American country. To escape the horrors of his reality, Molina retreats into his imagination and dreams about a female film star, Aurora (**Chita Rivera**), whose central role was as a spider woman with a fatal kiss. The plot shifts between the prison and Molina's dream world. Gradually Molina and Valentin become friends and eventually lovers. Upon his release, Molina agrees to try to get a message to Valentin's fellow rebels, but he is caught, tortured, and shot. In the final scene, which takes place in his imagination, he dances a tango with the Spider Woman and receives her kiss as the real-life bullet hits him. **Frank Rich** wrote long and thoughtful review for the *New York Times*, in which he was captivated by "the love affair that Mr. Prince masterminds between Chita Rivera and the audience." Rivera's show-stopping numbers included "Where You Are" and "Kiss of the Spider Woman." Extremely effective duets between Molina and his muse such as "Morphine Tango" and "Gimme Love" demonstrated Prince's innovative approach to staging. The theme of **social justice**, an important dimension of the show, is strongest in the anthem "The Day After That," the progeny of "One Day More" from *Les Misérables*. *See also* HOMOSEXUALITY.

KLEBAN, EDWARD (1939–1987). Lyricist for *A Chorus Line* (1975), a show that won **Tony Awards**, the **Pulitzer Prize**, and other honors. In 2000, the musical *A Class Act*, a musical biography of Kleban featuring songs with music and lyrics by its subject, opened at the Manhattan Theatre Club. It transferred to Broadway in 2001, and 14 years after his death, Kleban received a Tony nomination for Best Original Score.

KLINE, KEVIN (1947–). Actor whose performance in the 1981 revival of *The Pirates of Penzance* earned him a **Tony Award**. Other musical credits include Jamie Lockhart in *The Robber Bridegroom* (1975) and Bruce Granit in *On the Twentieth Century* (1978). He played **Cole Porter** in the 2004 biopic *De-Lovely*.

KNICKERBOCKER HOLIDAY **(19 OCTOBER 1938, ETHEL BARRYMORE, 168 PERFORMANCES).** Music by **Kurt Weill**, lyrics and book by **Maxwell Anderson**, staged by **Joshua Logan**. Based on Washington Irving's *The History of New York by Diedrich Knickerbocker*, *Knickerbocker Holiday* is most famous today for the hit "September Song." Anderson was a fine playwright (*High Tor*), but seems to have lacked the necessary lightness of spirit for **musical comedy**. *Knickerbocker Holiday* starred Walter Huston as Pieter Stuyvesant, the famed governor of 17th-century Manhattan. He is part of a love triangle, and at the end lets the woman leave with the other man, whom he has saved from the gallows. The character of Washington Irving (**Ray Middleton**) appeared as a narrator. The book took satirical views of the New Deal and rise of Fascism, and according to **Brooks Atkinson** in the *New York Times*, Weill's score was "lively and theatre-wise."

KUHN, JUDY (1958–). Classically trained soprano who played several roles in *The Mystery of Edwin Drood* (1985) and Bella Cohen in *Rags* (1986) before creating Cosette on Broadway in *Les Misérables* (1987) and receiving a **Tony Award** nomination. She reprised the role in the 10th Anniversary Concert production at the Royal Albert Hall in London. Kuhn also played Florence in *Chess* (1988) and Amalia Blash in the 1993 **revival** of *She Loves Me*.

– L –

LA CHIUSA, MICHAEL JOHN (1962–). Composer whose musical language is characterized by a sophisticated, nearly operatic, and at times harmonically dissonant complexity. His Broadway musicals include *Marie Christine* (1999), produced by **Lincoln Center Theater**, and *The Wild Party* (2000). Through his carefully constructed and musically integrated scores, he effectively captures the tragic themes and personalities that fill his shows.

LADY, BE GOOD! **(1 DECEMBER 1924, LIBERTY, 330 PERFORMANCES).** Music by **George Gershwin**, lyrics by **Ira Gershwin**, book by **Guy Bolton** and **Fred Thompson**, produced by **Alex A. Aarons** and **Vinton Freedley**. A show that has reached iconic status for having **Fred** and **Adele Astaire** in the cast and the inclusion of several Gershwin hits, especially "Fascinating Rhythm." After being evicted from their apartment, the brother-and-sister dance team, Dick and Susie (played by the Astaires), have a series of comic adventures. Far more important than the plot was the ecstatic reception of the Astaires and a score that came to represent the "Jazz Age" for the white audiences that frequented Broadway musicals. In addition to "Fascinating Rhythm," the score included "So Am I" and the title song. The show originally included "The Man I Love," but the song did not survive tryouts. The unnamed *New York Times* critic noted that the score included "a number of tunes that the unmusical and serious-minded will find hard to get rid of."

LADY IN THE DARK (23 JANUARY 1941, ALVIN, 467 PERFOR-MANCES). Music by **Kurt Weill**, lyrics by **Ira Gershwin**, book and staging by **Moss Hart**, produced by **Sam H. Harris**. An enduring myth of Broadway is that the **musical play** sprang nearly to life in *Show Boat* in 1927, and then remained dormant until *Oklahoma!* in 1943. This fallacy ignores a number of shows from between these milestones with solid integration of plot and music, including *Lady in the Dark*. The show was especially noteworthy for the manner in which musical numbers were integrated into the storyline and for its modern plot concerning psychoanalysis.

Liza Elliott (**Gertrude Lawrence**) is a fashion editor who cannot make up her mind either about what to choose for a particular magazine cover or whom she wants to marry. She visits a therapist, Dr. Brooks (Donald Randolph), and together they investigate her feelings about the four men in her life: Kendall Nesbitt (Bert Lytell), the married man with whom she lives; Randy Curtis (Victor Mature), a superficial Hollywood star; Randall Paxton (**Danny Kaye**), the fashion photographer at her magazine; and Charlie Johnson (Macdonald Carey), her feisty advertising manager. Liza confesses to the therapist that she has been having disturbing dreams and that a song keeps playing in her mind, "My Ship." With the exception of this recurring song, all of the show's musical numbers occur during staged dream sequences. The "Circus Dream" featured two of the show's extraordinary songs. First, Kaye performed "Tchaikovsky," a tour-de-force patter routine in which he recited the tongue-twisting names of 54 Russian composers in a mere 38 seconds. Lawrence followed immediately with the ballad "Jenny" in a rendition filled with sexual innuendo. The two performers competed night after night on who received the greater applause for their respective numbers. Liza finally decides that Charlie is her true love, since he is the only one who can complete her song "My Ship." ("Ah, Sweet Mystery of Life" fulfills a similar function in **Victor Herbert**'s *Naughty Marietta*.) **Brooks Atkinson** raved in his *New*

York Times review, calling Hart's book "a dramatic story about the anguish of a human being," leavened by the author's typical humor. He did not think that anyone except Lawrence "could play a virtuoso part of such length and variety."

THE LADY OF THE SLIPPER (28 OCTOBER 1912, GLOBE, 232 PERFORMANCES). Music by **Victor Herbert**, lyrics by James O'Dea, book by Anne Caldwell and Lawrence McCarty, produced by **Charles Dillingham**. A version of the Cinderella story conceived for its stars, *The Lady and the Slipper* ran the longest of any of Herbert's shows on Broadway. Elsie Janis played the young lady who wants to go to the ball, and among her assistants were Punks (Dave Montgomery) and Spooks (Fred Stone), said to be "from the cornfield," recalling the characters that the famous team played in *The Wizard of Oz* (1903). The three lead actors were hardly the best of singers and were more famous as dancers, so Herbert wrote to their various talents, and there was plenty of dancing. The unsigned *New York Times* reviewer praised many aspects of the production and called Stone a "marvel of agility" who does things without regard to safety, including grabbing the ascending curtain, taking a swan dive, and "reversing himself only just in time to avoid the hard knock in the place where they kill rabbits." The critic panned the book as "humorless," but liked the show overall. Notable songs in the score included "A Little Girl at Home," "Princess of Far Away," "All Hallowe'en," and "Meow! Meow! Meow!"

LAHR, BERT (BORN IRVING LAHRHEIM, 1895–1967). Known for playing the Cowardly Lion in the 1939 film *The Wizard of Oz*, Lahr was a star of Broadway **revues** and **musical comedies**. Credits included *Hold Everything!* (1928), *Flying High* (1930), *Life Begins at 8:40* (1934), *George White's Scandals* (1935), *The Show Is On* (1936), *Du Barry Was a Lady* (1939), *Seven Lively Arts* (1944), *Two on the Aisle* (1951), *The Girls Against the Boys* (1959), and *Foxy* (1964). He won a **Tony Award** for *Foxy*.

LA, LA, LUCILLE (26 MAY 1919, HENRY MILLER, 104 PERFORMANCES). Music by **George Gershwin**, lyrics by Arthur J. Jackson and **B. G. De Sylva**, book by Fred Jackson. Famous as the first Broadway show with a complete score by Gershwin, *La, La, Lu-*

cille seemed headed to a successful run but was canceled due to an Actor's Equity strike. In the show, creditors hound dentist John Smith (Jack Hazzard) to pay his bills. His aunt, who objects to his marriage to Lucille (Janet Velie), supposedly dies, and her will stipulates that John will inherit a fortune if he will divorce Lucille. The couple decides to divorce and then remarry, but runs into comical problems as they try to feign John's unfaithfulness. The aunt shows up alive, saying that she had only been testing the couple. Gershwin's score actually figured little in the reviews of the show. The anonymous reviewer for the *New York Times* described the show as "the incarnation of jazz," but did not mention the composer's name. Major songs were "The Best of Everything" and "Nobody But You."

LANE, BURTON (1912–1997). Composer whose melodic gifts are particularly evident in his scores for *Finian's Rainbow* (1947) and *On a Clear Day You Can See Forever* (1965). He also contributed to the *Earl Carroll Vanities* (1931) and wrote the ill-fated musical *Carmelina* (1979) with Alan Jay Lerner.

LANE, NATHAN (1956–). Comic singing actor whose portrayal of Nathan Detroit in the 1992 revival of *Guys and Dolls* garnered him tremendous praise. He won a **Tony Award** for playing Prologus/Pseudolus in *A Funny Thing Happened on the Way to the Forum* (1996 revival) and another for his creation of Max Bialystock in *The Producers* (2001), a role he reprised in the 2005 film version. He played Dionysos in the **Lincoln Center Theater**'s production of **Stephen Sondheim**'s *The Frogs* (2004), which carried the remark, "even more freely adapted by Nathan Lane."

LANSBURY, ANGELA (1925–). British actress who had a prolific career in Hollywood before becoming a major Broadway star in the 1960s. She made her Broadway musical debut in **Stephen Sondheim**'s *Anyone Can Whistle* (1964), and went from success to success, starring in *Mame* (1966), *Dear World* (1969), *Gypsy* (1974 revival), and *Sweeney Todd: The Demon Barber of Fleet Street* (1979). A four-time **Tony Award** winner, Lansbury emphasizes the human qualities of her characters, and uses her flexible character voice to give musical distinction to the roles she plays.

LAPINE, JAMES (1949–). Director and librettist who worked with **Stephen Sondheim** on *Sunday in the Park with George* (1984), *Into the Woods* (1987), and *Passion* (1994) and with **William Finn** on *Falsettos* (1992). He and Sondheim shared a **Pulitzer Prize** for *Sunday*. Lapine received a **Tony Award** for *Into the Woods* and created new staging for the show's 2002 **revival**. He also directed *Amour* (2002), the Michel Legrand French-themed musical, and *The 25th Annual Putnam County Spelling Bee* (2005).

LARSON, JONATHAN (1960–1996). Composer, lyricist, and librettist whose passions for rock music and musical theater culminated in *Rent*. During rehearsals for a production of *Rent* at the New York Theatre Workshop, Larson died suddenly and tragically of a brain aneurysm. His untimely death drew great media attention, and *Rent*, with its rave **off-Broadway** reviews, raced to Broadway that year. Larson received the **Pulitzer Prize** and **Tony Awards** for Best Book, Best Score, and Best Musical, all posthumously. His autobiographical musical *tick . . . tick . . . BOOM* played off-Broadway in 2001.

THE LAST SWEET DAYS OF ISAAC **(26 JANUARY 1970, EAST SIDE, 485 PERFORMANCES).** Music by Nancy Ford, lyrics and book by Gretchen Cryer. Despite the success of *Hair*, Broadway creators were slow to incorporate rock music in subsequent shows. **Rock musicals** were more plentiful off-Broadway, such as the successful *The Last Sweet Days of Isaac*. The show's concept included strong social commentary, with its characters imprisoned in an elevator during the first act and in a prison cell during the second. It was not depressing, however, with the appealing Austin Pendleton and Fredricka Weber playing the leads. Isaac believes that life has not been lived unless it has been recorded, so he constantly carries a movie camera and tape recorder. An on-stage rock band, The Zeitgeist, added to the show's atmosphere. **Clive Barnes**, writing in the *New York Times*, called the music "tuneful and appealing" and the musical "one of the most preposterous shows in New York and yet also one of the happiest."

LAURENTS, ARTHUR (1918–). Playwright, librettist, and director who created the books for *West Side Story* (1957), *Gypsy* (1959), *Anyone Can Whistle* (1964), *Do I Hear a Waltz?* (1965), *Hallelujah,*

Baby! (1967), *The Madwoman of Central Park West* (1979), and *Nick & Nora* (1991), and received a **Tony Award** for *Hallelujah, Baby!* He directed *I Can Get It for You Wholesale* (1962), *Anyone Can Whistle*, *Gypsy*, *The Madwoman of Central Park West*, *La Cage aux Folles* (1983), and *Nick & Nora*, and won a Tony for *La Cage aux Folles*. His memoir, *Original Story By*, was published in 2000.

LAWRENCE, CAROL (1934–). Lawrence created the youthful role of Maria in *West Side Story* (1957) on Broadway days after her 23rd birthday. She had previously appeared in revues (*Leonard Sillman's New Faces of 1952*, *Ziegfeld Follies* of 1957) and musical comedy as a dancer and singer. Post-Maria roles include Clio Dulaine in *Saratoga* (1959), *Subways Are for Sleeping* (1961), **replacement** She (Agnes) in *I Do! I Do!* (1966), and replacement Spider Woman/ Aurora in *Kiss of the Spider Woman* (1993). The expressiveness and purity of her voice elicited tremendous praise.

LAWRENCE, GERTRUDE (1898–1952). English-born singing actress who created the title role in **George Gershwin**'s *Oh, Kay!* (1926) and introduced such standards as "Someone to Watch Over Me" and "Do, Do, Do." After appearing in straight plays, many with **Noel Coward**, she returned to the world of the Broadway musical with *Lady in the Dark* (1941, music by **Kurt Weill**) as Liza Elliott, singing "My Ship" and "Jenny." In 1951, she created Anna in *The King and I*, a role **Rodgers and Hammerstein** created especially for her. Lawrence had a commanding stage presence that made her one of the leading actresses of her generation.

LAYTON, JOE (1931–1994). Director and choreographer whose credits include *The Sound of Music* (1959), *Once Upon a Mattress* (1959), *Tenderloin* (1960), *No Strings* (1962), *George M!* (1968), *Dear World* (1969), and *Barnum* (1980). He appeared as Greenwich Villager in *Wonderful Town* (1953) and understudied Wreck. He conceived and directed *Two by Two* (1970) and *Bring Back Birdie* (1981, a sequel to *Bye Bye Birdie*). He also directed special performances on Broadway, including *Bette Midler's Clams on the Half Shell Revue* (1975), *An Evening with Diana Ross* (1976), and *An Evening with Harry Connick Jr. and His Orchestra* (1990).

LEAVE IT TO JANE (28 AUGUST 1917, LONGACRE, 167 PER-FORMANCES). Music by **Jerome Kern**, lyrics and book by **Guy Bolton** and **P. G. Wodehouse**. Based on George Ade's play *The College Widow*, *Leave It to Jane* was another successful show from the creators of the famous **Princess Theatre musicals**. Jane (Edith Hallor) is the daughter of the president of Atwater College. As the big football game approaches, Atwater's star player, Billy Bolton (Robert G. Pitkin), seems ready to defect to rival Bingham College. Jane not only wins Billy back to Atwater, for whom he plays on Saturday, but also wins his heart. Kern's score included among its hits the title song, "The Crickets Are Calling," "Cleopatra," and "The Siren's Song."

LEAVE IT TO ME! (9 NOVEMBER 1938, IMPERIAL, 291 PER-FORMANCES). Music and lyrics by **Cole Porter**, book by **Bella and Samuel Spewack**, staged by Samuel Spewack and George Smith, dances and ensemble arranged by **Robert Alton**. Based on the Spewacks' 1932 play *Clear All Wires*, *Leave It to Me!* was a combination of straight **musical comedy** and political satire. **Victor Moore** played Alonso P. Goodhue, a bathtub salesman from Topeka, Kansas, whose ambitious wife (Sophie Tucker) made a large donation to Roosevelt's reelection campaign that resulted in her husband being named Ambassador to the U.S.S.R. Goodhue is unhappy with the new job and tries to cause an international incident so that he gets recalled. When he kicks the Nazi ambassador and tries to shoot a Romanoff (instead hitting a counterrevolutionary), he instead receives tremendous praise. He finally becomes comfortable in the position and works for world peace, and it is because of this agenda that the State Department recalls him. The cast also included **William Gaxton** as an American journalist who tries to discredit Goodhue, and **Mary Martin**, in her Broadway debut, as his secretary. Martin sang "My Heart Belongs to Daddy," a minor striptease number with lyrics filled with double entendres. A fur-clad male chorus (which included **Gene Kelly**) surrounded her on stage. Another highlight was the act 1 finale, during which Walter Armin, as a comic version of Josef Stalin, danced to "The Internationale." Porter's score also included "From Now On" and "Most Gentlemen Don't Like Love." **Brooks Atkinson** liked the show, quipping that the plot might cause problems with Germany and Russia, but "that is a small price to pay for a tumultuous comedy prank in music."

LEHÁR, FRANZ (1870–1948). Composer of Viennese **operetta** whose *The Merry Widow*, when it first appeared in an English-language adaptation on Broadway in 1907, caused a huge sensation and reinvigorated American audiences' interest in Viennese-style operetta. Other Lehár works to appear on Broadway (with the years of their Broadway premieres) include *Gypsy Love* (1911), *The Count of Luxembourg* (1912, 1930), and *Frederika* (1937).

LEIGH, MITCH (BORN IRWIN MICHNICK, 1928–). A composition student of Paul Hindemith at Yale and a jazz musician, Leigh won a **Tony Award** for his most successful Broadway score, *Man of La Mancha* (1965). He also wrote the less-successful musicals *Cry for Us All* (1970), *Saravà* (1979), *Chu Chem* (1989), and *Ain't Broadway Grand* (1993). Leigh has also been active as a director and producer.

***LEND AN EAR* (16 DECEMBER 1948, NATIONAL, 460 PERFORMANCES).** Music, lyrics, and sketches by Charles Gaynor; choreography by **Gower Champion**. A witty **revue** that introduced new stars to Broadway, *Lend an Ear* was a throwback to an earlier Broadway era with its humorous sketches and spoofs. The cast was young and not well known, but included several people who later became stars, including Yvonne Adair, **Carol Channing**, William Eythe, and Gene Nelson.

***LENNON* (14 AUGUST 2005, BROADHURST, 49 PERFORMANCES).** Music and lyrics by John Lennon, book by Don Scardino. Short-lived **jukebox musical** in which a nine-member ensemble and 10-piece onstage band tell the story of John Lennon's life using the legend's own words and music. The show included unpublished songs in addition to well-known numbers such as "Give Peace a Chance" and "Imagine."

LENYA, LOTTE (BORN KAROLINE WILHELMINE BLAMAUER, 1898–1981). Austrian-born actress and wife of **Kurt Weill**

who played Jenny in the 1928 production of *Die Dreigroschenoper* (*The Threepenny Opera*). She won a **Tony Award** when she reprised the role on Broadway in **Marc Blitzstein**'s 1954 adaptation. Lenya created the part of Fraulein Schneider in *Cabaret* (1966) and was known for her distinctive speech-singing style.

LERNER, ALAN JAY (1918–1986). Librettist and lyricist most famous for his collaborations with composer **Alan Jay Lerner** in a team popularly known as **Lerner and Loewe**. Lerner came from a wealthy family, the owners of Lerner Shops, a women's clothing chain. Alan Jay Lerner received a high-quality education at Juilliard, Harvard, and Oxford. His lyrics and librettos possess an extraordinarily fine literary quality and reflect their creator's romantic impulses and utopian vision. Lerner's words move smoothly between spoken dialogue (libretto) and singing (lyrics). He worked with composers other than Lerner, including **Kurt Weill** (*Love Life* [1948]), **Burton Lane** (*On a Clear Day You Can See Forever* [1965] and *Carmelina* [1979]), André Previn (*Coco* [1969]), **Leonard Bernstein** (*1600 Pennsylvania Avenue* [1976]), and **Charles Strouse** (*Dance a Little Closer* [1983]). **Andrew Lloyd Webber** asked Lerner to create lyrics for *The Phantom of the Opera* (1986), but the wordsmith's declining health prohibited him from accepting the offer.

LERNER AND LOEWE. The collaboration of librettist and lyricist **Alan Jay Lerner** and composer **Frederick Loewe** resulted in seven Broadway musicals: *What's Up?* (1943), *The Day Before Spring* (1945), *Brigadoon* (1947), *Paint Your Wagon* (1951), *My Fair Lady* (1956), *Camelot* (1960), and *Gigi* (1973, four new songs for the stage version of their 1958 film musical). Lerner and Loewe musicals possess a strong bond between story and music, and the appearance of Lerner's name before that of Loewe in their collective name reflects the central importance they gave to words in their creative process.

LET 'EM EAT CAKE **(21 OCTOBER 1933, IMPERIAL, 90 PERFORMANCES).** Music by **George Gershwin**, lyrics by **Ira Gershwin**, book by **George S. Kaufman** and **Morrie Ryskind**, book staged by Kaufman, produced by Sam H. Harris. An unsuccessful sequel to *Of Thee I Sing*, *Let 'Em Eat Cake* was still satirical, but the targets were too broad and the mood too dour. President John P. Wintergreen (**William Gaxton**) and Vice President Alexander Throttlebottom (**Victor Moore**) seek reelection but lose. Observing the fascist movements in Italy and Germany with their black and brown shirts, they stage their own revolution with "Maryblue" shirts sewn by Mary Wintergreen (Lois Moran). In act 2, Throttlebottom umpires a baseball game between the Supreme Court and the League of Nations. His calls prove so unpopular that he might face the guillotine, but Mary saves the day by diverting attention with a fashion show. **Brooks Atkinson** of the *New York Times* enjoyed aspects of the show and even called for another sequel, but was distressed by the tone. He wrote that the show "is not the hearty, guffawing burlesque" of *Of Thee I Sing*, and compared it to "a rowdy improvisation in one bitter, hysterical mood."

LET'S FACE IT! (29 OCTOBER 1941, IMPERIAL, 547 PERFORMANCES). Music and lyrics by **Cole Porter**, book by **Herbert** and **Dorothy Fields**, produced by **Vinton Freedley**. Based on the play *Cradle Snatchers* (1925), *Let's Face It!* combined workmanlike efforts from some fine Broadway creators and the inspired clowning of **Danny Kaye** to run for more than 15 months. Three wives (**Eve Arden**, **Vivian Vance**, and Edith Meiser) hire three soldiers (Kaye, Benny Baker, and Jack Williams) to take them around town because they believe their husbands are having affairs. Their husbands, of course, show up and begin to date the soldiers' girlfriends. Silly excuses and creative lying save the day for everyone as the loved ones reunite. A young **Nanette Fabray** also appeared in the show. **Brooks Atkinson**, writing in the *New York Times*, called it a "wonderfully joyous musical show," and cited "Jerry, My Soldier Boy," "You Irritate Me," "Farming," and "Let's Not Talk about Love" (a patter song of considerable difficulty for Kaye) as outstanding songs. Porter actually allowed interpolations, including "Melody in Four F" and "Fairy Tale" by Sylvia Fine (Kaye's wife) and Max Liebman. Atkinson praised director MacGregor for the show's speed and humor, and for making "no concessions to favorites," meaning that he did not allow Kaye to dominate the proceedings.

LIBRETTO/LIBRETTIST. The plot of a musical, or "book," is often called a libretto, while the person who creates the story and writes the spoken dialogue is the librettist. Most Broadway musical librettos have some sort of love story as their primary focus. Successful musical librettos have included social or political satires (*Of Thee I Sing* [1931], *Urinetown* [2001]), literary adaptations (*A Tree Grows in Brooklyn* [1951], *Wicked* [2003]), and works based on films (*A Little Night Music* [1973], *Thoroughly Modern Millie* [2002]). Many librettists are also noted lyricists, including **Rida Johnson Young, Dorothy Donnelly, Otto Harbach, Oscar Hammerstein II, Betty Comden** and **Adolph Green, Dorothy Fields, Alan Jay Lerner, Alain Boublil,** and **Lynn Ahrens.** Several well-known playwrights, such as **P. G. Wodehouse, Neil Simon,** and **Terrence McNally,** have written musical librettos. *See also* ADAMS, LEE; ANDERSON, MAXWELL; ASHMAN, HOWARD; ATTERIDGE, HAROLD; BLOSSOM, HENRY; BOLTON, GUY; BRICUSSE, LESLIE; BUCK, GENE; BURROWS, ABE; CAESAR, IRVING; COLEMAN, CY; COMPOSER; CROUSE, RUSSEL; DE SYLVA, B. G. "BUDDY"; DONNELLY, DOROTHY; EBB, FRED; FIELDS, HERBERT; FIELDS, JOSEPH; FINN, WILLIAM; GILBERT, W. S.; HART, MOSS; HOYT, CHARLES H.; JONES, TOM; KERR, WALTER; LAPINE, JAMES; LARSON, JONATHAN; LAURENTS, ARTHUR; LINDSAY, HOWARD; LYRICS/LYRICIST; MC-GOWAN, JOHN; RADO, JAMES; RAGNI, GEROME; RYSKIND, MORRIE; SAIDY, FRED; SCHMIDT, HARVEY; SCHWAB, LAURENCE; SCHWARTZ, ARTHUR; SIMON, NEIL; SMITH, EDGAR; SMITH, HARRY B.; SMITH, ROBERT B.; STEIN, JOSEPH; STEWART, MICHAEL; STONE, PETER; WEIDMAN, JOHN; WHEELER, HUGH; WILDHORN, FRANK.

LIFE BEGINS AT 8:40 **(27 AUGUST 1934, WINTER GARDEN, 237 PERFORMANCES).** Music by **Harold Arlen,** lyrics by **Ira Gershwin** and **E. Y. Harburg,** sketches provided by many authors, production devised and staged by **John Murray Anderson,** dances arranged by Robert Alton, produced by the **Shuberts.** An effective **revue** with an impressive cast, *Life Begins At 8:40* managed a run of about seven months. The title was a play on Walter Pitkin's book *Life Begins at Forty.* The impressive cast included **Bert Lahr, Ray Bolger,** Frances Williams, and Luella Gear. The finale saw Lahr as the new Mayor Fiorello LaGuardia, Gear as Eleanor Roosevelt, and Bolger and Williams as the former Mayor Jimmy Walker and his wife. Songs included "Fun to Be Fooled," "What Can You Sing in a Love Song?" and "Let's Take a Walk around the Block."

THE LIGHT IN THE PIAZZA (**18 APRIL 2005, VIVIAN BEAU-MONT, 504 PERFORMANCES**). Music and lyrics by **Adam Guettel**, book by Craig Lucas. Based on the novel by Elizabeth Spencer, *The Light in the Piazza* is a sophisticated musical version of the heartfelt story about a mother and daughter traveling in Italy. The daughter, Clara (**Kelli O'Hara**), falls in love with an Italian, Fabrizio Naccarelli (Matthew Morrison), but her mother, Mrs. Johnson (**Victoria Clark**), is concerned about her daughter's developmental disabilities, which are the result of a childhood accident. During the show, Mrs. Johnson confronts her own marital woes (in the moving "Dividing Day") and ultimately all ends happily at the wedding of Clara and Fabrizio. Guettel's dramatically evocative and compositionally advanced (when considering Broadway norms) music, along with the brilliant lighting design by Christopher Akerlind, scenic design by Michael Yeargan, and use of the Italian language (without supertitles or translation) make this show in many ways a hybrid between a typical Broadway musical and **opera**. Among the many notable musical numbers are the opening number, "Statues and Stories," as well as "The Beauty Is," "Say It Somehow," and "The Light in the Piazza." The show won **Tony Awards** for Best Score (Guettel), Best Actress in a Musical (Clark), Best Orchestrations (Bruce Coughlin, Guettel, and Ted Sperling), Best Scenic Design (Yeargan), Best Costume Design (Catherine Zuber), and Best Lighting Design (Akerlind).

LI'L ABNER (**15 NOVEMBER 1956, ST. JAMES, 693 PERFOR-MANCES**). Music by Gene de Paul, lyrics by **Johnny Mercer**, book by Norman Panama and Melvin Frank, directed and choreographed by **Michael Kidd**. Based on Al Capp's popular comic strip, the creators of *Li'l Abner* brought sufficient depth to Dogpatch's simple characters to make a genial show that ran for most of two years. The title character, played by Peter Palmer, is pursued by Daisy Mae (**Edith Adams**). Complications arise from other suitors, and the show included many other famous occupants of Dogpatch, including Marryin' Sam (**Stubby Kaye**). The town faces destruction because the government wants to test an atomic bomb there, but the community saves itself by showing that Abraham Lincoln had declared Dogpatch a national treasure. **Brooks Atkinson**, writing for the *New York Times*, praised Michael Kidd for his direction and dances, discussing in detail the mating-race, which Kidd "has made something exciting and hilarious." Atkinson admitted that it is hard to fashion an effective book out of characters with "hearts of gold," but also "not very bright in the upper story"; still, he described the score as "pleasant" with "entertaining lyrics" and remarked about the effectiveness of "Jubilee T. Cornpone," "Namely You," and "The Country's in the Very Best of Hands."

LILLIE, BEATRICE (BORN CONSTANCE SYLVIA MUNSFIRD, ALSO KNOWN AS LADY PEEL, 1894–1989). Canadian-born **revue** star who appeared in *André Charlot's Revue of 1924*, *Walk a Little Faster* (1932), *At Home Abroad* (1935), *The Show Is On* (1936), *Set to Music* (1939), *Seven Lively Arts* (1944), *Inside U.S.A.* (1948), and *Ziegfeld Follies* of 1957. She created the role of Madame Arcati in *High Spirits* (1964).

LINCOLN CENTER THEATER. Reestablished in 1985, Lincoln Center Theater produces musicals and plays at the 1,100-seat Vivian Beaumont Theater (which is considered a Broadway house), the 299-seat Mitzi E. Newhouse Theater, and other venues. In addition to notable revivals of shows such as *Anything Goes* (1987), Lincoln Center Theater is known for mounting dramatically and musically innovative and challenging shows such as *Parade* (1998), *Marie Christine* (1999), and *The Light in the Piazza* (2005).

LINDEN, HAL (1931–). Actor who won a **Tony Award** for his portrayal of Mayer Rothschild in *The Rothschilds* (1970). Other credits include *Bells Are Ringing* (1956, understudy and **replacement** for Jeff), *The Education of H*Y*M*A*N K*A*P*L*A*N* (1968), *The Pajama Game* (1973 **revival**), and *Cabaret* (1998 revival, replacement Herr Schultz [2002]).

LINDSAY, HOWARD (1889–1968). Director, librettist, producer, and actor with a long list of credits for both musical and nonmusical Broadway shows. He staged and performed in the **revue** *The '49ers* (1922) before achieving fame in the realm of **musical comedy** in the 1930s by staging shows such as *Anything Goes* (1934), for which he also revised the book with **Russel Crouse**, and *Red, Hot and Blue!* (1936), the book of which he cowrote with Crouse. He and Crouse also cowrote the books *Call Me Madam* (1950) and *The Sound of Music* (1959).

LINDSAY, ROBERT (1949–). English actor who won a **Tony Award** for his performance in *Me and My Girl* (1986), having starred in the London revival the previous year. **Frank Rich**'s *New York Times* review raved about the actor, who "at times recalls **[Gene] Kelly** and [James] Cagney."

THE LION KING **(13 NOVEMBER 1997, NEW AMSTERDAM, 3,803 PERFORMANCES AS OF 31 DECEMBER 2006; MOVED TO THE MINSKOFF THEATRE ON 13 JUNE 2006).** Music by **Elton John**, lyrics by **Tim Rice**, additional lyrics and music by others, book by Roger Allers and Irene Mecchi; adapted from the screenplay by Mecchi, Jonathan Roberts, and Linda Woolverton; direction and costumes by Julie Taymor; choreography by Garth Fagan; mask and puppet design by Taymor and Michael Curry; presented by **Disney Theatrical Productions**. Adapted from Disney's popular animated feature, *The Lion King*'s imaginative staging merges human actors with various types of puppets and gives the show an enchanting look and appeal.

The fundamental story from the animated film remains. Simba (Scott Irby-Ranniar), son of King Mufasa (Samuel E. Wright), will inherit the kingdom; however, his evil uncle, Scar (John Vickery), kills Mufasa and blames Simba, who flees into the jungle. As he matures, Simba realizes what his uncle has done and returns to reclaim his kingdom. **Heather Headley** played Nala, Simba's love interest. The stage version included all of the beloved moments from the film and a great deal more, since the running length increased by well more than an hour. The new music (including songs such as "The

Lioness Hunt" and "Rafiki Mourns") carried more of an African feel than did the songs from the film, just one aspect of a production that featured a sincere attempt to deal with the multicultural aspects of the story. Some felt that the show was too long and had some slow moments, but this was minor criticism of what became one of New York's great tourist attractions. Reviewing the show in the *New York Times*, **Ben Brantley** raved about the "transporting magic" of the opening "Circle of Life," when all of the animals parade in front of the audience as "creatures of air and light and even a touch of divinity." Brantley was somewhat less sanguine about other aspects of the show, but credited Taymor with bringing to Broadway "a whole new vocabulary of images." Regarding the new numbers, he heard "an irresistible pull to this music," especially as the performers came down the aisles with their puppets. *The Lion King* inaugurated the Disney-owned and renovated New Amsterdam Theatre, an important part of the rebirth of **Times Square** in the late 1990s.

LITHGOW, JOHN (1945–). Actor who won a **Tony Award** for his first lead role in a Broadway musical, J. J. Hunsecker in *The Sweet Smell of Success* (2002). He also created the role of Lawrence in *Dirty Rotten Scoundrels* (2005).

LITTLE, CLEAVON (1939–1992). African American actor who played the title role in *Purlie* and won a **Tony Award** for his performance.

LITTLE JOHNNY JONES **(7 NOVEMBER 1904, LIBERTY, 52 PERFORMANCES).** Music, lyrics, book, and direction by **George M. Cohan**, produced by **Sam H. Harris**. One of the most storied shows in Broadway history, *Little Johnny Jones* reveled in its creator's popular brand of American patriotism; and its score included some of Cohan's greatest songs, including "The Yankee Doodle Boy," "Give My Regards to Broadway," and "Life's a Funny Proposition After All." Although the original Broadway run was short, *Little Johnny Jones*, like many shows of the time, went on an extended tour and returned to New York. The cast included Cohan's wife, Ethel Levey, as his romantic interest and both of his parents in prominent roles. Cohan advertised the show as a "musical play," and it did bear a somewhat serious plot based loosely on "Tod" Sloan's recent experiences as an American jockey in England. Johnny Jones (George M. Cohan) is supposed to ride in the English Derby. He refuses an offer to throw the race, but then the villain, Anthony Anstey (Jerry Cohan), spreads the word that he lost on purpose. Johnny's name is cleared at the end of act 1. In act 2, Anstey kidnaps his love, Goldie Gates, and takes her to San Francisco. Johnny, of course, frees her and takes appropriate revenge on Anstey. The unnamed critic in the *New York Times* seemed unaware that history was being made. He criticized both Cohan and Levey for reciting rather than singing their songs but admitted that both "dance well."

LITTLE MARY SUNSHINE (18 NOVEMBER 1959, ORPHEUM, 1,143 PERFORMANCES). Music, lyrics, and book by Rick Besoyan. A hugely successful off-Broadway show, *Little Mary Sunshine* spoofed 1920s **operetta**, especially **Rudolf Friml**'s *Rose Marie*. Eileen Brennan played the title character, owner of a Colorado Rocky Mountains inn and adoptee of the Kadota Indians, a tribe with only three surviving members. She loves Captain Jim (William Graham) of the Rangers, but an opera star, Mme. Ernestine von Liebedich (Elizabeth Parrish), who visits the inn, and the Native American criminal, Yellow Feather (Ray James), complicate matters. The lovers sang "Colorado Love Call" (a direct parody of *Rose Marie*'s "Indian Love Call"), and the diva sang of exotic Central Europe with the ridiculously titled "In Izzenschnooken on the Lovely Essenzook Zee." Mary Sunshine sang of her optimism in "Look For a Sky of Blue." Louis Calta, writing a review for the *New York Times*, called the show "a merry and sprightly spoof" that treated operetta with more of a "light cartoon treatment" than a "sharp wit." *See also* REFLEXIVE REFERENCES/REFLEXIVITY.

LITTLE ME (17 NOVEMBER 1962, LUNT-FONTANNE, 257 PERFORMANCES). Music by **Cy Coleman**, lyrics by Carolyn Leigh, book by **Neil Simon**, staged by **Cy Feuer** and **Bob Fosse**, choreography by Fosse, presented by Feuer and Ernest H. Martin. Based on the novel by Patrick Dennis, *Little Me* was primarily a vehicle for Sid Caesar, who made his return to Broadway in the show after an absence of 14 years. A huge television star famous for his ability to play many characters, Caesar, in *Little Me*, portrayed a string of lovers for Belle (Virginia Martin). She is from the proverbial "wrong side of the tracks," but rises to social prominence and wealth. Caesar played a rich boy, an aged miser, a French music hall singer, a foolish soldier, a German director working in Hollywood, and a gambling Slavic prince. Neither the book nor the score garnered much admiration, but many wished to see Caesar, allowing an eight-month run. **Howard Taubman**, writing for the *New York Times*, compared the show to an "ordinary wine" that will inspire some admiration in a "nonvintage year" for musicals, and admired the songs "Deep Down Inside," "Be a Performer!," and "I've Got Your Number."

THE LITTLE MILLIONAIRE **(25 SEPTEMBER 1911, GEORGE M. COHAN, 192 PERFORMANCES).** Music, lyrics, book, directed, and produced by **George M. Cohan**. Audiences knew what to expect from a Cohan show when they saw *The Little Millionaire*, and Cohan fulfilled their wishes. The star played Robert Spooner, and his father, Jerry Cohan, was Henry Spooner. The father and son must both marry in order to fulfill the conditions of their late wife and mother's will, and do so by the end of the show. Two outstanding songs in Cohan's score were "Oh, You Wonderful Girl" and "The Musical Moon," the latter a satirical look at love songs. No music appeared in the second of the show's three acts; that segment consisted mainly of farce. The show had a great deal of dancing by soloists and ensembles, encompassing, among other things, a military drill with Cohan's requisite flag-waving and the final wedding scene enacted as a dance pantomime. The unnamed reviewer for the *New York Times* wrote that the show "represents" Cohan "at his very best," but also admits "there was often something of bad taste." He continued that "The Dancing Wedding" brought "the final note of novelty to an entertainment in which novelties abound."

LITTLE NELLIE KELLY **(13 NOVEMBER 1922, LIBERTY, 276 PERFORMANCES).** Music, lyrics, book, directed, and produced by **George M. Cohan**. A later show in Cohan's Irish vein, *Little Nellie Kelly* enjoyed a fine nine-month run. Nellie (Elizabeth Hines), fitting the New York Irish stereotype, is a policemen's daughter who works at a department store. Jack Lloyd (Barrett Greenwood) is a wealthy man who courts her but loses her to a poor Irish boy, Jack Conroy (Charles King). In the show, Cohan lampooned the mysteries then popular on Broadway. Conroy stands accused of stealing jewels from Lloyd's family, but clears his name. The unsigned review in the *New York Times* deals with the show jovially and also shows admiration for Cohan's abilities. When trying to find the show's "new turns," the critic observes "this time it is Nellie that is the most wonderful name in the world." The show has the "wild dancing, music . . . and the sentimentality" one expects but also more humor than sometimes found in a Cohan show. Not listed by name in the cast, Cohan was on stage, and, according to the *Times*, would talk to the audience about the plot and promise to speed it up. The show's notable songs include "The Voice in My Heart," "You Remind Me of My Mother," and "Nellie Kelly, I Love You."

A LITTLE NIGHT MUSIC (**25 FEBRUARY 1973, SHUBERT, 600 PERFORMANCES**). Music and lyrics by **Stephen Sondheim**, book by **Hugh Wheeler**, directed by **Harold Prince**, presented by Prince in association with **Ruth Mitchell**. Following Sondheim and Prince's memorable collaboration on *Company* (1970) and *Follies* (1971), the pair struck gold with *A Little Night Music*, a show that garnered rave reviews and has remained in the repertory of both theater and opera companies. Hugh Wheeler loosely based his book on Ingmar Bergman's film *Smiles of a Summer Night*, a frothy farce about adults trying to find physical and emotional love. Fredrik Egerman (**Len Cariou**), a middle-aged Swedish lawyer, marries Anne (Victoria Mallory), who is his son's age. Given her innocence, she remains a virgin even after 11 months of marriage. In desperation, Fredrik looks up his old mistress, Desirée Armfeldt (**Glynis Johns**), who, although married, remains interested in Fredrik. The lawyer's son, Henrik (Mark Lambert), is hopelessly in love with his stepmother. Everyone converges on the country home of Desirée's mother, Madame Armfeldt (Hermione Gingold), for the second act. Henrik elopes with Anne and Fredrik ends up with Desirée, and Madame Armfeldt dies peacefully after helping to arrange for this happy ending. **Clive Barnes**, in his enthusiastic *New York Times* review, reserved special praise for Prince, calling this his "particular triumph," succeeding here in bringing a serious element into the musical in a way that he did not in either *Follies* or *Company*. He called the score "a celebration of time, an orgy of plaintively memorable waltzes," all wonderfully nostalgic. He likened Sondheim to Gustav Mahler, a telling comment, and dubbed the lyrics "breathtaking" in the vein of **Cole Porter**. The score is filled with fine songs. Act 1 highlights include the memorable trilogy "Now," "Later," and "Soon," Fredrik and Desirée's hilarious yet touching "You Must Meet My Wife," and Mme. Armfeldt's "Liaisons," in which she describes her libidinous memories. The second act included, among other delights, the ensemble's "A Weekend in the Country" and Desirée's emotive soliloquy "Send in the Clowns," Sondheim's most famous song.

LITTLE SHOP OF HORRORS (OFF-BROADWAY: 27 JULY 1982, ORPHEUM, 2,209 PERFORMANCES; BROADWAY: 2 OCTOBER 2003, VIRGINIA, 372 PERFORMANCES). Music by **Alan Menken**, lyrics, book, and direction by **Howard Ashman**. Based on producer Roger Corman's campy 1960 film of the same name, *Little Shop of Horrors* initially ran **off-Broadway**. The spoof of horror movies features a bloodthirsty, talking plant named Audrey II, created by a nerd, Seymour (Lee Wilkof). Seymour suffers in silence in his love for Audrey (Ellen Greene), who works with him in a Skid Row floral shop. They put Audrey II in the shop window, and the plant becomes a tourist attraction, but its keepers must resort to murder to keep feeding the plant. When needed, however, Audrey II will eat rare roast beef. Mel Gussow, reviewing the original off-Broadway production for the *New York Times*, admits that this is an unusual show, but he calls it "as entertaining as it is exotic." The plant is "a cross between an avocado and a shark," and dramatically it proves "a scene-stealer." Wilkof bears "an affable, offhanded manner" for a murderer, while Greene is "sweetly guileless." The score is an eclectic tour through rock, pop, and Latin styles. Typically outrageous numbers from the show are the finale, "Don't Feed the Plants," and the catchy title song. Although the 2003 production was the first time the show played on Broadway, it was considered a **revival** because of the successful 1986 film version and the popularity of various regional productions.

THE LITTLE SHOW **(30 APRIL 1929, MUSIC BOX, 321 PER-FORMANCES).** Music mostly by **Arthur Schwartz**, lyrics by Howard Dietz. A witty **revue** featuring several stars, *The Little Show* ran for almost 10 months, helped make a star of **Fred Allen**, and introduced the team of Howard Dietz and Arthur Schwartz. Sketches encompassed such silliness as Fred Allen playing a hot-cross bun designer who works only one day per year. The best episode, though, was **George S. Kaufman**'s "The Still Alarm," in which Romney Brent and **Clifton Webb** played two men in a burning hotel who are so proper that they cannot decide what to wear on the fire escape. The firemen (Allen and Harold Moffet) appear, and they are also in no hurry and very polite. Allen finally plays "Keep the Home Fires Burning" on his violin. Musical highlights included Libby Holman singing "Can't We Be Friends?" (music by Paul James and **Kay Swift**), and, with Webb, "Moanin' Low" (music by Ralph Rainger). **J. Brooks Atkinson**, in his *New York Times* review, praised the show as "unfailingly diverting," more interested in amusing the audience than providing "abdominal laughter." He called the show "gay, sardonic, trifling and remarkably good fun," and found the small cast to be "all . . . uncommonly busy."

LITTLE WOMEN **(23 JANUARY 2005, VIRGINIA, 137 PERFOR-MANCES).** Music by Jason Howland, lyrics by Mindi Dickstein, book by Allan Knee. The lavish, nearly operatic treatment of Louisa May Alcott's famous novel starred **Sutton Foster** as Jo and Maureen McGovern as Marmee. The score includes emotive ballads, duets, and ensembles, an extensive use of melodrama (spoken dialogue above music), songs whose primary purpose is to move the story forward, numbers in the style of 19th-century dances, and lush orchestrations by Kim Schamberg that infuse the show with a sense of warmth and sophistication. Musical highlights include Jo's character-defining "Astonishing," Beth and Jo's touching duet "Some Things Are Meant to Be," and Jo and Professor Bhaer's lighthearted yet sentimental number "Small Umbrella in the Rain."

LLOYD WEBBER, ANDREW (1948–). British composer whose works have become among the most important Broadway musicals of the last quarter of the 20th century. Lloyd Webber's style ranges from rock to operatic, and many of his works helped define the **megamusical**. Lloyd Webber's earliest shows featured Biblical characters in search of redemption: *Joseph and the Amazing Technicolor Dreamcoat* (1968, London; 1982, New York) and *Jesus Christ Superstar* (1971, New York). This theme continued in *Evita* (1978, London; 1979, New York), where now it was the character of Eva Perón who was seeking redemption and immortality. Two "competition" musicals followed in which nonhuman characters try to win something. Various felines want to be the one chosen to ascend to the Heaviside Layer in *Cats* (1981, London; 1982, New York), while trains seek to win the race and find "The Light at the End of the Tunnel" in *Starlight Express* (1984, London; 1987, New York). The stage spectacle associated with these shows led to *The Phantom of the Opera* (1986, London; 1988, New York), Lloyd Webber's greatest stage success, and what is in many ways its gender-reversed version based on a classic Billy Wilder film, *Sunset Boulevard* (1993, London; 1994, New York). Not everything Lloyd Webber does involves tremendous stage effects. The first act of *Song and Dance* (1982, London; 1985, New York) consists of a one-woman show, while the second features a solo dancer. Lloyd Webber's more intimate shows such as *Aspects of Love* (1989, London; 1990, New York) and *The Woman in White* (2004, London; 2005, New York) have not fared well on Broadway.

LOESSER, FRANK (1910–1969). Songwriter, wordsmith, and pianist best known for the musicals for which he crafted music and lyrics, including *Where's Charley?* (1948), *Guys and Dolls* (1950), *The Most Happy Fella* (1956, for which he also wrote the libretto), and *How to Succeed in Business without Really Trying* (1961). Through his music and words, he created some of Broadway's most memorable and beloved characters, employing specific musical idioms for these highly individualistic personas. Loesser's musical palate ranged from classic **musical comedy** in *Guys and Dolls* to **opera** in *The Most Happy Fella*.

LOEWE, FREDERICK (1901–1988). Berlin-born child prodigy pianist who, after failing to establish himself as a classical pianist in New York, formed a partnership with librettist and lyricist **Alan Jay Lerner**, popularly known as **Lerner and Loewe**, that resulted in seven Broadway musicals, including *My Fair Lady* (1956). Loewe's European-inspired music was well matched for Lerner's romantic lyrics.

LOGAN, JOSHUA (1908–1988). Director whose career began in writing and acting and whose directorial credits for Broadway musicals include *Knickerbocker Holiday* (1938), *Annie Get Your Gun* (1946), and *South Pacific* (1949). Logan possessed an ability to elicit truth and interest from a variety of stories.

LORING, EUGENE (BORN LEROY KERPESTEIN, 1911–1982). Choreographer and dancer whose choreographic credits include *Carmen Jones* (1943) and *Silk Stockings* (1955).

LOST IN THE STARS **(30 OCTOBER 1949, MUSIC BOX, 273 PERFORMANCES).** Music by **Kurt Weill**, words by **Maxwell Anderson**, staged by **Rouben Mamoulian**. Billed as a "musical tragedy," *Lost in the Stars* was Weill's last work for the musical theater. He died during its run. An uncompromising work with operatic overtones, strong social commentary, and limited commercial possibilities, the show was a musicalization of Alan Paton's novel *Cry, the Beloved Country*, set in South Africa under apartheid. **Todd Duncan** played Stephen Kumalo, a preacher married to Grace (Gertrude Jeannette). They are worried about their son, Absalom (Julian Matfield), who has moved to Johannesburg and is living in poverty with his pregnant lover. During a robbery, he kills a young white man who is against apartheid. Stephen comes to Johannesburg, learns about what has happened, and marries his son and his son's girlfriend. After Absalom tells the truth, he receives the death penalty. The father of the murder victim, James Jarvis (Leslie Banks), a white conservative, sees how honorable the preacher and his son are and befriends Stephen. Weill and Anderson made frequent use of a chorus that commented upon the action in such dramatic numbers as "Fear," in which whites and blacks articulate the intense level of their fears. Among the show's powerfully dramatic musical numbers are the title song and "Cry, the Beloved Country." **Brooks Atkinson**, writing in the *New York Times*, called the musical's climax "a grand and enlightening scene with unadorned beauty" and described the score as "overflowing with the same compassion that Mr. Paton brought to this novel."

LOUDON, DOROTHY (1933–2003). Comic actress with a belt voice who won back-to-back **Tony Awards** for her portrayal of the evil Miss Harrigan in *Annie* (1977) and Bea Asher in *Ballroom* (1978). She was a **replacement** Mrs. Lovett in the original production of *Sweeney Todd: The Demon Barber of Fleet Street* (1979), succeeding **Angela Lansbury**. A decade earlier, in 1969, she played Lillian Stone in *The Fig Leaves Are Falling*, a show that only ran four performances but nonetheless garnered her a Tony nomination.

LOUIE THE 14th (3 MARCH 1925, COSMOPOLITAN, 319 PERFORMANCES). Music by **Sigmund Romberg**, book and lyrics by Arthur Wimperis, produced by **Florenz Ziegfeld**. The **musical comedy** about an American Army cook, Louie Ketchup, who remains in France after World War I, was conceived as a vehicle for *Ziegfeld Follies* star Leon Errol. Ketchup's superstitious employer invites the title character to be the 14th guest at a dinner party, afraid of having only 13 attendees, since that would be an unlucky number. Among the score's highlights was the nostalgic male choral number "Homeland."

LOUISIANA PURCHASE (28 MAY 1940, IMPERIAL, 444 PERFORMANCES). Music and lyrics by **Irving Berlin**, book by **Morrie Ryskind**, ballets arranged by **George Balanchine**, produced by **B. G. De Sylva**. *Louisiana Purchase*, though not groundbreaking, had quality material presented by a great cast, allowing it to run more than a year. **Victor Moore** played United States Senator Oliver P. Loganberry, who goes to Louisiana to investigate alleged corruption by the Louisiana Purchase Company. Possible inspiration came from the assassination of Louisiana's real Senator and Governor Huey Long, but Ryskind did not write high satire here. **William Gaxton** played the company's lawyer, Jim Taylor, who attempts to have the senator discredited by placing a photograph of Marina Van Linden (Vera Zorina) in his lap and then sending Madame Bordelaise (Irene Bordoni) to his hotel room at night. Loganberry, however, hilariously muddles through each possible scandal, as one might expect from the clown

Moore. The score did not include any of Berlin's greatest songs, but the title number was memorable and "Sex Marches On" was a notable comic piece. *New York Times* critic **Brooks Atkinson** wrote a workmanlike review of *Louisiana Purchase*, finding little wrong with it but also feeling that it did not represent the creators' best work.

LOVE LIFE (7 OCTOBER 1948, 46TH STREET, 252 PERFOR-MANCES). Music by **Kurt Weill**, lyrics and book by **Alan Jay Lerner**, staged by Elia Kazan, choreography by **Michael Kidd**. Billed as a **vaudeville**, *Love Life* was an unusual show that prefigured aspects of the **concept musical** two decades before the idea became popular. The plot followed a couple, Sam (**Ray Middleton**) and Susan Cooper (**Nanette Fabray**), and their children from 1791 through the next 150 years of American history. Interspersed between scenes telling the story were moments of vaudeville meant to comment on the plot, not unlike the nightclub acts in *Cabaret*. **Brooks Atkinson**, writing for the *New York Times*, described "a feeling of general disappointment" surrounding what he called "a general gripe masquerading as entertainment." He called Weill's work "flexible and idiomatic" and Kidd's ballets "beguiling." He complained, however, that the vaudeville elements are unrelated to Lerner's thoughts about marriage and are "generally inferior." Memorable songs included the lovely "Here I'll Stay," the joyful "Green-Up Time," and the satirical "Progress" and "Economics."

LUKER, REBECCA (1961–). Operatic-style soprano who created the role of Lily in *The Secret Garden* (1991). She starred in several important revivals, including **Hal Prince**'s *Show Boat* (1994), *The Sound of Music* (1998), and **Susan Stroman**'s *The Music Man* (2000), and played Mrs. Banks in the Broadway version of *Mary Poppins* (2006).

LUPONE, PATTI (1949–). Versatile singing actress whose array of vocal styles, which ranges from belt to the nearly operatic, allows her to bring a tremendous interpretive depth to the roles she plays. She won a **Tony Award** for her riveting portrayal of the title role in *Evita* (1979), followed by accolades as Nancy in the 1984 **revival** of *Oliver!*, Reno Sweeney in the 1987 revival of *Anything Goes*, and

Mrs. Lovett in **John Doyle**'s innovative 2005 reenvisioning of *Sweeney Todd: The Demon Barber of Fleet Street*, in which she also played tuba. In 1993, she created Norma Desmond in *Sunset Boulevard* in London, though Glenn Close played the part on Broadway.

LYNNE, GILLIAN (1927–). Dancer and choreographer whose choreographic credits include *Cats* (1981, London; 1982, New York) and *The Phantom of the Opera* (1986, London; 1998, New York), two of **Andrew Lloyd Webber**'s biggest successes, as well as *Chitty Chitty Bang Bang* (2002, London; 2005, New York).

LYRICS/LYRICIST. The words to the songs in a Broadway musical/the person who creates the words. Lyricists come from a variety of backgrounds and employ a range of approaches. Many are also composers. In the **musical comedies** of the early 20th centuries, creators such as **Ira Gershwin**, **Lorenz Hart**, and **Cole Porter** employed intricate rhyme and alliteration schemes in their lyrics, while others, such as **Oscar Hammerstein II**, illuminated dimensions of their characters' personalities through the words they sing and tended to avoid cleverness for its own sake. Hammerstein was especially known for his ability to create dialect in lyrics for shows such as *Show Boat* (1927), *Carmen Jones* (1941), and *South Pacific* (1949), among others. Several prominent lyricists have been women, and it is as lyricists that women have made the most significant contributions as creators for Broadway musicals. Lyricists from the middle decades of the 20th century onward, such as **Betty Comden** and **Adolph Green**, **Alan Jay Lerner**, **Dorothy Fields**, **Stephen Sondheim** (also a composer), and **Fred Ebb** possess a keen awareness of the intricacies of the English language, its theatrical possibilities, and its potential for character portrayal. *See also* ADAMS, LEE; ADLER, RICHARD; AHRENS, LYNN; ALLEN, PETER; ASHMAN, HOWARD; ATTERIDGE, HAROLD; BART, LIONEL; BLITZSTEIN, MARC; BLOSSOM, HENRY; BOLTON, GUY; BOUBLIL, ALAIN; BRICUSSE, LESLIE; BROWN, LEW; BUCK, GENE; CAESAR, IRVING; CHARNIN, MARTIN; COHAN, GEORGE M.; COMPOSER; DE SYLVA, B. G. "BUDDY"; DONNELLY, DOROTHY; DUNBAR, PAUL LAWRENCE; FINN, WILLIAM; FORREST, GEORGE "CHET"; GILBERT, W. S.; HAR-

BACH, OTTO; HARBURG, E. Y.; HARNICK, SHELDON; HER-
MAN, JERRY; HOYT, CHARLES H.; JONES, TOM; KLEBAN,
EDWARD; LARSON, JONATHAN; LIBRETTO/LIBRETTIST;
LOESSER, FRANK; MALTBY, RICHARD, JR.; MERCER,
JOHNNY; MERRILL, BOB; NORMAN, MARSHA; RADO,
JAMES; RAGNI, GEROME; RICE, TIM; ROBIN, LEO; ROME,
HAROLD J.; ROSE, BILLY; RYSKIND, MORRIE; SCHWARTZ,
ARTHUR; SCHWARTZ, STEPHEN; SMITH, EDGAR; SMITH,
HARRY B.; SMITH, ROBERT B.; SOUSA, JOHN PHILIP;
STROUSE, CHARLES; WODEHOUSE, P. G.; WRIGHT,
ROBERT; YAZBEK, DAVID; YOUNG, RIDA JOHNSON.

– M –

MACDERMOT, GALT (1928–). Canadian-born composer whose
rock musical scores include *Hair* (1968), *Two Gentlemen of Verona*
(1971), *Dude* (1972), and *Via Galactica* (1972); the first two succeeded while the latter two failed. With *Hair*, MacDermot proved
that rock could be a viable style on Broadway.

MACKINTOSH, CAMERON (1946–). British producer frequently
associated with the **megamusical** who is known for creating vivid
theatrical experiences without a reliance on highly recognizable stars.
His most notable successes include *Cats* (1981, London; 1982, New
York), *Song and Dance* (1982, London; 1985, New York), *Les Misérables* (1985, London; 1987, New York), *The Phantom of the
Opera* (1986, London; 1988, New York), *Miss Saigon* (1989, London; 1991, New York), and *Mary Poppins* (2005, London; 2006,
New York), the last a coproduction with **Disney Theatrical Productions**, which Mackintosh cocreated. He also produced the Broadway
revivals of *Oliver!* (1984) and *Carousel* (1994), both of which originated in London.

***MADAME SHERRY* (30 AUGUST 1910, NEW AMSTERDAM, 231
PERFORMANCES).** Music by **Karl Hoschna**, lyrics and book by
Otto Hauerbach (later **Otto Harbach**). Based on a French vaudeville
of the same name by Maurice Ordonneau, the New York version

included plot changes and a new score. It ran in New York City for about eight months before touring. The complicated story involved Edward Sherry (Jack Gardner), whose rich, eccentric Uncle Theophilus (Ralph Herz) lives in Greece, and his Uncle's niece (but not Edward's blood cousin), Yvonne (Lina Abarbarnell). The unsigned review in the *New York Times* glowed with praise, starting with the polka "Every Little Movement," which is reprised throughout the show. The critic described the show as a combination of Viennese **operetta**, French **vaudeville**, and American **musical comedy**, and found that the "plot plays a much more important role than it usually does in an American musical comedy." The reviewer praised the "hodgepodge" of a score, singling out "I'm All Right," "The Dublin Rag," and the waltz "The Birth of Passion."

***THE MAGIC SHOW* (28 MAY 1974, CORT, 1,920 PERFORMANCES).** Music and lyrics by **Stephen Schwartz**, book by Bob Randall. Primarily a vehicle for illusionist Doug Henning, *The Magic Show* was a treat for those who enjoyed frightening feats of magic. The thin plot concerned the Top Hat nightclub in Passaic, New Jersey, which was in decline until its owners found a splendid magician who could fill the seats. **Clive Barnes**, writing in the *New York Times*, was agog at Henning's prowess, noting that he "could not see how one single trick was done." Among other feats, Henning burned a girl to a skeleton and impaled himself on a falling ceiling of spikes. Barnes found Schwartz's songs too similar and the book poor, but it did not really matter because *The Magic Show* had Doug Henning (and fine replacement magicians) and ran for four and a half years.

***MAKE MINE MANHATTAN* (15 JANUARY 1948, BROADHURST, 429 PERFORMANCES).** Music by Richard Lewine, lyrics and sketches by Arnold B. Horwitt. A pleasant and witty **revue**, *Make Mine Manhattan* boasted a cast that included David Burns, Sid Caeser, and Joshua Shelley. The latter sang "Subway Song" while playing a man who is dating a woman who lives at the far end of the subway line. In another sketch, Caeser was a Hollywood director with a fake German accent who was shooting a film in New York City. Burns drove him crazy as a passerby telling him how to shoot the film. Caeser also appeared in a parody of **Richard Rodgers** and

Oscar **Hammerstein II**'s *Allegro*, where he makes absurd moral choices. *New York Times* critic **Brooks Atkinson** called it a "very pleasant musical revue" about "Manhattan foibles" such as the qualifications of newspaper drama critics. He found Caeser to be the "most original" member of the cast, but "he is hardly versatile enough yet to carry . . . a whole evening."

MALTBY, RICHARD, JR. (1937–). Lyricist for *Baby* (1983), *Miss Saigon* (1991), *Nick & Nora* (1991), and *Big* (1996) and director for *Ain't Misbehavin'* (1978), *Baby*, *Song and Dance* (1985), *Fosse* (1999), and *Ring of Fire* (2006). He conceived *Ain't Misbehavin'* and wrote additional lyrics for the show, prepared the American adaptation of *Song and Dance* and supervised the production, conceived *Fosse*, and served as production consultant for *Bea Arthur on Broadway* (2002). He won a **Tony Award** for Best Director for *Ain't Misbehavin'*.

MAME **(24 MAY 1966, WINTER GARDEN, 1,508 PERFORMANCES).** Music and lyrics by **Jerry Herman**, book by Jerome Lawrence and Robert E. Lee, choreography by **Onna White**. Based on Patrick Dennis's novel *Auntie Mame* and Lawrence and Lee's play of the same name, *Mame* was a triumph for **Angela Lansbury** and ran for almost four years. Lansbury played the irrepressible title character, a Manhattan socialite who becomes guardian to her 10-year-old nephew, Patrick (Frankie Michaels). Mame is a hopeless mother—she urges Patrick to live life to the fullest, just as she does. The Depression leaves her penniless, so she marries a rich southerner, who dies years later (while climbing an Alp) and leaves Mame again rich. Her best friend is Vera Charles (**Beatrice Arthur**). At the end, Patrick (now played by Jerry Lanning) is grown and married, and Mame starts to work her wiles on his young son. Some felt that Herman's score for *Mame* sounded too much like *Hello, Dolly!*, but the songs worked within the plot. Hits included the celebratory title tune, "Open a New Window," the hope-filled "We Need a Little Christmas," "The Man in the Moon," "If He Walked into My Life," and the insult-ridden "Bosom Buddies," one of the classic female duets of the musical theater. Stanley Kauffmann, writing for the *New York Times*, found the score "strongly rhythmic and sufficiently tuneful," admired the direction and production values, but also found the show a bit over-long and predictable. **Lucille Ball** and Beatrice Arthur starred in the 1974 film version, and Lansbury reprised her role in the short-lived 1983 Broadway revival.

MAMMA MIA! **(18 OCTOBER 2001, WINTER GARDEN, 2,166 PERFORMANCES AS OF 31 DECEMBER 2006).** Music and lyrics by Benny Andersson and Björn Ulvaeus, some songs with Stig Anderson, book by Catherine Johnson. Originally produced in London in 1999, *Mamma Mia!* is a celebratory **jukebox musical** featuring the music of ABBA. The thin plot, set on a Greek island, concerns a girl, Sophie, who is about to get married. She does not know who her father is, and invites three men from her mother's past to her wedding, hoping that one of them will turn out to be her father. Her mother, meanwhile, has invited two friends with whom she used to perform to the wedding. All ends happily, of course, and the show is fundamentally a reason to hear classic ABBA songs such as "Money, Money, Money," "Dancing Queen," "S.O.S.," "Knowing Me, Knowing You," "The Winner Takes It All," and the title song.

MAMOULIAN, ROUBEN (1897–1987). An important figure in the full integration of the musical, Mamoulian was director for several elegant Broadway shows, including *Porgy and Bess* (1935), *Oklahoma!* (1943), *Carousel* (1945), and *Lost in the Stars* (1949).

MANDEL, FRANK (1884–1958). He began his career as a journalist, and wrote librettos for **musical comedies** before teaming up with **Lawrence Schwab** on *No, No, Nanette!* (1925). Mandel and Schwab produced a series of successful shows in the 1920s, including the sports-themed musical comedies *Good News!* (1927) and *Follow Thru* (1929) and the operettas *The Desert Song* (1926) and *The New Moon* (1928). They continued to produce operettas with scores by **Sigmund Romberg** in the 1930s, including *East Wind* (1931) and *May Wine* (1935), but after the failure of these shows, Mandel went to Hollywood, where he directed films until his retirement in 1942. Mandel and Schwab helped inaugurate a new type of **operetta**, one that was not purely escapist in nature but rather addressed contemporary social issues and in many ways prefigured the "musical drama" so closely associated with the work of **Richard Rodgers** and their own collaborator, **Oscar Hammerstein II**.

MANN, TERRENCE (ALSO CREDITED AS TERRENCE V. MANN, 1951–). Actor, singer, and dancer who created the role of Rum Tum Tugger in *Cats* (1981). Other credits include Saul in *Rags* (1986), Javert in *Les Misérables* (1987), The Beast in *Beauty and the Beast* (1994), and Chauvelinin in *The Scarlet Pimpernel* (1997). His rich baritone voice and commanding stage presence infuse a sense of authority into his roles.

MANNING, IRENE (1912–2004). Classically trained singer whose Broadway credits include Eulalie Bland in *Susanna, Don't You Cry* (1939) and Katherine Townsend in *The Day before Spring* (1945). Manning appeared in numerous musical films; among her most famous roles was that of **Fay Templeton** in the **George M. Cohan** biopic *Yankee Doodle Dandy* (1942).

MAN OF LA MANCHA **(24 MAY 1965, ANTA WASHINGTON SQUARE, 2,328 PERFORMANCES).** Music by **Mitch Leigh**, lyrics by Joe Darion, book by Dale Wasserman. A daring musicalization of Cervantes' novel *Don Quixote de la Mancha, Man of La Mancha* became one of the favorite shows of the 1960s and has remained popular. The musical had a clever framing device: The author Miguel de Cervantes and his servant are thrown in an Inquisition dungeon. They have a large chest, and other prisoners start to steal their possessions and put Cervantes "on trial," but he placates them by offering entertainment. He tells the story of Don Quixote through simple props and suggestion, aided by the prisoners. The show's intensity came partly from the lack of an intermission, but also from truly violent emotions, especially in a startling rape scene. As Cervantes and Don Quixote, **Richard Kiley** gave a stunning performance. His sidekick, Sancho (Irving Jacobson), brought the same doses of comedy and reality found in the original novel. Aldonza (**Joan Diener**), identified by Don Quixote as his lady, Dulcinea, is nothing more than a kitchen strumpet, and she pays dearly when she starts to accept the mad knight's dreams. The Innkeeper (**Ray Middleton**) watches as Don Quixote turns his establishment upside down, and then dubs him

Knight of the Woeful Countenance. The Padre (**Robert Rounseville**) tries to help Don Quixote's family deal with his madness. The fantasy's ending was unforgettable, as Don Quixote, Sancho, and Aldonza briefly revive the dream before the knight's death. At the end of the show, Cervantes is called before the Inquisition, and his fellow prisoners exhort him to "dream the impossible dream."

Howard Taubman, writing in the *New York Times*, gave the show a somewhat mixed review, finding a "remarkable spirit," despite vulgar and trite moments. He was taken with Kiley, calling him "admirably credible—a mad, gallant, affecting figure who has honestly materialized from the pages of Cervantes," and describing his performance at great length. Taubman found Jacobson's Sancho "sympathetic," but noted how close the actor remained to his Yiddish theater background. Taubman seemed less than impressed with the music, admitting that Leigh and Darion sought to integrate the songs with the plot and characters, but that "their muse . . . does not always soar." Many disagreed with Taubman's verdict on the music. Several tunes alternate between 6/8 and 3/4, which many hear as a Spanish sound. This may be found, for example, in "Man of La Mancha," "Dulcinea," and "Aldonza." The orchestra included multiple guitarists, adding to the Spanish effect. The score's biggest hit was Don Quixote's "The Impossible Dream," a soaring ballad to a Latin beat. Secondary characters also had engaging music, including the Padre's "To Each His Dulcinea" and Sancho's "I Really Like Him." The 1972 film version starred Peter O'Toole, Sophia Loren, and James Coco, and the 2002 Broadway **revival** featured **Brian Stokes Mitchell**, Mary Elizabeth Mastrantonio, and Ernie Sabella.

MARIE CHRISTINE (2 DECEMBER 1999, VIVIAN BEAU-MONT, 42 PERFORMANCES). Music and words by **Michael John La Chiusa**, directed and choreographed by **Graciela Daniele**. A retelling of the legend of Medea set in New Orleans and Chicago during the 1890s, *Marie Christine* was an ambitious work built around the considerable talents of **Audra McDonald**, who played the title role. Marie Christine is a young woman of mixed race who carries her mother's talents for sorcery. Her lover is sea captain Dante Keyes (**Anthony Crivello**), and the show is told in flashback, beginning and ending in the women's prison where Marie Christine is incarcerated for murdering her children. The work represented a shift in the Broadway musical toward extremely serious themes and a sophisticated musical score, which included such notable numbers as Marie Christine's "Beautiful," the female nearly operatic duet "Way Back to Paradise," the moving lullaby "I Will Love You," Dante's "Your Name," and the finale, "Innocence Dies."

MARSH, HOWARD (?–1969). One of the leading Broadway **operetta** singers of the 1920s. His lyrical voice and impressive range garnered him tremendous praise. He created the roles of Franz Schober in *Blossom Time* (1921), the title character in *The Student Prince in Heidelberg* (1924), Ned Hamilton in *Cherry Blossoms* (1927), and Gaylord Ravenal in *Show Boat* (1927). He starred in numerous **Gilbert and Sullivan** revivals on Broadway during the 1930s.

MARSHALL, KATHLEEN (1962–). Choreographer who won **Tony Awards** for the **revivals** of *Wonderful Town* (2004) and *The Pajama Game* (2006).

MARSHALL, ROB (1960–). Imaginative dancer, choreographer, and director whose choreography for **revivals** of *She Loves Me* (1993), *Damn Yankees* (1994), *Company* (1995), *A Funny Thing Happened on the Way to the Forum* (1996), *Cabaret* (1998), and *Little Me* (1999), the last two of which he also directed, garnered him tremendous critical acclaim. He also choreographed *Victor/Victoria* (1995) on Broadway and directed the 2002 film version of *Chicago*.

MARTIN, MARY (1913–1990). Legendary Broadway star whose immediate "Everywoman" quality made her an audience favorite as well as one of **Rodgers and Hammerstein**'s most famous leading ladies. Her first major appearance was in 1938 in **Cole Porter**'s *Leave It to Me!*, where she did a mock striptease atop a trunk in "My Heart Belongs To Daddy." She introduced the **Kurt Weill** song "Speak Low" in *One Touch of Venus* (1943), and played the lead in a **touring production** of *Annie Get Your Gun*, a show which, though written by **Irving Berlin** and **Dorothy Fields**, was produced by Rodgers and Hammerstein. She captivated the legendary team with her commanding stage presence, and they wrote their next show, *South Pacific* (1949), for her. As Nellie Forbush, she brought a no-nonsense sensibility to the Arkansas nurse who overcomes her racial prejudices to marry Emile De Beque. She delighted audiences and critics with songs such as "Wonderful Guy," "I'm Gonna Wash That Man Right Outa My Hair" (during which she shampooed her hair on stage), and "Honey Bun" (performed in male drag), as well as the duets with her operatic costar **Ezio Pinza** such as "Twin Soliloquies." Rodgers and Hammerstein wrote for her again in 1959, this time creating *The Sound of Music* in which Martin played Maria, a nun who eventually leaves her order, marries Captain von Trapp, and becomes stepmother to his children. Martin worked with the real-life Maria von Trapp while preparing the role and sang such classics as "The Sound of the Music," "My Favorite Things," and "Do Re Mi." Martin won **Tony Awards** for *South Pacific* and *The Sound of Music*. She was also well known for her portrayal of the title role in *Peter Pan* (1954), both on stage and in television productions. Her pure voice, ability to portray a wide range of emotions, and physical appearance helped epitomize her as one of the leading Broadway actresses of the 20th century.

MARVENGA, ILSA. German-born **operetta** soprano best remembered for creating the role of Kathie in **Sigmund Romberg's** *The Student Prince* (1924). Her fine singing and physical appeal made her an audience favorite. She also starred in revivals of the classic operettas *Naughty Marietta* (1929, 1931) and *The Firefly* (1931).

MARY POPPINS **(16 NOVEMBER 2006, NEW AMSTERDAM, 53 PERFORMANCES AS OF 31 DECEMBER 2006).** Music and lyrics by Richard M. Sherman, Robert B. Sherman, George Stiles, and Anthony Drewe, book by Julian Fellowes, directed by Richard Eyre. Based on the P. L. Travers *Mary Poppins* stories and the 1964 Walt Disney film (with **Julie Andrews**, **Dick Van Dyke**, and **Ed Wynn**), the stage version of *Mary Poppins*, coproduced by **Disney Theatrical Productions** and **Cameron Mackintosh**, opened in London in 2004. On Broadway, Ashley Brown, a **replacement** Belle in *Beauty and the Beast*, played the title role, and Gavin Lee reprised his acclaimed London performance as Bert. Songs from the film were given new dramatic contexts, and new songs by George Stiles and Anthony Drewe appeared alongside those the Sherman brothers wrote for the film. Among the new songs were Mary Poppins's "Practically Perfect" and Mrs. Banks's emotive "Being Mrs. Banks," sung by **Rebecca Luker**. Visual effects include flying entrances and exits for Mary Poppins, "Supercalifragilisticexpialidocious" signed letter by letter by the ensemble, and Bert dancing on all four walls of the proscenium during "Step in Time."

MAYTIME (16 AUGUST 1917, SHUBERT, 492 PERFOR-MANCES). Libretto by **Rida Johnson Young** with assistance by Cyrus Wood, music by **Sigmund Romberg**. When the **Shuberts** decided to adapt Walter Kollo's immensely popular German **operetta** *Wie einst im Mai* for American audiences, they faced a tremendous challenge: World War I. Knowing that the work's German setting and source material would be major liabilities on Broadway, they had Rida Johnson Young transfer the action to New York City (from its original Berlin) and Sigmund Romberg create an entirely new score. This was Romberg's first complete score, and it proved to be one of his most successful. The story, which takes place over a 60-year period, begins with the forbidden love of Richard Wayne (**Charles Purcell**) and Ottilie van Zandt (**Peggy Wood**). Richard, or Dick, is from a poor family, and Ottilie's wealthy father will not allow his daughter to marry beneath her class. In the operetta's fourth and final act, the grandchildren of the thwarted lovers (played by the same actors who appear as Richard and Ottilie in the first three acts) meet and fall in love. In the operetta's bittersweet ending, the grandchildren realize the love their grandparents were denied. Romberg unifies the score through a recurring waltz duet, "Will You Remember," also known by the first two words of its refrain, "Sweetheart, Sweetheart." The song appears in each act as a symbol of the undying love between Richard and Ottilie. The *New York Times* reviewer called it "a work of extraordinary skill," and *Maytime*'s nostalgic and romantic atmosphere made it among the most popular musical theater offerings of its time. A film version starring Jeanette MacDonald and Nelson Eddy appeared in 1937, though the story was completely changed and the only song retained from the original was "Will You Remember."

MAY WINE (5 DECEMBER 1935, ST. JAMES, 213 PERFORMANCES). Music by **Sigmund Romberg**, lyrics by **Oscar Hammerstein II**, book by **Frank Mandel**, produced by **Laurence Schwab**. The long-running Depression-era musical began with Professor Johann Volk (**Walter Slezak**), a Viennese psychologist, confessing to murdering his wife. The story unfolds in flashback, and ends with the revelation that Volk, who had been the subject of a malicious plan devised by Baron Kuno Adelhurt, only shot a mannequin. Songs were treated as psychological soliloquies and included such evocative numbers as "I Built a Dream," "Dance, My Darlings," "Somebody Ought to Be Told," and an ode to a one-night stand titled "Once Around the Clock."

MAZZIE, MARIN (1960–). Lyrical singing actress who created the roles of Clara in *Passion* (1994) and Mother in *Ragtime* (1998) and brought a sympathetic portrayal to both parts. She played Lili/Katharine opposite **Brian Stokes Mitchell** in the 1999 **revival** of *Kiss Me, Kate*. **Replacement** roles include Aldonza/Dulcinea in the revival of *Man of La Mancha* (in 2003) and The Lady of the Lake in *Monty Python's Spamalot* (in 2006).

MCARDLE, ANDREA (1963–). Actress who played the title role in *Annie* (1975) when she was 12, and whose Broadway career continued to flourish as she reached adulthood. She appeared in *Starlight Express* (1987), *Les Misérables* (**replacement** Fantine, 1993), *Beauty and the Beast* (replacement Belle, 1999), and created the role of Margy Frake in the Broadway version of *State Fair* (1996).

MCDONALD, AUDRA (BORN AUDRA ANN MCDONALD, 1970–). Juilliard-trained soprano who won the **Tony Award** for Best Supporting Actress in a Musical for her first original role on Broadway, Carrie in the 1994 revival of *Carousel*. She won the Tony for Best Supporting Actress in a Play for *Master Class* (1995), in which she sang an aria from Verdi's opera *Macbeth*. She created Sarah in *Ragtime* (1998), for which she won her third Tony, this one for Best Actress in a Musical, and the title role in *Marie Christine* (1999). In addition to her work in musical theater, she has appeared in concert, on television, and in legitimate plays on Broadway. McDonald is known for her strong dramatic and vocal talents and the ability to use them in order to create multidimensional characters.

MCDOWALL, RODDY (BORN RODERICK ANDREW ANTHONY JUDE MCDOWALL, 1928–1998). British-born film, television, and stage actor who created the role of Mordred in *Camelot* (1960) and introduced "The Seven Deadly Virtues."

MCGOWAN, JOHN (ALSO KNOWN AS JACK MCGOWAN, 1894–1977). Librettist, director, and producer who began his Broadway career as a performer. He was involved with creating the librettos for the **musical comedies** *Hold Everything!* (1928), *Flying High* (1930), and *Girl Crazy* (1930).

MCHUGH, JIMMY (ALSO KNOWN AS JAMES MCHUGH, 1894–1969). Prolific composer of popular song whose Broadway credits include *Blackbirds of 1928* (with lyricist **Dorothy Fields**, his first major collaborator), *The International Revue* (1930, lyrics by Fields, included "On the Sunny Side of the Street"), *Keep Off the Grass* (1940), and *As the Girls Go* (1948). Since he envisioned songs as discreet entities, his work appeared mostly in **revues** and occasionally in **musical comedies**. His music was featured in *Sugar Babies* (1979), *Ain't Misbehavin'* (1988), and numerous **jukebox musicals**.

MCKECHNIE, DONNA (1942–). Singer and dancer who created the roles of Kathy in *Company* (1970) and Cassie in *A Chorus Line* (1975). She also played Emily Arden in the stage version of *State Fair* (1996).

MCNALLY, TERRENCE (1939–). Playwright and librettist who collaborated with composer **John Kander** and lyricist **Fred Ebb** on *The Rink* (1984) and *Kiss of the Spider Woman* (1993). He also created the librettos for *Ragtime* (1998), *The Full Monty* (2000), and *Chita Rivera: The Dancer's Life* (2005). He won four **Tony Awards**, two for Best Book of a Musical (*Kiss of the Spider Woman* and *Ragtime*) and two for Best Play (*Love! Valour! Compassion!* [1995] and *Master Class* [1995]). His work is characterized by strong characters and often controversial subject matter.

ME AND JULIET **(28 MAY 1953, MAJESTIC, 358 PERFOR-MANCES).** Music by **Richard Rodgers**, lyrics and book by **Oscar Hammerstein II**, directed by **George Abbott**, choreography by **Robert Alton**, produced by Rodgers and Hammerstein. For Rodgers and Hammerstein's sixth show, Rodgers wanted to create a **musical comedy** similar to *Pal Joey*, one of his later shows with Lorenz Hart, which had a successful revival in 1952. Rodgers and Hammerstein consciously wrote songs in an older style and hired the great musical comedy director George Abbott and choreographer Robert Alton. The plot was a backstage story about the preparation of a musical with a love story between second assistant stage manager George (Randy Hall) and a chorus girl, Jeanie (Isabel Bigley). Opening in Cleveland because no theater in New Haven (the usual tryout town) could accommodate the large set, *Me and Juliet* looked like a hit. This was not the case, however. The show opened to disappointing reviews, including that of **Brooks Atkinson** in the *New York Times*, where he commented that although captivating, it looked liked a rehearsal: "beautiful, talented, full of good things but still disorganized." Problems included Hammerstein's original play (never his forte), its weak "play-within-a-play" premise, and the overdomination of the set. "No Other Love," with its Latin rhythmic underpinning, was the only song from the score that became popular. (The melody was also used in the television series *Victory at Sea*.)

ME AND MY GIRL **(10 AUGUST 1986, MARQUIS, 1,420 PER-FORMANCES).** Music by **Noel Gay**, lyrics and book by L. Arthur Rose and Douglas Furber, book revised by Stephen Fry. A West End hit from 1937 and successfully revived there in 1985, *Me and My Girl* enjoyed a fine run on Broadway with star **Robert Lindsay** reprising his role from the London revival. He played Bill Snibson, a Cockney from Lambeth who inherits an earldom. In order to collect his legacy, he requires manners and breeding, but delights in shocking aristocrats at every possible opportunity by stealing, handling women inappropriately, and making fun of servants. He has a true love from his own class, Sally Smith (Maryann Plunkett). Some of Gay's songs for the original score were exchanged for other hits, but others, including the title tune and "The Lambeth Walk," remained.

MEGAMUSICAL. A type of musical theater especially popular from the late 1970s through the 1990s in which everything—sets, costumes, singing, choreography, musical style, emotion—are impressively grandiose. Many British imports, especially those associated with producer **Cameron Mackintosh**, are exemplars of the approach. **Andrew Lloyd Webber** and Claude-Michel Schönberg are two composers whose work helped define the style. Notable megamusicals include *Les Misérables* (1985, London; 1987, New York) and *The Phantom of the Opera* (1986, London; 1988, New York). *See also CATS*; *MISS SAIGON*; *THE SCARLET PIMPERNEL*; *SUNSET BOULEVARD*; *TITANIC*.

MENKEN, ALAN (1949–). Composer for film and stage whose Broadway scores include *Little Shop of Horrors* (1986, **off-Broadway**; 2003, Broadway) and *Beauty and the Beast* (1994). He is best known for his songs in Disney animated features and has worked with lyricists **Howard Ashman**, **Tim Rice**, and **Stephen Schwartz**.

***THE ME NOBODY KNOWS* (18 MAY 1970, ORPHEUM, 208 PERFORMANCES; BROADWAY: 18 DECEMBER 1970, HELEN HAYES, 378 PERFORMANCES).** Music by Gary William Friedman, lyrics by Will Holt. Based on Stephen M. Joseph's book of the same name, *The Me Nobody Knows* told the story of 12 young people who live in New York City slums. Joseph played the teacher who assigns them to write essays on their lives, and then turns their compelling stories into the basis for the musical. According to **Clive Barnes**'s review in the *New York Times*, the show had no plot but told many stories. He loved the show's "understanding and compassion" and praised the "eloquent music" and "tersely apt yet poetic lyrics," which allowed the show to be "both bitter and joyous." He compared the show to *Hair* in its effective introduction to a way of life.

MENZEL, IDINA (1971–). Actress known for her convincing and sympathetic portrayals of morally ambiguous characters. She created the role of Maureen Johnson in *Rent* (1996, which she reprised in the 2005 film version) and won the **Tony** for Best Actress in a Musical for her portrayal of Elphaba in *Wicked* (2003). In green makeup, Menzel brought a sensitive pathos to the character who later became the Wicked Witch of the West in *The Wizard of Oz*. She uses her rich pop-oriented voice to bring an extremely high level of dramatic intensity to her musical interpretations.

MERCER, JOHNNY (ALSO KNOWN AS JOHN MERCER, 1909–1976). Lyricist, singer, and composer who created lyrics for *St. Louis Woman* (1946, music by **Harold Arlen**) and *Li'l Abner* (1956, music by Gene de Paul). Most of his successful songs were written for Hollywood films. Mercer believed in the primacy of the song and integrated colloquial aspects of his southern upbringing to his lyrics. His lyrics have appeared in many **jukebox** and **dance musical**s, including **Bob Fosse**'s *Dancin'* (1978), *Sophisticated Ladies* (1981, featuring the music of Duke Ellington), *Dream* (1997, based on Mercer's lyrics), and *Fosse* (1999).

MERMAN, ETHEL (BORN ETHEL AGNES ZIMMERMAN, 1909–1984). Celebrated actress whose iconic belt voice established her as one of the leading Broadway singers from the 1930s through the 1950s. She made her Broadway debut as the saloonkeeper's wife in *Girl Crazy* (1930), introducing the **Gershwin** standard "I Got Rhythm." During the 1930s and 1940s, she starred in five musicals by **Cole Porter**: *Anything Goes* (1934), *Red, Hot and Blue!* (1936), *Du Barry Was a Lady* (1939), *Panama Hattie* (1940), and *Something for the Boys* (1943). A favorite of **Irving Berlin** in his later years, she starred in his *Annie Get Your Gun* (1946) and *Call Me Madam* (1950). Her already legendary career reached new heights when she created the role of Mama Rose in **Jule Styne** and **Stephen Sondheim**'s *Gypsy* (1959). She introduced musical theater classics such as "I Get a Kick Out of You," "Blow, Gabriel, Blow," "They Say It's Wonderful," "Doin' What Comes Naturally," "There's No Business Like Show Business," "Some People," "Everything's Coming up Roses," and "Rose's Turn," songs that remain closely associated with the genre-defining actress.

MERRICK, DAVID (1911–2000). One of Broadway's most flamboyant producers and showmen, Merrick's list of hits is long and varied, and includes *Gypsy* (1959), *Carnival* (1961), *Oliver!* (1963), *Hello, Dolly!* (1964), *Promises, Promises* (1968), and *42nd Street* (1980).

MERRILL, BOB (1921–1998). Composer and lyricist who wrote pop songs during the 1940s and 1950s (including "How Much Is That Doggie in the Window" and "Mambo Italiano") before beginning his career on Broadway. He created music and lyrics for *New Girl in Town* (1957), *Take Me Along* (1959), and *Carnival!* (1961), and lyrics for *Funny Girl* (1964) and *Sugar* (1972). He brought the sensibility from his popular song career to his work for Broadway and wrote some of the musical stage's most memorable lyrics, such as *Funny Girl*'s "Don't Rain on My Parade" and "People."

THE MERRY MALONES **(26 SEPTEMBER 1927, ERLANGER'S, 208 PERFORMANCES).** Music, lyrics, book, and produced by **George M. Cohan**. Another show in which Cohan exhibited his Irish heritage, *The Merry Malones* included all of Cohan's usual markers. It opened the new Erlanger Theater and was the last time that Cohan appeared in one of his own shows. Joe Westcott (Alan Edwards), a millionaire's son, is in love with Molly Malone (Polly Walker) from the Bronx but cannot marry her until he disinherits himself. He accomplishes his task, but his father convinces Molly to accept his money. Cohan ended up playing Molly's father because the actor hired for the part died while the show was in Boston. None of the songs achieved popularity outside of the show. The unsigned review in the *New York Times* characterized it as a "shamrock-studded harlequinade" and reported that, as always, Cohan waved the flag, but the evening's main message was "that God is good to the Irish."

THE MERRY WIDOW **(21 OCTOBER 1907, NEW AMSTERDAM, 416 PERFORMANCES).** Music by **Franz Lehár**, lyrics by Adrian Ross, book by Victor Léon and Leo Stein with English translation by Basil Hood. One of the most famous pieces of light musical theater, *The Merry Widow* came to New York after triumphing in European capitals. It premiered in Vienna as *Die lustige Witwe* on 30 December 1905, and Basil Hood's translation into English for London was fairly loyal to the original libretto. *The Merry Widow* opened in London on 8 June 1907, running there for 778 performances. The same version came to New York. Its fabulous popularity led to touring companies, a reinvigoration of Viennese-style **operetta** in the United States, endless commercial tie-ins, and the increased popularity of the waltz on Broadway.

The plot and some character names were slightly altered in the English-language version. The title character is now Sonia (Ethel Jackson), a wealthy widow from the fictional, tiny country of Marsovia. Her fellow Marsovians worry that she might marry a foreigner. This would remove her fortune from the national bank, and their economy would collapse. They encourage Prince Danilo (Donald Brian) of Marsovia to woo Sonia, which he does, but his heart is with the ladies who frequent Maxim's in Paris. Danilo, however, comes to love Sonia, saving Marsovia. The sets of the Marsovian Embassy and Maxim's were glorious, and the score became hugely popular in New York. Lehár was a gifted waltz composer, and filled *The Merry Widow* with numbers intended for singing and dancing. Among the hits were "The Merry Widow Waltz" (also called "I Love You So"), "Maxim's," "Vilja," "A Dutiful Wife," and "The Women." The show's popularity was unaffected by the bank panic that started two days after it opened in New York.

Theater and classical music critics raved about *The Merry Widow*. The unsigned *New York Sun* review (probably written by noted music critic W. J. Henderson) called *The Merry Widow* far superior to the "lamentable rot and debasing rubbish" that usually bears the name "comic opera." The show provides "excellent comedy" and calls for "genuine acting ability." **Reginald De Koven**, in the *New York World*, praised the show's "dramatic purpose and coherency, the artistic sincerity." The unsigned review in the *New York Times* describes a packed theater and assures the reader that *The Merry Widow* has lost none of it "gayety in crossing the ocean." *The Merry Widow* returned to Broadway in 1921, 1929, 1931, and 1943 and regularly appears on opera stages.

MEXICAN HAYRIDE **(28 JANUARY 1944, WINTER GARDEN, 481 PERFORMANCES).** Music and lyrics by **Cole Porter**, book by **Herbert** and **Dorothy Fields**, produced by Michael Todd. A vehicle for Bobby Clark, *Mexican Hayride* was an approachable **musical comedy** in the time-honored mold. Clark played Joe Bascom, an American fugitive in Mexico. He meets Lombo Compos (George Givot) and sets up a numbers racket. Among those trying to track down Bascom is the American chargé d'affaires, David Winthrop (Wilbur Evans). Winthrop's love interest is an American female bullfighter, Montana (June Havoc). Clark and Givot use several ridiculous disguises and are finally caught, while Winthrop and Montana end up together. Lewis Nichols, writing in the *New York Times*, enjoyed the show. He found Clark "upholding the tradition of Broadway comedy," the book "harmless," and Porter's score "satisfactory." He praised most aspects of the production and many in the cast, calling June Havoc "pert and attractive" and noting that Wilbur Evans "has an unusually good voice." Basically, "everything is in order." The best songs were "I Love You" and "Count Your Blessings."

MIDDLETON, RAY (1907–1984). Lyrical singing actor whose leading roles include John Kent in *Roberta* (1933), Washington Irving in *Knickerbocker Holiday* (1938), Frank Butler in *Annie Get Your Gun* (1946), Sam Cooper in *Love Life* (1948), and The Innkeeper in *Man of La Mancha* (1967). He was a **replacement** Emile De Beque in the original production of *South Pacific* (1949).

MILK AND HONEY (10 OCTOBER 1961, MARTIN BECK, 543 PERFORMANCES). Music and lyrics by **Jerry Herman**, book by Don Appell. The first Broadway musical to take place in Israel and Jerry Herman's first Broadway score, *Milk and Honey* ran for about 16 months but reportedly made no profit. **Robert Weede** played Phil, an American businessman separated from his wife and visiting his daughter and her husband on an Israeli kibbutz. He meets fellow American Ruth (**Mimi Benzell**) and they fall in love, but finally Ruth decides to go back to the United States and wait for Phil to divorce his wife. The comedy revolved around Clara Weiss (Molly Picon), an older American in Israel trying to find a husband, which she does in Mr. Horowitz (Reuben Singer). Herman's delightful score possessed an engaging combination of Jewish musical ideas and traditional Broadway writing. In his *New York Times* review, **Howard Taubman** praised the show's "heartwarming integrity" and "respect for human beings," but found that the "comedy is not sparkling." Among the show's best songs are "Shalom" and "I Will Follow You."

MILLER, ANN (BORN JOHNNIE LUCILLE ANN COLLIER, 1919–2004). Dancer, known especially for her remarkable tap dancing, bouffant hairdos, and belt voice who appeared in *George White's*

Scandals (1938) before achieving tremendous fame in Hollywood film musicals during the 1940s and 1950s. In 1969, she took over the title role in the original production of *Mame* and also appeared in *Sugar Babies* (1979).

MILLER, MARILYN (ALSO KNOWN AS MARILYNN MILLER, BORN MARY ELLEN REYNOLDS, 1898–1936). Tap-dancing singer who appeared in numerous **revues**, including editions of *The Passing Show* and *Ziegfeld Follies*. As a result of her commanding stage presence and tumultuous romantic relationship with **Florenz Ziegfeld**, she starred in several of his **musical comedies**, including *Sally* (1920), *Sunny* (1925), and *Rosalie* (1928). She also appeared in the 1933 **Irving Berlin** revue *As Thousands Cheer*.

MINNELLI, LIZA (1946–). The daughter of **Judy Garland** and Vincente Minnelli, she won her first **Tony Award** for the title role in **John Kander** and **Fred Ebb**'s *Flora, the Red Menace* (1965). She built her reputation singing the work of Kander and Ebb, substituting for **Gwen Verdon** in *Chicago* (1975), then starring in *The Act* (1977) and subsequently winning a second Tony. She can move almost indistinguishably between speech and song, and uses her dramatic vocal capabilities to portray the full range of human emotion.

LES MISÉRABLES **(12 MARCH 1987, BROADWAY, 6,680 PERFORMANCES).** Music by Claude-Michel Schönberg, English lyrics by Herbert Kretzmer after French text by **Alain Boublil** and Jean-Marc Natel, adapted and directed by **Trevor Nunn** and John Caird, presented by **Cameron Mackintosh**. Based on Victor Hugo's novel, *Les Misérables*, billed as "the world's most popular musical," as of 2006 has played in 223 cities in 38 countries in 21 languages and has been seen by more than 51 million people worldwide. After *Les Misérables* opened in Paris, Cameron Mackintosh supervised its adaptation for the London stage, which became the basis for all subsequent productions, including the American one. Several members of the London cast re-created their roles in New York, including **Colm Wilkinson** as the hero Jean Valjean and **Terrence Mann** as Javert. The large cast included several important roles played by Randy Graff (Fantine), David Bryant (Marius), Frances Ruffelle

(Eponine), **Judy Kuhn** (Cosette), Michael Maguire (Enjolras), Leo Burmester (Thénardier), and Jennifer Butt (Mme. Thénardier). These varied characters participate in a tapestry of events surrounding the unsuccessful French Revolution of 1832, with students and radicals dying on the barricades. The **megamusical** includes themes of human love, sacrifice, redemption, and **social justice**, set to a sung-through score filled with soaring ballads, stirring marches, and even some comic numbers.

New York Times critic **Frank Rich** raved about the show, noting that anyone who doubts whether the "contemporary musical theater can . . . yank an audience right out of its seats" should see the act 1 finale. Rich goes on to describe this ensemble finale, where several points of the story are woven into the song "One Day More." He also describes how the production helps make the number work, concluding that the success of such a scene shows how well this European work has transferred to Broadway. He warns those who love the entirety of Hugo's novel that many favorite scenes are missing, but "the thematic spirit of the original is preserved." Although most critics liked the show, Howard Kessel of the *Daily News* disliked the spectacle and called the music "drivel." *Les Misérables* owes as much to the tradition of 19th-century grand opera as it does the modern musical theater. The stage spectacle is overwhelming, with two enormous towers that lower into position to become the barricades manned by the doomed students, although for most of the three-hour show, sets are minimal. Famous songs include "At the End of the Day," "I Dreamed a Dream," "Who Am I?," "Master of the House," "Do You Hear the People Sing?," "One Day More," "On My Own," "Bring Him Home," and "Empty Chairs at Empty Tables." One of the show's most memorable moments is Valjean's solo "Bring Him Home," when he prays for the safe return of the young revolutionary, Marius. A limited-run Broadway revival opened on 9 November 2006.

MISS LIBERTY **(15 JULY 1949, IMPERIAL, 308 PERFOR-MANCES).** Music and lyrics by **Irving Berlin**, book by Robert E. Sherwood, staged by **Moss Hart**, dances and musical numbers staged by **Jerome Robbins**. With a score by America's most successful songwriter, a book by a fine playwright, and other luminaries among the creators, one might have expected *Miss Liberty* to soar, but the show misfired. The plot involved France's famous gift to the United States, and also encompassed a romantic triangle, a search for the sculptor's model, and a newspaper turf war. The stars included **Eddie Albert**, Allyn McLerie, and Mary McCarty. Berlin's score featured "Let's Take an Old-Fashioned Walk," "Homework," and the famous setting of Emma Lazarus's poem "Give Me Your Tired, Your Poor." **Brooks Atkinson** pulled no punches in his *New York Times* review. He opened by stating "'Miss Liberty' is a disappointing musical comedy . . . put together without sparkle or originality." He calls the book "a pedestrial tale" and the score "not one of Mr. Berlin's most memorable." Atkinson liked the cast, however, especially Albert.

MISS SAIGON **(11 APRIL 1991, BROADWAY, 4,092 PERFORMANCES).** Music by Claude-Michel Schönberg; lyrics by **Richard Maltby Jr.** and **Alain Boublil**, adapted from original French lyrics by Boublil; directed by Nicholas Hytner; musical staging by Bob Avian; presented by **Cameron Mackintosh**. The first musical to be set during the Vietnam War and bearing a close resemblance to Giacomo Puccini's opera *Madama Butterfly*, *Miss Saigon* gave the creators of *Les Misérables* another international hit. After opening successfully in London, Mackintosh announced that he intended to bring *Miss Saigon* to New York with **Lea Salonga** (Kim) and **Jonathan Pryce** (The Engineer) reprising their London roles. The Asian-American actors in Actor's Equity tried to bar Pryce, a Caucasian, from playing an Asian role. Mackintosh canceled the production and Actors' Equity backed down, providing *Miss Saigon* with additional publicity.

In the story, Kim is a prostitute in Saigon, working for The Engineer, a pimp. Chris, an American soldier stationed in Vietnam, and Kim fall in love, but he is forced to leave as Saigon falls, not knowing that she is carrying his child. Thuy (Barry K. Bernal) tries to blackmail Kim because of her son, and, in one of the show's most dramatic moments, she shoots him. The Engineer has thoughts of going to America, the land of capitalist opportunity, and shares his vision in the spectacular "The American Dream." After the war, Chris's friend, John (**Hinton Battle**), takes interest in the plight of the Bui-Doi, the children fathered by American soldiers in Vietnam who are outcasts in their own country. (This is the show's theme of **social justice**.)

Through John, Chris learns of his son. However, Chris is now married to Ellen (Liz Calloway), and the couple goes to Vietnam, where Ellen meets Kim. The only way Kim can guarantee that her son will return with his father to America is to kill herself, which she does.

Critical response in New York was mixed. **Frank Rich**, writing in the *New York Times*, concluded that "however sanitizing the words and corny the drama of 'Miss Saigon,' the real impact of the musical goes well beyond any literal reading." The score, like that of *Les Misérables*, includes some fine music, and the overall influence of rock is stronger in *Miss Saigon* than in *Les Mis*. This is understandable, considering that Schönberg uses musical styles of the 1970s to evoke the decade. Especially effective are the opening nightclub number "The Heat Is On In Saigon," the love duet between Chris and Kim "Sun and Moon," and Chris's anthem "Bui Doi," accompanied by visual images of dispossessed and interned children.

MITCHELL, BRIAN STOKES (1958–). Singing actor with a rich and resonant baritone voice who created the role of Coalhouse Walker in *Ragtime* (1998) and won the 2000 **Tony Award** for Best Actor in a Musical for his portrayal of Fred/Petruccio in the revival of *Kiss Me, Kate*. He starred in the 2002 revival of *Man of La Mancha* and played Emile De Beque in the 2005 Carnegie Hall concert version of *South Pacific*, broadcast on PBS. His strong acting ability and malleable singing voice allow him to convincingly play a wide variety of characters.

MITCHELL, JULIAN (ca. 1854–1926). Director who rose from the ranks of dancers and choreographers, and worked on many shows in the decades around 1900, including *A Trip to Chinatown* (1891), *Babes in Toyland* (1903), and early editions of *Ziegfeld Follies*.

MITCHELL, RUTH (ca. 1919–2000). Stage manager, assistant, and producer who worked closely with **Hal Prince** and **Stephen Sondheim**. She won a **Tony Award** for *Cabaret* (1966) and a Special Tony Award for the 1974 **revival** of *Candide*.

MITCHELL, THOMAS (1892–1962). Comic actor, writer, and director who won a **Tony Award** for Best Actor in a Musical for creating

Dr. Downer in *Hazel Flagg* (1953). Directorial credits include the **revues** *Calling All Stars* (1934) and *At Home Abroad* (1935).

***MLLE. MODISTE* (25 DECEMBER 1905, KNICKERBOCKER, 202 PERFORMANCES).** Music by **Victor Herbert**, lyrics and book by **Henry Blossom**. Conceived for opera singer **Fritzi Scheff**, *Mlle. Modiste* ran for almost seven months in New York and toured for three years. Scheff played Fifi, a hat shop clerk who loves Captain Etienne de Bouvray (Walter Percival). Her paramour's uncle, a Count, does not want the officer to marry below his station, and her boss, Madame Cecile, wants her to marry her son. An American millionaire, Hiram Bent (Claude Gillingwater) meets Fifi and learns that she wants a stage career. He pays for her voice lessons and helps her career flourish, and the Count removes his objections to the union. Herbert's score included the hit waltz "Kiss Me Again" (a tune associated with Scheff for the rest of her career) and the cleverly titled "I Want What I Want When I Want It."

***MONTE CRISTO, JR.* (12 FEBRUARY 1919, WINTER GARDEN, 254 PERFORMANCES).** Music by **Sigmund Romberg** and Jean Schwartz, book and lyrics by **Harold Atteridge**. Similar in concept to the **Al Jolson** vehicles in that a framing story surrounded what was in essence a **revue**, *Monte Cristo, Jr.* starred **Charles Purcell**, a singer known for his work in **operetta**, as Monte, who falls asleep and dreams that he is Dante, the actor who is playing the lead in a stage adaptation of Alexandre Dumas's *The Count of Monte Cristo*.

***MONTY PYTHON'S SPAMALOT* (17 MARCH 2005, SHUBERT, 749 PERFORMANCES AS OF 31 DECEMBER 2006).** Lyrics and book by Eric Idle, music by John Du Prez and Eric Idle. Although billed as a "musical lovingly ripped off from *Monty Python and the Holy Grail*," the show included other Monty Python references and songs and numerous reflexive references to the world of the Broadway musical, including a pastiche of a 1990s-style ballad in "The Song That Goes Like This" (sung by Galahad [Christopher Sieber] and The Lady of the Lake [**Sara Ramirez**]) with visuals that parody the journey to the underground lake in **Andrew Lloyd Webber**'s *The Phantom of the Opera*) and the musical-theater obsession of Sir Robin (David Hyde Pierce). American references abound, including a Las Vegas-style number where Arthur's (**Tim Curry**) Round Table becomes a roulette wheel, and, in a 21st-century twist to the Arthurian tale, Lancelot (Hank Azaria) is gay. The show won the 2005 **Tony Award** for Best Musical.

MOORE, GRACE (1898–1947). Operatic soprano who appeared in revues, including *Hitchy-Koo* (1920), the 1923 and 1924 editions of **Irving Berlin**'s *Music Box Revues*, and the *Ziegfeld Follies* of 1931. She also appeared in film, including *New Moon* (1930), the first film version of **Sigmund Romberg**'s *The New Moon*.

MOORE, MELBA (BORN MELBA HILL, 1945–). Rhythm-and-blues and gospel singer and actress who played Dionne in the original production of *Hair* (1968), won a **Tony Award** for Best Featured Actress in a Musical for her portrayal of Lutiebelle in *Purlie* (1970), and starred as Marsinah in *Timbuktu!* (1978). She created incidental music and lyrics for the play *Inacent Black*, in which she also appeared, and in 1995 was a **replacement** Fantine in *Les Misérables*.

MOORE, ROBERT (1927–1984). Director with a gift for comedy whose Broadway musical credits include *Promises, Promises* (1968), *Lorelei* (1974), *They're Playing Our Song* (1979), and *Woman of the Year* (1981).

MOORE, VICTOR (1876–1962). Performer who epitomized the concept of **musical comedy**. He created numerous memorable characters, including "Shorty" McGee in *Oh, Kay!* (1926), Herbert in *Funny Face* (1927), Vice President Alexander Throttlebottom in *Of Thee I Sing* (1931) and its sequel, *Let 'Em Eat Cake* (1933), Moonface Martin (Public Enemy No. 13) in *Anything Goes* (1934), bathtub salesman Alonzo P. Goodhue in *Leave It to Me!* (1938), and Senator Oliver P. Loganberry in *Louisiana Purchase* (1940). He performed the music of **George Gershwin** and **Cole Porter** and appeared onstage with the likes of **Gertrude Lawrence**, **Ethel Merman**, and **Mary Martin**.

MORGAN, HELEN (1900–1941). Musical theater star who created the role of Julie in **Jerome Kern**'s *Show Boat* (1927) and forged an iconic image by sitting on top of an upright piano while singing

"Bill." Two years later, Kern created *Sweet Adeline* as a vehicle for her.

MORISON, PATRICIA (1915–). After appearing in several films and a handful of short-lived Broadway shows, Morrison achieved a career success as the original Lilli Vanessi/Katherine in **Cole Porter**'s *Kiss Me, Kate* (1948). In the role, she aptly demonstrated her strong sense of comic timing and wide-ranging vocal abilities, from near vaudevillian to coloratura.

MORROW, DORETTA (BORN DORETTA MARANO, 1927–1968). Singing actress whose creamy vocal timbre brought her praise as Tuptim in *The King and I* (1951), in which she sang "My Lord and Master," "We Kiss in a Shadow," and "I Have Dreamed," and Marsinah in *Kismet* (1953), which featured her in "Baubles, Bangles and Beads," "Stranger in Paradise," and "And This Is My Beloved." Prior to these successes, she played Kitty Verdun in the **musical comedy** *Where's Charley?* (1948).

MORSE, ROBERT (1931–). Singing actor who won a **Tony Award** for his portrayal of corporate-ladder-climbing J. Pierrepont Finch in *How to Succeed in Business without Really Trying* (1961) and reprised the role in the 1967 film. Other roles include Richard in *Take Me Along* (1959), Jerry in *Sugar* (1972), and David in the short-lived *So Long, 174th Street* (1976).

MOSTEL, ZERO (1915–1977). Vivacious actor with a commanding stage presence who won **Tony Awards** for his portrayals of Pseudolus in *A Funny Thing Happened on the Way to the Forum* (1962) and Tevye in *Fiddler on the Roof* (1964). Mostel was able to move seamlessly between speaking and singing, and integrated the two types of vocal production in his performance style.

***THE MOST HAPPY FELLA* (3 MAY 1956, IMPERIAL, 676 PERFORMANCES).** Music, lyrics, and book by **Frank Loesser**. Producing an opera is unusual on Broadway, but Frank Loesser basically wrote one in *The Most Happy Fella*. Derived from Sidney Howard's play *They Knew What They Wanted*, Loesser endowed the show with more than 40 musical numbers and included very little dialogue. The story involves a lonely, middle-aged Italian owner of a Napa Valley winery, Tony (**Robert Weede**). He has set his eye on the waitress at a San Francisco eatery, and writes her, asking for her photograph. Rosabella (Jo Sullivan) complies, but requests a picture in return. Tony sends one of a younger hired hand, Joe (Art Lund). She comes to the ranch and discovers the deception, but before she can leave Tony is injured, and she remains with him out of compassion. Tony and Rosabella marry, but not before she has an affair with Joe and becomes pregnant. Tony accepts the child and promises to raise it. Critics were divided on the show, mostly because of its widely disparate tone. Loesser wrote primarily operatic music for Weede (such as "My Heart Is So Full of You") but more traditional Broadway ballads for Rosabella (such as "Somebody, Somewhere"). There are also pure musical comedy numbers, such as the perennially popular "Standing On The Corner (Watching All the Girls Go By)" and "Big D." Loesser himself called the show an "extended musical comedy." **Brooks Atkinson**, writing in the *New York Times*, found *Fella* "a profoundly moving dramatic experience," and stated that "Loesser has range and depth enough to give it an overwhelming musical statement." Ultimately, though, he concluded that Loesser and director Joseph Anthony's attempt to combine "music drama" and "Broadway entertainment" was unsuccessful.

MOVIN' OUT **(24 OCTOBER 2002, RICHARD RODGERS, 1,303 PERFORMANCES).** Music and lyrics by Billy Joel, conceived, directed, and choreographed by **Twyla Tharp**. Director-choreographer Twyla Tharp conceived the spectacular **jukebox musical** featuring Billy Joel songs. The plot of the **dance musical** followed a group of five friends from their high school graduation in the 1960s, through Vietnam and its aftermath, to their reunion years later. The story is told through Tharp's choreography, and, as opposed to *Contact* with its prerecorded music, *Movin' Out* uses live music, led by piano-playing Michael Cavanagh. Tharp won a **Tony Award** for Best Choreography, and Billy Joel and Stuart Malina won the Tony for Best **Orchestrations**.

MR. PRESIDENT (20 OCTOBER 1962, ST. JAMES, 265 PERFORMANCES). Music and lyrics by **Irving Berlin**, book by **Howard Lindsay** and **Russel Crouse**, staged by **Joshua Logan**, choreography by Peter Gennaro. Irving Berlin's Broadway swan song, *Mr. President* was a disappointment and ran for only eight months. Reminiscent of the Kennedys, who were then occupying the White House, the show starred Robert Ryan and **Nanette Fabray**. The Russians ruin President Henderson when they cancel his goodwill visit to Moscow as he is en route. The President arrives in the middle of the night and is ignored; he loses the next election because of the humiliation. In act 2 he turns down a seat in the Senate on reasons of principle, but then serves the next president. A subplot involved a relationship between the couple's daughter (Anita Gillette) and a Secret Service agent (Jack Haskell). In his *New York Times* review, Howard Taubman panned the book, calling it "remnants of lame topical allusions, pallid political jokes and stale gags," and described the whole show as "mechanical in an old-fashioned way." He called Berlin's contribution as below his best efforts, but cited notable songs such as "Pigtails and Freckles" and "Empty Pockets Filled with Love."

MR. WONDERFUL (22 MARCH 1956, BROADWAY, 383 PERFORMANCES). Music and lyrics by **Jerry Bock**, Larry Holofcener, and George Weiss, book by **Joseph Stein** and Will Glickman, conceived by **Jule Styne**. A vehicle for nightclub performer **Sammy Davis Jr.**, *Mr. Wonderful* ran for nearly a year. Davis played Charlie Welch, a nightclub entertainer whose friends convince him to try out his act in Miami. Act 2 was essentially the nightclub act that Davis had been doing with his father and uncle, Sammy Davis Sr. and Will Mastin. **Brooks Atkinson**, writing for the *New York Times*, described the show as "redundant" because all it did was demonstrate that Sammy Davis Jr. is a talented nightclub performer. The critic states that the show opens "with an explosion of mediocrity" that is exciting but "corny." The two best songs in the show were "Too Close for Comfort," which Davis sang, and the title song, performed by Olga James.

THE MULLIGAN GUARDS' BALL (13 JANUARY 1879, THEATRE COMIQUE, 153 PERFORMANCES). Music by David

Braham, lyrics and book by **Edward Harrigan**. One of the early musical comedies from the team of **Harrigan and Hart**, *The Mulligan Guards' Ball* brought together stereotypical characters and situations that Harrigan and Hart had previously used in shorter skits. Harrigan and Hart mined their Irish heritage, and included other ethnic character types as well, including Germans and **African Americans**, who were treated with sensitivity and dignity. *The Mulligan Guards' Ball* was not a full-length piece and was always offered along with a **vaudeville** act. The "guards" in the title referred to a group of men who, organized by a local politician, paraded in uniforms and drank large amounts of beer. Dan Mulligan (Harrigan), leader of such a group named after him, fights off younger men who desire to take over. An African American group has double-booked the hall he rented for their ball, and the African Americans move to a room directly above the Mulligans. The upstairs merry-making becomes so wild that revelers come tumbling through the floor. Meanwhile, Dan's son has fallen in love with a German girl; the children elope, and the families accept their marriage upon their return. Popular songs included "The Babies on Our Block" and "Paddy Duffy's Cart," as well as **interpolations**.

MURPHY, DONNA (1958–). Her heartfelt portrayals of Fosca in *Passion* (1994) and Anna in a revival of *The King and I* (1996) brought her **Tony Awards** for Best Actress in a Musical. She played Ruth Sherwood in a revival of *Wonderful Town* (2003) that demonstrated her versatility as an actress and singer.

MUSICAL COMEDY. A comic play with inserted songs and dances, especially those written for Broadway and London's West End since the 1890s. Its antecedents included **vaudeville, minstrel shows**, and **burlesque**. Of the Broadway genres popular at the beginning of the 20th century, the musical comedy was the most American, combining a lighthearted plot with Tin Pan Alley songs and popular dances, often rendered by a scantily clad female chorus. Among the first true musical comedies was *A Trip to Chinatown* (1891), praised for its fast pace and based on vaudeville routines with language close to natural American speech. The leading musical comedy figure in the first two decades after 1900 was **George M. Cohan**, who crafted rapid-fire entertainment and formed the prototype for a musical comedy star: a genial actor who could sing (or at least declaim songs) and dance, and might have other specialty acts that would be worked into every show. The golden decade for the musical comedy was the 1920s, and featured such fine songwriters as **Richard Rodgers** and **Lorenz Hart**, the **Gershwin** brothers, and **Jerome Kern**. Dozens of musical comedies opened each year, and the most successful ran just over a year. Audiences enjoyed high production values and high profile stars who could nearly guarantee a show's success. Musical comedies remained similar in the 1930s, but economic realities caused fewer shows to open. The advent of film talkies brought the genre to the screen, and a number of Broadway creators moved to Hollywood.

Broadway genres changed forever with *Oklahoma!* (1943), which included many musical comedy conventions amidst greater concern for integration. Even some shows from the 1940s that strongly resembled the musical comedy, such as *On the Town* and *Annie Get Your Gun*, showed more of a sense of integration. Closer to old-time musical comedies were *High Button Shoes* and *Gentlemen Prefer Blondes*. In the 1950s, many shows represented a true synthesis of the traditional musical comedy and strong elements of the **musical play**. Characters in *Guys and Dolls*, for example, were New York types familiar from earlier musical comedies, but the songs advanced the plot and described characters. Much the same could be said for *The Pajama Game* and *Damn Yankees*, both directed by **George Abbott**, the musical comedy's acknowledged master. The trend continued in the 1960s with shows such as *Hello, Dolly!*. Musical comedy elements remained in shows from the 1980s and beyond as a means to recall earlier times and styles, as is evident in *42nd Street*, *My One and Only*, *Crazy for You*, *Thoroughly Modern Millie*, *The Producers*, and *Monty Python's Spamalot*. *See also* MUSICAL PLAY; OPERETTA.

MUSICAL PLAY. A show in which the musical numbers and sequences, and perhaps the dances, play major roles in advancing the plot; the genre is sometimes referred to simply as the "musical." Movement toward the musical play began in the first half of the 20th century, and by about 1950, audiences expected musicals to be integrated. Almost every **musical comedy** and **operetta** shows some degree of plot/music integration. An early step toward an intentional integration of plot and music may be seen in the so-called **Princess Theatre musicals** by **Jerome Kern**, **P. G. Wodehouse**, **Guy Bolton**, and others in the mid-1910s. In *Oh, Boy!* (1917), for example, Kern and his collaborators combined a witty book with careful song placements. An important musical play was Kern and **Oscar Hammerstein II**'s *Show Boat* (1927), in which the creators combined a serious plot with musical conventions from both musical comedy and operetta. All of the songs advance the plot and add depth to the characterization. *Girl Crazy* (1930), for example, often cited as a typical musical comedy, includes a number of songs that at least comment upon the plot or add some depth to characterization. The plot, however, is silly, serving only as a vehicle for **George Gershwin**'s delightful songs. Another significant step was the innovative *Lady in the Dark* (1941) with music by **Kurt Weill**, lyrics by **Ira Gershwin**, and book by **Moss Hart**. A landmark work in the genre is **Rodgers and Hammerstein**'s *Oklahoma!* (1943), whose plot includes a dangerous character and his death on stage, elements alien to musical comedy. Rodgers and Hammerstein placed their songs carefully within the plot, deciding from the beginning what moments would be told best through dialogue, song, or dance.

The musical play could be seen as an attempt to move a commercial medium toward a more artistic product. Rodgers and Hammerstein confirmed their approach in *Carousel* (1945), then in almost all of their subsequent shows. Other creators rushed to include lengthy musical sequences and ballets that advanced the plot; **Alan Jay Lerner** and **Frederick Loewe** wrote their first musical play in *Brigadoon* (1947). The genre's commercial importance was clear by 1950; in subsequent years almost every show that has had a long run bears some of its characteristics. Canonic musical plays include *The King and I* (1951), *My Fair Lady* (1956), *West Side Story* (1957), *Gypsy* (1959), *Fiddler on the Roof* (1964), and *Man of La Mancha* (1965). Important examples of the genre from the 1990s and 2000s include *Ragtime* (1998) and *Wicked* (2003).

MUSIC BOX REVUE (MUSIC BOX: 22 SEPTEMBER 1921, 313 PERFORMANCES; 23 OCTOBER 1922, 272 PERFORMANCES; 22 SEPTEMBER 1923, 273 PERFORMANCES; 1

DECEMBER 1924, 184 PERFORMANCES). A notable series of **revues** that **Irving Berlin** and **Sam H. Harris** initiated to help launch their new theater, the *Music Box Revue* ran for four years. The Music Box was smaller than some Broadway houses, allowing for an intimacy that many revues lacked. The *Music Box Revue* became famous for its opulent production numbers and spectacular stage effects. The first edition boasted a winning score that included "Say It With Music," which became the title tune each year; "Everybody Step," a number with Sam Bernard and Rene Riano that lampooned dance marathons; "They Call It Dancing"; "I'm a Dumbbell," during which Riano nearly tied herself in knots; and "Eight Notes," where eight women representing the notes of the scale surrounded Berlin. An unnamed reviewer for the *New York Times* asserted that the production established "The Music Box as the pre-eminent home of rich and gorgeous revue in America." Charlotte Greenwood had a major hit in the second edition with "Pack Up Your Sins (And Go to the Devil)," during which she sent impersonators of jazz musicians and popular entertainers to the lower regions. In that edition, John Steel sang "Lady of the Evening," and the production numbers were huge, especially the finale "Porcelain Maid." The third edition included "What'll I Do," added after the show opened and sung by Steel and **Grace Moore** before she became a famous opera star. The edition's biggest production number was "An Orange Grove in California," which featured countless orange-colored lights and orange scent misted into the audience. For the fourth and final edition, the host was Rip Van Winkle (Joseph McCauley), who slept through most of the show. Berlin wrote 20 songs, not one of them a hit. He added "All Alone," sung by Moore and Oscar Shaw from either end of the stage into telephones. **Fannie Brice** sang "Don't Send Me Back to Petrograd" and, with Bobby Clark, "I Want to Be a Ballet Dancer." The "Tokio Blues" was a major production number. It was clear that interest in huge annual revues was waning, so Berlin and Harris closed the series.

MUSIC IN THE AIR **(8 NOVEMBER 1932, ALVIN, 342 PERFORMANCES).** Music by **Jerome Kern**, lyrics and book by **Oscar Hammerstein II**, staged by Kern and Hammerstein. Five years after *Show Boat*, Kern and Hammerstein again tried to integrate music and plot, this time in a work set in Europe and with strong **operetta** overtones. **Brooks Atkinson** noticed, opening his *New York Times* review with "At last the musical drama has been emancipated." The plot took place in a small Bavarian hamlet and in Munich. Working with the elderly music teacher, Dr. Walther Lessing (Al Shean), Karl Reder (**Walter Slezak**) writes a song. They decide to get it published in Munich, where they go with Karl's girlfriend, Sieglinde (Katherine Carrington), and the Edendorf Walking Club. Karl meets a prima donna who becomes Sieglinde's rival, and Sieglinde finds a composer who wants to write an operetta for her. The Edendorfers finally decide that they prefer their small town. The musical score featured "I've Told Ev'ry Little Star," "Egern on the Tegern See," and "When Spring Is in the Air." Atkinson called the show "a fable that flows naturally out of a full-brimming score" and praised Hammerstein's story as "an effortless piece of craftsmanship."

THE MUSIC MAN (**19 DECEMBER 1957, MAJESTIC, 1,375 PERFORMANCES**). Music, lyrics, and book by **Meredith Willson**. Americans adore nostalgic looks at their past, and few shows captured such sentiment better than *The Music Man*. Meredith Willson grew up in a small town in Iowa at the time the musical takes place, the early 20th century. He took the audience back to fictional River City, Iowa, to meet realistic, entertaining people. Professor Harold Hill (**Robert Preston**, in his Broadway musical debut) is a con man who sells band instruments and uniforms to unsuspecting locals, skipping town before being discovered. He romances the town's librarian and piano teacher, Marian Paroo (**Barbara Cook**), but his plan unwinds when they fall in love. Marian lives with her mother (Pert Kelton) and younger brother, Winthrop (Eddie Hodges). The shy boy lisps, but the purchase of a shiny cornet helps bring him out of his shell. Despite her doubts, Marian has feelings for Hill and destroys evidence that could expose his fraud. The town's many memorable citizens include the school board, which forms a barbershop quartet. Hill must produce a band by the end, which he does. Parents ignore the cacophonous results when they see their beloved children in their uniforms.

Brooks Atkinson described the show in the *New York Times* "as American as apple pie and a Fourth of July oration." Willson brought great imagination and skill to his score, producing tunes of varied types, with most songs sounding like they belonged to the period. The big hit was "Seventy Six Trombones," a rollicking march in the Sousa tradition. Willson transformed the melody into a sentimental waltz for "Goodnight, My Someone," allowing for a dramatic duet between Harold and Marian. The opening song, in which traveling salesmen chant about their livelihood and the scourge of con men like Hill to the rhythm of a speeding and slowing train, is most effective. Hill lures the people of River City into his gambit with the patter song "Trouble." "Till There Was You" is another fine love duet. The nostalgic glow that surrounds *The Music Man* still thrills audiences almost five decades after its premiere. Preston appeared with Shirley Jones in the 1962 film version. The 2000 Broadway revival starred Craig Bierko and **Rebecca Luker** with direction and choreography by **Susan Stroman**, while the 2003 television version, broadcast on *The Wonderful World of Disney*, featured **Matthew Broderick** and **Kristin Chenoweth**.

MY FAIR LADY **(15 MARCH 1956, MARK HELLINGER, 2,717 PERFORMANCES).** Music by **Frederick Loewe**, lyrics and book by **Alan Jay Lerner**, directed by **Moss Hart**, choreographed by Hanya Holm. A smash-hit adaptation of George Bernard Shaw's play *Pygmalion*. Although he was deceased by the time this masterwork appeared, the creation of *My Fair Lady* depended upon the persistence of Hungarian producer Gabriel Pascal. He bought film rights from Shaw for several of his plays and musical rights for *Pygmalion*. Starting in the early 1950s, Pascal pitched the project to every major Broadway creator or creative team. Like **Rodgers and Hammerstein** and others, Lerner and Loewe turned it down because of the unusual plot. In July 1954, Lerner read that Pascal had died and reconsidered *Pygmalion*. He now decided to adapt it into a musical without adding any characters or subplots. Lerner convinced Loewe of his approach, and the team began working on the show before securing rights from Pascal's estate. Lerner retained as many of Shaw's lines as possible and used others as inspirations for songs, depending more on Shaw's script for the 1930s film version than the original play. Lerner and Loewe's concern for integration is especially clear in the songs, which represent fine situational writing. They knew the identity of their major actors early on and wrote specifically for them.

Seldom have songwriters captured personalities and characterizations as well as they did for **Rex Harrison** as Henry Higgins, **Julie Andrews** as Eliza Doolittle, or Stanley Holloway as Alfred P. Doolittle. They describe Higgins's character beautifully in the songs "Why Can't the English" and "A Hymn to Him." His final song, "I've Grown Accustomed to Her Face" is a multi-sectioned musical scene of uncanny power. The song is ready proof of Lerner's ability to capture Shaw's voice in poetry, and Loewe effectively switches musical moods. Mr. Doolittle's easygoing nature is captured brilliantly in "With a Little Bit of Luck" and "Get Me to the Church on Time," pieces that Loewe based on the English music hall style. Eliza's complex character plays out well in her songs, from the hopefulness of "Wouldn't It Be Loverly," the anger of "Without You" and "Show Me," the playful happiness of "I Could Have Danced All Night," and the triumphant defiance of "Without You." Other songs are similarly successful, such as the understated comedy of the "Ascot Gavotte" and hilarity of "The Rain in Spain." Perhaps the most notable quality of *My Fair Lady* was the way that so many distinctive talents came together on the right project at the right time.

***MY MARYLAND* (12 SEPTEMBER 1927, JOLSON'S, 312 PERFORMANCES).** Music by **Sigmund Romberg**, lyrics and book by **Dorothy Donnelly**, produced by the **Shuberts**. Based on a play by Clyde Fitch that romanticized the Civil War legend of Barbara Frietchie, *My Maryland* ran for about nine months in Philadelphia and for a similar period in New York City. Soprano **Evelyn Herbert** played the main character, a lovely young Southern woman who finds herself with two suitors: Jack Negly, with Confederate sympathies, and Captain Trumbull (Nathaniel Wagner) of the Union Army. Romberg's score included "Won't You Marry Me?," "The Same Silver Moon" (the show's principal waltz), "Mother," and "Your Land and My Land," a male-choral march that quotes "Battle Hymn of the Republic" at the end of the refrain.

***MY ONE AND ONLY* (1 May 1983, St. James, 767 performances).** Music by **George Gershwin**, lyrics by **Ira Gershwin**, book by

Peter Stone and Timothy S. Meyer, staged and choreographed by Thommie Walsh and **Tommy Tune**. Intended as a revival of *Funny Face*, *My One and Only* went through a difficult creative period but emerged as a success. Tommy Tune played Captain Billy Buck Chandler, whose dream is to be the first pilot to fly solo from New York to Paris. He finds his efforts complicated by Edith Herbert (Twiggy), a famous swimmer of the English Channel. Tune and Thommie Walsh provided a true dancing spirit with contemporary interpretations of traditional tap dancing, as in the witty finale to "Kicking the Clouds Away," when Billy and Edith marry in a Harlem chapel. Other songs in the score included "'S Wonderful," "High Hat," "Funny Face," "Strike Up the Band," and "Nice Work If You Can Get It."

– N –

NAPIER, JOHN (1944–). British set and costume designer who won five **Tony Awards** for his work on Broadway, four of which were for musicals. Broadway musical credits include *Cats* (1982, Tony for Best Costume Design), *Les Misérables* (1987, Tony for Best Scenic Design), *Starlight Express* (1987, Tony for Best Costume Design), *Miss Saigon* (1991), *Sunset Boulevard* (1994, Tony for Best Scenic Design), and *Jane Eyre* (2000).

NATIONAL TOUR. *See* ROAD COMPANIES.

NAUGHTON, JAMES (1945–). Singing actor who played Wally in *I Love My Wife* (1977), Stone in *City of Angels* (1989), and Billy Flynn in the 1996 revival of *Chicago*. He won **Tony Awards** for *City of Angels* and *Chicago*.

NAUGHTY MARIETTA (7 NOVEMBER 1910, NEW YORK, 136 PERFORMANCES). Music by **Victor Herbert**, lyrics and book by **Rida Johnson Young**. Commissioned by opera impresario Oscar Hammerstein for his Manhattan Opera Company, *Naughty Marietta* was one of Herbert's finest scores, written for some of the best voices ever to appear in any of his shows. **Emma Trentini** played the title role, a young noblewoman who flees a bad marriage by going to

Louisiana. There, she meets Captain Richard Warrington (Orville Harrold). They are attracted to each other, but decide they cannot be lovers. She also meets Etienne Grandet (Edward Martindell), who is also the murderous pirate "Bras Prique." Warrington leads a search for the pirate, and finally wins Marietta's attention, but she will only fall in love with a man who can finish a mysterious melody that has haunted her for years. Warrington does this by singing "Ah, Sweet Mystery of Life." Other highlights included the coloratura "Italian Street Song," the romantic "I'm Falling in Love with Someone," and the march "Tramp, Tramp, Tramp." The unsigned review in the *New York Times* called Trentini "phenomenal," Herbert having written her a part that "would tire any prima donna to sing every night." The 1935 film version, with a radically altered plot, starred Jeanette Mac-Donald and Nelson Eddy.

NEUWIRTH, BEBE (BORN BEATRICE NEUWIRTH, 1958–). Dancer, singer, and actress who made her Broadway debut as a **replacement** Sheila in the original production of *A Chorus Line*, joining the cast in 1980. She played Boom Boom Girl in the 1982 revival of *Little Me*, Nickie in the 1986 revival of *Sweet Charity* (for which she won a **Tony Award** for Best Featured Actress in a Musical), and Lola in the 1994 revival of *Damn Yankees* before dazzling audiences as Velma Kelly in the 1996 revival of *Chicago*, a role that won her a Tony Award for Best Actress in a Musical. On 31 December 2006, she returned to the still-running *Chicago* revival, this time as Roxie Hart. Neuwirth has also appeared on film and television, her most famous role being Dr. Lilith Sternin on *Cheers* and its spinoff, *Frasier.*

NEW FACES OF 1952 (16 MAY 1952, ROYALE, 365 PERFOR-MANCES). Music and words mostly by Ronny Graham, June Carroll, Arthur Siegel, **Sheldon Harnick**, and Michael Brown; sketches mostly by Graham, Peter DeVries, and Melvin Brooks; entire production devised and staged by **John Murray Anderson**. Broadway **revues** often launched the careers of young performers, but few have included as many future luminaries as *New Faces of 1952*. The cast included Robert Clary, Alice Ghostley, Ronny Graham, Eartha Kitt, **Carol Lawrence**, and Paul Lynde. Among the sketches were send-ups of *Death of a Salesman* and Gian Carlo Menotti's opera *The*

Medium, the Oliviers forgetting which play they were acting, and an impersonation of Truman Capote. **Brooks Atkinson**, writing for the *New York Times*, observed that "summer nights may not be so desolate after all." He found Ghostley "a funny ballad singer and clown" and Kitt "looks incendiary but she can make a song burst into flames." He also praised the show's literate qualities and staging.

NEW GIRL IN TOWN **(14 MAY 1957, 46TH STREET, 431 PER-FORMANCES).** Music and lyrics by **Bob Merrill**, book and staging by **George Abbott**, dancers and musical numbers directed by **Bob Fosse**. Eugene O'Neill's play *Anna Christie* was hardly the typical source material for a musical, but Abbott and his fellow creators made *New Girl in Town* sufficiently interesting to allow it to run more than a year. **Gwen Verdon** played the title role of Anna, a prostitute trying to recover from tuberculosis and get out of her profession while living with her father, the barge captain Chris (Cameron Prud'homme). Anna falls in love with Irish seaman Mat (George Wallace), but he deserts her when he learns of her former life, although they reconcile by the final curtain. Thelma Ritter played Marthy, Chris's comic companion. **Brooks Atkinson**, writing in the *New York Times*, fretted about the show's ambiguous tone. He described the musical portions as "lively and gay," but the show also reminded him that O'Neill's play "is a wonderful bit of American stage literature." Merrill wrote some "illuminating songs," especially three for Verdon: "It's Good to Be Alive," "If That Was Love," and "Did You Close Your Eyes?" Atkinson found Ritter "extraordinarily funny" and thought that Fosse's dances brought "revelry when the musical comedy formula needs it."

THE NEW MOON **(19 SEPTEMBER 1928, IMPERIAL, 518 PER-FORMANCES).** Music by **Sigmund Romberg**, lyrics by **Oscar Hammerstein II**, book by Hammerstein, **Frank Mandel**, and **Laurence Schwab**, produced by **Mandel** and **Schwab**. The last of the great **operettas** of the 1920s, *The New Moon* was set in 1780s Louisiana, echoing the time and place of **Victor Herbert's** *Naughty Marietta*. Robert Misson (**Robert Halliday**), a French aristocrat charged with treason for not supporting the monarchy, escapes to New Orleans, where he falls in love with Marianne Beaunoir (**Eve-**

lyn Herbert), the daughter of the landowner on whose plantation he works. Robert rallies other dispossessed men around him in the rousing march "Stouthearted Men," and, after overtaking a bride ship, eventually establishes a democracy on the Isle of Pines. Marianne finally admits her love for Robert in the concluding scene as French envoys arrive to announce that France is now a republic, and the entire company offers a stirring reprise of "Stouthearted Men." Romberg wrote some of his most famous music for *The New Moon*, including the love duet "Wanting You," Marianne's waltz "One Kiss," and the evocative "Lover, Come Back to Me." Another of the score's hits was the tango "Softly, as in a Morning Sunrise," sung by Philippe as an expression of the scorning power of love. Robert's valet, Alexander (Gus Shy) and Marianne's maid, Julie (Marie Callahan), provided comedy in fast-paced songs such as "Gorgeous Alexander," as did Clotilde (Esther Howard), the polygamist leader of the bride ship who tattoos her name across the chests of her husbands. Two film versions of the operetta exist, both entitled *New Moon*, one from 1930 starring opera stars Lawrence Tibbett and Grace Moore, and the other from 1940 with Nelson Eddy and Jeanette MacDonald.

NEW YORK DRAMA CRITICS' CIRCLE AWARDS. Annual awards for best play, best musical, and best foreign play (although the exact categories vary depending upon the season) offered by a group of 20 drama critics from daily newspapers, magazines, and wire services in the New York metropolitan area. The group's founding came in 1935 with awards the following year, but the first citation for the best musical did not come until 1945–46, when *Carousel* won. The Drama Critics' Circle does not give an award if they do not consider there to be a show worthy of the prize. *See also* DRAMA DESK AWARDS; PULITZER PRIZE; TONY AWARDS.

***THE NEW YORKERS* (8 DECEMBER 1930, BROADWAY, 168 PERFORMANCES).** Music and lyrics by **Cole Porter**, book by **Herbert Fields**. Based on a story by E. Ray Goetz and Peter Arno, *The New Yorkers* had all of the makings of a successful musical comedy, but it only ran about five months, partly because of the deepening Great Depression. The cast included several major names, including

Hope Williams, Charles King, **Ann Pennington**, Richard Carle, **Marie Cahill**, and **Jimmy Durante**. Fred Waring and his Pennsylvanians were also part of this potpourri.

The show included amoral characters and a nightclub atmosphere, prefiguring *Pal Joey*. The cynical plot revolves around New York socialite Alice Wentworth (Williams), who falls in love with the bootlegger Al Spanish (King). **J. Brooks Atkinson** reported in the *New York Times* that the show is "as overpoweringly funny as a weak-muscled theatregoer can endure." He described several of Durante's stunts, noting that he "delivers a knockout blow every ten seconds and ruins all the props in sight." Porter's score included the suggestive "Love for Sale," "The Great Indoors," and "Let's Fly Away."

NIELSEN, ALICE (ca. 1871–1943). Soprano for whom **Victor Herbert** wrote principal roles in his operettas *The Serenade* (1897), *The Fortune Teller* (1898), and *The Singing Girl* (1899). Her Broadway success established, she embarked on an operatic and concert career.

THE NIGHT BOAT **(2 FEBRUARY 1920, LIBERTY, 313 PERFORMANCES).** Music by **Jerome Kern**, lyrics and book by Anne Caldwell, produced by **Charles Dillingham**. Based on a French farce by Alexandre Bisson, *The Night Boat* had a fine score and ran for almost 10 months. Bob White (John E. Hazzard) is a husband who pretends to pilot a night boat up the Hudson River to Albany, when he really was having an extramarital fling. One night his suspicious wife (Stella Hoban) and mother-in-law (Ada Lewis) sail on the craft to check out his story. White steals a uniform from a captain with the same name, but his story breaks down elsewhere. The unnamed reviewer in the *New York Times* found the story "conventional," but it "moves briskly and breezily." The critic noted that Hazzard looks "more like William Jennings Bryan than ever" and that Lewis "is a terrifying if grotesque mother-in-law." Kern provides tunes "which will be popular" such as "Left All Alone Again Blues," "Whose Baby Are You?" and "A Heart for Sale."

NINA ROSA **(20 SEPTEMBER 1930, MAJESTIC, 137 PERFORMANCES).** Music by **Sigmund Romberg**, lyrics by **Irving Caesar**, book by **Otto Harbach**, directed by **J. J. Shubert**. Set in Peru, the operetta was the tale of Nina Rosa Stradella (Ethelind Terry) and attempts to take over her gold mine. The score's highlights included "Nina Rosa," "Payador," and a created version of an Incan religious ceremony.

NINE **(9 MAY 1982, 46TH STREET, 729 PERFORMANCES).** Music and lyrics by **Maury Yeston**, book by Arthur Kopit, directed by **Tommy Tune.** Based on Italian director Federico Fellini's film *8 1/2*, *Nine* was one of director-choreographer Tune's most ambitious efforts. The show was about a film director, Guido Contini (**Raul Julia**), who struggles through a midlife crisis, spent largely in his head where he analyzes his relationships with females. Besides a boy playing young Guido and some playmates, the remainder of the cast consisted of 21 women, including Guido's dead mother (Taina Elg); his wife, Luisa (Karen Akers); his mistress, Carla (Anita Morris); and the woman who sexually initiated Guido, Saraghina (Kathi Moss). The set consisted of a white-tiled spa; each woman had her own pedestal. Guido solves his problems as the audience watches his memories, dreams, and thoughts come alive in routines reminiscent of the *Folies Bergère* and comic operas, with generous amounts of sexual imagery. **Frank Rich** of the *New York Times* gave *Nine* a mixed review, noting that anyone interested in Broadway will have to see the show for the "rich icing" of the imaginative musical sequences, but called it a "complex mixture of ecstatic highs and crass lows." He described Yeston's score as "a literate mixture" of traditional Broadway songs and opera, but his lyrics can be "pedestrian." Antonio Banderas starred in the 2003 Broadway revival.

NO, NO, NANETTE **(16 SEPTEMBER 1925, GLOBE, 321 PERFORMANCES).** Music by **Vincent Youmans**, lyrics by **Irving Caesar** and **Otto Harbach**, book by Harbach and **Frank Mandel.** One of the most famous musical comedies of the 1920s with huge hits from its score and a successful revival in 1971, *No, No, Nanette* had extended runs in a number of cities prior to its arrival in New York. Louise Groody played the title role, an independent-minded young woman. Her guardian is Jimmy Smith (**Charles Winninger**), a Bible publisher with sidelights that are less than scriptural. Nanette's boyfriend is Tom Trainor (Jack Barker), who finds himself stretched by her thinking. All confusion relents when Smith's wife (Eleanor Dawn) shows up and cleans up her husband's act and makes sure that Tom and Nanette get to the altar. The show nearly died in Detroit, but was improved with a new cast and fresh material, including two hugely popular songs: "Tea for Two" and "I Want to Be Happy." The unsigned review in the *New York Times* is brief but illustrates why *No, No, Nanette* was so popular: The plot was secondary to the songs and the "energetic cast of well selected comedians."

NO STRINGS **(15 MARCH 1962, 54TH STREET, 580 PERFOR-MANCES).** Music and lyrics by **Richard Rodgers**, book by Samuel Taylor, staged and choreographed by **Joe Layton**, presented by Rodgers in association with Taylor. Famous as the one show for which Rodgers wrote both music and lyrics, *No Strings* was a critical success that ran for about 17 months. **Diahann Carroll** played Barbara Woodruff, a successful **African American** fashion model in Paris. She meets and falls in love with David Jordan (**Richard Kiley**), an American novelist who has spent six unproductive years in Paris since winning the Pulitzer Prize. They break up briefly when Jordan discovers that Woodruff has a wealthy admirer, but they are soon back together. The writer decides, however, that he must return to his native Maine to be able to write again. He does not wish to attempt to have a biracial romance in the United States, nor does she want to leave her lucrative career. David Hays designed stylish scenery and lighting inspired by photographic props. The show opened and closed with "The Sweetest Sounds," sung by Carroll and Kiley, a lovely tune that served as an effective framing device. Other memorable songs included the title song, "Nobody Told Me," and "Look No Further." Ralph Burns's orchestrations included no strings, not only keeping with the title but also giving the orchestra a distinctive sound. **Howard Taubman** raved in the *New York Times*, noting that Rodgers as a lyricist "is good enough to walk—and sing—alone." He found the music enchanting, but Taylor's book too lightweight and sentimental. Carroll "brings glowing personal beauty to the role . . . and her singing captures many moods." He especially praised her rendition of the angry blues, "You Don't Tell Me." Kiley was "forthright and warm-hearted," and Taubman praises other members of the cast as well.

NORMAN, MARSHA (1947–). Writer and lyricist who won the 1991 **Tony Award** for Best Book of a Musical for *The Secret Garden* (1991). She also wrote the book and lyrics for the short-lived *The Red Shoes* (1993) and the book for *The Color Purple* (2005). Norman won the 1983 **Pulitzer Prize** for Drama for her play *'night, Mother.*

NUNN, TREVOR (1940–). British director whose work with the Royal Shakespeare Company and the Royal National Theatre has earned him tremendous respect. He brought many of his British productions—both musical and nonmusical—to Broadway. Nunn created a major Broadway **dance show** with choreographer **Gillian Lynne** in *Cats* (1982), and cultivated the operatic muse in *Les Misérables* (1987), *Sunset Boulevard* (1994), and *The Woman in White* (2005). Other Broadway credits include *Starlight Express* (1987), *Chess* (1988), *Aspects of Love* (1990), and *Oklahoma!* (2002 revival). His lyrics appeared in the **revue** *André DeShield's Haarlem Nocturne* (1984).

***NUNSENSE* (12 DECEMBER 1985, CHERRY LANE, 3,672 PERFORMANCES).** Music by Michael Rice, written and directed by Don Goggin. A light, delightful piece poking gentle fun at Catholicism, nuns, and life in general, *Nunsense* became the second longest-running show in **off-Broadway** history (after the perennial *The Fantasticks*) and extremely popular around the country. The premise is thin, but entertaining. The Little Sisters of Hoboken throw a variety show to pay for the multiple funerals of their late colleagues, all of whom died of food poisoning in the school cafeteria. The show contained ample puns and gags. The variety show and act of putting it on provides opportunities for singing, dancing (ballet and otherwise), clowning, and even ventriloquism, the latter performed by one sister with her dummy, a likeness of the Reverend Mother. Herbert Mitgang of the *New York Times* was appreciative, if perhaps a bit surprised at the show's silliness. For including such stunts "as putting a Carmen Miranda fruitbowl hat over a nun's wimple" he suggested that the writer should "do penance." The 1994 sequel, *Nunsense II,* pushed the concept too far and only ran for 149 performances.

– O –

OFF-BROADWAY. Officially, in terms of Actors Equity union contracts, an "off-Broadway" theater is one with between 100 and 499 seats. An "off-off-Broadway" theater has fewer than 100 seats, and is often a large room or other multiuse facility. Despite the fact that the term sounds like a designation of location, technically an off-Broadway theater can be in the Broadway district (midtown Manhattan, around Times Square, between about 40th and 60th Streets). Smaller theaters can present experimental works that are not economically viable at larger theaters. Off-Broadway productions figure prominently in the musical's history, and some fans do not make important distinctions about a show's origin. *The Fantasticks*, for example, is often called a "Broadway musical," despite its extraordinary off-Broadway run of 17,162 performances. Musicals that did not run on Broadway as part of their initial runs but became important representatives of the genre include, among others, *The Fantasticks*, **Little Shop of Horrors**, **Nunsense**, and **Assassins**.

OF THEE I SING **(26 DECEMBER 1931, MUSIC BOX, 441 PERFORMANCES).** Music by **George Gershwin**, lyrics by **Ira Gershwin**, book by **George S. Kaufman** and **Morrie Ryskind**, stage direction by Kaufman, produced by **Sam H. Harris**. A brilliant satire that became the first Broadway musical to win the **Pulitzer Prize** for drama (with George Gershwin's name excluded since it was a literary award), *Of Thee I Sing* is one of the genre's most storied creations from the 1930s. The Gershwin brothers first tried their hands at musical satire with George S. Kaufman in *Strike Up the Band!*, which failed out of town in 1927 but became a hit in 1930. The targets for barbs in *Of Thee I Sing* were presidential politics and American governance. A political party seeks an issue to galvanize the electorate and chooses "love." Nobody can recall the vice presidential candidate's name (Alexander Throttlebottom, played by **Victor Moore**), but they know they want to elect John P. Wintergreen **(William Gaxton)** as president, and will run him on a "platform of love." The party leaders decide that Wintergreen will marry the winner of an Atlantic City beauty contest. The winner is a southern belle, Diana Deveraux (Grace Brinkley), but Wintergreen has already fallen in love with the pageant's secretary, Mary Turner (Lois Moran). She bakes excellent corn muffins, somehow without even using corn. Wintergreen wins the election and marries Mary Turner during the inauguration ceremony. Diana interrupts with her tale of woe, but the Supreme Court rejects her suit, ruling that corn muffins are more important than justice. The title song, cleverly titled "Of Thee I Sing, Baby," closes act 1. In act 2, the French ambassador comes to Diana's rescue because she is "the illegitimate daughter of an illegitimate son of an illegitimate nephew of Napoleon." Congress tries to impeach Wintergreen, but cancels the proceedings when Mary says that she is pregnant. Further French threats come to nothing when Wintergreen realizes that the vice president fills in for him when he cannot fulfill a duty, meaning that Throttlebottom marries Diana, and all ends happily.

Although conceived early in the Depression, this rich and pointed satire holds up remarkably well. No major institution in Washington is spared, but the blows are softened and made more delightful by the outrageous silliness. The Senate's willingness to impeach President Wintergreen, for example, is callous and opportunistic, but it is rendered absurd by Throttlebottom's sung insistence that he will only call for votes from states whose names rhyme. It is remarkable to hear how much of the story occurs during the music, with entire scenes told mostly in song. The score is one of the Gershwin brothers' best, providing many lyrical highlights and winning melodies. The opening "Wintergreen for President," a gem of a lyric from Ira Gershwin, benefits from George Gershwin's haunting melody. "Some Girls Can Bake a Pie," "A Kiss for Cinderella," and "Who Cares" function well in the show and boast unforgettable melodies. George Gershwin made excellent use of special effects as well, such as the whole tone scale that introduces the Supreme Court, and quoting his own *An American in Paris* at the arrival of the French ambassador. **Brooks Atkinson** wrote in the *New York Times* that the musical was "funnier than the government, and not nearly as dangerous," while Burns Mantle, writing in the *Daily News*, called it "the newest, maddest and brightest of musical satire."

OH, BOY! **(20 FEBRUARY 1917, PRINCESS, 463 PERFOR-MANCES).** Music by **Jerome Kern**, lyrics by **P. G. Wodehouse**, book by Wodehouse and **Guy Bolton**. One of the famed **Princess Theatre musicals** of the 1910s that Broadway historians look back on as significant steps in the integration of music and plot, *Oh, Boy!* was a smash hit that followed its 14-month run with a five-year tour. George Budd (Tom Powers) has just married Lou Ellen (Marie Carroll), but learns that his Aunt Penelope (Edna May Oliver) is coming to try to prevent the marriage and fears that his aunt will discontinue his allowance. Lou Ellen leaves for the time being, but things become much more complicated when Jackie (Anna Wheaton) enters his home. She flees from a policeman that she struck, and during the remainder of the show Jackie finds herself playing either George's wife or his aunt. When the real aunt arrives, she accepts George's marriage after drinking spiked lemonade. Kern's score was of very high quality and included "'Til the Clouds Roll By," "An Old-Fashioned Wife," "You Never Knew about Me," and "Nesting Time in Flatbush." Critics were ecstatic. The *New York Times* review stated: "You might call this a musical comedy that is as good as they make them if it were not palpably so much better." According to the *Sun*, if such a category existed, then surely *Oh, Boy!* was one of the "masterpieces of musical comedy." Alan Dale wrote in the *American* that "there are so many delightful musical numbers that it is next to impossible to mention all of them." *See also* PRINCESS THEATRE MUSICALS.

OH, KAY! **(8 NOVEMBER 1926, IMPERIAL, 256 PERFORMANCES).** Music by **George Gershwin**, lyrics by **Ira Gershwin**, book by **Guy Bolton** and **P. G. Wodehouse**, produced by **Alex A. Aarons** and **Vinton Freedley**. A **musical comedy** featuring **Gertrude Lawrence** in her first lead role in the United States and some great Gershwin songs. The story involved an English Duke (Gerald Oliver Smith) who bootlegs liquor to assist with his cash flow problems. Lawrence played his sister, Kay, who becomes the love interest of Jimmy Winter (Oscar Shaw), on whose estate the Duke hides his supply of liquor. **Victor Moore** played "Shorty" McGee, the Duke's butler. **J. Brooks Atkinson** opened his *New York Times* review by stating that "Musical comedy seldom proves more intensely delightful than 'Oh, Kay!'" Gershwin wrote songs with both his brother and Howard Dietz, the latter uncredited. Lawrence and Shaw sang "Maybe" and "Do, Do, Do," and the entire cast performed the memorable "Clap Yo' Hands." The huge hit from the show was "Someone to Watch Over Me," sung by Lawrence.

O'HARA, KELLI. Operatically trained soprano who created the roles of Susan in *Sweet Smell of Success* (2002), Lucy Westenra in *Dracula, the Musical* (2004), and Clara in *The Light in the Piazza* (2005). She played Babe Williams in the 2006 revival of *The Pajama Game* opposite Harry Connick Jr.

O'HORGAN, TOM (1926–). Director best known for musicals with rock-based scores, including *Hair* (1968), *Jesus Christ Superstar* (1971), and *Dude* (1972). He also conceived *Jesus Christ Superstar* for the stage. *See also* ROCK MUSICALS.

***OKLAHOMA!* (31 MARCH 1943, ST. JAMES, 2,212 PERFOR-MANCES).** Music by **Richard Rodgers**, lyrics and book by **Oscar Hammerstein II**, orchestrations by **Robert Russell Bennett**, directed by **Rouben Mamoulian**, choreographed by **Agnes de Mille**, produced by Lawrence Langner and Theresa Helburn. Rodgers and Hammerstein's first collaboration and one of the most important shows in the history of Broadway for its close integration of plot, music, and dance. When the curtain rose on opening night to an almost bare stage and the simple waltz "Oh, What a Beautiful Morning'" was heard offstage, musicals would never be the same.

The show's deceptively simple story focused on Laurey Williams (Joan Roberts) and which boy should accompany her to the box social: the "good" cowboy, Curly (**Alfred Drake**), or the "bad" farmhand, Jud Fry (**Howard Da Silva**). Curly teases Laurey about taking her in "The Surrey with the Fringe on Top," in which the clip-clop of the team of horses is heard in the orchestra. Their courtship follows with the "maybe" love duet in "People Will Say," one of the year's most popular songs. Curly tries to dissuade Jud in the dirge-like "Poor Jud," the lyrics of which include some of Hammerstein's blackest humor. In the somber "Lonely Room," Jud reveals his true nature. The comic romance for the secondary leads between Ado Annie (**Celeste Holm**) and Will Parker (Lee Dixon) is complicated by the presence of peddler Ali Hakim (Yiddish comic Joseph Buloff) because Ado Annie admits, "I Can't Say No." Laurey dreams about her decision concerning her suitors, and in the dramatic "Dream Ballet" that concludes act 1, finds Jud Fry's world terrifying. In act 2, Curly and Laurey marry, but Jud returns to cause trouble and Curly kills him in self-defense. "Evil" has been defeated, and the couple and the cast sing about their hope in the future in "Oklahoma!" This song marked the emotional peak of the show when the cast walks to the front of the stage with a jubilant "Yeow!," an affirmation of community and the desire for statehood.

Oklahoma! originated in 1942 when Lawrence Langner and Theresa Helburn of the **Theatre Guild** dreamed of reviving *Green Grow the Lilacs* and adding typical Western songs and square dancing. The Guild approached Rodgers, who for the first time collaborated with Hammerstein. The lyricist had not had a hit in a decade, but Rodgers still wanted to work with the man who had written *Show Boat*. They hired Agnes de Mille, who had just created the Western ballet *Rodeo* to Aaron Copland's music, as choreographer. For *Oklahoma!*, she fashioned the dream ballet, as well as using elements of vernacular dance, and even a tap solo, minimizing the obvious square dancing. Hammerstein originally wanted her dream sequence to be a circus ballet, but de Mille answered that was not what young naive girls dream about, so she brought the world of Jud Fry's French postcard women to life. Still entitled *Away We Go!*, the show opened in New Haven, where it received a good reception, before moving to Boston. During the Boston tryout, Laurey and Curly's duet "Oklahoma!" became an ensemble number, and a reprise of "People Will Say" replaced "Boys and Girls Like You and Me." *Oklahoma!* received a special **Pulitzer Prize**, and in 1953 the title song became the state song of Oklahoma. Notable revivals include the National Theatre's production in London, which starred **Hugh Jackman** and subsequently transferred to Broadway in 2002 with Patrick Wilson and ran for 338 performances. The 1955 film starred Gordon MacRae and Shirley Jones.

OLIVER! (6 JANUARY 1963, IMPERIAL, 774 PERFORMANCES). Lyrics, music, and book by **Lionel Bart**; staged by Peter Coe; presented by **David Merrick** and Donald Albery. Based on Charles Dickens's novel *Oliver Twist*, *Oliver!* was disliked by critics, but appreciative audiences came to see it for almost two years, and it has remained in the repertory. Bart kept the novel's basic story and even included some of Dickens's dialogue. Familiar characters were given musical treatments, including Oliver Twist (Bruce Prochnik), Mr. Bumble (Willoughby Goddard), Fagin (Clive Revill), Artful Dodger (David Jones), Nancy (Georgia Brown), and Bet (Alice Playten). Critics found fault with the overly happy nature of the show and the excision of some of the story's horror. **Howard Taubman**, for example, writing for the *New York Times*, wondered how Fagin's "odious diggings" could become "a jolly rumpus room." He deplored the fact that Fagin had been made a "complacent low comedian," and that Dickens, with his "burning social conscience" had been reduced to "modern show business." Two songs, "As Long As He Needs Me" and "Consider Yourself," became popular outside of the theater, and among the show's other delightful tunes were the jaunty title song, "Food, Glorious Food," "You've Got to Pick a Pocket or Two," and "Who Will Buy?"

ON A CLEAR DAY YOU CAN SEE FOREVER **(17 OCTOBER 1965, MARK HELLINGER, 280 PERFORMANCES).** Music by **Burton Lane**, lyrics and book by **Alan Jay Lerner**, staged by Robert Lewis, dances and musical numbers staged by Herbert Ross. Based on an original story by Lerner, *On a Clear Day You Can See Forever* struggled because of a weak book. Lerner originally planned to write the show with **Richard Rodgers**, but their collaboration never bore fruit. Lerner retained rights to the story and produced many lovely songs with Burton Lane, including a title number that is one of Broadway's most enduring tunes. A great asset was the star **Barbara Harris**, who played Daisy Gamble, a nervous young woman with ESP. She goes to a psychiatrist, Dr. Mark Bruckner (**John Cullum**), for help to stop smoking. He discovers her psychic gifts and learns that she has lived another life in the 18th century as Melinda Wells. Bruckner falls in love with Melinda. Daisy discovers how he has used her to reach Melinda, but she is unable to leave him, and as the show ends they continue to work together. **Howard Taubman** reviewed the show for the *New York Times*, and although he admired Harris and the songs, he described Lerner's book as "labored and creaky." **Barbra Streisand** and Yves Montand starred in the 1970 film version.

ON THE TOWN **(28 DECEMBER 1944, ADELPHI, 463 PERFOR-MANCES).** Music by **Leonard Bernstein**, lyrics and book by **Betty Comden** and **Adolph Green**, entire production directed by **George Abbott**, musical numbers and choreography staged by **Jerome Robbins**. Based on Jerome Robbins's original concept that first found a home in the ballet *Fancy Free* (also with music by Bernstein), *On the Town* was a fleshed-out version of the story that became a brilliant **musical comedy**. Three sailors hit Manhattan for a 24-hour leave, looking for girls and fun. Ozzie (Adolph Green) finds his hands full with Claire de Loon (Betty Comden), an anthropology student. Chip (Chris Alexander) meets a randy cab driver named Hildegard Esterhazy (**Nancy Walker**). Chip wants to see the sights, but Hildy just wants to take him to her apartment. Gaby (John Battles) falls in love with a subway poster of "Miss Turnstiles" (Sono Osato) and spends his leave looking for her. The show was a valentine to New York City, taking place in a number of famous places. The three couples, of course, find out that 24 hours is not long enough to get to know each other, and they sing "Some Other Time" as they part. Three more sailors then burst out of the Brooklyn Naval Yard, ready for action. *On the Town* was nearly the perfect show for its time and place. New York City experienced a constant flow of soldiers and sailors on leave, and the public knew of *Fancy Free*'s riotous success.

In the short time since *Oklahoma!*, dance had become an expected part of the plot in progressive musicals, and Robbins, if anything, made the dance even more important in *On the Town* than it was in *Oklahoma!*. Osato was a ballet dancer by training and was featured in most of the important dance numbers. Bernstein's score was sophisticated and dissonant by Broadway's standards, but it was ebullient and included convincing references to popular styles. Among the many highlights were the opening "New York, New York," the lovely ballad "Lonely Town," the humorous "Carried Away," the naughty and hysterical "I Can Cook, Too," and the nostalgic "Some Other Time." Bernstein also wrote his own dance music for the show; usually an arranger took care of this task. The show's publicist could have quoted almost any line in Lewis Nichols's rave review in the *New York Times*. Nichols called it "the freshest and most engaging musical . . . since the golden day of 'Oklahoma!'" The book is "literate," one that the audience can actually enjoy. Nichols recalled

Bernstein's recent triumphs in the concert music work and wrote that the music "has humor and is unpedantic," praised the principals, found the show's "charm" in its totality, and called *On the Town* one of Abbott's "perfect jobs."

ON THE TWENTIETH CENTURY (19 FEBRUARY 1978, ST. JAMES, 449 PERFORMANCES). Music by **Cy Coleman**, lyrics and book by **Betty Comden** and **Adolph Green**, directed by **Hal Prince**. Based on the play *Twentieth Century* by Ben Hecht and Charles MacArthur, which also became a movie starring John Barrymore and Carole Lombard, *On the Twentieth Century* was a funny and spirited musical that fell a few feet short of smash hit. **John Cullum** played Oscar Jaffe, a theatrical producer who badly needs a hit and hopes to convince Lily Garland (**Madeline Kahn**), a Hollywood star who used to work with him, to help him and perhaps become romantically interested in him. He woos her on the Twentieth Century, the luxury train from New York to Chicago. Also on board are Letitia Primrose (**Imogene Coca**), a screwball millionaire who runs all over the train affixing "Repent" stickers to everything, and Bruce Granit (**Kevin Kline**), Lily's lover. The four stars delivered very strong performances, as did Robin Wagner's ingenious set, which presented the train from a number of different views. Some critics believed that the set overwhelmed the show; the *Variety* review opened with the line, "It's ominous when an audience leaves a musical whistling the scenery." Richard Eder, however, writing in the *New York Times*, gave the show a positive review, calling it "funny, elegant and totally cheerful" but with some "rough spots." He noted that scenic designer Wagner "manages all kinds of extraordinary things" and that Coleman's music always managed "to heighten the spirit of the production." Songs included the title number, "Repent," and "We've Got It All."

ON YOUR TOES (11 APRIL 1936, IMPERIAL, 315 PERFORMANCES). Music by **Richard Rodgers**, lyrics by **Lorenz Hart**, book by Rodgers, Hart, and **George Abbott**, staged by Worthington Miner, choreography by **George Balanchine**. Based on an original story by Rodgers and Hart, *On Your Toes* had a major ballet component, notable integration of music and plot, and a winning performance by **Ray Bolger** as Phil Dolan 3rd, the son of two vaudeville performers who helped him get an education. He now is a music professor at the WPA's (Works Progress Administration) Knickerbocker University, but would rather be a dancer. His love interest is Frankie Frayne (Doris Carson), but Phil begins to assist a Russian ballet company and starts to fancy himself as a consort for the prima ballerina, Vera Barnova (Tamara Geva). Phil helps put on a jazz ballet, and dances the male lead himself when that dancer disappears. Gangsters are after the dancer, and they mistake Bolger's character for him and intend to kill him. Frankie warns Phil, and he realizes his foolishness and returns to her. Balanchine choreographed two major ballets for the show: act 1's "Princess Zenobia," a satirical look at classical ballets, and act 2's famous "Slaughter on Tenth Avenue," in which the male lead pays the owner of a seedy bar to spend time with a stripper. The jealous owner shoots the girl, and then the lead male dancer shoots the owner. The ballet music was an impressive effort from Rodgers, one of the few instrumental works in the history of Broadway to become famous in the concert hall. The ballet did not advance the show's plot, but it was an early, substantive use of ballet in a musical. **Brooks Atkinson**, in his *New York Times* review, described it as "sophisticated," but hoped that the reader would not find that word too "unpalatable." He was impressed by the show's "uniformity of viewpoint," with its "mocking book" and "raised eyebrows." He suggested that because of the show's musical and literary allusions, one might want to look into Beethoven and Rimsky-Korsakov, and found the show somewhat elitist. Among the show's songs were "There's a Small Hotel," "It's Got to Be Love," "Glad to Be Unhappy," "The 3 B's," and "Too Good for the Average Man."

ONCE UPON A MATTRESS **(11 MAY 1959, PHOENIX, 460 PER-FORMANCES).** Music by **Mary Rodgers**, lyrics by Marshall Barer, book by Jay Thompson, Barer, and Dean Fuller, staged by **George Abbott**, choreography by **Joe Layton**. A musical version of "The Princess and the Pea," *Once Upon a Mattress* ran for almost 14 months and launched **Carol Burnett**'s career. Jane White played the formidable queen who wishes to test any princess who might want to marry her son, Prince Dauntless (Joe Bova). Before subjecting Princess Winnifred (Burnett) to the famous test, she forces her to swim a moat and serve as a maid. Jack Gilford worked in pantomime as he played the mute king. The music was by **Richard Rodgers**'s daughter Mary and is the score for which she remains best known. **Brooks Atkinson** reviewed the show for the *New York Times*, offering substantial praise for Burnett and for Rodgers's music. He found the show "full of good music" that sounds nothing like the composer's father, asserting that Mary Rodgers "has a style of her own" and is a good melodist. He noted Burnett's "metallic voice" and "ironic gleam," and her excellent feeling for "the comic gesture." Musical highlights included "Shy," "The Swamps of Home, "Happily Ever After," "Man to Man Talk," and "Yesterday I Loved You." The 1996 revival starring Sarah Jessica Parker ran for almost six months.

110 IN THE SHADE **(24 OCTOBER 1963, BROADHURST, 330 PERFORMANCES).** Music by **Harvey Schmidt**, lyrics by **Tom Jones**, book by N. Richard Nash, choreography by **Agnes de Mille**, presented by **David Merrick**. Based on Nash's play *The Rainmaker*, *110 in the Shade* included a score by the creators of *The Fantasticks* and managed a 10-month run. Inga Swenson played Lizzie Curry, a plain young woman who is unsuccessful in finding a husband. She lives in the drought-ridden West, and a young con man named Bill Starbuck (Robert Horton) offers to produce a rainstorm for $100. Lizzie is suspicious, but the family is desperate and pays Starbuck. She falls in love with him, and Starbuck confesses to her that he is a fraud. Another potential suitor for Lizzie is the sheriff (**Stephen Douglass**), but she does not want him to arrest Starbuck. Finally it rains, to everyone's surprise, and Starbuck leaves a more confident Lizzie who might spark more interest from the sheriff. The songs did not become popular outside of the show but worked well within it. Some of the more effective were "Hungry Men," "Rain Song," and "Love, Don't Turn Away." **Howard Taubman**, in the *New York Times*, described the show as "dry as the parched land outside the Broadhurst Theater," and all of the theatrical effects available "cannot substitute for warmth, humor or enchantment." He remarked that all Inga Swenson seemed to do was weep, and understood why she might.

ONE TOUCH OF VENUS **(7 OCTOBER 1943, IMPERIAL, 567 PERFORMANCES).** Music by **Kurt Weill**, lyrics by Ogden Nash, book by S. J. Perelman and Nash, staged by Elia Kazan, choreography by **Agnes de Mille**, presented by **Cheryl Crawford**. With a plot suggested by F. Anatey's novella *The Tinted Venus* (1885), *One Touch of Venus* was Weill's biggest hit written for the American stage and **Mary Martin**'s first major lead role. She played the goddess who is brought to life from a statue when barber Rodney Hatch (Kenny Baker) places the engagement ring he purchased for his girlfriend on the statue's finger. Venus tries to take Rodney for herself, but stops when she realizes the mundane nature of life in suburban Ozone Heights. She again becomes a statue, and Rodney then meets a young lady in the museum who looks much like Venus. The show's book was literate, and Ogden Nash's lyrics were outstanding. Weill's score, which he orchestrated himself, showed his uncanny ability to write theatrical music appropriate to any subject, even in this, the closest thing he ever wrote to a conventional **musical comedy**. The score included one of his greatest hits, "Speak Low," and "That's Him" also enjoyed popularity. Agnes de Mille produced two memorable ballets. The first depicted "Forty Minutes for Lunch," a droll look at the midday business of Rockefeller Center. The second, "Venus in Ozone Heights," was the dream ballet that convinced the goddess she is better off as a statue. Critics thought that *One Touch of Venus* was the best Broadway musical since *Oklahoma!* more than six months earlier. Lewis Nichols reviewed the show for the *New York Times*. He called Nash's lyrics "soft and sweet," but at times "a shade confused," and noted that several of Weill's songs should become popular. Nichols proclaimed Mary Martin "a lady of high charm" who can "toss a song over the footlights."

THE ONLY GIRL **(2 NOVEMBER 1914, 39TH STREET, 240 PERFORMANCES).** Music by **Victor Herbert**, lyrics and book by **Henry Blossom**. Based on **Frank Mandel**'s comic play *Our Wives*, *The Only Girl* combined a solid score and a book somewhat better than that of the average **musical comedy**. The story involved four bachelors who have forsworn marriage, all of whom are married by the end of the show. A musical librettist, Alan "Kim" Kimbrough (Thurston Hall), needs a composer and hears a delightful tune being played upstairs. The composer turns out to be pretty, young Ruth Wilson (Wilda Bennett). They decide to work together and avoid romantic connections, but Ruth quickly falls for Kim. Meanwhile, the other three bachelors get married. Kim tries to remain single, but in the end falls for Ruth. Another major character was Patrice La Montrose (Adele Rowland), the female comic. Blossom used lofty and more archaic language in the romantic tunes and words with a more contemporary twist in Rowland's songs, the latter including "The More I See of Others, Dear, the Better I Like You." The unnamed reviewer for the *New York Times* wrote that Herbert's music "has just the right swing to be exceedingly popular." The critic cautioned that this was not a show for tired businessmen but rather "a very wide-awake person" who desires "a thoroughly enjoyable evening."

OPERA. A musical theater work usually sung straight through with arias, recitatives, and ensemble numbers, recognizably part of the international operatic tradition including works by such composers as Wolfgang Amadeus Mozart and Giuseppe Verdi. The most famous reference to opera and Broadway is **Oscar Hammerstein II**'s quip that opera is something that loses money on Broadway. Famous operas have actually been produced on Broadway. The Society of American Singers produced several operas in repertory for seven months during the 1918–19 season, as did the San Carlo Opera Company in the springs of 1944 and 1948. Other European operas on Broadway have included Benjamin Britten's *The Rape of Lucretia* (1948–49) and Giacomo Puccini's *La Bohème* (2002–03), in addition to a Verdi spoof (*Ill Treated Il Trovatore*, 1880) and the updated *My Darlin' Aida* (1952–53). Several American composers have had operas produced in Broadway theaters, including, for example, **George Gershwin (*Porgy and Bess*, 1935)**, **Mark Blitzstein** (*Regina*, 1949), **Leonard Bernstein** (*Trouble in Tahiti*, part of *All in One*, 1955), and Gian Carlo Menotti, who has had the most success in this category (*The Telephone*, 1947; *The Medium*, 1950; *The Consul*, 1950; *The Saint of Bleecker Street*, 1954–55; and *Maria Golovin*, 1958). Operas have also inspired Broadway shows, such as ***Rent*** (1996), an updating of *La Bohème*, and ***Aida***, with a new score by **Elton John** and **Tim Rice**. A fascinating opera on Broadway was ***Carmen Jones*** (1943), Oscar Hammerstein II's revision of Georges Bizet's *Carmen* placed in the American South with an African American cast.

Opera has strongly influenced the American musical theater. Light operas by Austrian, French, and English composers had a huge effect on the American **operetta**, and many staging techniques used in musicals were first explored in opera houses. Despite the creators' unwillingness to label the works as such, opera has made a major comeback on Broadway since the 1970s in such sung-through shows as *Jesus Christ Superstar* (1971), *Les Misérables* (1987), *The Phantom of the Opera* (1988), *Miss Saigon* (1991), *Marie Christine* (1999), and *The Light in the Piazza* (2005). Musical styles range from that of Giacomo Puccini to pop, but these works share with earlier operas their use of recitative-like passages, memorable melodies, and demanding writing for singers.

OPERETTA. Musical theater genre dominated by its score, which usually requires a variety of voice types, ranging from the operatic to the comic. Operettas often took place in a foreign land, typically an imaginary Central European kingdom, Asia, or South America, but also were set in familiar European and North American locales. Glorious, expansive, and emotive music filled operettas; waltzes, marches, and ensemble numbers were plentiful. A coloratura soprano and a rousing baritone were the typical romantic leads. The history of operetta is rooted in Europe, but the genre had become a Broadway institution by the late 19th century. European works frequently appeared on Broadway stages, and newly written American works played alongside them. Among the most successful American works of the time were **Reginald De Koven**'s *Robin Hood* (1891) and **Victor Herbert**'s *The Fortune Teller* (1898). In 1907, **Franz Lehár**'s *The Merry Widow*, a Viennese import, captivated American audiences and catapulted the operetta genre to tremendous popularity. Three composers became closely identified with the genre on Broadway: Herbert, **Rudolf Friml**, and **Sigmund Romberg**. Herbert's *Naughty Marietta* (1910) and *Sweethearts* (1913); Friml's *The Firefly* (1912), *Rose Marie* (1924), and *The Vagabond King* (1925); and Romberg's *Maytime* (1917), *Blossom Time* (1921), *The Student Prince* (1924), *The Desert Song* (1926), and *The New Moon* (1928) became classics of the genre. With the stock market crash and Great Depression, operetta faded in popularity on Broadway due to production costs and changing audience attitudes. However, the genre found new life during the 1930s and 1940s in Hollywood as film adaptations of popular stage works and original film operettas graced movie screens throughout the world. *See also* OPERA.

ORBACH, JERRY (1935–2004). Actor who was the original El Gallo in *The Fantasticks* (1960) and introduced "Try to Remember." His Broadway roles included Paul in *Carnival* (1961), where he sang "Her Face"; Chuck in *Promises, Promises* (1968), where he introduced "I'll Never Fall in Love Again" and for which he won a **Tony Award** for Best Actor in a Musical; Billy Flynn in *Chicago* (1975), immortalizing "Razzle Dazzle" and "All I Care About"; and Julian Marsh in *42nd Street* (1980), singing the title song and "Lullaby of Broadway." He is also known for his roles in the film *Dirty Dancing* (1987) and the television series *Law and Order* (1992–2004).

ORCHESTRATOR/ORCHESTRATIONS. The person who creates the orchestral parts in a Broadway musical, the orchestrations. Often, after the composer creates the songs for voice(s) and piano, the music is given to the orchestrator, who assigns various parts to various instruments. One of the most important Broadway orchestrators was **Robert Russell Bennett**, who frequently worked with **Rodgers and Hammerstein**. Orchestrators often created the overtures and other instrumental numbers in Broadway musicals. A **Tony Award** for Best Orchestrations was established in 1997. *See also* TUNICK, JONATHAN.

ORIENTALISM. A cultural phenomenon with strong Broadway manifestations. Following the seminal work of scholars such as Edward V. Said, Orientalism concerns how and why the Western world created an image of the Orient (Asia), often for colonialist purposes. Asia and Asians were often portrayed as being somehow inferior to their European counterparts. Orientalist attitudes frequently appeared on Broadway stages in the 20th century, including scenes in **revues** and entire shows such as *Katinka* (1915), *The Desert Song* (1926), *East Wind* (1931, music by **Sigmund Romberg**, lyrics by **Oscar Hammerstein II**), *The King and I* (1951), *Kismet* (1953), and *Flower Drum Song* (1958). **Stephen Sondheim**'s *Pacific Overtures* (1976) even went so far as to incorporate Japanese stage and acting conventions. At the turn of the 21st century, Orientalism acquired a broader definition as the appropriation of Western musical styles and techniques by creators of Asian origin. Two examples are Chinese-American David Henry Hwang's reworked book for the 2002 **revival** of *Flower Drum Song* and Indian composer **A. R. Rahman**'s score for *Bombay Dreams* (2004). *See also AVENUE Q*; *CHERRY BLOSSOMS*; *SOUTH PACIFIC*; *THOROUGHLY MODERN MILLIE*.

– P –

PACIFIC OVERTURES **(11 JANUARY 1976, WINTER GARDEN, 193 PERFORMANCES).** Music and lyrics by **Stephen Sondheim**, book by **John Weidman**, directed by **Harold Prince**, presented by Prince in association with Ruth Mitchell. Based on Weidman's play about Commodore Perry's 1853 voyage that opened commerce between Japan and the United States, the musical version included conventions of the Kabuki theater and an entirely Asian cast. Writing in the *New York Times*, **Clive Barnes** was most taken with Sondheim's score, calling it "Japonaiserie" but with a "carefully applied patina of pastiche." He was willing to forgive problems in the show, however, because the concept was "so bold" and "fascinating." Broadway audiences were not as open to the experiment, however, and *Pacific Overtures*, in its original run, was a noble failure. Musical highlights included "Chrysanthemum Tea," "A Bowler Hat," and the dramatic finale, "Next." The 2004 Broadway revival starred B. D. Wong as the Reciter, and was based on Amon Miyamoto's 2000 production at the New National Theatre in Tokyo. *See also* ORIENTALISM.

PAGE, KEN (1954–). Singer with a large, comforting voice who made his Broadway debut as a **replacement** Lion in *The Wiz* and played Nicely-Nicely Johnson in an all-black **revival** of *Guys and Dolls* (1976). He created the roles of Fats Waller in *Ain't Misbehavin'* (1978) and Old Deuteronomy in *Cats* (1982), reprising the latter for the show's 1998 video release.

PAINT YOUR WAGON **(12 NOVEMBER 1951, SHUBERT, 289 PERFORMANCES).** Music by **Frederick Loewe**, lyrics and book by **Alan Jay Lerner**, choreographed by **Agnes de Mille**, produced by **Cheryl Crawford**. Lerner enjoyed Bret Harte's stories of the old West and conceived a story about the "life and death of a ghost town," desiring more realism than the Western folksiness of *Oklahoma!* Lerner's story involves a town inhabited entirely by men, except for one woman. The show's creation was difficult because Lerner's quest for untheatrical realism made problems with the book insoluble. Tryout runs in both Philadelphia and Boston were extended for rewrites. The show opened in New York to mixed critical reaction. **Brooks Atkinson**, writing in the *New York Times*, was impressed, calling *Paint Your Wagon* "a bountiful and exultant jamboree" but noting that it did not meet the "artistic standard of *Brigadoon*." Loewe captured the spirit of Western folk songs in his settings of Lerner's descriptive lyrics, as in the songs "They Call the Wind Maria" and "I Talk to the Trees." Lerner constructed a new plot for the 1969 film.

THE PAJAMA GAME **(13 MAY 1954, ST. JAMES, 1,063 PERFORMANCES).** Music and lyrics by **Richard Adler** and **Jerry Ross**, book by **George Abbott** and Richard Bissell, staged by Abbott and **Jerome Robbins**, choreography by **Bob Fosse**. Based on Richard Bissell's novel *7 1/2 Cents*, *The Pajama Game* was a delightful romp and Adler and Ross's first score for a **book musical**. George Abbott assisted Bissell in adapting his novel, providing delightful comedy and situations for musical numbers. The lead comic was Eddie Foy Jr., who played Hines, the efficiency expert at the Sleep-Tite Pajama Factory. He has decided, with the help of management, to speed up the machines. The union's grievance officer, Babe Williams (Janis Page), goes to the factory superintendent, Sid Sorokin (**John Raitt**), and demands a raise of seven and a half cents per hour. Sid quickly falls for Babe, and after many complications, the two are together at the final curtain. Slanted significantly on the workers' side, the show worked because the tone remained light and the cast was superb. The show was the first time Bob Fosse choreographed a major musical, and his dance "Steam Heat" became one of his most famous numbers. **Brooks Atkinson**, in the *New York Times*, found the score "exuberant . . . in any number of good American idioms without self-consciousness." The score included several memorable songs, including "Hernando's Hideaway," a mock sexy tango "Steam Heat," the love ballad "Hey There," and the comic numbers "I'll Never Be Jealous Again" and "Think of the Time I Save." The 2006 Broadway revival starred **Kelli O'Hara** and Harry Connick Jr.

PAL JOEY **(25 DECEMBER 1940, ETHEL BARRYMORE, 374 PERFORMANCES).** Music by **Richard Rodgers**, lyrics by **Lorenz Hart**, book by John O'Hara, staged and produced by **George Abbott**. Based on John O'Hara's fictional letters about the title character that were published in *The New Yorker*, *Pal Joey* was one of Broadway's groundbreaking musicals. **Gene Kelly** played Joey, a heel loaded with ambition and the superficial charm to get others to pay for his dreams. He has begun to date the innocent, young Linda English (Lelia Ernst), but dumps her quickly when he has the chance to become a gigolo for Vera Simpson (**Vivienne Segal**), a bored but wealthy middle-aged married woman. She sees right through Joey, but wants to have fun and pays for everything until Joey becomes a problem. Linda, whose feelings for Joey have cooled, warns Vera that he plans to blackmail her about their affair. Vera cuts Joey loose, and he starts looking for a new patsy. Many were not ready for the frank story and character, but the show's wonderful score and Gene Kelly's engaging nature softened its less-appealing aspects. **Brooks Atkinson**, for one, found *Pal Joey* hard to swallow. He concluded his *New York Times* review with a famous question about this "expertly done" show, "Can you draw sweet water from a foul well?" He admits the show's glories: the score, effective dances, wonderful scenery and costumes, and a fine cast. But O'Hara's book is "a pitiless portrait of his small-time braggart," a role that Kelly plays "with remarkable accuracy." One can only revel, however, in the show's score. Joey sang "I Could Write a Book," one of the great Broadway ballads. Vera sang "Bewitched, Bothered, Bewildered," her coy, sexy admission of her feelings for Joey, set to an especially memorable melody. A nightclub performer sang "Zip" during a striptease, a parody of Gypsy Rose Lee's monologues. There were a number of other fine songs, such as "You Mustn't Kick It Around," and others sung in nightclub routines. The 1952 revival starred Segal and Harold Lang, while the 1957 film version featured Frank Sinatra, Rita Hayworth, and Kim

Novak. **Patti LuPone, Peter Gallagher**, and **Bebe Neuwirth** appeared in the **City Center** *Encores!* 1995 production.

PANAMA HATTIE **(30 OCTOBER 1940, 46TH STREET, 501 PERFORMANCES).** Music and lyrics by **Cole Porter**, book by **Herbert Fields** and **B. G. De Sylva**. An original story conceived as a vehicle for **Ethel Merman**, *Panama Hattie* featured Merman as Hattie Maloney, a singer who works in a bar in the Panama Canal Zone. Among her songs was "Make It Another Old-Fashioned, Please." Three sailors spend much of the show searching for girls, but Hattie falls for Nick Bullett (James Dunn), who is from a respectable Philadelphia family. He asks Hattie to marry him, but she insists that his young daughter, Geraldine (Joan Carroll), must first accept her. By the end of the show, Hattie and Geraldine sing "Let's Be Buddies." **Brooks Atkinson** of the *New York Times* found that "everything is noisy, funny and in order" but criticized the show's bawdy theme. He found Merman to be a "coarse-timbered entertainer with a heart of gold," playing a part she "rolls through . . . with the greatest gusto."

PAPP, JOSEPH (1921–1991). Innovative producer who was founding director of the New York Shakespeare Festival in Central Park and brought many of his shows from there, as well as from the Public Theatre, to Broadway, including *Hair*, *Two Gentlemen of Verona*, *A Chorus Line*, the 1981 revival of *The Pirates of Penzance*, and *The Mystery of Edwin Drood*.

PARADE **(17 DECEMBER 1998, VIVIAN BEAUMONT, 85 PERFORMANCES).** Music and lyrics by Jason Robert Brown, book by Alfred Uhry, coconceived by **Harold Prince**. Based on the historic 1913 "Trial of the Century," *Parade* was the story of Leo Frank **(Brent Carver)**, a New York Jew living in Atlanta who is falsely accused of killing young Mary Phagan, found guilty, and sentenced to be hung. His wife, Lucille (Carolee Carmello), launches a campaign on his behalf and convinces the Governor to overturn her husband's death decree, only to have a group of vigilantes break into the prison in the midst of night and lynch the innocent man. Musical highlights include the opening "The Old Red Hills of Home" (which is reprised as the finale) and the powerful duets for the Franks, "This Is Not

Over Yet" and "All the Wasted Time." The show won **Tony Awards** for Best Book and Best Original Score.

PARDON MY ENGLISH **(20 JANUARY 1933, MAJESTIC, 46 PERFORMANCES).** Music by **George Gershwin**, lyrics by **Ira Gershwin**, book by **Herbert Fields**, produced by **Alex A. Aarons** and **Vinton Freedley**. A commercial failure, the show, in its final form, was a vehicle for Jack Pearl, famous as Baron Munchausen on the radio, here playing a Dresden police commissioner who wrongfully arrests two Americans in a show that tested the limits of sexual content for the day. **Brooks Atkinson** noted in the *New York Times* that the show "rolled around in the gutter." The score included the songs "Lorelei," "My Cousin in Milwaukee," and "Isn't It a Pity."

PARKER, DOROTHY (1893–1967). Noted author, playwright, and screenwriter who wrote lyrics for *Candide* (1956). She was known for her sharp wit and clever one-liners.

THE PASSING SHOW **(WINTER GARDEN: 22 JULY 1912, 136 PERFORMANCES; 24 JULY AND 29 SEPTEMBER 1913, 116 PERFORMANCES; 1 JUNE 1914, 133 PERFORMANCES; 29 MAY 1915, 145 PERFORMANCES; 22 JUNE 1916, 140 PERFORMANCES; 26 APRIL 1917, 196 PERFORMANCES; 25 JULY 1918, 124 PERFORMANCES; 23 OCTOBER 1919, 280 PERFORMANCES; 29 DECEMBER 1920, 191 PERFORMANCES; 20 SEPTEMBER 1922, 85 PERFORMANCES; 14 JUNE 1923, 118 PERFORMANCES; 3 SEPTEMBER 1924, 93 PERFORMANCES).** A **Shubert**-produced series of **revues** that began in 1912 to compete with the success of *Ziegfeld Follies*, they were filled with topical humor and satirical looks at contemporary culture. The Shuberts took the name from what is generally considered to be the first American revue, George W. Lederer's *The Passing Show* (1894). Productions were elaborate, but the Shuberts were unwilling to match Ziegfeld's salaries, so they offered young talent that soon moved on. The 1912 edition starred Charlotte Greenwood and also introduced the brothers Eugene and **Willie Howard**. The *New York Times* praised how the chorus girls and principals "romped through a jumble of things politic, theatric, and social, leaping from comedy scenes to elaborate musical numbers with an agility inspired by an unusually energetic stage director." **Marilyn Miller** starred in *The Passing Show*s of 1914 and 1915, the latter considered one of the best with the Howards mocking Charlie Chaplin and Shakespeare, and Miller appearing as Mary Pickford. **Ed Wynn** headlined in 1916, parodying Theodore Roosevelt's bellicose calls for war. The show also included live horses on treadmills facing the audience, imitating a cavalry charge.

Harold Atteridge usually wrote the books and lyrics for *The Passing Show*. The music that such composers as **Sigmund Romberg** and Jean Schwartz wrote for the annual shows included few hits and was generally in the slightly syncopated style popular at the time, but in later editions some interpolations became quite popular. 1917 brought "Goodbye Broadway, Hello France," and the 1918 show featured the songs "Smiles" and "My Baby-Talk Lady!," along with a young **Fred** and **Adele Astaire**. Highlights of the later versions, as interest in the annual revues waned and the thrifty Shuberts became ever more conscious of the bottom line, included the song "I'm Forever Blowing Bubbles" in 1919, a young **Fred Allen** and the song "Carolina in the Morning" in 1922, and comedian George Jessel in 1923. Another Shubert revue that appeared with regularity was the racy *Artists and Models*.

PASSION **(9 MAY 1994, PLYMOUTH, 280 PERFORMANCES).** Music and lyrics by **Stephen Sondheim**, book and direction by **James Lapine**. A musical about obsessive love based on a French film, *Passion* showed another side of Sondheim and Lapine as collaborators. Their insistence on bringing art and ambivalent emotions to the Broadway musical was already clear in *Sunday in the Park with George* and *Into the Woods*, but in *Passion* they plunged into deeper emotional terrain. The handsome soldier Giorgio (Jere Shea) is happily involved with his married mistress, Clara (**Marin Mazzie**), but then the Italian army transfers him to an isolated outpost. There he meets Fosca (**Donna Murphy**), an unattractive invalid who falls completely in love with the uninterested Giorgio. He ends up fighting a duel with his colonel (Gregg Edelman), Fosca's cousin, and then has a nervous breakdown. After his recovery, he learns that Fosca died from her obsessive love for Giorgio. He finds himself moved and transformed by her feelings. Conceived in one act (but often performed with an intermission), the show is a rhapsody about the many dimensions of love, not all of which have happy resolutions. David Richards, in the *New York Times*, described the production as "ravishing" and believed that Sondheim and Lapine "achieved an uncommonly graceful intertwining of dialogue and music."

PATINKIN, MANDY (BORN MANDEL PATINKIN, 1952–). The versatile actor and singer's Broadway credits include Che Guevara in *Evita* (1979), George Seurat in *Sunday in the Park with George* (1986), and Archibald Craven in *The Secret Garden* (1991). He won a **Tony Award** for *Evita*. Patinkin uses his distinctive falsetto tenor and ability to create a musical line to bring emotional life to every song he sings and intensity and depth to every role he plays.

PEGGY-ANN **(27 DECEMBER 1926, VANDERBILT, 333 PERFORMANCES).** Music by **Richard Rodgers**, lyrics by **Lorenz Hart**, book by **Herbert Fields**. Based on *Tillie's Nightmare*, a musical vehicle for Marie Dressler that premiered in 1910, *Peggy-Ann* featured **Helen Ford** in the title role as a young woman who has glorious dreams about her life, but never gets past her dreams and nightmares. The show incorporated some Freudian thinking, as well as a Cinderella-like plot. Although it appeared early in Rodgers and Hart's career, the *New York Times*'s unnamed critic noted the "freshness" of the team's shows, and believes here that "they travel a little further along their road." The critic especially praised the song "Where's That Rainbow?"

PENNINGTON, ANN (1893–1971). Diminutive dancer, actress, and singer who starred in multiple editions of *Ziegfeld Follies* and *George White's Scandals* in the 1910s and 1920s. She was especially known for the "Black Bottom" dance, which she introduced in the 1926 edition of *George White's Scandals*. Pennington created the role of Lola McGee in *The New Yorkers* and also achieved success in silent and sound motion pictures.

PETER PAN **(20 OCTOBER 1954, WINTER GARDEN, 152 PERFORMANCES).** Music by Mark Charlap, lyrics by Carolyn Leigh, additional music by **Jule Styne**, additional lyrics by **Betty Comden** and **Adolph Green**, direction and choreography by **Jerome Robbins**. A musicalization of J. M. Barrie's famous children's play, *Peter Pan* had a disappointing initial run but became popular through various television productions and stage versions. It was conceived as a vehicle for **Mary Martin**, who engagingly brought to life the adolescent male hero. Cyril Ritchard was an effective Captain Hook, and also played Mr. Darling. Other leading cast members included Margalo Gillmore as Mrs. Darling, Sondra Lee as Tiger Lily, and Kathy Nolan as Wendy. Jerome Robbins wrote the book (without credit) and for the first time served as both director and choreographer. Robbins Americanized the story and had the idea to cast the pirates with children. The show opened first in San Francisco with a score by Leigh and Charlap, but more and different music was need for Broadway, and Comden, Green, and Styne entered the project. **Brooks Atkinson**'s review of the original version in the *New York Times* was mixed, lauding it as "a bountiful, good-natured show," but also lamenting that the huge production might "look ponderous toward the end." He called Martin "the liveliest Peter Pan in the record book," flying with abandon and performing "with skill and enjoyment." Some of the songs in *Peter Pan* have entered the popular consciousness, at least among children, especially "I Gotta Crow" and "I'm Flying," both by Leigh and Charlap. Comden, Green, and Styne wrote the fine "Captain Hook's Waltz" and "Never Never Land."

PETERS, BERNADETTE (BORN BERNADETTE LAZZARO, 1948–). One of the most distinctive musical theater actresses of her generation, Peters brings a depth of character to her roles that is rarely matched. She originated the roles of Mabel in *Mack and Mabel* (1974), Dot in *Sunday in the Park with George* (1983), Emma in *Song and Dance* (1985), the Witch in *Into the Woods* (1987), and Marsha in *The Goodbye Girl* (1993). In addition to her original roles, she brought new and riveting interpretations to revivals as Annie in *Annie Get Your Gun* (1999) and Rose in *Gypsy* (2003).

***THE PHANTOM OF THE OPERA* (26 JANUARY 1988, MAJESTIC, 7,893 PERFORMANCES AS OF 31 DECEMBER 2006).** Music by **Andrew Lloyd Webber**, lyrics by Charles Hart, additional lyrics by Richard Stilgoe, book by Stilgoe and Lloyd Webber, musical staging and choreography by **Gillian Lynne**, directed by **Harold Prince**, presented by **Cameron Mackintosh** and **The Really Useful Theater Company**. Based on the famous novel by Gaston Leroux, *The Phantom of the Opera* became the longest-running Broadway musical of all time on 9 January 2006, with 7,486 performances, surpassing the previous record holder, *Cats*, another Lloyd Webber show. *Phantom* and other **megamusicals** have raised public interest in spectacle and musical opulence, changing the essential thrust of the popular musical theater. At its core, *The Phantom of the Opera* concerns the love triangle of the murderous title character (**Michael Crawford**); Christine Daae, a dancer in the chorus (**Sarah Brightman**); and Raoul, a friend from her youth. The disfigured Phantom wants to achieve immortality through Christine, and ensures (through threats and murders) that she will have a starring role at the Paris Opera. The show's staging is extraordinary: the falling chandelier (in the house), the underground lake with rising candelabra, the Phantom's lair, and scenes from three created operas provide unforgettable theatrical effects. The score is likewise grandiose and expansive. Several of *Phantom*'s songs have become well known outside of the show, including the title number, "Music of the Night," "Wishing You Were Somehow Here Again," "Think of Me," and "Angel of Music." The septet "Prima Donna," "Masquerade," and opera sequences (including the modernist *Don Juan Triumphant*) are works of considerable skill.

Frank Rich's review in the *New York Times* is instructive. Widely viewed as dismissive of megamusicals, especially those by Lloyd Webber, Rich's reaction to *Phantom* is varied. There are aspects, particularly the staging, that he found extraordinary. He described the show as "a characteristic Lloyd Webber project—long on pop professionalism and melody, impoverished of artistic personality and passion" and found its most convincing love story to be that which the creators have with "the theater itself." Rich was astonished by the opening sequence, when the theater transforms instantly from something ready to be torn down to glorious life. Rich found the story "skeletal," but copiously praised Crawford's performance, even through the iconic mask. The 2004 film version starred Gerard Butler and Emmy Rossum, and in 2006, a 95-minute version opened in a purpose-built theater at the Venetian Resort-Hotel-Casino in Las Vegas.

PINKINS, TONYA (1962–). Noted **African American** actress whose roles include Anita in *Jelly's Last Jam* (1992), Kate in *The Wild Party*, and Caroline Thibodeaux in *Caroline, or Change* (2004). She brings a dramatic depth to her characters through her commanding stage presence and versatile vocal technique.

THE PINK LADY **(13 MARCH 1911, NEW AMSTERDAM, 312 PERFORMANCES).** Music by **Ivan Caryll**, lyrics and book by C. M. S. McLellan. Based on the French farce *Le Satyre* by Georges Berr and Marcel Guillemand, *The Pink Lady*'s unlikely but enjoyable plot involved a satyr running through the Forest of Compiègne, where he steals hugs and kisses from young ladies. In the human world, Lucien Garidel (William Elliott) is to marry Angèle (Alice Dovey) in six weeks, but seeks one last fling with Claudine (Hazel Dawn), a former girlfriend and the so-called "Pink Lady." Lucien and Angele reconcile in the end, Claudine is alone, and the satyr turns out to be a disguised antique dealer. The *New York Times* critic was most impressed with the book and the "dash" of a full plot that all takes place in a single day. Songs included "On the Saskatchewan," "My Beautiful Lady," "Hide and Seek," and "Donny Did, Donny Didn't."

PINS AND NEEDLES **(27 NOVEMBER 1937, LABOR STAGE, 1,108 PERFORMANCES).** Music and lyrics by **Harold Rome**, sketches by Arthur Arent, **Marc Blitzstein**, Emanuel Eisenberg, Charles Friedman, and Rome, directed by Friedman, produced by Labor Stage, Inc. under the sponsorship of the International Ladies Garment Workers Union. A **revue** acted by members of the union, the only originally scheduled performances of *Pins and Needles* were for the opening weekend. Nightly performances did not start until 3 January 1938, by which time the show had become very popular. It ran at the old Princess Theatre, renamed the Labor Stage for the event, part of the show's leftist stance. The review in the *New York Times*, signed by "J.G.," noted that the players "do not miss any plugs for the anti-fascism cause and for the working man in general," but their message is all part of the entertainment. Harold Rome did his first significant work for Broadway in *Pins and Needles*, providing such songs as "Sing Us a Song with Social Significance," "Doin' the Reactionary," "Four Little Angels of Peace Are We," and "One Big Union for Two." The *Times* critic remarked that the show "is certainly a revue out of the ordinary." The low budget helped the show enjoy a long run, and material was changed as current events demanded it.

PINZA, EZIO (1892–1957). Operatic bass-baritone who played Emile De Beque in *South Pacific* (1949) and won a **Tony Award** for his performance. He also starred as César in *Fanny* (1954).

PIPE DREAM **(30 NOVEMBER 1955, SHUBERT, 246 PERFORMANCES).** Music by **Richard Rodgers**, lyrics and book by **Oscar Hammerstein II**, directed by Harold Clurman, produced by Rodgers and Hammerstein. Rodgers and Hammerstein's seventh show and their least successful, *Pipe Dream* was the team's grittiest work. Set in a Cannery Row brothel, the story dealt with softhearted Madame Fauna (opera singer Helen Traubel) who brings together hard-edged Suzy (Judy Taylor) and impoverished marine biologist Doc (William Johnson). Based on John Steinbeck's novel-in-progress *Sweet Thursday*, Rodgers and Hammerstein wrote the show as Steinbeck delivered his book to them chapter by chapter. *New York Times* critic **Brooks Atkinson** found the play "sweet, pleasant and enjoyable," but Rodgers and Hammerstein were "in a minor key." Traubel sang "The Bum's Opera," "Sweet Thursday," "The Happiest House on the Block," and "How Long?," and the act 1 finale, "All at Once You Loved Her," enjoyed fame outside the theater.

PIPPIN **(23 OCTOBER 1972, IMPERIAL, 1,944 PERFORMANCES).** Music and lyrics by **Stephen Schwartz**, musical comedy by Roger O. Hirson, directed and choreographed by **Bob Fosse**. Considered a triumph for Fosse, *Pippin* was a musical with simple content that found its audience and enjoyed a long run. The plot concerned a search for identity by Pepin (respelled for the American audience), son of the medieval Emperor Charlemagne. John Rubinstein played Pippin, but **Ben Vereen**, as The Leading Player, stole the show. Pippin experiences the challenges of war, sex, revolution, and quiet living with his wife and family. Nothing satisfies him, but after he is offered the chance to be burned to death in a flaming hoop, domesticity suddenly looks acceptable, and there the musical ends. Many criticized the underdramatic story, but Fosse's staging carried them all away. During rehearsals, Fosse literally took over the show, inserting a racy tone that contradicted what Hirson and Schwartz had planned. The cast functioned much like a commedia dell'arte troupe with some in clown makeup and The Leading Player in modern dress. Fosse gave the show what Clives Barnes (in the *New York Times*) called "the pace of a roller derby and the finesse of a conjuror." Barnes dismissed the book as "feeble" and the music as "bland," but admitted that Schwartz wrote some "memorable" ballads. One was "Colors of the Sky," a fine song in the accessible pop idiom that Schwartz had used so successfully in *Godspell*. Barnes and other critics missed the appeal the show had for the younger generation. A search for one's identity was a popular theme in the early 1970s, and Schwartz's music carried enough of a rock beat to capture the youngsters. *Pippin* benefited from the first intensive television campaign for a Broadway musical, and many also probably enjoyed its naughtiness.

THE PIRATES OF PENZANCE (8 JANUARY 1981, URIS, 772 PERFORMANCES). Music by **Arthur Sullivan** and adapted by William Elliott, lyrics by **W. S. Gilbert**, choreography by **Graciela Daniele**, presented by **Joseph Papp**, a New York Shakespeare Festival production. A witty rethinking of this popular **operetta**, this rendition first appeared in Central Park the previous July. Aspects of the updating included Elliott's new orchestrations, which did away with the strings and gave the accompaniment a brassier sound, and casting rock stars Linda Ronstadt and Rex Smith as the young lovers. The Pirate King was **Kevin Kline**, who brought a maniacal quality to the role, and **George Rose** delightfully played Major General Stanley. The show provided many memorable moments, especially Rose's "I Am the Very Model of a Modern Major General" and several unexpected moments of dancing, such as a kick line inspired by the finale of *A Chorus Line* as the show ended. **Frank Rich**, writing in the *New York Times*, was charmed. He applauded the union of "civilized British wit and American show-biz" and praised most members of the cast, such as George Rose, who is "having so much devilish fun it's indecent." Of the musical numbers, he liked Ronstadt's singing of "Poor Wandering One," which "somehow merges pure sex with virginal rapture." Kline, however, occupied "a class by himself" with all of the elements of a star's performance. The show ran for nearly two years and also toured.

PLAIN AND FANCY **(27 JANUARY 1955, MARK HELLINGER, 461 PERFORMANCES).** Music by Albert Hague, lyrics by Arnold B. Horwitt, book by **Joseph Stein** and Will Glickman. Based on an original story that took two New Yorkers into Pennsylvania Amish country, *Plain and Fancy* managed a run of more than 13 months before disappearing almost completely. Ruth Winters (Shiri Conway) and Dan King (Richard Derr) go to Lancaster County to sell a farm that Dan has inherited. A possible buyer is Papa Yoder (Stefan Schnabel), whose daughter, Katie (Gloria Marlowe), is to marry Ezra Reber (Douglas Fletcher Rodgers). Katie, however, loves Ezra's brother, Peter, who has left the community and been shunned. Peter proves his worthiness and Katie agrees to marry him about the time the two New Yorkers declare their love for each other. **Brooks Atkinson**, writing in the *New York Times*, appreciated act 1, but thought that act 2 relied excessively on "the old staples of Broadway." Atkinson's favorite song was "Plain We Live," a declaration of Amish values. "Young and Foolish," sung by Katie and Peter, also achieved some popularity.

PLUMMER, CHRISTOPHER (1927–). Actor primarily known for his dramatic roles who played Cyrano de Bergerac in *Cyrano* (1973) and won a **Tony Award** for his performance. In musical theater circles, he is perhaps most famous for playing Captain von Trapp in the 1965 film version of *The Sound of Music*.

POOR LITTLE RITZ GIRL **(28 JULY 1920, CENTRAL, 119 PERFORMANCES).** Music by **Richard Rodgers** and **Sigmund Romberg**; lyrics by **Lorenz M. Hart** and Alex Gerber, book by George Campbell and **Lew Fields**, produced by Fields. The first Broadway **musical comedy** for which **Rodgers and Hart** wrote a complete score, the neophyte team was shocked and embarrassed on opening night, when they learned eight of their songs had been re-placed during the tryout period with new ones by Romberg and Gerber. The plot involved a chorus girl, Annie Farrell (Florence Webber), who sublets a luxury Riverside Drive apartment, only to have its bachelor owner, William Pembroke (**Charles Purcell**), return. He does not know about the sublet, but agrees to let her stay there until the farce in which she is performing, *Poor Little Ritz Girl*, is over. They, of course, fall in love. Rodgers and Hart's songs were more in the line of musical comedy, while Romberg's contributions, including the waltz "When I Found You," were closer to **operetta**.

POPPY (3 SEPTEMBER 1923, APOLLO, 346 PERFOR-MANCES). Music by Stephen Jones and Arthur Samuels, lyrics and book by **Dorothy Donnelly**. Although unknown today, *Poppy* ran for an entire season, most unusual at the time. This was largely because of **W. C. Fields**, already famous for his work in *Ziegfeld Follies*, who played Professor Eustace McGargle, a traveling showman who comes to a Connecticut town and discovers that his daughter, Poppy McGargle (Madge Kennedy), is a long-lost heiress. Luella Gear sang "What Do You Do Sundays, Mary?" and "Alibi Baby," two **interpolations** by Howard Dietz and Arthur Samuels.

PORGY AND BESS (10 OCTOBER 1935, ALVIN, 124 PERFOR-MANCES). Music by **George Gershwin**, lyrics by DuBose Heyward and **Ira Gershwin**, libretto by Heyward, directed by **Rouben Mamoulian**, produced by the **Theatre Guild**. Billed as "An American Folk Opera," *Porgy and Bess* premiered on Broadway because there was no place else to perform it in New York City at that time. Gershwin approached the project with different intentions than he did in his other Broadway projects. He spent more than a year composing it and traveled to South Carolina to hear African Americans sing the music that he imitated in the score. The novel *Porgy* by DuBose Heyward appeared in 1925, and Gershwin was soon interested in an operatic treatment. The next version was the play *Porgy* by Dorothy and DuBose Heyward, produced by the Theatre Guild (1927). Heyward then chose Gershwin's operatic proposal over a musical starring **Al Jolson** (perhaps with music by **Jerome Kern**). Heyward drafted the libretto and sent each finished scene to Gershwin. Heyward was supposed to create the lyrics, but that summer Ira Gershwin entered the project and wrote many of the words. Heyward argued for spoken dialogue with songs, but Gershwin wanted a "grand **opera**" and wrote recitatives. African American characters sing almost every line, while whites can only speak. The creators found a fine cast of African Americans. **Todd Duncan** and Anne Wiggins Brown took the title roles, while John W. Bubbles made an inspired Sportin' Life, the smarmy pimp and drug pusher.

Early in the show, Bess's man, Crown (Warren Coleman), kills Robbins (Henry Davis) and leaves Catfish Row. Bess moves in with Porgy, and they fall in love. Later, Porgy kills Crown in a fight and, after being jailed, manages to convince the police of his innocence. He returns to find that Sportin' Life has tempted Bess with cocaine, her nemesis, and taken her to New York to be a prostitute. Porgy leaves Charleston for New York on his goatcart as the chorus sings "O Lawd, I'm on My Way." Gershwin's score is loaded with gems, many of them jazz- and blues-inflected songs like he had been writing for years, but now with far greater vocal demands. Among the show's highlights are "Summertime," "My Man's Gone Now," "It Ain't Necessarily So," "Bess, You Is My Woman Now," and "I Got Plenty of Nothin'." How well Gershwin actually captured the African American musical style has been a matter of some debate, but few can question the quality of the score or its melodic inspiration. The critical reaction to the original production was mixed. It only managed a 124-performance run and was a financial failure. As has been often noted, however, this is a very long run for an opera. For the next few decades, *Porgy and Bess* remained controversial, especially among African Americans, who resented their portrayal by white creators. Perhaps its vindication on Broadway came in the 1976 Houston Grand Opera production, when the musical quality of the score became brilliantly clear with a superb cast and splendid production. *See also* AFRICAN AMERICAN MUSICALS.

PORTER, COLE (1891–1964). Composer and lyricist of tremendous sophistication, Porter came from a wealthy family and enjoyed social and financial privilege throughout his troubled life. His music possesses an advanced harmonic style atypical of American popular song of his time while his lyrics are filled with clever word plays, ingenious rhyme schemes, and delightful double entendres. Although his first full score for Broadway, *See America First* (1916), was a failure, he kept persevering with relatively successful shows during the 1920s, including *Fifty Million Frenchmen* (1929), before achieving true success with *Anything Goes* (1932), starring **Ethel Merman**. He had a string of hits in the 1930s and early 1940s, several of which featured Merman, including *Red, Hot and Blue!* (1936), *Du Barry Was a Lady* (1939), *Panama Hattie* (1940), and *Something for the Boys* (1943). Hits continued to appear, with *Kiss Me, Kate* (1948), *Can-Can* (1953), and *Silk Stockings* (1955). In the midst of these successes, Porter suffered a personal trauma: a riding accident in 1937 left him in almost constant pain, and the injuries to his right leg led to its amputation in 1958. Porter loved Paris, and references to the city, such as the song "I Love Paris" from *Can-Can* and "Paris Loves Lovers" from *Silk Stockings*, regularly appear in his work. Porter struggled throughout his life with his **homosexuality**, an aspect of his life omitted from the biopic *Night and Day* (1946), in which Cary Grant played Porter, but addressed in the subsequent film celebration of Porter and his music, *De-Lovely* (2004), which starred **Kevin Kline** as the legendary songwriter.

POWELL, ELEANOR (1912–1982). Exuberant solo tap dancer and actress known primarily for her work in Hollywood. Her Broadway credits include Molly in *Follow Thru* (1929) and Miss Hunter in *Fine and Dandy* (1930). She performed "Got a Bran' New Suit" and "The Lady with the Tap" in the **revue** *At Home Abroad* (1935).

PRESTON, ROBERT (ROBERT PRESTON MESERVEY, 1918–1987). The legendary creator of Professor Harold Hill in *The Music Man* (1957), for which he won a **Tony Award**, Preston had a dramatic bass-baritone voice that was immediately recognizable for its clarity, depth, and expressive qualities. He reprised Hill in the 1962 film version of *The Music Man*, and won a second Tony for his portrayal of Michael in *I Do! I Do!* (1966). He also created Mack in *Mack and Mabel* (1974).

PRINCE, HAROLD (HAL PRINCE, 1928–). Prince started his Broadway career as a producer, working with partner Robert E. Griffith on various shows directed by **George Abbott**. Early production credits include *The Pajama Game* (1954) and *West Side Story* (1957). In the 1960s he began to produce **Stephen Sondheim**'s shows, often working in conjunction with Ruth Mitchell. His debut as a Broadway director was with *Cabaret* (1966), and this aspect of his craft has included major contributions to the **concept musical** in such shows as *Company* (1970) and *Follies* (1971). Taking a page from French grand opera, and lacking a background in dance, Prince has gravitated to weighty set designs as a concept around which to base a show, evident in *Follies*, *Sweeney Todd: The Demon Barber of Fleet Street* (1979), and *The Phantom of the Opera* (1986). Prince worked with significant choreographers, including **Jerome Robbins** in *Fiddler on the Roof* (1964) and **Michael Bennett** in *Company* and *Follies*, but many of his shows since the late 1970s have not included significant dance components. He has won 10 **Tony Awards**, two for Best Producer and eight for Best Director. In 2006, he received a Special Tony Award for Lifetime Achievement in the Theatre.

PRINCESS FLAVIA **(2 NOVEMBER 1925, CENTURY, 152 PERFORMANCES).** Music by **Sigmund Romberg**, book and lyrics by **Harry B. Smith**, produced by the Messrs. **Shubert**. The **operetta** adaptation of Anthony Hope's *The Prisoner of Zenda* was in many ways a gender-reversed remake of *The Student Prince*, Romberg's hit from the previous year. **Evelyn Herbert** and Harry Welchman played the romantic leads. The score's primary love song was "I Dare Not Love You," the refrain of which is extremely similar to that of *The Student Prince*'s "Deep in My Heart, Dear."

THE PRINCESS PAT **(29 SEPTEMBER 1915, CORT, 158 PERFORMANCES).** Music by **Victor Herbert**, lyrics and book by **Henry Blossom**. Billed as a "comic opera," *The Princess Pat* combined a charming musical score with a Long Island setting, different than the typical **operetta** with its exotic locales. The cast, however, remained European in type. The show starred Eleanor Painter as the Princess di Montaldo, who is married to Prince Antonio (Joseph R. Lertora). She pretends to elope with another man to save her friend from marrying him, and also to incite her husband's jealousy. The unnamed *New York Times* critic adored Painter, going on for more than a paragraph about her singing, acting, and dancing. Although the critic found Herbert's score very much like his earlier work, including "whole stretches . . . amusingly reminiscent of 'The Only Girl' [from the previous season]," this score "is prettier." He compared Herbert to **Arthur Sullivan** but did not believe that Blossom was ready to be the librettist for this "American Savoy." The score included the hits "Love Is the Best of All" and "Neapolitan Love Song."

PRINCESS THEATRE MUSICALS. A series of **musical comedies** from the late 1910s that appeared at the 299-seat Princess Theatre in which songs—rooted in everyday idioms—were integrated into the narrative, comedy grew out of the plot, storylines were believable, and the lavish production values of the revue were avoided. **Jerome Kern**, **Guy Bolton**, and **P. G. Wodehouse** are credited with creating this new approach in works such as *Very Good Eddie* (1915), *Oh, Boy!* (1917), and *Oh, Lady! Lady!!* (1918). These shows had a significant impact on the development of musical comedy in the 1920s, evident in the work of **George Gershwin**, **Richard Rodgers**, and **Vincent Youmans**, among others.

PRODUCER. The member(s) of a creative team responsible for raising money, signing the talent, and overseeing the show in terms of business and ensuring that people can work together. Sometimes a producer will also be the director and/or a writer. Most producers decide whether a proposal is affordable. Producers have come from a variety of theatrical professions and other businesses, and the list of those who have had lengthy, successful careers is not long. When one acquires a reputation for raising money and supervising the egos and challenging personalities that inhabit the theatrical world, that person's career as a producer can last for decades.

The early 20th century was the era of luminary producers such as the **Shuberts**, **George White**, and **Florenz Ziegfeld**, who collectively created the awe and sense of power associated with the title "producer." In the middle of the century, **Rodgers and Hammerstein**, in addition to creating musicals, also produced them. **George Abbott** and the **Theatre Guild** were also major producers of the time. **Cameron Mackintosh**, **Andrew Lloyd Webber**'s the **Really**

Useful Company, and **Disney Theatricals** are among the corporate producers active in the early 21st century. The role of the producer is central to the plot of Mel Brooks's *The Producers* (2001). *See also* AARONS, ALEXANDER A.; ADLER, RICHARD; AVIAN, BOB; BERLIN, IRVING; BROWN, LEW; CAESAR, IRVING; COHAN, GEORGE M.; DE SYLVA, B. G. "BUDDY"; DILLINGHAM, CHARLES; DIRECTOR; FEUER, CY; FIELDS, LEW; FREEDLEY, VINTON; GORDON, MAX; HARRIGAN, EDWARD "NED"; HARRIS, SAM H.; HAYWARD, LELAND; KELLY, GENE; KIDD, MICHAEL; LEIGH, MITCH; LINDSAY, HOWARD; McGOWAN, JOHN; MERRICK, DAVID; MITCHELL, RUTH; PAPP, JOSEPH; PRINCE, HAROLD; RICE, EDWARD E.; ROSE, BILLY; SCHWAB, LAURENCE; SCHWARTZ, ARTHUR; WEBER, JOSEPH; WHEATLEY, WILLIAM.

***THE PRODUCERS* (19 APRIL 2001, ST. JAMES, 2,374 PERFORMANCES AS OF 31 DECEMBER 2006).** Music and lyrics by Mel Brooks, book by Brooks and Thomas Meehan, directed and choreographed by **Susan Stroman**. A stage version of Mel Brooks's classic comic film, the show starred **Nathan Lane** as producer Max Bialystock and **Matthew Broderick** as accountant-turned-producer Leo Bloom. Others in the outstanding cast included Roger Bart as Carmen Ghia, **Gary Beach** as Roger De Bris, Cady Huffman as Ulla, and Brad Oscar (who took over the role of Max Bialystock) as Franz Liebkind. The film's musical showpiece, "Springtime for Hitler," is expanded into a massive production number and includes a soliloquy for Hitler, "Heil Myself." Other new songs include "We Can Do It," "I Wanna Be a Producer," "Keep It Gay," "That Face," "Where Did We Go Right?," "Betrayed," and "'Til Him." The show won a record 12 **Tony Awards**, including Best Musical, Best Book, Best Original Score, Best Actor in a Musical (Lane), Best Featured Actor in a Musical (Beach), Best Featured Actress in a Musical (Huffman), Best Costume Design (William Ivey Long), Best Choreography (Stroman), and Best Direction of a Musical (Stroman). It also won 11 **Drama Desk Awards**. The 2005 film adaptation of the musical, directed by Stroman, starred Lane and Broderick and featured Uma Thurman as Ulla.

PROMISES, PROMISES (1 DECEMBER 1968, SHUBERT, 1,281 PERFORMANCES). Music by Burt Bacharach, lyrics by Hal David, book by **Neil Simon**, staged by **Robert Moore**, choreography by **Michael Bennett**, presented by **David Merrick**. Based on Billy Wilder's popular movie *The Apartment, Promises, Promises* took a modern and amoral, but also humorous and touching, look at the American business world. Neil Simon's book was filled with clever one-liners, but also expressed real emotions. Chuck Baxter (**Jerry Orbach**) is a junior executive who lets his bosses use his apartment for their romantic trysts in hopes that this might help advance his career. J. D. Sheldrake (Edward Winter) makes frequent use of the apartment with Fran Kubelik (Jill O'Hara), until he dumps her there and she attempts suicide. Baxter tries to help Fran, and they fall in love. Together they give Sheldrake what he deserves and find their own happiness. **Clive Barnes** raved about *Promises, Promises* in the *New York Times*, admitting that he would rather "send . . . a congratulatory telegram than write a review." He called Simon's book "one of the wittiest . . . a musical has possessed in years," and Burt Bacharach's "music excitingly reflects today." The cast was "virtually perfect," especially Orbach and O'Hara. Barnes also extravagantly appreciates Moore's direction and Bennett's dances. There is no question that Bacharach's and David's score helped the show's immediate appeal. Bacharach was hugely popular, and brought his great sensitivity for the pop style to *Promises, Promises*, heard especially in the title song and the hit "I'll Never Fall in Love Again," sung by Fran to Baxter after he and a doctor have saved her from her suicide attempt. Bacharach also provided fine music for the production numbers, such as the memorable "Turkey Lurkey Time" that closes act 1. The show worked as both comedy and satire and ran for about three years.

PRYCE, JONATHAN (1947–). British dramatic and musical actor who won a **Tony Award** for his portrayal of the Engineer in *Miss Saigon* (1991). He played Lawrence in *Dirty Rotten Scoundrels* for six months in 2006.

PULITZER PRIZE. Annual awards for journalistic achievement established by Joseph Pulitzer (1847–1911), publisher of the *New York*

World and *St. Louis Post Dispatch*. Announcement of the first prizes came in 1917. Columbia University, where Pulitzer endowed the School of Journalism, administers the awards. Pulitzer originally established four literary prizes, including one for the outstanding play written by an American in a particular year. Seven Broadway musicals have been honored with Pulitzer Prizes for Drama: *Of Thee I Sing* (1931), *South Pacific* (1949), *Fiorello!* (1959), *How to Succeed in Business without Really Trying* (1961), *A Chorus Line* (1975), *Sunday in the Park with George* (1984), and *Rent* (1998). The selection committee is not obligated to award a prize in each category every year. *See also* DRAMA DESK AWARDS; NEW YORK DRAMA CRITICS' CIRCLE AWARDS; TONY AWARDS.

PURCELL, CHARLES (1883–1962). Baritone who was one of the leading **operetta** stars of the 1910s, but whose career extended into the 1940s. His created the role of Richard Wayne in **Sigmund Romberg**'s *Maytime* (1917), which catapulted him to fame. He starred in three other Romberg shows during the years that immediately followed: *The Melting of Molly* (1918), where he played a physically attractive weight-loss doctor; *Monte Cristo, Jr.* (1919), a show following the **Al Jolson** model at the Winter Garden Theatre; and *The Magic Melody* (1919), an operetta in which he played the dual roles of an Italian composer and his son, who was adopted and raised by an English couple. He also appeared in the **musical comedies** *Poor Little Ritz Girl* (1921) and *Dearest Enemy* (1925). In the 1930s, he appeared in **revivals** of *The Chocolate Soldier*, and made his final Broadway appearance in 1946 in the musical comedy *Park Avenue*.

PURLIE (15 MARCH 1970, BROADWAY, 688 PERFORMANCES). Music by Gary Geld, lyrics by Peter Udell, book by Ossie Davis, Philip Rose, and Udell; staged and presented by Rose. Based on the 1961 play *Purlie Victorious* by Ossie Davis, *Purlie* was a humorous high-energy musical that ran for about 20 months. **Cleavon Little** played the title role, a black preacher of the post-Civil War era who wants to organize a church and bring better lives to the sharecroppers who work on Ol' Cap'n Cotchipee's (John Heffernon) plantation. Purlie triumphs against all obstacles, many of them erected by Cotchipee, and wins the hand of Lutiebelle (**Melba Moore**) in the process. Purlie even receives help from Ol' Cap'n's son, Charlie (C. David Colson). The show opens at Ol' Cap'n's funeral, where there is general rejoicing, and then the flashback begins. **Clive Barnes** of the *New York Times* called the show "the most successful and richest of all black musicals" for "the depth of the characterizations and the salty wit of the dialogue." He raved about Moore and Little, both of whom won **Tony Award**s. The score included the gospel hymn "Walk Him up the Stairs," Purlie's "New Fangled Preacher Man," and Lutiebelle's declaration, "I Got Love." A revival in late 1972 ran only 14 performances. *See also* AFRICAN AMERICAN MUSICALS.

– Q –

***QUEEN HIGH* (8 SEPTEMBER 1926, AMBASSADOR, 378 PERFORMANCES).** Music by Lewis E. Gensler, lyrics by **B. G. De Sylva**, book by **Lawrence Schwab** and De Sylva. A show whose success was based partly on the popularity of the song "Cross Your Heart," *Queen High* also boasted a fine story and quality characters. T. Boggs Johns (Charles Ruggles) and George Nettleton (Frank McIntyre) jointly own a garter manufacturer, but they do not get along and settle their problems in a poker game. The winner runs the company, and the loser must serve as the winner's butler for one year. Nettleton wins, but he must now suffer watching Johns try to be his servant. Their children, Richard Johns (Clarence Nordstrom) and Polly Nettleton (Mary Lawlor), of course, fall in love, which eventually causes the partners to reconcile. Edwin Michaels played Jimmy, the show's main dancer, and Luella Gear provided additional comedy as Coddles. Reviewing *Queen High* in the *New York Times*, **J. Brooks Atkinson** described it as "a delightful evening in the theatre." He found the plot unusually fine for a **musical comedy**, noting that the show "keeps a ridiculous, volatile story running constantly," and praised the cast, especially Lawlor and Nordstrom, who sing "Cross Your Heart."

– R –

RACE RELATIONS/RACISM. Issues of race relations have been part of the Broadway musical for virtually its entire existence. Relations between **African Americans** and whites provided plots or subplots in shows such as *Show Boat* (1927), *Porgy and Bess* (1935), *Finian's Rainbow* (1947), *Street Scene* (1947), *Big River* (1985), *Ragtime* (1998), *Parade* (1998), *The Wild Party* (2000), and *Hairspray* (2002). *Lost in the Stars* (1949) directly addressed South African apartheid. Native Americans, invented through stereotypes, appeared in *Rose Marie* (1924) and *Annie Get Your Gun* (1946), often in unflattering lights. Relations between whites and Asians and Pacific Islanders were central to the plots of *South Pacific* (1949), *The King and I* (1951), and *Miss Saigon* (1989, London; 1991, New York). Broadway songs that directly address racism include "You've Got to Be Carefully Taught" from *South Pacific* and "Everyone's a Little Bit Racist" from *Avenue Q* (2003). Issues of race and racism are addressed in a broad sense in *Wicked* (2003), where Elphaba is ostracized because of her skin's green color. *See also* ORIENTAL-ISM.

RADO, JAMES (BORN JAMES RADOMSKI, 1932–). Lyricist and librettist with **Gerome Ragni** for the **rock musical** *Hair* (1968), in which he created the role of Claude.

RAGNI, GEROME (1935–1991). Lyricist and librettist for the **rock musicals** *Hair* (1968, with **James Rado**) and *Dude* (1972) who also created the role of Berger in *Hair*.

RAGTIME (18 JANUARY 1998, FORD, 861 PERFORMANCES). Music by **Stephen Flaherty**, lyrics by **Lynn Ahrens**, book by **Terrence McNally**, directed by Frank Galati, musical staging by **Graciela Daniele**. Based on E. L. Doctorow's 1975 novel of the same name, *Ragtime* considers the lives of three different groups in the United States at the dawn of the 20th century. The upper middle-class WASPs from New Rochelle are emotionally repressed and not even given names; they are tellingly called Mother (**Marin Mazzie**) and Father (**Mark Jacoby**). An Eastern European Jewish immigrant,

Tatch (Peter Friedman), trying to find the American dream with his nameless daughter, eventually becomes a movie director. Coalhouse Walker Jr. (**Brian Stokes Mitchell**) is a black ragtime pianist with a pregnant girlfriend, Sarah (**Audra McDonald**). Famous historical figures also appear, such as Henry Ford, Booker T. Washington, Emma Goldman, Harry Houdini, and Evelyn Nesbit. The three groups—WASPs, immigrants, and **African Americans**—come into contact in various ways throughout the show. For example, after Father is killed, Mother begins a liaison with Tatch. Mother also takes Sarah into her home. Coalhouse is jailed, the result of racism, and Sarah, when trying to inform the president of the injustice, is suspected of trying to assassinate him and is killed. **Ben Brantley** wrote a huge, informative review of *Ragtime* for the *New York Times*, which he opened by saying the show has "beauty, ambition, a smashing wardrobe *and* a social conscience," but in the end he found it "utterly resistible." Brantley called the characters "identikit personages," and other critics complained about too much political correctness, with despicable whites, somewhat more admirable Jews, and saintly African Americans. The show's musical highlights and stunning performances were many, including the opening "Prologue: Ragtime," a cleverly staged depiction of the three principal ethnic groups in the show; "New Music," in which Coalhouse celebrates ragtime; the hope-filled anthem "'Til We Reach That Day"; and the full-throated duet "Wheels of a Dream," sung by Coalhouse and Sarah on a picnic after they drove Coalhouse's *Ford* automobile on the stage of the newly created *Ford* Center for the Performing Arts on 42nd Street. *See also* RACE RELATIONS; SOCIAL JUSTICE/INJUSTICE.

RAHMAN, A. R. (BORN A. S. DILEEP KUMAR, CHANGED HIS NAME TO ALLAH RAKHA RAHMAN, 1966–). Indian composer known for his Bollywood films whose first musical, ***Bombay Dreams*** (2002, London; 2004, New York), includes Indian ethnic and popular music styles alongside characteristic musical theater songs.

***RAISIN* (18 OCTOBER 1973, 46TH STREET, 847 PERFORMANCES).** Music by Judd Woldin, lyrics by Robert Britten, book by Robert Nemiroff and Charlotte Zaltzberg, directed and choreographed by Donald McKayle. Based on Lorraine Hansberry's famed

1959 play *Raisin in the Sun*, *Raisin* was a rousing success that ran for two years. The plot involves the Younger family, led by matriarch, Lena (Virginia Capers), who harbors a dream to use her late husband's $10,000 in life insurance money to move her family to a better neighborhood. Her son, Walter Lee (Joe Morton), is married to Ruth (Ernestine Jackson), and they have a son, Travis (Ralph Carter). Lena also has a daughter, Beneatha (Deborah Allen), a college student who wants to become a doctor and is in love with an African exchange student. Through considerable difficulty, the Youngers manage to realize Lena's dream, and at the final curtain find their new home in a white neighborhood, filled with solidarity and hope. **Clive Barnes**, writing in the *New York Times*, loved the show, noting "it warms the heart and touches the soul" and found the show's race issues perhaps less important than the "tremendous story" about a family's struggle. He concluded that was a musical that anyone should love, even those who dislike the genre. The score is an eclectic mix of African American musical styles with large doses of jazz, blues, and especially gospel. Although the songs are not strikingly original, each fits beautifully into its dramatic situation and most help propel the story forward. Walter's anger at his lot in life appears movingly in "Runnin' to Meet the Man," and his wife, Ruth, confronts him effectively in "Sweet Time" with memories of the tenderness they once shared. "He Come Down This Morning" is a fine, characteristic gospel tune for the church scene that opens act 2. Lena urges her daughter to regard Walter Lee's entire character in "Measure the Valleys," a profoundly lovely and emotional song. "Not Anymore" is a catchy and witty ensemble reaction to a visit by leaders of the white community where the Youngers hope to move. *See also* AFRICAN AMERICAN MUSICALS; RACE RELATIONS.

RAITT, JOHN (1917–2005). Raitt's background in opera served him well when he played Curly McLain in the 1944 national tour of *Oklahoma!* and subsequently originated the role of Billy Bigelow in *Carousel* (1945). He later created Sid Sorokin in *The Pajama Game* (1954). He avoided excessive operatic mannerisms in his singing, which remained consistently natural and clear throughout his career.

RAMIREZ, SARA (1976–). Mexican-born actor whose credits include *The Capeman* (1998) and *A Class Act* (2001). She received the

2005 **Tony Award** for Best Supporting Actress in a Musical for her portrayal of The Lady of the Lake in *Monty Python's Spamalot*, a comedic role that demanded the full range of vocal styles, including belt, Las Vegas lounge, and lyrical ballads.

RASCH, ALBERTINA (1896–1967). Austrian-born dancer and choreographer whose "Albertina Rasch Dancers" and "Albertina Rasch Girls" appeared in many Broadway musicals during the 1920s and 1930s. Her choreography, which was tied to dramatic narrative, integrated classical ballet technique with uniform ensemble dancing. Her credits include *Rio Rita* (1927), *The Three Musketeers* (1928), *The Cat and the Fiddle* (1931), and *Lady in the Dark* (1941).

REALLY USEFUL COMPANY. Company established by **Andrew Lloyd Webber** in 1977, which includes the Really Useful Theatre Company (the producer for Lloyd Webber musicals), Really Useful Films, Really Useful Records, Really Useful Theatres (which owns houses in London's West End), and Really Useful Music Publishing. The company also controls merchandise and marketing for Lloyd Webber shows.

REAMS, LEE ROY (1942–). Lyrical tenor and virtuoso dancer who created the roles of Duane Fox, a gay hairdresser, in *Applause* (1970); Henry Spofford in *Lorelei* (1974), appearing opposite **Carol Channing**; and Billy Lawler in *42nd Street* (1980). He was choreographer-director for the 1995 revival of *Hello, Dolly!*

REDHEAD (5 FEBRUARY 1959, 46TH STREET, 452 PERFOR-MANCES). Music by Albert Hague; lyrics by **Dorothy Fields**; book by **Herbert** and Dorothy **Fields**, Sidney Sheldon, and David Shaw; directed and choreographed by **Bob Fosse**. Inspired by Jack the Ripper's murderous spree in London, *Redhead* was a dancing show that provided an effective star vehicle for **Gwen Verdon**. She played Essie Whimple, an actress at the turn of the 20th century who becomes a potential victim for a serial killer preying on actresses. Her love interest was Tom Baxter (**Richard Kiley**), a strongman whose female partner has already been murdered. The murderer is revealed, and Essie remains with Tom at the end of the show. *Redhead* included some of Fosse's finest dances, such as the "Pick Pocket Tango" and

"The Uncle Sam Rag." Writing in the *New York Times*, **Brooks Atkinson** compared the latter to the "Ascot Gavotte" from *My Fair Lady*. He found the score "genial," but the book is too complex. *Redhead* ran for more than a year on the strength of Verdon's performance and Fosse's dances, a monument to the new importance of the director-choreographer. Atkinson concluded his review with the insightful remark that perhaps only choreographers should create musical comedies.

RED, HOT AND BLUE! **(29 OCTOBER 1936, ALVIN, 183 PERFORMANCES).** Music and lyrics by **Cole Porter**, book by **Howard Lindsay** and **Russel Crouse**, directed by Lindsay. After the great success of *Anything Goes* the previous season, the creators conceived *Red, Hot and Blue!* for the same cast, but **Victor Moore** and **William Gaxton** proved unavailable. The plot involved "Nails" O'Reilly Duquesne (**Ethel Merman**), a wealthy woman who holds a contest, the winner of which will be the person who finds the long-lost love of Bob Hale (**Bob Hope**). She can be identified by distinctive marks left on her derriere from an accident with a hot waffle iron. Assisting in the search are prison parolees, including "Policy" Pinkle (**Jimmy Durante**). Bob's former love comes forth, but he no longer finds her of interest, so, of course, marries Nails. The cast featured several fine clowns, and Porter's score included the standard "It's De Lovely." Writing in the *New York Times*, **Brooks Atkinson** finds the show, most of all, funny, reporting, "Most of us were laughing outrageously last evening." He found the book to be less coherent than that of *Anything Goes*, and raved about Durante, whose comedy and singing "makes for boisterous revelry in a vein of clowning thermodynamics." Merman remained the musical theater's "most commanding minstrel," and Hope was "generally cheering." He thought Porter's score was a mixed success, but commented positively on Durante's rendition of "A Little Skipper from Heaven Above" and Merman's singing of "Down in the Depths, on the Ninetieth Floor" and "Ridin' High."

THE RED MILL **(24 SEPTEMBER 1906, KNICKERBOCKER, 274 PERFORMANCES).** Music by **Victor Herbert**, lyrics and book by **Henry Blossom**. *The Red Mill* was more **musical comedy** than **operetta**, and starred the famed comic team of David Montgomery and Fred Stone as Kid Conner and Con Kidder, two Americans in Europe. They are penniless and arrive in Katwyk-ann-Zee, Holland, where they talk their way into staying at the inn on the main square. Dominating the stage was a large red mill, symbolic of the locale and an important part of the plot. Katwyk-ann-Zee has a fierce burgomaster (Edward Begley) who wishes his daughter, Gretchen (Augusta Greenleaf), to marry Zeeland's governor, but she loves a sea captain (Joseph M. Ratliff). Amidst many complications, the burgomaster imprisons his daughter in the mill, but Montgomery and Stone acrobatically rescue her through the use of the mill's sails. She and her sea captain finally unite, with the famous comedians appearing throughout the evening in such disguises as Italian musicians and Sherlock Holmes and Dr. Watson. Herbert's score was one of his finest, and included the standards "The Streets of New York" and "Everyday Is Ladies' Day to Me," both considerably more like Tin Pan Alley tunes than the more vocally demanding songs that Herbert wrote for his operettas. The unsigned review in the *New York Times* lauded every aspect of the show, noting that the music, lyrics, Montgomery and Stone's "droll extravagance," and the fine cast and lovely production "cheer the heart, delight the eye, charm the ear, tickle the fancy, and wreath the face in smiles."

REFLEXIVE REFERENCES/REFLEXIVITY. A practice in musical theater where references to the genre itself or to a specific show appear in another show. Examples include **Cole Porter** listing "a **Berlin** ballad" among the superlatives in "You're the Top" from *Anything Goes* (1934), Little Sally's remarks to Officer Lockstock in *Urinetown* (2001), **Joel Grey** re-creating his stage persona as the Master of Ceremonies in *Cabaret* (1966) while playing the Wizard of Oz in *Wicked* (2003), or the many references to musical theater in *The Producers* (2001) and *Monty Python's Spamalot* (2005). *See also LITTLE MARY SUNSHINE.*

REFRAIN. Many Broadway songs, especially those from the early and middle parts of the 20th century, have a two-part construction. The first part, the **verse**, is often closer to speech singing and in many instances establishes the dramatic context or mood of the song. The refrain, often the most familiar part of the song, follows. Refrains themselves possess a variety of forms: the most common is AABA, where the A sections have similar or identical music and the B section (also known as the bridge) is recognizably different. The four sections are typically of equal length.

REINKING, ANN (1949–). Dancer and choreographer whose stage credits included *Coco* (1969) and *Pippin* (1972) before taking over the roles of Cassie in *A Chorus Line* and Roxie Hart in *Chicago* in their original Broadway productions. She received a **Tony Award** for Best Choreography for her imaginative dances in the 1996 revival of *Chicago*, which she modeled after **Bob Fosse**'s originals. She also contributed to *Fosse* (1999) as codirector and cochoreographer, and, late in the run, as a dancer.

RENT **(29 APRIL 1996, NEDERLANDER, 4,441 PERFOR-MANCES AS OF 31 DECEMBER 2006).** Music, lyrics, and book by **Jonathan Larson**, directed by Michael Greif, choreography by Marlies Yearby. A winner of numerous awards, including a **Pulitzer Prize** for Drama, *Rent* is an imaginative retelling of the story of Giacomo Puccini's *La Bohème* set in New York's East Village. Mimi Marquez (Daphne Rubin-Vega), a dancer at a sadomasochism club, meets Roger Davis (Adam Pascal), a songwriter who wants to create one famous work before he dies. Both are HIV-positive. Other memorable characters include writer Mark Cohen (Anthony Rapp); performance artist Maureen Johnson (**Idina Menzel**); a transvestite who dies of AIDS, Angel Schunard (Wilson Jermaine Hereida); and Maureen's lesbian lover, the lawyer Joanne Jefferson (Fredi Walker). The characters all emerge as flesh-and-blood personalities about whom the audience cares.

The show takes place between two successive Christmas Eves. Roger and Mimi meet when she comes to his apartment to light her candle during a power outage. On the next Christmas Eve, Mimi is still alive, unlike in Puccini's opera. Mimi and Roger are gritty survivors, showing that you must live each day as though it might be your last. As author, lyricist, and composer, Larson received much of the credit for the show's success. Tragically, he died from an aortic aneurysm on the night of the final dress rehearsal. The show was a huge success off-Broadway and then moved to the Nederlander Theater. When **Ben Brantley** reviewed the show for the *New York Times* after the Broadway opening, he already knew the show. His impressions, therefore, were more along the lines of how the show was doing and what it was like after it transferred to a larger theater. He found the cast "even better," with more energy in the larger venue. Also, the "ingenuity and dexterity of Mr. Larson's rock-pop score . . . are, in fact, more evident now." He called *Rent* "a sentimental triumph," and placed it in the tradition of such shows as ***Carousel*** or ***South Pacific*** because of its basic "good will and . . . optimism."

Larson's score is a mixture of rock and pop styles, making the designation "**rock musical**" problematic. The rock sound naturally depends upon a prominent electric bass and drum line, and one finds that in the title song and "Out Tonight," the latter an anthem celebrating Mimi's desire to experience clubs and dancing. Other songs such as "Life Support," "Without You," "Your Eyes," and "Will I?" project more of a soft rock sensibility with the use of acoustic guitar. The act 1 finale, "La Vie Bohème," is the only real dance number in the show, and, along with the famous "Seasons of Love," carries a gospel appeal. "I'll Cover You" is a very emotional song in a moderate tempo that speaks of the friends's mutual support. Despite the rock instrumentation and obvious amplification, Larson wanted every word to be understood, a major challenge for the sound designers. In his lyrics, **Stephen Sondheim**'s influence is clear; Larson was one of his protégés. Larson's gift for word play and clever rhyme schemes is fetching, harkening back to much earlier days on Broadway. A frank show, *Rent* offends some, but for those interested in artists living on the edge, and in the continuing necessity for interpersonal communication and support, it is in some ways a very traditional Broadway show with a comforting message. Many of the original cast members appeared in the 2005 film version.

REPLACEMENT. An actor or actress who takes over a role during a show's run. Replacement casts can consist of both known and unknown performers. Sometimes, a celebrity is cast as a replacement as a means to increase ticket sales during a long run.

REPRISE. A common technique in musicals where a song heard earlier in the show is brought back later for dramatic and/or musical effect, often in an abridged fashion. The most typical case is for a song from act 1 to return in act 2.

REVIVAL. The return of a show to Broadway after its original production has closed. Revivals have existed throughout the 20th century, but became especially prolific in the last decades of the 20th century. Revivals can basically be restagings of original productions, revisions of original productions in terms of book, musical arrangements, orchestrations, choreography, and so forth, or radical restructurings and reconceptions of original material. Producers often find them to be safer investments than new shows, since audiences who are already familiar with the material and know they like it, are keen to attend them. Revivals often feature famous performers in lead roles, such as **Bernadette Peters** in *Annie Get Your Gun* (1999) and *Gypsy* (2003) or Harry Connick Jr. in *The Pajama Game* (2006). Director-designers such as **John Doyle** are bringing a new dimension to revivals through radical restagings of shows such as *Sweeney Todd: The Demon Barber of Fleet Street* (2005) and *Company* (2006). A **Tony Award** for Best Musical Revival was established in 1994.

REVUE. A show that includes a series of songs, skits, and dances, sometimes based on a central theme, and often including scantily clad female dancers or models, like the French works from the *Folies Bergère* on which the genre was based. Along with **musical comedy** and **operetta**, revue was one of the three main genres cultivated on Broadway from the 1890s until about 1930. The revue did not carry on after 1930 with nearly the same intensity. Revues were star-centered productions, and many famous actors and dancers appeared in them. Shows often appeared in series that boasted annual "editions," such as *The Passing Show*, *Ziegfeld Follies*, *Earl Carroll Vanities*, *The Garrick Gaieties*, *George White's Scandals*, *Greenwich Village Follies*, and the *Music Box Revue*. Producers also mounted revues that were not part of a series, such as *Yip! Yip! Yaphank!* (1918), *Blackbirds of 1928*, *The Little Show* (1929), *Pins and Needles* (1937), *Hellzapoppin'* (1938), *This Is the Army* (1942), *Call Me Mister* (1946), and *New Faces of 1952*. The revue's progeny at the end of the 20th century and beginning of the 21st century includes new revues such as *The Will Rogers Follies* (1991), shows such as *Cats* (1981) with a variety of musical styles and a thin plot, **concept musicals**, **jukebox musicals**, and television variety programs.

REYNOLDS, DEBBIE (BORN MARY FRANCES REYNOLDS, 1932–). Known primarily for her screen and television work, Reynolds's Broadway musical credits include Irene O'Dare in the 1973 **revival** of *Irene* and a **replacement** Tess Harding in *Woman of the Year* (1981).

RICE, EDWARD E. (ca. 1849–1924). Producer and stage director who wrote the music and the libretto for the **burlesque** *Adonis* (1885). He served as director, producer, and music director for *The Show Girl* (1902).

RICE, TIM (1944–). Lyricist whose early collaborations with **Andrew Lloyd Webber** included *Joseph and the Amazing Technicolor Dreamcoat* (1968–1972), *Jesus Christ Superstar* (1971), and *Evita* (1978), which established him among the leading wordsmiths of his generation. All three shows concern important religious figures, whether biblical or contemporary, who search for freedom from suffering. He also wrote lyrics for *Chess* (1988) and three musicals produced by **Disney Theatrical Productions**: *Beauty and the Beast* (1994), *The Lion King* (1997), and *Aida* (2000).

RICH, FRANK (1949–). Chief theater critic for the *New York Times* during the 1980s, Rich, in addition to offering brutally honest reviews, drew connections between popular culture and current political events. His reviews were published in 1998 as *Hot Seat: Theater Criticism for the New York Times, 1980–1993.*

THE RINK **(9 FEBRUARY 1984, MARTIN BECK, 204 PERFORMANCES).** Music by **John Kander**, lyrics by **Fred Ebb**, book by **Terrence McNally**. A edgy musical about the problems between a mother (**Chita Rivera**) and a daughter (**Liza Minnelli**), as well as the family rollerskating rink in a doomed American fairground, the show's innovative aspects included a clever and frequent use of flashbacks to depict crises in the lives of the female protagonists. Musical highlights included the opening waltz "Colored Lights," the carnivalesque "Under the Roller Coaster," the wistful "What Happened to the Old Days?," the ballad "Marry Me," the jaunty title song, and the powerful final numbers "All the Children in a Row" and "Coda."

RIO RITA (2 FEBRUARY 1927, ZIEGFELD, 494 PERFOR-MANCES). Music by **Harry Tierney**, lyrics by Joseph McCarthy, book by **Guy Bolton** and Fred Thompson, staged and produced by **Florenz Ziegfeld**. An elaborate **operetta** that opened the new Ziegfeld Theater on 6th Avenue at 54th Street, reviewers focused as much with the space as the show, for New York had never seen anything quite like the monument to Art Deco elegance designed by **Joseph Urban**. *Rio Rita* took place in Mexico, where the Texas Rangers seek a notorious renegade known as Kinkajou. Their leader, Jim (J. Harold Murray), loves Rio Rita (Ethelind Terry), but Kinkajou challenges Jim for her affections. Bert Wheeler and Robert Woosley provided the comedy. The production was pure Ziegfeld, with more than 100 young women on stage in various dance numbers, lavish costumes, and Urban's distinctive set designs. Harry Tierney provided music appropriate for an operetta, quite different from his usual fare. The men's chorus was "The Rangers' Song" and the love song "If You're in Love, You'll Waltz," bringing into play the quintessential operetta dance. **J. Brooks Atkinson**, writing in the *New York Times*, opens with effusive praise for the new theater. He found the show's plot incomprehensible, noting that finding it is a "detective's job." He cataloged the many forces that cross the stage, including the Central American Marimba Band, and deemed Urban's set designs "a feast to the eye."

RITTMANN, TRUDE (1908–2005). Dance and vocal arranger whose credits include *Carousel* (1945), *Brigadoon* (1947), *Finian's Rainbow* (1947), *Gentlemen Prefer Blondes* (1949), *South Pacific* (1949), *The King and I* (1951), *Peter Pan* (1954), *My Fair Lady* (1956), *The Sound of Music* (1959), and *Camelot* (1960).

RIVERA, CHITA (BORN DOLORES CONCHITA FIGUEROA DEL RIVERO, 1933–). Rivera had chorus parts in several Broadway shows before being cast as Anita in *West Side Story* (1957), a role that showcased her strong dancing abilities. Other roles she created include Rose Grant in *Bye Bye Birdie* (1960), Velma Kelly in *Chicago* (1975), the mother character in *The Rink* (1984), and the title role in *Kiss of the Spider Woman* (1993). She appeared as Liliane La Fleur in the 2003 revival of *Nine*. She received **Tony**

Awards for *The Rink* and *Kiss of the Spider Woman* in addition to many other career accolades. Rivera does not limit herself to any one vocal technique, but uses her wide dynamic and timbral range to bring added depth and drama to any character she plays. Her dancing and acting abilities parallel her supreme vocal artistry. She returned to Broadway in 2005 with a one-woman show, *Chita Rivera: A Dancer's Life*, in which she reprised some of her legendary songs as well as introducing new material.

ROAD COMPANIES. Touring productions of musicals, often designed to take a close approximation of the Broadway version on the road. National tours form a significant part of the Broadway legacy, for they bring live musical theater to a large audience. Early in the 20th century, Broadway productions were often simply part of a tour, as was the case, for example, with **George M. Cohan**'s *Little Johnny Jones* (1904) and **Victor Herbert**'s *Naughty Marietta* (1910), which had limited New York runs but toured for months. Broadway histories include scant mention of road companies, but some shows have played for years on the road. The demand for *The Student Prince* (1924) was so strong at one point that there were nine separate companies, and the show's touring lasted for about 25 years. **Rodgers and Hammerstein** formed a national touring company for *Oklahoma!* in 1943, the year that the show opened, and it played for 10 years in 250 cities. When the show closed in New York in 1948, two more companies visited 70 cities in the next year. Other companies toured with the show internationally. Road companies have sometimes helped confirm an actor's virtual ownership of a role, allowing audiences outside of New York to see them work. **Yul Brynner**, for example, not only originated the King in *The King and I* (1953) on Broadway and later revived it there, but also performed it in thousands of tour performances. **Carol Channing** had similar success with the title role in *Hello, Dolly!* (1964); she was still appearing in touring productions of the show almost four decades after it first opened. Twenty-first century Broadway musicals such as *Thoroughly Modern Millie*, *Wicked*, *The 25th Annual Putnam County Spelling Bee*, and *Monty Python's Spamalot* have had successful national tours.

THE ROAR OF THE GREASEPAINT—THE SMELL OF THE CROWD **(16 MAY 1965, SHUBERT, 232 PERFORMANCES).** Music, lyrics, and book by **Leslie Bricusse** and **Anthony Newley**, staged by Newley, choreography by **Gillian Lynne**, presented by **David Merrick**. Following the great success of *Stop the World—I Want to Get Off* (1962), Bricusse and Newley wrote this show, but it was too similar to its predecessor to develop a life of its own. Newley played Cocky, a "little guy" pushed around by his bigger **vaudeville** partner, Sir (Cyril Ritchard). The show took on a number of serious issues, such as those listed by **Howard Taubman** in his *New York Times* review: "Playing the game, religion, hunger, work, love, the ladder of success, death, the Negro and rebellion." Taubman, however, did not find this topicality successful because of the "obviousness of the treatment" and "vulgarity of the humor." The show's score included two hits: "Who Can I Turn To" and "A Wonderful Day Like Today."

ROBBINS, JEROME (BORN JEROME RABINOWITZ, 1918–1998). Choreographer, director, and dancer who worked with **Leonard Bernstein** on the ballet *Fancy Free* (1944), which evolved into the musical *On the Town* (1945). His stylish choreography for shows such as *High Button Shoes* (1947), *Miss Liberty* (1949), *Call Me Madam* (1950), and *The King and I* (1951, with its famous "The Small House of Uncle Thomas" ballet) established him as one of the undisputed leaders in his field. As a choreographer-director, he brought to life such visionary shows as *The Pajama Game* (1954), *Peter Pan* (1954), *Bells Are Ringing* (1956), *West Side Story* (1957), *Gypsy* (1959), *A Funny Thing Happened on the Way to the Forum* (1962), *Funny Girl* (1964), and *Fiddler on the Roof* (1964). He returned to Broadway in 1989 with the celebratory *Jerome Robbins' Broadway*, an **anthology show** in which he re-created some of his legendary dance sequences. Robbins won five **Tony Awards** and was also a significant figure in the fields of ballet and cinema.

ROBERTA **(18 NOVEMBER 1933, NEW AMSTERDAM, 295 PERFORMANCES).** Music by **Jerome Kern**, lyrics and book by **Otto Harbach**, staged and lighted by **Hassard Short**, produced by Max

Gordon. Based on Alice Duer Miller's novel *Gowns by Roberta*, *Roberta* combined an excellent score by Jerome Kern—his last for Broadway—with a sumptuous mounting. **Ray Middleton** played John Kent, a college football player who inherits a Parisian dress shop run by his Aunt Minnie (**Fay Templeton**), whose trade name is Roberta. Kent becomes interested in Stephanie (Tamara), who works in the shop, but things become complicated when Sophie Teale (Helen Gray), his college girlfriend, arrives in Paris. Kent chooses Stephanie, who turns out to be an exiled Russian princess. **Bob Hope** was the male comic, Huckleberry Haines, director of an orchestra. The show possessed several scenic highlights, such as a lovely fashion show with gowns by Kiviette and a dance for the models in the act 1 finale. **Brooks Atkinson**, writing in the *New York Times*, gloried in the first-act finale but found problems elsewhere. He praised several songs, such as "You're Devastating," "Smoke Gets in Your Eyes," and "The Touch of Your Hand." The critic, of course, could not have known that "Smoke" would become one of the most popular of American songs.

ROBIN HOOD **(28 SEPTEMBER 1891, STANDARD, 40 PERFORMANCES).** Music and lyrics by **Reginald De Koven**, book by **Harry B. Smith** and De Koven. A production of the Boston Ideal Opera Company, which developed its repertory in Boston, then took it on tour, including New York, *Robin Hood* basically followed the famous legend. The Sheriff of Nottingham (Henry Clay Barnabee) steals the lands of Robert, Earl of Huntington (Tom Karl), and gives them to Guy of Gisborne (Peter Lang). He also allows Guy to marry Maid Marian (Caroline Hamilton). Robert takes to Sherwood Forest and, as Robin Hood, leads a gang of thieves. The Sheriff captures Robin Hood and forces him to watch Guy marry Maid Marian. At the same ceremony, the Sheriff tries to marry Annabel (Lea Van Dyke), the lover of Alan-a-Dale (Jessie Bartlett Davis), against her will. The merry band comes to the rescue, bearing a pardon for Robin Hood from King Richard. The contemporary dialogue eschewed the archaic theatrical speech of the time. The Boston Company invested little money in *Robin Hood* before its New York appearance, but with its success they made the production a good bit more lavish. Seven

New York revivals appeared before 1944, indicative of the show's popularity. *Robin Hood* included one of the most popular songs ever to appear in an **operetta**: "Oh, Promise Me." Sung by Alan-a-Dale (a trouser role for a woman) to Annabel before her threatened marriage to the Sheriff of Nottingham, the tune became a favorite at weddings well into the 20th century. Another hit from the show was "Brown October Ale," a drinking song led by Little John featuring the male chorus that anticipated other famous Broadway drinking songs such as "Drinking Song" in **Sigmund Romberg**'s *The Student Prince*.

ROBIN, LEO (1900–1984). Lyricist for several **musical comedies**, including *Hit the Deck* (1927) and *Gentlemen Prefer Blondes* (1949). His most prolific work was in Hollywood, where he wrote more than 50 hit songs with composer Ralph Rainger, including "Thanks for the Memory," made famous by **Bob Hope** in *The Big Broadcast of 1938* and later as his theme song.

***ROBINSON CRUSOE, JR.* (17 FEBRUARY 1916, WINTER GARDEN, 139 PERFORMANCES).** Music by **Sigmund Romberg** and James Hanley, book and lyrics by **Harold Atteridge** and Edgar Smith. In this **Al Jolson** vehicle, the actor played his famous blackface character, Gus. The framing tale concerned a wealthy Long Island resident, Hiram Westbury, who falls asleep and dreams that he—and his chauffeur, Gus—have landed in Daniel Defoe's novel. Although Romberg was listed as the show's main composer, Jolson did not sing any of Romberg's music in the extravaganza, but instead performed **interpolations**, including the famous "Where Did Robinson Crusoe Go with Friday on Saturday Night?" (music by George W. Meyer, lyrics by Sam M. Lewis and Joe Young).

ROCK MUSICAL. A musical that includes a significant amount of rock music in its score. Notable examples include *Hair* (1968), *Jesus Christ Superstar* (1971), *Little Shop of Horrors* (1982), *The Who's Tommy* (1993), *Rent* (1996), *Mamma Mia!* (2001), and *Spring Awakening* (2006). In addition to musical style, many aspects of the rock genre, including loud decibel levels, lighting, and the use of hand microphones or headsets, are part of the theatrical aesthetic. *See* *also DUDE*; *EVITA*; *THE FULL MONTY*; *JERSEY BOYS*; MacDER-MOT, GALT; RADO, JAMES; RAGNI, GEROME; *THE ROCKY HORROR SHOW*; *TWO GENTLEMEN OF VERONA*; *YOUR OWN THING*.

THE ROCKY HORROR SHOW (10 MARCH 1975, BELASCO, 45 PERFORMANCES). Music, lyrics, and book by Richard O'Brien. When the British stage phenomenon about an all-American couple who take refuge in a remote castle inhabited by an unusual assortment of characters, including Frank 'n' Furter (**Tim Curry**), a "sweet transvestite from Transexual, Transylvania," transferred to Broadway, it failed miserably. Ironically, when the 1976 film version, *The Rocky Horror Picture Show*, appeared, it did well in the United States but not in Great Britain. O'Brien's score evoked the sound and popular music styles of the 1950s. The 2000 revival (15 November 2000, Circle in the Square, 437 performances) was far more successful than the original production. *See also* ROCK MUSICALS.

RODGERS AND HAMMERSTEIN. The legendary team of **Richard Rodgers** (music) and **Oscar Hammerstein II** (lyrics) collaborated on nine Broadway musicals: *Oklahoma!* (1943), *Carousel* (1945), *Allegro* (1947), *South Pacific* (1949), *The King and I* (1951), *Me and Juliet* (1953), *Pipe Dream* (1955), *Flower Drum Song* (1958), and *The Sound of Music* (1959). They helped define the **musical play**, one of the archetypical Broadway musical forms from the appearance of *Oklahoma!* onward. In their working relationship, Hammerstein usually created the lyrics first, since they had to propel the storyline, after which Rodgers set them to music. The team also wrote one film musical, *State Fair* (1945), later made into a stage musical, and one television musical, *Cinderella* (1957). Although they wrote for many leading performers of the day, two hold especially significant places in their legacy: **Mary Martin**, the star of *South Pacific* and *The Sound of Music*, and **Gertrude Lawrence**, who commissioned them to create *The King and I* for her. Rodgers and Hammerstein were also active as producers; among the notable works by creators other than themselves that they produced was *Annie Get Your Gun* (1946).

RODGERS AND HART. The songwriting team of **Richard Rodgers** and **Lorenz Hart** helped define the Broadway **musical comedy** of the 1920s and 1930s. They collaborated on 26 original Broadway productions, in addition to works for London's West End, amateur productions, nightclubs, and film. The team created some of the most popular theater songs of the time, including "Thou Swell" from *A Connecticut Yankee* (1927), "There's a Small Hotel" from *On Your Toes* (1936), "My Funny Valentine" and "The Lady Is a Tramp" from *Babes in Arms* (1937), "Falling in Love with Love" from *The Boys from Syracuse* (1938), and "Bewitched, Bothered, Bewildered" and "I Could Write a Book" from *Pal Joey* (1940). Their final song together was the murderously entertaining "To Keep My Love Alive," written for **Vivienne Segal** to sing in the 1943 revival of *A Connecticut Yankee*.

RODGERS, MARY (1931–). Wrote music for *Once Upon a Mattress* (1959), *Hot Spot* (1963), and *Working* (1978). Her songs appeared in the revue *From A to Z* (1960) and the musical *The Madwoman of Central Park West* (1979). She is the daughter of **Richard Rodgers** and the mother of composer **Adam Guettel** and actress Kim Beaty.

RODGERS, RICHARD (1902–1979). Genre-defining Broadway composer whose professional career spanned more than half a century, from songs for *The Garrick Gaieties* (1925), including "Manhattan," to *I Remember Mama* (1979). His catalogue includes more than 1,000 songs for 40 different shows. Rodgers grew up in an affluent Jewish family, attended Columbia University, and worked on the amateur theatrical circuit before finding success on Broadway in a long-term collaboration with lyricist **Lorenz Hart**. The team of **Rodgers and Hart** was among the most important creators of **musical comedy** from the 1920s through the early 1940s. After Hart expressed his desire to quit writing songs in 1942, Rodgers found a new collaborator in **Oscar Hammerstein II**. **Rodgers and Hammerstein** not only were the main composer-lyricist team on Broadway during the 1940s and 1950s but also were active as producers. They were significant in the development of the **musical play**, where the music and dance were central to *how* the story was told and how characters were defined. After the death of Hammerstein in 1960, Rodgers continued to write for Broadway. He created both the music and the lyrics for *No Strings* (1962), which included "The Sweetest Sounds." **Stephen Sondheim** provided lyrics for *Do I Hear a Waltz?* (1965), and Martin Charnin did the same for *Two by Two* (1970). Neither of Rodgers's last two shows, *Rex* (1976, lyrics by **Sheldon Harnick**) and *I Remember Mama* (1979, lyrics by Charnin), were successes. Rodgers received many accolades and awards throughout his career, including elections to the Songwriters Hall of Fame in 1971 and to the Theatre Hall of Fame in 1972. He was a Kennedy Center Honoree in 1978.

ROGERS, GINGER (BORN VIRGINIA KATHERINE MCMATH, 1911–1995). Actress, singer, and dancer who, at age 19, played Molly Gray in **George** and **Ira Gershwin**'s *Girl Crazy* (1930), introducing the classic songs "Embraceable You" and "But Not for Me." In 1966, she was a **replacement** Dolly in the original production of *Hello, Dolly!* Rogers had a spectacular Hollywood career that included 73 films, including the 10 she made with **Fred Astaire** that transformed the film musical genre.

ROGERS, WILL (BORN WILLIAM PENN ADAIR ROGERS, 1879–1935). Performer, broadcaster, newspaper columnist, lecturer, and author who appeared in several editions of *Ziegfeld Follies* between 1917 and 1925. He was born in Indian Territory (what became Oklahoma), and was known for his witticisms and rope tricks as well as his genuine love for humanity. His life and work were the inspirations for *The Will Rogers Follies* (1991).

ROMBERG, SIGMUND (BORN SIEGMUND ROSENBERG, 1887–1951). Hungarian-born composer and pianist who arrived in the United States in 1909, and made his Broadway debut in 1914 writing for the **Shubert**-produced **revue** *The Whirl of the World*. He worked closely with the Shuberts during the 1910s and early 1920s, contributing music to various revues, including editions of *The Passing Show*, and **musical comedies**, among them the **Al Jolson** vehicles *Robinson Crusoe, Jr.* (1916), *Sinbad* (1918), and *Bombo* (1921). At the same time, he adapted Central European **operettas** for the Shuberts, and achieved tremendous fame with *The Blue Paradise*

(1915), *Maytime* (1917), and *Blossom Time* (1921). *The Student Prince* (1924), with book and lyrics by **Dorothy Donnelly**, was the longest-running Broadway musical of the 1920s, with 608 performances. In this string of Shubert-produced shows, Romberg developed a formula for American operetta: a story with a bittersweet ending (the principal lovers are not together at the end) is unified through a recurring waltz with nostalgic lyrics. Romberg left the Shuberts in the mid-1920s, and working with producers **Lawrence Schwab** and **Frank Mandel** and lyricist **Oscar Hammerstein II**, developed a new paradigm for American operetta—one in which the principal lovers were together at the end and in which various popular music styles of the era, such as tangos and ballads, received the same musical importance as the waltzes—in shows such as *The Desert Song* (1926), *The New Moon* (1928), and *Nina Rosa* (1930). In the 1930s and 1940s, Romberg experimented with new approaches to the musical theater in works such as *May Wine* (1935), a show in which songs were treated as dramatic internal soliloquies, and the **Rodgers and Hammerstein**-influenced *Up in Central Park* (1945, lyrics by **Dorothy Fields**), in which ballads constituted the principal musical material and the "Currier and Ives Ballet" was integrated into the show's plot.

ROME, HAROLD J. (1908–1993). Composer and lyricist who excelled at writing **revues** and **musical comedies** from the 1930s through the 1960s. He created music, book, and lyrics for *Pins and Needles* (1937) before focusing only on music and lyrics for the revues *Sing Out the News* (1938), *Let Freedom Sing* (1942), *Call Me Mister* (1946), *Alive and Kicking* (1950), and *Bless You All* (1950). His book musicals include *Wish You Were Here* (1952), *Fanny* (1954), *Destry Rides Again* (1959), *I Can Get It for You Wholesale* (1962), and *The Zulu and the Zayda* (1965).

ROONEY, MICKEY (BORN JOE YULE JR., 1920–). Hollywood child star who, as an adult, starred in *Sugar Babies* (1979) and in the early 1990s was a **replacement** Clem Rogers in *The Will Rogers Follies*.

***ROSALIE* (10 JANUARY 1928, NEW AMSTERDAM, 335 PERFORMANCES).** Music by **George Gershwin** and **Sigmund**

Romberg, lyrics by **Ira Gershwin** and **P. G. Wodehouse**, book by William Anthony McGuire and **Guy Bolton**, produced by **Florenz Ziegfeld**. A vehicle for **Marilyn Miller**, the plot for *Rosalie* drew upon two news events of the time: Charles Lindbergh's solo flight across the Atlantic and the visit of Queen Marie of Romania to the United States. American pilot Richard Fay (Oliver McLennan) flies to Romanza to be with the woman he loves, the Crown Princess Rosalie. Afterward, the Romanzan royal family visits America. Since Rosalie is of royal blood, she cannot marry a commoner. In the final scene, her father, the King of Romanza (Frank Morgan), abdicates so that the young lovers can be together. The show was set in both a mythical **operetta** kingdom and contemporary America. As such, its score included numbers in the spirit of operetta by Romberg such as "Hussar March" and "Kingdom of Dreams" and others in the style of **musical comedy** by Gershwin such as "Say So!" and "Oh Gee! Oh Joy!" Neither Romberg nor Gershwin had time to write a complete score for *Rosalie*, for Romberg was working on *The New Moon* and Gershwin on *Funny Face*. The 1936 film version did not include any music from the original stage production but rather featured an entirely new score by **Cole Porter**.

ROSE, BILLY (BORN WILLIAM SAMUEL ROSENBERG, 1899–1966). Lyricist, producer, and theater owner whose musical productions included *Jumbo* (1935), *Carmen Jones* (1943), and the **revue** *Seven Lively Arts* (1944).

ROSE, GEORGE (1920–1988). Actor who won **Tony Awards** for Best Actor in a Musical for his portrayal of Henry Higgins in the 1976 revival of *My Fair Lady* (as **Rex Harrison** had done in the original) and again in 1986 for *The Mystery of Edwin Drood*.

ROSE MARIE **(2 SEPTEMBER 1924, IMPERIAL, 557 PERFORMANCES).** Music by **Rudolf Friml** and **Herbert Stothart**, lyrics by **Otto Harbach** and **Oscar Hammerstein II**, produced by **Arthur Hammerstein**. Capitalizing on the era's fascination with Native Americans, *Rose Marie*, set in Canada, was the story of Rose Marie La Flamme (Mary Ellis), a singer who is in love with fur trapper Jim Kenyon (**Dennis King**). Ed Hawley, one of Rose Marie's suitors, frames Jim for murdering Black Eagle. The real killer was Black Eagle's wife, Wanda, who was having an affair with Ed. The show featured the male chorus, an **operetta** trademark, as the Mounties, who boisterously sang the rousing march "The Mounties." Other musical highlights included the famous "Indian Love Call," the waltz "The Door of My Dreams," "Totem Tom-Tom," a spectacular ensemble number led by Wanda, and the lilting title song. Friml incorporated Indianist musical identifiers such as drone fifths and melodic chromaticism at various points in the score. In *Rose Marie*, the creators strove for an integration of music and plot and included the famous note in the playbill: "The musical numbers in this play are such an integral part of the action that we do not think we should list them as separate episodes." Two sound film versions appeared, both with revised plots, the first in 1936 with Jeanette MacDonald and Nelson Eddy and the second in 1954 with Howard Keel and Ann Blyth.

THE ROTHSCHILDS (19 OCTOBER 1970, LUNT-FONTANNE, 507 PERFORMANCES). Music by **Jerry Bock**, lyrics by **Sheldon Harnick**, book by Sherman Yellen, directed and choreographed by **Michael Kidd**. Based on Frederic Morton's biography of the 18th-century Jewish banking family, *The Rothschilds* found some success and gave **Hal Linden** a **Tony Award**-winning performance as the head of the family, Mayer Rothschild. Mayer rises from the Frankfurt Jewish ghetto through the success of his rare coin shop, enters banking, and establishes his successful firm with the help of his five sons. The featured son is Nathan (Paul Hecht), who goes to London and wins the heart of Hannah Cohen (**Jill Clayburgh**). Keene Curtis played four roles in the show, managing what **Clive Barnes** called in the *New York Times* a "virtuoso display." Barnes called Linden's role "one of the best musical performances now on Broadway." The score was by the creators of *Fiddler on the Roof* (which was still playing when *The Rothschilds* opened), and Barnes noted that the music "blends period pastiche with a gentler, more cultivated version of those Jewish folk melodies" found in *Fiddler*. No hit song emerged from the score.

ROUNSEVILLE, ROBERT (1914–1974). Classically trained tenor who created the roles of Andrew Munroe in *Up in Central Park* (1945), Candide in *Candide* (1958), and Padre Perez in *Man of La*

Mancha (1965). In addition to his work on Broadway, he also appeared in opera, on film, and in regional theater.

RUPERT, MICHAEL (ALSO KNOWN AS MIKE RUPERT, 1951–). Singing actor who made his Broadway debut at age 16 as Bibi Bonnard in *The Happy Time*. He took over the lead role in the long-running *Pippin*, won a **Tony Award** for his portrayal of Oscar in the 1986 revival of *Sweet Charity*, and led the cast as Marvin in *Falsettos*. He composed and costarred in the **off-Broadway** hit *Three Guys Naked from the Waist Down* (1985).

RUSSELL, LILLIAN (BORN HELEN LOUISE LEONARD, 1860–1922). One of the leading **operetta** singers of the late 19th century, Russell had a gorgeous voice, classic beauty, and a commanding stage presence. After suffering vocal problems and appearing in nonmusical comedies, she returned to **burlesque** and **musical comedy** after the turn of the century. Her signature tune of later years, and the only song she is known to have recorded, was "Come Down Ma Evenin' Star," which she introduced in *Twirly Whirly* (1902).

RUSSELL, ROSALIND (1911–1976). Comic stage and screen actress with a distinctively low singing voice who won a **Tony Award** for creating Ruth Sherwood in *Wonderful Town* (1953), a musical based on her film *My Sister Eileen* from a decade earlier, in which she also played Ruth.

RYSKIND, MORRIE (1895–1985). Librettist and lyricist who collaborated with **George S. Kaufman** on the books for the Marx Brothers' comedy *Animal Crackers* (1928) and the political satires *Strike Up the Band* (1930), *Of Thee I Sing* (1931), and *Let 'Em Eat Cake* (1933), the latter three with music by **George Gershwin** and lyrics by **Ira Gershwin**. He also wrote the libretto for *Louisiana Purchase* (1940), **Irving Berlin**'s show about political corruption.

– S –

SAIDY, FRED (1907–1982). Librettist who worked as a journalist and screenwriter before coauthoring the book for *Bloomer Girl* (1944) with Sig Herzig, then creating, on his own, the librettos for *Finian's Rainbow* (1947), *Flahooley* (1951), and *Jamaica* (1957).

SALLY (21 DECEMBER 1920, NEW AMSTERDAM, 570 PER-FORMANCES). Music by **Jerome Kern** and **Victor Herbert**, lyrics by Clifford Grey, book by **Guy Bolton**, produced by **Florenz Ziegfeld**. A vehicle for **Marilyn Miller**, *Sally* was one of the biggest hits of the period. Miller played the title role, one of a group of young women who come looking for work at the Elm Tree Alley Inn in Greenwich Village. She becomes a dishwasher, meets Blair Farquar (Irving Fisher), who is from a wealthy family, and marries him at the end of the show. Sally is an excellent dancer, and replaces the main dancer at an evening of entertainment. By the end of the show, she finds out that she will dance in the *Ziegfeld Follies*. A late addition to the show was comic **Leon Errol**, who was given an unnecessary but entertaining part at Ziegfeld's insistence. Kern's score included a number of standards: "Look for the Silver Lining," "Wild Rose," "Whip-poor-will," "You Can't Keep a Good Girl Down," and "The Church around the Corner." Herbert supplied *Sally*'s ballet music. **Alexander Woollcott** reviewed the show for the *New York Times* and called it "an amusing and tuneful diversion." He found Errol "comical" and Miller "a jewel." The true star, however, was Ziegfeld, who "knows a little more than any of his competitors the secret of bringing beauty to his stage."

SALONGA, LEA (BORN MARIA LEA CARMEN IMUTAN SA-LONGA, 1971–). Filipino actress who created the role of Kim in *Miss Saigon* in both London (1989) and New York (1990), winning a **Tony Award** for her Broadway performance. She sang Eponine in *Les Misérables* in early 1992 and reprised the role for the 10th Anniversary Concert version of the musical at the Royal Albert Hall. She played Mei-Li in the heavily revised 2002 **revival** of *Flower Drum Song*.

SARAFINA! (25 OCTOBER 1987, NEWHOUSE/CORT, 597 PER-FORMANCES). Music by Ngema and Hugh Masekela, conceived, written, and directed by Mbongeni Ngema. A protest musical concerning South African apartheid, *Sarafina!* opened off-Broadway but ended up at the Cort Theater, where it ran for about eighteen months. The show celebrated *mbaqanga* music, a rock-based style popular in the black townships in South Africa that inspired Paul Simon in his *Graceland* album. Ngema auditioned young people from the townships and selected two dozen of them for his tight-knit ensemble. The show is set at Morris Isaacson High School in Soweto, where student protests took place in 1976. The students create a play that tells their school's story, including the presence of secret police and police massacre of schoolchildren, but also had some light moments. **Frank Rich** reviewed *Sarafina!* for the *New York Times* and appreciated most the music, noting that the "company becomes a single entity, a rolling human wave," singing close harmonies or dancing "in angular leaps coordinated even to the slightest flicks of elbows or index fingers." *See also* SOCIAL JUSTICE/INJUSTICE.

SATURDAY NIGHT FEVER **(21 OCTOBER 1999, MINSKOFF, 501 PERFORMANCES).** Music by the Bee Gees, based on the Paramount/RSO Picture and a story by Nik Cohn, screenplay adaptation by Nan Knighton, in collaboration with Arlene Philips, Paul Nicholas, and Robert Stigwood, directed and choreographed by Philips. Another attempt to transfer a hit movie nearly intact to the stage, *Saturday Night Fever* received poor notices from critics but still ran for about 15 months because of a huge advance sale and its famous name. According to **Ben Brantley**, writing in the *New York Times*, the show "achieves the distinction of turning the two dimensions provided by celluloid into one dimension onstage," and its creators decided to "imitate, rather than reconceive." He did not think that the star, James Carpinello as Tony, had the charisma that John Travolta brought to the film.

THE SCARLET PIMPERNEL **(9 NOVEMBER 1997, MINSKOFF, 772 PERFORMANCES).** Music by **Frank Wildhorn**, lyrics and book by Nan Knighton, directed by Peter Hunt. Based on the famous novel by Baroness Orczy, the musical had horrible reviews but ran for almost two years with two breaks for major alterations. Douglas Sills played the dual role of Percy/Scarlet Pimpernel, **Christine Andreas** was his wife, Marguerite, and **Terrence Mann** created the villian Chauvelin. The creators showed the domestic relationship between

Percy and Marguerite and added heat by making Marguerite a former lover of Chauvelin, who is now executing aristocrats, except for those whom the Scarlet Pimpernel rescues. The score followed the lyrical ballad model associated with **megamusicals**, and like many megamusicals, has enjoyed tremendous worldwide popularity and has been translated into many languages.

SCHEFF, FRITZI (1879–1954). Viennese-born operatic soprano for whom **Victor Herbert** created the roles of Fifi in *Mlle. Modiste* (1905), Mlle. Athenee in *The Prima Donna* (1908), and Rose in *The Duchess* (1911).

SCHMIDT, HARVEY (1929–). Composer who collaborated with librettist-lyricist **Tom Jones** on *110 in the Shade* (1963), *I Do! I Do!* (1966), and *Celebration* (1969). The team also collaborated on the legendary long-running **off-Broadway** musical *The Fantasticks* (1960).

SCHWAB, LAURENCE (1893–1951). Producer and librettist whose partnership with **Frank Mandel** resulted in a string of hits beginning with *No, No, Nanette* (1925).

SCHWARTZ, ARTHUR (1900–1984). Composer, producer, librettist, and lyricist who created music for the **revues** *The New Yorkers* (1927), *The Little Show* (1929), *Three's a Crowd* (1930), *The Band Wagon* (1931, included "Dancing in the Dark" with lyrics by Howard Dietz), *Flying Colors* (1932, included "Louisiana Hayride" with lyrics by Dietz), *Revenge with Music* (1934, included "You and the Night and the Music" with lyrics by Dietz), *At Home Abroad* (1935), *The Show Is On* (1936), and *Inside U.S.A.* (1948). He also wrote the scores for the **book musicals** *A Tree Grows in Brooklyn* (1951) and *By the Beautiful Sea* (1954).

SCHWARTZ, STEPHEN (1948–). Composer whose most important Broadway works include *Godspell* (1971), *Pippin* (1972), and *Wicked* (2003). After writing the title song for the play *Butterflies Are Free* (1969), Schwartz demonstrated his ability to compose memorable music in a variety of pop idioms in his score to *Godspell*, which ran for more than 2,500 performances. *Pippin* appeared the next season, with another lively score and direction by **Bob Fosse**. Schwartz's score for *The Magic Show* (1974) was overshadowed by Doug Henning's magic, but, like *Pippin*, the show ran for more than four years. Schwartz's other Broadway work has included several songs for *Working* (1978), lyrics for *Rags* (1986, music by **Charles Strouse**), and the score for *Wicked*. In the latter, Schwartz demonstrates his expanded range as a composer, incorporating a wider palette of musical influences and a motivically unified score.

Schwartz's work away from Broadway has included a show that closed out of town (*The Baker's Wife*, 1976) that he has reworked, a Biblical musical (*Children of Eden*, 1991) that premiered in London and is becoming popular among regional groups, and the English lyrics for Leonard Bernstein's *Mass* (1971). Schwartz wrote the lyrics for **Alan Menken**'s music in the Disney animated features *Pocahontas* (1995) and *The Hunchback of Notre Dame* (1996). Schwartz wrote both words and music for the animated feature *The Prince of Egypt* (1998) and the Disney television special *Geppetto* (2000). In 2006, Schwartz turned the latter into a stage musical, *Disney's Geppetto & Son*.

SCREEN ADAPTATIONS. Broadway musicals have been taken to the silver screen since the advent of talkies. An early adaptation was the first film version of *Show Boat* (1929), which included some songs from the Broadway show. Comparison of a stage musical with its screen version is complicated because they exist in essentially different media, and what works on a stage might not make for good cinema. Films, for example, can be made on location, providing many possibilities that do not exist on stage. Films also include close-ups, but the cinema often lacks the spontaneity of live theater. When a Hollywood studio makes a musical out of a Broadway property, changes are inevitable, not only because of the transfer between media and time constraints (films are generally shorter than stage musicals), but also because different creators usually work on the film. For example, MGM's adaptation of **Lerner and Loewe**'s *Brigadoon* (1954), which starred **Gene Kelly** and Cyd Charisse, was much more of a dancing show than its 1947 stage version. MGM's *A Chorus Line* (1985), directed by Richard Attenborough, included a rethought plot and songs were given different meanings.

Other reasons for major changes in screen adaptations include the presence of Hollywood stars for whom material is rewritten, and also a studio's desire to own the film's music, usually not possible for a Broadway show. A good example of a property changing for a particular star is *Hello, Dolly!* (MGM, 1969), where **Barbra Streisand** took over **Carol Channing**'s Broadway role. Streisand remade the role, a major reason the movie carried a hugely different feel than the stage version. A good example of Hollywood's desire for commercial control of the music is *On The Town* (MGM, 1949), in which most of **Leonard Bernstein**'s original songs were removed, replaced with new ones that lyricists **Betty Comden** and **Adolph Green** wrote with Roger Eden.

Many Broadway shows, however, became films from which the viewer receives an accurate, if cinematic, idea of the stage show. This was certainly the case with such **Rodgers and Hammerstein** films as *Oklahoma!* (Rodgers and Hammerstein Productions, 1955), *Carousel* (20th Century Fox, 1956), and *The King and I* (20th Century Fox, 1956). Other faithful transcriptions include *Show Boat* (MGM, 1936), *My Fair Lady* (Warner Bros., 1964), *1776* (Columbia, 1972), *Chicago* (Miramax, 2002), and *The Producers* (Universal, 2005). Some stage musicals have been effectively reimagined for the screen, showing substantial changes but still conveying much of the Broadway version's intention. In the film version of *Guys and Dolls* (Samuel Goldwyn Company, 1955), for example, major roles were adapted to the talents of Frank Sinatra and Marlon Brando, but **Vivian Blaine** and **Stubby Kaye** re-created their Broadway parts. *West Side Story* (MGM, 1961), brought the gritty story into the streets where it takes place along with **Jerome Robbins**'s choreography, but some songs were moved and the cast was completely different. *The Sound of Music* (20th Century Fox, 1965), was a Rodgers and Hammerstein property that became one of the most successful films ever, with the stage version adapted effectively to the screen through lovely use of views of Salzburg and its surrounding countryside and two new songs with music and lyrics by **Richard Rodgers**. The film version of *Cabaret* (Warner Bros., 1972) was directed by **Bob Fosse**, who expanded on **Hal Prince**'s concept of cabaret acts that mirror the larger society. The role of Sally Bowles, expanded because of **Liza Minnelli**'s talents, helped to create a film that differed substantially from the stage original, while **Joel Grey**'s presence as the Master of Ceremonies brought an important, original Broadway conception to the screen. Joel Schumacher's version of **Andrew Lloyd Webber**'s *The Phantom of the Opera* (Warner Bros., Really Useful Films/Scion Films, 2004) included a frame story that surrounded the plot of the stage musical.

Broadway musicals have also been transferred to the small screen, in versions for either television or direct-to-video/DVD. Bette Midler starred in the 1993 television version of *Gypsy*, while the 2001 television adaptation of *South Pacific* starred Glenn Close, who also was one of the project's executive producers. Several adaptations featuring noted Broadway personalities have been broadcast on *The Wonderful World of Disney*, including *Annie* (1999, with Kathy Bates, **Alan Cumming**, **Audra McDonald**, **Kristin Chenoweth**, and Victor Garber) and *The Music Man* (2003, starring **Matthew Broderick** and Chenoweth). Several **Andrew Lloyd Webber** shows have been released in specially made versions for video/DVD, including *Cats* (1998), *Joseph and the Amazing Technicolor Dreamcoat* (1999), and *Jesus Christ Superstar* (2000).

SECAUCUS WAREHOUSE. In 1982, a treasure trove of forgotten and presumably lost materials for Broadway shows from the early part of the 20th century was discovered at the Warner Bros. warehouse in Secaucus, New Jersey. It included songs by **George** and **Ira Gershwin**, **Victor Herbert**, **Jerome Kern**, **Cole Porter**, **Richard Rodgers**, and **Sigmund Romberg**, among others. The material has been used in several **revivals** and recordings, and some of the songs were featured in *Crazy for You* (1992).

THE SECRET GARDEN **(25 APRIL 1991, ST. JAMES, 709 PERFORMANCES).** Music by **Lucy Simon**, lyrics and book by **Marsha Norman**, directed by Susan H. Schulman. A groundbreaking musical in that all of its principal creators were women, *The Secret Garden* was a musicalization of the famous novel by Frances Hodgson Burnett. Daisy Eagan played Mary Lennox, an orphan who comes to live with her mysterious uncle in Yorkshire, Archibald Craven (**Mandy Patinkin**). Through her sickly cousin, Colin (John Babcock), and a magnificent garden, Mary helps everyone come to grips with a sad past and move together into the future. The musical had an elaborate set and ghosts who crossed the stage at opportune moments, effects very much in the world and mood of the original story. **Rebecca Luker**, as Archibald's dead wife, Lily; **Robert Westenberg**, as his brother, Neville; Alison Fraser, as the chambermaid Martha; and **John Cameron Mitchell,** as her brother, Dickon, completed the list of principals. Reviewing the show for the *New York Times*, **Frank Rich** offered a detailed picture of a production that he found too laden with symbolism, noting that the creators "explore the meaning of the novel's every metaphor." The score included a wide variety of styles, including the operatic duet "Lily's Eyes" for the two brothers, Dickon's folksy "Wick," Martha's wise "Hold On," Archibald's impassioned "Where in the World," and Lily and Archibald's emotive "How Could I Ever Know."

SEGAL, VIVIENNE (1897–1992). Singing actress who made her Broadway debut in the **Sigmund Romberg operetta** *The Blue Paradise* (1915). She achieved tremendous fame as an operetta heroine in the 1920s, starring in *The Desert Song* and *The Three Musketeers*. After a time in Hollywood, she returned to Broadway in 1938 as Countess Peggy Palarffi in *I Married an Angel*, and two years later, triumphed as Vera Simpson in *Pal Joey*, singing the sexually charged "Betwitched, Bothered, and Bewildered." She played Morgan le Fey in the 1943 revival of *A Connecticut Yankee*, introducing "To Keep My Love Alive," written expressly for her by **Richard Rodgers** and **Lorenz Hart**. Her far-ranging acting abilities and broad range of vocal styles allowed her to play a wide variety of roles.

SEUSSICAL **(30 NOVEMBER 2000, RICHARD RODGERS, 198 PERFORMANCES).** Music by **Stephen Flaherty**, lyrics by **Lynn Ahrens**, book by Ahrens and Flaherty, conceived by Ahrens, Flaherty, and Eric Idle. Based on the literary creations of Dr. Seuss, the musical featured The Cat in the Hat (David Shiner) as the M.C. in the musical retelling of *Horton Hears a Who*. The eclectic score included the vibrant gospel-inspired "Oh, the Things You Can Think," the Caribbean-influenced "Horton Hears a Who," the Broadway ballad "Alone in the Universe," and the **vaudeville**-evoking "How Lucky You Are." According to Flaherty and Ahrens, they wanted the sound of the Whos, represented in songs such as "Here on Who," to resemble "marching bands on helium." The show has become popular in a one-act version geared toward children. *See also* FAMILY MUSICALS.

1776 **(6 FEBRUARY 1969, 46TH STREET, 1,217 PERFORMANCES).** Music and lyrics by Sherman Edwards, book by **Peter Stone**, staged by Peter Hunt, musical numbers staged by **Onna White**. Although the musical theater is not usually a good way to deal with history, the creators of *1776* managed to tell the story of the adoption of the Declaration of Independence. Conceived by Sherman Edwards, a history teacher and songwriter, and with Stone's **Tony Award**-winning book, *1776* brings suspense to a plot where everybody knows how it ends. Stone reduced the number of congressmen and came up with plot devices that allowed a feminine presence. He shows John Adams (William Daniels) conversing in his imagination with his wife, Abigail (Virginia Vestoff), and brings Martha Jefferson (**Betty Buckley**) to Philadelphia to keep her husband, Thomas (Ken Howard), content while he drafted the Declaration. The latter never happened. The show takes place between early May and July 4, 1776; time passes as a clerk rips numbers off a large wall calendar. Spirited debate precedes the Declaration's writing, followed by even more contentious consideration of the document. Those opposing independence change their minds through various devices — some based on actual history — and the South finally agrees once Jefferson's antislavery clause is deleted. They sign the Declaration to the tolling of the Liberty Bell. **Clive Barnes**, a native Englishman who wrote a review for the *New York Times*, noted that the show is a "most striking, most gripping musical . . . with style, humanity, wit and passion." He admitted that history has been "bent" a bit, but "the genuine thrust" is there. He found Stone's book "literate, urbane and . . . very amusing" and Edwards's music "apt, convincing and enjoyable."

Every song in the score helped advance the drama. We meet the irrepressible John Adams and his frustrated colleagues in "Sit Down, John." The effective musical scene continues as we learn more of Adams and his wife in "Piddle, Twiddle and Resolve" and "'Til Then." In "The Lees of Old Virginia," Richard Henry Lee explains why he can promise an independence resolution. Perhaps the cleverest song is "But, Mr. Adams," when the Declaration Committee decides who will draft the document. Martha Jefferson tells what drew her to her husband in "He Plays the Violin," and the conservative faction in Congress sings the self-congratulatory "Cool, Cool, Considerate Men." "Momma Look Sharp" is a haunting ballad about war sung by a military messenger visiting Congress. In "The Egg," Adams, Benjamin Franklin (**Howard Da Silva**), and Jefferson debate possible national birds, their choices based on the writings of each man. After the South walks out, Adams plaintively asks "Is Anybody There?" Soon after, all are "there," and the vote for independence is unanimous. The film version appeared in 1972.

SHE LOVES ME **(23 APRIL 1963, EUGENE O'NEILL, 301 PERFORMANCES).** Music by **Jerry Bock**, lyrics by **Sheldon Harnick**, book by Joe Masteroff, staged by **Harold Prince**, choreography by **Carol Haney**, presented by Prince and others. Based on the Hungarian play *Parfumerie* by Miklós László, which became the film *The Shop around the Corner*, *She Loves Me* was a charming combination of story and music that told the tale of Amalia Balash (**Barbara Cook**) and Georg Nowack (Daniel Massey), who both work in a music box shop in Budapest. They have been corresponding as pen pals but have never met and do not realize that they work together. The letter writers decide to meet, but Georg arrives and realizes it is Amalia, and keeps his identity secret. Later, however, he falls in love with her and begins to quote his letters, and she confesses her love as well. **Howard Taubman** reviewed the show for the *New York Times*, comparing it to several sweet desserts but stating "you find yourself relishing nearly all of them." Masteroff's book makes "a virtue of sentiment" and maintains a fine consistency in its style. He finds that the songs have been integrated unusually well with the plot. Only the show's title song gained much popularity outside of the theater. **Judy Kuhn** starred in the 1993 Broadway **revival**.

SHELTON, REID (1924–1997). Singing actor who made his Broadway debut as Joe in *Wish You Were Here* (1952). He also appeared in *My Fair Lady* (1956), *Canterbury Tales* (1969), the replacement cast for *The Rothschilds* (1970), and *1600 Pennsylvania Avenue* (1976) before creating the role of Oliver Warbucks in *Annie* (1977).

SHENANDOAH **(7 JANUARY 1975, ALVIN, 1,050 PERFOR-MANCES).** Music by Gary Geld, lyrics by Peter Udell, book by James Lee Barrett, Udell, and Philip Rose. Based on the 1965 film of the same name, *Shenandoah* was a mixed bag for critics but sufficiently liked by audiences to run for about two and a half years. In one of his greatest roles, **John Cullum** played Charles Anderson, a farmer who has lost his wife after they had seven sons and one daughter. He lives in Virginia's Shenandoah Valley during the Civil War, but prefers not to be involved and tries to keep his sons out of the Confederate Army. When the Union Army kidnaps the youngest son, the family's attitude changes. **Clive Barnes**, writing in the *New York Times*, found Cullum a huge presence, stating that none of his previous Broadway roles "has extended him so well and to such splendid advantage," and comparing him to **Richard Kiley** as an actor and singer. Unfortunately Barnes does not appreciate most aspects of the staging, and he believes that the film's screenplay "was richer and more interesting than the present book." The score gave Cullum a strong soliloquy in which he sings of his wife and all of the children they had, but concludes with his desire for isolationism. A good ensemble number was the country-western sounding number for the boys, "Next to Lovin', I Like Fightin' Best." A 1989 revival lasted less than a month.

SHORT, HASSARD (1887–1956). English actor who served as director for more than 40 Broadway musicals, including three of the *Music Box Revues* (1921–23), *As Thousands Cheer* (1933), and *Carmen Jones* (1943). Short was especially known for his lighting and stage effects.

SHORT, MARTIN (1950–). Comedian who made his Broadway musical debut in *The Goodbye Girl* (1993) opposite **Bernadette Peters**. He won a **Tony Award** for his work in the 1998 revival of *Little Me*, and conceived, wrote the book for, and starred in the sketch-filled "comedy musical" *Martin Short: Fame Becomes Me* (2006).

SHOW BOAT **(27 DECEMBER 1927, ZIEGFELD, 575 PERFOR-MANCES).** Music by **Jerome Kern**, lyrics and book by **Oscar Hammerstein II**, produced by **Florenz Ziegfeld**. A seminal show in

Broadway history, *Show Boat* was a conscious effort by Kern and Hammerstein to take the American musical theater to a new level of integration between plot and music. At a time when musicals tended to be created in a few to several months and dozens of new shows opened every year, Kern and Hammerstein spent an entire year creating *Show Boat*. Based on Edna Ferber's popular novel of the same name, *Show Boat* tells a sprawling story involving fascinating characters who live and work on and around a showboat. The plot's principal love interests are Magnolia, or "Nola" (**Norma Terris**), daughter of the showboat *Cotton Blossom*'s owners, and Gaylord Ravenal (**Howard Marsh**), a riverboat gambler who falls in love with her at first sight. The primary actors on the boat are the married couple, Julie (**Helen Morgan**) and Steve (Charles Ellis). Julie is part **African American** but can pass for white. Their mixed-raced marriage, however, is illegal in places along the boat's route, and they are forced to leave the show boat. Gaylord arrives, and he and Nola become the lead actors. Other major characters include Cap'n Andy (**Charles Winninger**) and Parthy Ann Hawkes (Edna May Oliver), Magnolia's parents, and the boat's leading African American servants, Joe (**Jules Bledsoe**) and Queenie (Aunt Jemima). Six years pass, and Nola and Gaylord are at the 1893 Chicago Exposition with their young daughter, Kim. Gaylord, though he loves his family, has amassed large debts and leaves his wife and daughter. Nola auditions at a club where the alcoholic singer, who is none other than Julie, has been threatening to quit. When Julie spies her beloved Nola, she leaves. Despite problems at first, Magnolia wins the crowd over that night, thanks to her father's encouragement. The show ends in 1927; in a major departure from the novel, Hammerstein brings most of the main characters back for the finale. Kim is now an established singing star, Gaylord returns, and Joe gives a final reprise of one of the show's most famous songs, "Ol' Man River."

Realization of *Show Boat*'s special status in Broadway history came fairly quickly. Even the unsigned *New York Times* review the next morning said it was "an excellent musical comedy." The critic does not use the term "musical play," which is how Ziegfeld advertised *Show Boat*. The reviewer clearly believed Ziegfeld to be the most praiseworthy figure in the enterprise, called him the "maestro." The reviewer appreciated Hammerstein's "adaptation of the novel that has been intelligently made," and noted that *Show Boat* "has an exceptionally tuneful score," putting it among Kern's best with several sure hits. The critic applauded every aspect of the show and Ziegfeld's "unimpeachable skill and taste." *Show Boat's* score was a marvel of musicodramatic continuity and full of delightful melodies. Kern depended largely upon traditional song forms, such as 32-bar AABA refrains, but his melodies show great variety and care. "Make Believe" provides a fine musical introduction between Magnolia and Gaylord. "Ol' Man River," which rapidly became an American "folk song," is reprised throughout the show. "Can't Help Lovin' Dat Man" is critical to the plot, for it offers the first indication of Julie's African American heritage, and is also Julie's audition number in Chicago. "Why Do I Love You?" and "You Are Love" are the big love songs for Gaylord and Magnolia, the latter a waltz. Like "Ol' Man River," both numbers are reprised in various ways through the course of the show. Kern and Hammerstein also included "Bill," a song from *Oh, Lady! Lady!!*, for Julie's torch song in act 2. This was the song for which Helen Morgan sat atop the upright piano, creating one of Broadway's iconic images. They also interpolated "After the Ball," a huge hit from the 1890s to help set time and place for Chicago in 1893. Kern's score shows remarkable integration and unity. For example, the motive for the boat, *Cotton Blossom* is rearranged to become the identifier "Captain Andy" in the refrain of the same name, showing that Andy is captain of the *Cotton Blossom*. Kern turned the *Cotton Blossom* motive upside down, the result being the music for the title words of "Ol' Man River." The showboat and the river are closely linked, and Kern makes this clear through the music. The creators' close attention in adapting Edna Ferber's novel and the care with which they crafted the score produced a show that has been revived often and been filmed three times, in 1929, 1936, and 1951. The 1994 **Hal Prince** production starred **Mark Jacoby** and **Rebecca Luker**, with **Elaine Stritch** appearing as Parthy and singing "Why Do I Love You" as a lullaby to her infant granddaughter, Kim.

THE SHOW IS ON **(25 DECEMBER 1936, WINTER GARDEN, 237 PERFORMANCES).** Most music by **Vernon Duke**, most lyrics by Ted Fetter; sketches by David Freedman and **Moss Hart**, dances staged by **Robert Alton**, conceived, staged, and designed by Vincente

314 • SHUBERT ET AL.

Minnelli, produced by the **Shuberts**. One of the last of the great Broadway **revues**, *The Show Is On* starred **Beatrice Lillie** and **Bert Lahr** and sported contributions by a number of the theater's most distinguished creators. Other composers and lyricists included Hoagy Carmichael and Stanley Adams, the **Gershwins**, **Richard Rodgers** and **Lorenz Hart**, **E. Y. Harburg** and **Harold Arlen**, and **Howard Dietz** and **Arthur Schwartz**. Lillie and Lahr, while not on stage for every sketch, dominated the show. Lillie, among other things, took a satirical look at Josephine Baker, swung out over the audience while sitting on a moon and singing a parody of all of those songs about our nearest celestial neighbor, and went after the popular singers of the day with Rodgers and Hart's "Rhythm." Lahr sang Harburg and Arlen's "Song of the Woodman" to devastating effect, and took part in other spoofs. The Gershwins' "By Strauss" was the last number they wrote for Broadway before George's death; it was sung by Gracie Barrie and Robert Shafer with dancing by Mitzi Mayfair. As he had done in other revues, Vincente Minnelli assembled a beautiful production. **Brooks Atkinson**'s review in the *New York Times* was an unqualified rave. Given the Christmas Day opening, he thanked Kris Kringle and Minnelli for this "finest" of revues. He noted the many fine hands that wrote for the show, but stated that Minnelli pressed it all "into a luminous work of art."

SHUBERT/SHUBERT BROTHERS/SHUBERT ORGANIZA-TION/SHUBERT THEATRICAL CORPORATION/SHU-BERTS. At the dawn of the 20th century, three brothers, Lee (1875?–1953), Sam S. (1877?–1905), and Jacob J. (or J. J., 1879?–1963), established the Shubert Theatrical Corporation, which became the major theatrical business enterprise for the ensuing decades. During the second quarter of the century, the Shuberts owned, managed, operated, or booked nearly 1,000 theaters across the United States, in addition to controlling most of the major houses on Broadway. As producers of musicals and legitimate plays, they presented more than 500 works. Most important from a musical perspective were **revues**, including the series *The Passing Show*, *Artists and Models*, and *Greenwich Village Follies*; and **operetta**s, the most famous of which had scores by **Sigmund Romberg** and included *Maytime* (1917), *Blossom Time* (1921), *The Student Prince* (1924), and *My Romance* (1948). The Shubert Organization continues to be a major Broadway presence as a theater owner and producing body.

***SHUFFLE ALONG* (23 MAY 1921, 63RD STREET MUSIC HALL, 504 PERFORMANCES).** Music by **Eubie Blake**, lyrics by Noble Sissle, book by Flournoy Miller and Aubrey Lyles. Although not the first show conceived entirely by **African Americans** to reach Broadway, *Shuffle Along* was the first to become a hit. It came into being in Philadelphia after a meeting between two important African American entertainment duos. Noble Sissle and Eubie Blake were songwriters, and Flournoy Miller and Aubrey Lyles worked in **vaudeville**. The plot had to do with a mayoral election in Jimtown, where partners in owning a grocery, Steve Jenkins (Flournoy Miller) and Sam Peck (Aubrey Lyles), run against each other. Jenkins wins and appoints his partner police chief. Both are corrupt and ineffectual. Miller and Lyles also brought into the show one of their vaudeville specialties: a comic boxing match. Harry Walton (Roger Matthews) comes forward to help clean up the mess as a reformer, causing Jimtown to sing "I'm Just Wild about Harry." Jenkins and Peck leave in disgrace. The show was at a shabby theater north of most Broadway houses, but it became so popular that midnight performances were added on Wednesdays, and the show ran for a surprising 15 months. The cast included such future stars as **Josephine Baker**, Hall Johnson, and Florence Mills.

"I'm Just Wild about Harry" was only one of the great tunes in Blake's score, which was unlike anything Broadway had ever heard. Blake was a ragtime pianist who had mastered the intricacies of early jazz, and these he brought to *Shuffle Along*. Jazz was heard in many clubs in New York City, but it had not been heard in any amount from Broadway pits. The wildly syncopated rhythms thrilled audiences and seemed to make the dancers work all the harder, a point invariably noticed by white critics and audiences. Other fine songs in the score were "Love Will Find a Way" and "Bandana Days." "I'm Just Wild about Harry" became associated with U.S. President Harry S. Truman.

***SILK STOCKINGS* (24 FEBRUARY 1955, IMPERIAL, 478 PERFORMANCES).** Music and lyrics by **Cole Porter**, book by **George**

S. Kaufman, Leueen MacGrath, and Abe Burrows, directed by **Cy Feuer**, dances and musical numbers staged by **Eugene Loring**, presented by Feuer and Ernest Martin. Cole Porter's last Broadway show had a difficult gestation period, with Abe Burrows doing major rewrites on Kaufman and MacGrath's book, and Kaufman insisting on the removal of his name as director. The plot was "suggested" by the 1939 movie *Ninotchka*, which starred Greta Garbo. It was a lively Cold War story, but became a formulaic musical. A Soviet composer is in Paris considering offers from an American theatrical agent, Steve Canfield (Don Ameche). The Communists send a serious but pretty official, Ninotchka (Hildegard Neff), to lure the composer back, but she falls in love with him. She returns to Russia, but Canfield pursues her and they end up together in the West. Brooks Atkinson of the *New York Times* was taken with *Silk Stockings*. He noted that the show has "the wittiest dialogue of recent years" and placed it in the same class as *Guys and Dolls*. He found Porter's score "bold, ironic and melodious" with his typical "intricately worded lyrics." "All of You" was the score's major hit.

SILVERS, PHIL (1911–1985). Actor whose legendary **musical comedy** roles include Harrison Floy in *High Button Shoes* (1947), Jerry Biffle in *Top Banana* (1952), Hubert Cram in *Do Re Mi* (1960), and Prologus/Pseudolus in the 1972 revival of *A Funny Thing Happened on the Way to the Forum*. He won **Tony Awards** for *Top Banana* and *Forum*.

SIMON, LUCY (1940–). Popular music performer and composer whose first Broadway musical, *The Secret Garden* (1991), earned her a **Tony Award** nomination. Simon's evocative and eclectic score captures and accentuates the various narrative dimensions of Marsha Norman's libretto.

SIMON, NEIL (1927–). Prolific playwright and librettist known for his innate comic skills, one-liners, and the depth of his characters. He created the librettos for *Little Me* (1962), *Sweet Charity* (1966), *Promises, Promises* (1968), *They're Playing Our Song* (1979), and *The Goodbye Girl* (1993). He is also active as a screenwriter, and wrote the screenplay for the 1969 film version of *Sweet Charity*. Most of his stories concern New Yorkers and New York City.

SINBAD **(14 FEBRUARY 1918, WINTER GARDEN, 388 PER-FORMANCES).** Music by **Sigmund Romberg, Al Jolson**, and others, lyrics and dialogue by **Harold Atteridge**. A vehicle for Al Jolson, *Sinbad* ran for almost a year. The show's framing story concerned Long Island socialite Nan Van Decker (Virginia Fox Brooks), who consults a crystal ball and "sees" the extravagant Middle East and its inhabitants, including Inbad (Jolson), an Arabian incarnation of Gus, Jolson's blackface valet character. Jolson never performed Romberg's music in the show, leaving that to the rest of the cast. Instead, he delivered his own selection of songs, including "Rock-a-Bye Your Baby with a Dixie Melody," "My Mammy" (introduced while the show was on a national tour), and **George Gershwin**'s first hit, "Swanee" (for which **Irving Caesar** was lyricist).

SLEZAK, WALTER (1902–1983). Viennese baritone singer and actor who often played Central European characters. His Broadway credits include Karl Reder in *Music in the Air* (1932), Johann Volk in *May Wine* (1935), Harry Mischak Szigetti in *I Married an Angel* (1938), and Panisse in *Fanny* (1954). He won a **Tony Award** for his performance in *Fanny*.

SMITH, EDGAR (1857–1938). Librettist and lyricist who contributed to more than 60 Broadway shows in the late 19th and early 20th centuries. He wrote **burlesque** musicals for the team of **Joe Weber** and **Lew Fields** and also the libretto for *Robinson Crusoe, Jr.* (1916), an **Al Jolson** vehicle.

SMITH, HARRY B. (1860–1936). Prolific librettist and lyricist for 123 Broadway shows, some of which were adaptations of European works. Among his greatest successes were *Robin Hood* (1891, music by **Reginald De Koven**) and *The Fortune Teller* (1898, music by **Victor Herbert**). He also collaborated with Herbert on *The Serenade* (1897), *Cyrano de Bergerac* (1899), *Miss Dolly Dollars* (1905), *Sweethearts* (1913), and *The Century Girl* (1916), among others. Smith contributed to *Ziegfeld Follies*, and worked with composers such as **Jerome Kern** (*Very Good Eddie* [1915] and *Miss 1917* [1917]) and **Sigmund Romberg** (*Princess Flavia* [1925] and *Cherry Blossoms* [1927]).

SMITH, KATE (BORN KATHRYN ELIZABETH SMITH, 1907–1986). Radio and television singer and recording artist most famous for her version of **Irving Berlin**'s "God Bless America." Early in her career, she appeared on Broadway as Tiny Little (a comic title, considering Smith's ample figure) in *Honeymoon Lane* (1926) and Pansy Sparks in *Flying High* (1930).

SMITH, ROBERT B. (1875–1951). Lyricist and librettist who wrote the words for **Lillian Russell**'s hit, "Come Down Ma' Evenin' Star," from *Twirly Whirly* (1902). He also worked with **Victor Herbert** on *Sweethearts* and sometimes collaborated with his brother, **Harry B. Smith**.

SOCIAL JUSTICE/INJUSTICE. Many musicals have underlying themes concerning the pursuit of justice. This was evident in **operettas** from the 1920s through marches such as "Song of the Vagabonds" from *The Vagabond King* (1925) and "Stouthearted Men" from *The New Moon* (1928). In 1949, *South Pacific* and *Lost in the Stars* both dealt with **race relations**. Later, shows such as *West Side Story* (1957) and *Cabaret* (1966) included strong references to social problems. Anthems where either soloists or the chorus faces the audience and sing directly about societal problems became a feature of musicals from the 1980s and 1990s: "One Day More" and "Do You Hear the People Sing?" from *Les Misérables* (1985, London; 1987, New York) "Bui Doi" from *Miss Saigon* (1989, London; 1991, New York) and "The Day after That" from *Kiss of the Spider Woman* (1993) are four examples. Twenty-first century shows such as *Wicked* (2003) and *Caroline, or Change* (2004) continue the trend of addressing socially relevant issues in Broadway musicals. *See also* HOMOSEXUALITY.

SOMETHING FOR THE BOYS **(7 JANUARY 1943, ALVIN, 422 PERFORMANCES).** Music and lyrics by **Cole Porter**, book by **Herbert** and **Dorothy Fields**, staged by **Hassard Short**, dances arranged by **Jack Cole**, produced by Michael Todd. A spirited **musical comedy** that is now largely forgotten, *Something for the Boys* was created by fine Broadway professionals and starred **Ethel Merman**. Three cousins discover they have inherited a ranch in Texas and travel there. Merman played Blossom Hart, a former chorus girl who works in the wartime defense industry. Her cousins are salesman Harry Hart (Allen Jenkins) and nightclub singer Chiquita Hart (Paula Laurence). The ranch house is decrepit, and the local army base is using it, but they leave and the cousins turn it into a guesthouse for servicemen's wives. Accusations of the house's loose morals cause the army to declare it off-limits, but it turns out that Blossom can hear radio signals in her fillings. This helps save an airplane in distress, the army relents, and Blossom wins the sergeant with whom she has fallen in love. Lewis Nichols, writing for the *New York Times*, called the show "a big, fast glittering musical comedy" and said Michael Todd "has been lavish to the point of excellent good taste." The biggest hits were "Could It Be You?" and "Hey, Good Lookin'."

SOMETIME **(4 OCTOBER 1918, SHUBERT, 283 PERFOR-MANCES).** Music by **Rudolf Friml**, lyrics and book by **Rida Johnson Young**. Remembered mostly as a vehicle for **Ed Wynn**, who was a latecomer to the show, *Sometime* ran for about nine months. The plot was told in flashback. Enid Vaughn (Francine Larrimore) has not spoken to her fiancé in five years because she caught him in a compromising position with Mayme Dean (Mae West). As the last five years are retold, Enid discovers that she was wrong and the couple reunites. Wynn played Loney, who comes onstage to present his outrageous behavior, puns, and one-liners. The score's songs included Enid's "Sometime" and "Baby Doll," and Mayme's "Any Kind of Man," with which she stopped the show.

SONDHEIM, STEPHEN (1930–). Composer and lyricist who is an undisputed reigning figure in the American musical theater. A protégé of **Oscar Hammerstein II**, Sondheim also studied music with noted composer Milton Babbitt. He created the lyrics for *West Side Story* (1957) and *Gypsy* (1959), and the first Broadway musical for which he wrote both lyrics and music was *A Funny Thing Happened on the Way to the Forum* (1962). Each of his shows is unique. His songs are not only character driven but also plot specific; they often function as soliloquies that can only be sung by one character at one particular moment in the show. A motoric undercurrent typically appears in the orchestra under the singer's well-proportioned and goal-driven melodic lines. His ensembles are extremely complicated in terms of rhythm, pitch, and counterpoint. Sondheim's catalog for which he wrote music and lyrics includes such iconic works as *Company* (1970), *Follies* (1971), *A Little Night Music* (1973), *Pacific Overtures* (1976), *Sweeney Todd: The Demon Barber of Fleet Street* (1979), *Merrily We Roll Along* (1981), *Sunday in the Park with George* (1984), *Into the Woods* (1987), *Assassins* (1991), and *Passion* (1994). Sondheim has a stronger following among theater professionals, critics, and scholars than with the general public. The themes he addresses in his work—which include revenge (*Sweeney Todd*), creativity and the commercialization of art (*Sunday*), human psychology and social issues (*Into the Woods*, *Assassins*), and love that does not work out (*A Little Night Music*, *Passion*)—generally have limited popular appeal. In addition to numerous Broadway **revivals**, his work also appears regularly on opera stages and in regional and college/university theaters. In 2002, the Kennedy Center in Washington, D.C., hosted a high-profile festival dedicated to Sondheim.

SONG AND DANCE **(18 SEPTEMBER 1985, ROYALE, 474 PERFORMANCES).** Music by **Andrew Lloyd Webber**, lyrics by Dan Black, entire production supervised by **Richard Maltby Jr.** and Peter Martins, presented by **Cameron Mackintosh**. Although panned by critics, *Song and Dance* managed a reasonable run because of its popular composer and **Bernadette Peters**'s one-woman show in act 1. She played Emma, a young English hat maker living in New York who recalls her difficult love life through song. Frank Rich, writing in the *New York Times*, found Emma "a completely synthetic, not to mention insulting, creation whom no performer could redeem." He admitted, however, that Peters brought "vocal virtuosity, tempestuous fits and husky-toned charm" to the role. "Tell Me on a Sunday" (which was the title of act 1 when it was performed separately) was among the show's highlights. Act 2 consisted of a self-examining dance by one of the men in Emma's life, choreographed by Peter Martins. The music was Lloyd Webber's *Variations on a Theme by Paganini for Cello and Rock Band*.

SONG OF NORWAY **(21 AUGUST 1944, IMPERIAL, 860 PERFORMANCES).** Musical adaptation and lyrics by **Robert Wright** and **George Forrest**, book by Milton Lazarus, choreography and singing ensembles by **George Balanchine**. *Song of Norway* was a fictionalized story of the life of Edvard Grieg with songs based on the composer's music. Lawrence Brooks played Grieg, who is married to Nina (Helena Bliss). Grieg falls in love with an opera singer, Louisa Giovanni (Irra Petina), and follows her to Italy, but eventually he returns to his beloved wife and country. A subplot involved Henrik Ibsen (Dudley Clements) commissioning *Peer Gynt*, which becomes a ballet in *Song of Norway* and a major part of Balanchine's work for the show. The creators found good singers; Petina, for example, was on the Metropolitan Opera roster. Lewis Nichols, in the *New York Times*, welcomed *Song of Norway* as a "pleasant show." As for Wright and Forrest's work, the "lyrics are not particularly distinguished but they are cheerful enough." An example of their efforts was "Hymn of Betrothal," based on Grieg's "To Spring."

SONG OF THE FLAME **(30 DECEMBER 1925, 44TH STREET, 219 PERFORMANCES).** Music by **Herbert Stothart** and **George Gershwin**, lyrics and book by **Otto Harbach** and **Oscar Hammerstein II**, produced by **Arthur Hammerstein**. Billed as a "romantic opera" and loosely based on the Russian Revolution, *Song of the Flame* was a richly produced **operetta** in which Aniuta (Tessa Kosta) urges Russian peasants to overthrow their oppressors. In her red revolutionary disguise, she is called "The Flame." Prince Volodyn (Guy Robertson) falls in love with her, ignorant of her part in the rebellion. Later they meet in Paris and accept each other, despite the past. The Russian peasantry played a major role in the production, with several scenes including 53 voices, encompassing the regular chorus and the "Russian Art Choir." A similar number of dancers also appeared, offering, among other things, a ballet on the Russian seasons. The title number, most likely composed by Gershwin, was perhaps the best, but "Far Away" and the "The Cossack's Love Song" were also memorable. *Song of the Flame* represented a departure from Gershwin's usual kind of show. The show's spectacle impressed the unnamed *New York Times* critic, especially **Joseph Urban**'s "gay-colored, variegated settings," and the many groups who crossed the stage "with the beauty of bizarre costumes and hangings." He questioned the "literary propriety" of writing an operetta on the Russian Revolution so

soon after it happened, and wondered if the show might have benefited from a "more varied, lighter treatment."

SOPHISTICATED LADIES (1 MARCH 1981, LUNT-FONTANNE,
767 PERFORMANCES). Based on the music of Duke Ellington,
directed by Michael Smuin, musical staging and choreography by
Donald McKayle and Smuin, cochoreography and tap choreography
by Henry Le Tang. Conceived as a showpiece for Ellington's most famous songs, *Sophisticated Ladies* was a fine dancing show with
Ellington's band in the pit led by the composer's son, Mercer Ellington. The show's nine cast members included the brilliant tap dancer
Gregory Hines and female dancer Judith Jamison. Songs were
clothed in a lavish production that evoked the days of the Cotton
Club. Although Ellington never managed a hit on Broadway, *Sophisticated Ladies* gave that to him posthumously. **Frank Rich**, in the
New York Times, noted that the show "just won't quit until it has won
over the audience with dynamic showmanship." He described the
multitalented Hines as "the frisky Ellington spirit incarnate" and
Jamison, a dancer with Alvin Ailey's company, as "towering, charismatic." Rich thought the choreographers had found the "old-time
Harlem razzmatazz."

THE SOUND OF MUSIC (16 NOVEMBER 1959, LUNT-
FONTANNE, 1,443 PERFORMANCES). Music by **Richard
Rodgers**, lyrics by **Oscar Hammerstein II**, book by **Howard Lind-
say** and **Russel Crouse**, choreography by **Joe Layton**, directed by
Vincent J. Donehue, produced by Leland Hayward and Richard Hal-
liday, Rodgers and Hammerstein. Rodgers and Hammerstein's final
collaboration began with **Mary Martin**, as Maria, singing "The hills
are alive with the sound of music," providing a fitting epitaph to the
Rodgers and Hammerstein partnership. Sent by the Reverend Mother
(Patricia Neway) to be governess of the seven von Trapp children,
Maria enchants the children and their father, Captain von Trapp
(**Theodore Bikel**), filling them with her love of music ("Do-Re-Mi").
Fearful that she is falling in love with the already engaged captain,
Maria returns to the abbey where the Reverend Mother tells Maria
that she must face life ("Climb Ev'ry Mountain"). She returns to the
von Trapp villa and learns that the captain has broken his engagement

because of his fiancée's tolerance of the Nazi threat to Austria. The captain and Maria declare their love as "an ordinary couple," marry, and then escape the Nazis over Maria's beloved mountain. The oldest child, Leisl, who is "sixteen going on seventeen," and a local boy provide a romantic subplot. Captain Von Trapp and others sing of their Austrian homeland in "Edelweiss," the last song Rodgers and Hammerstein wrote, and one that was often mistaken for a genuine folksong.

Originally proposed by Howard Lindsay and Russel Crouse after viewing the German movie adaptation of *The Trapp Family Singers*, based on the autobiography of Maria von Trapp, the original musical concept was to use the von Trapp Family Singers' repertoire alongside new songs. Rodgers and Hammerstein, however, wanted to write the entire score and not compete with Mozart. On opening night, **Brooks Atkinson** of the *New York Times* was disappointed about the creators "succumbing to the clichés of **operetta**," and thought that their innovative string of musicals had lost some of its energy, but the show did include "melodies, rapturous singing and Miss Martin" and "is always moving. Occasionally it is also glorious." The 1965 film version starred **Julie Andrews** and **Christopher Plummer**. The show is part of popular culture, and in 2006, **Andrew Lloyd Webber** created a reality television show in Great Britain, "How Do You Solve a Problem Like Maria?" to cast the female lead in a new production. Twenty-three-year-old Connie Fisher was the winner, and she received tremendous praise from both critics and the general public for her performance.

SOUSA, JOHN PHILIP (1854–1932). Conductor, composer, and lyricist whose **operetta** *El Capitan* played on Broadway in 1896. His music has appeared in several shows, including the **dance musical** *Dancin'* (1978) and **Stephen Sondheim**'s *Assassins* (1991).

SOUTH PACIFIC **(7 APRIL 1949, MAJESTIC, 1,925 PERFORMANCES).** Music by **Richard Rodgers**, lyrics by **Oscar Hammerstein II**, book by Hammerstein and **Joshua Logan**, directed by Logan, produced by Rodgers and Hammerstein. Rodgers and Hammerstein's fourth show and one of their most avidly anticipated, *South Pacific* was also an important step in the development of the musical play. The first three notes of the overture to *South Pacific*, based on the opening of the song "Bali Ha'i," whisks one to the mystery and romance of an island paradise where ordinary Americans deal with romance and prejudice against the backdrop of World War II. Rodgers and Hammerstein based the show on three short stories from James Michener's *Tales of the South Pacific*, brought to their attention by Joshua Logan and Leland Hayward. Hammerstein did not feel completely comfortable with a play about the military, in which he had never served. Logan, a World War II veteran who had just co-written and directed *Mr. Roberts*, assisted him with the military mindset and earned part of the book credit.

The play opens with French planter Emile De Beque (Metropolitan Opera star **Ezio Pinza**) entertaining Navy nurse Ensign Nellie Forbush (**Mary Martin**). We learn about her character through the song "A Cockeyed Optimist," a taste of pure Americana with its AABA form and memorable melody. Though they know little about each other, they recognize their attraction, but realize they are from different worlds ("Twin Soliloquies"). Emile dreams of their future together in the sophisticated "Some Enchanted Evening." On the nearby naval base, Tonkinese souvenir merchant Bloody Mary (Juanita Hall) meets Lieutenant Joseph Cable (**William Tabbert**), whom she tells about her home, the mysterious island "Bali Ha'i." Seeking intelligence on Japanese fleet movements, Cable tries to enlist de Becque's help on a dangerous mission, who at first refuses because of his love for Nellie. She is, however, confused about her feelings for him, singing the delightful "I'm Gonna Wash That Man Right Outa My Hair," not long before she meets him again and sings "I'm in Love with a Wonderful Guy." These straightforward songs add effectively to her characterization. Cable goes to Bali Ha'i, where Bloody Mary's beautiful daughter, Liat, enchants him. Both stories involve racial prejudice, because Nellie runs away from Emile after meeting his two children of mixed race by his first, Tonkinese wife, and Cable realizes that he cannot take Liat back to his parents in Philadelphia. Nellie claims that she cannot explain herself because she was born with her prejudice. Emile does not accept this, and Cable replies that "You've Got to Be Taught." Afterward Emile agrees to help Cable with his mission, which succeeds, but Cable dies. Nellie overcomes her prejudices and accepts Emile's children as Emile enters just before the final curtain. The comedic subplot involved the ever-scheming Seabee Luther Billis (Myron McCormick) and his fellow Seabees, who sing rousing numbers such as "There's Nothing Like a Dame." The show included several lighthearted songs to balance the generally serious tone, including the act 2 opening, "Honey Bun," which featured Luther Billis's gyrating ship tattoo on his belly and Nellie dancing around in her wildly oversized sailor suit.

Brooks Atkinson of the *New York Times* found it "a tenderly beautiful idyll of genuine people inexplicably tossed together in a strange corner of the world" where all elements of the show contributed to the mood. *South Pacific* won eight **Tony Awards** and a **Pulitzer Prize**. The 1958 film version started Mitzi Gaynor and Rosanno Brazzi (with Giorgio Tozzi's voice), and the 2001 television version featured Glenn Close, Rade Sherbedgia, and Harry Connick Jr. *See also* RACE RELATIONS/RACISM.

SPAMALOT. See MONTY PYTHON'S SPAMALOT.

SPEWACK, BELLA AND SAMUEL (1899–1990; 1899–1971). Husband and wife creators of 35 plays, librettos, and film scripts who won a **Tony Award** for *Kiss Me, Kate* (1948), with music by **Cole Porter**. Both were reporters before embarking on their collaborative theatrical career. They also wrote the book for Porter's *Leave It to Me!* (1938), which they based on their play *Clear All Wires*.

SPRING AWAKENING **(10 DECEMBER 2006, EUGENE O'NEILL, 25 PERFORMANCES AS OF 31 DECEMBER 2006).** Music by Duncan Sheik, book and lyrics by Steven Sater. Based on the play by Frank Wedekind, *Spring Awakening* takes places in "a provincial German town in the 1890s" and focuses on the challenges of adolescence. Wendla (Lea Michele) and Melchior (Jonathan Groff) discover each other's bodies, and she becomes pregnant. When Melchior's best friend, Moritz (John Gallagher Jr.), commits suicide, blame falls on Melchior, and when Wendla's mother learns of the pregnancy, she arranges a back-alley abortion for her daughter. The haunting score encompasses a range of pop-rock styles, and a parental advisory label for explicit content appears on the original cast album. Musical numbers are presented as psychological soliloquies, and are thus distinguished from the main thrust of the ultimately tragic drama. *See also* ROCK MUSICALS.

STARLIGHT EXPRESS **(15 MARCH 1987, GERSHWIN, 761 PERFORMANCES).** Music by **Andrew Lloyd Webber**, lyrics by Richard Stilgoe, directed by **Trevor Nunn**. A musical about trains that was far more popular in London than in New York, *Starlight Express* was a visual extravaganza in which actors careened around tracks on roller skates. The plot concerned a boy and his train set. The steam engine, Rusty (Greg Mowry) wants to beat the diesel, Greaseball (Robert Torti), and does so, through the spiritual guidance of Starlight Express (portrayed as a disembodied voice and a bright off-stage light). **John Napier**'s complicated set featured three levels of train tracks, some of which went over and through the audience. **Frank Rich** panned the show in the *New York Times*, wondering for whom it was written and what part of the plot was most important. Among the score's most effective numbers is the gospel finale, "The Light at the End of the Tunnel."

STATE FAIR **(27 MARCH 1996, MUSIC BOX, 110 PERFOR-MANCES).** Music by **Richard Rodgers**, lyrics by **Oscar Hammerstein II**, book by Tom Briggs and Louis Mattioli after the screenplay by Hammerstein. After touring extensively, the stage version of Rodgers and Hammerstein's film musical (it was filmed twice, in 1945 and 1962), despite abysmal or somewhat unflattering reviews, managed to run through the summer. In addition to songs from the film, including "It's a Grand Night for Singing," other songs from the Rodgers and Hammerstein catalog were added to the show, including "The Man I Used to Be" from *Pipe Dream* and "That's the Way It Happens" from *Me and Juliet*.

STEEL PIER **(24 APRIL 1997, RICHARD RODGERS, 76 PER-FORMANCES).** Music by **John Kander**, lyrics by **Fred Ebb**, conceived by Scott Ellis, **Susan Stroman**, and David Thompson, directed by Ellis, choreographed by Stroman. Called "an American fable" and set on Atlantic City's Steel Pier in August 1933, *Steel Pier* captured the spirit of the Depression-era dance marathons, events where hope and perseverance could provide escape from the troubles of real life. The plot focuses on Rita Racine (**Karen Ziemba**), who wants to escape the world of her husband's dance marathons and begin a new life. Others in the cast included Gregory Harrison, Daniel McDonald, Debra Monk, and **Kristin Chenoweth**. Kander and Ebb's score evokes popular dance styles of the 1930s; "Somebody Dance," "Lovebird," and "Steel Pier" are among the outstanding musical numbers. Ben Brantley, writing in the *New York Times*, found *Steel Pier* lacking in a number of areas, especially in comparison to Kander and Ebb's *Cabaret* and *Chicago*.

STEIN, JOSEPH (1912–). Librettist whose credits include *Plain and Fancy* (1955), *Mr. Wonderful* (1956), *Take Me Along* (1959), *Zorba* (1968), and the 1973 revival of *Irene*. His greatest success, however, was *Fiddler on the Roof* (1964), for which he won a **Tony Award**.

STEWART, MICHAEL (1929–1987). Librettist for three influential musicals staged by **Gower Champion**: *Bye Bye Birdie*, *Carnival!*, and *Hello, Dolly!* He also wrote the books for *George M!*, and *42nd Street* and the lyrics for *I Love My Wife* and *Barnum*. He was an extremely gifted wordsmith, and many of his shows extol the joys and wonders of show business in various guises.

ST. LOUIS WOMAN **(30 MARCH 1946, MARTIN BECK, 113 PERFORMANCES).** Music by **Harold Arlen**, lyrics **by Johnny Mercer**, book by Arna Bontemps, production directed by **Rouben Mamoulian**. Based on Bontemps's novel *God Sends Sunday*, *St. Louis Woman* was a musical play created by a number of distinguished artists that failed to win an audience. Ruby Hill played Della Green, who loves any man who looks good at the moment. Her male friend is Biglow Brown (Rex Ingram) until Little Augie (Harold Nicholas), a winning jockey, comes along. Brown assaults Augie, but then another woman that Brown left shoots him. Brown curses Augie from his deathbed and the jockey starts to lose races and also Della, but she returns when he starts to win again. A notable character was a young **Pearl Bailey** as Butterfly. Mamoulian's staging was a highlight as was the dancing of brothers Harold and Fayard Nicholas. Lewis Nichols, writing in the *New York Times*, wrote a mixed review. He found "nice things," but "not enough of them," citing the show's plot as its problem. He believed that the original intention was to make the show a folk play like *Porgy and Bess*, but the writers dressed it up as a **musical comedy**, making it "a hybrid affair." He appreciated the cakewalk at the end of the act 1 and remarked that Pearl Bailey "can sing a song so that it stays sung." The tunes that Nichols named were those sung by Bailey: "Legalize My Name" and "A Woman's Perogative." Another fine song from the show was "Come Rain or Come Shine." *See also* AFRICAN AMERICAN MUSICALS.

STONE, PETER (1930–). Librettist who won three **Tony Awards** for Best Book: the first for *1776* (1969), the second for *Woman of the Year* (1981), and the third for *Titanic* (1997). Other librettos include *Two by Two* (1970), *Sugar* (1972), and *The Will Rogers Follies* (1991). Historic themes and events, such as Noah's Ark, the signing of the Declaration of Independence, or the sinking of the Titanic, are prevalent in his work, and re-creating the atmosphere of the past in the spirit of the present is one of his greatest talents.

STOP THE WORLD—I WANT TO GET OFF (3 OCTOBER 1962, SHUBERT, 555 PERFORMANCES). Music, lyrics, and book by Anthony Newley and **Leslie Bricusse**, directed by Newley, produced by **David Merrick**. A hit in London before its arrival on Broadway, *Stop the World—I Want to Get Off* was an allegorical and satirical show about a man making his way in the world. Its staging was circus-like, and the musical was rife with imaginative moments. Newley, in addition to creating most of the material with Bricusse, directed and starred as Littlechap. He was an "everyman" sort of figure, wearing baggy pants and makeup that suggested a clown. He begins the show as a mime but eventually starts to speak. Littlechap begins his professional career serving tea to executives, but eventually directs the company, gets elected to Parliament, and receives a noble title. He also marries the boss's daughter and has affairs with Russian,

German, and American women on his travels. Anna Quayle played all of the female roles, and the Greek chorus featured seven female dancers. **Howard Taubman**, reviewing the show for the *New York Times*, found it "a brave attempt" at a new type of musical theater, but that its use of allegory and satire were superficial. The tuneful score included "What Kind of Fool Am I," a major hit in the early 1960s. A revival in 1978 ran less than a month.

STOTHART, HERBERT (1885–1949). Music director and composer who worked with producer **Arthur Hammerstein** in the 1920s. His Broadway music usually appeared alongside that of other composers. Stothart contributed music for *Wildflower* (1923, with **Vincent Youmans**), *Rose Marie* (1924, with **Rudolf Friml**), *Song of the Flame* (1925, with **George Gershwin**), and *Good Boy* (1928, with Harry Ruby). He is best remembered for his work as a film composer and music director at MGM studios.

STRAUSS, JOHANN, JR. (1825–1899). Quintessential Viennese composer of **operettas** and waltzes whose works frequented Broadway stages in the first part of the 20th century. Among his works to play on Broadway in English-language adaptations (with the years of their Broadway productions) are *Vienna Life* (1901) and two works based on *Die Fledermaus—A Wonderful Night* (1929) and *Champagne, Sec* (1933). *The Great Waltz* (1934) featured Strauss and his father, also a composer, as characters and also included their music.

***STREET SCENE* (9 JANUARY 1947, ADELPHI, 148 PERFORMANCES).** Music by **Kurt Weill**, lyrics by Langston Hughes, book by Elmer Rice, staged by Charles Friedman, dances by Anna Sokolow. Based on Rice's Pulitzer Prize-winning play from 1929, *Street Scene* was a superior work of musical theater that proved too sophisticated for the commercial Broadway audience. One of the first works that Weill saw after moving to the United States was *Porgy and Bess*, and he had always dreamed of writing an American opera, which became *Street Scene*. It was billed as a "dramatic musical," but the audience would hardly have been fooled when singers came from the Metropolitan Opera and the pit orchestra had 35 musicians. Rice's play involves a short romance between Sam Kaplan (Brian

Sullivan) and Rose Maurrant (Anne Jeffreys), brought to a tragic end through the actions of Rose's mother, Anna (Polyna Stoska). They live along with other memorable characters in a row of brownstones. Weill found the play full of musical possibilities, and employed various styles for different characters. For example, the leads had operatic music, while African American characters sang in the style of blues. "Moon-Faced, Starry-Eyed" was the only song to achieve fame outside of the production. Hughes's lyrics were outstanding, universally praised for their honest emotion and plain language. **Brooks Atkinson**, reviewing the production for the *New York Times*, called *Street Scene* "a musical play of magnificence and glory." The cast was "superb," Weill "found notes to express the myriad impulses of Mr. Rice's poem," and Hughes's lyrics are "affectionate." The run of about 18 weeks was disappointing, but *Street Scene* is now alive in the opera repertory.

STREISAND, BARBRA (1942–). Singing actress who made her Broadway debut in *I Can Get It for You Wholesale*, stopping the show with "Miss Marmelstein." She played **Fanny Brice** in *Funny Girl*, performing "Don't Rain on My Parade" and "People." Streisand has also had a successful film, concert, and recording career. Her repertory on stage and on record includes Broadway standards, which she performs with her characteristic warm, stylized sound.

***STRIKE UP THE BAND* (14 JANUARY 1930, TIMES SQUARE, 191 PERFORMANCES).** Music by **George Gershwin**, lyrics by **Ira Gershwin**, book by **Morrie Ryskind**, based on the libretto by **George S. Kaufman**. One of the first purely satirical book musicals, *Strike Up the Band* closed in Philadelphia during its first production in 1927, but the revival in 1930 included important changes and became a success. The original plot involved a nonsensical war between the United States and Switzerland over an American tariff on Swiss cheese. An American cheese magnate convinces Congress to declare war on Switzerland; he offers to pay for the war if it is named after him. The war is a rollicking success, and even the Swiss profit from it with many American soldiers staying in their hotel rooms. At the end, the Russians and Americans are discussing the possibility of their own mutually beneficial war. The satire was simply too bitter for 1927, but once the Depression had begun, audiences became more receptive to such material. Morrie Ryskind reworked the book for the 1930 production, making the plot a staged dream of a tycoon (Dudley Clements), who awakens a reformed man. Cheese also became chocolate. The score included the title tune and several other hits: "Soon" and "I've Got a Crush on You." Writing in the *New York Times*, **Brooks Atkinson** found the score "an original contribution to the comic musical stage," but he noted that the show loses its edge over the course of the evening. *Strike Up the Band* directly paved the way for *Of Thee I Sing*.

STRITCH, ELAINE (1925–). Belt-singing actress who captivated audiences in revivals of *Pal Joey* (1952) and *On Your Toes* (1954) before being cast as Mimi Paragon in the **Noel Coward** musical *Sail Away* (1961) and singing "Why Do the Wrong People Travel?" She created the role of Joanne in *Company*, introducing "Ladies Who Lunch," and was Parthy in **Hal Prince**'s 1994 revival of *Show Boat*, in which she sang "Why Do I Love You?" as a touching lullaby to her granddaughter, Kim. She received the **Drama Desk Award** for Outstanding Solo Performance for her one-woman show *Elaine Stritch at Liberty* (2002).

STROMAN, SUSAN (1954–). Director-choreographer whose credits include **revivals** (*Show Boat*, 1994; *The Music Man*, 2000; *Oklahoma!*, 2002), shows based on older music (*Crazy for You*), and shows that emulate styles of the early part of the 20th century (*Steel Pier*, *The Producers*). She also was director-choreographer for the innovative **dance musical** *Contact*, for which she also developed the concept. Other credits include *Big*, *Thou Shalt Not*, and *The Frogs*. In her work, she approaches historical styles through contemporary means and creates dances that advance the plot. She often incorporates props as integral parts of her routines, as she did with aluminum walkers in "Along Came Bialy" from *The Producers*. Stroman is the recipient of five **Tony Awards** and five **New York Drama Desk Awards**, has worked in opera and ballet and on television, and was director-choreographer of the 2005 film version of *The Producers*.

STROUSE, CHARLES (1928–). Composer who collaborated with lyricist **Lee Adams** on *Bye Bye Birdie*, *Golden Boy*, and *Applause*,

Martin Charnin on *Annie*, and **Richard Maltby Jr.** on *Nick and Nora* (1991). He works firmly in the standard Broadway idiom, but adds musical dimensions appropriate to the setting of each show, such as a rock 'n' roll-inspired ensemble number ("A Lot of Livin' to Do") in *Bye Bye Birdie* or an anthem of hope sung by an orphan during the Great Depression ("Tomorrow") in *Annie*.

THE STUDENT PRINCE (2 DECEMBER 1924, JOLSON'S, 608 PERFORMANCES). Music by **Sigmund Romberg**, lyrics by **Dorothy Donnelly**, produced by the Messrs. **Shubert**. The longest-running Broadway musical of the 1920s is the tale of Karl Franz (**Howard Marsh**), a prince from mythical Karlsberg, who goes to study at Heidelberg University and falls in love with Kathie (**Ilsa Marvenga**), a waitress at the local beer garden, the Inn of the Three Golden Apples. When his grandfather the king, dies, Karl Franz must return to Karlsberg to become king and also to enter into an arranged marriage. The **operetta** ends with Karl Franz returning to Heidelberg and saying farewell to both Kathie and the days of his youth. The couple realizes that all they can keep of their first love is its memory. *The Student Prince* played a major role in the rehabilitation of Germany's reputation after World War I and also cemented the importance of the male chorus in not only Romberg's work but also the Broadway musical in general. The score included many famous songs, including the male choral numbers "Drinking Song," "Students Marching Song" and "Come, Boys, Let's All Be Gay, Boys" (with a coloratura obligato for Kathie); the waltzes "Deep in My Heart, Dear," "Golden Days," and "Just We Two"; and the famous "Serenade," in which Romberg demonstrates his originality with scoring by skillfully moving between a baritone solo, a male quartet, and a male chorus. The operetta is sometimes known by its longer title, *The Student Prince in Heidelberg*. A film version appeared in 1954 starring Edmund Purdom (with Mario Lanza's voice) and Ann Blyth.

STYNE, JULE (1905–1994). Classically trained pianist, bandleader, and vocal coach who became one of the most successful Broadway composers of the mid-20th century. His first success was *High Button Shoes* (1947), followed by *Gentlemen Prefer Blondes* (in which

Carol Channing sang "Diamonds Are A Girl's Best Friend"), additional music for *Peter Pan*, *Bells Are Ringing* (the **Judy Holliday** vehicle that included "The Party's Over"), *Gypsy* (in which **Ethel Merman** sang "Everything's Coming Up Roses" to **Stephen Sondheim**'s lyrics), *Do Re Mi*, *Funny Girl* (in which **Barbra Streisand** sang "People"), and *Fade In—Fade Out*. He won his only **Tony Award** for *Hallelujah, Baby!* (1967), and in 1972, wrote the score for *Sugar*, which starred **Robert Morse**. His last score was for *Red Shoes* (1993), a show that closed after only three performances. He also conceived *Mr. Wonderful* as a vehicle for **Sammy Davis Jr.** Styne wrote for some of Broadway's most impressive stars, and his songs simultaneously exude theatrical opulence and dramatic depth.

SUGAR (9 APRIL 1972, MAJESTIC, 505 PERFORMANCES). Music by **Jule Styne**, lyrics by **Bob Merrill**, book by **Peter Stone**, directed and choreographed by **Gower Champion**, presented by **David Merrick**. Based on the film *Some Like It Hot*, *Sugar* featured excellent performances by **Robert Morse**, Tony Roberts, Cyril Ritchard, and Elaine Joyce and ran for about 15 months. Morse and Roberts played Jerry and Joe, two musicians during Prohibition who witness a gang murder and hide in an all-girl band. Jerry draws unwanted attention from Osgood Fielding Jr. (Ritchard), an aging millionaire who proposes marriage, and Joe falls in love with "Sugar Kane" (Joyce), the part made famous by Marilyn Monroe in the film version. Many people did not believe that the film transferred well to the stage. **Clive Barnes**, writing for the *New York Times*, thought that "the performances may just about provide a reason to see 'Sugar'." He appreciated most Robert Morse, whose "acting shows a sharp insight into feminine psychology," but Tony Roberts is "hardly less effective." Ritchard and Joyce also drew considerable praise, and Champion directed the show with "demonic energy" in the midst of a fine production. Barnes despaired at the book, music, and lyrics, however, and admitted that his enjoyment of the performances came with free admission.

SUGAR BABIES (8 OCTOBER 1979, MARK HELLINGER, 1,208 PERFORMANCES). Music by **Jimmy McHugh** and others, lyrics by **Dorothy Fields** and **Al Dubin**, and others, conceived by Ralph G.

Allen and Harry Rigby. A tribute to **burlesque**, *Sugar Babies* included many of the genre's low comedy effects. The stars were the irresistible **Mickey Rooney** and **Ann Miller**. After playing on Broadway for three years, *Sugar Babies* toured until 1986. The show was the brainchild of Ralph G. Allen, a professor at the University of Tennessee, who was obsessed with the old, uproarious world of burlesque. Rooney was at his best when clowning in the skits, libidinously pursuing Miller in various settings. There were double entendres and costume gags galore, and Miller showed that her fabled ability as a tap dancer remained. **Walter Kerr**, reviewing the show for the *New York Times*, wrote copiously about Mickey Rooney and found him as "energetic and exactly as talented" as he was as a young child. Kerr thought him "at his funniest . . . in drag." He called Miller "in stunning shape at whatever age she must be."

SULLIVAN, ARTHUR (1842–1900). British composer whose Savoy operas, collaborations with librettist-lyricist **W. S. Gilbert**, have appeared on Broadway since the late 19th century. *H.M.S. Pinafore* (1879) actually received its world premiere in New York because of international copyright law. Other G&S works to appear on Broadway include *Trial by Jury*, *The Sorcerer*, *The Pirates of Penzance*, *Patience*, *Iolanthe*, *Princess Ida*, *The Mikado*, *Ruddigore*, *The Yeomen of the Guard*, and *The Gondoliers*. Gilbert and Sullivan's work had a tremendous influence on Broadway in terms of vocal style (virtuosic soprano writing), effusive marches, comic patter songs, lighthearted waltzes, and various combinations of recitatives, solos, duets, small ensembles, and choral numbers fused together into coherent musical-dramatic scenes.

SULLIVAN, JO. Lyric soprano who played Polly Peachum in **Marc Blitzstein**'s version of **Kurt Weill**'s *Threepenny Opera* (1954) and created Rosabella in *The Most Happy Fella* (1956), with a score by her husband, **Frank Loesser**. She served as "artistic associate" for the 1992 **Lincoln Center Theatre revival** of *The Most Happy Fella*.

SUNDAY IN THE PARK WITH GEORGE **(2 MAY 1984, BOOTH, 604 PERFORMANCES).** Music and lyrics by **Stephen Sondheim**, book and direction by **James Lapine**, presented by the **Shubert** Organization and Emanuel Azenberg, by an arrangement with Playwrights Horizons. A show about the creative process, *Sunday in the Park with George* looked to the enigmatic Georges Seurat and a modern artist (perhaps George's great-grandson). The show ran for well over a year and won a **Tony Award** and a **Pulitzer Prize**, partly because of its moments of magical beauty, but also, some would say, for its extensive coverage by the *New York Times*. Act 1 follows "George" (**Mandy Patinkin**) as he works on his masterpiece "Sunday Afternoon on the Island of La Grande Jatte," formed from thousands of dots. His model/girlfriend is cleverly called Dot (**Bernadette Peters**), but she barely understands her cerebral lover and his obsession with the painting and his revolutionary technique. Seurat goes to La Grande Jatte every Sunday afternoon to paint people and animals—the people he sees in the park become the images in the painting. The act 1 finale is the creation of the famous painting, and involves George positioning the other characters into their places, creating a living tableau of the painting in front of which an image of the painting drops as the act ends. Act 2 takes place in the 1980s at the Chicago Art Institute (where "Sunday Afternoon" hangs). George finds he can no longer be original, and questions the value of art in the extended musical scene "Putting It Together." His grandmother, Marie (Peters), tells him the story of Seurat and encourages him to travel to the site of "Sunday Afternoon." He does, experiences Dot's spirit, and they sing the impassioned "Move On." In the powerful finale, the characters from act 1 return, acknowledge George for creating them, and he likewise acknowledges them.

Writing in the *New York Times*, **Frank Rich** noted that Sondheim and Lapine asked the audience to completely change the way it regarded the Broadway musical. Rich called the set, designed by Tony Straiges, "an animated toy box complete with popups," the latter cutouts of George or other characters that appeared for dramatic and sometimes hilarious effect. Rich terms Patinkin's portrayal "a crucible of intellectual fire" and Peters "overflows with . . . warmth and humor." The other members of the cast provided delightful texture and memorable moments, but none emerged as fully developed as George or Dot. Rich finds the second act somewhat less effective, finding it more traditional concerning how "the modern George overcomes his crisis of confidence." Sondheim's score feels very much like a single work, showing the strong influence of French composers such as Maurice Ravel and constructed from many memorable phrases and motives, not unlike the innumerable dots that Seurat used in his painting. A highlight of the first act was "Finishing The Hat," a profound patter song of amazing economy of construction. The show's theme of moving toward an artistic whole is paralleled in the duets between George and Dot: the opening title song, "Color and Light," "We Do Not Belong Together," and "Move On." Other highlights include Dot's "Everybody Loves Louis," in which she contrasts the popularity of a pastry chef with the nonpopularity of an experimental artist, and the act 2 opening, "It's Hot up Here," sung by the hapless characters in the painting.

SUNNY (22 SEPTEMBER 1925, NEW AMSTERDAM, 517 PERFORMANCES). Music by **Jerome Kern**, lyrics and book by **Otto Harbach** and **Oscar Hammerstein II**, staged by **Hassard Short**, produced by **Charles Dillingham**. Conceived as a vehicle for the popular **Marilyn Miller**, *Sunny* combined the talents of some of Broadway's best creators and stage personalities. Although it opened the same week as *No, No, Nanette*, *Dearest Enemy*, and *The Vagabond King*, *Sunny* managed to run for 15 months. Miller played the title character, an American circus performer in England who wants to marry Tom Warren (Paul Frawley). He boards a ship to head home, and Sunny stows away to be near him, but to avoid the brig she must marry Tom's friend, Jim Denning (Jack Donahue). By the end of the show, she has divorced Denning and will marry Warren. The cast also included **Clifton Webb**, Cliff "Ukulele Ike" Edwards, and Mary Hay. Harbach and Hammerstein managed to assemble a workable book, and Kern wrote a lovely score. Along with Dillingham's sumptuous production, *Sunny* provided more than enough delights for an audience primarily coming out to see Marilyn Miller's winning dancing and captivating stage personality. The unsigned review in the *New York Times* was most positive, noting that the show "skipped gayly across the stage" for three hours. The critic praised how the show "has been skillfully pulled together" with a sense of "general excellence." There is an entire paragraph on Miller who, despite her stardom, "retains . . . an agreeable air of modesty and young beauty." Highlights of the score included the title song, "D'ye Love Me?," and "Who."

SUNSET BOULEVARD (17 NOVEMBER 1994, MINSKOFF, 977 PERFORMANCES). Music by **Andrew Lloyd Webber**, lyrics and book by Don Black and Christopher Hampton, directed by **Trevor Nunn**, musical staging by **Bob Avian**, produced by the **Really Useful Company**. Based on Billy Wilder's 1950 film of the same name starring Gloria Swanson, *Sunset Boulevard* featured a mesmerizing, **Tony Award**-winning performance by Glenn Close. She played Norma Desmond, a star of silent movies who desperately wants to make a comeback in modern Hollywood but has lost her grip on reality. She thinks she has found her ticket back when she meets Joe Gillis (Alan Campbell), a writer between jobs. He will write the screenplay that will make Norma a star again, and she takes him as a lover. Joe is also interested in Betty Schaefer (Alice Ripley), but this arouses Norma's jealousy and she shoots Joe. **George Hearn** played Max von Mayerling, Norma's ex-husband and now her faithful butler. The show opens with Joe's body floating in the swimming pool, viewed from the perspective of the drain, just one of the arresting images that John Napier brought to the stage. One of the show's greatest stars, though, was the magnificent staircase in Norma's mansion. At one point, the large-scale set rises from the stage floor to a more relaxed gathering of young people. The set was in the tradition of the **megamusical**, wowing the audience with stagecraft and spectacle. Critics were mixed about the show, but most agreed that Glenn Close was brilliant as "Norma," taking risks and making her a monster while avoiding campiness. David Richards, writing in the *New York Times*, found the show at times "outlandishly good" and at other times merely "big." Norma had some stunning music, including her opening numbers, "Surrender" and "With One Look," and the act 2 "As If We Never Said Goodbye." Joe's frenetic title number, "New Ways to Dream," "The Perfect Year," and "Eternal Youth Is Worth a Little Suffering" were other highlights of the score.

SWEENEY TODD: THE DEMON BARBER OF FLEET STREET (1 MARCH 1979, URIS, 557 PERFORMANCES). Music and lyrics by **Stephen Sondheim**, book by **Hugh Wheeler**, directed by **Harold Prince**. Based on the English legend and play by Christopher Bond, *Sweeney Todd* is a musical thriller that makes no concessions to popular taste or conventional Broadway fare. Sondheim always shied away from the simple and fashionable, but his psychological and musical exploration of an insane, vengeful barber was a huge gamble. It was one of his best scores, however, and enjoyed one of Sondheim's longer runs. Benjamin Barker (**Len Cariou**) was a happily married barber with a young daughter before the corrupt Judge Turpin and his beadle unjustly sent him to prison so they could have their way with the barber's wife. Fifteen years later, Barker returns as Sweeney Todd, who intends to reestablish himself as a barber to get revenge on the judge. He returns to his old neighborhood and meets Mrs. Lovett (**Angela Lansbury**), an eccentric proprietor of a meat-pie shop. Traveling with Todd is young Anthony Hope (**Victor Garber**), who falls in love with Johanna (Sarah Rice), Sweeney's daughter and now the judge's ward. Interrupted by Anthony just as he is about to slit the judge's throat, Sweeney decides to kill every visitor to his barber's chair. Disposing of bodies is no problem because Mrs. Lovett is always looking for fresh sources of meat; their cannibalistic specialty becomes one of the most popular meals in London. Sweeney helps Anthony hatch a plan that wins him Johanna, but as events career out of control, Sweeney kills his wife (now an unrecognizable madwoman), the judge, and then Mrs. Lovett, when he realizes she has lied to him. Tobias, a simple boy who has been helping with the meat pies until he realizes the source of the meat, finally kills Sweeney.

Harold Prince and his creative team placed this horrific tale into the cavernous Uris Theater with a huge steel set, the remains of a New England foundry, a grim reminder of the Industrial Revolution. The steam whistle came as well, startling the audience as the show's first sound. Richard Eder, writing in the *New York Times*, was overwhelmed: "There is more of artistic energy, creative personality and plain excitement in 'Sweeney Todd' . . . than in a dozen average musicals." Sondheim's score is a triumph of musicodramatic unification, a factor that has helped the work's acceptance as part of the operatic, as well as theatrical, repertory. The score includes a variety of styles, from the incessant "Ballad of Sweeney Todd" (with its quotation of the "Dies Irae" theme, representing death), the transcendent beauty of "Johanna" and "Finch and Linnet Bird," to Sweeney's terrifying "Epiphany," when he decides to kill whoever sits in his barber chair, followed by "A Little Priest," a lighthearted waltz whose pun-filled lyrics praise the delights of cannibalism, revealing some of the blackest humor ever to appear in a Broadway musical. The 2005 Broadway revival, directed and reimagined by **John Doyle** as a tale told by inmates in a mental asylum, starred **Patti LuPone** and **Michael Cerveris**.

SWEET ADELINE **(3 SEPTEMBER 1929, HAMMERSTEIN, 234 PERFORMANCES).** Music by **Jerome Kern**, lyrics and book by **Oscar Hammerstein II**, produced by **Arthur Hammerstein**. A worthy successor to *Show Boat*, *Sweet Adeline* had its run cut short by the Depression and never regained popularity. It was a vehicle for **Helen Morgan,** who played Addie Schmidt, a singer in her father's beer garden in Hoboken at the time of the Spanish-American War. She loses her first love to her sister and begins singing in a Bowery theater, eventually becoming a Broadway star. James Day (Robert Chisholm) helps her career, and they fall in love. The cast included the comedian Charles Butterworth, whose reactions to such events as a **burlesque** show were most memorable. Kern's score was perhaps not quite as glorious as that for *Show Boat*, but it bore "A Girl Is on Your Mind" and several hits that he wrote for Morgan: "Why Was I Born?" and "Here Am I." She was a master at singing bittersweet songs, and Kern made fine use of this ability. Hammerstein's book had its share of **musical comedy** silliness, but it also told a serious story about a flawed character. **J. Brooks Atkinson** reviewed the show for the *New York Times* and described it as "downright enjoyable all the while." He raved about the variety of sets and tied the appeal of Kern's score directly to Morgan, who is wonderful as she "sings in the pensive, gently melancholy mood" that many love.

SWEET CHARITY **(30 JANUARY 1966, PALACE, 608 PERFORMANCES).** Music by **Cy Coleman**, lyrics by **Dorothy Fields**, book by Neil Simon, conceived, staged, and choreographed by **Bob Fosse**. Based on Federico Fellini's 1957 film *Nights of Cabiria*, *Sweet Charity* was a vehicle for **Gwen Verdon**, who at the time was Fosse's wife, and her considerable star power was a major reason for the show's success. Fosse's staging and choreography had its usual punch and style. Verdon played Charity, a dance hostess at a cheap club in New York. She desires real love, and first finds an Italian movie star (James Luisi) whose date for the evening left him. Charity takes him back to her apartment, but his date returns, and Charity hides in the closet while they make love. She then meets Oscar (John McMartin), an accountant, and they start a promising relationship, but he is not the marrying type, and Charity ends up alone. Verdon, as usual, danced wonderfully in a variety of styles, sang distinctively, and exuded a mature sexiness and charm. Coleman and Fields's songs also included "Baby, Dream Your Dream" and "I'm a Brass Band." Fosse's dances encompassed the show's big hit "Big Spender," "The Rich Man's Drug," and "Rhythm of Life," and were reprised in *Dancin'* and *Fosse*. Stanley Kauffman, writing in the *New York Times*, missed much of the show's charm. He derided it as "The Show That Wants to Be Loved," designed too much to be a "heart-tugger," but called Fosse's work "superb," although he ultimately found *Sweet Charity* to be mostly a "theatrical device" and not a real show.

SWEETHEARTS (8 SEPTEMBER 1913, NEW AMSTERDAM, 136 PERFORMANCES). Music by **Victor Herbert**, lyrics by **Robert B. Smith**, book by Fred de Gresac and Smith. Boasting Herbert's fine score and a typical **operetta** story about misplaced European royalty, Herbert wrote the role of Sylvia specifically for Christie MacDonald, an excellent singer. She was the Crown Princess of Zilania, but during a war she was taken to the Laundry of the White Geese in Bruges for safety. Dame Paula (Ethel Du Fre Houston), also known as "Mother Goose," raises Sylvia along with her six daughters. Years later, Sylvia has two suitors, the evil Lieutenant Karl (Edwin Wilson) and Franz (Thomas Conkey), the "Heir Presumptive" of Zilania. She marries Franz, and they rule her homeland together. Most commentators found Herbert's score superior to the lyrics or book. The most famous song was the title number, but the score also included the love duet "The Angelus," the male chorus "Pretty as a Picture," and "Cricket on The Hearth." The unnamed critic for the *New York Times* approached the show with tongue placed firmly in cheek, extensively quoting the published plot synopsis to demonstrate its absurdity. He thought that Herbert "has provided a very well written score" with several songs "graced with those delightful touches of unexpectedness." Jeannette MacDonald and Nelson Eddy starred in the heavily revised 1938 film version, and a Broadway revival in 1947 ran for 288 performances.

SWIFT, KAY (BORN KATHERINE SWIFT, 1897–1993). Composer and pianist whose musical *Fine and Dandy* (1930) featured the first complete Broadway score written by a woman. She was **George Gershwin**'s assistant, musical adviser, and the woman who came closest to becoming the composer's wife. She was extremely involved with the creation of *Porgy and Bess* (1935). Swift attended the Institute for Musical Art (precursor to the Juilliard School), where she studied composition with Percy Goetschius. She wrote for Radio City Music Hall and was director of music for the 1939 World's Fair.

– T –

TABBERT, WILLIAM (ALSO KNOWN AS BILL TABBERT, 1921–). Singing actor who began his Broadway career in the **musical comedies** *What's Up* (1943), *Follow the Girls* (1944), and *Billion Dollar Baby* (1945). He also appeared in the **revue** *Seven Lively Arts* (1944) before creating the role of Lt. Joseph Cable in **Rodgers and Hammerstein**'s *South Pacific* (1949), where he introduced "Younger Than Springtime" and "You've Got to Be Taught." He also played Marius in *Fanny* (1954).

TAKE A CHANCE **(26 NOVEMBER 1932, APOLLO, 243 PERFORMANCES).** Music by **Herb Nacio Brown** and Richard Whiting with additional songs by **Vincent Youmans**, book and produced by **B. G. De Sylva** and **Laurence Schwab**. A fast-paced **musical comedy**, *Take a Chance* had a memorable cast that propelled the show to a run of more than seven months. The plot involved putting on a **revue** called *Humpty Dumpty*. Producer Kenneth Raleigh (Jack Whiting) works with two dishonest associates, Duke Stanley (**Jack Haley**) and "Louie Webb" (Sid Silvers). Kenneth falls in love with another backer, Toni Ray (June Knight), a star in the revue. **Ethel Merman** played Wanda Brill, not a large role, but she sang every hit song in the show, including "Eadie Was a Lady," "You're an Old Smoothie," and "Rise 'n' Shine." The first two were by Brown and Whiting, but the latter was by Youmans, one of his last Broadway songs. **Brooks Atkinson**, writing for the *New York Times*, captured the intent of *Take a Chance*. He simply stated: "Pay no attention to the plot," and goes on to describe the silliness of the proceedings, especially those for which Jack Haley and Sid Silvers were responsible. Atkinson noted that Ethel Merman has never before approached her songs with "quite so much abandon."

TAKE ME ALONG (22 OCTOBER 1959, SHUBERT, 448 PERFORMANCES). Music and lyrics by **Bob Merrill**, book by **Joseph Stein** and Robert Russell, directed by Peter Glenville, choreography by **Onna White**, produced by **David Merrick**. Based on Eugene O'Neill's play *Ah, Wilderness!*, *Take Me Along* boasted a strong cast. The plot took place in Centerville, Connecticut, around the turn of the century. Walter Pidgeon played Nat Miller, the newspaper editor. He watches his brother-in-law, Sid (**Jackie Gleason**), woo his sister, Lily (Eileen Herlie). Richard (**Robert Morse**), Nat's young son, is in love with Muriel Macomber (Susan Luckey). Lily manages to reform Sid, who has a serious drinking problem, and he promises to go on the wagon if she will marry him. Muriel's father drives her away from Richard, but the young man finds out that the breakup was her father's idea, and goes to college promising to wait for her. Merrill's score worked well within the show, but few songs were heard outside the theater. The best tunes were the title song, "Staying Young," and "Little Green Snake," the latter concerning the evils of drinking too much. Gleason's performance wowed the critics.

THE TAP DANCE KID (21 DECEMBER 1983, BROADHURST, 669 PERFORMANCES). Music by Henry Krieger, lyrics by Robert Lorick, book by Charles Blackwell. Based to an extent on Louise Fitzhugh's novel *Nobody's Family Is Going to Change*, *The Tap Dance Kid* featured Alfonso Ribeiro as Willie, a child in a middle-class African American family who dreams of becoming a tap dancer. His father, William (Samuel E. Wright), is a lawyer and bitterly opposes his son entering a profession that he sees as part of his race's demeaning past. He ignores, however, that the boy's grandfather was a tap dancer, his uncle is a dancer and choreographer, and his mother is a former dancer. The uncle, Dipsey (**Hinton Battle**), did some wonderful tap dancing during the show, and Willie joined his grandfather's ghost (Alan Weeks) in some routines. William remains stridently opposed to his son's dreams until the finale, but there the show has its joyful ending. **Frank Rich**, reviewing the premiere for the *New York Times*, had a mixed view. He found one of the glories to be choreographer Danny Daniels, who was capable "of raising yesteryear's routines to their fantastic apotheosis," but thought the show overall was a "plodding domestic drama." *See also* AFRICAN AMERICAN MUSICALS.

TARZAN **(10 MAY 2006, RICHARD RODGERS, 270 PERFOR-MANCES AS OF 31 DECEMBER 2006).** Music and lyrics by Phil Collins, book by David Henry Hwang, produced by **Disney Theatrical Productions**. A live-action version of Disney's 1999 animated film, *Tarzan* is best remembered for its athleticism, with cast members swinging from vines (bungee cords) throughout the show. *American Idol* alum Josh Strickland made his Broadway debut as the title character, and his pop-style voice was well suited for Collins's music.

TAUBMAN, HOWARD (1907–1996). He became music editor of the *New York Times* in 1935, and in 1955, was named chief music critic. From 1960 to 1965, he was chief drama critic. He was a consultant for the PBS series *Great Performances* and wrote eight books, seven about music and one about theater.

TELEVISION VERSIONS. *See* SCREEN ADAPTATIONS.

TEMPLETON, FAY (1865–1939). Comic contralto who worked in **burlesque** and **vaudeville** before playing Mary Jane Jenkins in **George M. Cohan**'s *Forty-five Minutes from Broadway* (1906) and introducing "Mary is a Grand Old Name." She appeared in several shows produced by **Joseph Weber** and **Lew Fields**, including *Fiddle-dee-dee* (1900) and *Hokey-Pokey* (1912). Decades later, she played Aunt Minnie in **Jerome Kern**'s *Roberta* (1933).

TENDERLOIN **(17 OCTOBER 1960, 46TH STREET, 216 PER-FORMANCES).** Music by **Jerry Bock**, lyrics by **Sheldon Harnick**, book by **George Abbott** and Jerome Weidman, staged by Abbott, choreography by **Joe Layton**, presented by Robert E. Griffith and **Harold S. Prince**. Based on Samuel Hopkins Adams's 1959 novel of the same name, *Tenderloin* was a fictionalized account of Reverend

Charles K. Pankhurst's attempt at the end of the 19th century to clean up the Tenderloin district near West 23rd Street. Created by the same team that produced *Fiorello!*, the show starred Maurice Evans as Reverend Brock. His supposed helper in this effort is Tommy (Ron Husmann), who actually works with a corrupt policeman, Lieutenant Schmidt (Ralph Dunn). They alter photographs to frame the pastor, but Tommy later admits his deeds through the influence of Laura (Wynne Miller). The authorities start to clean up the Tenderloin district. The score's highlights included "Artificial Flowers," "The Picture of Happiness," and "The Tenderloin Celebration."

TERRIS, NORMA (1904–1989). After appearing in the **musical comedy** *Queen O'Hearts* (1922) and several **revues**, Terris created the roles of Magnolia and Kim (as an adult) in *Show Boat* (1927). She reprised the role in the 1932 **revival**.

TESORI, JEANINE. Tesori's early Broadway credits were as a dance arranger for the 1995 revival of *How to Succeed in Business without Really Trying* and the 1998 revival of *The Sound of Music*. But it is as a composer of the scores for *Thoroughly Modern Millie* (2002) and *Caroline, or Change* (2004) that she has become best known. She also wrote the **off-Broadway** musical *Violet* (1998). Tesori's music matches the characters and situations for which she writes, whether it is the classic **musical comedy** style of *Thoroughly Modern Millie* or the nearly sung-through post-**Sondheim** approach of *Caroline, or Change*.

TESTA, MARY (1955–). Comic actress whose credits include Domina in the 1996 revival of *A Funny Thing Happened on the Way to the Forum*, Madame Maude in the 1998 revival of *On the Town*, and Maggie in the 2001 revival of *42nd Street*. In a radically different vein, she created the role of Magdalena in *Marie Christine*.

THARP, TWYLA (1941–). Legendary modern dancer who became a significant Broadway presence in the early 21st century with *Movin' Out* (2002), based on music by Billy Joel, and the Bob Dylan musical *The Times They Are a'Changin'* (2006). In her shows, Tharp conceives all aspects of the work without the aid of book writers.

THEATRE GUILD. The Theatre Guild, an organization established in 1919, was a respected producer of plays before it staged musicals such as *Porgy and Bess* (1935) and **Rodgers and Hammerstein**'s first three shows: *Oklahoma!* (1943), *Carousel* (1945), and *Allegro* (1947). Other musical productions include *Bells Are Ringing* (1956) and *The Unsinkable Molly Brown* (1960).

***THEY'RE PLAYING OUR SONG* (11 FEBRUARY 1979, IMPER-IAL, 1,082 PERFORMANCES).** Music by **Marvin Hamlisch**, lyrics by Carole Bayer Sager, book by **Neil Simon**, directed by **Robert Moore**. Said to have been based on Hamlisch's complicated relationship with Sager, *They're Playing Our Song* offered Simon's funny book, good songs, and goofy characterizations by Lucie Arnaz and Robert Klein. They played Sonia Walsk, a successful lyricist, and Vernon Gersch, a famous popular songwriter. They spend the show trying to deal with each other and their own neuroses, the latter often acted out for the audience by choruses of three men and three women, alter-egos for the stars. These eight people were the entire cast seen on stage, but there were also off-stage voices. Sonia and Vernon part at the end, perhaps to meet again. Simon made heavy use of several running gags, such as Sonia continually purchasing her clothes from defunct stage productions and phone messages from her hopeless ex-lover, Leon. Richard Eder, writing in the *New York Times*, was not convinced. He called the book "one of Mr. Simon's weakest" plays, but found Hamlisch's score "the show's main distinction." Among the songs are "Fallin'," "If He Really Knew Me," and the title number. The latter occurs in a restaurant, with both main players wildly overreacting when one of their songs is heard in the canned music.

***THIS IS THE ARMY* (4 JULY 1942, BROADWAY, 113 PERFOR-MANCES).** Music and lyrics by **Irving Berlin**, book by James Mac-Coll, directed by Ezra Stone, produced by Uncle Sam. Irving Berlin's World War II sequel to *Yip! Yip! Yaphank!*, *This Is the Army* was one of the most extraordinarily selfless, patriotic acts ever performed by a member of the American entertainment industry. Broadway has long waved the flag as a way of saluting the country and packing in audiences, but no Broadway figure ever gave as much to a national war effort as Berlin did during the two world wars. After selling out on Broadway for almost four months (after an announced run of four weeks), *This Is the Army* was filmed and then the live production went on a world tour that lasted until late 1945, playing to American servicemen in both theaters of the war. Berlin accepted no payment for his participation and dedicated all royalties from his hit-laden score to the Army Emergency Relief Fund, the charity that also benefited from the Broadway run. Like *Yip! Yip! Yaphank!*, *This Is the Army* was a **revue** presented entirely by soldiers, but in this case the cast was assembled from throughout the country and included such professional entertainers as Burl Ives, Gary Merrill, Julie Oshins, and Joe Cook Jr. Berlin framed the show with the title song "This Is the Army, Mr. Jones," sung by the 300-member cast. The opening skit continued with the songs "I'm Getting Tired So I Can Sleep," "I Left My Heart at the Stage Door Canteen," "My Sergeant and I," "The Army's Made a Man out of Me," and finally "Mandy," a hit from *Yip! Yip! Yaphank!* Other skits encompassed predictable references to the German and Japanese and men in drag. In the second act, Berlin and other veterans of the first show sang "Oh, How I Hate to Get Up in the Morning," called by the *New York Times* the "theme still regarded as undying among members of the lower military orders."

THOROUGHLY MODERN MILLIE (**18 APRIL 2002, MARQUIS, 903 PERFORMANCES**). New music by **Jeanine Tesori**, new lyrics by Dick Scanlan, book by Scanlan and Richard Morris, directed by Michael Mayer. Based on the 1967 film starring **Julie Andrews**, Mary Tyler Moore, and **Carol Channing**, *Thoroughly Modern Millie* is the tale of Millie Dillmount (**Sutton Foster**) and her experiences after moving to New York City in 1922, which include working as a secretary, exposing a kidnapping ring run by the proprietress of the hotel where she lives (under the auspices of a Chinese laundry), and finding true love. Songs from the film, including the title number and "Jimmy" appeared on stage, and Tesori and Scanlan's new numbers, including the opening "Not for the Life of Me," "Forget About the Boy," and Millie's 11:00 number "Gimme Gimme," endorsed the show's overall 1920s **musical comedy** style. The show won numerous **Tony Awards** in 2002, including Best Musical. *See also* ORIENTALISM.

***THE THREE MUSKETEERS* (13 MARCH 1928, LYRIC, 319 PER-FORMANCES).** Music by **Rudolf Friml**, lyrics by Clifford Grey, book by William Anthony McGuire, produced by **Florenz Ziegfeld**, choreographed by **Albertina Rasch**. Based on Alexandre Dumas's novel, the **operetta** included only three adventures from the book: the first meeting of d'Artagnan (**Dennis King**) and the Musketeers Athos, Porthos, and Aramis; d'Artagnan's romance with Constance (**Vivienne Segal**); and his efforts to protect the honor of the Queen (Yvonne D'Arle) from the evil Cardinal Richelieu (Reginald Owen). The score included the lyrical "Ma Belle," "One Kiss," "My Dreams," and "My Sword and I" and the heroic marches "All for One and One for All" and "March of the Musketeers." The show capitalized on the 1920s' love of all things French and had a short-lived Broadway **revival** in 1984.

***THE THREEPENNY OPERA* (THEATRE DE LYS: 10 MARCH 1954, 96 PERFORMANCES; 20 SEPTEMBER 1955, 2,611 PER-FORMANCES).** Music by **Kurt Weill**, lyrics and book by Bertolt Brecht, translated by **Marc Blitzstein**. One of the most significant pieces of musical theater in a Western language from the first half of the 20th century, *The Threepenny Opera* premiered in Berlin as *Die Dreigroschenoper* in 1928. Brecht and Weill conceived the work during the Weimar Republic, and drew the story from *The Beggar's Opera*, a hit in London from exactly two centuries before that celebrated the lower classes and their struggle against oppression. In his libretto, Brecht borrowed techniques and stances from the agit/prop theater, but still showed more than one side of the characters and managed other nuances. The story involves the love between Polly Peachum and Macheath (Mack the Knife), and their relationships with others in a seedy district of Soho. Weill, a sophisticated composer with solid classical training, wrote a score in which he effectively mixed elements of popular and concert music. "Morität," known in English as "Mack the Knife," has been popular in several countries. *Die Dreigroschenoper* became far better known in the United States through an English translation by composer Marc Blitzstein that premiered at the Brandeis University Festival of the Creative Arts on 14 June 1952. **Leonard Bernstein**, then a Brandeis professor, directed the concert production, and **Lotte Lenya**, the composer's widow, played Jenny, reprising her role in the original 1928 production.

Blitzstein's translation opened almost two years later in a fully staged production at the Theatre de Lys, again with Lenya as Jenny. It only played 96 performances because of a previous commitment at the theater, but great interest caused it to reopen the next season. The run was at the time the longest in the history of the American musical stage. The 1954 opening was reviewed for the *New York Times* by "L.F.," who opens with a "heartfelt thanks" to Blitzstein for his "remarkable contribution" of placing the work in accessible English while retaining the "bite, the savage satire, the overwhelming bitterness." The cast featured, in addition to Lenya, Charlotte Rae (Mrs. Peachum), **Jo Sullivan** (Polly), **Beatrice Arthur** (Lucy), and Scott Merrill (Macheath). *The Threepenny Opera* has played several more times on Broadway, including the 2006 revival starring a black-leather-clad cast led by bisexually charged Macheath (**Alan Cumming**) and Jenny (Cyndi Lauper).

THREE'S A CROWD **(15 OCTOBER 1930, SELWYN, 271 PERFORMANCES).** Music and lyrics by Howard Dietz, **Arthur Schwartz**, and others, conceived and compiled by Dietz, staged by **Hassard Short**, produced by **Max Gordon**. A **revue** that is perhaps most famous for introducing the British hit "Body and Soul" to the United States, *Three's a Crowd* had a winning cast and fine material. Its three stars were comedian **Fred Allen**, singer Libby Holman, and singer-dancer **Clifton Webb**, each also a cast member in *The Little Show*, another revue to which this was a sort of sequel. Allen's material included a skit about an Admiral Byrd-like figure suggesting that the unemployed could be hired to shovel polar snow. The unnamed reviewer in the *New York Times* praised the revue for its "pleasant lightness, a sort of unforced gayety, and, for the most part, a quizzical, knowing point of view." He called attention to the innovative lighting, which used lights hung from the balcony rather than footlights.

TIERNEY, HARRY (ca. 1890–1965). Musical comedy composer of the late 1910s and 1920s whose most important scores include *Irene*

(1919) and *Rio Rita* (1927), two of his seven collaborations with lyricist Joseph McCarthy. He also contributed to **revues**, including various editions of *The Passing Show* and *Ziegfeld Follies*.

TIMES SQUARE. The crossroads of Broadway and 7th Avenue in the heart of Manhattan, originally called Longacre Square, was renamed Times Square in 1904, when the *New York Times* erected a building on the southern edge of the site. It was also in that year that the famous New Year's Eve celebrations began. During World War I, the area became the nexus of American theater, with 42 houses in a 13-block area. In the 1960s and 1970s, the area was filled with sex-oriented shows, films, and shops, particularly along 42nd Street, and the district became one of the most dangerous parts of New York City. At the turn of the 21st century, a tremendous Times Square renaissance took place, and the area was transformed into a family-friendly entertainment district. Sleaze shops closed and new theaters, hotels, attractions (such as MTV and Madame Tussaud's Wax Museum), and stores (including a Toys 'R Us) opened.

THE TIMES THEY ARE A'CHANGIN' **(26 OCTOBER 2006, BROOKS ATKINSON, 28 PERFORMANCES).** Music and lyrics by Bob Dylan, conceived, directed, and choreographed by **Twyla Tharp**. The Bob Dylan **jukebox musical** relied heavily on dance, following in the line of *Contact* and Tharp's *Movin' Out*.

TIP-TOES **(28 DECEMBER 1925, LIBERTY, 192 PERFORMANCES).** Music by **George Gershwin**, lyrics by **Ira Gershwin**, book by **Guy Bolton** and Fred Thompson, produced by **Alex A. Aarons** and **Vinton Freedley**. A hit musical that came a year after *Lady, Be Good!* and concerned a trio of **vaudeville** performers (Andrew Tombes, Harry Watson Jr., and Queenie Smith) who are stranded without money in Florida. Their female member, Tip-Toes (Smith), romances a wealthy glue magnate (Allen Kearns) with whom she genuinely falls in love. Despite many complications, including Tip-Toes's temporary amnesia, all ends happily. The score included a number of hits, such as "These Charming People," "That Certain Feeling," "Looking for a Boy," and, especially, "Sweet and Low Down," a production number staged with toy trombones and kazoos. Reviewers were very pleased with the show, including **Alexander Woollcott** of the *New York World*, who loved the score: "Gershwin's evening, so sweet and sassy are the melodies he has poured out . . . all told, the best score he has written in his days in the theater."

TITANIC **(23 APRIL 1997, LUNT-FONTANNE, 804 PERFOR-MANCES).** Music and lyrics by **Maury Yeston**, book by **Peter Stone**. Although few musicals have ever given critics such obvious phrases with which to pan it, *Titanic* survived a critical drubbing and ran for two years but did not earn back its costs. John Cunningham played Captain E. J. Smith, often urged by the managing director of the White Star Line, J. Bruce Ismay, to try for more speed. An elderly couple who remained devoted to each other, Isidore and Ida Straus (Larry Keith and Alma Cuervo), provided some of the show's human interest. The set, designed by Stewart Laing, was a masterpiece that showed all three classes of cabins simultaneously and tilted as the ship sank. At the climactic moment, the lights went out and survivors then appeared in blankets to finish the story. The bridge was near the top of the stage, and panels on either side showed the date, time, and positions of latitude and longitude. Following the model of a **mega-musical**, *Titanic* was mostly sung through. The score included the opening "In Every Age," sung by **Michael Cerveris** as Thomas Andrews, the ship's architect, followed immediately by the impressive multi-sectional "The Launching." Another outstanding number was "The Proposal/The Night Was Alive," a duet between the ship's radio operator and a stoker.

TONY AWARDS. The most prestigious Broadway award, sponsored by the American Theatre Wing, which founded the honors in 1947. The name honored Antoinette Perry (1888–1946), an actor, director, and producer who headed the American Theatre Wing during World War II. Until 1965, the award ceremonies took place in various large rooms and usually included some entertainment by Broadway stars. The event has been broadcast on television since 1967, first in theaters and, starting in 1997, from Radio City Music Hall. In the television era, the Tony broadcast has become known as a means whereby one can see a Broadway cast perform songs from current

shows. Awards are for shows that have opened during the current season, before the cut-off date in early May. The broadcast is in early
June. Approximately 750 eligible voters must attend all productions
nominated in a particular category in order to vote.

The award for Best Musical first appeared in 1949, when *Kiss Me,
Kate* won it. In 2006, there were 25 different categories, with the following that apply to musicals: Best Musical; Best Book of a Musical;
Best Original Score (music and/or lyrics) Written for the Theatre;
Best Choreography; Best Scenic Design for a Musical (split off in
2005 from the general category for any play); Best Costume Design
for a Musical (split off from the play category in 1960–61 and again
in 2005); Best Lighting Design for a Musical; Best Director of a Musical (separated from the play category in 1960); Best Performances
by a Leading Actor, Leading Actress, Featured Actor, Featured Actress; Best Orchestrations; and Best Revival of a Musical. The American Theatre Wing awards a Tony each year in all categories. As the
number of musicals produced each year has declined, sometimes
there are few possible competitors in various categories. *See also*
DRAMA DESK AWARDS; NEW YORK DRAMA CRITICS' CIR-
CLE AWARDS; PULITZER PRIZE.

TOO MANY GIRLS (18 OCTOBER 1939, IMPERIAL, 249 PER-
FORMANCES). Music by **Richard Rodgers**, lyrics by **Lorenz
Hart**, book by George Marion Jr., staged and produced by **George
Abbott**, dances arranged by **Robert Alton**. A Rodgers and Hart hit
based on Abbott's formula for a college musical, *Too Many Girls*
concerned a rich Easterner who sends his daughter, Consuelo Casey
(Marcy Wescott), to Pottawatomie College in New Mexico. She en-
joys a good party, so he also sends, unbeknownst to her, four body-
guards who play football. Consuelo falls in love with one of her pro-
tectors, Clint Kelley (Richard Kollmar), and wants to go home when
she discovers his real purpose, but all works out in the end. The show
had a sassy edge—**Brooks Atkinson** noted in the *New York Times*
that some of the humor is "too anatomical for quick enjoyment"—
and fine dancing. The score carried a popular Latin flavor, partly because one of the football players was Desi Arnaz. Atkinson liked the
show's "breezy impudence" and called it "humorous, fresh and ex-
hilarating." He thought the best tunes were a witty list song about

New York City, "Give It Back to the Indians," and "I Like to Recognize the Tune," the latter showing Rodgers's real-life disgust with what swing arrangements did to his songs. The score also bore the wonderful standard "I Didn't Know What Time It Was."

TREASURE GIRL (8 NOVEMBER 1928, ALVIN, 68 PERFOR-MANCES). Music by **George Gershwin**, lyrics by **Ira Gershwin**, book by Fred Thompson and Vincent Lawrence, produced by **Alex A. Aarons** and **Vinton Freedley**. Although this show brought back together creators of *Lady, Be Good!* and *Oh, Kay!*, including the star **Gertrude Lawrence**, it failed. Lawrence was Ann Wainwright, an unpleasant character who schemed ambitiously for a $100,000 treasure. The dancing of **Clifton Webb** and Mary Hay or comical efforts of Walter Catlett could not save the show, although the score included a number of fine songs, including "I've Got a Crush on You" and "Feeling I'm Falling." **Brooks Atkinson**, in the *New York Times*, found that Lawrence "embodies most of the qualities that make for versatility and splendor in musical comedy stars," but here she was an "evil thing."

A TREE GROWS IN BROOKLYN (19 APRIL 1951, ALVIN, 270 PERFORMANCES). Music by **Arthur Schwartz**, lyrics by **Dorothy Fields**, book by Betty Smith and **George Abbott**, staged by Abbott, choreography by Herbert Ross, produced by Abbott with Robert Fryer. Based on Betty Smith's popular novel by the same name, *A Tree Grows in Brooklyn* opened at the end of a season that had already included *Call Me Madam*, *Guys and Dolls*, and *The King and I*. **Shirley Booth** played Cissy, a woman who unknowingly married a bigamist years before and has a string of affairs. The young lovers Katie (Marcia Van Dyke) and Johnny Nolan (Johnny Johnston) have their own problems. Katie's love is true, but Johnny can neither accept responsibility nor stay sober. **Brooks Atkinson**, in his *New York Times* review, called the show "one of those happy inspirations that the theatre dotes on" and thought that Booth gave a "glowing performance" in her best role yet, finding her interpretation of "Love Is the Reason" "**musical comedy**" in its best form." The score also included the songs "That's How It Goes" and "I'll Buy You a Star."

TRENTINI, EMMA (1885–1959). Italian-born operatic soprano who Oscar Hammerstein brought to America in 1906 to sing in his Manhattan Opera Company. On Broadway, she created the title roles in **Victor Herbert**'s *Naughty Marietta* (1910), **Rudolf Friml**'s *The Firefly* (1912), and Friml's *The Peasant Girl* (1915). Herbert and Friml wrote demanding coloratura numbers especially for her.

A TRIP TO CHINATOWN **(9 NOVEMBER 1891, MADISON SQUARE, 657 PERFORMANCES).** Music by Percy Gaunt, lyrics and book by Charles Hoyt. One of the more storied shows in Broadway history, *A Trip to Chinatown* managed a record-breaking run of about 20 months. *A Trip to Chinatown* was a remarkably unified show for its time, with some songs adding to the plot development. The story, which bore some resemblance to Thornton Wilder's *The Matchmaker* (the basis for *Hello, Dolly!*), concerned two young men who wish to take their lady friends to a masquerade ball. They are afraid that Uncle Ben will forbid such an evening, so they tell him they are going on a tour of Chinatown (the only reference to it in the entire plot) and invite a widow, Mrs. Guyer, to chaperone the party. Misunderstandings ensue, but all is well at the end. For his book, Hoyt largely depended upon standing gags and **vaudeville** routines, and some of his characters were stock figures. Of the songs that he wrote with Gaunt, "The Bowery" is easily the most famous, but there were also many **interpolations**, such as Charles K. Harris's famous "After the Ball." Songs could also change according to need; for example, when a drinking song was required, almost any might be used. The show included plenty of dances. The unnamed critic for the *New York Times* wrote that the show was "simply a lot of impossible people doing wildly absurd things" in various settings.

TRYOUT. The practice of producing a show first in a city outside of New York in order to identify problems before an audience and fix them with cuts and rewrites. For many musicals, the out-of-town tryout has been replaced by previews at the New York theater for which audiences can buy tickets, with the understanding that cuts and rewrites may go on until the announced premiere. Frequent tryout cities included New Haven, Boston, Philadelphia, Washington, and Baltimore, also at times including Cleveland, Detroit, and Toronto.

Some shows are developed in theaters such as the Goodspeed Opera House in East Haddam, Connecticut, and the La Jolla Playhouse in San Diego, then brought to Broadway. Several Broadway musicals, such as *Godspell* and *Rent*, have had their "tryouts" as **off-Broadway** shows.

TUNE, TOMMY (1939–). Eclectic dancer, actor, director, and choreographer who received nine **Tony Awards** in four different categories, including Best Supporting Actor for *Seesaw* (1973); Best Actor for *My One and Only* (1983); Best Choreographer for *My One and Only*, *A Day in Hollywood, A Night in the Ukraine* (1980) *Grand Hotel* (1989), and *The Will Rogers Follies* (1991); and Best Director for *Nine* (1982), *Grand Hotel*, and *The Will Rogers Follies*. He also choreographed and codirected *The Best Little Whorehouse in Texas* (1978). Tune draws imaginatively on American dance and entertainment traditions and never forgets to delight the audience.

TUNICK, JONATHAN. Orchestrator for many musicals by **Stephen Sondheim**, including *Company* (1970), *Pacific Overtures* (1976), *Sweeney Todd: The Demon Barber of Fleet Street* (1979), *Into The Woods* (1987), and *Passion* (1994), as well as *A Chorus Line* (1975), *Nine* (1982), *Titanic* (1997), *Marie Christine* (1999), and *The Color Purple* (2005). Tunick is known for creating a wide array of instrumental colors that complement the show's dramatic development from a relatively small, amplified ensemble. He won **Tony Awards** for *Passion* and *Titanic*.

THE 25th ANNUAL PUTNAM COUNTY SPELLING BEE (2 MAY 2005, CIRCLE IN THE SQUARE, 697 PERFORMANCES AS OF 31 DECEMBER 2006). Music and lyrics by **William Finn**, book by Rachel Sheinkin, conceived by Rebecca Feldman, directed by **James Lapine**. Based on the play *C-R-E-P-U-S-C-U-L-E*, the one-act show capitalized on the American fascination with spelling bees. Set at a spelling bee, the students, all of whom have their own stories to tell and challenges to overcome, compete for the coveted prize. Several audience members who do well on a preshow spelling test are invited on stage to join the festivities, creating some humorous moments in the choreography when the actors leave the audience participants on their own and stand by to watch. Among the more memorable students are William Barfee (Dan Fogler, who won a **Tony Award** for his performance), who spells out words with his foot before reciting the spelling, and Logainne Schwartzandgrubenierre (Sarah Saltzberg), the daughter of a gay couple. The score included many fine songs, including the title number, William Balfee's "Magic Foot," and Logainne's "Woe Is Me."

***TWO BY TWO* (10 NOVEMBER 1970, IMPERIAL, 352 PERFOR-MANCES).** Music by **Richard Rodgers**, lyrics by **Martin Charnin**, book by **Peter Stone**, conceived and directed by **Joe Layton**, presented by Rodgers. Conceived as a vehicle for **Danny Kaye**, who had not been on Broadway in decades, *Two by Two* was a musical retelling of Clifford Odets's 1954 play *The Flowering Peach*, where the story of Noah meets the Jewish humor and world of the Borscht Belt. Kaye played Noah and dominated the proceedings, creating a memorable stage persona that allowed a flawed show to run for more than 10 months. The cast also included his wife, Esther (Joan Copeland), his three sons and their wives, one of whom was played by **Madeline Kahn**. Not long after the show opened, Kaye tore a ligament and began to perform in a wheelchair or on crutches. He improvised extensively, angering Rodgers, but delighting audiences. Among the finer songs in the score is "I Do Not Know A Day I Did Not Love You."

***TWO GENTLEMEN FROM VERONA* (1 DECEMBER 1971, ST. JAMES, 613 PERFORMANCES).** Music by **Galt MacDermot**, lyrics by John Guare, adaptation by Guare and Mel Shapiro, directed by Shapiro, presented by New York Shakespeare Festival, **Joseph Papp**, producer. A musical version of Shakespeare's play, *Two Gentlemen from Verona* opened in Central Park in the summer of 1971. Its transfer to the St. James Theater tried to retain the spirit and informality of the outdoor staging. Clifton Davis and **Raul Julia** played Valentine and Proteus, the title characters, while Jonelle Allen and Diana Davila were their love interests, Silvia and Julia. Ming Cho Lee's set consisted of scaffolding of different levels and colors placed in front of a rear wall painted sky blue, an effective background for the boisterous tale. **Clive Barnes** reviewed the musical for the *New York Times*, and he loved it, calling it "a lovely fun show." He praised the show's "New York feel" with its music "a mixture of rock, lyricism and Caribbean patter," lyrics that are "spare, at times even abrasive," and its "sense of irreverence." Barnes remarked that MacDermot has grown as a composer since *Hair*, and now uses more instruments and possesses a greater range in his songs.

– U –

UGGAMS, LESLIE (1943–). **African American** singer and television actress who won a **Tony Award** for her portrayal of Georgina in *Hallelujah, Baby!* (1967). She was a **replacement** Reno Sweeney in the 1987 **Lincoln Center Theatre revival** of *Anything Goes* and in 2003 and 2004, played Muzzy Van Hossmere in *Thoroughly Modern Millie*.

THE UNSINKABLE MOLLY BROWN **(3 NOVEMBER 1960, WINTER GARDEN, 532 PERFORMANCES).** Music and lyrics by **Meredith Willson**, book by Richard Morris, choreography by Peter Gennaro. Based on the life of a plucky woman who rose from poverty in Hannibal, Missouri, to wealthy society in Denver and then survived the sinking of the *Titanic*, *The Unsinkable Molly Brown* featured **Tammy Grimes** in the title role. **Howard Taubman**, writing in the *New York Times*, admitted the presence of "pleasant things," such as Willson's score, effective comedy, interesting moments of theater, pleasant performers, and attractive costumes and scenery, but "only one fresh, appealing character" with Grimes as the "buoyant interpreter." Willson's score included "Dolce Far Niente," "My Own Brass Bed," "Beautiful People of Denver," and "I'll Never Say No."

UP IN CENTRAL PARK **(27 JANUARY 1945, CENTURY, 504 PERFORMANCES).** Music by **Sigmund Romberg**, lyrics by **Dorothy Fields**, book by Dorothy and **Herbert Fields**, choreographed by Helen Tamiris, presented by Michael Todd. A late success in Romberg's career, the nostalgic show about *New York Times* reporter John Matthews (Wilbur Evans), who is investigating Boss Tweed's ring and falls in love with Rosie Moore (Maureen Cannon), the daughter of one of Tweed's men, included some splendid ballads, including "When She Walks in the Room" and "Close as Pages in a Book." The lavish dance sequence, "Currier and Ives Ballet," was one of the show's highlights, as was its rousing celebratory anthem of Central Park, "The Big Back Yard." The production opened at a theater near Central Park, and the opening night festivities included horse-drawn carriage rides through the park. Deanna Durbin and Dick Haymes starred in the 1948 film version.

URBAN, JOSEPH (ALSO KNOWN AS JOSEF URBAN, 1872–1933). Viennese-born set designer most famous for envisioning the iconic staircases associated with *Ziegfeld Follies*. He created scenic designs for many of **Florenz Ziegfeld**'s productions, including *Sally* (1923), *Rio Rita* (1927), and *Show Boat* (1927). Urban also designed for the Metropolitan Opera and was active as an architect.

URINETOWN **(20 SEPTEMBER 2001, HENRY MILLER'S, 965 PERFORMANCES).** Music and lyrics by Mark Hollmann, lyrics and book by Greg Kotis, directed by John Rando. Its Broadway opening postponed because of the September 11 terrorist attacks, *Urinetown* is a biting social satire, set in a place where, because of a water shortage, people must pay to urinate. The show addresses issues such as corporate corruption and monopolies, crooked politicians, environmental concerns, and the divide between rich and poor. Bruce Coughlin's lean orchestrations and the declamatory nature of the songs give an edge to the score (evident in the title song) that enhances the show's political cartoonesque quality, culminating in the freedom-extolling gospel-tinged anthem finale, "I See a River." As with many shows of the early 21st century, the show includes many **reflexive references**. *See also* SOCIAL JUSTICE/INJUSTICE.

– V –

THE VAGABOND KING **(21 SEPTEMBER 1925, CASINO, 511 PERFORMANCES).** Music by **Rudolf Friml**, lyrics and book by Brian Hooker and W. H. Post. Based on Justin Huntly McCarthy's 1901 play *If I Were King*, *The Vagabond King* featured one of Rudolf

Friml's finest scores and was a hugely lavish production. After he insults King Louis XI (Max Figman), François Villon (**Dennis King**) is made king for a day, and must win the heart of the king's niece Catherine de Vaucelles (Carolyn Thomson) or be killed. That day, the Burgundians attack Paris, and Villon leads the French and defeats the enemy. Villon's former lover, the prostitute Huguette (Jane Carroll), dies saving Villon. Friml's score included the famous love song "Only A Rose," the rousing march "Song of the Vagabonds," the waltz "Love Me Tonight," Catherine's exquisite "Some Day" and Huguette's earthy "Love for Sale" and "Huguette's Waltz." Two film versions exist: the first starring King and Jeanette MacDonald (1929) and the second with the Maltese tenor Oreste, Kathryn Grayson, and Rita Moreno (1956).

VALLEE, RUDY (BORN HUBERT PRIOR VALLÉE, 1901–1986). Popular singer, actor, and bandleader who appeared in the 1931 and 1935 editions of *George White's Scandals* and, later in life, created the role of J. B. Biggley in *How to Succeed in Business without Really Trying* (1961).

VANCE, VIVIAN (1909–1979). Musical comedy actress who made her Broadway debut in *Music in the Air* (1932), played Babe in *Anything Goes* (1934), Vivian in *Red, Hot and Blue!* (1936), Stephanie Stephanovich in *Hooray for What!* (1937), and Nancy Collister in *Let's Face It!* (1941). She also played Mrs. Mister in the 1947 **revival** of *The Cradle Will Rock*. Vance is best remembered for her work on television as Ethel Mertz in *I Love Lucy* (1951–1957) and Vivian Bagley in *The Lucy Show* (1962–1965), appearing alongside **Lucille Ball**. Vance occasionally showcased her musical talents in both series.

VAN DYKE, DICK (1924–). The talented song-and-dance man won a Theatre World Award for his multiple roles in the **revue** *The Girls against the Boys* (1959) and a **Tony Award** for his portrayal of manager Albert Peterson in *Bye Bye Birdie* (1960). He achieved tremendous fame as the star of the television sitcom *The Dick Van Dyke Show* (1961–1966) and the film musicals *Mary Poppins* (1964) and *Chitty Chitty Bang Bang* (1968), both of which have been made into live stage musicals. After nearly 19 years away from Broadway, he returned to play Harold Hill in **Michael Kidd**'s 1980 revival of *The Music Man.*

VAUDEVILLE. Theatrical genre that peaked from the 1880s through the 1920s and featured a wide spectrum of entertainment, including musical numbers, comic routines, magic tricks, lectures, animal acts, operatic and dramatic excerpts, and athletic feats of various sorts. Vaudeville grew out of "variety," and differed from its predecessor by having a mixed-gender audience, promoting cultural values of the Progressive Era, and catering to the rising middle class. The penultimate place in the program went to the "headliner," the star who was the focus of publicity efforts and the main audience draw. Many leading Broadway stars began their theatrical careers in vaudeville. The first self-proclaimed "clean" vaudeville took place in New York on 24 October 1881, under the auspices of Tony Pastor. Acts were usually booked on regional and national circuits, theatrical alliances that prefigured the system frequently used for **road companies** of Broadway shows.

THE VELVET LADY **(3 FEBRUARY 1919, NEW AMSTERDAM, 136 PERFORMANCES).** Music by **Victor Herbert**, lyrics by **Henry Blossom**, book by Fred Jackson. Based on Jackson's farce *A Full House, The Velvet Lady*'s title character, nightclub singer Vera Vernon (Fay Marbe), does not appear until the last 15 minutes of the show, but in terms of characters she was the highlight. George Howell (Ray Raymond) heads to Boston to recover letters that his sister's fiancé once wrote to Vera. On the train back, George accidentally picks up a bag of stolen jewels rather than the letters, considerably confusing his wife, Ottilie (Marie Flynn), but the Velvet Lady appears to set things aright. John Corbin, reviewing the show for the *New York Times*, suggested that the show's "velvet," until the last 15 minutes, "was mainly supplied by Victor Herbert," especially by his waltzes "in the very best mood of the Viennese composers." At the end, however, the Velvet Lady came on stage bearing "a radiance of charm" and carried the show. The hit song was "Life and Love."

VERDON, GWEN (GWYNETH EVELYN VERDON, 1925–2000). The versatile actress and dancer's Broadway credits include Claudine in *Can-Can*, Lola in *Damn Yankees,* Anna Christie in *New Girl in Town*, Essie Whimpole in *Redhead*, Charity Hope Valentine in *Sweet Charity*, and Roxie Hart in *Chicago*. Verdon's realistic portrayal of strong females came in large part through her ability to have her singing voice emerge naturally and barely perceptibly from her speaking voice.

VEREEN, BEN (1946–). African American actor, singer, and dancer who created the roles of Judas Iscariot in *Jesus Christ Superstar* (1971) and Leading Player in *Pippin* (1972), winning a **Tony Award** for the latter. Notable **replacement** roles include Chimney Man in *Jelly's Last Jam* and The Wonderful Wizard of Oz in *Wicked*. He also appeared as a replacement in *Fosse*.

VERSE. Many Broadway songs, especially those from the early and middle parts of the 20th century, are constructed in two fundamental parts, the verse and the **refrain**. The refrain is the "famous tune" that people tend to remember, while the verse is the part of the song that sets up the mood and dramatic situation for the refrain. The musical style is often closer to speech-singing, and verses are often omitted in **reprises**. The verse's associative nonmelodiousness (though this is certainly not always the case) is referred to in "You're the Top" from *Anything Goes*. Verses can range from being fairly simple to small-scale scenes (as in "Deep in My Heart, Dear" from *The Student Prince*).

VERSE-REFRAIN FORM. The most common design for Broadway songs. A **verse**, which is close to speech-singing and often sets the mood for the song, is followed by the **refrain**, the part of the song that normally contains the memorable melody.

***VERY GOOD EDDIE* (23 DECEMBER 1915, PRINCESS, 341 PERFORMANCES).** Music by **Jerome Kern**, lyrics by Schuyler Greene, book by **Guy Bolton** and Philip Bartholomae. Based on Bartholomae's farce *Over Night*, *Very Good Eddie* was an early show to include a somewhat believable plot and the integration of songs with the dramatic action. Set aboard the Hudson River Day Liner *Catskill* and at the Rip Van Winkle Inn, the plot involves two honeymooning couples: Eddie and Georgina Kettle (Ernest Truex and Helen Raymond) and Percy and Elsie Darling (John Willard and Alice Dovey). Complications ensue, causing the hotel clerk to eventually declare, "Very good, Eddie." Among the songs were "Isn't It Great to Be Married?," "Wedding Bells Are Calling Me," "If I Find the Girl," "Babes in the Wood," and "Size Thirteen Collar," the latter Eddie's lament for his small size. "Babes in the Wood" became the biggest hit. The critics gave *Very Good Eddie* a mixed reception. The critic for the *World* called it "very, very good only in the acting," and the *Press* noted that the show "is not going to set any fashions in musical comedies." Heywood Broun, writing for the *Tribune*, said the music "is not pretentious, and no muses leaped and clapped their hands when the book was written, but for all of that it is an agreeable entertainment." The 1975 revival featured different songs and a campy presentation. *See also* PRINCESS THEATRE MUSICALS.

VICTOR/VICTORIA **(25 OCTOBER 1995, MARQUIS, 734 PERFORMANCES).** Music by Henry Mancini and **Frank Wildhorn**, lyrics by **Leslie Bricusse**, book and direction by Blake Edwards, choreography by **Rob Marshall**. A stage version of Blake Edwards's successful musical film, *Victor/Victoria* brought **Julie Andrews** back to Broadway after an absence of more than 30 years. She played Victoria Grant, an English singer whose career has failed. She finds herself in Paris, where a gay friend, Carroll Todd (Tony Roberts) cooks up the wild scheme that she can become a man who works as a female impersonator. The plan succeeds, and she wows Paris of the 1930s as a nightclub entertainer. An American gangster, King Marchan (Michael Nouri), finds himself strangely attracted to this creature that he believes to be a man, but they do get together in the end after the confusion has been resolved. Marchan's girlfriend is Norma Cassidy, played as a ditsy, blonde bombshell by Rachel York. The cast was excellent, but many criticized other aspects of the show, including a director who was more comfortable in film. Writing in the *New York Times*, Vincent Canby raved about Andrews, writing that she still "looks terrific and sings with a sweet purity." He also praised her diction, which survived the amplification, and her "grandly funny stage presence." Since Henry Mancini, who wrote the music for the film, died before finishing the new score, Wildhorn collaborated with original lyricist Bricusse on some new songs. The most memorable songs, however, were those from the film, including the production number "Jazz Hot" and "You and Me," the latter a soft-shoe number for Andrews and Roberts. *See also* HOMOSEXUALITY.

– W –

WALKER, GEORGE (1873–1911). African American comedian, singer, and dancer who formed a **vaudeville** act with **Bert Williams**, and the two starred together in three Broadway musicals: *In Dahomey*, *Abyssinia*, and *Bandana Land* (1907). Walker had to leave *Bandana Land* in 1909 because of illness, and his wife, Ada Overton Walker, a leading performer with the company, took over his role.

WALKER, NANCY (BORN ANNA MYRTLE SWOYER, 1922–1992). Actress known for her dry comic delivery who made her Broadway debut in the **musical comedy** *Best Foot Forward* (1941) before creating the randy taxi driver Hildy Esterhazy in *On the Town* (1944). She appeared in various **revues** and musical comedies during the 1940s and 1950s, and starred as long-suffering Kay Cram in *Do Re Mi* (1960).

WALSTON, RAY (1914–2001). Comic actor who played Mac in *Me and Juliet* (1953), Captain Jonas in *House of Flowers* (1954), and who won a **Tony Award** for creating Applegate in *Damn Yankees* (1956). He played Luther Billis in the 1958 film version of *South Pacific* and created the lovable Uncle Martin in the television comedy *My Favorite Martian* (1963–1966).

***WATCH YOUR STEP* (8 DECEMBER 1914, NEW AMSTERDAM, 175 PERFORMANCES).** Music and lyrics by **Irving Berlin**, book by **Harry B. Smith**. The first show to have a score entirely by Irving Berlin, who had released "Alexander's Ragtime Band" three years before, *Watch Your Step* occupied the nether region between **musical comedy** and **revue**. Jabez Hardacre has died and left his fortune to whichever male relative has never been in love, engaged, or married.

Two of his family members are investigated on and off for the remainder of the evening. In the meantime, however, entertainers appear on the scene, including dancers Vernon and Irene Castle and the African American Frank Tinney, who until recently had been working in Europe. Berlin composed a huge score of 20 songs, including "The Syncopated Walk," "Show Us How to Do the Fox Trot" and "Simple Melody." A grand opera spoof, done to the irritation of Giuseppe Verdi's ghost, dominated act 2. The reviewer in the *New York Times* called *Watch Your Step* "hilarious fun" and termed Berlin's contribution "a score of mad melodies, nearly all of them of the tickling sort."

WATERS, ETHEL (1900–1977). African American singing actress known for her work in **vaudeville** and **revue**. As a star in **Irving Berlin**'s *As Thousands Cheer* (1933), she introduced "Heat Wave" and "Supper Time" and portrayed **Josephine Baker**. She also appeared in *At Home Abroad* (1935), another revue, before playing Petunia Jackson in **Vernon Duke**'s *Cabin in the Sky* (1940). She reprised the role in the 1943 film. In 1953, she starred in the retrospective *At Home with Ethel Waters*.

WEBB, CLIFTON (1891–1966). Fine dancer and singer (a tenor) with an elegant stage presence who appeared in *Sunny* (1925), *Treasure Girl* (1928), *The Little Show* (1929), *Three's a Crowd* (1930), and *As Thousands Cheer* (1933). He introduced the **George** and **Ira Gershwin** standard "I've Got a Crush on You" in *Treasure Girl*.

WEBER, JOSEPH (1867–1942). He formed a popular **vaudeville** partnership with **Lew Fields**; the duo became the quintessential "Dutch" (a corruption of "Deutsch"—German) act and spawned many imitators. The team opened a theater on Broadway in 1896, offering **burlesques** and parodies of popular hits (much like *Forbidden Broadway* in the late 20th and early 21st centuries). After dissolving the partnership in 1904, Weber remained active as a performer and a producer.

***THE WEDDING SINGER* (27 APRIL 2006, AL HIRSCHFIELD, 285 PERFORMANCES).** Music by Matthew Sklar, lyrics by Chad

Beguelin, book by Beguelin and Tim Herlihy, directed by John Rando. Based on the 1998 film, the lighthearted romantic show with plenty of dancing was filled with references to the 1980s in its plot, jokes, and music, including the high-energy "Wedding Day." Stephen Lynch made his Broadway debut in the title role.

WEEDE, ROBERT (BORN ROBERT WIEDEFELD, 1903–1972). One of the finest American baritones of the 20th century, Weede was equally at home on opera and musical theater stages. He created Tony in *The Most Happy Fella* (1956), stating that the part was as vocally demanding as any opera role. Subsequent Broadway credits included *Milk and Honey* (1961) and *Cry for Us All* (1970).

WEIDMAN, JOHN (1946–). Librettist whose collaborations with **Stephen Sondheim** include *Pacific Overtures* (1976) and *Assassins* (1991). He also created a new book for the 1987 **Lincoln Center Theatre revival** of *Anything Goes* and the libretto for *Big: The Musical* (1996). He conceived and created the book for **Susan Stroman**'s **dance musical** *Contact* (2000).

WEILL, KURT (1900–1950). To avoid Nazi persecution, Weill and his wife, **Lotte Lenya**, immigrated to the United States in 1935. His Broadway scores include *Knickerbocker Holiday* (1938), *Lady in the Dark* (1941), *One Touch of Venus* (1943), *Street Scene* (1947), *Love Life* (1948), and *Lost in the Stars* (1949). His *Die Dreigroschenoper* (1928) appeared on Broadway as *The Threepenny Opera* (1954). Weill successfully combined tuneful music, serious dramatic themes, and aspects of **social justice** in his shows. His music is closely wedded to the plot. He strove to bridge the divide between **opera** and Broadway, and many of his roles require classically trained singers. In the early 21st century, his works are performed by both theater and opera companies.

WESTENBERG, ROBERT (ALSO KNOWN AS BOB WESTENBERG, 1953–). Singing actor with a resonant baritone voice who made his Broadway debut as Nikos in the 1983 **revival** of *Zorba*. He played Alex and the Soldier in **Stephen Sondheim**'s *Sunday in the Park with George* (1984) and was a **replacement** George. He created

Cinderella's Prince and Wolf in Sondheim's *Into the Woods* (1987) and Dr. Neville Craven in *The Secret Garden* (1991).

WEST SIDE STORY (26 SEPTEMBER 1957, WINTER GARDEN, 732 PERFORMANCES). Music by **Leonard Bernstein**, lyrics by **Stephen Sondheim**, book by **Arthur Laurents**, choreographed and directed by **Jerome Robbins**, presented by Robert E. Griffith and **Harold S. Prince**. A modern retelling of Shakepeare's *Romeo and Juliet* set among youth gangs in New York City, *West Side Story* represents a high level of artistic integration between plot, music, and dance. Robbins first conceived the idea in 1949, basing it upon conflict between Irish Catholics and Jews. He brought Laurents and Bernstein into the project, but they were too busy and work ceased. They resumed discussions in the mid-1950s and created the show while Bernstein simultaneously worked on *Candide*. The composer intended to write the lyrics, but finally asked the young Sondheim to join his first Broadway creative team. Robbins, Bernstein, Sondheim, and Laurents worked closely together, drawing song placements from Laurents's spare plot and telling much of the story through Robbins's expressive dances. The significance of dance in the show becomes clear in the "Prologue," which effectively introduces the plot in dance and pantomime. Although the show's parallels to *Romeo and Juliet* are many, Laurents made a number of changes, especially the ending, where he gave the surviving female lead a powerful, spoken plea for reason.

Robbins insisted that the entire cast should be dancers, except for Tony and María, who sing the most, but even the romantic leads dance. The cast was composed largely of unknowns—including **Larry Kert** (Tony), **Carol Lawrence** (María), and **Chita Rivera** (Anita)—allowing Robbins to forge a tight ensemble. He insisted that dancers develop personalities for every character and rigidly maintain their gang identities, even during rehearsal breaks. Robbins more or less choreographed the entire show, allowing inarticulate characters to express themselves through dance. Bernstein's score shows a sense of musicodramatic unification and sophistication rare on Broadway to that point. It is unified musically by the frequent use of the tritone and melodic and rhythmic motives. The score's gritty realism comes from a mixture of vernacular references, especially various types of jazz and Latin music, the latter very popular in contemporary dance halls. Bernstein's music for the romantic leads is often based on Latin or Caribbean rhythms, and includes some of his most inspired melodies, such as "María," "Tonight," and "One Hand, One Heart." The musical representation of the gangs, heard in the "Prologue," "Jet Song," "Rumble," "Cool," and other pieces, was violent and dissonant, and based upon models such as Igor Stravinsky, Woody Herman, Dizzy Gillespie, and Milt Jackson. The score had a brilliant comic song in "Gee, Officer Krupke" and the winning, energetic "America" was a Mexican *huapango*. In later years Sondheim expressed displeasure with his lyrics for the show, believing them too clever, but others have found honest emotion in them. Although the show now has iconic status, the initial critical reception was mixed. **Brooks Atkinson** summed it up in the opening of his *New York Times* review: "Although the material is horrifying, the workmanship is admirable." He found early moments of the show to be "facile and a little forbidding," but was won over by the "tender and affecting" balcony scene featuring the "perfectly cast" Larry Kert and Carol Lawrence and then found the remainder of the show "incandescent."

WHAT MAKES SAMMY RUN? **(24 FEBRUARY 1964, 54TH STREET, 540 PERFORMANCES).** Music and lyrics by Ervin Drake, book by Budd and Stuart Schulberg. Based on Budd Schulberg's 1941 novel of the same name, *What Makes Sammy Run?* featured Steve Lawrence, a popular nightclub performer, as Sammy Glick, a jerk who rises in Hollywood by stealing other people's work and jobs. He meets a nice secretary (**Sally Ann Howes**), but leaves her to romance the chairman of the board's daughter, Laurette Harrington (Bernice Massi). **Howard Taubman**, writing in the *New York Times*, asked, "Are you willing to wait until a puppet like Sammy runs through . . . a hard-nosed musical and becomes a human figure?" The outstanding songs included "A Room without Windows" and "My Hometown."

WHEATLEY, WILLIAM (1816–1876). Actor, producer, and manager who is credited with assembling *The Black Crook* (1877), an extravaganza that was so successful it allowed Wheatley to retire two years after its debut.

WHEELER, HUGH (1912–1987). English-born librettist, playwright, and author who won a **Tony Award** for *A Little Night Music* (1973) with a score by **Stephen Sondheim**. He continued his collaboration with Sondheim, contributing material to *Pacific Overtures* (1976) and writing the Tony Award-winning libretto for *Sweeney Todd: The Demon Barber of Fleet Street* (1979). He created a new book for the 1973 **revival** of *Irene* and won a Tony Award for his adaptation of *Candide* the following year.

***WHERE'S CHARLEY* (11 OCTOBER 1948, ST. JAMES, 792 PER-FORMANCES).** Music and lyrics by **Frank Loesser**, book adapted and directed by **George Abbott**, dances directed by **George Balanchine**. Adapted from Brandon Thomas's farce *Charley's Aunt*, *Where's Charley* had the benefit of a well-known story and humorous expectations. The other most significant aspects of the production were its director, a master at whipping a **musical comedy** into a fast-paced frolic, and **Ray Bolger**, one of Broadway's biggest stars. Bolger careened through his role as Charley Wykeham, who cross-dresses, sings, and dances with great spirit. Other cast members included Doretta Morrow as Kitty Verdun, Allyn Ann McLerie as Amy Spettigue, and Jane Lawrence as Donna Lucia d'Alvadorez, Charley's real aunt. **Brooks Atkinson**, writing in the *New York Times*, opened by commenting that Ray Bolger makes "a mediocre musical show . . . enjoyable." When dancing, Bolger translates "love into leaps, whirls and comic staggers." Atkinson commented on Loesser's varied score, calling it "lively" and showing many different influences. The critic noted that the "ballets are cultivated," but "you can enjoy them," and mentions Abbott's usual "organization and tempo." One of the most famous moments in the show was the song "Once in Love with Amy," which Bolger performed in front of the closed curtain as a sing-along with the audience.

WHITE, GEORGE (1890–1968). Producer, director, and dancer who got his start in **vaudeville** and later as a dancer in *Ziegfeld Follies*. Ziegfeld fired White when the dancer told the producer that the quality of the dances in the *Follies* could be improved. White then produced his own series of **revues**, *George White's Scandals*, which lasted from 1919 to 1939, and gave Ziegfeld some stiff competition.

WHITE, ONNA (1922–2005). Choreographer and dancer whose dance sequences seem like natural extensions of everyday body movements. After working as an assistant to **Michael Kidd**, she choreographed *The Music Man* (on stage in 1957 and on film in 1962), *Mame* (1966), *1776* (1969), *I Love My Wife* (1977), and *Working* (1978).

WHOOPEE **(4 DECEMBER 1928, NEW AMSTERDAM, 379 PERFORMANCES).** Music by Walter Donaldson, lyrics by Gus Kahn, book by William Anthony McGuire, produced by **Florenz Ziegfeld**. Based on Owen Davis's play *The Nervous Wreck* from five years earlier, *Whoopee* was a popular vehicle for comedian **Eddie Cantor** within one of Ziegfeld's lavish productions. Cantor was Henry Williams, a hypochondriac who marries Sally Morgan (Frances Upton) so that she can escape marrying a man she dislikes and "save" herself for Waonenis (Paul Gregory). They go to an Indian reservation because Waonenis is said to be part Native American. He is not, but Sally still gets her man, and Williams goes back to his nurse, Mary Custer (Ethel Shutta). Ruth Etting played Leslie Daw, a movie star who came on occasionally to sing songs that had nothing to do with the plot. There were also the usual Ziegfeld beauties who appeared as, among other things, Native Americans riding actual horses. **J. Brooks Atkinson**, writing in the *New York Times*, noted that "Mr. Cantor has never been so enjoyable as a comedian." He appeared in the show in both blackface and without, accomplishing the former once by bursting out of a gas stove oven. The critic praised the score, noting composer "Walter Donaldson has composed an appropriate score worthy of better singing." Songs included "Love Is the Mountain," "Love Me or Leave Me," and the perennially popular "Makin' Whoopee."

THE WHO'S TOMMY **(22 APRIL 1993, ST. JAMES, 899 PERFORMANCES).** Music and lyrics by Peter Townshend, book by Townshend and Des McAnuff, additional music and lyrics by John Entwistle and Keith Moon, directed by McAnuff, choreography by Wayne Cilento. Based on the rock group The Who's 1969 double album that the group presented in various concert performances and made into a film in 1975, *The Who's Tommy* brought the story and music into a fully realized Broadway musical. As a four-year-old, Tommy watches his father come home from World War II and kill his mother's lover; the trauma leaves him deaf, mute, and blind. He becomes a world-renowned pinball wizard and recovers his lost senses at age 18 when his mother smashes the mirror in which he saw the murder. His celebrity evaporates, but his family remains. In *The Who's Tommy*, the title character appears at three different ages, with **Michael Cerveris** playing him at 18. He faces a distant father (Jonathan Dokuchitz), a mother (Marcia Mitzman) who ignores him, an uncle (Paul Kandel) who is sexually abusive, and numerous thugs. As **Frank Rich** noted in the *New York Times*, these characters make "'Tommy' a poster-simple political statement reflecting the stark rage of the Vietnam era." Des McAnuff's production included many special lighting effects, video screens, and an exploding pinball machine; at one point, he turned the entire theater into the inside of a pinball machine. Rich called the show "the authentic **rock musical**," a phenomenon that had eluded Broadway for 20 years. He found the show "not merely an entertainment juggernaut," but "surprisingly moving" and "completely alive in its own moment."

WICKED (30 OCTOBER 2003, GERSHWIN, 1,324 PERFOR-MANCES AS OF 31 DECEMBER 2006). Music and lyrics by **Stephen Schwartz**, book by Winnie Holzman, directed by Joe Mantello, choreographed by Wayne Cilento. A successful and imaginative adaptation of Gregory Maguire's novel of the same name, *Wicked* played on the continued American fascination with L. Frank Baum's fantasy *The Wonderful Wizard of Oz*. The creators drew characters, situations, and basic story from Maguire, but filled in many details of their own. Maguire turns the Oz story on its head, portraying the Wizard as an amoral interloper from another world who unifies the people of Oz against its talking animals. In the musical Glinda (**Kristin Chenoweth**) and the future Wicked Witch of the West, Elphaba (**Idina Menzel**), whose name is derived from L. Frank Baum's name, are college roommates and overcome their initial mutual dislike to become friends. Glinda, although occasionally realizing the Wizard's true nature, follows a conventional path for success and eventually parts company with Elphaba, whose crusade to help the animals leads her into conflict with authorities and gets her branded "wicked." The results of her "death" bring down the Wizard. Both Chenoweth and Menzel worked with the production for months before it opened, and their considerable vocal talents and rich stage personalities heavily influenced the writers. **Joel Grey** was the Wizard and Carole Shelley played Madame Morrible, his partner in evil. Production values were high, with a large set and stage effects, but the human element remained paramount, and the female protagonists stole the evening. A not-so-subtle subplot was how the problems of Oz might parallel those of early 21st-century America.

Wicked found great popularity with audiences but had less success with some critics. The tone of **Ben Brantley**'s review in the *New York Times*, "There's Trouble in Emerald City," accurately summarizes his review. He rhapsodized about Kristin Chenoweth, noting that "it's amazing how she keeps metamorphosing before your eyes and ears" as a singer and actor. He called her performance of the song "Popular" "a master class in musical phrasing." Schwartz's score exists primarily in the pop world, especially in the power ballads with rhythm-and-blues associations that he wrote for Idina Menzel, but there are also a host of classical references and moments conditioned by his love for earlier Broadway shows, and his lyrics are witty and helpful to the characterization. Schwartz also unified the score with several telling motifs. Menzel was unforgettable in the hopeful "The Wizard and I" and the powerful act 1 finale, "Defying Gravity." Chenoweth showed how ambivalent and deep Glinda could be in "I Couldn't Be Happier," and her duet with Menzel at the end, "For Good," is one of the show's most moving songs. Schwartz wrote a wonderful "falling into hate" number in "What Is This Feeling," sung by the two women soon after they meet. *See also THE WIZ; THE WIZARD OF OZ.*

WILDCAT **(16 DECEMBER 1960, ALVIN, 171 PERFOR-MANCES).** Music by **Cy Coleman**, lyrics by Carolyn Leigh, book by N. Richard Nash, staged by **Michael Kidd**. Based on Nash's original story, *Wildcat* remains in the Broadway consciousness only because it starred **Lucille Ball** in her only lead role in a musical, and for the stirring march "Hey, Look Me Over!" Ball played Wildcat Jackson, a rough-and-ready gal who comes to Centavo City in 1912 with her disabled sister, Jane (Paula Stewart), to strike it rich in oil. She meets and falls in love with Joe Dynamite (Keith Andes) and makes him the foreman of her well. After many failed attempts, they finally strike oil. The best notices went to the star. **Howard Taubman**, writing for the *New York Times*, noted that *Wildcat* "had as much spirit and excitement as a tame, old tabby," but that Ball gave it her best, "singing and dancing with zest and reading her lines with an expert's timing."

WILDFLOWER (7 FEBRUARY 1923, CASINO, 477 PERFORMANCES). Music by **Herbert Stothart** and **Vincent Youmans**, lyrics and book by **Otto Harbach** and **Oscar Hammerstein II**. A vehicle for **Edith Day**, *Wildflower* was an extremely successful if pedestrian show that ended up being Day's final work before she left for London. She played Nina Benedetto, who inherits a small fortune on the condition that she has no displays of temper for six months. A cousin tempts her sorely, but she wins the legacy and her lover, Guido (Guy Robertson). The *New York Times* panned the book as "practically never funny, and now and then even a little dull," but "the songs are worked into the piece with not a little cleverness." Youmans's songs, his first for Broadway, included the hit "Bambalina."

WILDHORN, FRANK (1958–). Composer whose Broadway debut consisted of new songs with lyrics by **Leslie Bricusse** for *Victor/Victoria* (1995). His Broadway scores include *Jekyll and Hyde* (lyrics by Bricusse), *The Scarlet Pimpernel* (book and lyrics by Nan Knighton), *The Civil War* (1999, for which he was colibrettist), and *Dracula* (2004, book and lyrics by Don Black and Christopher Hampton). His music is rooted in a lush romantic style that adds emotional depth to the stories he sets.

THE WILD PARTY (13 APRIL 2000, VIRGINIA, 68 PERFORMANCES). Music and lyrics by **Michael John La Chiusa**, book by La Chiusa and George C. Wolfe. Based on the notorious 1928 poem by Joseph Moncure March, *The Wild Party* addresses the urban alienation, disorientation, and ambivalence of not only the late 1920s, the setting of the musical, but also the turn of the 21st century. Decadence, American Modernism, and interactions between whites and **African Americans** are central to the show, which includes aspects of **concept musical**, **vaudeville**, and **revue**. The plot concerns the tragic events surrounding a party hosted by Queenie (Toni Collette), a blond vaudeville dancer, and her live-in lover Burrs (**Mandy Patinkin**), a comedian prone to violence. The score is a vivid pastiche of American music styles of the late 1920s. La Chiusa's musical was the second *Wild Party* to appear in New York in 2000; an **off-Broadway** musical with the same title and source material, with book, music, and lyrics by Andrew Lippa, opened at the Manhattan Theatre Club City Center Stage I on 24 February 2000 and played for 88 performances.

WILKINSON, COLM (1944–). Irish-born singing actor who created the role of Jean Valjean in the London (1985) and Broadway (1987) productions of *Les Misérables*. His dramatic voice and acting ability have caused many fans of the show to dub him the "definitive Valjean." He was a member of the 1970s Irish band "The Action" and represented Ireland in the 1978 Eurovision Song Contest. After *Les Mis*, he sang the title role in the Toronto production of *The Phantom of the Opera* (1989), a part he originated in 1985 at one of **Andrew Lloyd Webber**'s Sydmonton workshops.

WILLIAMS, BERT (1874–1922). African American singer, dancer, and comedian who began his career in minstrel shows, in blackface, and later refused to make fun of his race. He formed a **vaudeville** act with **George Walker**, and the two starred together in three Broadway musicals: *In Dahomey*, *Abyssinia*, and *Bandana Land* (1907). Williams appeared in *Ziegfeld Follies* from 1910 to 1919, and was the first African American to appear alongside whites in a major Broadway production and the first African American to receive star billing in a white-oriented show.

WILLIAMS, VANESSA (1963–). The pop singer who was the first **African American** Miss America was a **replacement** Spider Woman/Aurora in *Kiss of the Spider Woman* in 1994, and played the Witch in the 2002 **revival** of *Into the Woods*.

***THE WILL ROGERS FOLLIES* (1 MAY 1991, PALACE, 981 PERFORMANCES).** Music by **Cy Coleman**, lyrics by **Betty Comden** and **Adolph Green**, book by **Peter Stone**, directed and choreographed by **Tommy Tune**. A show said to be "inspired by the words of Will and Betty Rogers," *The Will Rogers Follies* combined a biographical treatment of this noted American humorist with a modern version of the *Ziegfeld Follies*, in which Rogers performed. Keith Carradine played the title character, and Paul Ukena Jr. played Wiley Post, the pilot with whom Rogers died in a plane crash in 1935. In the show, Post keeps asking if Rogers if he would like to fly with him. Between segments about Rogers, Tune re-created the effect of the *Ziegfeld Follies*, with its variety of acts and female chorus clad in dazzling costumes. **Frank Rich**, writing in the *New York Times*, did not know what to do with the show, which he called "the most disjointed musical of this or any other season." He described Carradine as "beguiling," but simply did not understand combining Rogers's life story with the Ziegfeld numbers. Rich found a musical about an entertainer who neither sang nor danced a strange idea, and Stone's "book is longer on exposition than humor," but the Ziegfeld-inspired numbers included "breathtaking" costumes and show Tune to be "a master of his particular art." Musical highlights included "Willamania," "Our Favorite Son," and "Never Met a Man I Didn't Like."

WILLSON, MEREDITH (ROBERT MEREDITH REINIGER, 1902–1984). His triumphal Broadway debut was as creator of music, book, and lyrics for *The Music Man* (1957). Two other musicals, *The Unsinkable Molly Brown* (1960) and *Here's Love* (1963), followed, although neither achieved the popularity of *The Music Man*. Willson knew firsthand about bands and the Midwest, two central aspects of *The Music Man*, for he played flute and piccolo in John Philip Sousa's band (and later, the New York Philharmonic) and grew up in Mason City, Iowa. His music demonstrates an appealing blend of popular and sophisticated styles.

WINNINGER, CHARLES (1884–1969). Vaudeville actor, singer, and dancer whose comic antics and acrobatic abilities made him an audience favorite. He created the character of Jimmy Smith in *No, No, Nanette* (1925) and ended "I Want to Be Happy" with a back flip. His greatest fame was as Cap'n Andy Hawks in *Show Boat* (1927), a role he reprised on Broadway in 1932 and on film in 1936.

WISH YOU WERE HERE **(25 JUNE 1952, IMPERIAL, 598 PER-FORMANCES).** Music and lyrics by **Harold Rome**, book by Arthur Kober and **Joshua Logan**, directed by Logan. Based on Arthur Kober's 1937 play *Having a Wonderful Time*, *Wish You Were Here* was a lavishly produced show about fun and romance at a Jewish summer camp. The set included an actual swimming pool and outdoor scenery, but problems with content caused the opening to be postponed several times. The elaborate set made out-of-town tryouts impossible, so there were previews in New York City. The critical response was devastating, but popular singer Eddie Fisher recorded the title song and turned it into a hit. This, and a good advance sale, gave the show some commercial appeal. The plot involved a romance between Teddy Stern (Patricia Marand) and Chuck Miller (**Jack Cassidy**) at Camp Karefree. Doubts arise about Teddy's fidelity, but she clears her name. Rome's score included the fine title song, the ballad "Where Did the Night Go?," and some good comedy songs sung by Sidney Armus as Itchy Flexner, the camp's social director.

THE WIZ **(5 JANUARY 1975, MAJESTIC, 1,672 PERFOR-MANCES).** Music and lyrics by Charlie Smalls, book by William F. Brown, direction and costumes by Geoffrey Holder, choreography and musical numbers staged by George Faison. An **African American** adaptation of L. Frank Baum's famous fantasy *The Wonderful Wizard of Oz*, *The Wiz* rode a vibrant pop score and memorable sense of style to a long run. The plot was closer to Baum's original story than the famous MGM movie. Here Dorothy was Stephanie Mills, a 15-year-old whom **Clive Barnes** described in the *New York Times* as "having a really wonderful voice, unusually mature." The Scarecrow (**Hinton Battle**), Tinman (Tiger Haynes), and Lion (Ted Ross) were part of an "admirable" cast, and "the singing throughout was first rate," especially that of Mabel King as Evillene and Dee Dee Bridgewater as Glinda. Bridgewater won a **Tony Award** for her role and went on to a significant career as a jazz singer. The visual impact of the production was striking, with "vibrantly colored and wackily imaginative costumes by Geoffrey Holder." The music was largely in rock, gospel, and soul styles. The one song that became famous outside of the production was the lively "Ease on Down the Road." *See also WICKED; THE WIZARD OF OZ.*

THE WIZARD OF OZ **(20 JANUARY 1903, MAJESTIC, 293 PER-FORMANCES).** Music by Paul Tietjens and A. Baldwin Sloan, lyrics and book by L. Frank Baum. Long before the famous MGM musical, there was a successful Broadway musical with lyrics and book by the original story's author. Baum changed the story substantially for this staged version, but Dorothy (Anna Laughlin) was still blown to Oz from her native Kansas, now with her cow. Fred Stone, the Scarecrow, and his vaudeville partner Dave Montgomery, the Tin Man, stole the show and launched their highly successful Broadway careers. The Cowardly Lion was relegated to a minor role. The scenery and other aspects of the production raised considerable comment as well, especially the cyclone. The score produced no hits, and the only songs that received commentary were **interpolations**. The unsigned review in the *New York Times* includes praise for the principal members of the cast. Anna Laughlin is "charmingly girlish and graceful," singing "with pretty humor." Stone and Montgomery raise considerable admiration, especially as dancers. As the Scarecrow, Stone managed "musical nonsense wherever he went." Montgomery, despite his ungainly costume, was "clever and characteristic" when hoofing. *See also WICKED*; *THE WIZ*.

WODEHOUSE, P. G. (PELHAM GRENVILLE WODEHOUSE, 1881–1975). English comic novelist, lyricist, and librettist, who, with **Guy Bolton** and **Jerome Kern**, created the legendary **Princess Theatre musicals**, which included *Oh, Boy!* (1917). Bolton and Wodehouse worked with **George** and **Ira Gershwin** on *Oh, Kay!* (1926) and with **Cole Porter** on the first script for *Anything Goes* (1934). He created the famous Jeeves and Wooster characters, which were the basis for **Andrew Lloyd Webber**'s *By Jeeves* (2001).

THE WOMAN IN WHITE **(17 NOVEMBER 2005, MARQUIS, 109 PERFORMANCES).** Music by **Andrew Lloyd Webber**, lyrics by David Zippel, book by Charlotte Jones, directed by **Trevor Nunn**. "Loosely based on the novel by Wilkie Collins," *The Woman in White* is the tale of Anne Catherick (Angela Christian), the title character, who has a secret that will cause the downfall of Sir Percival Glyde (Ron Bohmer). The show's protagonists are Marian Halcombe (Maria Friedman, a noted British actress in her Broadway debut), the art teacher, Walter Hartright (Adam Brazier), and Marian's half-sister, Laura Fairlie (Jill Paice). In the musical, a love triangle occurs between the three protagonists that does not exist in Collins's novel. The manipulative Count Fosco (**Michael Ball**) dazzled the audience with his sociopathic "You Can Get Away with Anything." The production was changed from its original London version, with many of the subtleties made obvious, and a new, happier ending appended. The show did not fare well on Broadway, perhaps because of its nearly operatic music and Lloyd Webber's sophisticated use of **reprise** or else its source material, which was largely unknown to American audiences. The set consisted principally of video projections designed by William Dudley, which simultaneously created a sense of mystery and grandeur alongside the plot's tremendous intimacy. The score's highlights include the soaring ballad "I Believe My Heart," Laura's emotive "If I Could Only Dream This World Away," and Marian and Fosco's tango, "The Seduction."

WOMAN OF THE YEAR (**29 MAY 1981, PALACE, 770 PERFORMANCES**). Music by **John Kander**, lyrics by **Fred Ebb**, book by **Peter Stone**, directed by **Robert Moore**. Based on the famous MGM movie starring Katherine Hepburn and Spencer Tracy, the musical *Woman of the Year* was conceived as a vehicle for **Lauren Bacall**. Bacall played Tess Harding, a famous television journalist, and her paramour was Sam Craig (Harry Guardino), a successful cartoonist. Bacall's notices were luminous. Writing in the *New York Times*, **Frank Rich** rhapsodized about "her class . . . angular physique, her big, sensuous eyes and that snapdragon of a voice . . . she remains not only mesmerizing, but also completely fresh." Rich was not nearly so sanguine about the remainder of the show. He called Kander's score "tuneful," Ebb's lyrics "routine," Stone's book not sufficiently funny, and thought that the production lacked opulence. It is possible that Rich and other reviewers missed the show's essential strengths, because when Bacall left the production, it continued running with Raquel Welch in the starring role. The score included the song "The Grass Is Always Greener."

WONDERFUL TOWN (**25 FEBRUARY 1953, WINTER GARDEN, 559 PERFORMANCES**). Music by **Leonard Bernstein**, lyrics by

Betty Comden and **Adolph Green**, book by Joseph Fields and Jerome Chodorov, choreographed by Donald Saddler, staged by **George Abbott**. A vehicle for **Rosalind Russell**, Abbott and Fryer held an option for the star to appear in a musical version of the play *My Sister Eileen* by Fields and Chodorov, but the first musical team dragged its feet on the score, and Abbott convinced Bernstein, Comden, and Green to write the songs, which they did in six weeks. The creators brilliantly evoked the 1930s in this story of two sisters who leave Columbus, Ohio, to move to Greenwich Village, where they seek their fortunes. Their success is nebulous, but the many hysterical comic situations were adequate fodder for the inspired clowning of Russell and **Edie Adams**, who played her sister. **Brooks Atkinson** fawned over Adams, calling her "absolutely perfect," but Russell was even better: "she makes the whole city wonderful." He noted that the writers, composer, and choreographer "settled down joyfully to the creation of a beautifully organized fandango." The score included a number of gems, among them "Christopher Street," "Wrong Note Rag," "Conversation Piece," "Ohio," "Conga!," "Pass the Football," "One Hundred Easy Ways," "It's Love," and "A Little Bit in Love." The 2003 revival, which sparked a renewed interest in the show, including a touring production, starred **Donna Murphy**.

WOOD, PEGGY (1892–1979). Wood achieved tremendous fame as Ottilie in **Sigmund Romberg**'s *Maytime*, and created the role of Sarah Millick in the original London production of **Noel Coward**'s *Bitter Sweet.* Her stunning looks and clear soprano voice made her a fine **operetta** heroine. Late in life, she played the Mother Abbess in the 1965 film version of *The Sound of Music*, but her singing had to be dubbed.

WOOLLCOTT, ALEXANDER (1887–1943). One of the most prolific drama critics for the *New York Times* during the 1920s, Woollcott was known for his caustic wit and florid writing style. He also wrote the "Shouts and Murmurs" column for the *New Yorker* magazine and numerous books, including one about **Irving Berlin** (*The Story of Irving Berlin*, 1925). He was a member of the Algonquin Round Table, a group of writers that included **Dorothy Parker**, and was one of the most quoted writers of his generation.

WRIGHT, ROBERT (1914–2005). Composer and lyricist whose work with **George Forrest** began in Los Angeles nightclubs before they wrote songs for 58 different films. On Broadway, their best-known shows featured adaptations of famous melodies by earlier composers. These included *Song of Norway* (1944, Edvard Grieg), *Gypsy Lady* (1946, **Victor Herbert**), *Kismet* (1953, Alexander Borodin), and *Anya* (1964, Sergei Rachmaninoff). Their original musical *Grand Hotel*, which closed out of town during its **tryout** in 1958, finally arrived on Broadway in 1989, directed by **Tommy Tune** and with additional music by **Maury Yeston**.

WYNN, ED (1886–1966). Comic actor who appeared in numerous **revues**, including *Ziegfeld Follies*, *Over the Top* (1917), and, decades later, *Laugh Town Laugh* (1942). He led the cast in **Rudolf Friml**'s **musical comedy** *Sometime* (1918). Wynn was an important star of early radio and television, and played Uncle Albert in the 1964 film *Mary Poppins*, delighting audiences with "I Love to Laugh," a testimony to his long and illustrious career.

– Y –

YAZBEK, DAVID (1960–). Composer and lyricist for *The Full Monty* (2000) and *Dirty Rotten Scoundrels* (2005) who possesses an intrinsic ability to work in multiple popular music styles. Yazbek has also released rock albums, written for late-night talk show host David Letterman, composed commercial jingles and music for children's television shows, and been active as a record producer.

A YEAR WITH FROG AND TOAD **(13 APRIL 2003, CORT, 73 PERFORMANCES).** Music by Robert Reale, book and lyrics by Willie Reale. Based on the "Frog and Toad" books by Arnold Lobel, the 90-minute **family musical** received strong reviews in the *New York Times* and yielded an original cast recording, despite its short run. Mark Linn-Baker and Jay Goede played the title characters.

YESTON, MAURY (1945–). Composer of *Nine* (1982), additional songs for *Grand Hotel* (1989), and *Titanic* (1997), Yeston taught at

Yale University and is the author of two music theory books, *The Stratification of Rhythm* and *Readings in Schenker Analysis and Other Approaches*. His music is characterized by a strong sense of design, lyrical expansiveness, and a notable ability to create a sense of time and place through musical means. He also wrote music for *Phantom* (1991), a version of the same tale immortalized in music by **Andrew Lloyd Webber**. Yeston's *Phantom* did not appear on Broadway.

YIP! YIP! YAPHANK! (2 SEPTEMBER 1918, CENTURY, 32 PERFORMANCES). Music and lyrics by **Irving Berlin**. In an effort to make his army hitch more palatable, Berlin convinced the brass at Camp Upton to allow him to put on a **revue** with his mates at the camp, the proceeds slated for building a camp community building. There were several memorable aspects to the show, not the least of which were the large size of the cast and the outrageous chorus "girls," all soldiers in drag. The content included a send-up of a possible visit to camp by the *Ziegfeld Follies* cast, with soldiers impersonating **Eddie Cantor** and **Ann Pennington**, a boxing demonstration by Benny Leonard, a famed prizefighter and camp instructor, and a juggler. Berlin's score, of course, helped make *Yip! Yip! Yaphank!* famous because it included the ironic number based on a bugle call, "Oh, How I Hate to Get Up in the Morning," one of the most famous songs to come out of World War I and among Berlin's biggest hits. Berlin sang the song himself in the revue. Another song was "Mandy," but it did not become a hit until Ziegfeld used it in the next *Follies*. The unsigned review in the *New York Times* was kind and positive, noting that the servicemen benefited "with the professional hand of Berlin at the helm." The revue "is vastly better" than "the average Broadway piece," and it also has the commercial advantage that it does not require a professional cast. The chorus provides "one long laugh," and the audience's favorite song was "Berlin's classic bugler lyric."

YOUMANS, VINCENT (1898–1946). A leading composer of **musical comedy**, Youmans's most famous shows include *Wildflower* (1923), the genre-defining *No, No, Nanette* (1925, including "Tea For Two"), *Hit the Deck* (1927), and the **Ethel Merman** vehicle *Take a*

Chance (1932). His music exuded rhythmic energy and melodic freshness, while his life was filled with trials and tribulations that were exacerbated by the success of his shows and his penchant for hedonism and alcohol.

YOUNG, RIDA JOHNSON (1869–1926). Librettist, lyricist, and playwright who created words for two genre-defining **operettas** of the 1910s, *Naughty Marietta* (1910, music by **Victor Herbert**) and *Maytime* (1917, music by **Sigmund Romberg**).

YOUR ARMS TOO SHORT TO BOX WITH GOD **(22 DECEMBER 1976, LYCEUM, 429 PERFORMANCES IN ORIGINAL RUN).** Music and lyrics by Alex Bradford and Micki Grant, book by Vinnette Carroll. An African American telling of the Holy Week narrative from the Gospel of Matthew, this show by the creators of *Don't Bother Me, I Can't Cope* was developed for the 1975 Spoleto Festival. The dominant musical style was gospel, a contrast to the fairly recent *Jesus Christ Superstar*. **Clive Barnes** observed in the *New York Times* that the Lloyd Webber-Rice show "was all trash and glitter," but *Your Arms Too Short* possesses "something of the emblematic simplicity of a medieval morality play." He called the show "funny and fervent." The show takes place in a chapel with a robed choir, and the cast changes into biblical costumes to tell the story. The story is sacred, but Barnes identifies many "rogues" in the plot as well. After telling their story, the cast returns to the choir robes for a tribute to famous gospel singers. Barnes praises the "infectious happiness" that the music and dancing bring the show. Among the cast he cited Jesus (Stanley Perryman), Judas (Héctor Jaime Mercado), and the singer Delores Hall, whose "I Love You So Much Jesus" stopped the show. *See also* AFRICAN AMERICAN MUSICALS.

YOU'RE A GOOD MAN, CHARLIE BROWN **(7 MARCH 1967, THEATER 80 ST. MARKS, 1,597 PERFORMANCES).** Music, lyrics, and book by Clark Gesner. A spectacular success as an off-Broadway show, this musical based on the popular *Peanuts* comic strip did not fare so well on Broadway. The original cast was superior to the Broadway actors, and the show lost its intimacy in a larger theater. The 1999 revival introduced **Kristin Chenoweth**, who won a

Tony Award for her portrayal of Sally. *You're a Good Man, Charlie Brown* offers a disjointed romp through typical *Peanuts* personalities and situations with pleasant songs and delightful characterizations, such as Snoopy's "Suppertime," Linus's "My Blanket and Me," and "Happiness Is."

YOU'RE IN LOVE (**6 FEBRUARY 1917, CASINO, 167 PERFOR-MANCES**). Music by **Rudolf Friml**, book and lyrics by **Otto Harbach** and Edward Clark, produced by **Arthur Hammerstein**. The shipboard **musical comedy** included colorful characters such as Georgianna, the sleepwalking heroine (Marie Flynn), her Auntie Payton, who has had three failed marriages (Florine Arnold), and Wix, a family friend who turns out to be Auntie's third husband (Al Roberts). Musical highlights included Auntie Payton's "Keep Off the Grass," Georgianna's sleepwalking song, "I'm Only Dreaming," and the syncopated title song.

YOUR OWN THING (**13 JANUARY 1968, ORPHEUM, 933 PER-FORMANCES**). Music and lyrics by Hal Hester and Danny Apolinar, book and staging by Donald Driver. Based on Shakespeare's *Twelfth Night*, *Your Own Thing* played off-Broadway for more than two years and spawned numerous touring companies. It was a simplified version of the story with only the lovers remaining. Orsino, or Orson (Tom Ligon) runs a rock group, while Olivia (Marian Mercer) owns a discothèque. The twins, Sebastian (Rusty Thacker) and Viola (Leland Palmer), cause their usual confusion, and in the end the right couples (Viola and Orson, Sebastian and Olivia) are together. The show took place in "Manhattan Island, Illyria," in other words, New York City. A major part of the show took place on screens, where famous commentators such as John Wayne, Humphrey Bogart, the pope, Shirley Temple, Shakespeare, Queen Elizabeth, and God as depicted in Michelangelo's Sistine Chapel ceiling offer barbs on the action. The music was in the rock style, but with a soft edge and allusions to other musical styles. **Clive Barnes** reviewed the show for the *New York Times*, pronouncing it "blissfully irreverent to Shakespeare and everything else." He called the show's humor "light-fingered and light-hearted" and praised the "vitality and charm" as "terrific." He noted that the script quotes the Bard, perhaps most effectively in the songs "Come Away Death" and "She Never Told Her Love." Barnes found delightful modern touches, such as when Orson starts to have feelings for Viola, whom he believes to be male, and investigates his possible latent **homosexuality**.

– Z –

ZIEGFELD, FLORENZ, JR. (ALSO KNOWN AS FLORENZ ZIEGFELD, 1867–1932). One of Broadway's legendary producers and impresarios, Ziegfeld shows were known for their opulence and quality. His series of **revues**, *Ziegfeld Follies*, epitomized the genre, and Ziegfeld assembled a creative team of the era's finest performers, composers, and lyricists for the legendary productions. **Joseph Urban** was responsible for many of the spectacular sets, including the elaborate staircases on which the long-legged chorus girls would appear. Ziegfeld also produced significant **book musicals**, including *Rio Rita* (1927, which opened his Ziegfeld Theater), the history-making *Show Boat* (1927), *Rosalie* (1928), *The Three Musketeers* (1928), *Whoopee* (1928), and *Bitter Sweet* (1929). His common-law wife was French music hall star **Anna Held**, whom he left in 1913 to marry comedienne Billie Burke.

ZIEGFELD FOLLIES **(JARDIN DE PARIS/LIBERTY/GRAND OPERA HOUSE: 8 JULY 1907, 70 PERFORMANCES; JARDIN DE PARIS/NEW YORK: 15 JUNE 1908, 120 PERFORMANCES; JARDIN DE PARIS: 14 JUNE 1909, 64 PERFORMANCES; 20 JUNE 1910, 88 PERFORMANCES; 26 JUNE 1911, 80 PERFORMANCES; MOULIN ROUGE: 21 OCTOBER 1912, 88 PERFORMANCES; NEW AMSTERDAM: 16 JUNE 1913, 96 PERFORMANCES; 1 JUNE 1914, 112 PERFORMANCES; 21 JUNE 1915, 104 PERFORMANCES; 12 JUNE 1916, 112 PERFORMANCES; 12 JUNE 1917, 111 PERFORMANCES; 18 JUNE 1918, 151 PERFORMANCES; 16 JUNE 1919, 171 PERFORMANCES; 22 JUNE 1920, 123 PERFORMANCES; 21 JUNE 1921, 119 PERFORMANCES; 5 JUNE 1922, 424 PERFORMANCES; 20 OCTOBER 1923, 333 PERFORMANCES; 24 JUNE 1924, 401 PERFORMANCES [IN-**

**CLUDING 1925 VERSION THAT FOLLOWED IMMEDI-
ATELY AND SOME SCHOLARS DO NOT LIST AS A SEPA-
RATE SHOW]; 16 AUGUST 1927, 167 PERFORMANCES;
GLOBE: 24 JUNE 1926, 108 PERFORMANCES; ZIEGFELD: 1
JULY 1931, 165 PERFORMANCES; WINTER GARDEN: 4
JANUARY 1934, 182 PERFORMANCES; 1 MARCH 1957, 123
PERFORMANCES; 30 JANUARY 1936, 115 PERFOR-
MANCES; WINTER GARDEN/IMPERIAL: 1 APRIL 1943, 553
PERFORMANCES).** (Notes about performances: "Ziegfeld" was
added to the title in 1911. In 1926, Ziegfeld legally enjoined from us-
ing "Follies" name; title of this show variously reported as *Ziegfeld's
American Revue* and *Ziegfeld's Revue "No Foolin'"*; usual name returned in 1927.) **Florenz Ziegfeld**, one of the Broadway's most significant producers, codified the **revue** with his long series of eponymous editions that lasted from 1907 until well past his death in 1932,
when the **Shubert** Brothers took over the name and irregularly produced shows for another quarter century. Ziegfeld hired prominent
lyricists and composers and brought to his stage Broadway's biggest
stars with the most lavish of sets and costumes. Many anecdotes exist on how much Ziegfeld spent for seemingly meaningless details of
scenery and costumes, but such extravagance was part of his brand
name. The cost of a production was part of his publicity campaign:
the 1921 edition was said to have cost more than $250,000. A major
part of the costume expense was what Ziegfeld used to "glorify the
American girl," a process so famous that the appellation "Ziegfeld
Girl" became an important measure of beauty. His "girls" formed his
large choruses, who often paraded down apparently endless staircases in scant costumes and full plumage.

Ziegfeld's common-law wife, **Anna Held**, suggested that a New
York City audience might enjoy a Parisian style revue. Ziegfeld was
more the manager of the first several editions, finally becoming producer in 1915. The so-called "Jardin de Paris" was the roof of the
New York Theatre with folding chairs and a corrugated iron roof,
open at the sides for ventilation. The 50 chorus girls were called the
"Anna Held Girls," and Ziegfeld's first featured beauty was
Annabelle Whitford dressed as the "Gibson Bathing Girl." Featured
dancers, singers, and comics filled out the evening, and the success
spawned future versions. The succession of stars who appeared in the

Follies over the years is a veritable who's who of entertainment: Mae Murray, Lillian Lorraine, **Bert Williams** (making him the first African American to appear in a Broadway revue), **Fannie Brice**, Vera Maxwell, **Ann Pennington**, **Ed Wynn**, W. C. Fields, **George White** (who started his own *Scandals* in 1919), Will Rogers, Frances White, Marion Davies, Justine Johnstone, **Eddie Cantor**, **Marilyn Miller**, Mary Eaton, **Leon Errol**, Gilda Gray, Gallagher & Shean, Louise Brown, Ray Dooley, Ruth Etting, Claire Luce, and **Helen Morgan**.

In the shows after Ziegfeld's death, a number of the stars who became famous in the *Follies* returned for the Shubert Brothers' editions, including Brice in 1933. New names included **Bob Hope**, **Eve Arden**, **Josephine Baker**, Gypsy Rose Lee, Milton Berle, **Fred Astaire**, and **Beatrice Lillie**. Through 1925, Gene Buck wrote many of the scripts and found many of the singers, dancers, and comics; Ziegfeld concentrated on the search for beauty. Austrian designer **Joseph Urban** worked on many of the editions from 1915 and helped create Ziegfeld's opulent look. His importance to the formula could be seen in his fee for the designs, which rose gradually from $5,000 to $30,000. Ziegfeld often produced a smaller floor show called *Midnight Frolic Roof* on top of the New Amsterdam Theater, sometimes bringing the successful acts from that venue into the *Follies*. Some suggest that Ziegfeld was somewhat less concerned about the music in his shows, but he routinely hired some of the best song-writing talent available. Composers who worked with him over the years included, among others, Maurice Levi, Gus Edwards, **Jerome Kern**, **Irving Berlin**, Louis Hirsch, **Victor Herbert**, **Rudolf Friml**, and **B. G. De Sylva**. Few entire scores were the work of a single composer, but **Irving Berlin** did write all of the songs for the 1927 edition. Songs that originated in the *Follies* included such hits as "Shine on Harvest Moon" (1908), "Row Row Row" (1912), "Have a Heart" (1916), and "A Pretty Girl Is Like a Melody" (1919, and thereafter the *Follies* anthem).

ZIEMBA, KAREN (1957–). Singer and dancer who took over roles in the original productions of *A Chorus Line* (1975), *42nd Street* (1980), and *Crazy for You* (1992) before creating the part of Rita Racine, a marathon dancer, in *Steel Pier* (1997). She also starred in the "Did You Move?" sequence of *Contact* (1999) as a housewife who imagines herself in lavish dance fantasies, winning the **Tony Award** for Best Featured Actress in a Musical for her performance.

ZIEN, CHIP (1947–). Singing actor with a particular gift for comic roles. He created the Baker in *Into the Woods* (1987), Mendel in *Falsettos* (1992), Dromio of Ephesus in the 2002 **revival** of *The Boys from Syracuse*, and Goran in *Chitty Chitty Bang Bang* (2005).

ZORBA THE GREEK **(17 NOVEMBER 1968, IMPERIAL, 305 PERFORMANCES).** Music by **John Kander**, lyrics by **Fred Ebb**, book by **Joseph Stein**, production staged and presented by **Harold Prince**. Based on the novel *Zorbá the Greek* by Nikos Kazantzakis and following a popular film starring Anthony Quinn, this musical included winning performances by Herschel Bernardi and other members of the cast. Ebb, Kander, and Prince had previously worked together on *Cabaret*, as had Stein and Prince on *Fiddler on the Roof*. *Zorba* was not the equal of those shows, but it was a good musical play with laudable points. In the title role, Bernardi played a Greek who lives life like he might die at any moment, all intuition and acting on instantaneous desires. He teaches Nikos (John Cunningham) his philosophy, helping this far more deliberate man through some very tough times, including his girlfriend's murder. The stage action included a singer in black leading two musicians playing bouzoukis and an authentic Greek chorus.

Appendix

Winners of the Tony Award for Best Musical, 1949–2006

1949	*Kiss Me, Kate*
1950	*South Pacific*
1951	*Guys and Dolls*
1952	*The King and I*
1953	*Wonderful Town*
1954	*Kismet*
1955	*The Pajama Game*
1956	*Damn Yankees*
1957	*My Fair Lady*
1958	*The Music Man*
1959	*Redhead*
1960	*The Sound of Music* and *Fiorello!* (tie)
1961	*Bye Bye Birdie*
1962	*How to Succeed in Business without Really Trying*
1963	*A Funny Thing Happened on the Way to the Forum*
1964	*Hello, Dolly!*
1965	*Fiddler on the Roof*
1966	*Man of La Mancha*
1967	*Cabaret*
1968	*Hallelujah, Baby!*
1969	*1776*
1970	*Applause*
1971	*Company*
1972	*Two Gentleman of Verona*
1973	*A Little Night Music*
1974	*Raisin*
1975	*The Wiz*
1976	*A Chorus Line*
1977	*Annie*

1978	*Ain't Misbehavin'*
1979	*Sweeney Todd: The Demon Barber of Fleet Street*
1980	*Evita*
1981	*42nd Street*
1982	*Nine*
1983	*Cats*
1984	*La Cage aux Folles*
1985	*Big River*
1986	*The Mystery of Edwin Drood*
1987	*Les Misérables*
1988	*The Phantom of the Opera*
1989	*Jerome Robbins' Broadway*
1990	*City of Angels*
1991	*The Will Rogers Follies*
1992	*Crazy for You*
1993	*Kiss of the Spider Woman*
1994	*Passion*
1995	*Sunset Boulevard*
1996	*Rent*
1997	*Titanic*
1998	*The Lion King*
1999	*Fosse*
2000	*Contact*
2001	*The Producers*
2002	*Thoroughly Modern Millie*
2003	*Hairspray*
2004	*Avenue Q*
2005	*Monty Python's Spamalot*
2006	*Jersey Boys*
2007	*Spring Awakening*

Bibliography

CONTENTS

INTRODUCTION

The literature on the Broadway musical is a rapidly growing commodity. As a burgeoning area of scholarship among music, theater, and literary scholars, many specialist studies are now appearing, in addition to the general surveys, photographic essays, and laudatory tributes to the genre and its most distinguished practitioners.

The most important chronologies are Gerald Bordman's extensive *American Musical Theatre: A Chronology*, which is replete with details and contexts for shows, and Stanley Green's *Broadway Musicals Show by Show*, which includes half-page or full-page entries on the most important shows, most with photographs.

For histories and surveys, Cecil Smith's *Musical Comedy in America* and Stanley Green's *The World of Musical Comedy*, though dated, provide valuable information and insights on the Broadway musical during the late 19th and early-to-mid 20th centuries. Alan Jay Lerner's *The Musical Theatre: A Celebration* offers a creator's view of the genre, while Kurt Gänzl's *The Musical* and Andrew Lamb's *150 Years of Popular Musical Theatre* place the Broadway musical in the larger context of popular musical theater. Geoffrey Block's *Enchanted Evenings: The Broadway Musical from "Show Boat" to Sondheim* remains the benchmark for musicological studies on the genre, and Raymond Knapp's two books, *The American Musical and the Formation of National Identity* and *The American Musical and the Performance of Personal Identity*, offer thematic approaches to the genre. In these volumes, Knapp discusses specific shows that reflect particular historical, sociological, or psychological topics. Ethan Mordden, in his decade-by-decade survey, provides extremely subjective commentary on the state of the Broadway musical from the 1920s to the end of the 20th century. Michael Kantor and Laurence Maslon's *Broadway: The American Musical*, a companion book to the acclaimed six-part PBS series, is replete with lavish illustrations, as is *The Shuberts Present*, a book written by the staff of the Shubert Archive.

Biographies on people associated with the Broadway musical are plentiful; some focus on the lives of the subjects, others on their art. Titles in the Yale Broadway Masters series, published by Yale University Press, focus on works by seminal Broadway composers and are intended for a musically literate audience as well as a general readership; as of mid-2007, books have appeared on Richard Rodgers (by Geoffrey Block), Andrew Lloyd Webber (by John Snelson), Jerome Kern (by Stephen Banfield), and Sigmund Romberg (by William A. Everett). Many people connected to Broadway have written autobiographies, including Moss Hart (*Act One*), Arthur Laurents (*Original Story by Arthur Laurents*), Alan Jay Lerner (*The Street Where I Live*), Mary Martin (*My Heart Belongs*), and Richard Rodgers (*Musical Stages*). An especially laudatory work concerning a composer's own words is Mark Eden Horowitz's *Conversations with Sondheim*, which consists of transcripts of interviews with Stephen Sondheim. As additional sources of biographical information, Oxford University Press has published collections of source readings regarding Broadway composers in their Readers on American Composers Series, including *The Richard Rodgers Reader* (edited by Geoffrey Block) and *The George Gershwin Reader* (edited by Robert Wyatt and John Andrew Johnson).

Video material related to the Broadway musical is becoming increasingly available. Particularly noteworthy is the six-episode *Broadway: The American Musical*, broadcast on PBS and available in a three-disc set that includes archival material not included in the broadcast. The three volumes of *Broad-*

way's Lost Treasures include scenes from musicals shown on the annual Tony Awards broadcasts. Most excerpts feature original cast members.

Of the current internet resources for the Broadway musical, the Internet Broadway Database (ibdb.com) allows researchers to find listings of runs of shows, cast and crew, and awards. The "Advanced Search" feature allows access to multiple lists, including long-running shows. Musicals101.com boasts a variety of information on the American musical theater, and contains both encyclopedic entries and prose essays.

Primary source material for the study of the Broadway musical exists in libraries and archives throughout the world. Among the most important repositories in the United States are the Library of Congress, the New York Public Library for the Performing Arts (Lincoln Center, especially the Billy Rose Theatre Collection), the Museum of the City of New York, the Shubert Archive, and the Harvard Theatre Collection.

Not included in this list are the numerous recordings of Broadway musicals. These can take the form of original cast recordings, studio recordings, and "hits" albums by singers whose focus includes musical theater (Julie Andrews, Kristin Chenoweth, Audra McDonald, Brian Stokes Mitchell), pop styles (Harry Connick, Jr., Barbra Streisand), or opera (Thomas Hampson, Jerry Hadley, Kiri Te Kanawa, Dawn Upshaw). Many musicals are also available in video versions based on stage productions (as opposed to true Hollywood film adaptations). Among these are *Oklahoma!* (starring Hugh Jackman) and *Kiss Me, Kate* (with Brent Barrett and Rachel York), as well as many shows by Stephen Sondheim (*Sweeney Todd, Sunday in the Park with George, Into the Woods, Passion*). Several Andrew Lloyd Webber shows, including *Cats, Joseph and the Amazing Technicolor Dreamcoat*, and *Jesus Christ Superstar* have appeared in made-for-video productions. Furthermore, several concert versions of Broadway musicals are also available on DVD, including performances of *Les Misérables, Sweeney Todd, Candide*, and *South Pacific*.

Also not contained in this bibliography are works on individual shows, which include not only scholarly studies but also published librettos, photographic essays, and "making of" books. For a list of this material that appeared before 2004, see William A. Everett's *The Musical: A Research and Information Guide*.

ANNOTATED BIBLIOGRAPHIES

Everett, William. *The Musical: A Research and Information Guide*. New York: Routledge, 2004.
Wildbihler, Hubert, and Sonja Völkline. *The Musical: An International Annotated Bibliography*. Munich: K. G. Saur, 1986.

CHRONOLOGIES

Bordman, Gerald. *American Musical Theatre: A Chronicle.* 3rd ed. New York: Oxford University Press, 2001.

Green, Stanley. *Broadway Musicals Show by Show.* 5th ed. Revised and updated by Kay Green. Milwaukee, Wis.: Hal Leonard, 1996.

Norton, Richard C. *A Chronology of American Musical Theater.* 3 vols. New York: Oxford University Press, 2002.

DICTIONARIES AND ENCYCLOPEDIAS

Bloom, Ken. *American Song: The Complete Musical Theatre Companion, 1900–1984.* 2nd ed. 2 vols. New York: Schirmer, 1996.

——. *Broadway: Its History, People, and Places, An Encyclopedia.* London: Routledge, 2003.

——. *The Routledge Guide to Broadway.* London: Routledge, 2006.

Bunnett, Rexton S., Michael Patrick Kennedy, and John Muir. *Guide to Musicals.* Glasgow: HarperCollins, 2001.

Cullen, Frank. *Vaudeville, Old and New: An Encyclopedia of Variety Performers.* 2 vols. London: Routledge, 2006.

Gänzl, Kurt. *The Encyclopedia of the Musical Theatre.* 2nd ed. 3 vols. New York: Schirmer, 2001.

Green, Stanley. *Encyclopedia of the Musical Theatre.* New York: Dodd, Mead & Company, 1976.

Larkin, Colin, ed. *The Guinness Who's Who of Stage Musicals.* Enfield, U.K.: Guinness, 1994.

Larkin, Colin, and John Martland, eds. *The Virgin Encyclopedia of Stage and Film Musicals.* London: Virgin, 1999.

Suskin, Steven. *More Opening Nights on Broadway: A Critical Quotebook of the Musical Theatre 1965 through 1981.* New York: Schirmer, 1997.

——. *Opening Night on Broadway: A Critical Quotebook of the Golden Era of the Musical Theatre, "Oklahoma" (1943) to "Fiddler on the Roof (1964).* New York: Schirmer, 1990.

——. *Show Tunes: The Songs, Shows, and Careers of Broadway's Major Composers.* Rev. and expanded 3rd ed. Foreword by Michael Feinstein. Oxford: Oxford University Press, 2000.

HISTORIES, SURVEYS, AND CRITICAL STUDIES

Alpert, Hollis. *Broadway! 125 Years of Musical Theatre.* New York: Arcade, 1991.

Banfield, Stephen. "Popular Song and Popular Music on Stage and Film." In *The Cambridge History of American Music,* edited by David Nicholls, pp. 309–44. Cambridge: Cambridge University Press, 1998.

BBC Music Magazine. Special Issue: The Golden Age of Musicals, 1999.

Bernstein, Leonard. "American Musical Comedy." In *The Joy of Music.* New York: Simon and Schuster, 1959, pp. 152–79. Reprint, New York: Anchor Books, Doubleday, 1994, pp. 164–91.

Block, Geoffrey. "The Broadway Canon from *Show Boat* to *West Side Story* and the European Operatic Ideal." *Journal of Musicology* 11 (1993): 525–44.

———. *Enchanted Evenings: The Broadway Musical from "Show Boat" to Sondheim.* Oxford: Oxford University Press, 1997.

Botto, Louis. *At This Theatre: 100 Years of Broadway Shows, Stories and Stars,* edited by Robert Viagas. New York: Applause and Playbill, 2002.

Bowers, Dwight Blocker. *American Musical Theater: Shows, Songs, and Stars.* Washington, D.C.: Smithsonian Collection of Recordings, 1989.

Bradley, Ian. *You've Got to Have a Dream: The Message of the Musical.* Louisville, Ky: Westminster John Knox Press, 2005.

Brantley, Ben, ed. *The New York Times Book of Broadway.* New York: St. Martin's Press, 2001.

Bryer, Jackson R., and Richad A. Davison, eds. *The Art of the American Musical: Conversations with the Creators.* New Brunswick, N.J.: Rutgers University Press, 2005.

Clark, John R., and William E. Morris. "Scherzo, Forte, and Bravura: Satire in America's Musical Theatre." *Journal of Popular Culture* 12, no. 3 (1978): 459–81.

Engel, Lehman. *The American Musical Theater: A Consideration.* New York: CBS Legacy Collection, Macmillan, 1967. Rev. ed. New York: Macmillan, 1975.

———. *Words with Music: Creating the Broadway Musical Libretto.* Updated and rev. by Howard Kissel. New York: Applause, 2006.

Everett, William A., and Paul R. Laird, eds. *The Cambridge Companion to the Musical.* Cambridge and New York: Cambridge University Press, 2002.

Flinn, Denny Martin. *Musical! A Grand Tour.* New York: Schirmer, 1997.

Frommer, Myrna Katz, and Harvey Frommer. *It Happened on Broadway: An Oral History of the Great White Way.* New York: Harcourt Brace & Company, 1998.

Furia, Philip, and Michael Lasser. *America's Songs: The Stories Behind the Songs of Broadway, Hollywood, and Tin Pan Alley.* London: Routledge, 2006.

Gänzl, Kurt. *The Musical: A Concise History.* Boston, Mass.: Northeastern University Press, 1997.

Gottfried, Martin. *Broadway Musicals.* New York: Abradale/Abrams, 1979.

——. *More Broadway Musicals: Since 1980*. New York: Abrams, 1991.

Gottlieb, Jack. *Funny, It Doesn't Sound Jewish: How Yiddish Songs and Synagogue Melodies Influenced Tin Pan Alley, Broadway, and Hollywood*. Albany: State University of New York Press in Association with the Library of Congress, 2004.

Grant, Mark N. *The Rise and Fall of the Broadway Musical*. Boston, Mass.: Northeastern University Press, 2004.

Green, Stanley. *The World of Musical Comedy*. New York: Grosset & Dunlap, 1960. Revised and enlarged 4th ed., San Diego: A. S. Barnes, 1980. Reprint, New York: Da Capo, n.d.

Henderson, Amy, and Dwight Blocker Bowers. *Red Hot & Blue: A Smithsonian Salute to the American Musical*. Washington, D.C.: Smithsonian, 1986.

Hirst, David. "The American Musical and the American Dream: From *Show Boat* to Sondheim." *New Theatre Quarterly* 1, no. 1 (February 1985): 24–38.

Hischak, Thomas S. *Through the Screen Door: What Happened to the Broadway Musical When It Went to Hollywood*. Lanham, Md.: Scarecrow, 2004.

Jones, John Bush. *Our Musicals, Ourselves: A Social History of the American Musical Theatre*. Hanover, N.H.: Brandeis University Press, 2003.

Kantor, Michael, and Laurence Maslon. *Broadway: The American Musical*. New York: Bulfinch, 2004.

Kasha, Al, and Joel Hirschhorn. *Notes on Broadway: Conversations with the Great Songwriters*. Chicago: Contemporary Books, 1985.

Kirle, Bruce. *Unfinished Show Business: Broadway Musicals as Works-in-Process*. Carbondale: Southern Illinois University Press, 2005.

Kislan, Richard. *The Musical: A Look at the American Musical Theatre*. Englewood Cliffs, N.J.: Prentice-Hall, 1980. Rev. ed. New York: Applause, 2000.

Knapp, Raymond. *The American Musical and the Formation of National Identity*. Princeton, N.J.: Princeton University Press, 2004.

——. *The American Musical and the Performance of Personal Identity*. Princeton, N.J.: Princeton University Press, 2006.

LaChiusa, Michael John. "Genre Confusion." *Opera News*, August 2002, 12–15, 73.

Lamb, Andrew. "From *Pinafore* to Porter: United States-United Kingdom Interactions in Musical Theater, 1879-1929." *American Music* 4, no. 1 (1986): 34–49.

——. *150 Years of Popular Musical Theatre*. New Haven, Conn.: Yale University Press, 2000.

Lawson-Peebles, Robert, ed. *Approaches to the American Musical*. Exeter, U.K.: University of Exeter Press, 1996.

Lerner, Alan Jay. *The Musical Theatre: A Celebration*. New York: McGraw-Hill, 1986. Reprint, New York: Da Capo, 1989.

Lewis, David H. *Broadway Musicals: A Hundred Year History*. Jefferson, N.C.: McFarland, 2002.

Loney, Glenn, ed. *Musical Theatre in America: Papers and Proceedings of the Conference on the Musical Theatre in America*. Westport, Conn.: Greenwood, 1984.

Mandelbaum, Ken. *Not Since Carrie: 40 Years of Broadway Musical Flops*. New York: St. Martin's, 1991.

Mast, Gerald. *'Can't Help Singing': The American Musical on Stage and Screen*. Woodstock, N.Y.: Overlook Press, 1987.

McMillin, Scott. *The Musical As Drama: A Study of the Principles and Conventions Behind Musical Shows from Kern to Sondheim*. Princeton, N.J.: Princeton University Press, 2006.

Miller, Scott. *Deconstructing Harold Hill: An Insider's Guide to Musical Theatre*. Portsmouth, N.H.: Heinemann, 2000.

——. *From "Assassins" to "West Side Story": The Director's Guide to Musical Theatre*. Portsmouth, N.H.: Heinemann, 1996.

——. *Rebels with Applause: Broadway's Groundbreaking Musicals*. Portsmouth, N.H.: Heinemann, 2001.

——. *Strike Up the Band: A New History of Musical Theatre*. Portsmouth, N.H.: Heinemann, 2007.

Mordden, Ethan. *Beautiful Mornin': The Broadway Musical in the 1940s*. Oxford: Oxford University Press, 1999.

——. *Better Foot Forward: The History of the American Musical Theatre*. New York: Grossman, 1976.

——. *Broadway Babies: The People Who Made the American Musical*. Oxford: Oxford University Press, 1983.

——. *Coming Up Roses: The Broadway Musical in the 1950s*. Oxford: Oxford University Press, 1998.

——. *Make Believe: The Broadway Musical in the 1920s*. Oxford: Oxford University Press, 1997.

——. *One More Kiss: The Broadway Musical in the 1970s*. New York: Palgrave, 2003.

——. *Open a New Window: The Broadway Musical in the 1960s*. New York: Palgrave, 2001.

——. *Sing for Your Supper: The Broadway Musical in the 1930s*. New York: Palgrave, 2005.

Most, Andrea. *Making Americans: Jews and the Broadway Musical*. Cambridge, Mass.: Harvard University Press, 2004.

Portantiere, Michael, ed. Foreword by Jerry Herman. *The Theater Mania Guide to Musical Theater Recordings*. New York: Back Stage Books, 2004.

Sennett, Ted. *Song and Dance: The Musicals of Broadway*. New York: Metrobooks, 1998.

Shubert Archive (Maryann Chach, Reagan Fletcher, Mark E. Swartz, and Sylvia Wang). *The Shuberts Present: 100 Years of American Theater*. New York: Abrams, in association with the Shubert Organization, Inc., 2001.

Singer, Barry. *Ever After: The Last Years of Musical Theater and Beyond*. New York: Applause, 2004.

Smith, Cecil. *Musical Comedy in America*. New York: Theatre Arts Books, 1950.

Smith, Cecil, and Glenn Litton. *Musical Comedy in America*. 2nd ed. New York: Theatre Arts Books, 1981.

Sondheim, Stephen. "The Musical Theater." *Dramatists Guild Quarterly* 15, no. 3 (1978): 6–29.

Stempel, Larry. "The Musical Play Expands." *American Music* 10, no. 2 (1992): 136–69.

Steyn, Mark. *Broadway Babies Say Goodnight: Musicals Then & Now*. New York: Routledge, 1999.

Suskin, Steven. *Second Act Trouble: Behind the Scenes at Broadway's Big Musical Bombs*. New York: Applause, 2006.

Swain, Joseph P. *The Broadway Musical: A Critical and Musical Survey*. New York and Oxford: Oxford University Press, 1990. Revised and expanded 2nd ed., Lanham, Md.: Scarecrow Press, 2002.

Verdino-Süllwold, Carla Maria. "Opera, Operetta, or Musical? Vanishing Distinctions in 20th Century Musical Drama." *Opera Journal* 23, no. 4 (1990): 31–43.

Wilk, Max. *They're Playing Our Song: From Jerome Kern to Stephen Sondheim—The Stories Behind the Words and Music of Two Generations*. New York: Atheneum, 1973.

GENDER STUDIES AND HOMOSEXUALITY

Clum, John M. *Something for the Boys: Musical Theater and Gay Culture*. New York: St. Martin's, 1999.

Feder-Kane, Abigail Miriam. "'Anything You Can Do, I Can Do Better': Transgressive Gender Role Performance in Musical Theater and Film, 1930–1950." Ph.D. diss., Northwestern University, 1999.

Miller, D.A. *A Place for Us [Essay on the Broadway Musical]*. Cambridge, Mass.: Harvard University Press, 1998.

Vincentelli, Elisabeth. "The Queen and I: True Confessions of a Lesbian Lover of Show Tunes." *Village Voice* 41, no. 37 (10 September 1996), 45, 50, 56.

Wolf, Stacy. *A Problem Like Maria: Gender and Sexuality in the American Musical*. Ann Arbor: University of Michigan Press, 2002.

BUSINESS AND COMMERCIAL STUDIES

Adler, Steven. *On Broadway: Art and Commerce on the Great White Way.* Carbondale: Southern Illinois University Press, 2004.

Rosenberg, Bernard, and Ernest Harburg. *The Broadway Musical: Collaboration in Commerce and Art.* New York and London: New York University Press, 1993.

Wollman, Elizabeth L. "The Economic Development of the 'New' Times Square and Its Impact on the American Musical." *American Music* 20, no. 2 (winter 2002): 445–65.

GENRES

African American Musical

Graziano, John. "Black Musical Theater and the Harlem Renaissance Movement." In *Black Music in the Harlem Renaissance: A Collection of Essays*, edited by Samuel A. Floyd, Jr., pp. 87–100. New York: Greenwood, 1990.

Peterson, Bernard L. Jr. *A Century of Musicals in Black and White: An Encyclopedia of Musical Stage Works By, About, or Involving African Americans.* Westport, Conn.: Greenwood, 1993.

Riis, Thomas L. *Just Before Jazz: Black Musical Theater in New York, 1890–1915.* Washington, D.C.: Smithsonian Institution Press, 1989.

——. *More Than Just Minstrel Shows: The Rise of Black Musical Theatre at the Turn of the Century.* Brooklyn: Institute for Studies in American Music, 1992.

Woll, Allen L. *Black Musical Theatre: From "Coontown" to "Dreamgirls."* Baton Rouge: Louisiana State University Press, 1989.

——. *Dictionary of the Black Theatre: Broadway, Off-Broadway, and Selected Harlem Theatres.* Westport, Conn.: Greenwood, 1983.

Megamusical

Sternfeld, Jessica. *The Megamusical.* Bloomington: Indiana University Press, 2006.

Vermette, Margaret. *The Musical World of Boublil and Schönberg: The Creators of "Les Misérables," "Miss Saigon," "Martin Guerre," and "The Pirate Queen."* New York: Applause, 2006.

Musical Comedy

Bordman, Gerald. *American Musical Comedy: From "Adonis" to "Dreamgirls."* Oxford: Oxford University Press, 1982.

Operetta

Bordman, Gerald. *American Operetta: From "H.M.S. Pinafore" to "Sweeney Todd."* Oxford: Oxford University Press, 1981.

Traubner, Richard. *Operetta: A Theatrical History.* Garden City, N.Y.: Doubleday, 1983. Oxford: Oxford University Press, 1989. Rev. ed., London: Routledge, 2003.

Revue

Bordman, Gerald. *American Musical Revue: From "The Passing Show" to "Sugar Babies."* Oxford: Oxford University Press, 1985.

Davis, Lee. *Scandals and Follies: The Rise and Fall of the Great Broadway Revue.* New York: Limelight, 2000.

Knapp, Margaret M. "Theatrical Parodies in American Topical Revues." *Journal of Popular Culture* 12, no. 3 (1978): 482–90.

Rock Musical

Wollman, Elizabeth L. *The Theater Will Rock: A History of the Rock Musical, From "Hair" to "Hedwig."* Ann Arbor: University of Michigan Press, 2006.

COMPOSERS

Irving Berlin

Barrett, Mary Ellin. *Irving Berlin: A Daughter's Memoir.* New York: Simon & Schuster, 1994.

Furia, Philip, with the assistance of Graham Wood. *Irving Berlin: A Life in Song.* New York: Schirmer, 1998. Songography by Ken Bloom.

Hamm, Charles. *Irving Berlin: Songs from the Melting Pot: The Formative Years, 1907–1914.* Oxford: Oxford University Press, 1997.

Jablonski, Edward. *Irving Berlin: American Troubadour.* New York: Henry Holt, 1999.

Magee, Jeffrey. "'Everybody Step': Irving Berlin, Jazz, and Broadway in the 1920s." *Journal of the American Musicological Society* 59, no. 3 (2006): 697–732.

——. "Irving Berlin's 'Blue Skies': Ethnic Affiliations and Musical Transformations." *Musical Quarterly* 84, no. 4 (2000): 537–80.

Leonard Bernstein

Burton, Humphrey. *Leonard Bernstein.* New York: Doubleday, 1994.

Laird, Paul R. *Leonard Bernstein: A Guide to Research.* London: Routledge, 2002.

Secrest, Meryle. *Leonard Bernstein.* New York: Knopf, 1994.

Eubie Blake

Rose, Al. *Eubie Blake.* New York: Schirmer, 1979.

Marc Blitzstein

Gordon, Eric A. *Mark the Music: The Life and Work of Marc Blitzstein.* New York: St. Martin's, 1989.

Lehrman, Leonard J. *Marc Blitzstein: A Bio-Bibliography.* Westport, Conn.: Praeger, 2005.

George M. Cohan

McCabe, John. *George M. Cohan: The Man Who Owned Broadway.* Garden City, N.Y.: Doubleday, 1973.

Noel Coward

Citron, Stephen. *Noel & Cole: The Sophisticates.* Oxford: Oxford University Press, 1993.

Coward, Noel. *Autobiography.* With an introduction by Sheridan Morley. London: Methuen, 1986.

Morley, Sheridan. *A Talent to Amuse: A Biography of Noël Coward.* Garden City, N.Y.: Doubleday, 1969.

George Gershwin

Gilbert, Stephen. *The Music of Gershwin*. New Haven: Yale University Press, 1995.

Jablonski, Edward. *Gershwin: A Biography*. New York: Doubleday, 1988. Reprint, New York: Da Capo, 1998.

Pollack, Howard. *George Gershwin: His Life and Work*. Berkeley: University of California Press, 2006.

Rosenberg, Deena. *Fascinating Rhythm: The Collaboration of George and Ira Gershwin*. New York: Dutton, 1991.

Schwartz, Charles. *Gershwin: His Life and Music*. New York: Bobbs-Merrill, 1973. Reprint, New York: Da Capo, 1979.

Wyatt, Robert, and John Andrew Johnson, eds. *The George Gershwin Reader*. New York: Oxford University Press, 2004.

Victor Herbert

Kaye, Joseph. *Victor Herbert*. New York: Watt, 1931.

Waters, Edward N. *Victor Herbert: A Life in Music*. New York: Macmillan, 1955.

Jerry Herman

Citron, Stephen. *Jerry Herman: Poet of the Showtune*. New Haven, Conn.: Yale University Press, 2004.

Herman, Jerry, with Marilyn Stasio. *Showtune: A Memoir*. New York: Donald I. Fine, 1996.

John Kander and Fred Ebb

Kander, John, and Fred Ebb, as told to Greg Lawrence. *Colored Lights: Forty Years of Words and Music, Show Biz, Collaboration, and All that Jazz*. New York: Faber and Faber, 2003.

Jerome Kern

Banfield, Stephen. *Jerome Kern*. Yale Broadway Masters. New Haven, Conn.: Yale University Press, 2006.

Bordman, Gerald. *Jerome Kern: His Life and Music*. New York and Oxford: Oxford University Press, 1980.

Andrew Lloyd Webber

Coveney, Michael. *Cats on a Chandelier: The Andrew Lloyd Webber Story*. London: Hutchinson, 1999. Paperback ed., *The Andrew Lloyd Webber Story*. London: Arrow, 2000.

Richmond, Keith. *The Musicals of Andrew Lloyd Webber*. London: Virgin, 1995.

Snelson, John. *Andrew Lloyd Webber*. Yale Broadway Masters. New Haven, Conn.: Yale University Press, 2004.

Walsh, Michael. *Andrew Lloyd Webber: His Life and Works, A Critical Biography*. New York: Abrams, 1989. Rev. and enlarged ed., New York: Abrams, 1997.

Frank Loesser

Loesser, Susan. *A Most Remarkable Fella: Frank Loesser and the Guys and Dolls in His Life*. New York: Donald I. Fine, 1993.

Sobran, Joseph. "Adult Entertainment." *National Review* 44, no. 10 (25 May 1992), 46–48.

Cole Porter

Kimball, Robert, ed. *Cole*. Biographical essay by Brendan Gill. New York: Holt, Rinehart & Winston, 1971.

McBrien, William. *Cole Porter: A Biography*. New York: Knopf, 1998. Paperback ed., New York: Vintage, 2000.

Richard Rodgers

Block, Geoffrey. *Richard Rodgers*. Yale Broadway Masters. New Haven, Conn.: Yale University Press, 2003.

——. *The Richard Rodgers Reader*. Oxford: Oxford University Press, 2002.

Hyland, William G. *Richard Rodgers*. New Haven, Conn.: Yale University Press, 1998.

Maslon, Laurence. *Richard Rodgers: The Sweetest Sounds*. American Masters. DVD. CentreStage WHE73153 (2001).

Rodgers, Richard. *Musical Stages: An Autobiography*. New York: Random House, 1975. Richard Rodgers Centennial Edition, with an updated introduction by Mary Rodgers and a new afterword by John Lahr, New York: Da Capo, 1995. 2nd ed., New York: Da Capo, 2002.

Secrest, Meryle. *Somewhere for Me: A Biography of Richard Rodgers*. New York: Knopf, 2001.

Wood, Graham. "The Development of Song Forms in the Broadway and Hollywood Musicals of Richard Rodgers, 1919–1943." Ph.D. dissertation, University of Minnesota, 2000.

Richard Rodgers et al.

Goldstein, Richard M. "'I Enjoy Being a Girl': Women in the Plays of Rodgers and Hammerstein." *Popular Music and Society* 13, no. 1 (1989): 1–8.

Green, Stanley, ed. *Rodgers and Hammerstein Fact Book*. New York: Lynn Farnol Group, 1980.

Marx, Samuel, and Jan Clayton. *Rodgers and Hart: Bewitched, Bothered, and Bedevilled*. London: W. H. Allen, 1977.

McConachie, Bruce A. "The 'Oriental' Musicals of Rodgers and Hammerstein and the U.S. War in Southeast Asia." *Theatre Journal* 46, no. 3 (1994): 385–98.

Mordden, Ethan. *Rodgers & Hammerstein*. New York: Abrams, 1992.

Sigmund Romberg

Arnold, Elliott. *Deep in My Heart*. New York: Duell, Sloan and Pearce, 1949.

Everett, William A. *Sigmund Romberg*. Yale Broadway Masters. New Haven, Conn.: Yale University Press, 2007.

——. "Sigmund Romberg and the American Operetta of the 1920s." *Arti musices* 26, no. 1 (1995): 49–64.

Stephen Sondheim

Adler, Thomas P. "The Musical Dramas of Stephen Sondheim: Some Critical Approaches." *Journal of Popular Culture* 12, no. 3 (winter 1978): 513–25.

Banfield, Stephen. *Sondheim's Broadway Musicals*. Ann Arbor: University of Michigan Press, 1993.

Goodhart, Sandor, ed. *Reading Stephen Sondheim: A Collection of Critical Essays*. New York: Garland, 2000.

Gordon, Joanne. *Art Isn't Easy: The Theatre of Stephen Sondheim*. New York: Da Capo, 1992.

Horowitz, Mark Eden. *Sondheim on Music: Minor Details and Major Decisions*. Lanham, Md.: Scarecrow, in association with the Library of Congress, 2002.

Leithauser, Brad. "A Funny Thing Happened on the Way to Broadway." *New York Review of Books*, 10 February 2000, 35–38.

Lipton, James. "The Art of the Musical: Stephen Sondheim." *Paris Review* 39, no. 142 (spring 1997), 258–78.

Rich, Frank. "Conversations with Sondheim." *New York Times Magazine*, 12 March 2000, 38–43, 60–61, 88–89.

Secrest, Meryle. *Stephen Sondheim: A Life*. New York: Knopf, 1998.

Swayne, Steve. *How Sondheim Found His Sound*. Ann Arbor: University of Michigan Press, 2005.

Kay Swift

Ohl, Vicki. *Fine and Dandy: The Life and Work of Kay Swift*. New Haven, Conn.: Yale University Press, 2004.

Kurt Weill

Drew, David. *Kurt Weill: A Handbook*. Berkeley: University of California Press, 1987.

Hirsch, Foster. *Kurt Weill on Stage: From Berlin to Broadway*. New York: Knopf, 2002.

Kowalke, Kim H., ed. *A New Orpheus: Essays on Kurt Weill*. New Haven, Conn.: Yale University Press, 1986.

Vincent Youmans

Bordman, Gerald. *Days to Be Happy, Years to Be Sad: The Life and Music of Vincent Youmans*. Oxford: Oxford University Press, 1982.

LYRICISTS AND LIBRETTISTS

Engel, Lehman. *Their Words Are Music: The Great Theatre Lyricists and Their Lyrics*. New York: Crown, 1975.

Furia, Philip. *The Poets of Tin Pan Alley: A History of America's Great Lyricists*. Oxford: Oxford University Press, 1990.

Gottlieb, Robert, and Robert Kimball, eds. *Reading Lyrics*. New York: Pantheon Books, 2000.

Hischak, Thomas S. *Word Crazy: Broadway Lyricists from Cohan to Sondheim*. New York: Praeger, 1991.

——. *Boy Loses Girl: Broadway's Librettists*. Lanham, Md.: Scarecrow, 2002.

Betty Comden and Adolph Green

Baer, William. "Singin' in the Rain: A Conversation with Betty Comden and Adolph Green." *Michigan Quarterly Review* 41, no. 1 (2002): 1–20.

Comden, Betty. *Off Stage*. New York: Simon & Schuster, 1995.

Robinson, Alice M. *Betty Comden and Adolph Green: A Bio-Bibliography*. Westport, Conn.: Greenwood, 1994.

Dorothy Fields

Winer, Deborah Grace. *On the Sunny Side of the Street: The Life and Lyrics of Dorothy Fields*. With a foreword by Betty Comden. New York: Schirmer, 1997.

Ira Gershwin

Furia, Philip. *Ira Gershwin: The Art of the Lyricist*. Oxford: Oxford University Press, 1996.

Jablonski, Edward. "What About Ira?" In *The Gershwin Style: New Looks at the Music of George Gershwin*, edited by Wayne Schneider, pp. 255–77. New York: Oxford University Press, 1999.

Oscar Hammerstein II

Citron, Stephen. *The Wordsmiths: Oscar Hammerstein 2nd and Alan Jay Lerner*. Oxford: Oxford University Press, 1995.

Fordin, Hugh. *Getting to Know Him: A Biography of Oscar Hammerstein II*. New York: Random House, 1977. Introduction by Stephen Sondheim. Reprint ed., New York: Ungar, 1995.

Edgar Yip Harburg

Lahr, Jon. "The Lemon-Drop Kid." *New Yorker* 72, no. 29 (30 September 1996): 68–74.

Meyerson, Harold, and Ernie Harburg. *Who Put the Rainbow in "The Wizard of Oz"?: Yip Harburg, Lyricist*. Ann Arbor: University of Michigan Press, 1993.

Lorenz Hart

Nolan, Frederick. *Lorenz Hart: A Poet on Broadway*. Oxford: Oxford University Press, 1994.

Moss Hart

Bach, Steven. *Dazzler: The Life and Times of Moss Hart*. New York: Knopf, 2001.

Brown, Jared. *Moss Hart: A Prince of the Theatre*. New York: Back Stage Books, 2006.

Hart, Moss. *Act One: An Autobiography*. New York: Random House, 1959. Reprint ed., New York: Vintage, 1976.

Alan Jay Lerner

Citron, Stephen. *The Wordsmiths: Oscar Hammerstein 2nd and Alan Jay Lerner*. Oxford: Oxford University Press, 1995.

Jablonski, Edward. *Alan Jay Lerner: A Biography*. New York: Henry Holt, 1986.

Lerner, Alan Jay. *On the Street Where I Live*. New York: Norton, 1978.

Johnny Mercer

Furia, Philip. *Skylark: The Life and Times of Johnny Mercer*. New York: St. Martin's, 2003.

Tim Rice

Rice, Tim. *Oh, What a Circus*. London: Hodder and Stroughton, 1999. Paperback ed., London: Hodder and Stroughton, 2000.

OTHER CREATORS

Michael Bennett

Mandelbaum, Ken. *"A Chorus Line" and the Musicals of Michael Bennett*. New York: St. Martin's, 1989.

Robert Russell Bennett

Robert Russell Bennett. *"The Broadway Sound": The Autobiography and Selected Essays of Robert Russell Bennett,* ed. George J. Ferencz. Rochester, N.J.: University of Rochester Press, 1999.

Ferencz, George J. *Robert Russell Bennett: A Bio-Bibliography*. Westport, Conn.: Greenwood, 1990.

Lew Fields

Fields, Armond, and L. Marc Fields. *From the Bowery to Broadway: Lew Fields and the Roots of American Popular Theater*. Oxford: Oxford University Press, 1993.

Bob Fosse

Gottfried, Martin. *All His Jazz: The Life and Death of Bob Fosse*. New York: Bantam, 1990.

Grubb, Kevin Boyd. *Razzle Dazzle: The Life and Works of Bob Fosse*. New York: St. Martin's, 1989.

Cameron Mackintosh

Morley, Sheridan, and Ruth Leon. *Hey Mr Producer! The Musical World of Cameron Mackintosh*. Preface by Andrew Lloyd Webber. London: Weidenfeld & Nicholson and New York: Backstage Books, 1998.

Hal (Harold) Prince

Hirsch, Foster. *Harold Prince and the American Musical Theatre*. Cambridge: Cambridge University Press, 1989.

Ilson, Carol. *Harold Prince: From "Pajama Game" to "Phantom of the Opera" and Beyond*. Foreword by Sheldon Harnick. Ann Arbor: UMI Research Press, 1989. New ed., New York: Limelight, 1992.

Jerome Robbins

Conrad, Christine. *Jerome Robbins: That Broadway Man, That Ballet Man*. London: Booth-Clibborn, 2000.

Lawrence, Greg. *Dance with Demons: The Life of Jerome Robbins*. New York: Putnam, 2001.

Sam, Lee, and J. J. Shubert

Hirsch, Foster. *The Boys from Syracuse: The Shuberts' Theatrical Empire*. Carbondale: Southern Illinois Press, 1998. Paperback ed., New York: Cooper Square, 2000.

McNamara, Brooks. *The Shuberts of Broadway: A History Drawn from the Collections of the Shubert Archive*. Foreword by Beverly Sills. Oxford: Oxford University Press, 1990.

Florenz Ziegfeld

Higham, Charles. *Ziegfeld*. Chicago: Henry Regnery, 1972.
Lasser, Michael. "The Glorifier: Florenz Ziegfeld and the Creation of the American Showgirl." *American Scholar* 63, no. 3 (1994): 441–48.

PERFORMERS

Julie Andrews

Windeler, Robert. *Julie Andrews: A Life on Stage and Screen*. New York: Citadel, 1997.

Theodore Bikel

Bikel, Theodore. *Theo: An Autobiography of Theodore Bikel*. New York: HarperCollins, 1994.

Fanny Brice

Goldman, Herbert G. *Fanny Brice: The Original Funny Girl*. New York and Oxford: Oxford University Press, 1992.
Grossman, Barbara W. *Funny Woman: the Life and Times of Fanny Brice*. Bloomington: Indiana University Press, 1991.

Yul Brynner

Brynner, Rock. *Yul: The Man Who Would Be King*. New York: Simon & Schuster, 1989.

Carol Channing

Channing, Carol. *Just Lucky I Guess: A Memoir of Sorts*. New York: Simon & Schuster, 2002.

W. C. Fields

Curtis, James. *W. C. Fields: A Biography*. New York: Knopf, 2003.

Al Jolson

Fisher, James. *Al Jolson: A Bio-Bibliography*. Westport, Conn.: Greenwood, 1994.

Goldman, Herbert G. *Jolson: The Legend Comes to Life*. Oxford: Oxford University Press, 1988.

Angela Lansbury

Gottfried, Martin. *Balancing Act: The Authorized Biography of Angela Lansbury*. Boston, Mass.: Little, Brown, 1999.

Mary Martin

Martin, Mary. *My Heart Belongs*. New York: William Morrow, 1976.

Ethel Merman

Bryan, George B. *Ethel Merman: A Bio-Bibliography*. Westport, Conn.: Greenwood, 1992.

Thomas, Bob. *I Got Rhythm!: The Ethel Merman Story*. New York: Putnam, 1985.

DVD ANTHOLOGIES

Broadway: The American Musical. Directed by Michael Kantor. 3 DVDs. PBS Home Video 88571 (2004).

Broadway: The Golden Age. Directed by Rick McKay. DADA Films/RCA Victor/BMG 62876 65441 8 (2004).

Broadway's Lost Treasures: 22 Rare Performances from Broadway's Greatest Musicals. Acorn Media AMP-6706 (2003). (from Tony Awards television broadcasts)

Broadway's Lost Treasures II: 18 Rare Performances from Broadway's Greatest Musicals. Acorn Media AMP-7303 (2004). (from Tony Awards television broadcasts)

Broadway's Lost Treasures III, The Best of the Tony Awards: 23 Rare Performances from Broadway's Greatest Musicals. Acorn Media AMP-8008 (2005). (from Tony Awards television broadcasts)

INTERNET RESOURCES

American Theater Web: www.americantheaterweb.com
Internet Broadway Database: www.ibdb.com
Musical Heaven: www.musicalheaven.com
Musicals 101: www.musicals101.com
Playbill: www.playbill.com
SIBMAS, International Association of Libraries and Museums of the Performing Arts: www.theatrelibrary.org

About the Authors

William A. Everett is associate professor and coordinator of musicology at the University of Missouri–Kansas City's Conservatory of Music and Dance, where he also serves as chair of the Division of Composition, Music Theory, and Musicology. Prior to his appointment at UMKC, he taught at Washburn University in Topeka, Kansas, for 12 years. At Washburn, he was co-music director and conductor for productions of *Assassins* and *Once on This Island*. His musicological research focuses on the American musical theater, particularly American operetta of the 1910s and 1920s, and relationships between music and national identity. He is the author of *British Piano Trios, Quartets, and Quintets, 1850–1950: A Checklist* (2000), *The Musical: A Research and Information Guide* (2004), *Sigmund Romberg* (2007), and *Rudolf Friml* (forthcoming).

Paul R. Laird is professor of musicology and director of the Musicology Division at the University of Kansas, where he teaches undergraduate and graduate courses in music history and directs the Instrumental Collegium Musicum. His research interests include the Spanish villancico, Leonard Bernstein, the Broadway musical, and early string instruments. He is the author of *Towards a History of the Spanish Villancico* (1997), *Leonard Bernstein: A Guide to Research* (2002), *The Baroque Cello Revival: An Oral History* (2004), and *Leonard Bernstein's "Chichester Psalms"* (forthcoming). He is also active as a Baroque cellist, playing with the Spencer Consort.

Everett and Laird have coedited *The Cambridge Companion to the Musical* (2002, 2nd edition in progress) and *On Bunker's Hill: Essays on Music in Honor of J. Bunker Clark* (2007).